HOSPITALITY IN REVIEW
A CAPSTONE TEXT

Complete with Senior and Graduate-Level Projects

Edited By

Michael M. Lefever

University of Massachusetts, Amherst

KENDALL/HUNT PUBLISHING COMPANY
4050 Westmark Drive   Dubuque, Iowa 52002

Cover photos courtesy of ITT Sheraton Corporation

Pictured from top to bottom are Sheraton Moana Surfrider, Honolulu, HI;
The Palace Hotel, San Francisco, CA; Princeville Hotel, Kauai, HI.

Copyright © 1996 by Kendall/Hunt Publishing Company

ISBN 0-7872-0251-7

Library of Congress Catalog Card Number: 95-77371

Printed in the United States of America
10 9 8 7 6 5 4 3 2 1

A special thanks
to Terry Cloonan
for her assistance with
this project.

CONTENTS

PREFACE

HOSPITALITY EDUCATORS have long recognized the value of the senior-level project or capstone course. Almost every four-year program requires the equivalent of a senior-year capstone course that summarizes or integrates the many topics found in the hospitality curriculum. Until now, however, there has been no single resource from which to draw for educators who seek to offer their students the opportunity to apply their cumulative knowledge in a manipulative, or hands-on, learning experience.

This book is the first attempt to locate and compile forward-looking curriculum ideas and proven projects that can be used in a capstone setting. In its design and content, this volume collects the wisdom of thirty-two leading experts from twenty-one U.S. hospitality programs. These educators collectively designed and contributed to the twenty-six curricular components of this book. They recommended the most current and advanced readings available, selecting these items both for breadth and depth. These experts also contributed their most effective term projects for each section. The educators using these projects report considerable success in integrating and applying curricular components.

In Chapter 26 we are pleased to share the details of the graduate-level integrative project offered at Cornell University's School of Hotel Administration. We feel this particular project has far-reaching value at upper and graduate levels by bringing theory into practice with substantial verisimilitude. The topics raised in this and other sections of the book also provide nascent hospitality researchers and graduate students with dozens of topics that can serve as springboards for thesis work.

A successful book is always the result of a collective effort. This is especially the case here. Special thanks go to all the contributing editors and to their students, who over the years have tested, cut, and polished the integrative projects presented in this book.

Michael M. Lefever

Contributing Editors

Howard Adler
Purdue University
(Chapter 11)

Elizabeth B. Barrett
Kansas State University
(Chapter 3)

Cherylynn F. Becker
Kansas State University
(Chapter 18)

Sandra K. Boothe
Cornell University
(Chapter 26)

John T. Bowen
University of Nevada - Las Vegas
(Chapter 16)

Patricia M. Bowman
Johnson & Wales University
(Chapter 2)

James J. Buergermeister
University of Wisconsin - Stout
(Chapter 8)

Agnes L. DeFranco
University of Houston
(Chapter 15)

H. A. "Andy" Divine
University of Denver

James W. Dougan
Pennsylvania State University
(Chapter 13)

Linda K. Enghagen
University of Massachusetts - Amherst
(Chapter 21)

A. Neal Geller
Cornell University
(Chapter 26)

Nancy S. Graves
University of Houston
(Chapter 1)

Lynn M. Huffman
Texas Tech University
(Chapter 6)

Thomas Jones
University of Nevada - Las Vegas
(Chapter 12)

Mahmood A. Khan
Virginia Polytechnic Institute and State
  University
(Chapter 17)

Stephen M. LeBruto
University of Central Florida
(Chapter 14)

Linda L. Lowry
University of Massachusetts - Amherst
(Chapter 23)

Frankie F. Miller
University of Delaware
(Chapter 24)

David V. Pavesic
Georgia State University
(Chapter 5)

Charles G. Partlow
University of South Carolina

Richard H. Penner
Cornell University
(Chapter 26)

Emily C. Richardson
Widener University

Carol W. Shanklin
Kansas State University
(Chapter 4)

Sandra K. Strick
University of South Carolina
(Chapter 22)

David L. Tucker
Widener University
(Chapter 10)

W. Terry Umbreit
Washington State University
(Chapter 9)

Carl W. Vail
California State Polytechnic University—
    Pomona & Cini-Little International, Inc.
(Chapter 7)

Gary K. Vallen
Northern Arizona University
(Chapter 25)

Glenn Withiam
Cornell University
(Chapter 26)

Robert H. Woods
Michigan State University
(Chapter 19)

Peter M. Yersin
Pennsylvania State University
(Chapter 20)

1

NUTRITION

Nutrition: Consumers Still Split into Three Camps

Renee Iwamuro

The proportion of consumers who are nutrition-conscious and who order healthy items when dining at restaurants has plateaued, while the percentage of consumers who are concerned about nutrition but who are more taste-driven and occasion-driven when eating out has risen.

THE NATIONAL RESTAURANT Association conducted its first nationwide survey to assess consumer attitudes toward health and nutrition in 1986. In 1989, and again in 1992, the association conducted follow-up surveys.

Study Highlights

▶ Two-thirds of adults overall reported restricting their diets in the previous year to maintain health. Weight control was the next most frequently cited reason for restricting diet. Forty-one percent of consumers reported restricting their diets to lose weight, while 38 percent did so to maintain their weight.

▶ Roughly one out of three adults (32 percent) restricted their diets to control blood cholesterol, while 18 percent did so to control high blood pressure.

▶ Of those who consciously restricted their diets to control blood cholesterol or high blood pressure, the majority did so on a doctor's recommendation. In contrast, the majority of people who restricted their diets during the previous year to control their weight or maintain overall health did so on their own initiative.

▶ Nearly three out of four respondents (71 percent) reported consciously restricting their consumption of foods high in fat, while 64 percent restrict their intake of foods high in cholesterol.

▶ More than half of consumers consciously restrict their consumption of salt (58 percent), sugar (52 percent), eggs (52 percent) and red meat (51 percent).

▶ Consumers are least likely to restrict their consumption of poultry (10 percent) or fish/seafood (17 per-

cent)—not surprising given the reputation of these items as being relatively low in fat and calories.

▶ The majority of consumers reported consciously eating more vegetables (76 percent), fruits (70 percent), starchy foods such as rice, pasta and whole-grain breads (61 percent) and foods high in fiber (57 percent).

▶ A slight majority (55 percent) of adults reported paying attention to the nutritional content of the food they eat. However, a similar proportion said that they eat what they want whenever they feel like it (51 percent) and select food based on taste rather than nutrient content (50 percent).

▶ Nearly three out of 10 adults reported eating a diet high in fruits, vegetables and grains; low in foods from animal sources; and

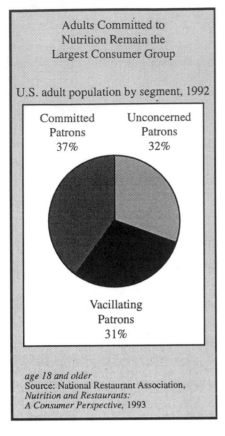

with olive oil as the principal fat. Meanwhile, 23 percent said their diet includes many items containing sugar substitutes and/or fat substitutes.

► Twenty-two percent of adults describe themselves as either a vegetarian (6 percent) or almost a vegetarian (16 percent).

► Many consumers eat differently at restaurants than they do at home. A majority (62 percent) of adults say that when they eat out, they eat foods that are different from the foods they eat at home, while 55 percent of consumers report that when eating out for a special occasion, they are less concerned about the nutritional value of the food they eat.

► Nevertheless, 47 percent make a point of ordering foods that are nutritious when eating out, and 39 percent look for low-fat foods when eating out. One out of two consumers would order a main dish at a restaurant that didn't include meat, poultry or fish, while 36 percent say they would order vegetarian dishes at restaurants if they were available.

► For the most part, restaurants are seen as being accommodating to consumers' health and nutrition needs. Seven out of 10 consumers agree that restaurants are usually responsive to special requests from patrons, such as serving sauce or salad dressing on the side.

► However, only 41 percent of consumers believe that it's easy to eat healthy at most tableservice restaurants.

The Three Consumer Segments

The three studies show the nation's adult population dividing into three distinct consumer segments regarding their attitudes toward health and nutrition:

► Unconcerned Patrons
► Committed Patrons
► Vacillating Patrons

Unconcerned Patrons are generally not concerned about nutrition and health. They describe themselves as "meat and potatoes" people and profess to eat whatever they want whenever they want. Their eat-

ing behavior is consistent with their attitude.

The second group, identified as Committed Patrons, consists of individuals who believe that a good diet plays a role in the prevention of serious illness and are committed to good nutrition when eating away from home.

Vacillating Patrons, the third group of consumers, are concerned about health and nutrition but are driven primarily by taste and occasion when dining out.

Percentage of Unconcerned Patrons Plateaus

The proportion of the adult population who are Unconcerned Patrons regarding nutrition plateaued from 1989 to 1992 at 32 percent. This followed a decline from 1986 to 1989, when the proportion of Unconcerned Patrons dropped from 38 percent to its current level of 32 percent.

There were approximately 60.4 million Unconcerned Patrons in 1992 (according to Census Bureau data for the adult population age 18 and older in conjunction with association survey results). Overall, the number of Unconcerned Patrons has declined by 7.0 million since 1986, when Unconcerned Patrons numbered 67.4 million.

Committed Patrons Dip

After increasing from 35 percent in 1986 to 39 percent in 1989, the proportion of the adult population identified as Committed Patrons dipped to 37 percent in 1992.

However, Committed Patrons remain the largest of the three consumer groups, representing 69.8 million adults in 1992, down from a peak of 71.5 million in 1989. The ranks of Committed Patrons have grown by nearly 8 million persons since the first survey was conducted in 1986.

More Vacillating Patrons

The proportion of Vacillating Patrons has risen steadily since the first survey was conducted in 1986 and is now almost equal in size to Unconcerned Patrons. In 1986, Vacillating Patrons represented the smallest consumer group, accounting for 27 percent of the U.S. adult population (about 47.9 million persons). By 1989, Vacillating Patrons had increased to 29 percent of adults, an increase of some 5.3 million from 1986.

A similar gain in the number of Vacillating Patrons was evident from 1989 to 1992, with Vacillating Patrons accounting for 31 percent of the adult population. Overall, the ranks of Vacillating Patrons swelled by roughly 10.7 million between 1986 and 1992, with Vacillating Patrons numbering more than 58.5 million in 1992.

Who Are Unconcerned Patrons?

Unconcerned Patrons are more likely than average to be

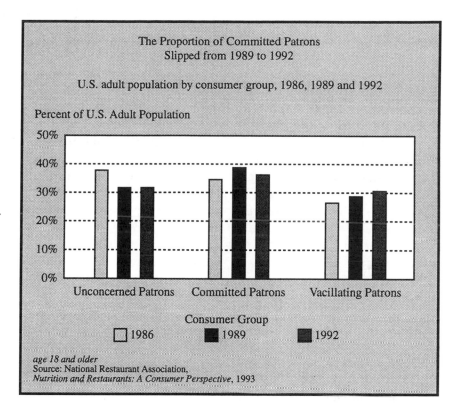

The Proportion of Committed Patrons Slipped from 1989 to 1992

U.S. adult population by consumer group, 1986, 1989 and 1992

Percent of U.S. Adult Population

Consumer Group

☐ 1986   ■ 1989   ■ 1992

age 18 and older
Source: National Restaurant Association,
Nutrition and Restaurants: A Consumer Perspective, 1993

men age 18 to 34 with average incomes. These consumers are also more likely than average to live in the South.

Unconcerned Patrons identified themselves as being less concerned about nutrition in 1992. Approximately two-thirds of Unconcerned Patrons described themselves as "meat and potatoes" people, a proportion which has increased steadily since 1986 (55 percent) and 1989 (61 percent).

In addition, Unconcerned Patrons are more likely than ever to have no restrictions on when or what they eat. The proportion of Unconcerned Patrons who report eating whatever they want whenever they feel like it has risen steadily, from 68 percent in 1986 to roughly three-quarters in 1992.

Unconcerned Patrons show a preference for convenient

dining options. These consumers are more likely to be frequent patrons of fast-food restaurants and to order carryout or delivery from fast-food or tableservice establishments. Unconcerned Patrons are more likely than average to order regular soft drinks, fried chicken, french fries, rich desserts, hamburgers, fried fish or seafood, steak or roast beef, premium ice cream, and Mexican, Latin American, French or Italian dishes.

In 1992, 48 percent of Unconcerned Patrons indicated that they are often concerned about their health, down from nearly two-thirds in 1986. In addition, the proportion of Unconcerned Patrons who believe that good diet and nutrition play a role in the prevention of serious illness such as heart disease and cancer has slipped steadily from a high of 71 percent in 1986 to approximately two-thirds in 1992.

Unconcerned Patrons were more likely to say that foods that are good for you usually don't taste good in 1992 (25 percent) compared with 1986 (18 percent), although the proportion who agreed that low-calorie means less taste has remained steady throughout the six-year period at roughly 25 percent.

Profile of Committed Patrons

Eighty-five percent of Committed Patrons in 1992 reported paying attention to the nutritional content of the food they eat. The proportion of Committed Patrons who say they eat what they want whenever they feel like it fell to 13 percent in 1992 from 21 percent in 1989.

Committed Patrons are more likely than average to be women age 35 to 54 and to have graduated from college or have some graduate school education. Consequently, Committed Patrons also have above-average incomes and tend to live in metropolitan areas.

Committed Patrons are more likely to be frequent patrons of moderately priced (average check less than $10) tableservice establishments.

Their concern with health and nutrition is revealed by their food preferences. Committed Patrons are more likely than average to order calorie-controlled entrees, vegetarian pizza, low-fat frozen yogurt, low-fat fruit-based dessert, vegetables seasoned only with herbs and lemon, reduced-calorie salad dressing, whole-grain muffins, diet soft drinks, food cooked without salt, a raw vegetable appetizer, caffeine-free coffee, and a main-dish salad with vegetables and grains.

The proportion of Committed Patrons who are often concerned about their health remained steady at approximately 80 percent from 1986 to 1992.

NO SURPRISE: COMMITTED PATRONS PREFER NUTRITIOUS FOODS			
Most popular foods ordered in the previous year by each consumer group, 1992			
Most Popular Foods	**Unconcerned Patrons**	**Committed Patrons**	**Vacillating Patrons**
1	Hamburgers	Fresh fruit	Steak or roast beef
2	Steak or roast beef	Broiled/baked fish or seafood	Hamburgers
3	French fries	Chinese dishes	French fries
4	Regular soft drink	Fruit salad	Fresh fruit
5	Italian dishes	Poultry without skin*	Broiled/baked fish or seafood
6	Fried fish or seafood	Italian dishes	Poultry without skin
7	Fresh fruit	Hamburger	Regular soft drink
8	Fried chicken	Low-fat frozen yogurt	Fried chicken*
9	Mexican dishes	Whole-grain muffins*	Fruit salad
10	Rich desserts	Main-dish salad with vegetables and grains	Chinese dishes

*tied with above
Note: Based on a list of 38 items
Source: National Restaurant Association, *Nutrition and Restaurants: A Consumer Perspective*, 1993.

Seventy-eight percent of Committed Patrons in 1992 agreed that fried food is bad for you, a proportion which has risen steadily from 69 percent in 1986. This belief is reflected in the finding that 90 percent of Committed Patrons in 1992 said they prefer broiled foods to fried foods.

Committed Patrons are a somewhat ambivalent group when it comes to the taste of healthy and nutritious foods. Although the proportion of Committed Patrons who believe that foods that are good for you usually don't taste good declined from 13 percent in 1986 to 8 percent in 1992, a higher proportion of Committed Patrons equated low-calorie with less taste in 1992 (14 percent) than in 1986 (8 percent).

Roughly one out of four Committed Patrons are tired of hearing about what's good and bad for them when it comes to food, up from 19 percent in 1989.

Profile of Vacillating Patrons

Vacillating Patrons are more likely than average to be over 45 years old, have below-average incomes, have a high school degree or less education and live in the Northeast.

The proportion of Vacillating Patrons who reported watching their caloric intake dropped 7 percentage points from 1989 to 1992, to 48 percent. Meanwhile, 35 percent of Vacillating Patrons paid attention to the nutritional content of the food they eat, a de-

cline of 7 percentage points from 1986.

However, the proportion of Vacillating Patrons who describe themselves as "meat and potatoes" people has been declining steadily since 1986. In 1986, roughly two-thirds of Vacillating Patrons described themselves as such, a proportion which dropped to 59 percent in 1989 and 54 percent in 1992. In addition, the proportion of Vacillating Patrons who reported eating whatever they want whenever they felt like it dipped from 74 percent in 1986 to 71 percent in 1992.

Vacillating Patrons are more likely than average to frequently patronize fast-food restaurants and self-serve cafeterias or buffets. These consumers are more likely to order both nutritious foods and items high in fat and calories—reflecting their conflicting attitudes towards health and nutrition. For instance, Vacillating Patrons are more likely to order steak or roast beef, fried chicken, premium ice cream, hamburgers, fried fish or seafood, and french fries—but they're also more likely to order caffeine-free soft drinks, food cooked without salt, whole-grain muffins and reduced-calorie salad dressing.

Vacillating Patrons Shift Away from Healthy Eating

Nearly all (96 percent) Vacillating Patrons in 1992 agreed that good diet and nutrition play a role in the prevention of serious illness. However, the proportion of

Vacillating Patrons who say they are often concerned about their health has declined steadily from a peak of 86 percent in 1986 to 78 percent in 1989 and 74 percent in 1992.

In addition, 69 percent of Vacillating Patrons in 1992 agreed that fried food is bad for them, down from a peak of 72 percent in 1989. Although a greater proportion of these consumers believe fried food to be bad for them, the proportion who say they prefer broiled foods to fried foods has remained relatively steady at 80 percent.

The proportion of Vacillating Patrons who say they are tired of hearing about what's good and bad for them when it comes to food rose to 64 percent in 1992, from 57 percent in 1989.

Trends in Menu Items Ordered

Unconcerned Patrons were more likely to order rich desserts, poultry without skin and regular soft drinks in 1992 compared with 1989. These items posted double-digit gains in the proportion of Unconcerned Patrons who reported ordering the item during the previous year.

Unconcerned Patrons may be receptive to being offered more healthful dishes. This group was more likely in 1992 than in 1989 to have ordered vegetables seasoned only with herbs or lemon juice, food cooked without salt and calorie-controlled entrees (all up 7 percentage points since 1989). On the other hand, these individuals were less likely to order whole-grain muffins and fruit ices or sorbets.

Although Committed Patrons remain committed to good nutrition, these adults were more likely to order rich desserts in 1992 than in 1989 (up 13 percentage points). However, the proportion of Committed Patrons who reported ordering rich desserts in 1992 (51 percent) remains lower than the 60 percent of all consumers who ordered rich desserts.

In addition, vegetables seasoned only with herbs and lemon juice posted a 12 percentage point gain among Committed Patrons during the same period. What's more, the food items that Committed Patrons are less likely to order in 1992 include nutrition-conscious items. Committed Patrons are slightly less likely to order broiled or baked fish or seafood, a diet soft drink, sugar substitutes and raw fish or shellfish (all down 4 percentage points from 1989).

Not surprisingly, the items that Vacillating Patrons were more likely to order in 1992 include a mix of healthy and nutritious items as well as items that are higher in fat or calories. Items that posted double-digit gains since 1989 included low-fat frozen yogurt and poultry without skin, as well as regular soft drinks and fried chicken.

What Operators Can Do

A substantial proportion of consumers would like to see restaurants do more to accommodate their health and nutrition concerns. For instance, 78 percent of adults think that restaurants ought to offer different size portions for different size appetites, while 64 percent wish that more restaurants offered menu items for health-conscious customers.

Nearly six out of 10 consumers (59 percent) wish that more restaurants in their area offered food for people on restrictive diets. Specifically, consumers would like to see items made with low-fat substitutes like low-fat cheese or low-fat mayonnaise (54 percent), menu items cooked without salt (40 percent) and organic fruits and vegetables (38 percent) made available at more restaurants. In fact, a significant minority of consumers (25 percent) say they would eat out more often if it weren't so fattening.

CHARACTERISTICS OF THE THREE HEALTH AND NUTRITION CONSUMER GROUPS, 1992

	Unconcerned Patrons	Committed Patrons	Vacillating Patrons
Demographic Characteristics	Men 18 to 34 years old Average income Work full-time High school graduate/some college education Have children under 18 living in home Live in Southern states	Women 35 to 54 years old Above-average income Married Work part-time or not at all College graduate or graduate school education Live in metropolitan areas	Over 45 years old Below-average income Widowed No children under 18 in home High school graduate or less education Live in Northeastern states
Behavioral Characteristics (Members of all three groups come from all demographic and behavior segments. The characteristics presented here represent those where greater proportion than average occurs.)	Patronize fast-food restaurants Order carryout and delivery Not concerned about health Unlikely to order light and healthy menu items Do not diet for health reasons or to lose weight Do not restrict salt, additives, sugar, foods high in cholesterol or foods high in fat Do not consciously restrict foods consumption of red meat, eggs and dairy products Do not consciously consume more foods high in fiber and calcium or starchy foods, vegetables and fruits or beans and peas	Patronize moderately priced tableservice establishments Are concerned about health Likely to order light and healthy menu items Restrict diet to lose or maintain weight and to control blood cholesterol or maintain health Restrict use of salt, additives, sugar and foods high in cholesterol and fat Restrict consumption of red meet, eggs and dairy products Consume foods high in fiber as well as starchy foods Consciously eat more vegetables and fruits	Patronize fast-food restaurants and self-serve cafeteria/buffets Are concerned about health Diet to control high blood pressure and cholesterol Do not consciously restrict red meat Consume foods high in fiber and calcium Consciously eat more beans and peas
Foods Likely to Order in Restaurant (Members of all groups are likely to order any foods covered by the survey. The ones here are foods that group members have a greater likelihood of ordering compared to all consumers. Foods are shown in descending order based on the difference in mean score between the group and total consumers.)	Regular soft drink Fried chicken French fries Rich desserts Hamburger Fried fish or seafood Steak or roast beef Premium ice cream Mexican dishes Latin American dishes French dishes Italian dishes	Calorie-controlled entree Vegetarian pizza Low-fat frozen yogurt Low-fat, low-calorie fruit dessert Vegetables seasoned with herbs, lemon Reduced-calorie salad dressing Whole-grain muffins Diet soft drink Food cooked without salt Raw vegetable appetizer Caffeine-free coffee Main-dish salad with vegetables and grains	Steak or roast beef Fried chicken Caffeine-free soft drink Premium ice cream Food cooked without salt Hamburger Fried Whole-grain muffins Reduced-calorie salad dressing French fries

Source: National Restaurant Association, *Nutrition and Restaurants: A Consumer Perspective*, 1993

EAT RIGHT AMERICA: YOUR GUIDE TO ACHIEVING A LOWFAT LIFESTYLE

Evelyn Tribole

Different Folks with Different Forks

INSTEAD OF "YOU ARE WHAT you eat," it might be more fitting to say, "What you eat is because of who you are." Our eating habits and nutrition needs are influenced by our ethnicity, age, genetics, sex, lifestyle, health history and beliefs.

The effect of diet on health is not a myth. Several landmark reports, including one issued by the U.S. Surgeon General, have shown a clear relationship between what we eat and chronic disease.

Yet, despite wide acceptance of the importance of eating right, backgrounds and lifestyles can sometimes get in the way of healthy intentions. NATIONAL NUTRITION MONTH® is a good time to reassess your eating habits. Let's explore your eating style. Whatever your eating style, you can eat right and eat well. The articles in this supplement will help you make healthy choices to work in concert with the way you live.

Whether you are chasing fast food, have the urge to splurge or can savor a gourmet meal, you can eat right and love it.

What's Inside

- ▶ Your guide to eating right
- ▶ Facts and fallacies about good nutrition
- ▶ How to determine your fat allowance
- ▶ Lowfat cooking tips
- ▶ How to beat brain drain on the job
- ▶ The pleasure principle of eating right
- ▶ Steps to make meal preparation easier

About The American Dietetic Association

With a membership of 61,000, The American Dietetic Association is the largest group of food and nutrition professionals in the world. The ADA is dedicated to the promotion of optimal health and nutrition of the population.

WHAT KIND OF EATER ARE YOU?	
Eating Style	**Lifestyle**
Gulp 'n Go	Life in the fast lane. Juggling schedules and deadlines.
Gourmet/Connoisseur	Pleasure principle guides your palate. You take time to enjoy more leisurely eating.
Melting Pot	One day you're hectic, the next you have time to savor the flavors.

From Supplement to the JOURNAL OF THE AMERICAN DIETETIC ASSOCIATION, Vol. 92 by Evelyn Tribole, MS, RD. Copyright 1992 by the American Dietetic Association. Reprinted by permission.

THE BASIC FOOD GUIDE
Your Guide To Eating Right

Food Group	Suggested Daily Servings	Serving Sizes
Bread, cereals and other grain products Whole grain or enriched	6–11	1 slice bread 1 oz. ready to eat cereal 1/2 c. cooked cereal 1/2 c. pasta, rice or grits
Fruit Citrus, melons, berries, all other fruit	2–4	Whole piece of fruit 1/2 c. juice 1/4 melon or 1/2 grapefruit 1/2 c. cooked or canned fruit 1/4 c. dried fruit
Vegetables Dark green leafy, deep yellow, starchy, all other vegetables	3–5	1/2 c. cooked or chopped raw vegetable 1 c. leafy raw vegetable
Meat, poultry, fish and shellfish Egg whites, yolks, (limit yolks to 4 per week) Dried beans and peas, peanut butter	2–3 (A daily total of about 6 ounces)	2–3 oz. cooked lean meat fish or poultry 2 eggs, 4 egg whites 1 c. cooked dried beans or peas 2 tbs. peanut butter
Lowfat milk, cheese, yogurt	Children: 3–4 Teens: 3–4 Women up to 25: 3–4 Women over 25: 2–3 Men: 2–3	1 c. lowfat or skim milk 1 c. lowfat yogurt 1 1/2 oz. lowfat cheese
Fats (unsaturated) Vegetable oils, salad dressings, spreads, nuts	3–6	1 tsp. spreads and vegetable oils 1 tbs. salad dressing 1 oz. nuts
Sweets and alcoholic beverages	Consume in moderation	If you drink alcoholic beverages, health authorities recommend: Women: No more than 1 per day Men: No more than 2 per day

These food groups are the basis for your food foundation. Ironically, in the 1991 ADA Survey of American Eating Habits, only 28% of those surveyed rated themselves knowledgeable about these basic guidelines. What about you—is your food foundation solid, or could it stand some improvement?

The quality of your food choices makes a significant impact on your path to optimal nutrition and health, especially when it comes to fat and cholesterol.

Eating Like a "10"

Whether you rate your eating habits as poor or good—a "1" or a "10"—there is usually room for improvement. To build a solid foundation, arm yourself with the basic food and nutrition facts.

First, there are no "good" or "bad" foods. You can enjoy your favorite foods. What is important is to eat a wide variety of foods in moderation. Making small changes in portion sizes and giving more careful thought to what you eat over the course of a day can reap big dividends.

"As you read the guidelines in this section, just remember it is progress—not perfection—that counts," states Judy Dodd, M.S., R.D., President of The American Dietetic Association. "As long as you make some progress, you are a step ahead. So while you may strive to be a "10," focus on small steps and consistency."

Learn the Facts, Forget the Fallacies

Much has been written about the dangers of eating a diet high in fat and cholesterol. Frightening and often misleading headlines have led many to believe that drastic changes in their diets are necessary. But dietitians say there is no need to stop eating favorite foods and exist solely on bran and broccoli.

Here are the facts:

▶ **Fat Facts:** Fat is found in meat, poultry, eggs, nuts, whole-fat dairy products and vegetable oils. It is a naturally occurring substance and necessary for human life. Too little fat in your diet can be as undesirable as too much fat.

All fats contain twice as many calories as equal amounts of protein or carbohydrates, about 9 calories per gram or 120 calories per tablespoon.

Fats are made up of substances called fatty acids. Much has been learned in the past 15 years about how different fatty acids affect our overall body chemistry. The most significant finding is that eating foods high in saturated fatty acids raises blood cholesterol levels. While saturated fat is the major culprit, current research indicates that too much of any type of fat in the diet can raise the amount of cholesterol in your blood.

NOTE: All fats are high in calories that contribute to excess weight. Being overweight is in itself a risk factor for heart disease.

▶ **Saturated Fats:** Saturated fats are found primarily in meats and whole-fat dairy products. There are also some vegetable sources of saturated fats. They include palm, coconut, and palm kernel oils.

▶ **Polyunsaturated Fats:** This type of fat comes primarily from vegetable sources like corn, safflower, soybean and cotton seed oils.

▶ **Monounsaturated Fats:** These are found in large amounts in plant oils such as olive oil, canola oil, and peanut oil.

▶ **Cholesterol Facts:** CHOLESTEROL IS NOT FAT—FAT IS NOT CHOLESTEROL. Cholesterol is a substance produced by the liver and found naturally in animals, including humans. Cholesterol found in food is called dietary cholesterol. Dietary cholesterol comes from animal sources, including whole-milk dairy products, egg yolks, meats, poultry and seafood.

Plants do not contain cholesterol. However, they do contain saturated fat which can raise blood cholesterol.

Determining Your Fat Allowance

Experts recommend limiting dietary fat intake to 30% of calories. Currently, the average person gets 37–40% of their calories from fat. To understand your fat limit, you need to know your calorie limit. If you are a moderately active woman, 2,000 calories a day is a good rule; for moderately active men, 2,500 to 3,000 calories. To determine a 30% fat allowance, use the formula below.

**30% x 2,000 calories = 600 calories
divided by 9 calories per gram of fat = 66.66
or 67 grams of total fat allowable per day**

The chart below lists grams of total fat recommended per day at several different calorie levels.

Calories	Grams Of Total Fat To Stay Within 30% Limit
1,200	40
1,500	50
2,000	67
2,500	83
3,000	100

Lowfat Cooking Tips

Here are some simple tricks you can use to lighten up your home cooking without skimping on flavor.

➤ Roast, bake, grill, braise or broil meat, poultry and fish.
➤ Fry and sauté less often. Use a minimum of oil. Invest in nonstick cookware and use an aerosol cooking spray.
➤ Baste meats and poultry with stock or broth and a minimum of butter or margarine.
➤ Use marinades of lemon juice, flavored vinegars or fruit juices mixed with herbs when grilling or broiling and to tenderize leaner cuts of meat.
➤ Create sauces by adding stock or broth to pan juices and thicken by boiling rapidly for a few minutes. Season with herbs and a touch of wine.

➤ Substitute plain lowfat yogurt in dips or sauces calling for sour cream or mayonnaise. Also use lowfat yogurt to top baked potatoes and chili.
➤ Try stir-fry. Use a nonstick wok or sauté pan and a small amount of oil.
➤ Rely on your microwave to reheat left-overs and cook fish, vegetables, and poultry with a minimum of fat.
➤ Use small amounts of flavorful oils, such as olive, sesame and chili oil, to season vegetables, meats, sauces, stir-fry and sautéed dishes. Also, season cooked vegetables with herbs, lemon juice or stock.
➤ Skim fat from homemade soups by chilling and removing the fat layer that rises to the surface.
➤ Make favorite cheese-based casseroles with lowfat or reduced-fat cheese. Top with a sprinkling of sharp cheese or grated Romano for more flavor.
➤ Use ground turkey or extra lean ground beef for casseroles, spaghetti sauce, chili and skillet dishes.

The Pleasure Principle of Eating Right

Nutritious eating doesn't doom you to "nutrition martyrdom"—eating flavorless foods that taste like cardboard. Yet, there is a prevailing attitude that if it tastes good, it must not be good for you. If these thoughts mirror your attitude, you are not alone. In a 1990 Gallup Poll, a majority of adults(56%) said they didn't find eating pleasurable at

times because they worried about fat and cholesterol.

Remember, progress not perfection. One food will not make or break your health or waistline—it is what you eat on a consistent basis that matters.

Thanks to the creativity of diets and innovative dietitians, trendy, tasty foods that also are good for you seem to be popping up everywhere. A National Restaurant Association poll showed that nearly 40% of the restaurants surveyed offer menu items that are lower in calories, fat and cholesterol.

Here are some palate-pleasing examples from a variety of settings:

Fine Dining:

Herbed Grilled Swordfish

Linguini with Clam Sauce

Vegetarian Pizza

Grilled Vegetable Platter

Family Restaurant:

Soup and 1/2 Turkey Sandwich

Salad Bars

Teriyaki Grilled Chicken Breast

Seafood Stir-Fry

Fast Food:

Marinated Grilled Chicken Breast Sandwich

Tossed Salad with Seafood

Grilled Fish Sandwich

10 Ways to Beat Brain Drain on the Job

1. Don't leave home without it—breakfast.
2. Space your meals throughout the day. Go no longer than five hours without eating.
3. Snack on lowfat foods when there's no time for lunch.
4. Pack your desk and briefcase with snacks such as lowfat crackers, pretzels or juice boxes.
5. Drinks lots of water. Also, contribute to your daily water needs (minimum eight cups) by drinking herbal teas or hot water with a twist of lemon.
6. Limit coffee to two cups a day. Too much coffee can drain vital fluids. Caffeine is a diuretic which causes the body to lose water.
7. Pass on the doughnuts, except as a special treat. Try bagels and fresh fruit for a breakfast on the run.
8. Keep power lunches light. Overeating during midday can cause drowsiness.
9. Take five—a five-minute walk or stress break beats eating to ease stress.
10. Keep the office kitchen stocked with energizing snacks such as nonfat yogurt, snack-size cereals, lowfat cheeses and single servings of water-packed tuna.

Quick Shopping Smart Shopping

Whether you are a frequent grocery shopper or an "only by necessity" drop-in, here are some quick tips for adding a health advantage to your shopping cart.

▶ **Produce:** Fruits and vegetables are low in fat and high in fiber. Buy the freshest possible produce for top nutrition.

▶ **Cereals:** Whole-grain cereals are a good choice for fiber and nutrition. Check labels. Some cereals, such as granola, may have hidden fat.

▶ **Dairy Case:** Choose skim milk, buttermilk, evaporated skim milk, nonfat dry milk and lowfat plain yogurt. Look for lower fat variations of cheese favorites including ricotta, pot or farmer cheese, skim-milk mozzarella and cottage cheese. Check the labels of new lowfat cheeses to be sure they fit your nutrition standards.

▶ **Frozen Foods:** Choose frozen fruits and vegetables without sauces, lowfat frozen yogurt, ice milk, and fruit-juice bars. Check the labels of frozen entrées and select items that fit within your daily fat allowance. Limit fried foods, cream sauces and high-fat baked items such as puff pastry, croissants and doughnuts.

▶ **Meats:** All cuts should be lean and trimmed of visible fat.

Choose the following:

Beef—round, loin, sirloin and extra lean ground beef

Lamb—leg, arm, loin, rib

Pork—tenderloin, leg, shoulder

Turkey/Chicken—skinless

Fish and Shellfish

▶ **General:** Stock up on pasta, noodles and rice, especially some of the whole-grain selections. Try incorporating cornmeal, bulgur, barley and other grains into recipes. Include dried and canned beans, split peas, lentils and chickpeas. Supplement fresh fruits and vegetables with frozen fruits, vegetables and juices.

▶ **Breads:** Along with enriched white products, add the flavor and nutrition Of whole-grain breads, English muffins, bagels and crackers. Remember the available variety of rice cakes, lower fat muffins and Pita bread.

▶ **The Deli:** Select sliced turkey or chicken, lean ham, turkey-based substitutes and lowfat cheeses, instead of the usual "luncheon meats." Limit use of high-fat, high-sodium processed sausages and meats, hot dogs, bacon and salami.

▶ **Fats and Oils:** All of these choices should be used sparingly. Select unsaturated vegetable oils for cooking and reduced or lowfat salad dressings and lowfat mayonnaise. Limit use of butter, cream cheese and margarine.

Family Ties: Who's Doing the Cooking?

If Ozzie and Harriet reflected today's family eating style, Harriet would be arriving home from a full day's work and one of the Nelson boys would have shopped for the week's groceries. Instead of eating dinner together every night, the Nelson family would be sitting down together for only two out of three suppers.

The typical American family is changing. Consider these statistics:

► Among children aged 6 to 14, 65% prepare food for themselves at least once a week.
► In 70% of households where both (or single) parents work, teenagers do much of the grocery shopping.
► 44% of all grocery shoppers are men and 85% of them shop for the family.

So, who's doing the cooking? Rather than Mom slaving over a hot stove, meals may come from fast-food restaurants, supermarket take-out or the family freezer. It is no surprise that frozen dinner and entrée sales are expected to increase by 48% to reach $7.5 billion by the end of the century. Whether you eat out or order in, remember your food basics and choose wisely.

Simple Strategies to Save Time

► **Planning:** It's an essential key. Delegate tasks among family members, each taking responsibility to plan at least one meal per week. Not only will it save you time, it will teach organizational skills to younger family members. Even preschoolers can be involved in the planning process. Let them choose the vegetable or side dish.

► **Shopping:** Begin with a grocery list, then try any of these options:

Divide and conquer: Shop as a family. Consider using two shopping carts and cover separate areas of the store to cut your time in half.

Delegate: Assign the shopping to one person and take turns.

Delivery: Take advantage of stores where you can phone or fax in an order.

► **Preparation and Cooking:** Cook together: Try do-it-yourself meals with homestyle taco bars or build-your-own salads, where everyone can customize his or her own meal.

Batch cook: Make several casseroles or a big pot of soup—serve that night and freeze extra in family-size or individual servings.

► **Stock Up on "Grab-and-Eat" Foods:** Have plenty of fruit and cut-up raw vegetables on hand. Freeze fresh breads and rolls to be quickly defrosted for fast, fresh sandwiches made with lean sliced meats from the deli. Juice bars and frozen yogurt make quick, healthy desserts.

10 Ways to Reduce Dietary Fat

1. Drink skim milk. If you drink whole milk, wean yourself gradually to 2% to 1% to skim.

2. Use jam, jelly or marmalade on bread and toast instead of butter or margarine.
3. Buy whole-grain and freshly baked breads and rolls. They have more flavor and do not need butter or margarine to taste good.
4. Eat more pasta, rice, potatoes, grains and vegetables. Use these foods as the centerpiece of your meals.
5. Choose lean meat, fish and poultry. Remove skin from chicken.
6. Choose a vegetarian entrée at least once a week.
7. Top your salads with lowfat or fat-free salad dressings.
8. Snack on fresh fruit and vegetables, plain popcorn, pretzels or rice cakes instead of fried chips and cookies.
9. For dessert, choose fruit, angel food or sponge cake. Use fruit purées to top cake.
10. Substitute lowfat frozen yogurt or sherbet for ice cream. Try frozen juice bars.

Remember the Basics

Eating right means having a wide variety of foods in moderation every day. There are no good or bad foods. There are only bad eating habits.

Puzzled by Nutrition?

It's easy to be confused about nutrition. Scientists are continually discovering new benefits in some foods and causes for concern in others. A registered dietitian is the food and nutrition expert who can separate facts from fads and translate the latest scientific breakthroughs into practical food choices.

Your life already is touched by registered dietitians in more ways than you may realize. They work with food companies to develop new products, with restaurants to create healthy menus, and with the media to communicate nutrition-smart information. You'll find them in healthcare, business, and education. They're in hospitals and health clubs, colleges and cafeterias, research labs and private practices, daycare facilities and senior centers.

The letters "R.D" after a person's name signify that she or he has at least a baccalaureate degree and training in dietetics or a related area at an accredited college or university, and has demonstrated competency in a national registration examination. Many registered dietitians also hold advanced degrees.

To find a registered dietitian, contact your physician, local hospital, state or local dietetic association, or write to the National Center for Nutrition and Dietetics at 216 West Jackson Boulevard, Suite 800, Chicago, Illinois 60606-6995.

10 Tips for Successful Waist Management

1. Start with a commitment. (A goal to lose ten pounds for a class reunion is not a long-term commitment.)
2. Identify your major problem area. A food journal logging when, where, what and why you eat would be helpful.
3. Be realistic. Don't expect to lose ten pounds of fat in one week. (This would require a daily deficit of 5,000 calories!)
4. Fight the "quick-fix" temptation of crash diets. They usually don't work and result mostly in water-weight loss.
5. Don't put your lifestyle on hold to "go on a diet"; it ignores the real challenges such as sweet attacks, eating out, alcohol, and exercise.
6. Choose a plan you could realistically follow for a lifetime. Be sure it includes foods you like.
7. Exercise—but choose an activity you enjoy.
8. Remember that weight plateaus are normal. Focus on your progress and remember where you started.
9. Keep in mind that one food indiscretion does not make or break your weight. It is what you eat on a regular basis that counts.
10. Don't skip meals. Skipping meals can make you hungrier and you may end up overeating, regardless of your intentions.

12 SECRETS OF PEAK NUTRITION: THE DOCTORS' EATING PLAN FOR TOTAL HEALTH

Susan Zarrow

THERE IS CERTAINLY NO shortage of self-proclaimed nutrition "experts" out there, from fitness gurus who make millions selling worthless supplement powders and pills to next-door neighbors who claim that eating white bread will send you to an early grave.

Who has the time to weigh all the contradictory advice, much less judge the validity of its source? Not you. And anyway, that's what you pay us for.

To get straight answers for our readers, we surveyed 300 of the nation's top nutrition experts—not the self-appointed kind, but the ones doing important research at major hospitals and universities. Medical Consensus Surveys™, a research arm of Rodale Press, asked the experts to rate 44 nutritional actions (all purported to benefit health) as follows: Extremely Important, Very Important, Important, Not Important, or Probably Worthless.

What we were after was a list of priorities, a simple guide to making smart nutritional choices. For example, should you put a lot of energy into reducing the amount of cholesterol in your diet? The amount of salt? Or is it more important to avoid pesticides, irradiated food or alcohol?

The nutritionists' responses were then compiled and statistically weighted to create a list of dietary priorities that's both clear and practical. "We could easily have an enormous advance in the health of America if we could simply follow these guidelines," says George L. Blackburn, M.D., Ph.D., chief of the Nutrition/Metabolism Laboratory at New England Deaconess Hospital in Boston.

Here, in order of importance, are the nutritional steps most vital to your healthy diet, and the stuff that's not worth worrying about:

Get the fat out. The experts were almost unanimous in putting weight control at the top of the list—97 percent of them gave it high priority.

"If everybody in the United States maintained his ideal weight, the incidence of type-II diabetes would be greatly reduced, hypertension would be much less common and so would coronary disease," says Meir Stampfer, M.D., associate professor of epidemiology at Harvard School of Public Health.

Nearly 24 percent of American men are overweight for their age and build, which makes obesity one of the country's biggest health problems.

How do the experts recommend we lose weight? Seventy-five percent said that cutting calories is Extremely Important or Very Important; 70 percent said the same about controlling fat intake. The two go hand in hand: If you cut calories, you'll cut fat. The number of calories you eat ultimately determines how much you'll weigh, but reducing fat is important for other reasons: It slashes the risk of heart disease by keeping arteries from choking with plaque, and it may reduce the risk of some forms of cancer.

Eat and run (. . . or walk, or bike). Strictly speaking, exercise isn't a nutritional habit, but we included it in our survey because physical activity has a direct bearing on how much we eat and on what happens to food once we've taken it in. The experts affirmed this view, and then some. Eighty-four percent gave high priority to exercising more. "It's hard to reduce your weight by controlling calories alone," says Dr. Stampfer. "If you exercise as well, you're more likely to be able to maintain the weight loss in the long run."

Exercise boosts your metabolism, allowing you to eat more without putting on more pounds. It also helps relieve stress and keep your heart, bones and circulatory system in top form.

Most people can fill their exercise quota with 20 minutes of brisk walking three times a week. Adding a regimen of resistance weight training fires up your metabolism to its calorie-burning peak.

If you don't like it, don't eat it. Giving up all your favorite foods and switching to a very healthy but very boring diet won't work. Kelly Brownell, Ph.D., professor of psychology at Yale University and a top obesity researcher, says he and others have worked with dieters and found that the most punishing methods inevitably fail.

Nobody is going to eat food they don't enjoy for very long. If you want to eat healthy, you either have to find low-fat prepared foods that taste great or learn to cook your own.

Keep it balanced, but lean. You've heard the old nutritionist's creed: Balance your diet among the four food groups and make sure you get the Recommended Dietary Allowance (RDA) of vitamins and minerals. These concepts are certainly not passé; roughly 90 percent of those surveyed said they're still high priority. Yet those notions now clearly take a back seat to cutting fat and controlling weight

The weakness of the four-food-groups approach is that it doesn't provide enough guidance to prevent you from eating too much fat and amassing it on your body.

If you make fat-fighting your number-one priority, however, it quite naturally leads you toward fulfilling those other guidelines. "If you phase out the high-calorie, high-fat foods in your diet, you're going to have to replace them with something low-fat—cereals, fruits and vegetables," says Dr. Blackburn. An emphasis on those foods moves you closer to meeting your RDA for vitamins and minerals. It can also move you closer to balancing your diet, which for most Americans is overladen with high-fat meat and dairy products.

Don't sweat the technicalities. If you've never been able to keep straight the difference between saturated, unsaturated, monounsaturated and polyunsaturated fats, here's good news: You don't have to. The trendy notion that you should trade saturated fats for heart-smarter mono-and polyunsaturated ones is "putting

the cart before the horse," according to Dr. Blackburn. Most of the foods that are highest in total fat—ice cream, cheeseburgers and doughnuts, for example—are also highest in saturated fat. So if you simply cut down on all fatty foods, you'll cut down on saturated fat as well.

How much fat should you eat? The nutritionists advise following the American Heart Association's recommendation that total dietary fat be limited to no more than 30 percent of calories.

Let cholesterol take care of itself. Cutting cholesterol scored surprisingly low. Only 14 percent of the experts rated it Extremely Important. It's not that cholesterol is insignificant but, again, if you follow the priorities outlined above, you'll have already taken care of it. Those polled felt that excessive concern about this issue to the exclusion of all others could lead you to eat foods that are low in cholesterol but still dangerously high in fat. For example, potato chips fried in vegetable oil contain no cholesterol, but 72 percent of their calories are from fat

Don't fear saying "cheers"—occasionally. The nation's top nutritionists plainly don't support prohibition. But they're staunch believers in moderation when it comes to alcohol. "There's no evidence, unless you are driving, that drinking alcohol in limited quantities is bad for you," says Judith S. Stern, Sc.D., RD., professor of nutrition at the University of California-Davis. Alcohol in excess (more than two drinks per day) is another story: It may destroy livers as well as lives.

Practice safe eating. While many people are worried about pesticides on fruit and vegetables, the experts rated it 34 out of 44 on their list of priorities.

More than three-quarters of the nutritionists thought it wise to avoid raw foods, particularly eggs, meat and seafood. Raw eggs and chicken can harbor salmonella bacteria, a common cause of food poisoning. Raw seafood can harbor viruses or parasites. Buy only from a reputable dealer or avoid raw seafood altogether.

Get more fiber. Insoluble or soluble? It doesn't matter how you get your fiber. What's important is just that you do get it. "People eat so little fiber, we'll take anything," says Dr. Blackburn. "Whatever you can find—some peas in your stew—put them in!"

A high-fiber diet fills you up without filling you out, keeps you regular, helps lower your cholesterol level and may help reduce the risk of colon cancer. The nutritionists advocate getting at least 20 grams per day. A breakfast of oatmeal, whole-wheat toast, a pear and a banana would give you more than half that amount. The highest-fiber foods are fruits, vegetables, whole grains and legumes.

Eat more surf, less turf. Fish is lower in saturated fat than meat, and the oil in fish—especially cold-water varieties such as salmon and mackerel—helps your cardiovascular system by keeping blood from clotting and preventing hardening of the arteries. If you do eat meat, the experts recommend limiting portions to 3 or 4 ounces, choosing lean cuts such as flank steak, and using low-fat cooking methods such as broiling and braising.

Don't join the Scare-of-the-Month Club. Many nutrition hazards you read or hear about on the 11 o'clock news aren't worth paying attention to, according to our experts. For example, avoiding trans-fatty acids (found in stick margarine) and tropical oils drew only moderate priority ratings from the nutrition authorities, despite their getting big play in the news. Again, it's much more important to lower *total* fat intake.

The experts also said most of us need not worry about sugar. It's a problem for people who are obese (it's got lots of calories but little nutrition) or diabetic (they can't metabolize it properly). For the rest of us, though, avoiding sugar is only of moderate importance.

Rated among the lowest was avoiding irradiated food—68% percent of respondents put this among the Probably Worthless, right down there with avoiding charred or

FOOD FACTS, FOOD FADS

How our experts rated nutrition strategies

Score	High Priority
79	Control calories to control weight
76	Reduce all dietary fats
71	Increase physical activity
71	Enjoy your food
70	Eat a balanced diet
69	Get the RDAs of vitamins and minerals
65	Reduce saturated fats
65	Limit alcohol intake
63	Avoid raw eggs, meat and seafood
62	Boost fiber to 20 grams per day
61	Eat fish instead of meat
	Low Priority
16	Make breakfast the biggest meal
14	Avoid irradiated foods
13	Avoid charred or blackened foods

The numbers indicate how valuable our 300-plus experts think these actions are for a healthy diet. The higher the number, the greater the action's importance.

blackened foods. Apparently these nutritionists feel neither poses any significant health risk.

Stop watching the clock. Our experts gave only a moderate Priority rating to avoiding snacks and eating three square meals a day. It seems the nutrition masters are trying to tell us something: What you eat is much more important than how or when you eat.

Write and present a marketing plan to a General Manager of a Hotel or Resort to improve the existing menu by incorporating six new "healthy" menu items and writing a fitness plan for guests and employees.

Evaluation Criteria
for the Integration of a Healthy Menu
and Activities for
Guests and Employees

Presentation

Introduction: interesting beginning and overview
Body: 1) analysis of key marketing factors
        2) general objectives
        3) strategies to take advantage of the marketing factors and achieve the objectives
Conclusion: a summary of the high points in the body of the presentation.

Length of time of the presentation
Vocal variety
Body language during the presentation
Professional: what type of visual aids were used?
Creative, 1–10?
Sound research backing the plan?

Written Report

Were each of the items listed below identified and analyzed?

1. Nutritional analysis of the current menu. A summary of the recipes and menu items to include the total calories, grams of protein, fat, and carbohydrates, and milligrams of cholesterol and sodium. The nutrients may be analyzed manually or by the use of a computer. Guideline: offer 700 to 800 calories, 12–15 percent protein, less than thirty percent fat, 50 to 60 percent carbohydrates, less than 1000 milligrams of cholesterol, and less than 1200 milligrams of Sodium.

2. Nutritional analysis of six new menu items. A summary of the recipes and menu items to include the total calories, grams of protein, fat and carbohydrates, and milligrams of cholesterol and sodium. The nutrients may be analyzed manually or by the use of a computer. Guideline: offer 700 to 800 calories, 12–15 percent protein, less than thirty percent fat, 50 to 60 percent carbohydrates, less than 1000 milligrams of cholesterol, and less than 1200 milligrams of Sodium.

3. Fitness Plan. Report existing opportunities. Develop new opportunities to supplement existing fitness opportunities.

4. Executive summary of the marketing plan, is it focused?

5. Internal analysis; is material supplied concerning the current marketing, management and finance strategies?

6. Environmental analysis; is there a remote and operating analysis?

7. SWOT analysis; what are the: strengths, weaknesses, opportunities, and threats at this property?

8. Opportunities, problems, and issues, what are they?

9. Objectives; quantify them, are they stated succinctly?

10. Strategies; how is the marketing plan going to be positioned with the marketing mix variables?

11. Marketing action plan; are the following questions answered: what, when, where, budget and responsibility of the plan. Are tactics in place to achieve the strategy?

This project focuses on the dietary habits of different ethnic groups. Choose two different ethnic groups to study. Library references such as books and journals will be useful to gather data. Personal interviews with several people from each of the cultures is also important. International student groups or Consulates would be good locations to meet people from a variety of cultures. Students should write a report about the dietary habits of each of the cultures studied. The report should be supported with several journal articles and interviews. Supply references to your paper.

Examples of possible questions to ask during an interview.

What were the indigenous foods to this culture?

What changes have taken place to these indigenous foods?

What words accurately describe the tastes, aromas, flavors, colors and textures of the food from this culture?

What impact does religion or religious festivals have on food?

Are there any food taboos?

What food preparation and eating habits are common in this culture?

What are the food differences between your own culture and the ethnic culture you are studying?

Are there different dining traditions at home versus in a public site?

How much importance is placed on nutrition?

2

SANITATION

The Seven Steps in a HACCP System
HACCP Reference Book

Battling Aids
Jennifer Batty

Project 1

Project 2

The Seven Steps in a HACCP System

*Steps 1–2 help you design your system; Steps 3–5 help you implement it;
Steps 6–7 help you maintain it and verify its effectiveness.*

Step 1: Assessing Hazards

IDENTIFY THE POTENTIALLY hazardous foods in your recipes. To assess the danger that a foodborne illness might occur, review your operation's capacity to handle these foods safely.

1.1 Identify Potentially Hazardous Foods

Review your menus and recipes and identify the potentially hazardous foods you serve, as shown in Exhibit 1. Remember that potentially hazardous foods may be served as separate items and as ingredients in recipes. For example, meat is often served as an ingredient in chili or sauces as well as a separate item.

1.2 Recognizing the Flow of Food

The *flow of food* is the path that foods travel in your operation. The sequence may include the:

- ► Decision to include an item on the menu.
- ► Development of the recipe.
- ► Purchase of ingredients and supplies.
- ► Delivery of ingredients and supplies.
- ► Storage of ingredients and supplies.
- ► Preparation—thawing, processing, and cooking.
- ► Holding or display of food.
- ► Service of food.
- ► Cooling and storing food.
- ► Reheating for service.

As this list shows, the flow of food begins well before the food is prepared for service and involves many decisions as well as actions. To help you focus on the hazards, the HACCP system provides a series of steps for setting up controls.

1.3 Identify Hazards

Now that you have selected foods in your operation, you need to discover any hazards (contamination, survival, growth) that could develop from the ingredients and the way these foods are handled and used in your recipes. So start with your recipe (see Exhibits 2 and 3 on pages 29 and 30, respectively). In addition to the information you gather from studying recipes, observe your employees in action, seek additional facts by interviewing employees, measure temperatures, test foods, and review records.

1.4 Estimate Risks

Review your operation's capacity to control the hazards involved in the foods you serve. If you serve a large number of potentially hazardous foods and use complicated recipes to prepare them, several factors can increase the chance of foodborne illness:

1. **Type of Customer.** Who are your customers? Young, elderly, or immuno-suppressed customers may have very low resistance to foodborne illness. You need to assess who your customers are and plan accordingly.
2. **Suppliers.** You need reputable, and in some cases certified, suppliers for all

EXHIBIT 1—SAMPLE INSTITUTIONAL MENU

Dinner
St. Andrew's Hospital

(Please Check ✔ Your Selections)

Soup

☐ *Hearty Beef Noodle*   ☐ *New England-Style Clam Chowder*

Salads and Dressings

☐ Great Garden Salad—mixed greens,   ☐ Fresh seasonal fruits—strawberries,
green and black olives, tomatoes,   green grapes, and apple slices
chives, and *hard-boiled egg*

Dressing— ☐ Raspberry vinaigrette, ☐ Peppered Ranch, ☐ Spicy French, ☐ Oil and vinegar

Entrées (Select one)

☐ *Baked Pork Chop* with Hot Apple Compote   ☐ *Swiss Steak* with *French-cut Green Beans*
☐ *Poached Salmon* with Lemon Butter Sauce   ☐ *Vegetarian Lasagna* with Garlic Bread

Breads and Spreads

☐ White Bread   ☐ Whole Wheat   ☐ Chale
☐ *Whipped Butter*   ☐ Margarine   ☐ Apple Butter

Sweet Treats

☐ *Frozen Strawberry Yogurt*   ☐ Apple Crumb Cake
☐ *Vanilla Ice Cream*   ☐ Lemon Sherbet

Beverages

☐ Coffee   ☐ Decaffeinated coffee   ☐ Iced Tea
☐ *Whole Milk*   ☐ *Low Fat Milk*   ☐ Non-Dairy Creamer

Hot Tea ☐ Orange Pekoe   Herbal Tea ☐ Chamomile   ☐ Sparkling Water
        ☐ Black   ☐ Apple Spice

Seasonings

☐ Salt   ☐ Pepper   ☐ Sugar   ☐ Lemon
☐ Ketchup   ☐ Mustard   ☐ Mayonnaise

Name _____   Room _____

Potentially hazardous food are italicized.

EXHIBIT 2—NEW ENGLAND-STYLE CLAM CHOWDER

Yield: 3 gallons (11.36 l)

Ingredients	Weights and Measures	
Chowder Soup Base (frozen)	2 1/4 gal	8.52 l
Clams (canned)	4—15 oz cans	425 g cans
Vegetables (pre-cut, washed)	6 lbs	2.72 kg

Preparation
1. Thaw base under refrigeration.
2. Drain clams.
3. Combine thawed base, clams, and vegetables in a stockpot.

Cooking
4. Simmer ingredients. Stir frequently and skim surface as necessary.

Serving and Holding
5. Serve immediately, or hold for service.

Recipe adapted with permission from *The New Professional Chef,* Fifth Edition. Copyright © 1991 by the Culinary Institute of America. Published by Van Nostrand Reinhold, NY.

potentially hazardous items, such as exotic fish. Shellfish, in particular, must be purchased only from suppliers that appear on public health service Food and Drug Administration lists of Certified Shellfish Shippers or on lists of state-approved sources. In addition, processors of food should employ verified HACCP systems.

3. **Size and Type of Operation.** You need proper equipment and facilities if you plan to serve complicated or multi-step recipes. Check your equipment for its capacity and ability to maintain or produce proper temperatures. You may decide that if the recipe is too difficult to handle from scratch, you may purchase it in a pre-prepared form.

4. **Employees.** Employees need to be trained in the proper handling and preparation of food. It is also necessary to provide them with the proper equipment and materials to do their job well.

Step 2: Identifying Critical Control Points

Your analysis probably revealed a number of potential hazards of varying risk. The next step in developing a HACCP system is to identify critical control points in the flow of food and in your recipes (see Exhibit 3).

In determining critical control points, draw a flowchart of the preparation of each ingredient and the combined mixture.

2.2 Designing Your Flowcharts

A visual way to follow the flow of food in your establishment is to create a diagram called a *flowchart* (see Exhibit 4 on page 31). This chart is very helpful in analyzing your procedures. It illustrates the flow of food and critical control points in a one-page format. A flowchart follows a recipe item from the point where the ingredients are received to service.

Critical control points differ for each kind of food and method of preparation. Although critical control points are not necessary at every stage in the flow of food, they are necessary at one or more stages. For example, raw chicken may carry *Salmonella* when it is received—even if it is received at the proper temperature. Because the *Salmo-*

EXHIBIT 3—NEW ENGLAND-STYLE CLAM CHOWDER WITH CCPs ADDED

Yield: 3 gallons (11.36 l)

Ingredients	Weights and Measures	
Chowder Soup Base (frozen)	2 1/4 gal	8.52 l
Clams (canned)	4—15 oz cans	425 g cans
Vegetables (pre-cut, washed)	6 lbs	2.72 kg

Preparation

1. Thaw base under refrigeration.
2. Drain clams.
3. Combine thawed base, clams, and vegetables in a stockpot.

Cooking

CCP 4. Simmer ingredients **until a final product temperature of 140°F (60°C) is reached.** Stir frequently and skim surface as necessary.

Serving and Holding

CCP 5. Serve immediately, or **hold for service at 140°F (60°C) or higher.** Do not mix new product with old.

Transporting

CCP 6. **Hold for transporting at 140° (60°C) or higher** for no longer than 30 minutes.

Cooling

CCP 7. **Cool to 45°F (7.2°C) or lower within 4 hours** in shallow pans with a product depth of 2 inches or less.

8. Store at a product temperature of 45°F (7.2°C) or lower in refrigerated unit. Cover.

Reheating

CCP 9. **Reheat chowder to a product temperature of 165°F (73.9°C) or higher within 2 hours.**

Sanitation Instructions: Measure all temperatures with a thermocouple. Wash hands before handling food, after handling raw foods, and after any interruption that may contaminate hands. Wash, rinse, and sanitize all equipment and utensils before and after use. Return all ingredients to refrigerated storage, if preparation is interrupted.

CCPs are highlighted in boldface.

Recipe adapted with permission from *The New Professional Chef, Fifth Edition.* Copyright © 1991 by the Culinary Institute of America. Published by Van Nostrand Reinhold, NY.

Exhibit 4—Flowchart for Clam Chowder (Institutional)

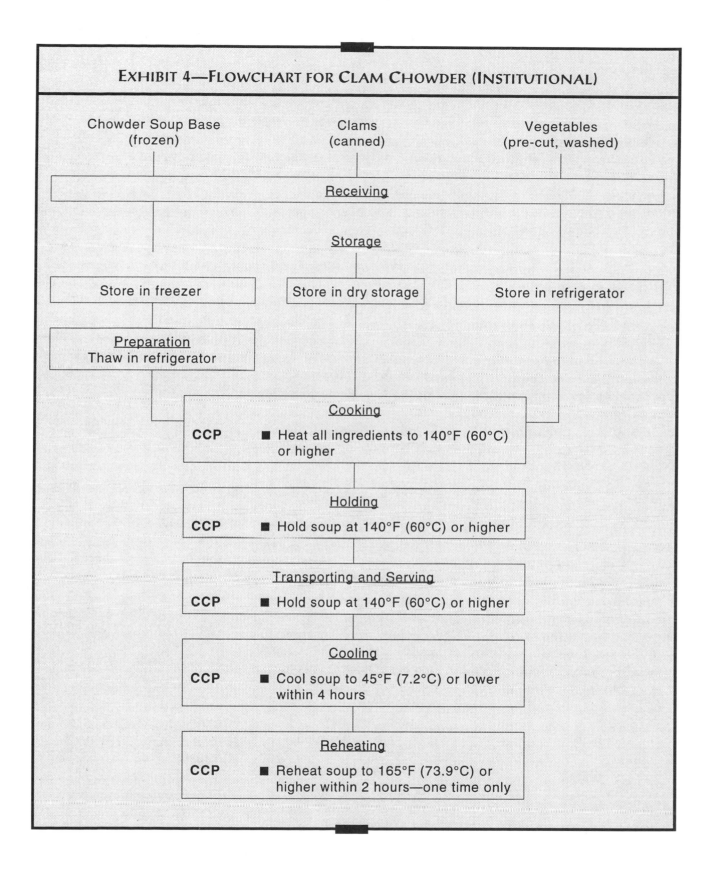

Chowder Soup Base (frozen)   Clams (canned)   Vegetables (pre-cut, washed)

Receiving

Storage

Store in freezer   Store in dry storage   Store in refrigerator

Preparation
Thaw in refrigerator

Cooking

CCP ■ Heat all ingredients to 140°F (60°C) or higher

Holding

CCP ■ Hold soup at 140°F (60°C) or higher

Transporting and Serving

CCP ■ Hold soup at 140°F (60°C) or higher

Cooling

CCP ■ Cool soup to 45°F (7.2°C) or lower within 4 hours

Reheating

CCP ■ Reheat soup to 165°F (73.9°C) or higher within 2 hours—one time only

nella, at receiving, may not be eliminated, reduced, or minimized, receiving is only a control point at which you check for proper temperatures and keep the time the product is kept out of storage to a minimum. It is later in the flow of food—during the cooking process—that the *Salmonella* is eliminated, which makes cooking a critical control point.

Step 3: Setting Up Control Procedures and Standards for Critical Control Points

At this step in the process, you establish the standards (criteria) that must be met for each critical control point. Remember that, in order to keep food safe, there may be more than one standard for each critical control point. To be effective, each of your standards should be:

▶ Based on proven facts from experience, research data, or food regulations.
▶ Appropriate for the food in question under the normal working conditions in the restaurant, such as equipment temperatures, number of employees, and number of orders to be filled.
▶ Focused on a measurable or observable criteria to be monitored, such as temperature and time.
▶ Specific. Use precise nouns and action verbs and include exact criteria for meeting the standard. For example, a standard for reheating chili should be "Heat rapidly on stove top to an internal temperature

of 165°F (73.9°C) within two hours."

In addition to standards established for critical control points, you should develop standards to prevent contamination at other points in the flow of food. For example, while preparing a baked whitefish dish, a standard to prevent cross-contamination from other food items being prepared at the same time may read "Use clean and sanitized utensils (that have not been used for raw food) to handle cooked fish."

Step 4: Monitoring Critical Control Points

Monitoring (checking to see that criteria are met) is one of the most important aspects and activities involved in the HACCP system. Having critical control points is meaningless without monitoring.

In monitoring, you should:

▶ Focus on critical control points throughout the flow of food.
▶ Determine whether criteria are being met.
▶ Involve employees responsible for following the procedures and monitoring. For example, you need to observe your chef's food preparation procedures for any differences between the procedures you have designed into the recipes and what the cook is actually doing.

Step 5: Taking Corrective Actions

When you discover that criteria for a critical control point are not being met, a corrective action must be carried out **immediately**. Many corrective actions are very simple and limited, such as to sanitize a utensil, or continue heating food to a specified temperature. Other corrective actions may be more involved, such as rejecting a shipment.

To be effective, corrective actions must adjust the procedure to meet the criteria listed above for standards: they must be applicable in daily operations, focused on measurable factors, and clearly worded. For example, the standard for holding baked chicken breast may read:

▶ Hold baked chicken breast at 140°F (60°C) or higher until served.

The corrective action if the standard is not met may read:

▶ If held over two hours, discard; if less than two hours and temperature falls below 140°F (60°C), reheat to 165°F (73.9°C).

Step 6: Setting Up a Record-Keeping System

The records your employees need to keep should be accessible, simple, something they can do quickly, and scheduled so they are able to maintain them. Possible systems include:

- Blank forms and a clipboard to be used when following the flow of food and documenting corrective actions (see Exhibit 5).
- Notebook to be used to store documentation and refer to corrective actions.
- Regular monitoring for times and temperatures.
- HACCP systems, flowcharts and recipes kept up-to-date and easily available to the employees. These materials can also be put in a notebook or fastened to the wall near work areas.
- Written logs that are completed at the time the process considered a critical control point is carried out.

Accurate records have at least two important benefits. First, they provide a source of information about daily operations and long-term trends. Second, by showing that criteria are being met and that your operation is addressing problems, you create a record that may be valuable if a food-borne illness should occur.

The HACCP System

After you have developed your flowcharts and added CCPs to your recipes, it is time to create your written HACCP system. (See Exhibit 6 on page 35 for a sample section of a HACCP System.) However, this does not involve as much time and effort as it may seem at first. Similar recipes requiring similar procedures for handling and preparation, can be combined or use basically the same information in several systems. For example, the procedures for preparing chicken noodle soup and beef noodle soup are similar.

Seven types of information identified in HACCP systems are:

- Operational Step (purchasing, receiving, storage, preparation, cooking, holding, cooling, and reheating).
- Hazards (bacterial growth or survival, cross-contamination, chemical or physical contamination).
- Critical Control Points.
- Standards (criteria).
- Types of Monitoring.
- Corrective Actions.
- Records.

Step 1

Document your findings in a list that identifies each potentially hazardous food and its use as a separate item or as an ingredient in a recipe.

Identify the possible hazards at each step. Consider possible contaminants that may possibly be on or in each ingredient and that may be introduced at any handling procedure. Also consider possible bacterial growth during storage or holding and possible survival during cooking and reheating.

Watch present preparation practices; measure temperatures of foods during and at the completion of thawing, cold storage, cooking, hot holding, cooling, and reheating to identify additional hazards and estimate risks. Remember that employees may modify practices, while being watched. Repeat observation

as necessary. Confirm any doubts or questions that come to mind during recipe review. Foodservice managers may consider replacing potentially hazardous ingredients or items, simplifying recipes, monitoring and verifying control measures, or purchasing pre-prepared items from a reputable source that employs HACCP systems.

Step 2

Insert CCPs into your flowchart and system for each recipe. Enter the hazards that must be controlled.

Step 3

Add standards. Instruct your employees to begin following the procedures specified in the flowcharts and revised recipes. Be sure you and your supervisors are available to answer questions and help solve problems your employees may encounter.

Step 4

Decide on monitoring procedures for each critical control point. Monitor whether standards are being met.

Step 5

Be sure to implement any corrective actions promptly. After a corrective action has occurred, document it to make your system more effective.

EXHIBIT 5. SAMPLE LOG FOR HACCP RECORD KEEPING

Hazard Analysis Critical Control Point Worksheet

Date: [mo.] [day] [yr.] TIME: Start [ ] : [ ] A.M./P.M. End [ ] : [ ] A.M./P.M.

Product _____

Ingredients _____
_____

Sources _____
_____

Time	Temp	Procedure/Observation	Comment/Interpretation

Time/Temperature (°F) Chart

Product Flow Chart

Name of Inspector/Manager _____

Time in Hours

Source: Adapted from New York State Department of Health, Bureau of Community Sanitation and Food Protection. Albany, NY.

Step 6

Set up a record-keeping system. Document monitoring critical control points, occasions when criteria are not met, and all corrective actions taken.

Step 7: Verifying That the System Is Working

Once your system is implemented, you need to *verify* (confirm) that it is effective over time. Both internal (quality control) and external (health department) verifications are useful.

Deciding to Revise Your System

You need to return to your HACCP systems and revise as necessary. You may decide at this time to purchase a pre-prepared item because even revising the recipe and flow-chart will not correct the problems that are occurring. You should check to see if you have:

▶ Listed operations sequentially.
▶ Identified and assessed all hazards.
▶ Selected critical control points.
▶ Set criteria.
▶ Selected monitoring procedures and specified times of monitoring.
▶ Specified corrective actions.
▶ Decided on procedures and forms for recording monitoring data.
▶ Determined procedures to verify that monitoring is being done effectively.
▶ Determined procedures for employees if they are not following criteria and decided if additional training is needed.
▶ Noted any flaws or omissions in procedures.

EXHIBIT 6. A HACCP SYSTEM FOR CLAM CHOWDER					STEP: COOKING	
Operational Step	Hazard	CCP	Standard (Criteria)	Type of Monitoring	Corrective Action if Standard Not Met	Records
Cooking Soup	Bacterial survival due to inadequate cooking	CCP	Cook all ingredients to 165°F (73.9°C) or higher.	Cook will measure final cooking temperature with a thermocouple.	Continue cooking soup to 165°F (73.9°C) or higher.	Chef's cooking log
	Contamination from cook's hands or mouth		Use proper tasting procedures.	Observation	Discard contaminated product.	
				Supervision and one-on-one training	Review proper procedure with cook, and verify cook's training record.	
	Cross-contamination		Use clean and sanitized utensils for stirring.	Observation	Discard contaminated product.	
				Observation	Wash, rinse, and sanitize all utensils in accordance with standard operating procedures.	
				Supervision and one-on-one training.	Review proper procedure with cook, and check cook's training record.	

➤ Calibrated monitoring equipment.

Typical Challenges to a HACCP System

A HACCP food safety system is meant to be continually updated. For example, you may need to make changes when:

➤ Changes in customers, suppliers, employees, menu items, or equipment and facilities create new hazards or make some of your criteria or corrective actions become obsolete.

➤ Menus need to be up-dated with new recipe items.

➤ Employee commitment and diligence in food safety needs reinforcement. You may find examples of *dry lab*, the entering of data without taking actual measurements. You may need to change supervisory techniques or increase your own involvement.

Internal Resources

These include the documentation system you have developed and information collected from your employees. You need to review this information on a regular basis.

External Resources

In addition to continuing monitoring and verification by your own employees, experts recommend that you consider other sources as well. Form working relationships with outside consultants, food suppliers, equipment dealers, and governmental agencies who can offer advice and verification about HACCP procedures and sanitation regulations.

Action: Draw up and document plans for ongoing evaluation of your system.

When designing your own HACCP System, refer to Sections 3 and 4 for illustrations and examples.

BATTLING AIDS

Jennifer Batty

The story of a restaurant industry veteran's struggle—and one company's resolve—show that courage is needed in the fight against AIDS.

IN 1987, JON STANLEY Szumigala counted 325 friends' patches sewn onto the AIDS Memorial Quilt. Then he stopped counting. Now Szumigala is fighting against having his own patch threaded into the ever-expanding quilt.

When the NAMES Project AIDS Memorial Quilt was first displayed in Washington DC on October 11, 1987, Szumigala was an executive chef at the Smithsonian, working for the contract-feeding arm of DAKA International, Inc. Szumigala gave out 500 gallons of coffee that day to volunteers unfurling the quilt, which serves as a loving monument to people who have died of AIDS. The coffee was a small gesture of support from DAKA, hinting at the future public stance the company would take as the AIDS epidemic worsened.

More than a quarter of a million Americans have been diagnosed with AIDS and more than 1 million Americans are currently estimated to be infected with HIV, the vi-rus that causes AIDS, according to the National Leadership Coalition on AIDS.

The chances of employing a person who has HIV or AIDS has increased, changing AIDS from a remote tragedy into a personal struggle for many, as it begins to take on the faces of valued friends and co-workers, like Szumigala.

20 Years as Foodservice "Mechanic"

"I chose the foodservice profession because working with food gives you the immediate gratification of a job well done. It's a constant challenge to pull off a big event or special dinner in a limited amount of time," says Szumigala (pronounced "zoom-a-galla"). "I ended up being a 'mechanic.' If someone needed something fixed, they'd call Szum. I'd go in and set up the standards and say, 'This is what I want, and I won't compromise.' My standards with food were high, and I was really proud of my work."

Szumigala started his foodservice career scrubbing mussels and opening clams in a Philadelphia restaurant. His 20-year career has encompassed almost every aspect of the industry: He has been a waiter, a chef, a hotel foodservice director and an independent owner/operator of a restaurant in Denver. During his stint at the Massachusetts-based DAKA International, which operates the Fuddruckers chain and 500 contract-feeding operations nationwide, he was executive chef at the Smithsonian American History Museum, director of catering for five of the Smithsonian museums, foodservice director for Triton College in Chicago and supervising corporate travel chef at Gallaudet University in Washington DC.

Last April, during exam week at Triton College, Szumigala's T-cell count plummeted, an indicator of the onset of AIDS. "It was one of our busiest times, and I was so fatigued I could barely function. In May the doctors said, 'You've got it.' It was difficult coming to a screeching halt after being so active," he says.

But Szumigala says he's been luckier than most with AIDS. "I have not had any opportunistic infections; the doctors think I'm from Krypton," he says with a laugh.

To help bolster his body's defenses, Szumigala is on an intensive vitamin and nutrition program, and takes various medications to lessen the chance of contracting an opportunistic infection.

"I'm still experiencing some weight loss, which is disturbing, and sometimes even cleaning around the house is hard for me. The fatigue level is there," he says. "I have seen friends die excruciating deaths; it is difficult to face your mortality on a daily basis."

Being diagnosed with AIDS has given Szumigala a new perspective on life. "It's odd to say this, but I think this disease coming into my life has done a lot for me. You see a sunrise differently or smell a cup of coffee differently. 'Thank you' becomes very important; you just appreciate everything more," he says.

Szumigala continues to use his foodservice expertise to contribute to the community and the industry. He is putting together a handbook on hospitality for his church, he assists DAKA with its AIDS education program, and he acts as "mechanic" for the company,

helping to fine-tune recipes and the like.

A Courageous Corporate Culture

"DAKA has given me the opportunity to do many different jobs in the industry. The company has been very good to me, and they have stood by me throughout this whole thing," says Szumigala. "They weren't afraid to care."

DAKA's courage in caring enough about its employees to address the issue of AIDS in the workplace was recognized this year by the Business Enterprise Trust. The Trust annually honors "acts of social vision and moral leadership in American business."

The company earned the award, according to the Trust, "for its courage in implementing an aggressive AIDS education program in an industry highly vulnerable to public fears and misconceptions about the disease."

DAKA began its AIDS education program in 1987. The program now includes an AIDS counseling office, an 800-number hotline for employees, a flexible sick-leave and disability policy, a supportive benefits package, and AIDS education seminars for all employees and managers.

The company's chairman and CEO, William Baumhauer, is personally committed to combating the AIDS crisis, not just in his operation, but in the community as a whole. Baumhauer is a member of the board of the National Leadership Coalition on AIDS and has been invited to

speak on the topic on numerous occasions.

Baumhauer is so focused on educating his employees about AIDS in part because of what he read in the *Employee Attitudes About AIDS* survey by the National Leadership Coalition on AIDS. The report showed that 50 percent of employees reported AIDS as the health problem they were most concerned about and that 34 percent of employees said they knew someone with HIV or AIDS.

"It is obviously a workplace issue. Employees look to the employer as a legitimate source of information on controversial issues such as AIDS," he says.

In order to properly address the issue, the company has a three-part plan:

▶ a policy stating that DAKA won't discriminate against anyone because of illness
▶ an AIDS education program including training and the 800 number
▶ a corporate-wide attitude set by management that engenders trust from employees through its visibility.

"From myself on down, we're not afraid to talk about the subject and make clear what our policy is towards AIDS. We truly try to be a resource to our associates and build a relationship of trust," says Baumhauer.

That trust is earned through such company policies as notifying people only on a need-to-know basis that an associate has HIV or AIDS. "People ask me all the time how many people we have working for us who are HIV-infected and I can't tell them. I honestly don't know, because I don't need to know," says Baumhauer.

It took a lot of courage and trust for Szumigala to pick up the phone and call the benefits office to notify Louise Faucher, who was then DAKA's AIDS program coordinator, about his condition. "She said, 'This is completely confidential. Who do you want to know?' I left it up to her, and I don't think she told anyone for the first three months," says Szumigala. "I also told my executive chef and my executive assistant at Triton College, and they helped me through any bad days."

Szumigala left Chicago to assume his post at Gallaudet University in Washington DC but was only able to work for four weeks before exhaustion forced him to go on short-term disability leave for six months, after which he went on permanent disability.

"DAKA has been tremendously supportive. I have heard horror stories about other people in the industry being bounced from their jobs because they were suspected of having AIDS and employers were worried about how the other employees and the public would react if word got out," he says.

Fighting the Stigma Within

Operators who seek to address the controversial issue of AIDS may find they have to combat the fears, concerns and prejudices of their employ-ees first, before tackling those of their customers.

"We've had one extreme to the other when our associates found out a co-worker had AIDS. We've had a threatened boycott, had people say they were going to quit or that they wouldn't work next to that person anymore," says Baumhauer.

When faced with such a situation, Baumhauer says they counsel the employee who feels uncomfortable working with the person who has AIDS. "Usually it is simply fear or lack of knowledge that makes the person react that way. Counseling has been very effective in remedying the situation," he says.

If educational efforts fail to convince the employee that it is safe to work with someone with AIDS, then DAKA transfers that employee. "We will not compromise the infected person's integrity; we will transfer their co-worker if we can," he says. "But we really try to combat the issue with education first."

According to the survey by the National Leadership Coalition on AIDS, simply distributing AIDS literature to employ-ees without further educational efforts was more likely to actually increase employee anxiety about AIDS. A more comprehensive program tended to reduce that anxiety. "You can't just get a video and show it once a year. That's not good enough; you have to have follow-up or you could create even more fear and misunderstanding about AIDS," says Baumhauer.

Employees at DAKA view an AIDS video, receive an AIDS brochure, go through training and also get periodic payroll stuffers on the issue.

"In all companies, it's the intangibles that create a team. Our associates respect our courageous stance on AIDS and appreciate that we take the time and effort to educate them on the subject," says Baumhauer. "A lot of good-will comes from this, and morale goes up."

In fact, Baumhauer says that DAKA's AIDS-awareness program has improved the company by minimizing the escalating business costs of AIDS and by cementing DAKA's reputation as a progressive and caring employer, thus reducing employee turnover.

The program has also succeeded in creating a more compassionate work environment for employees. "I never felt any bad vibes at any time from my coworkers at DAKA," says Szumigala. "I know of people in other companies who were pressured to quit or resign because they had AIDS. Their boss might make their work load heavier to get them to quit. For example, they might be told to make two soups instead of one or made to stay late to prep for a banquet after already working a full shift.

"When other employees see their employer react that way, then they feel that they have to hide it if they have HIV or AIDS. And the stress of hiding the disease will hurt you more than any opportunistic infection," he says.

AVOIDING A PUBLIC CRISIS

In the National Restaurant Association's new tape, "The AIDS Issue Guidelines for the Foodservice Manager," it is recommended that foodservice operators adopt a four-step approach to preventing a crisis that could occur when it becomes known that an employee has AIDS.

Develop an AIDS policy statement. Create a policy statement that spells out the company's position for the public as well as employees. When creating a policy, address in legal terms the following issues: confidentiality, health education, eligibility for medical benefits, and the ability of infected employees to continue to work. A sample policy statement is given in "The AIDS Tape."

Educate employees. Examples of ways to educate your employees include conducting seminars with local health experts; distributing literature about AIDS treatment, prevention and confidentiality to employees; and providing access to professional counsel and treatment. Holding a seminar with a local health expert after showing employees the association's tape "HIV and AIDS: What You Need to Know" would help alleviate the fears and misconceptions your employees may have about AIDS and create a better working environment.

Assemble a crisis team. This group will have the authority to control and minimize loss in the restaurant from any crisis—from fire to an AIDS incident. Form this group well in advance of any crisis, don't wait until the crisis occurs.

This group should include the owner/operator or someone who can make company-wide decisions, a team leader who is responsible for keeping other team members updated on the crisis, a spokesperson to make statements to the media, an employee representative to act as liaison between management and the employees, and (perhaps from outside the company) a legal representative and a healthcare expert.

Develop an AIDS communication strategy. Your response to an AIDS incident will help shape public perception. The crisis team's spokesperson should be media savvy and should be the only person to communicate to the media about the incident.

Of course, with your crisis team assembled and your education program in place, you may be able to avoid an incident that requires talking to the media. But if one does occur, you will be well prepared to handle it.

Remember that any approach to handling the AIDS crisis in your operation should be safe, legal and compassionate.

Fighting Customers' Fears

DAKA was honored by the Business Enterprise Trust for its courage. And it is indeed courageous for a company, especially one in the foodservice industry, to step to the forefront on such a sensitive issue as AIDS. The stigma surrounding AIDS in the context of food has resulted in a sort of ostrich reaction from many operators—hiding their heads from the inevitable impact of the epidemic.

Fears about interactions with infected persons persist even though the Centers for Disease Control (CDC) in Atlanta has repeatedly told the public that HIV cannot be contracted through everyday contact with infected people. Nor can a person get the virus from phones, toilet seats, forks, cups or other utensils that someone with HIV or AIDS has used. It is not transmitted through sweat or tears. And most important for the foodservice industry, a person cannot get the virus from eat-

ing food prepared by someone with HIV or AIDS. Still, misconceptions haunt the industry.

"Can the fact that someone in your operation has AIDS affect your business? The answer is 'yes.' But then you have to ask yourself, 'Do you only have the courage of your convictions as long as it doesn't impact on you financially?'" asks Baumhauer.

Baumhauer was amazed at how much media attention he got when he first spoke out on the AIDS issue. "They said I was one of the few CEOs to admit that this is a problem in the business world," he says.

Szumigala acknowledges that there is a strong stigma attached to AIDS and the food-service industry. "I respect the fact that a small operator could lose business if word slips out that his chef or bartender has AIDS. But even though a small operator doesn't have the financial resources that a large corporation does, they can still have compassion for their employees," he says.

Out of necessity, more and more foodservice operators will be following in DAKA's risk-taking wake in the near future. According to the National Leadership Coalition on AIDS survey, an estimated two-thirds of large businesses (with more than 2,500 employees) and nearly one in 10 small businesses (with fewer than 500 employees) already have encountered employees with HIV or AIDS in their workplaces.

There are legal reasons for developing an AIDS strategy as well. Employees with HIV or AIDS are now protected under the new regulations set up by the passage of the Americans with Disabilities Act (ADA). Employees who are HIV-infected cannot be discriminated against under Title I of the ADA. Currently, any employer with 25 or more employees has to comply with the ADA's regulations. By July 26, 1994, any employer with 15 or more employees must comply, meaning that not only large corporations but many mom-and-pop operations will have to address the issue as well.

Turning Condemnation into Compassion

"Often the problem with HIV and AIDS is that people view it as a moralistic disease; it is not. I've never heard of a manager asking an employee how they got cancer, but that's often the first question asked of someone with AIDS," says Baumhauer.

Szumigala says that DAKA's educational efforts are good because they are setting an example for other food-service operations.

Baumhauer says, "I don't think everybody has to get on a soapbox and say, 'I care.' We just have to educate our employees and provide a compassionate work environment."

Szumigala plans to continue his work with DAKA's AIDS education program and to remain active in his church and with local and national AIDS education efforts. He is also writing a novel. But he admits that he misses the action of the restaurant industry. "Whenever I go to a corporate function, I still rearrange the napkins or straighten the sugar packets."

"Most of us would like to think we'll work in the industry until the day we drop, because when you're in this business, and you love it like I do, you're in it for good," says Szumigala. "But your priorities change when you find out you have a terminal disease. I told my staff when I left, 'Don't waste time, because you never know what's going to hit you.'"

Using your sanitation course book, class notes, industry experience, personal research, and personal interviews, develop a sanitation maintenance training program manual for a property of your choice. This property can be one that you currently work in, one you have worked in or a fictitious one.

This maintenance program manual should be a revolving document; one that can be updated with very little inconvenience as the local, city, state or federal laws change. It should provide both corporate/management policies as well as serve as a training manual for all employees.

Areas that should be incorporated into the manual: **NOTE:** This is not a complete list.

➤ Front and back of the house
➤ Public guest areas
➤ Restrooms, both public and employee
➤ Manager's office
➤ Employee break room
➤ Time clock area
➤ Cautionary signage
➤ Employee procedures, rules and regulations
    ie.: eating on the job
    smoking on the job
    uniform
    storage/handling of personal belongings
    personal hygiene
    calling in sick
    hand washing procedures
➤ Daily, weekly, monthly, yearly cleaning schedules
➤ Employee training exams, pre and post test with the answer sheet provided
➤ Employee Right the Know Law as it pertains to the organization
➤ MSDS forms for all chemicals used
➤ An AIDS/Infectious Disease policy statement

Remember to make this project as realistic as possible. This program must be able to be implemented by someone other than yourself. Therefore, it would be a good idea to get someone else's opinion of the final manual before it is submitted for a grade.

Paper Requirements

Length: minimum 30 pages
Sources: at least 5, including interviews
Word processed using the MLA format

PROJECT 2

Using your course book, class notes, hand outs, industry experiences and references, and the following example pages, develop a Hazard Analysis Critical Control Point (HACCP) file using the criteria listed below:

1. Obtain a menu from a restaurant or food service operation of your choice.

2. After reviewing the menu, collect a recipe for each of the menu selections.

3. Design a flow chart outlining the flow of food for ten of the menu selections using the following criteria:

   a. Identify all Critical Control Points

   b. Identify each of the Hazards

   c. Explain the Standard to be met

   d. Define the Corrective action to be taken if the standard is not met

4. After the flow chart is complete for each of the ten selections, rewrite the recipes and insert the Critical Control Point into the procedures of the recipe.

5. Requirements of the project

   1. All materials should be word processed

   2. The original menu must be submitted

   3. All original recipes must be submitted along with complete bibliographical information

   4. Length: 20–30 pages

3

FOOD PRODUCTION

Basic Cooking Principles
Wayne Gisslen

Sous Vide: What's All the Excitement About?
Betsy Baird

Project 1

Project 2

BASIC COOKING PRINCIPLES

Wayne Gisslen

NO WRITTEN RECIPE CAN BE 100% accurate. No matter how carefully a recipe is written, the judgment of the cook is still the most important factor in making a preparation turn out well. A cook's judgment is based on experience, on an understanding of the raw materials available, and on knowledge of basic cooking principles.

This chapter deals with basic principles. You will learn about what happens to food when it is heated, about how food is cooked by different cooking methods, and about rules of seasoning and flavoring. It is important to understand the theories so that you can put them into practice successfully in the kitchen.

After reading this chapter, you should be able to:

► Name the most important component of foods and describe what happens to them when they are cooked.
► Describe the ways in which heat is transferred to food in order to cook it.
► List the factors that affect cooking times.

► Explain the differences between moist-heat cooking methods, dry-heat cooking methods, and dry-heat methods using fat.
► Describe each basic cooking method used in the commercial kitchen.
► List the rules for achieving good quality in deep-fried foods.
► Understand the basic principles for using seasoning and flavorings to create good-tasting foods.

Heat and Food

To cook food means to heat it in order to make certain changes in it. Skillful cooks know exactly what changes they want to make and what they have to do to get them right. To learn these cooking skills, it is important for you to know why foods behave as they do when heated. For this you have to study a little theory to support your practice in the kitchen.

Perhaps not all the parts in this section will make sense to you at first. But they should

become clearer to you after you have thought about them in relation to specific techniques, as demonstrated by your instructor. Later in your studies, when you are learning about cooking meats, fish, vegetables, and other foods, review this section from time to time. Not only will you understand it better, but it should help you make more sense out of the procedures you are learning and practicing.

Effects of Heat on Foods

Foods are composed of proteins, fats, carbohydrates, and water, plus small amounts of other compounds such as minerals (including salt), vitamins, pigments (coloring agents), and flavor elements. It is important to understand how these components react when heated or mixed with other foods. You will then be better equipped to correct cooking faults when they occur and to anticipate the effects of changing cooking methods, cooking temperatures, or ingredient proportions.

In other words, when you know *why* foods behave as they do, you can then understand *how* to get them to behave as you want them to.

Proteins

1. Protein is a major component of meats, poultry, fish, eggs, milk, and milk products. It is present in smaller amounts in nuts, beans, and grains
2. *Coagulation.* As proteins are heated, they become firm, or *coagulate.* As the temperature increases, they shrink, become firmer, and lose more moisture. Exposure of proteins to excessive heat toughens them and makes them dry. Most proteins complete coagulation or are "cooked" at 160 to 185°F (71 to 85°C).
3. *Connective tissues* are special proteins that are present in meats. Meats with a great deal of connective tissue are tough, but some connective tissues are dissolved when cooked slowly with moisture. By cooking tough meats properly, therefore, they can be made more tender.
4. *Acids,* such as lemon juice, vinegar, and tomato products, do two things to proteins:
   a. They speed coagulation.
   b. They help dissolve some connective tissues.

Carbohydrates

1. Starches and sugars are both carbohydrates. Both compounds are present in foods in many different forms. They are found in fruits, vegetables, grains, beans, and nuts. Meats and fish also contain a very small amount of carbohydrate.
2. For the cook, the two most important changes in carbohydrates caused by heat are caramelization and gelatinization.
   a. *Caramelization* is the browning of sugars. The browning of seared meats and sautéed vegetables and the golden color of bread crust are forms of caramelization.
   b. *Gelatinization* occurs when starches absorb water and swell. This is a major principle in the thickening of sauces and in the production of breads and pastries.

      Acids inhibit gelatinization. A sauce thickened with flour or starch will be thinner if it contains acid.

Fruit and Vegetable Fiber

1. Fiber is the name for a group of complex substances that give structure and firmness to plants. This fiber cannot be digested.
2. The softening of fruits and vegetables in cooking is in part the breaking down of fiber.
3. Sugar makes fiber more firm. Fruit cooked with

sugar keeps its shape better than fruit cooked without sugar.
4. Baking soda (and other alkalis) make fiber softer. Vegetables should not be cooked with baking soda because they become mushy and lose vitamins.

Fats

1. Fats are present in meats, poultry, fish, eggs, milk products, nuts and whole grains, and, to a lesser extent, in vegetables and fruits. Fats are also important as cooking mediums, as for frying.
2. Fats can be either solid or liquid at room temperature. Liquid fats are called oils. Melting points of solid fats vary.
3. When fats are heated, they begin to break down. When hot enough, they deteriorate rapidly and begin to smoke. The temperature at which this happens is called the *smoke point,* and it varies for different fats. A stable fat—one with a high smoke point— is an important consideration in deep-fat frying.

Minerals, Vitamins, Pigments, and Flavor Components

1. Minerals and vitamins are important to the nutritional quality of the food. Pigments and flavor components are important to a food's appearance and taste and may determine whether the food is appetizing enough to eat. So it

is important to preserve all these elements.

2. All of these components may be leached out, or dissolved away, from foods during cooking.
3. Vitamins and pigments may also be destroyed by heat, by long cooking, and by other elements present during cooking.
4. It is important, then, to select cooking methods that preserve, as much as possible, a food's nutrients and appearance. This will always be a consideration when cooking techniques are explained in the remainder of this book.

Heat Transfer

In order for food to be cooked, heat must be transferred from the heat source (such as a gas flame or an electric element) to and through the food. Understanding the ways in which heat is transferred and the speed at which it is transferred helps the cook control the cooking process.

Heat is transferred in three ways: conduction, convection, and radiation.

Conduction

Conduction occurs in two ways:

1. When heat moves directly from one item to something touching it. For example: from the top of the range to a soup pot placed on it, from the pot to the broth inside, and from the broth to the solid food items in it.

2. When heat moves from one part of something to an adjacent part of the same item. For example: from the exterior of a roast to the interior, or from a sauté pan to its handle.

Different materials conduct heat at different speeds. Heat moves rapidly through copper and aluminum, more slowly in stainless steel, slower yet in glass and porcelain. Air is a very poor conductor of heat.

Convection

Convection occurs when heat is spread by the movement of air, steam, or liquid (including hot fat). There are two kinds of convection:

1. *Natural.* Hot liquids and gases rise, while cooler ones sink. Thus in any oven, kettle of liquid, or deep-fat fryer there is a constant, natural circulation that distributes heat.
2. *Mechanical.* In convection ovens and convection steamers, fans speed the circulation of heat. Thus, heat is transferred more quickly to the food, and the food cooks faster.

Stirring is a form of mechanical convection. Thick liquids cannot circulate as quickly as thin ones, so the rate of natural convection is slower. This explains in part why it is so easy to scorch thick soups and sauces. The heat is not carried away from the bottom of the pan quickly enough, so it stays concentrated on the bottom and scorches the food. Stirring redistributes the heat and helps

prevent this. (Using heavy pots made of a material that conducts heat well also helps prevent scorching, because the pot conducts the heat more quickly and evenly all across the bottom and up the sides.)

Radiation

Radiation occurs when energy is transferred by waves from the source to the food.

The waves themselves are not actually heat energy, but are changed into heat energy when they strike the food being cooked. (Light waves, radio waves, and X rays are examples of radiation not used for cooking.)

Two kinds of radiation are used in the kitchen:

1. *Infrared.* Broiling is the most familiar example of infrared cooking. In a broiler, an electric element or a ceramic element heated by a gas flame becomes so hot that it gives off infrared radiation, which cooks the food. There are also high-intensity infrared ovens designed to heat food rapidly.
2. *Microwave.* In microwave cooking, the radiation generated by the oven penetrates part way into the food, where it agitates the molecules of water. The friction caused by this agitation creates heat, which cooks the food.
   a. Because microwave radiation affects only water molecules, a completely waterless material will not heat up in a microwave oven. Plates become

hot only when heat is *conducted* to them by hot foods.

b. Because most microwaves penetrate no more than about 2 inches into foods, heat is transferred to the center of large pieces of food by *conduction*, just as in roasting.

Cooking with microwaves is discussed in more detail later in this chapter.

Cooking Times

It takes time to heat a food to a desired temperature, the temperature at which a food is "done" (meaning that the desired changes have taken place). This time is affected by three factors:

1. *Cooking temperature.* This means the temperature of the air in the oven, the fat in the fryer, the surface of a griddle, or the liquid in which a food is cooking.
2. *The speed of heat transfer.* Different cooking methods transfer heat at different rates, as shown by these examples:

    Air is a poor conductor of heat, while steam is much more efficient. A jet of steam (212°F/100°C) will easily burn your hand, but you can safely reach into an oven at 500°F (260°C). This is why it takes longer to bake potatoes than to steam them.

    A convection oven cooks faster than a conventional oven, even if both are set at the same temperature. The forced air movement transfers heat more rapidly.

3. *Size, temperature, and individual characteristics of the food.* For example:

    A small beef roast cooks faster than a large one.

    A chilled steak takes longer to broil than one at room temperature.

    Fish items generally cook more quickly than meats.

Because there are so many variables, it is very difficult or even impossible to determine exact cooking times in most recipes. Different ovens, fryers, and steamers, for example, may transfer heat more or less efficiently or have different recovery times. Roasting charts that give cooking times for various cuts of meat can be used only as guidelines, and the cook must use his or her judgment to make the final determination of doneness.

Cooking Methods

Cooking methods are classified as "moist heat" and "dry heat."

Moist-heat methods are those in which the heat is conducted to the food product by water (including stock, sauces, etc.) or by steam.

Dry-heat methods are those in which the heat is conducted without moisture, that is, by hot air, hot metal, radiation, or hot fat. We usually divide dry-heat methods into two categories: without fat and with fat.

Different cooking methods are suited to different kinds of foods. For example, some meats are high in connective tissue and will be tough unless this tissue is broken down slowly by moist heat. Other meats are low in connective tissue and are naturally tender. They are at their best and juiciest when cooked with dry heat to a rare or medium-done stage.

There are many other factors to consider when choosing cooking methods for meats, fish, and vegetables, such as the flavor and appearance imparted by browning, the flavor imparted by fats, and the firmness or delicacy of the product.

The basic cooking methods are summarized here. Practical application to different foods will be discussed in detail in the remainder of the book and reinforced by your instructors' demonstrations and your own experience and practice.

Moist-Heat Methods

Poach, Simmer, and Boil

To poach, simmer, and boil all mean to cook a food in water or a seasoned and flavored liquid. The temperature of the liquid determines the method.

1. To *boil* means to cook in a liquid that is bubbling rapidly and is greatly agitated. Water boils at 212°F (100°C) at sea level. No matter how high the burner is turned, the temperature of the liquid will go no higher.

Boiling is generally reserved for certain vegetables and starches. The high temperature would toughen the proteins of meats, fish, and eggs, and the rapid bubbling breaks up delicate foods.

2. To *simmer* means to cook in a liquid that is bubbling very gently. Temperature is about 185 to 205°F (85 to 96°C).

   Most foods cooked in a liquid are simmered. The higher temperatures and intense agitation of boiling are detrimental to most foods. The word "boiled" is sometimes used as a menu term, as when simmered fresh beef is called "boiled beef."

3. To *poach* means to cook in a liquid, usually a small amount, that is hot but not actually bubbling. Temperature is about 160 to 180°F (71 to 82°C).

   Poaching is used to cook delicate foods such as fish and eggs out of the shell. It is also used to partially cook foods such as variety meats, in order to eliminate undesirable flavors and to firm up the product before final cooking.

4. A rule of thumb: whether a food is to be simmered or boiled, the liquid is often brought to a full boil at first. This compensates for the lowering of the temperature when the food items are added. The heat is then adjusted to maintain a steady temperature.

5. *To blanch* means to cook an item partially and very briefly, usually in water, but sometimes by other methods (as when french fries are blanched in deep fat).

   There are two ways of blanching in water:
   a. Place the item in cold water, bring to a boil, simmer briefly. Cool the item by plunging it into cold water.

   Purpose: to dissolve out blood, salt, or impurities from certain meats and bones.

   b. Place the item in rapidly boiling water and return the water to the boil. Remove the item and cool in cold water.

   Purpose: to set the color and destroy harmful enzymes in vegetables, or to loosen the skins of tomatoes, peaches, and similar items for easier peeling.

6. Altitude note: The boiling point of water decreases as altitude above sea level is increased. At 5000 feet (1500 meters) above sea level, water boils at about 203°F (95°C). Thus it takes longer to boil foods at high altitudes, because the temperature is lower.

Steam

To *steam* means to cook foods by exposing them directly to steam.

1. In quantity cooking, this is usually done in special steam cookers, which are designed to accept standard-size pans. Steaming can also be done on a rack above boiling water. This method is more cumbersome, however, and is only occasionally used in food service. Cooking in a steam-jacketed kettle is not steaming, because the steam does not actually touch the food.

2. Steaming also refers to cooking an item tightly wrapped or in a covered pan, so that it cooks in the steam formed by its own moisture. This method is used in cooking items *en papillote,* wrapped in parchment paper (or foil). "Baked" potatoes wrapped in foil are actually steamed.

3. Steam at normal pressure is 212°F (100°C), the same as boiling water. However it carries much more heat than boiling water and cooks very rapidly. Cooking times must be carefully controlled to avoid overcooking.

4. A *pressure steamer* is a steam cooker that holds in steam under pressure. The temperature of the steam then goes higher than 212°F (100°C), as the following chart shows:

Pressure	Steam Temperature
5 psi (pounds per square inch)	227°F (106°C)
10 psi	240°F (116°C)
15 psi	250°F (121°C)

Because of these temperatures, pressure steaming is an extremely rapid method of cooking and must be very carefully controlled and timed.

5. Steaming is widely used for vegetables. It cooks them rapidly, without agitation, and minimizes the dissolving away of nutrients that occurs when vegetables are boiled.

Braise

To *braise* means to cook covered in a small amount of liquid, usually after preliminary browning. In almost all cases, the liquid is served with the product as a sauce.

1. Braised meats are usually browned first using a dry-heat method such as pan-frying. This gives a desirable appearance and flavor to the product and to the sauce.
2. Braising also refers to cooking some vegetables, such as lettuce or cabbage, at low temperature in a small amount of liquid, without first browning in fat, or with only a light preliminary sautéing.
3. Foods being braised are usually not completely covered by the cooking liquid. The top of the product is actually cooked by the steam held in the covered pot. Pot roasts, for example, are cooked in liquid that covers the item by one-third to two-thirds. The exact amount depends on how much sauce is needed for service. This

method yields a flavorful, concentrated sauce.

4. In some preparations, especially of poultry and fish, no liquid is added. This is still considered braising, since steam is trapped by the cover and the item cooks in its own moisture and in the moisture of other ingredients such as vegetables.
5. Braising may be done on the range or in the oven. Oven-braising has three major advantages:
   a. Uniform cooking. The heat strikes the braising pot on all sides, not just the bottom.
   b. Less attention required. Foods braise at a low, steady temperature, without having to be checked constantly.
   c. Range space is free for other purposes.

Dry-Heat Methods

Roast and Bake

To *roast* and to *bake* means to cook foods by surrounding them with hot, dry air, usually in an oven. Cooking on a spit in front of an open fire is also roasting.

Roasting usually applies to meats and poultry.

Baking applies to breads, pastries, vegetables, and fish. It is a more general term than roasting.

1. Cooking *uncovered* is essential to roasting. Covering holds in steam, changing the process from dry-heat to moist-heat

cooking, such as braising or steaming.

2. Meat is usually roasted on a rack (or, if it is a rib roast, on its own natural rack of bones). The rack prevents the meat from simmering in its own juices and fat. It also allows hot air to circulate all around the product.
3. When roasting in a conventional oven, the cook should allow for uneven temperatures by occasionally changing the position of the product. The back of the oven is often hotter because heat is lost at the door.
4. To *barbecue* means to cook with dry heat created by the burning of hardwood or by the hot coals of this wood. In other words, barbecuing is a roasting or grilling technique requiring a wood fire.

Authentic, traditional American barbecue is done in wood-burning ovens or pits, but these are not really practical for the average restaurant that wants to add some barbecued items to the menu. So today, most barbecuing is done in specially designed smoke ovens or cookers. In principle, these units work like regular ovens, except that they also have devices that heat small pieces of hardwood to produce smoke. Foods should be suspended in the ovens or placed on racks so that the smoke can contact all surfaces.

Technically, the foods cooked in these units cannot be said to be barbecued, since the heat is created by electric or gas burners. But because of the wood smoke, the results can be nearly identical.

Broil

To *broil* means to cook with radiant heat from above.

NOTE: The terms broiling, grilling, and griddling are sometimes confused. Grilling (see below) is often called broiling, and griddling is called grilling. This book uses the terms that refer to the equipment used. Thus, broiling is done in a broiler, grilling on a grill, and griddling on a griddle.

---

1. Broiling is a rapid, high-heat cooking method that is usually used only for tender meats, poultry, and fish and for a few vegetable items.
2. Note the following rules of broiling:
   a. Turn heat on full. Cooking temperature is regulated by moving the rack nearer to or farther from the heat source.
   b. Use lower heat for larger, thicker items, and for items to be cooked well done. Use higher heat for thinner pieces and for items to be cooked rare. This is done so that the inside and outside are done at the same time. It takes practice and experi-

ence to cook foods of different thickness to the right degree of doneness inside with the desired amount of surface browning.
   c. Preheat the broiler. This helps to sear the product quickly, and the hot broiler will make the desired grill marks on the food.
   d. Dip foods in oil to prevent sticking and to minimize drying. (This may not be necessary if the food is high in fat.) Care should be taken, as too much oil on a hot broiler grate may cause a fire.
   e. Turn foods over only once, to cook from both sides but to avoid unnecessary handling.
3. A low-intensity broiler called a *salamander* is used for browning or melting the top of some items before service.

Grill, Griddle, and Pan-broil

Grilling, griddling, and pan-broiling are all dry-heat cooking methods that use heat from below.

1. *Grilling* is done on an open grid over a heat source, which may be charcoal, an electric element, or a gas-heated element. Cooking temperature is regulated by moving the items to hotter or cooler places on the grill. Grilled meats should be turned to achieve desired grill markings, just as in broiling.

2. *Griddling* is done on a solid cooking surface called a griddle, with or without small amounts of fat to prevent sticking. The temperature is adjustable and is much lower (around 350°F/ 177°C) than on a grill. In addition to meats, items such as eggs and pancakes are cooked on a griddle.
   Grooved griddles have a solid top with raised ridges. They are designed to cook like grills, but to create less smoke. Meats cooked on a grooved griddle do not have the "charcoal-grilled" flavor imparted by smoke from burning fats.
3. *Pan-broiling* is like griddling, except it is done in a sauté pan or skillet instead of on a griddle surface. Fat must be poured off as it accumulates, or the process would become pan-frying. No liquid is added, and the pan is not covered, or else the item would steam.

Dry-Heat Methods Using Fat

Sauté

To *sauté* means to cook quickly in a small amount of fat.

1. The French word *sauter* means "to jump," referring to the action of tossing small pieces of food in a sauté pan. However, larger foods, such as slices of meat and pieces of chicken, are sautéed with-

out actually being tossed in the pan.

2. Note these two important principles:
   a. Preheat the pan before adding the food to be sautéed. The food must be seared quickly, or it will begin to simmer in its own juices.
   b. Do not overcrowd the pan. Doing so lowers the temperature too much, and again the food is not seared but begins to simmer in its own juices.
3. Meats to be sautéed are often dusted with flour to prevent sticking and to help achieve uniform browning.
4. After a food is sautéed, a liquid such as wine or stock is often swirled in the pan to dissolve browned bits of food sticking to the bottom. This is called *deglazing*. This liquid becomes part of a sauce served with the sautéed items.

Pan-Fry

To *pan-fry* means to cook in a moderate amount of fat in a pan over moderate heat.

1. Pan-frying is similar to sautéing, except that more fat is generally used and the cooking time is longer. The method is used for larger pieces of food, such as chops and chicken pieces, and the items are not tossed by flipping the pan as they often are in sautéing.
2. Pan-frying is usually done over lower heat than

sautéing, because of the larger pieces being cooked.
3. The amount of fat depends on the food being cooked. Only a small amount is used for eggs, for example, while as much as an inch or more may be used for pan-fried chicken.
4. Most foods must be turned at least once for even cooking. Some larger foods may be removed from the pan and finished in the oven, to prevent excessive surface browning. This method of finishing in the oven is also used to simplify production when large quantities of foods must be pan-fried.

Deep-Fry

To *deep-fry* means to cook a food submerged in hot fat. Quality in a deep-fried product is characterized by the following properties:

Minimum fat absorption

Minimum moisture loss (that is, not overcooked)

Attractive golden color

Crisp surface or coating

No off flavors imparted by the frying fat

Many foods are dipped in a breading or batter before frying. This forms a protective coating between food and fat and helps give the product crispness, color, and flavor. Obviously, the quality of the breading or batter affects the quality of the finished product.

Guidelines for Deep-Frying

1. *Fry at proper temperatures.* Most foods are fried at 350 to 375°F (175 to 190°C). Excessive greasiness in fried foods is usually caused by frying at too low a temperature.
2. *Don't overload the baskets.* Doing so greatly lowers the fat temperature.
3. *Use good quality fat.* The best fat for frying has a *high smoke point* (the temperature at which the fat begins to smoke and to break down rapidly).
4. *Replace about 15 to 20 percent of the fat with fresh after each daily use.* This extends frying life.
5. *Discard spent fat.* Old fat loses frying ability, browns excessively, and imparts off flavors.
6. *Avoid frying strong and mild-flavored foods in the same fat, if possible.* French fries should not taste like fried fish.
7. *Fry as close to service as possible.* Do not leave foods in the basket above the fry kettle, and do not hold under heat lamps for more than a few minutes. The foods' moisture quickly makes the breading or coating soggy.
8. *Protect fat from its enemies:*

   Heat. Turn fryer off or to a lower holding temperature (200 to 250°F/95 to 120°C) when not in use.

   Oxygen. Keep fat covered between services, and try to aerate the fat as little as possible when filtering.

Water. Remove excess moisture from foods before frying. Dry baskets and kettle thoroughly after cleaning. Keep liquids away from the fryer to prevent accidental spills.

Salt. Never salt foods over the fat.

Food particles. Shake loose crumbs off breaded items before placing over fat. Skim and strain fat frequently.

Detergent. Rinse baskets and kettle well after cleaning.

Pressure Frying

Pressure frying means deep-frying in a special covered fryer that traps steam given off by the foods being cooked and increases the pressure inside the kettle.

In a standard fryer, even though the fat may be at 350°F (175°C), the temperature inside the food will not rise above 212°F (100°C), the boiling point of water. Just as in a pressure steamer, a pressure fryer raises this temperature and cooks the food more quickly, without excessive surface browning. At the same time, the fat temperature can be lower, 325°F (165°C) or less.

Pressure frying requires accurate timing, because the product cannot be seen while it is cooking.

Microwave Cooking

Microwave cooking refers to the use of a specific tool rather than to a basic dry-heat or moist-heat cooking method. This equipment is used mostly for heating prepared foods and for thawing either raw or cooked items. However, it can be used for primary cooking as well.

Different models of microwave ovens range in power from about 500 watts up to about 2000 watts. The higher the wattage, the more intense the energy it puts out and the faster it will heat foods. Some models have switches that allow you to cook at different power levels.

One of the most important advantages of the microwave oven in à la carte cooking is that it enables you to heat individual portions of many foods to order quickly and evenly. Instead of keeping such foods as stews hot in the steam table, where they gradually become overcooked, you can keep them refrigerated (either in bulk or in individual portions) and reheat each order as needed. This is perhaps the main reason why most restaurants have one or more microwave ovens, even though they may not use them for primary cooking.

Because the microwave oven is a unique tool in food service, the cook should observe the following special points regarding its use:

1. Small items will not brown in a standard microwave. Large roasts may brown somewhat from the heat generated in the item itself. Some models of microwave ovens have added browning elements that use conventional heat.

2. Watch timing carefully. Overcooking is the most common error in microwave use. High-energy levels cook small items very rapidly.

3. Large items should be turned once or twice for even cooking.

4. An on-off cycle is often used for large items to allow time for heat to be conducted to the interior.

5. If your equipment has a defrost cycle (which switches the oven to lower power), use this cycle rather than full power to thaw frozen foods. Lower power enables the item to thaw more evenly, with less danger of partially cooking it. If your oven does not have this feature, use an on-off cycle.

6. Sliced, cooked meats and other items that are likely to dry out in the microwave should be protected either by wrapping them loosely in plastic or wax paper or by covering them with a sauce or gravy.

7. Because microwaves act only on water molecules, foods with a high water content, such as vegetables, heat faster than denser, drier foods, such as cooked meats.

8. Foods at the edge of a dish or plate heat faster than foods in the center. This is because they are hit by rays bouncing off the walls of the oven as well as by rays directly from the energy source. Therefore,
   a. Depress the center of casseroles so that the

food is not as thick there as at the edges. This will help it heat more evenly.

b. When you are heating several foods at once on a plate, put the moist, quick-heating items like vegetables in the center and the denser, slower-heating items at the edges.

9. Because microwaves do not penetrate metal, aluminum foil and other metals shield foods from the radiant energy. For example, a potato wrapped in foil will not cook in a microwave oven.

With older machines, it was a general rule not to put any metal in the oven, since the radiation could bounce off the metal and damage the magnetron (the oven's generator). With newer machines, it is possible to heat foods in foil pans and to shield certain parts of the food by covering them with pieces of foil, so that they do not overheat. Follow the procedures recommended by the manufacturer.

Because microwaves cook so rapidly, they will not break down the connective tissues of less tender meats. Slow, moist cooking is necessary for dissolving these connective tissues.

The more food that is placed in a microwave at once, the longer the cooking time. Thus the primary advantage of microwave cooking—speed—is lost with large roasts and other large quantities.

Summary of Cooking Terms

The following is an alphabetical list of terms that describe ways of applying heat to foods. Basic cooking methods described earlier are included, as well as more specific applications of these basic methods.

BAKE. To cook foods by surrounding them with hot, dry air. Similar to ROAST, but the term *baking* usually applies to breads, pastries, vegetables, and fish.

BARBECUE. (1) To cook with dry heat created by the burning of hardwood or by the hot coals of this wood. (2) Loosely, to cook over hot coals, such as on a grill or spit, often with a seasoned marinade or basting sauce.

BLANCH. To cook an item partially and very briefly in boiling water or in hot fat. Usually a prepreparation technique, as to loosen peels of vegetables, fruits, and nuts, to partially cook french fries or other foods before service, to prepare for freezing, or to remove undesirable flavors.

BOIL. To cook in water or other liquid that is bubbling rapidly, about 212°F (100°C) at sea level and at normal pressure.

BRAISE. (1) To cook covered in a small amount of liquid, usually after preliminary browning. (2) To cook (certain vegetables) slowly in a small amount of liquid without preliminary browning.

BROIL. To cook with radiant heat from above.

DEEP-FRY To cook submerged in hot fat.

DEGLAZE. To swirl a liquid in a sauté pan, roast pan, or other pan to dissolve cooked particles of food remaining on the bottom.

DRY-HEAT COOKING METHODS. Methods in which heat is conducted to foods without the use of moisture.

FRY. To cook in hot fat.

GLAZE. To give shine to the surface of a food, by applying a sauce, aspic, sugar, or icing, and/or by browning or melting under a broiler or salamander or in an oven.

GRIDDLE. To cook on a flat, solid cooking surface called a griddle.

GRILL. To cook on an open grid over a heat source.

MOIST-HEAT COOKING METHODS. Methods in which heat is conducted to foods by water or other liquid (except fat) or by steam.

PAN-BROIL. To cook uncovered in a skillet or sauté pan without fat.

PAN-FRY. To cook in a moderate amount of fat in an uncovered pan.

(EN) PAPILLOTE. Wrapped in paper (or sometimes foil) for cooking, so that the food is steamed in its own moisture.

PARBOIL. To cook partially in a boiling or simmering liquid.

PARCOOK. To cook partially by any method.

POACH. To cook very gently in water or other liquid that is hot but not actually bubbling, about 160 to 180°F (71 to 82°C).

REDUCE. To cook by simmering or boiling until the quantity of liquid is decreased, often done to concentrate flavors.

ROAST. To cook foods by surrounding them with hot, dry air, in an oven or on a spit in front of an open fire.

SAUTÉ. To cook quickly in a small amount of fat.

SEAR. To brown the surface of a food quickly at a high temperature.

SIMMER. To cook in water or other liquid that is bubbling gently, about 185 to 205°F (85 to 96°C).

STEAM. To cook by direct contact with steam.

STEW. To simmer a food or foods in a small amount of liquid, which is usually served with the food as a sauce.

SWEAT. To cook slowly in fat without browning, sometimes under a cover.

The Art of Seasoning and Flavoring

People eat because they enjoy the flavors of good food, not just because they must fill their stomachs to stay alive. Appearance, texture, and nutrition are important, too, but good taste is the first mark of good cooking.

Enhancement and adjustment of flavors is one of a cook's most critical tasks, a task requiring experience and judgment. Unfortunately, the fine art of seasoning and flavoring is too often one of the most abused.

The most important flavors of a particular preparation are the flavors of its main ingredients. Roast beef should taste like roast beef, green beans like green beans, sole stuffed with crabmeat like sole and crabmeat. It's a fact of life, however, that plain foods generally are a little bland to most palates, so the cook's job is to perk up the taste buds with a few added ingredients, so that the beef tastes more like beef, the green beans more like green beans.

Seasoning and Flavoring Defined

Strictly speaking, there is a difference between seasoning and flavoring.

Seasoning means enhancing the natural flavor of the food, without significantly changing its flavor. Salt is the most important seasoning ingredient.

Flavoring means adding a new flavor to a food, changing or modifying the original flavor.

The difference between seasoning and flavoring is often one of degree. For example, salt is usually used only to season, not to flavor. But in the case of potato chips or pretzels the salt is so predominant that it can be considered an added flavoring. On the other hand, nutmeg is normally used for its distinctive flavor, but just a dash can perk up the flavor of a cream sauce without actually being detectable to most people.

Basic Rule of Seasoning and Flavoring

Your main ingredients are your main sources of flavor. Use good-quality main ingredients, handle all foods with care, and employ correct cooking procedures.

Badly prepared foods cannot be rescued by a last minute addition of spices. The function of spices, herbs, and seasonings is to heighten and to give extra interest to the natural flavors of foods, not to serve as main ingredients or to cover up natural flavors.

When to Season and Flavor

Seasoning

1. The most important time for seasoning liquid foods is at the end of the cooking process.

   The last step in most recipes, whether written or not, is "adjust the seasoning." This means that you have to first taste and evaluate the product. Then you must decide what should be done, if anything, to improve the taste. Often a little salt in a stew or a dash of fresh lemon juice in a sauce is enough.

   The ability to evaluate and correct flavors takes experience, and it is one of the most important skills a cook can develop.

2. Salt and other seasonings are also added at the beginning of cooking, particularly for larger pieces of food, when seasonings added at the end would not be absorbed or blended in, but would just sit on the surface.
3. Adding some of the seasoning during the cooking process also aids in evaluating the flavor at any step along the way.
4. Do not add very much seasoning if it will be concentrated during cooking, as when a liquid is reduced.

Flavoring

Flavoring ingredients can be added at the beginning, middle, or end, depending on the cooking time, the cooking process, and the flavoring ingredient.

1. Only a few flavorings can be added successfully at the end of cooking. Fresh (not dried) herbs, sherry or flamed brandy, and condiments like prepared mustard and Worcestershire sauce can be.
2. Most flavorings need heat to release their flavors and time for the flavors to blend.
   a. Whole spices take longest.
   b. Ground spices release flavors more quickly and thus don't require as long a cooking time.
3. Too much cooking results in loss of flavor. Most flavors, whether in spices or in main ingredients, are *volatile,* which means they evaporate when heated.

That is why you can smell food cooking.

We can conclude that herbs and spices should cook with the foods long enough to release their flavors but not so long that their flavors are lost. If cooking times are short, you can generally add spices and herbs at the beginning or middle of cooking time. On the other hand, if cooking times are long, it is usually better to add them in the middle or toward the end of cooking time.

Common Seasoning and Flavoring Ingredients

Any food product can be used as a flavoring ingredient, even meat (as when crumbled bacon is added to sautéed potatoes, or diced ham is included in a mirepoix). Sauces, which are compound preparations containing many flavoring ingredients, are themselves used as flavorings for meats, fish, vegetables, and desserts.

We obviously cannot treat all possible flavoring ingredients here, but we discuss some of the most important ones as follows. A survey of herbs and spices is provided in Table 1.

1. *Salt* is the most important seasoning ingredient. Don't use too much. You can always add more, but you can't take it out.
2. *Pepper* comes in three forms: white, black, and green. They are actually the same berry but processed differently. (Black

pepper is picked unripe; white is ripened and the hull is removed; green peppercorns are picked unripe and are preserved before their color darkens.)
   a. Whole and crushed *black pepper* is used primarily in seasoning and flavoring stocks and sauces, and sometimes red meats. Ground black pepper is used in the dining room by the customer.
   b. Ground *white pepper* is more important as a seasoning in the food service kitchen. Its flavor is slightly different from that of black pepper, and it blends well (in small quantities) with many foods. Its white color makes it undetectable in light-colored foods.
   c. *Green peppercorns* are fairly expensive and are used in special recipes, primarily in luxury restaurants. The types packed in water, brine, or vinegar (those in water and in brine have better flavor) are soft. Wet-pack peppercorns are perishable; water-packed peppercorns will keep only a few days in the refrigerator after they are opened, while the others will keep longer. Green peppercorns are also available freeze-dried.
3. *Red pepper* or *cayenne* is completely unrelated to black and white pepper. It belongs to the same family

as paprika and fresh sweet bell peppers. Used in tiny amounts, it gives a spicy hotness to sauces and soups, without actually altering the flavor. In larger amounts, it gives both heat and flavor to the spicy foods of Mexico and India.

4. *Lemon juice* is an important seasoning, particularly for enlivening the flavor of sauces and soups.

5. *Parsley, chives,* and sometimes *mint* and *dill* are usually the only *fresh herbs* available to most food service operations. The fresh products should be used instead of the dried whenever possible. Their flavor is greatly superior. Parsley, both whole leaf and chopped, is also important as a garnish.

6. *Onion, garlic, shallots,* and other members of the onion family, as well as *carrots* and *celery*, are used as flavorings in virtually all stations of the kitchen except the bakeshop. Try to avoid the use of dried onion and garlic products. They have less flavor and the fresh product is always available.

7. *Wine, brandy,* and other alcoholic beverages are used to flavor sauces, soups, and many entrées. Brandy should be boiled or flamed to eliminate the high percentage of alcohol, which would be unpleasant in the finished dish. Table wines usually need some cooking or reduction (either separately or with other ingredients) to produce the desired flavors. Fortified wines like sherry and madeira, on the other hand, may be added as flavorings at the end of cooking.

8. *Prepared mustard* is a blend of ground mustard seed, vinegar, and other spices. It is used to flavor meats, sauces, and salad dressings and as a table condiment. For most cooking purposes, European styles such as Dijon (French) or Dusseldorf (German) work best, while the bright-yellow American ballpark style is more appropriate as a table condiment than as a cooking ingredient. There is also a coarse, grainy style that is sometimes called for in specialty recipes.

9. Grated *lemon and orange rind* are used in sauces, meats, and poultry (as in duckling a l'orange), as well as in the bakeshop. Only the colored outer portion, called the *zest*, which contains the flavorful oils, is used. The white pith is bitter.

10. *MSG,* or *monosodium glutamate,* is a flavor enhancer widely used in oriental cooking. MSG doesn't actually change the flavor of foods but acts on the taste buds. It has a bad reputation for causing chest pains and headaches in some individuals.

Using Herbs and Spices

Definitions

Herbs are the leaves of certain plants that usually grow in temperate climates.

Spices are the buds, fruits, flowers, bark, seeds, and roots of plants and trees, many of which grow in tropical climates.

The distinction is often confusing, but it is not as important to know which flavorings are spices and which are herbs as it is to use them skillfully.

Guidelines for Using Herbs and Spices

1. Be familiar with each spice's aroma, flavor, and effect on food. Looking at a spice chart, including the one in this book, is no substitute for familiarity with the actual product.

2. Store spices in a cool place, tightly covered in opaque containers. Heat, light, and moisture deteriorate herbs and spices rapidly.

3. Don't use stale spices and herbs, and don't buy more than you can use in about 6 months. Whole spices keep longer than ground, but both lose much flavor after 6 months.

4. Be cautious after you have replaced old spices. The fresher products are more potent, so the amount you used before might now be too much.

5. Use good-quality spices and herbs. It doesn't pay to economize here. The dif-

ference in cost is only a fraction of a cent per portion.

6. Whole spices take longer to release flavors than ground spices, so allow for adequate cooking time.
7. Whole herbs and spices for flavoring a liquid are tied loosely in a piece of cheesecloth (called a *sachet*) for easy removal.
8. When in doubt, add less than you think you need.

You can always add more, but it's hard to remove what you've already added.

9. Except in dishes like curry or chili, the spices should not dominate. Often they should not even be evident. If you can taste the nutmeg in the creamed spinach, there's probably too much nutmeg.
10. Herbs and spices added to uncooked foods such as salads and dressings need

several hours for flavors to be released and blended.

11. Taste foods before serving, whenever possible. How else can you "adjust the seasoning"?

Table 1 is not a substitute for familiarity with the actual products. Eventually you should be able to identify by aroma, taste, and appearance any spice on your shelf without looking at the label.

TABLE 1. HERBS AND SPICES			
Product	**Market Forms**	**Description**	**Examples of Use**
Allspice	Whole, ground	Small brown berry; flavor resembles blend of cinnamon, cloves, and nutmeg	Sausages and braised meats, poached fish, stewed fruits, pies, puddings
Anise seed	Whole, ground	Small seed; licorice flavor	Cookies, pastries, breads
Basil	Crushed leaves	Aromatic leaf; member of mint family	Tomatoes and tomato dishes, pesto (Italian basil sauce), egg dishes, lamb chops, eggplant, peas, squash
Bay leaves	Whole	Stiff, dark green, oblong leaves; pungent aroma	One of the most important herbs; used in stocks, sauces, stews, braised meats
Caraway seed	Whole	Dark brown, curved seed; familiar rye bread seasoning	Rye bread, cabbage, sauerkraut, pork, cheese spreads, eastern European dishes
Cardamom	Whole pod, ground seed	Tiny brown seeds inside white or green pod; sweet and aromatic; expensive	Pickling, Danish pastries, curries
Cayenne (red pepper)	Ground	Ground form of hot red pepper; looks like paprika, but is extremely hot	In small amounts in many sauces, soups, meat, fish, egg, and cheese dishes (see p. 59)

TABLE 1. (CONT.)

Product	Market Forms	Description	Examples of Use
Celery seed	Whole, ground, ground mixed with salt (celery salt)	Tiny brown seeds with strong celery flavor	Salads, cole slaw, salad dressings, tomato products
Chervil	Crushed leaves	Herb with mild flavor of parsley and tarragon	Soups, salads, sauces, egg and cheese dishes
Chili powder	Ground blend	Blend of spices including cumin, chili peppers, oregano, garlic	Chili and Mexican dishes, egg dishes, appetizers, ground meat
Chives	Fresh, dried, frozen	Grasslike herb with onion flavor	Salads, egg and cheese dishes, fish, soups
Cinnamon	Sticks, ground	Aromatic bark of cinnamon or cassia trees	Pastries, breads, desserts, cooked fruits, ham, sweet potatoes, hot beverages
Cloves	Whole, ground	Dried flower buds of a tropical tree; pungent, sweet flavor	Whole: marinades, stocks, sauces, braised meats, ham, pickling; ground: cakes, pastries, fruits
Coriander	Whole, ground	Round, light brown, hollow seed; slightly sweet, musty flavor	Pickling, sausage, pork, curried dishes, gingerbread
Cumin seed	Whole, ground	Small seed resembling caraway, but lighter in color	Ingredient of curry and chili powders; sausages and meats; egg and cheese dishes
Curry powder	Ground blend	A mixture of 16 to 20 spices, including red pepper, turmeric, cumin, coriander, ginger, cloves, cinnamon, black pepper; different brands vary greatly in flavor and hotness	Curried dishes, eggs, vegetables, fish, soups, rice
Dill	Crushed leaves (called "dill weed"), whole seed	Herb and seed with familiar "dill pickle" flavor; seed is more pungent than the herb	Seed: pickling, sauerkraut, soups; herb: salads, cheese dishes, fish and shellfish, some vegetables
Fennel	Whole seed	Greenish-brown seeds similar in flavor to anise, but larger size	Italian sausage, tomato sauce, fish
Garlic	Fresh: whole bulbs; dried: granulated, powder, and mixed with salt	Strong, aromatic member of onion family; fresh bulbs composed of many small cloves	Wide variety of foods

TABLE 1. (CONT.)

Product	Market Forms	Description	Examples of Use
Ginger	Whole, ground (also fresh and candied or crystallized)	Light brown, knobby root of ginger plant	Baked goods and desserts, fruits, curried dishes, braised meats; fresh: in Chinese and other oriental dishes
Juniper berries	Whole	Slightly soft, purple berries with "piney" flavor; principal flavoring of gin	Marinades, game dishes, sauerkraut
Mace	Whole ("blade"), ground	Orange outer covering of nutmeg; similar flavor, but milder	Baked goods, desserts, fruits, sausages, pork, fish, spinach, squash, other vegetables
Marjoram	Crushed leaves	Grey-green herb with pleasant aroma and slightly minty flavor, similar to oregano but much milder	Pâtés and ground meats, braised meats, sauces, roast lamb, poultry and poultry stuffings
Mint	Leaves	Aromatic herb with familiar cool flavor; two varieties: spearmint and peppermint	Lamb, fruits, tea and fruit beverages, peas, carrots, potatoes
Mustard seed	Whole, ground (also prepared mustard; see p. 59)	Very pungent seed in two varieties: white or yellow, and brown. Brown is stronger.	Cheese and egg dishes, pickling, meats, sauces and gravies
Nutmeg	Whole, ground	Sweet, aromatic kernel of nutmeg fruit	Soups, cream sauces, chicken, veal, many vegetables (spinach, mushrooms, squash, potatoes), desserts, custards, breads, pastries
Oregano	Leaves, ground	Pungent herb, known as the "pizza herb"	Italian and Mexican dishes, tomato products
Paprika	Ground	Ground form of a dried, sweet red pepper. Spanish variety is brighter in color, mild in flavor; Hungarian is darker and more pungent.	Spanish: used (or overused) primarily as garnish on light-colored foods; Hungarian: goulash, braised meats and poultry, sauces
Parsley	Fresh: whole sprigs, in bunches; dried: in flakes	Most widely used herb. Dark green curly or flat leaves with delicate, sweet flavor.	Almost all foods (see p. 59)
Pepper, black and white	Whole (peppercorns); ground fine, medium, or coarse	Small black or creamy white, hard berry. Pungent flavor and aroma.	Most widely used spice (see p. 58)

TABLE 1. (CONT.)

Product	Market Forms	Description	Examples of Use
Pepper, red	(see cayenne)		
Poppy seed	Whole	Tiny blue-black seeds with faint but distinctive flavor	Garnish for breads and rolls, buttered noodles; ground: in pastry fillings
Rosemary	Whole	Light green leaves resembling pine needles	Lamb, braised meats and poultry, soups, tomato and meat sauces
Saffron	Whole (threads)	Red stigma of saffron crocus. Gives bright yellow color to foods. Mild, distinctive flavor. Very expensive.	Should be steeped in hot liquid before use. Rice dishes, poultry and seafoods, bouillabaisse, baked goods.
Sage	Whole, rubbed (finer consistency than whole leaves), ground	Pungent grey-green herb with fuzzy leaves	Pork, poultry, stuffings, sausage, beans, tomatoes
Savory	Crushed leaves	Fragrant herb of mint family; summer savory is preferred to winter	Many meat, poultry, fish, egg, and vegetable dishes
Sesame seeds	Whole (hulled or unhulled)	Small yellowish seed with nutlike taste. Familiar hamburger bun garnish. High oil content.	Bread and roll garnish
Tarragon	Crushed leaves	Delicate green herb with a flavor that is both minty and licoricelike	Béarnaise sauce, tarragon vinegar, chicken, fish, salads and dressings, eggs
Thyme	Crushed leaves, ground	Tiny brownish-green leaves; very aromatic	One of the most important and versatile of herbs; stocks, soups, sauces, meats, poultry, tomatoes
Turmeric	Ground	Intense yellow root of ginger family; mild but distinctive peppery flavor	A basic ingredient of curry powder; pickles, relishes, salads, eggs, rice

Sous Vide: What's All the Excitement About?

Betsy Baird

A REVOLUTIONARY METHOD of food processing has been developed in France and imported into the United States, generating a lot of excitement in the American foodservice industry in the process. The method, called *sous vide,* is expected to provide fresher food with better taste in less preparation time using fewer high-priced cooks.

Why does this matter? On the one hand, the consumer wants fresh or nearly fresh products with a minimum of processing. Consumers are more nutrition conscious than ever. On the other hand, Americans who are living their lives in the fast lane have less time to spend in traditional kitchen preparation. There are more women in the workplace, more single households, and more senior citizen households; these demographic categories all prefer convenience to spending much time in food preparation. The microwave has been a major factor in changing how America eats. Speed and convenience—but safe foods providing good nutrition—are today's consumer demands.

Sous vide appears to meet this criteria. This report explains what sous vide is and discusses some of the advantages and disadvantages of the process.

What Is Sous Vide?

The literal French meaning is "under vacuum." It is a technologically advanced method of cooking whereby fresh food is vacuum sealed in impermeable plastic pouches, cooked at length at a low temperature in circulating water, then chilled and held at refrigerated temperatures for up to three weeks. The term "sous vide" is used for both the processing method and the final food product. According to information obtained from the Vie de France Company, it was developed in France during the 1970s when a French chef and a university food scientist were seeking a better way to prepare foie gras.

Vacuum cooking allows the food to cook in its own juices. All the nutrients, flavor, texture, and aroma of the food are locked in, thereby enhancing the quality. Natural fibers soften, leaving proteins such as beef quite tender, and there is much less need for seasonings such as salt. There is uniform consistency, little food shrinkage, and shelf-life is lengthened. It is a very clean operation. Properly prepared, the quality of sous vide food is equal to, and often superior to, that of conventionally prepared foods. Thus, sous vide offers high-quality convenient foods to consumers and a wide variety of marketing and cost savings to foodservice operators, supermarkets, and other retailers.

Restaurants, hotels, banquet halls, take-out—any foodservice operation of any size will benefit from using the process. Labor shortages are of major concern in the foodservice industry; this process can eliminate the need for expensive chefs and large kitchen staffs, even large kitchens. It puts all the elements of food quality, expert preparation, equipment, training, transportation, and packaging into a single support service and product concept. Virtually anyone with a refrigerator, a pot of hot water, and a sharp implement can be taught to prepare high quality meals using sous vide products.

Process

The process begins with very fresh, high quality ingredients. These are sorted by size and thickness, and like sizes are packaged under vacuum in special thermoretractable pouches. The sealed pouches are then placed in circulating hot water and slowly cooked at a low temperature for up to four hours. Strict controls are maintained during cooking to monitor cooking temperatures. The slow cooking is critical to the process, as it breaks down the connective tissue of meat, thus tenderizing it, and also ensures that nutrients and flavor are locked in. Once cooked, the product is then held in a refrigerated or frozen state until ready to be served.

Food Safety

Since sous vide contains no preservatives, strict precautions must be taken during the procurement, manufacture, distribution and storage of the product. Because of the danger of mishandling, sous vide must be manufactured and distributed under Hazard Analysis and Critical Control Point procedures, or HACCP. While vacuum-packed foods taste better, there is some concern

that conventional food processing may provide greater protection against food poisoning. For one thing, the near oxygen-free atmosphere of this process can provide a breeding ground for harmful bacteria, particularly those responsible for deadly forms of food poisoning. For another, unless strict sanitation controls are maintained, it is too easy to contaminate the product anywhere in the preparation/distribution process. And the food itself may not exhibit any signs of spoilage such as odor or discoloration.

The answer appears to lie in strict controls throughout the entire process from the supplier of the fresh ingredients to the consumer who eats the finished product. In France, the Ministry of Agriculture has issued specific guidelines for products prepared by the sous vide method. In England, the preparation of these products falls under existing chilled food regulations, which are currently under review. In the U.S., however, there are no specific regulations for sous vide. According to the July 1990 issue of *Supermarket News,* the FDA is worried that the practice of packaging fresh food by reduced oxygen techniques is dangerous, and the agency is preparing guidelines to regulate the process. Currently, the general approach is to process within current USDA and FDA guidelines for meat, poultry, and seafood items.

In all countries, the major problem appears to be within the distribution system, not the in-plant processing. Great

care must be taken that the products are properly chilled from manufacture to consumption. In the United States, sous vide may include freezing the finished product, whereas in Europe sous vide is generally a chilled food product. Sous vide preparation has been widely used for several years in France, England, and other European countries; reports are that the technology has caused virtually no problems with foodborne illness providing the food has been properly refrigerated at all times.

Besides refrigeration concerns, the sous vide producer must:

▶ Know his supplier. He must know his sources, what kind of fertilization was used for raw vegetables; what kind of feed went into livestock, how clean his operation is.
▶ Maintain a hygienic preparation plant. Employees must wash their hands thoroughly and frequently, wear latex gloves, and otherwise be properly dressed. Illness or open sores must not be tolerated in the preparation environment.

A compartmentalized approach to plant design was undertaken at Vie de France's new sous vide plant in Alexandria, Va., which prepares 70,000 meals per day. Seafood, meat, and vegetables are each prepared in separate rooms to avoid cross-contamination. Temperature controls in each room maintain temperature at 42°F; cleaning stations are located in each room; chemical baths are located between rooms for plant personnel to walk through and through which carts are wheeled; and plant personnel wear sanitary disposable clothing, including hats and shoes.

In terms of safety, the processor must check the preparation of sous vide at every stage by using the HACCP system. This system consists of:

▶ determining the hazards and assessing their severity and risks;
▶ identifying the critical control points;
▶ developing criteria for control and applying preventive/control measures;
▶ monitoring each critical control point;
▶ establishing immediate corrective action wherever the established criteria are not met; and
▶ verifying that controls are adequate.

The amount of toxin in food is a function of time, temperature, and what pathogens are present. Of these, temperature has the greatest effect on the shelf life of the product. New systems are being developed now which will indicate the presence of toxins in foods;

one promising new development is an indicator which changes color as it is exposed to temperature.

Is All the Excitement Valid?

After the development of canning, then frozen food, it would seem that this newest, "third generation" method of food preparation is here to stay. Its greatest value currently is in the commercial preparation of food; not until safety considerations can be worked out will it be generally available to the homemaker, except through takeout purchases. To succeed, the sous vide processor first needs good quality ingredients; and then must handle those ingredients properly to limit contamination, using the HACCP system at every stage; use appropriate storage and refrigeration methods; and include a time/temperature indicator to assure that the product is used within its limited shelf-life period.

The sous vide distribution chain still does not have sufficient technology to adequately handle vacuum-chill foods on a broad scale. In addition, the cooking process for sous vide kills some of the harmless mi-

croorganisms whose odor warns of spoilage, but does not kill many microbes that cause botulism and other deadly illnesses. New methods are being tested, however, and the process is continually being adapted to meet these concerns.

Advantages of the process are that sous vide does not require the large labor force of conventional food preparation, which reduces cost and space considerations. It looks good, it tastes good, and it is applicable to a wide variety of foods. There is greater menu flexibility. Supermarkets have discovered the advantages of offering freshly prepared food to the consumer. Military foods are greatly improved with this method; they taste better and are simpler to prepare in the field, a consideration that is particularly important today.

Some specialists are forecasting that the chilled foods market, including sous vide, will become the fresher alternative to shelf-stable and frozen foods. If you eat out and find your food to be palatable, tender, nutritious, and still reasonably priced, chances are you are eating sous vide.

Your group (three to four persons) is to simulate that of the Food and Beverage director in a large metropolitan hotel. This hotel's foodservice operations include a fine dining restaurant; an informal eatery that serves breakfast, lunch, and dinner; a Chinese restaurant, banquets and catering (on and off premises) and room service. All meals are prepared primarily from one large facility. The food and beverage department employs 120 to 130 persons. The employee turnover for this department is 150% and labor cost has risen from 25 to 35% in the last year. You are having a difficult time employing trained personnel who are knowledgeable about basic food preparation. Therefore, you must develop a comprehensive training program for new employees.

As a group, select either the moist heat (poach, simmer, boil, steam, braise) or dry heat (roast, bake, broil, grill, griddle, and pan broil) method of food production and develop a training module based on these concepts. (It should take more than one training session). Additional information for each method should include sanitation, nutrition as it relates to each method, equipment used, and types of controls (recipe, costs). The module should include but not be limited to:

1. A primary goal of the training.

2. Specific objectives which should be written in measurable terms. Examples are: objectives for your operation (i.e., reduce turnover); objectives for the employees (i.e, prepare an excellent poached fish).

3. A training outline for each of the sessions—key concepts, food items pertaining to each method, training technique (lecture, OJT), time frame (no longer than 30 minutes for each session). Remember to include sanitation, nutrition, equipment, and controls.

4. Detailed lesson plans for each training session with handouts or overheads and one learning project or assignment for employees (be creative).

5. Pre and post tests to measure knowledge gained.

6. Methods for appraising practical application of knowledge (observation checklist, etc.).

Use a three-hole punched folder for final project. It must be word processed and in the order cited above. References must be cited using APA (American Psychological Association) style. Points will be deducted for grammar and spelling errors.

This project is due three weeks from date assigned. Team grading will be based on content, creativity, and completeness of project. Team members will award individual grades to fellow team members.

The purpose of this project is to determine if the Sous Vide method of production would be feasible and applicable to a specific foodservice operation. Through completing the following assignments, you should complete this goal.

1. Develop a scenario for a foodservice operation you want to manage—full service, casual, institution, hotel food and beverage etc. Include the location, a brief description of menu items, general costs of menu items, number of seats, customer demographics (age, gender, occupation, income status, family status), number of customers per year, number of employees (front and back of the house), employee basic food production skills, employee turnover rate, average check (lunch and dinner), annual sales, annual expenses (food, labor, direct and indirect), profit if applicable. As you do this determine that employee turnover is high, employees lack basic food production skills, labor and food costs have increased in the last year, and profits are declining. As a result of this study you decide to study the feasibility of incorporating sous vide production into your operation.

2. Due to menu flexibility, you choose to make the sous vide products in your operation rather than purchase from a distributor. From a systems perspective, outline in detail the steps to implement sous vide production in your operation. This should entail menuing, recipes, purchasing, equipment, sanitation and safety, service, employee training, etc. (Consider all the systems in your operation).

3. What would be the major advantages and disadvantages of implementing sous vide into your operation? Explain why.

4. Determine the start-up costs for implementing sous vide (include equipment and training costs). At this point, select wage rates for your employees. Conduct a cost-benefit analysis to calculate if it would be less or more expensive to use the sous vide method of production. Calculate a break-even point for recouping start-up (equipment, new menus, training, etc.) costs.

5. What would be the major considerations for selecting sous vide production? Design a chart or table that would demonstrate each step in the decision process. From the research conducted, what would be your final decision? Or can you make one at this time? Why or why not?

To complete this project, begin by conducting research on sous vide production. Include an annotated bibliography for each resource (use APA style). To conduct the cost-benefit analysis and the break-even refer to an accounting text. Include the references. This project will take a great deal of research, thinking, and creativity on your part. **IT IS NOT A PROJECT THAT CAN BE STARTED AT THE LAST MINUTE!!!**

This project will be due at the end of the semester and must be word-processed. Points will be deducted for grammar and spelling errors. Grading will be based on thoroughness, originality, and creativity.

4

PURCHASING

PURCHASING

B. A. Byers, C. W. Shanklin and L. C. Hoover

Introduction

FOOD PURCHASING PLAYS an essential role in meeting customer needs and ensuring the success of the health care food service operation. Aside from being well versed in product selection and food quality standards, the purchasing agent (or buyer) should be knowledgeable about product availability, trends directing customer expectations, the purchasing process, market conditions, production demand, and purchasing methods. The buyer/purchasing agent provides leadership in establishing partnerships with distributors and serves on the product evaluation team. Knowledge of the food distribution system, the structure of wholesale markets in which purchasing occurs, and ethical issues that arise in purchasing also is important to the buyer role.

This chapter will discuss trends that influence purchasing decisions and the purchasing process. Specific trends explored are continuous quality improvement, technology, dis-tributors' changing product line, and the changing role of distributors' sales representatives.

Food marketing and wholesaling will be examined within the context of a larger food distribution system that tracks the flow food from its place as a raw product grown by a farmer to an item for consumer consumption in the health care environment. The intermediary points—food assembly, grading, storing, processing, transport, and the like—are translated to the food service area and expedited to buyer and distributor.

A 10-step procurement model will be broken down into its component parts and examined, starting with assessing needs for a new product, service, or piece of equipment, and ending with receipt and distribution of items throughout the production area in a food service operation. Buyers and department directors will be able to adapt the model to suit their individual needs. The buyer's responsibilities and optimum qualifications needed to perform the functions of procurement will be delineated.

Methods of "power-purchasing" strategies will be described. Some of these are group purchasing organizations, just-in-time purchasing, one-stop purchasing, and prime vendor agreements. Their advantages and disadvantages are explored, along with other distinctions—such as centralized versus noncentralized and contract versus noncontract purchasing.

The chapter will give an in-depth look at how vendors are selected, the buyer-vendor relationship, and ethics issues that can arise in the purchasing process. Finally, a brief "how-to" list of computer-assisted procurement will be given. (The term *buyer* will be used throughout this chapter to describe the individual primarily responsible for acquiring food products, equipment, and services for the health care food service department.)

Trends Influencing Purchasing Decisions

Like all other functions of the food service department, purchasing is influenced by, and must respond to, changes in the internal and external environments. Trends that will affect the purchasing function include:

▶ Continuous quality improvement
▶ Technology
▶ Distributors' changing product lines
▶ Changing role of distributors' sales representatives

Specific impact of these trends on the purchasing function is discussed below.

Continuous Quality Improvement

Purchasing is an area that should be integrated with continuous quality improvement (CQI). Because CQI is designed to be customer driven, it has a direct link with product selection. If food service is to provide products and services to meet the demands of different customers, it is imperative that feedback be obtained from the patients, employees, administrators, and guests. Unfortunately, data collected on what customers really want too often are ignored by food service staff who think they know better what customers desire. Instead of using information collected to identify new products and develop or modify specifications, the information is ignored.

Continuous quality improvement can be used to enhance the relationship between the food service department and brokers and distributors. This is particularly critical in a prime vendor arrangement. Open communication, sharing of information, and being customer focused are essential elements in the CQI process. Benefits include faster introduction of new products, provision of product information that will meet a specific operation's needs, and enhanced training on product use and marketing. (A more detailed discussion of vendor relations is presented later in this chapter.)

In addition to selecting and evaluating products, a product evaluation team should be empowered to identify the need for new products, select them, evaluate their acceptability, and recommend purchases. The team may be composed of food production employees, the production manager, the buyer, tray line and cafeteria employees, and customers.

Group purchasing organizations can implement CQI in providing services to their members. The process should help overcome some of the barriers described later in this chapter.

Technology

The most rapidly changing trend that affects food service distributors and health care operations is to be observed in technological developments, which will influence distributors' interactions with customers, order placement, and in-

ventory control. Predictions are that by the year 2000, electronic data interchange (EDI) will replace face-to-face meetings and other modes of communication such as the telephone, facsimile (fax) machine, and written message. Described as a totally automated process whereby data are transmitted, received, and processed by computers without direct interaction between sender and receiver, EDI already is processing orders. By the year 2000, 80 percent of all ordering will be done directly by the buyer using personal computers with software distributed by a specific distributor or generic direct-order-entry software application that processes purchase orders. Electronic data interchange will be used to monitor customers' buying habits and provide nutritional breakdown of all products in the distributor's line, as well as assess market outlook and menu suggestions.

Advantages to using EDI systems for food service order placement include immediate order confirmation; notification of out-of-stock items, with a list of suggested substitutions; automatic price updates; menu analysis; inventory control; and portion control. The expansion of cost-effective radio frequency (RF) communication systems will provide at least three benefits: immediate customer access to the distributor's computer while decreasing telephone expenses; the transfer of inventory data to a personal computer within the food service operation; and bar-code scanning that can facilitate deliveries and receiving. In the future, any member of the management team can use electronic data bases from the distributor to obtain product information including a color photo of the product, unit cost, and other data needed in planning menus and analyzing cost implications of different menu items and menu mixes. The use of electronic mail (e-mail) also is predicted to increase.

Distributors' Changing Product Line

Distribution will continue to be a people business in which service is the name of the game for distinguishing one distributor from another. The move toward "full-line" food service distribution is predicted to continue, with distributors' product mix expanding and the number of items available greater than ever before. Food distributors will become the primary source for supplies and equipment to food service operations. Specialty distributors in meat, poultry, paper products, and so on will be forced to expand their product line to compete with full-line distributors for national accounts. The specialty distributor of the 1980s will become the broad-line distributor of the 1990s. Distributors will place more emphasis on packaging relative to its impact on the environment and the "green movement." They will work in partnership with food service organizations and the packaging industry to develop packages that are less

dense and contain recycled materials.

To become more competitive, distributors are offering *value-added services,* those services that go beyond simply completing the delivery accurately and on time. Value-added services to providers include:

▶ Computerized services that incorporate EDI and advanced technology
▶ Advice on new products, nutrition information, food cost, and so on
▶ Continuing education seminars
▶ Menu development, merchandising, and marketing services
▶ Floral service
▶ Consulting services on design, layout, and equipment
▶ Coordination of a food service operation's recycling efforts

Today's competitive environment requires distributors and their sales representatives to continue to provide and expand value-added services to retain customers and acquire new ones.

Changing Role of Distributors' Sales Representatives

Distributors' sales representatives (DSRs) will become consultants and problem solvers rather than mere order takers. Because purchase orders will be processed using EDI, DSRs will be trained to be more customer oriented and to provide information on products, packaging, economics, environmental issues,

commodities, market trends, inventory control, conditions influencing costs, availability of products and supplies, and promotional and recipe ideas. Each DSR will need to have thorough knowledge of their accounts and of their company's product lines. In effect, they will provide value-added services as a strategy to increase customer loyalty.

Food Marketing and Wholesaling

The food distribution and marketing system is part of the food and fiber system, the largest industrial system in the United States. Using inputs of technology, capital, machinery, fertilizers, chemicals, petroleum, and labor, farmers produce the nation's supply of raw food and fiber products. They then wholesale these basic raw products to the marketing sector of the food and fiber system.

Marketing System

The American food marketing system serves the country's population by supplying farm products in the desired forms and at the appropriate times. The system assembles, grades, stores, processes, packages, transports, wholesales, retails, prices, takes risks on, controls the quality of, merchandises, exchanges ownership of, brands, regulates, develops, and tests most of the food products—old and new—consumed in the United States.

Food processors and manufacturers are a direct-market outlet for vast quantities of raw farm products as well as the source of supplies for hundreds of thousands of distributors. This large, complex system must mesh smoothly to overcome problems of food perishability, seasonal availability, volume, and logistics. To remain dynamic and responsive, the system must provide not only a means for product flow from producer to consumer, but also a communication system for the flow of information about consumer preferences and demands from consumer to producer.

The food marketing system includes more than half a million businesses that employ the equivalent of more than 5 million full-time employees. Persons employed by restaurants and other food service facilities make up almost half of that total. The output of farms in the United States combined with food products from other countries around the world are gathered by wholesalers and distributors within the market-ing system and processed to various degrees by the nation's food manufacturers and processors.

Wholesaling

Wholesaling is the link in the marketing system responsible for distributing food from the producer or processor to the retailer. The principal wholesaling activities involve gathering foods from many sources and distributing them to retailers, hotel and restaurant operators, and other institutions.

Because of the extensive number of products available and the variety of items stocked in relatively small amounts in food service operations, food service managers could not possibly search out and deal with the producers and processors of all the food products needed. Conversely, processors could not (in many instances) profitably provide the limited quantities needed by individual food service units. The job of the food wholesaler is to set up an efficient system for gathering the various products in sizable quantities from various producers and processors and then to sell them in smaller quantities to direct users of the materials.

As shown in Figure 1, the structure of a typical food distribution system, the food wholesaler (who buys and assembles the needed products) is the central figure in the distribution process. Some processors can perform the function of wholesaling through their sales offices and branch warehouses. The fact that processors' sales agents specialize in a limited product line means that they can concentrate their expertise and sales effort on fewer products. These agents do not take title, submit bills, or set prices for the goods sold. Some processors distribute a limited product line or a limited volume of

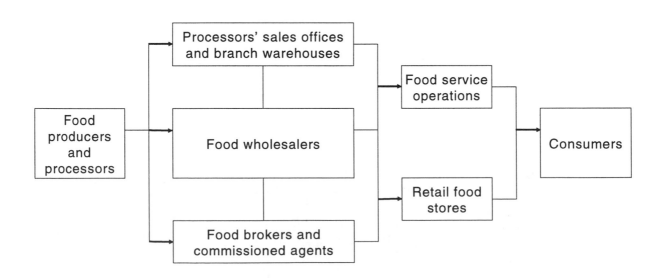

FIGURE 1. The Food Distribution System

products through food brokers and commissioned agents who act as their sales representatives. This group of intermediaries in the distribution system helps the processors by keeping them informed of current trade conditions and requirements of the market. In turn, the broker's sales staff provides goods and services for the retail and food service trade without taking actual possession of the products for sale. Brokers and commissioned agents are paid by the food processors for their services.

Food wholesalers are classified on the basis of their position and their activities in the marketing system. One category includes full-function wholesalers. *Full-function* wholesalers perform all the marketing functions in varying degrees. Their knowledge of the market, buying methods, and techniques for merchandising items to the best advantage is their strongest asset. Because wholesalers must be able to supply their customers with relatively small quantities at frequent intervals, they purchase large quantities of food and store the food and other goods in the form of stock in inventory. *Full-service* wholesalers extend credit to the customer and deliver goods when ordered. This type of wholesaler is the one most commonly used by food service operations.

In contrast, *limited-function* wholesalers carry a limited product line, may or may not extend credit, and establish order-size requirements for delivery. Processors' sales forces usually fall into this category.

Wholesalers also can be classified according to the types of products they handle. For example, wholesalers that stock a wide variety of goods so that the buyer can obtain a significant percentage of the items needed from one source are known as *general-line* wholesalers. There has been a trend toward expansion of the types and lines of products and services handled by institutional wholesalers so that volume feeding establishments can purchase virtually all their supplies from one wholesaler. This strategy is sometimes called *one-stop shopping*. (More information about this trend is provided later in this chapter.)

In contrast to general-line wholesalers, *specialty wholesalers* handle only one line or a few closely related lines of products. For example, some specialize in perishable products, such as fresh produce; they may handle some frozen fruits and vegetables and other related products as well. The number and economic importance of specialty wholesalers is declining in the American food distribution system.

The Procurement Process

Procuring products and services for the food service department is a complex process involving much more than the buyer simply acquiring products and services from reputable distributors and organizations. The term *procurement* involves a broad range of product selection and purchasing activities required to meet the needs of the food service department.

The process depends on a complex decision-making process that includes determining quality and quantity standards for the facility; specifying and ordering foods that meet those standards; and receiving, storing, and controlling the food supply inventory. Effective procurement requires that buyers have immediate access to a great deal of current and accurate information so as to make the best decision given the resources at their disposal.

Buyer's Responsibilities

Responsibility for the procurement process varies depending on the size and philosophy of the health care institution and on available expertise in the food service department. In smaller facilities, the food service director or manager often performs and/or coordinates procurement activities. Large organizations may employ an individual with special training or expertise in procurement. The buyer may be a food service employee if decentralized purchasing is used, or an employee of the purchasing department if the facility has centralized its purchasing activities. Responsibilities of the food buyer include:

▶ Determining food service department needs in terms of product, equipment, and services
▶ Selecting the method(s) of purchasing

- Selecting vendor(s)
- Soliciting and awarding bids or contracts
- Placing and following up on orders
- Training and supervising employees in receiving, storage, and issuance of food and supplies
- Establishing and maintaining an inventory control system
- Conducting research, including evaluating new products and conducting value analyses and make-buy studies
- Participating on the product evaluation team
- Maintaining effective vendor relations
- Assessing cost-benefit of value-added services provided by the distributor
- Providing product information such as cost data and nutrition information to others in the food service department
- Tracking changes in market and economic conditions through open communication with DSRs, attending trade and food shows, and keeping abreast of trends by reading trade and professional publications
- Utilizing current technology to facilitate the procurement process
- Maintaining open communication lines throughout the food service department and the larger institution

Buyer's Qualifications

Ideally, a buyer's educational and experiential qualifications should encompass the following areas: food quality; product specifications; computer skills, especially in spreadsheet applications and marketing and distribution channels in the food distribution system (see Figure 1); and accounting and other business activities associated with purchasing such as soliciting and awarding bids and contracts and performing make-buy analyses. Experience in food production and service also is beneficial. In addition, the buyer should possess certain managerial, interpersonal, and personal attributes. Some of these are organizational skills and a penchant for detail and accuracy; a team mind-set; initiative; good human relations and communication skills; and high ethical standards. Due to the complexity of activities performed, the buyer must be organized and follow through on tasks. Good human relations and communication skills are essential because he or she must meet the needs of several individuals in the food service department and communicate these needs to DSRs, members of group purchasing organizations (GPOs), and all other parties with whom the buyer interacts. Not only must the buyer demonstrate initiative in continuously assessing opportunities to increase or maintain food quality, but he or she must do so while decreasing cost whenever feasible. Attention to detail is critical because accuracy in purchase orders and inventory affects operating costs and service delivery. The buyer must maintain high ethical standards at all times, avoiding conflict of interest and kickbacks, for example. (More will be said on ethics in purchasing later in this chapter.)

No matter who has ultimate authority for the procurement function, a procurement specialist or the food service manager, the individual must maintain high standards in product quality. The buyer must continuously assess how to obtain products, equipment, and services to meet the needs of various components of the food service department while remaining within the financial constraints imposed on the operation.

Steps in the Food Service Procurement Process

As illustrated in Figure 2, the procurement process in a food service department is a 10-step sequence of activities. This process may be adjusted as needed to accommodate a particular facility or organizational structure. The following sections discuss the procurement-process steps.

Needs Assessment

The purpose of a needs assessment is to determine the operation's requirement for food, supplies, equipment, and services including quality, quantity, and required time frame. Information sources the buyer should rely on in completing the needs assessment include menu(s), standardized recipes, production demand forecasts, input from the product evaluation team and management staff, and the image the operation wants to project. Current and projected needs should be determined.

1. Complete needs assessment
   - Evaluate menu
   - Standardize recipe
   - Gather input from product evaluation team
   - Gather input from management staff
   - Forecast production demand
2. Select purchasing method(s)
   - Consider size and philosophy of operation
   - Determine purchase volume
   - Determine frequency of delivery
   - Consider distributor location
   - Evaluate department storage facilities
   - Determine available personnel
3. Develop approved vendor/distributor list
   - Decide whether to use a prime vendor
4. Establish and maintain inventory system
   - Just-in-time purchasing?
   - Perpetual inventory?
   - Physical inventory?
   - Consider value of inventory
   - Determine frequency of delivery
5. Determine order quantity
   - Forecast menu portions
   - Determine standard portions
   - Determine serving supplies
   - Assess food on hand
6. Obtain bid/price quotes
   - Develop specifications for each item
   - Obtain best prices/terms
7. Place order
   - Specify price
   - Specify quantity
   - Specify payment method
   - Distribute copies of order
8. Receive order
   - Request minimum number of shipments
9. Store Order
   - Consider type of food
10. Issue items

FIGURE 2. The Procurement Process

Maintaining a master calendar of catered functions and other special activities that would influence the procurement process is strongly recommended.

Selection of Purchasing Method

The next step in the process is selection of the procurement method(s) most appropriate for a particular facility. Factors influencing the decision may include size and philosophy of the food service operation, purchase volume, frequency of delivery desired, distributors' location, department storage facilities, available personnel and their skill levels, and type of purchasing system—centralized or decentralized, for example. Purchasing methods most frequently used by health care food service providers are discussed later in this chapter.

Approved Vendor/Distributor List

Identification of the vendor/distributor/suppliers with whom the organization will conduct business is a critical step of the procurement process. Specific factors to consider, which are discussed more fully later in this chapter, also may influence the selected method(s) of purchasing. These factors also may determine whether a distributor would meet a particular organization's needs or even conduct business with the facility.

Inventory System

The inventory system established will help determine

whether to implement just-in-time purchasing, a perpetual inventory, or a physical inventory (among other choices). It also will determine quantity of supplies maintained on hand, value of the inventory (in other words, how much money is tied up in inventory and unavailable for other uses), and frequency of delivery.

Order Quantity

The planned menu tells the buyer what kinds of food are needed, but only careful planning can ensure a supply of food sufficient for producing the anticipated number of meals with a minimum amount of leftovers. The quantities of food needed can be calculated by following four steps:

1. Forecast as accurately as possible the number of serving portions required for each item on the menu. When a selective menu is used, the forecast can be based on records of the number of selections previously made when the same combinations were served.
2. Determine a standard portion size for each food item. The standard portion size should correspond to the portion size stated on the standardized recipes to be used. Standardized recipes also should state the amount of each ingredient to be purchased for the stated yield.
3. Determine the quantities of food supplies required

for the number of serving portions needed.
4. Check the amount of food on hand in refrigerated, frozen, and dry storage areas and subtract that amount from the quantity needed for the planned menus. Prepare a list of supplies that must be purchased and a list of those to be requisitioned from the storeroom.

Regardless of the purchasing method used, order quantities should be large enough to make transactions economically worthwhile for vendors. The advantages of price comparison and product choice are lost if small orders are split among several vendors because of price.

Bid/Price Quotes, Order Placement, and Record Keeping

If purchasing is centralized, the food service department usually completes a purchase requisition form like the one shown in Figure 3 to inform the purchasing agent of the quantity and quality of specific foods to be ordered. The purchase requisition should contain complete specifications for each item, the unit of purchase (dozen or case, for example), the total quantity of each item, and the requested delivery date. In addition, a vendor and a price may be suggested; however, the purchasing agent is responsible for obtaining bids and awarding the purchase to the supplier quoting the best prices and terms. This approach works best when the director of the food service department and the

purchasing agent can pool their knowledge and communicate freely.

Administrative policy usually requires that purchase requisitions be approved by a designated person in the food service department before being sent to the purchasing department. The purchase requisition should be prepared in multiple copies, the number depending on the organization's record-keeping system. At least one copy should be kept on file in the food service department.

Whether purchasing is done by a purchasing department or by the food service department, a purchase order should always be used to inform the vendor of specific requirements. A purchase order is a legal document authorizing a supplier to deliver merchandise in accordance with the terms stated on the form. Purchase order forms, such as the example shown in Figure 4, are standardized by the institution and used by all departments.

The information contained in these forms includes the name and address of the supplier; a complete specification for each item, unless the vendor already has the specification on file (in which case the specification number can be used along with a brief description); the total quantity of each item ordered; the price per unit quoted by the vendor; the total price for the amount ordered; the terms of delivery; and the method of payment. The number of copies of the purchase order to be made varies among institutions, but because it is the record of merchandise ordered and the form used to check the receipt of deliveries, all departments dealing with supplies or with payments need copies.

Order Receipt, Storage, Issuance of Items

Delivery schedule requests should be considered carefully. Increased transportation costs will affect food costs if deliveries are requested more often than necessary. The delivery schedule required depends on the size of the institution, its geographic location, its storage facilities, and the size of the food service staff. In general, however, economy of food delivery and storage can be achieved as follows:

▶ Meat, poultry, and fish delivered once a week or less frequently, depending on whether the products are chilled or frozen
▶ Fresh produce delivered once or twice a week, depending on the storage space available and the quantities needed
▶ Canned goods and staples delivered weekly, semi-monthly, monthly, or quarterly, depending on the storage space available, quantities needed, and price quotes for specific volume
▶ Milk, milk products, bread, and baked goods delivered daily or every other day, although suppliers should be consulted because many dairies and bakeries have reduced delivery frequency
▶ Butter, eggs, and cheese delivered weekly

▶ Frozen foods delivered weekly or semimonthly, depending on the storage space available, usage rate, and price quotes for the quantities needed

Upon delivery, acceptance, and storage, items can be dispensed as needed to production areas.

Purchasing Methods

The purchasing method used by the buyer varies depending on the organization's size, philosophy and policies, purchasing volume, and financial stability, as well as the distributor's location and current environmental trends. The most common methods of purchasing used by health care food service facilities include group purchasing, consortium purchasing, prime vendor, one-stop purchasing, just-in-time purchasing, and formal (competitive) and informal (off-the-street) purchasing.

Group Purchasing Organizations

Some institutions are combining their buying power by forming purchasing cooperatives, or group purchasing organizations (GPOs), to effect cost savings. These units are also known as co-ops, buying groups, and purchasing support groups. Generally, the term *cooperative* is used to describe nonprofit organizations, whereas the term *group purchasing* describes the relationship among for-profit organizations that pool their pur-

chasing power. Regardless of which term is used, approximately 90 percent of all health care organizations belong to one or more of these groups. Compared with other health care departments, purchases by food service departments account for less than 10 percent of purchases made by the largest national and regional GPO.

The concept of group purchasing is based on the premise that several organizations have more purchasing power when negotiating collectively than any *one* entity alone. The organization of purchasing groups can occur on a local, state, regional, or national level. The requirements for membership and services provided vary. In most instances, members of the GPO pay a membership fee that is often based on bed count, dollar value of operating budget, or some other scale based on volume of purchases. These fees provide capital for operating the central office, employing procurement personnel, and legal services attendant to negotiating contracts. Some GPOs require members to purchase a specified volume of products, whereas others expect members to use their contractual agreements to their fullest potential.

Most GPOs have several characteristics in common. These include:

▶ At least one full-time procurement person who works with members to identify their needs and to negotiate contracts.

PURCHASE REQUISITION

To: Purchasing Office

Date: _____

From: _____

Requisition No.: _____

Purchase Order No.: _____

Date Required: _____

Unit	Total Quantity	Description	Suggested Vendor	Unit Cost	Total Cost

Requested by: _____   Approved by: _____   Date Ordered: _____

FIGURE 3. Example of a Purchase Requisition

PURCHASE ORDER

To: _____

_____

Purchase No.: _____
(Please refer to the above number on all invoices)

Date: _____

Requisition No.: _____

Department: _____

Date Required: _____

Ship to: _____F.O.B. _____   Via: _____ Terms: _____

Unit	Total Quantity	Description	Price per Unit	Total Cost

Approved by: _____

FIGURE 4. Example of a Purchase Order Form

- Members usually meet formally to establish or update policies and operating procedures, establish specifications, evaluate products, share information, and assess the GPO's function.
- Group purchasing organizations frequently function as agents for the members, acting on members' behalf when negotiating contracts.
- A membership fee is required.
- Many GPOs are currently establishing prime vendor programs requiring committed volume contracts. Members are required to purchase a minimum of 80 percent of their purchases from prime vendors with whom the GPO has contracts. In some instances, members are prohibited from joining other GPOs with prime vendor arrangements.
- Competitive bidding is the primary procedure used for determining pricing, terms, and contract conditions between the GPO and the supplier.
- Value-added services such as product quality testing, value analysis, computer systems and software, employee development seminars, recipe ideas, and menu planning may be provided to GPO members.

Savings in excess of 20 percent is the primary reason food service directors use group purchasing. Other benefits include product standardization, increased quality, decreased administrative cost for processing multiple purchase orders, and less time spent in purchasing products and supplies. Members also cite improved knowledge of new and existing products and enhanced networking as a result of participation in GPO meetings. Membership commitment and support of the GPO's philosophy are essential for success of the group.

Some barriers that influence the effectiveness and cost savings of participating in a GPO include difficulty in obtaining consensus on product specifications; loss of control over supplier selection, product variety, quality, and contract awards; and unwillingness of representatives of competing health care organizations to work as team members. Group members who join multiple GPOs decrease the negotiating power of the group because the volume of purchases is diminished. The group's purchasing power is increased only when volume is significantly more than it would be for each individual food service department.

When selecting a GPO, the buyer and food service director should adhere to certain guidelines. Among them:

- Select a group composed of members from organizations sharing similar characteristics.
- Interview current members and the GPO's employees to assess potential savings in excess of required fees.
- Answer the following questions:
  - What are membership requirements? Is a guarantee to purchase a specified quantity (%) or dollar volume through the GPO required?
  - How does the GPO operate?
  - What value-added services are provided to members?
  - Is a prime vendor contract used? If so, what product lines are available?
  - What is the GPO doing to obtain data on current market prices, new products, and trends?
- Discuss findings with food service management staff and members of the quality product evaluation team.
- Consult with the financial officer when evaluating the cost-benefit ratio of membership.
- Present a proposal for joining a GPO to the administration.

One-Stop Purchasing or Single Sourcing

One-stop purchasing or *single sourcing* is defined as the strategy of selecting and using a single supply source. This purchasing method is used by large and small health care facilities (including long-term care facilities). The method is based on a cooperative relationship between the food service department and the vendor.

One vendor (a full-line distributor) supplies the buyer with most of the food and supplies needed. The efficiency of food purchasing is improved by eliminating the time-consuming processes of placing bids and getting quotations. A substantial reduction in warehousing costs is possible if deliveries are made frequently. Lower net costs of products can result because the supplier knows relatively far in advance that certain food services will be needing specific products; thus the vendor can buy from wholesalers in larger quantities.

Certain disadvantages can arise with relying on one vendor exclusively. For one thing, backup suppliers might be difficult to find should the single-source vendor fail to deliver the supplies ordered. For another, the quality of available foods might be inferior or inconsistent. For larger food service departments, the number of distributors able to supply one-stop services may be limited; nonetheless, the supplier pool for this service provision is definitely growing. The effectiveness of one-stop purchasing is directly related to the efficiency and credibility of the supplier. Most food service departments generally have found this method to work very satisfactorily.

Prime Vendor Agreements

The *prime vendor* method involves a formal agreement between the food service department (buyer) and one vendor (supplier), whereby the buyer contracts with the vendor to supply a specified percentage of a given category (or categories) of product. The percentage ranges from 60 to 80, with 80 percent being more common today. The prime vendor contract, also referred to as a *systems con-*

tract, includes an agreement to purchase certain items for a specified time period and frequently specifies a minimum quantity of any or all items to be ordered during the contract period.

The steps involved in establishing a prime vendor relationship are outlined below. The bidding system is similar to contract purchasing, which is discussed later in this section.

1. Buyer completes an ABC analysis of purchases to determine which items make up the majority of purchases.
2. Food service solicits bid proposals from several distributors for an estimated, committed volume (annual or monthly usage), product specification and designated delivery, services, and inventory.
3. Food service director (or other buyer) reviews the bid and determines lowest bidder that meets all criteria.
4. Buyer negotiates and awards contract.
5. Food service department (via the director or other channel) provides feedback to the vendor on quality of service, delivery, and products. The food service representative can require the vendor to "open the books" and provide information on the structure of its cost and pricing data if this privilege is a condition of the contract. It is imperative that the purchasing agent

continue to track prices and market conditions.
6. Buyer develops secondary sources for products and supplies.

Benefits of a prime vendor agreement are increased competition and lower price; reduced cost of inventory, space, and order processing; and availability of value-added services. One value-added service that many health care food services utilize is computer systems provided by the prime vendor that allow the operations to place orders; obtain current price information and availability of products and supplies and product information (including nutrient analysis); and implement menu-planning and merchandising ideas. Some prime vendors provide a variety of software programs to their customers.

Disadvantages include potential gradual price increases, a decrease in competition, and a limited number of vendors with whom the operation conducts business. A reduction in service level can occur, especially in areas where only a limited number of vendors are available to conduct business. For the concept to be effective, continued enhancement of the vendor-buyer relationship is essential. The buyer must treat the DSRs and individuals delivering the product as partners rather than adversaries.

Just-in-Time Purchasing

Just-in-time (JIT) purchasing is a production planning strategy adopted by many manufacturing firms. The process involves purchasing products and supplies in the exact quantity required for a production run or limited time period and only as they are needed ("just in time"). Distributors deliver small quantities of supplies more frequently, and deliveries are timed more precisely based on production demand. Thus, just-in-time has an impact on both purchasing and inventory. Three goals are achieved with the JIT process: Inventory is decreased significantly as are related costs; space management is simplified; and problems must be resolved immediately as they occur. Unlike the manufacturing industry, each day food service operations produce a large number of perishable products in smaller quantities. The effectiveness of JIT warrants investigation because of potential cost reductions.

The ability to implement this method depends on several factors. These include complete support and cooperation of suppliers, commitment of all employees (including top administrators), accurate production demand forecasts, and changes in most aspects of the operation from menu planning through final service.

Locating food service distributors willing to provide frequent deliveries may be a challenge to some buyers, given that most distributors are requesting that customers accept fewer deliveries so as to decrease costs. Like the prime vendor concept, JIT requires building partnerships with distributors, and adoption of the JIT philosophy

could require a change in attitude regarding quantity of supplies to maintain in inventory. Just-in-time purchasing practices emphasize ordering smaller quantities rather than storing large quantities just in case additional product is needed.

Centralized Purchasing

With centralized purchasing, the most common method of purchasing used in health care institutions, a separate department in the institution specializes in purchasing the materials and supplies needed by the institution's various services and departments. In this system, the food service director (like all other department heads) requisitions supplies from the purchasing department. Only representatives from the purchasing department deal directly with outside vendors and suppliers. Vendors have direct contact with end users of the supplies only if new products or services are being brought into the purchasing system. In many institutions that use centralized purchasing, receiving and storage are also handled by the purchasing department rather than by the individual departments that use the supplies.

Contract and Noncontract Purchasing

Two other general methods of buying are contract purchasing and noncontract purchasing. *Contract purchasing* (sometimes called formal buying) involves a binding agreement between vendor and purchaser. With this process,

food service directors develop written specifications for each product and an estimate of the quantity needed for the designated bid period. A written notice of requirements, or a bid request (see Figure 5), is made available to vendors, who are invited to submit price bids based on the quality and quantity needed. The bid request includes instructions about the method of bidding, delivery schedule required, and frequency of payment; the date bids are due; the basis for awarding contracts; and any other information needed by buyer and seller. This process may be formal, with notices of intent to bid published under "Legal notices" in the local newspaper. Alternatively, it may be informal with copies of the bid distributed widely through the mail or by other means.

In addition to specifications for each item to be purchased, the bid request may include general provisions. For example:

▶ A performance bond by the seller
▶ Errors in the bid
▶ Alternate or partial bids
▶ A discount schedule
▶ Definition of the term of the contract
▶ Time frame for performance
▶ Requirements for the submission of samples
▶ Requirements for delivery points
▶ Inspection provisions
▶ Provisions for certification of quality
▶ Packing requirements
▶ Billing instructions
▶ Payment methods

BID REQUEST

Bids will be received until _____ for [indicate type of] delivery on the date indicated.

Issued by: _____   Address: _____

_____

Date Issued: _____

Date to Be
Delivered: [5–10 days after bid is awarded]

Increases in quantity up to 20 percent will be binding at the discretion of the buyer. All items are to be officially certified by the U.S. Department of Agriculture for acceptance no earlier than two days before delivery; costs of such service to be borne by the supplier.

Item No.	Description	Quantity	Unit	Unit Price	Amount
1	Chickens, fresh-chilled fryers, 2 1/2 to 3 lb., ready-to-cook, U.S. Grade A	500	Pound		
2	Chickens, fresh-chilled hens, 4 to 5 lb., ready-to-cook, U.S. Grade A	100	Pound		
3	Turkeys, frozen young toms, 20 to 22 lb., ready-to-cook, U.S. Grade A	100	Pound		
4	Eggs, fresh, large, U.S. Grade A, 30 dozen cases	150	Dozen		
5	Eggs, frozen, whole, inspected, six 4-pound cartons per case	60	Pound		

Vendor: _____

FIGURE 5. Example of a Bid Request

- Requirements for standard package size
- Cancellation clause

Obtaining firm, fixed prices for the specified bid period is desirable. However, when product prices fluctuate frequently or rise steadily, vendors may be unable (or unwilling) to quote firm prices for an extended period. Bid requests that state a maximum amount required, as well as a minimum quantity to be purchased from the successful bidder, allow some flexibility for both buyer and vendor when prices of the product needed are likely to fluctuate considerably. Although price is a major consideration in awarding the contract, the buyer should carefully consider quality of the product and ability of the vendor to meet the delivery schedules specified in the contract. In addition, the vendor's reputation, previous performance, and compliance with specifications and government regulations are important considerations. All bidders, including those not awarded the contract, should be informed when the contract has been awarded.

Noncontract purchasing (sometimes called informal buying) is done through verbal and written communications between buyer and vendor via telephone sales representatives. However, it may be handled without direct contact with the sales representative through the open market. Price quotations are obtained from two or more suppliers. Quotation sheets, or call sheets, such as those shown in Figure 6, are useful. A quotation sheet provides spaces for the name and description of food items, amount of food needed, and prices quoted by various suppliers. After the price quotes have been received, the service and quality record of the supplier that gave the lowest quotation is checked. If the supplier has a history of providing good-quality products on schedule, the order usually is placed there. Although small institutions may use this method to purchase most of their foods, larger ones may use it only for perishable fresh products or foods needed in limited quantities. One disadvantage of noncontract purchasing is the amount of time required to check and compare prices, interview sales representatives, and place orders. Problems also can result from verbal commitments to buy. Some of these problems, however, can be avoided by providing vendors with a list of accurate product specifications as a communication aid.

Vendor Selection and Relations

All distributor/vendors cannot meet the needs and expectations of all food service operations. Thus, it is imperative to select those compatible with a specific operation and with which the buyer can work cooperatively to obtain products that meet established standards and the operation's financial constraints. Quality, price, dependability, and service are factors that must dictate supplier selection. The buyer should strive to achieve the following objectives when evaluating potential vendors:

- Negotiate a fair price.
- Receive consistent quality and quantity as specified.
- Receive order on time.
- Develop relationships with vendors based on trust.
- Avoid internal conflicts over vendor relations.
- Build relationship with local vendors to develop goodwill within the community.

Achievement of these objectives is essential to the overall success of the procurement process.

Selection

Supplier selection involves a four-stage process, which is best remembered by the mnemonic SINE:

1. *S*urvey: Explore all possible sources of supply.
2. *I*nquiry: Compare and evaluate prospective vendors to identify qualifications, advantages, and disadvantages.
3. *N*egotiation and selection: Enter into effective and clear dialogue with candidates to secure the best price, quality, and delivery commitment.
4. *E*xperience: Monitor vendor service and product quality to ensure that what is promised is delivered.

The *survey stage* is devoted to identification of the need for new products, the need to investigate new suppliers, or

QUOTATION SHEET

Type of Product: __Fresh Produce__ Day: __Monday__ Date: __2/10/88__ Approved by: __DL__

Amount on Hand	Quantity	Unit	Description and Specifications	Supplier and Quotations per Unit			
				Smith	Brown		
21	23	50# bag	Carrots	11.40	13.85		
0	1	40# bag	Bananas, #4	12.00	13.40		

QUOTATION SHEET

Type of Product: __Canned goods__ Day: __Wednesday__ Date: __4/6/88__ Approved by: __DL__

Amount on Hand	Quantity	Unit	Description and Specifications	Supplier and Quotations per Unit			
				Smith	Brown		
3	6	Case	Applesauce, regular #10 can	10.09	10.83		
4	6	Case	Peas, early June, #10 can	11.39	13.46		

FIGURE 6. Examples of Quotation Sheets

the need to reevaluate current suppliers. Questions in this regard include:

▶ What is available on the market?
▶ Who can supply the product(s) or service(s)?
▶ Who can supply it (them) most (or more) economically within the required time period?
▶ Who are the distributors that service this area?

This stage results in a list of potential suppliers. The goal is to use the management information system (MIS) to identify as many sources as possible. A buyer who is new to an area must also network with other food service directors or buyers to assemble the list. Additional sources of information include past experience, interviews with DSRs, trade journals and shows, yellow pages, and buyer's guides.

In the *inquiry stage,* after identifying all potential sources the buyer must compare and analyze sources that appear capable of meeting the needs of the food service department. Criteria for evaluation include, but are not limited to, price, quality, service, delivery schedule, and available quantity. Also during this phase, the buyer should contact other buyers or managers for their feedback and experience with the suppliers from which they purchase. Sample questions that could be asked include:

▶ Is the firm reliable?
▶ Is quality consistently excellent?

▶ Are deliveries accurate and on time?
▶ How would you rate DSRs and other vendor employees with whom you have interacted?
▶ What additional value-added services do you use?
▶ How would you evaluate these services?
▶ What do you like most about this distributor?
▶ What problems, if any, have you experienced in conducting business with this vendor?

Another factor that must be evaluated is whether to use local or national vendors, each of which offers advantages and limitations. Additional criteria for comparing distributors are financial stability of the firm, technical expertise of the distributors' staff, and compatibility of business practices with regard to ethics standards. Business practices include strict adherence to delivery schedule, credit terms, minimum order requirement, lead time, return policy, and product line variety. If possible, a visit to the vendor's facility is recommended, especially if there has been no prior business relationship. After comparing all the potential distributors based on these criteria, the buyer narrows the options and prepares a second list called a qualified supplier list (QSL).

During the *negotiation and selection stage,* the buyer uses information obtained during the inquiry stage to issue an initial purchase order. Before doing so, however, he or she should meet with the suppliers

to discuss payment, delivery, and contract terms, if applicable.

During the *experience stage,* the buyer follows up to ensure that the chosen vendor is providing the type of service and quality of products previously agreed on. If problems occur, the buyer should document them and provide immediate feedback to the distributor so that corrective action can be taken. Any problems (and their resolution) should be documented for future reference and evaluation.

The goal of the supplier selection process is to establish several product, supply, and equipment sources that can consistently provide the quantity and quality of products required at the right price and the right time. Communication and feedback are critical ingredients for a long-term and effective buyer-vendor relationship.

Buyer-Vendor Relations

Sound business practices and well-stated purchasing policies are the bases for good purchasing decisions. Careful planning and an accurate statement of food needs are the starting points in building good buyer-vendor relations. As always, fairness and honesty are essential. Product requirements should be specified and complete information as to availability and prices should be obtained. The buyer should establish an appointment schedule with sales representatives and adhere to it. At no time should one vendor's price information be discussed with another vendor. Accepting gifts, favors, coupons, and other promotional offers can create a potentially unhealthy obligation to a vendor that can adversely affect the buyer's freedom to make objective vendor selections. Buyers should be familiar with and follow the fair business policies of their institutions. Special services that ordinarily would not be available from vendors should not be requested.

Basic Purchasing Guidelines

As a quick-reference tool, the following purchasing guidelines are summarized. They provide the fundamental "how-to's" of purchasing:

► Develop a specification for each food item. Government and industry specifications can provide a starting point to help food service managers and buyers develop their own. For some products, specifications can be quite brief, whereas others will require substantial detail.
► Make sure that a copy of specifications developed by the food service department is available to and used by the buyer. Many departments find it convenient to provide a complete set of their specifications (classified by commodity group and number) to vendors with which they routinely do business. This decreases the time required to get a price quotation.

► Compare food quality and yield in relation to price. A food of higher quality and a higher unit price may yield more serving portions of better quality and at a lower cost per serving than the same food of lower quality and price. Frequent studies of the net yield in serving portions and of the cost per serving of various brands make it possible to base buying decisions on cost per serving rather than on unit purchase price.
► Use bid requests or quotation sheets to get price quotations.
► Purchase only the types, quality, and quantities required for the planned menu and/or production forecasts. However, if a special buy becomes available and the quality is acceptable, a surplus of the product may be purchased if adequate storage space and conditions permit. For example, prices on the previous year's pack of canned or frozen fruit or vegetable items may be quite reasonable just before the new pack reaches the market.
► Purchase foods only from vendors known to maintain approved levels of sanitation and quality control in accordance with government regulations and recommended practices of food handling and storage.
► Purchase foods by weight, size, or count per container. The minimum weights acceptable for purchase units should be stated in the specifications.

► Establish a purchase and delivery schedule based on the storage life of various foods, the location of vendor in relation to the buying facility, delivery costs, storage space, inventory policies, and the food needs specified in the menu(s).
► Ensure that all purchases are inspected upon delivery. Rejection of an item should be done at the time of delivery unless there is a prior agreement that the vendor will give credit for any defective products or gross errors. Delivery sheets or invoices should not be initiated or signed until the quality and quantity of foods delivered have been checked against the purchase order.
► Maintain written purchase and receiving records for all foods and supplies ordered and received.

Standards of Ethics

Several ethics issues should be addressed when establishing purchasing policies. Along with responsibility for spending large quantities of money on behalf of an operation comes certain temptations that involve making ethics-based decisions. Implicit in the buyer role is the basic requirement to remain loyal to the employer and to the ethics standards established by the organization. This means avoiding conflicts of interest, whereby personal gain could be derived from conducting business with a specific vendor. Most organizations policies proscribe against accepting gifts or services from vendors with which the facility conducts business if such gifts or services are for personal use. Accepting bribes, kickbacks, and gifts in exchange for special ordering consideration, then, is not only unethical but illegal.

Many dilemmas will occur for which there is no one "right" or "wrong" action. When this happens, a buyer's personal ethics imperative and organizational policies must provide a framework for action. For example, sensitive issues that have occurred in food service and interfered with fair and honest business practice include the following:

▶ Gaining confidential information about a competitor from suppliers
▶ Accepting free trips, entertainment, and gifts beyond the dollar amount set by the organization
▶ Purchasing from suppliers favored by the administration
▶ Disclosing one vendor's quote to another vendor
▶ Using the organization's economic clout to force a vendor to lower prices

The best way to avoid these situations is to adhere to defined policies and procedures for conducting good and ethical business practices with vendors. The food service director may consider adopting the National Association of Purchasing Management's Principles and Standards of Purchasing Practices as a guide for everyone involved in the procurement process

(available from the NAPM, P.O. Box 22160, Tempe, AZ 85285-2160).

Computer-Assisted Procurement

Technology's impact on food service distributors and health care food service operations has already been discussed. Predictions of the role electronic data interchange will have on the procurement process also has been described.

This section provides a brief footnote to the earlier section so that buyers understand the fine points of computer-assisted procurement from actual practice. The steps enumerated below are intended as another quick-reference tool explaining computerized purchasing by buyers whose computer terminals are connected to a central processing unit (CPU).

1. The buyer calls up from the computer's files a listing for the product to be purchased. The computer record shows the specification for the product, its unit price, and a list of vendors who can supply the product.
2. The buyer selects the vendor, the quantities needed, and the desired delivery date and time.
3. After the products have been delivered and accepted, delivery confirmation is entered into the computer record and conveyed (or telecommunicated) to the vendor's computer.

4. The vendor's computer sends an invoice directly to the institution or to the institution's bank for payment for the products delivered. The invoice may be communicated by computer or with hard copy of the invoice printed out from the computer's record.
5. For an invoice communicated directly to the bank, the institution's bank automatically credits the vendor's account and debits the institution's account for the purchase.

In addition to the system described above, a number of spreadsheet applications might facilitate record keeping and provide current cost information. Examples include vendor evaluation, bid analysis, usage reports, and inventory analysis and valuation. Point-of-sale systems can be directly linked to a perpetual inventory.

Summary

Whether a health care facility hires a procurement specialist or charges the task of purchasing to the food service director or a centralized purchasing department, procurement activities ultimately have one objective. That objective is to ensure that everything needed to produce menu items is in place, on time, and within budget boundaries.

To accomplish this massive objective, buyers must survey supplier sources, inquire about prospective vendors, negotiate for the best selection at the most favorable price, and monitor selected vendor/suppliers to make sure they deliver what they promised when they promised it. Buyers must do this while minimizing leftovers, plate waste, and rampant overstocking. •

Certain trends affect these efforts significantly. For example, distributors no longer can rely on the traditional "sales call." Their service representatives—DSRs—now must promote value-added services to retain a buyer-client base they once could take for granted. Thus, technology such as direct computer linkups between buyers and distributors' product or service line can expedite the buyer's order process and inventory control methods. Such services provided by distributors create distributor-buyer alliances whose common goal is customer retention. What's more, this interaction can be accomplished without either party leaving his or her office.

References

Anasari, A., and Modarress, B. *Just-in-Time Purchasing.* New York City: Free Press, 1990.

Birkman, I. Food service needs controls to contain cost. *Hospitals* 54:79, Mar. 16, 1980.

Casper, C. A new way to manage inventory. *Institutional Distribution* 28(40):44–45, 48–49, Sept. 1, 1992.

Casper, C. Information 2000—computer wizardry will radically alter how distributors and their customers commu-

nicate. *Institution Distribution* 27(12):45–50, Dec. 1991.

Casson, J. The economic importance of the hospitality industry. In: A. Pizam, R. C. Lewis, and P. Manning, editors. *The Practice of Hospitality Management.* Westport, CT: AVI, 1982.

Coltman, M. M. *Hospitality Industry Purchasing.* New York City: Van Nostrand Reinhold, 1990.

Dion, P. A., Banting, P. M., Picard, S., and Blenkhorn, D. L. JIT implementation: a growth opportunity for purchasing. *Journal of Purchasing and Materials Management* 28(4):32–36, Fall 1992.

Hamann, T., Scott, W. G., and Conner, P. E. *Managing the Modern Organization.* 4th ed. Boston: Houghton Mifflin, 1982.

Heinritz, S., Farrel, P. V., Giuniperro, L., and Kolchin, M. Institutional purchasing. In: *Purchasing Principles and Application.* 8th ed. New York City: Prentice Hall, 1991.

Hoffman, M. DSRs in basic training. *The Food Service Distribution* 5(9):26–27, Aug. 1991.

King, P. In central Pennsylvania colleges. *Food Management* 28(4):98, Apr. 1993.

King, P. In nursing homes in New Hampshire. *Food Management* 28(4):102, Apr. 1993.

Lambert, H. R. Partnerships needed to create customer value. *Institutional Distribution* 28(1):16, Jan. 1992.

Murai, S. State of the industry: purchasing coopera-

tives. In: *Impact of Food Procurement on the Implementation of the Dietary Guidelines for Americans in Child Nutrition Programs Conference Proceedings.* University, MS: Food Service Management Institute, 1992.

National Association of Meat Purveyors. *The Meat Buyer's Guide.* McLean, VA: NAMP, 1984.

Newman, R. G. Single sourcing: short-term saving versus long-term problems. *Journal of Purchasing and Materials Management* 25(2):20–25, Summer 1989.

Ninemeir, J. D. *Purchasing, Receiving, and Storage: A Systems Manual for Restaurants, Hotels, and Clubs.* Boston: CBI Publishers, 1983.

Ouellette, R. P., Lord, N. W., and Cheremisinoff, P. N. *Food Industry Energy Alternatives.* Westport, CT: Food and Nutrition Press, 1980.

Reid, R. D., and Riegel, C. D. *Purchasing Practices of Large Food Service Firms.* Tempe, AZ: Center for Advanced Purchasing Studies/National Association of Purchasing Management, Inc., 1989.

Salkin, S. The growing clout of healthcare purchasing groups. *Institution Distribution* 28(2):101–5, Feb. 1992.

Salkin, S. Value added services add value, but you provide the service. *Institutional Distribution* 27(12):18, Dec. 1991.

Salkin, S. Why GPOs are booming. *Food Service Di-*

rector 59(3):60, Mar. 15, 1992.

Schechter, M., and Boss, D. Putting quality management to work. *Food Management* 57(11):102–4, 106, 110–13, Nov. 1992.

Schuster, K. In hospitals in California. *Food Management* 28(4):100, Apr. 1993.

Sneed, J., and Kresse, K. H. *Understanding Food Service Financial Management.* Gaithersburg, MD: Aspen, 1989.

Spears, M. C. *Foodservice Organizations: A Managerial and Systems Approach.* 2nd ed. New York City: Macmillan, 1991.

Stefanelli, J. M. *Purchasing: Selection and Procurement for the Hospitality Industry.* 2nd ed. New York City: John Wiley & Sons, 1985.

Trace, T. L., Lynch, J. F., Fischer, J. W., and Hummrich, R. C. Ethics and vendor relationships. In: S. J. Hall, editor. *Ethics in Hospitality Management: A Book of Readings.* East Lansing, MI: Educational Institute, 1992.

Weisburg, K. Why more hospitals eye group purchasing options. *Food Service Director* 65(3):65, Mar. 15, 1991.

Wetrich, J. G. Group purchasing: an overview. *American Journal of Hospital Pharmacy* 44(7):1581–92, July 1992.

Wolkenhauer, S. Selling something other than product at a price. *Institutional Distribution* 28(10):23, 90, Oct. 1992.

DSRS AND THE NEW TECHNOLOGY

Carol Casper

Is the Pen Mightier than the Keyboard?

THE TALK OF SALES technology a few years ago was whether computers would replace the pad and pen. Today, the focus of discussion has shifted to whether the pen will replace the computer keyboard.

No one is talking about pen and paper, however. The discussion is about pen computers, the latest wizardry to emerge from the PC revolution.

Pen computers, also called pad PCs, penpads, or tablets, are lightweight, high-powered, full-function personal computers with one important difference: an interactive screen. Instead of using a keyboard or mouse, users can write commands and other information directly onto the screen, using a special electronic pen. Some versions are also touch-sensitive, allowing one to interact with the computer by touching it.

While standard laptops have gained acceptance among foodservice distributors, several hail pen PCs as the wave of the future. Mobility and greater ease of use are the chief benefits cited by proponents such as Thoms Proestler Co., Davenport, Iowa.; Labatt Foodservice, San Antonio, Texas; and Pocahontas Foods USA, Richmond, Va.

New Ways to Enter Data

Applications for pen PCs usually incorporate handwriting recognition, so users can enter letters and numbers by simply writing on the screen. The system then converts the handwriting into data files. Graphics software enables the unit to capture elements like drawings and signatures as well.

"Think of the hardware as paper with brains," says a representative for GRiD Systems, Westlake, Texas, the computer manufacturer that introduced the first pad three years ago.

But, handwriting recognition is not the chief attraction of pen PCs. In fact, one drawback is that although the software continually improves, handwriting capture is still a cumbersome way to enter quantities of text.

What pen computers handle spectacularly are "point-and-shoot" operations, tasks that involve mainly selecting options from a screen. Proponents call pen PCs the perfect tool for applications that consist mainly of filling out forms or lend themselves to graphical user interfaces where either a mouse or arrow keys on a keyboard are used to position a cursor on a display.

For this reason, a growing number of distributors are looking to pen hardware as an alternative to the standard laptop PC. Most sales applications, from order-taking and recipe analysis to looking up account, inventory, and product information, involve little text entry but large amounts of positioning cursors and hitting enter and function keys— all of which can be replaced by simply touching pen to screen.

There are ways to enter text into penpads other than writing. Most applications include an option for displaying a keyboard diagram on half the screen so users can tap in letters. They can also pull up a calculator.

For salespeople who find a conventional laptop with keyboard intimidating, cumbersome, or more complicated than needed, pen PCs offer a powerful and appealing alternative.

Computing on the Run

"Mobility and accessibility were the main reasons Thoms Proestler opted for the pen format," vice president of sales and marketing James Hendrickson explains. "Pen PCs also eliminate much of the anxiety some people have as soon as you say the word computer."

Another factor was the sizzle.

"We were late coming into the laptop game compared with other distributors. Our thinking was, why come in with a me-too product? Let's do something to position us ahead of the competition. Not many customers in our market had seen or even heard of pen computers before we introduced them."

TPC spent over a year developing its own set of pen applications for its sales force and customers. It has phased reps onto the equipment since last spring and has customer test sites up. When the last group of DSRs completes training this month, TPC will begin selling the system to customers.

Similar to other distributor laptop programs, TPC's pen computers allow DSRs to build orders from customized order guides, look up items in its price book, check customer purchasing histories/accounts receivable/daily inventory, analyze recipes, and pull up expanded product files.

For customers, the software also includes an inventory-control system so they can take inventory as they walk through the storeroom and, using par levels, generate orders automatically.

One reason TPC opted for pen technology was the ease and directness with which DSRs and customers can perform these functions on screen, notes project manager Ed Haupt. To enter orders, a rep simply goes through the order guide on screen and taps desired products with the stylus. With one tap, the system automatically defaults to a quantity of one. To enter larger quantities, the rep can write in a numeral or tap a number from a display on the side of the screen.

Reps tap on-screen command lines to pull down menus of other options—to scan through the product catalog, figure portion costs, or check the total gross-profit dollars or commission they've generated so far that day. They can also jot down notes in customer files and a daily planner.

"Order input is three to four times quicker with the pen," Haupt says. "DSRs and customers are often intimidated by a keyboard and screen commands. With the pen PC, they just see what they want and point."

Gary Egel, the first TPC rep to work with the system, says that it "was so user-friendly I was able to begin using it immediately." Two other reps note that it took almost a month to get comfortable with the machine, but both believe that pen interface was easier to learn than a keyboard.

Ease of movement is the other key feature touted by pen enthusiasts. A DSR or operator can hold the pad PC comfortably in one hand and tap or write with the other while walking through a storeroom or kitchen.

"Mobility was the biggest factor in our decision," notes Tony Canty, Labatt's director of MIS. "Our reps don't generally sit down at a desk to take an order. Either they're chasing the chef around the kitchen, or going through the storeroom with the customer or by themselves."

Labatt chose IBMs Thinkpad hardware and OrderWriter software from Access International, Lansing, Ill., a company that specializes in remote order-entry and communications systems. The software is a new version of its OrderTaker program, rewritten for the pen environment.

"We added some features such as the ability to jot down notes while the rep is talking with the customer, but the basic product is the same whether running on a laptop, pen computer, or desktop," Access sales and marketing administrator Matthew Hook notes. TPC's software also runs in all three environments and accepts input from a keyboard, mouse, or pen.

More pen-software options will soon be available. Sales Partner Systems, Daytona Beach, Fla., is readying a pen-based inventory application, followed by a pen-enabled version of SPS-Link, its DSR laptop program.

American Eagle Software Integrators, Upland, Calif., plans a pen version of its laptop program by year's end. It expects the format to eventually supersede the keyboard for sales applications, manager of sales and marketing Gary Davis notes.

Keyboard Advocates

Some have reservations, however.

Joey Pierce, president of Advanced Data Systems, Richmond, Va., says, "We are concerned about reliability of the hardware and feel most of our customers still prefer a keyboard. However, we will probably offer a pen version of our laptop system as an option."

Sales Partner Systems president Larry Frank also voices concerns about jumping on the pen bandwagon too quickly. "The ability to do word processing is an advantage to most DSRs—for organizing notes, creating specialized promotions, writing thank-you letters, and other situations. These applications are easier with a keyboard."

A check of about a dozen distributors shows them divided on how sales reps actually work. David Dow, sales manager at Gordon Food Service, Grand Rapids, Mich., says that reps manage to follow customers through kitchen and stockroom comfortably with a notebook PC, although a pad might be easier. Others say such runaround selling today is the exception rather than the rule, and reps have no problems setting up at a desk with most customers.

Several also agree with Frank that word processing is of growing importance. "Our reps write reports and are responsible for their own letters," notes Bob Kranz, regional manager with Maines Paper and Food Service, Conklin, N.Y. "This gives them the ability to shine."

Some penpads allow a keyboard to be plugged in, so pen-equipped reps could still handle such functions.

The chief argument against pen PCs is the price. Hardware costs about twice as much as a laptop or notebook for comparable computing power. That means a tag of roughly $3,000 per unit. Prices will no doubt fall, though, as they have for laptops and notebooks.

For those uncomfortable with an either/or hardware choice, there is a third option: a combination laptop/penpad. GRiD Systems debuted such a unit, its Convertible, in November. A tablet equipped with a pull-out keyboard, it is designed to offer users the best of both worlds.

The Convertible is already generating interest among distributors. Frank says that such a design could be the best way to go, and Thoms Proestler is considering it for the extra flexibility.

Pocahontas started developing software for GRiD's Palm-Pad pen computer, but is now retooling to run on the Convertible, vice president of information systems Mark Johnson says.

Kathy Rhodes, director of data processing for Caro Produce and Institutional Foods, Houma, La., is impressed with the options it affords. Caro will likely be the first Pocahontas member to use the group's pen software.

Rhodes says that Caro waited for pen technology because management felt it would be easier for reps to learn and use than a laptop. However, she likes the idea of including a keyboard.

On the price tag, Rhodes comments, "The machine is more expensive than a laptop, but costs the same as we were willing to pay for a plain keyboard unit three years ago."

As numerous distributors note, waiting for hardware to stop evolving and prices to bottom out means never getting started.

How Much Will the Rep's Role Change?

With portable PCs now commonplace for sales reps and technologies like pen computers coming into play, it is a good time to re-examine questions posed when laptops first appeared in distribution three years ago.

How are computers changing the role of the DSR—or are they? Are PCs worth the investment or are they merely overpriced order-entry devices?

Also, with more companies marketing direct-order-entry

systems for customers, are DSR laptops just a phase? What will happen as more customers enter their own orders? Will sales reps become superfluous?

The reply to the last question, all executives interviewed agree, is a resounding no. The DSR will continue to play an important role, although one that is changing and may alter even more over the rest of the decade.

Several executives point out that technology is not responsible for changes in the DSR's role, although it does provide tools to help its evolution.

The rising costs of doing business dictate that salespeople must be more productive, generating higher sales and profits, several sales managers note. Greater profits, in particular, mean better account penetration and program selling. Laptops and direct-access systems for customers can help.

"If you just take an order-taker and give him a laptop, you still have an order-taker, only with better equipment," says Mike Teagle, president of Valley Food Service & Poultry, Norfolk, Va. "But, if a rep uses the menu planner, the portion-costing system, and other features, the tools can help him become a consultant."

Most executives say that their better DSRs recognize the advantages laptops provide and run with them. To others, laptops are just sophisticated order-entry terminals—although even in that limited role laptops offer benefits,

Teagle notes. These include reductions in manual labor and time to process orders, fewer errors, and even a boost in order size because on-screen order guides function as prompts.

Most executives stress sales reps' responsibility in effecting consultative selling, but Joe Bendix, president of CP Foodservice, Ormond Beach, Fla., asserts that the challenge really belongs to management.

"A lot of companies put in the technology, but keep all other processes the same," Bendix observes. "They don't invest in other systems to support the sales rep's new role. You have to provide resources such as product specialists, corporate chefs, and other services to enable your salespeople to act as consultants and problem-solvers."

Larry Frank, president of Sales Partner Systems, Daytona Beach, Fla., agrees that distributors need to conceptualize the big picture to get the most out of laptops and PC systems.

"People look at what their DSRs are doing and how the laptop can improve their performance in their current functions. Too few consider the whole picture from a systems approach. Simply designing a system around getting the order is not taking full advantage of the many capabilities laptops provide.

"We look at them as a means to equip reps for a whole new range of field-sales activities."

These include maintaining customer profiles, keeping notes, listing competitive prod-

ucts, sales tracking and analysis, menu consultation, recipe costing, and other functions Frank expects will be developed over the next few years.

In fact, as more customers begin keying in their own orders, Frank believes ordering will become a minor feature for DSRs, although the PC will be more rather than less important in their daily functioning as account managers.

Labatt Foodservice, San Antonio, Texas, has a view of the DSR's role that is reflected in the specific pen-PC system it chose.

"Increasing speed and shrinking errors are the two goals we want sales technology to accomplish," general manager Al Silva explains. "A customer can only give a rep so much time. If a DSR spends 40 percent of that solving problems from errors, and 40 percent on replenishment, that leaves only 20 percent for selling. So speeding up the order process and shrinking errors are key."

While agreeing that reps must become consultants, Labatt defines the role as packaging and selling distribution programs, rather than providing expertise on product, menu, and other aspects of restaurant management.

"Menu-analysis capabilities and similar tools are important to operators, and we provide them in customer systems. Our reps, however, don't have time to spend on menu analysis and customers don't expect it," Silva says.

Other distributors, though, think that tools like menu cost analysis and expanded product information can help reps become consultative account managers, which in turn will lead to increased sales and profits.

The big picture, says Jeff Braverman, president of Hawkeye Food Systems, Iowa City, Iowa, involves not just specific tools, but the whole array of ways that laptops contribute to reps' overall efficiency.

"We hoped to increase productivity by creating more selling time, decreasing the manual labor of order entry, and reducing errors," Braverman notes. Then, theoretically, reps could increase their consultative selling by showing the benefit of product features and helping customers manage food costs and turn inventory faster. All this, in turn, should result in improved gross-margin dollars per drop.

"That has happened since we installed laptops," Braverman says. "Our average order size has gone from the high $500s to nearly $700."

David Dow, sales manager at Gordon Food Service, Grand Rapids, Mich., agrees laptops have enabled reps to become more efficient. "The laptops have provided other cost savings by putting so much information right at DSRs' fingertips," he adds.

More Profitable Sales

An area where distributors say they see almost immediate improvement from laptops is gross profit.

"Laptops contributed to an increase in our gross profit margin because reps now see their results for each order," Bob Kranz, a regional sales manager with Maines Paper and Food Service, Conklin, N.Y., points out. "Average lines per order are also up."

Laptops also serve as sales-management tools, Kranz notes. "Regional managers track reps' daily and weekly sales in each product category and monitor gross profit. Product specialists also record each DSR's weekly sales in their category and if they see a drop, address it immediately."

James Hendrickson, vice president of sales and marketing at Thoms Proestler Co., Davenport, Iowa, says that as reps got pen PCs, most showed improvement in profit performance.

The company has been grooming reps to take on more of a consulting role, he adds, and PCs aid the process by giving them access to information that can help them help customers.

TPC rep Bill Brownson says, "If I want to help a customer make up a plate, I can substitute in different items and see how each affects food cost. The program also lets you set a desired food cost and then see what price the customer would have to charge with different items.

"I could do all that before manually, but it was much too time-consuming."

One point on which distributors agree is that as more customer systems are installed, street accounts will do more of this kind of analysis themselves, rather than looking to DSRs for help. They will also browse the product catalog themselves, pick up recipe ideas, and take advantage of whatever other information distributors provide.

However, most think that DSRs will still need the ability to provide these services since not all accounts will ever qualify for nor want such systems.

"Our Atlantic Access software is only designed for customers with a strong or program relationship with us," notes William C. Eacho 3d, chairman of Manassas, Va.-based Atlantic Food Services. "While customers like that are more common, I don't think you could characterize the majority of our accounts as falling into that type.'

Gene May, vice president of sales and marketing at Quality Foods, Little Rock, Ark., says that in several years, up to 30 percent of the company's orders will be entered directly by customers, up to 50 percent will be handled by telemarketing reps, and only some 20 percent will be entered by salespeople.

Dow says that reps may end up with primarily a merchandising function. "One of our customers sees their role growing into a kind of super broker, the difference being that our DSRs will have a much better handle on what each operation is all about."

Butch Hartman, who oversees laptop functions for Atlantic, sees successful DSRs "taking even a more active role with customers after we install an on-site system."

He agrees with Frank, who says that a DSR needs to stay closely involved with the account, not just set up a system and walk away

Atlantic rep Bob Yare, 17 of whose 30 accounts are on Atlantic Access, says, "Most of my job right now is acting almost as a computer-systems consultant. I spend about 40 percent of the day actually selling. The rest is spent teaching customers how to use the computer to become more profitable."

About 85 percent of Yare's dollar sales come in through his 17 customers on the Access system. "I run a support group for my customers on the system. Since I'm always getting new people on, I've recently broken it down into separate beginner, intermediate, and advanced classes."

Yare's daily routine starts with pulling up a routing summary each morning on his own PC.

"It shows who's on each truck, how much they've spent in each category, whether anything was shorted or substituted, and what time each customer is scheduled for delivery. If anything is shorted, I can call the customer before the truck arrives.

"I also get weekly and monthly reports showing what customers bought, the dollar amounts in each category, and any new items that were added or dropped from their purchases.

"I still see my clients at least once a week. I go over computer functions, sample products, and discuss ways they can improve sales and profits."

"The job has gotten more technical than in the old days," Yare notes.

The following projects can be assigned to individual students or a team of three students.

1. Interview a minimum of two distributors' sales representatives (DSRs) employed by foodservice distributors and a minimum of one sales representative employed by a foodservice broker organization. Obtain the following information: roles and responsibilities of a DSR and broker, differences between the two organizations within marketing chain, trends in purchasing specific to three different market segments of the foodservice and hospitality industry including use of technology in the procurement process, value-added services provided to the three market segments, and strategies to enhance working relationship between DSRs and foodservice/hospitality operations. Interview at least two operators from different market segments of the foodservice and hospitality industry regarding strategies to enhance working relationship between DSRs and brokers and their organization. Submit 10 page report which describes the roles and responsibilities of DSRs and brokers; summarizes results of the interviews; compares the responses of the DSRs, broker, and operators; and includes recommendations for enhancing partnerships between DSRs and foodservice operators and between brokers and foodservice operators.

2. Conduct a feasibility study to assess the implementation of prime vendor contract (single sourcing) in an independent foodservice operation. The study should include an in-depth analysis of the current procurement process including the specific methods currently used to purchase food, beverages, supplies, and equipment and to control the inventory. Arrange to observe the purchasing and inventory procedures. Select a minimum of ten (10) meat and ten (10) produce items and complete a cost analysis including labor time for purchasing the items using a prime vendor and at least one other method. Prices should be obtained from at least two foodservice distributors which have the product lines necessary to function as a prime vendor. At least one of the foodservice distributors should be classified as broadline distributor. Identify factors the operator must consider prior to implementing a prime vendor agreement. Determine minimum order required, frequency of delivery, and other conditions necessary to initiate a prime vendor agreement. Prepare a management report which includes description of current procurement process, detail cost comparisons including labor cost, description of factors which operator must consider before implementing a prime vendor agreement, pros and cons of prime vendor agreement specific to the operation being analyzed, and specific recommendations to the foodservice operator.

5

FOOD SERVICE MANAGEMENT

Positioning and Price: Merging Theory, Strategy, and Tactics
Margaret Shaw

Psychological Aspects of Menu Pricing
David V. Pavesic

Project 1

Project 2

Positioning and Price:
Merging Theory, Strategy, and Tactics

Margaret Shaw

Introduction

KEY FACTORS FOR A PRICING decision from an economic perspective are demand, competition, and cost: demand sets the ceiling, cost sets the floor, and competition determines where on this continuum the actual price will fall. Marketers, on the other hand, view price as one of the "four P's," a controllable part of the marketing mix that helps marketers sell their products or services (The four P's are: product, price, place, and promotion). The missing link is the consumer perspective. Though implicit in the approaches outlined above, what is lacking is placing the customer as the focal point for strategic and tactical pricing decisions.

It is the customer who really determines price. This concept is not new, yet direct customer input for pricing decisions often gets buried under cost, competition, and revenue considerations. A positioning approach for pricing decisions puts the customer front and center for strategic marketing and planning. Positioning, by one definition, is the customers' perception, real or perceived, of a product's value and worth to them. The price level of a product is perceived first by the buyer, followed by a perception of the product's actual price. Price level decisions, that is, minimum and maximum price positioning thresholds, are strategic pricing decisions. Actual price determination within the positioning threshold framework is tactical pricing. Thus, a positioning approach to price focuses first on price levels, then on actual price decisions for a specific product and/or product line.

The intent of this article is to address the issue of price from a strategic positioning viewpoint, that is, a price positioning framework for any and all final pricing decisions. The price positioning model presented incorporates a blending of economic theory, strategic management, and marketing tactics. It also captures recent contributions in the pricing literature drawn from several selected sources.

Approaches to the Pricing Dilemma

Various viewpoints and treatises on pricing abound. They range from the theoretical and applied scholarly approaches, to the strategic and tactical managerial perspectives. Selected key players include Zeithaml, Tellis, Nagle, and Renaghan. A brief overview of their contributions follows.

A Theoretical Perspective

Zeithaml (1988) addresses pricing from a theoretical perspective and demand orientation. Drawing on the research of others and her own insights, Zeithaml develops a conceptual consumer model relating price, quality, and value. Her model is essentially a series of progressive propositions leading to price, quality, and value relationships from a consumer perspective. For instance, Zeithaml distinguishes between intrinsic and extrinsic attributes as cues for the consumer for perceived quality and value of a product. Intrinsic cues are largely tangible and product specific, such as specific attributes of the product itself. Extrinsic cues are more intangible and generalized and serve largely as "value signals." Depending on the consumer and on the purchase situation, intrinsic and extrinsic attributes are used in varying degrees to help make the purchase decision.

The key point in Zeithaml's message is that the price of a product is largely an extrinsic indicator of perceived quality and value for numerous segments of the buying public, especially in the purchase of services. Implicit in her argument is that the perceived quality and value can be directly linked to the desired position of the product in the marketplace.

A Managerial Perspective

Tellis (1986) approaches pricing under the heterogeneous consumer assumption. Consumers differ with respect to (1) information costs, such as time, effort, and search costs; (2) price sensitivities or "reservation" prices; and (3) transaction costs such as obtaining funds, costs of uncertainty, and switching costs. Breaking away from Zeithaml's theoretical and consumer orientation, Tellis takes a more managerial perspective through his development of a taxonomy of pricing strategies. He offers 11 pricing strategies for management consideration when making pricing decisions, such as periodic discounting, penetration pricing, image pricing, price bundling, and so forth. Tellis's strategies are not necessarily mutually exclusive. Each is recommended relative to consumer characteristics, competitive position in the marketplace, and product-line considerations. Positioning implications in his taxonomy, however, are missing. Although Tellis offers a constructive critique of pricing strategy alternatives for management consideration when making pricing decisions, a direct linkage of pricing to the issue of positioning is needed for maximum benefit.

A Strategic Perspective

Nagle (1987) also takes a managerial perspective, yet his focus is more strategic. Strategic objectives of the firm are developed after demand, competition, and cost considerations have been analyzed. Nagle defines strategic objectives as "general aspirations toward which all activities in the firm, not only pricing, are directed" (p. 7). Once objectives have been established, goals and tactics, which include price and price policy, are determined. Differentiating between goals and objectives, Nagle cites strategic goals as being concrete and having deadlines. Implicit here is the positioning desires of the firm. His positioning concerns are imbedded in the objectives and goals development process.

Marketing Management Perspectives

Moving from strategic management to marketing management, classic marketing introduces price as one of the four P's of the marketing mix. These elements—product, price, place, and promotion—are the marketing tools practitioners have at their disposal to implement strategic marketing planning. The marketing mix approach treats price as a tactical decision, after strategic choices have been made. Yet pricing is also a strategic issue, that is, a positioning tool, and should be dealt with at the strategic level as well.

Renaghan (1981) proposed a new marketing mix specifically for the hospitality industry. Breaking away from the traditional "four P's," he offered a three-part product-service, presentation, and communication mix:

1. *The Product-Service Mix:* recognizing and emphasizing the total offering of the hospitality product;
2. *The Presentation Mix:* elements used to increase the tangibility of the product-service mix, that is, physical plant, location, atmosphere, employees, and price; and
3. *The Communications Mix:* further emphasis on making product-service attrib-

utes tangible and communicating the message through advertising, personal selling, direct mail, and so forth.

Of issue and importance here is the placement of price in this new marketing mix proposal. Renaghan clearly places price, along with other significant aspects of the product service, in the presentation mix. All are an integral part of the positioning of the hospitality product. Though perhaps not revolutionary, it is evolutionary to align price more closely with the presentation or positioning of hotels and other hospitality products.

Positioning and Price: Closing the Gap

None of the above approaches directly address the impact that pricing has on the *positioning* of a product in the marketplace. Recent developments, however, are helping to close this gap. Lewis and Seymour bring positioning and price closer to the forefront of strategic marketing and management thinking.

Lewis directly addresses the issue of positioning for hospitality. In an earlier article (1981) and in a more recent update (1990), Lewis articulates the point that positioning is concerned with building an image, differentiating the product and offering benefits to identified target markets. Another keypoint is Lewis's distinction between objective and subjective positioning.

Objective positioning focuses primarily on the objective attributes of a hotel or restaurant. Subjective positioning is more concerned with the consumer's perception of the product. As he notes, "[W]hen you try to influence peoples' perceptions of your operation, you are dealing with subjective positioning. The perceived image of your property does not belong to the product; it is connected with the consumer's mental processes." (Lewis, 1990, p. 86)

Lewis (1990) relates price to positioning by making the point that it is difficult to differentiate on price within a product class. Pricing "can play a larger role [as a positioning tool] in differentiating between different product classes" (p. 90). This role of price he identifies as objective positioning, such as Motel 6 offering low-cost accommodations to economy/budget market segments. It should be argued, however, that price can support both objective and subjective positioning statements. Price can help identify the product class in objective positioning. It can also enhance a consumer's perceived value for a particular purchase, such as a discounted weekend package rate, in subjective positioning. Both are strategic issues. It is the actual price set that is tactical.

Seymour (1989) also explicitly recognizes positioning as an area of strategic importance. He has developed a price planning framework from which actual price decisions can be made, Seymour notes:

The basic thrust of the planning framework is that management should choose a price that is consistent with the overall positioning of the product or service. The six stages of the product/service position represent a sequential set of decisions that act to frame or limit choices. . . . Each subsequent stage acts to further qualify the price decision and, consequently, enables their attention on a more manageable set of pricing options. (p. 8)

Seymour directly links pricing to positioning, a major step for strategic price management, Seymour's market niche stage explicitly recognizes positioning as giving upper and lower limits, or thresholds, for all pricing decisions that a firm has to make. Like Zeithaml, he recognizes that price is "used as a cue to infer the value of different product attributes" (Seymour, 1989, p. 11). He emphasizes this value inference especially when considering lower limit price decisions. There is a point when a consumer will say, "That price is too cheap, there must be something wrong with it."

This is true for all product classes, from the high-end Four Seasons product to the low-end Motel 6 product. Would you purchase a room at the motel for $10? Probably not. Even if this rate covered the variable costs, somehow a $10 room connotes a lack of credibility or lack of security.

HIGH → *DEMAND:* WHAT THE MARKET WILL BEAR

→ *MAXIMUM POSITIONING THRESHOLD*

COMPETITION: DEMAND RELATIVE TO SUPPLY IN THE MARKETPLACE

→ *MINIMUM POSITIONING THRESHOLD*

LOW → *COST:* VARIABLE COSTS OF "DOING" BUSINESS

STRATEGIC PRICING: PRICE LEVEL DETERMINATION SETTING MINIMUM AND MAXIMUM PRICE POSITIONING THRESHOLDS

TACTICAL PRICING: ACTUAL PRICE DETERMINATION WITHIN POSITIONING THRESHOLD FRAMEWORK

FIGURE 1. Price/Positioning Framework Model: A Strategic Choice

Positioning on Price: A Strategic Decision

Drawing on the theoretical, strategic, and managerial approaches to pricing presented thus far, and returning to the basic tenet of supply and demand, price and positioning are strategic decisions for hospitality management. From the economic or market perspective, demand, competition, and cost are key factors for pricing decisions.

As noted by Meek (1938), a renowned and respected leader in the field of hospitality:

The classical analysis explaining price in terms of supply and demand has passed through many examinations

and revisions, but still stands in its essential idea as the most satisfactory, most generally acceptable explanation of the phenomena of price determination. (p. 2)

Meek's statement, made more than 50 years ago, remains true today.

The strategic marketing perspective of the 1990s, however, mandates positioning in the marketplace as of great importance as well. An integration of these two perspectives can be used to develop a price positioning framework from which all pricing decisions can be made. Key aspects of this framework are shown in Figure 1.

Demand sets the ceiling for pricing decisions, that is, what

the market will bear. Costs, variable costs in particular, set the floor. From an accounting perspective and in the short term, any price set above the variable cost of doing business contributes something to the fixed cost of being in business. The competitive environment, or supply relative to demand for any given period, helps to determine where on this continuum actual prices will be set. During peak periods, when demand is greater than supply, higher prices are achieved. During off-peak periods, when supply is greater than demand, prices will fall. The debate centers on how high, or how low, the actual price should be. The concept of positioning helps resolve this debate.

Positioning is the customers' perception—real or perceived—of a product's value and worth to them. It provides the true minimum and maximum thresholds for initial price level decisions. A $250 room rate for a first class, full-service hotel in Toronto, for example, seems high but not outrageous. A $400 rate for the same accommodation *is* outrageous. There may be a few individuals who would pay this amount, but it defies good positioning for, say, a Four Seasons or Hyatt hotel. The primary target market willing to pay $250, but initially quoted $400, will probably book elsewhere. In this example, the $400 is the absolute ceiling set by demand, but the $250 more closely approximates the true maximum threshold from a positioning perspective.

Similarly, using the motel example mentioned earlier, minimum positioning thresholds will by-and-large be higher than the actual variable cost to produce the product or service. A discounted $10 room rate at Motel 6 or Journey's End, which serves the low-end budget/economy markets, is too low a rate even for these highly price-sensitive markets. This rate may very well cover variable costs, but it does not cover the perceived image of clean, safe, and secure lodging accommodations.

Thus, the true minimum and maximum thresholds for pricing, from both a managerial and consumer perspective, are the desired and perceived positioning, respectively. This is the strategic level for price de-cision-making. Within these thresholds are where tactical price decisions are made.

Consumers' Price Perceptions: A Pilot Study

Krim (1990) conducted a pilot study in western Massachusetts measuring consumers' price perceptions of economy/budget, mid-tier, and upscale hotel markets. Respondents were asked at what price a hotel room was cheap/too cheap and expensive/too expensive for each of the hotel market categories. This approach is a direct application of the minimum/maximum price positioning concept. Though the results are inconclusive because of the nature of the study, the data collected (from 122 respondents) demonstrate how the model can work from a broader industry perspective.

Figure 2 summarizes the high, the low, and the range of rates that the respondents gave for budget/economy, mid-tier, and upscale hotel accommodations. The initial results are not surprising. For budget/economy lodging accommodations the range was from $30–$62, for mid-tier from $40–$92, and for upscale from $60–$145. Upscale had the broadest range which also could be expected. The key point here is that each of the high/low points of resistance represents the minimum/maximum thresholds for price positioning for the three market categories. Strategic implications are that these points help "define" the product class through price positioning, and that price setting within each product class helps define the product. Tactical implications are where to set the price, given specific market conditions, within identified thresholds.

Prices can and do vary for the same core product, yet they lie within parameters set forth by the minimum and maximum positioning threshold framework. This positioning threshold concept lies within the economic prescription of demand, competition, and cost.

Managerial Implications

From an educator and/or practitioner perspective, the message is to think strategy first, that is, to consider positioning. Have you identified your minimum and maximum price positioning thresholds? If you're a first class, full-service hotel in downtown Toronto, for example, you may determine that $75 is your minimum threshold. Given the current economic conditions in the Northeast corridor, a maximum threshold might be set at $175. Once these thresholds have been identified, then specific (tactical) price decisions can be made for the various market segments targeted by this hotel. During peak demand periods the lowest rate, in all likelihood, will be well above the minimum threshold. Yet during off-peak demand periods, the maximum threshold of $175 may never be reached.

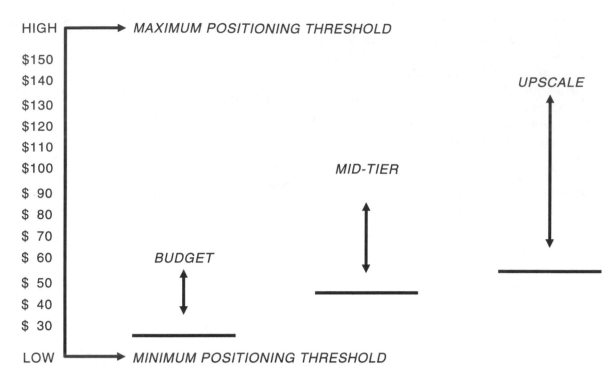

Note: From a pilot study conducted by Karen Krim, University of Massachusetts/Amherst, 1990, under the supervision of Dr. Margaret Shaw.

FIGURE 2. Consumers' Price Perceptions of Economy/Budget, Mid-Tier, and Upscale Hotel Markets: A Pilot Study

The model explicitly recognizes that positioning, and not contribution margin pricing, sets the minimum threshold for pricing decisions. If the variable cost for this hotel is $30–$40, contribution margin pricing would accept a short-term price of $40+; that is, at a minimum contribution margin pricing would recoup the variable cost and contribute something to fixed overhead. Positioning on price, however, in this example, raises the minimum level to $75. Any price below this threshold puts the hotel at too great a risk to undermine its overall position in the marketplace.

It should be noted that setting a minimum threshold too high can also be problematic in that potential revenues may be lost. Hotel management has to repeatedly ask where the "cut-off" is to maximize revenues yet minimize damage to the positioning statement of the hotel. There is no magic formula or crystal ball to turn to, but the question nonetheless needs to be addressed.

The positioning on price model supports the "art" and "science" of pricing. Contribution margin pricing is the science side and is well-grounded in the literature. Positioning on price (which is not widely written about) is the art side of pricing, a judgment decision based on a solid understanding of the marketplace. Both educators and operators often want neat, quanti-fiable formulas to arrive at final pricing decisions. The positioning on price model, however, promotes the notion that unquantifiable factors have a very prominent place in pricing decisions. Positioning decisions are not readily quantifiable, yet their strategic importance is imperative for effective pricing management.

Summary and Conclusions

Recently published in *Fortune,* Henkoff (1990) suggests that "[W]hen it comes to thinking and acting strategically, managers still have to depend, to some degree, on a few devil-ishly unquantifiable factors, like experience, instinct, guesswork, and luck" (p. 70). Positioning on price, indeed, involves a bit of instinct, guesswork, and luck. It is also a learned art separate and distinct from the tactical or scientific side of pricing decisions.

Positioning on price is a strategic level decision. The price level of a product is perceived first by the buyer, and price level helps define the product class category for the consumer. Actual price determination is a tactical decision. It supports the positioning decision and can be especially important for incremental sales consideration. Even lowering a price, as long as it is within the positioning threshold, can actually increase revenues in the short run. Overall positioning has not been thwarted, and increased customer satisfaction has been achieved. Again, the weekend package concept is an excellent example of discounting prices to secondary markets, yet pricing to be compatible with an operation's overall positioning to its primary target market(s).

Am I trying to oversimplify price? No. Am I trying to bring price into the strategic arena? Yes. Recognition of its importance as a strategic tool as well as a tactical tool, and distinguishing between these two perspectives is essential to the effective management of hospitality and pricing decisions.

References

Henkoff, R. (1990, December 31). How to plan for 1995. *Fortune,* pp. 70–79.

Krim, K. A. (1990). *Measuring the price sensitivity of consumers: a study in the hospitality industry.* Unpublished manuscript, University of Massachusetts, Amherst.

Lewis, R. C. (1981). The positioning statement for hotels. *The Cornell Hotel and Restaurant Administrative Quarterly, 22* (1), 51–61.

Lewis, R. C. (1990). Advertising your hotel's position. *The Cornell Hotel and Restaurant Administration Quarterly, 31* (2), 84–91.

Meek, H. B. (1938). *A theory of hotel room rates.* Ithaca, NY: Cornell University.

Nagle, T. T. (1987). *The strategy and tactics of pricing: a guide to profitable decision making.* Englewood Cliffs, NJ: Prentice Hall.

Renaghan, L. M. (1981). A new marketing mix for the hospitality industry. *The Cornell Hotel and Restaurant Administration Quarterly, 22* (2), 31–35.

Seymour, D. T. (Ed.) 1989. *The pricing decision: a strategic planner for marketing professionals.* Chicago: Probus Publishing.

Tellis, G. J. (1986). Beyond the many faces of price: an integration of pricing strategies, *Journal of Marketing, 50* (4), 146–160.

Zeithaml, V. A. (1988). Consumer perceptions of price, quality, and value: a means-end model and synthesis of evidence. *Journal of Marketing, 52,* 2–22.

PSYCHOLOGICAL ASPECTS OF MENU PRICING

David V. Pavesic

There are a number of "costless" considerations that must be taken into account when pricing menu items. Pricing cannot be reduced to a purely quantitative exercise as one must consider the subjective and psychological aspects of the customers' purchase decision.

Introduction

REGARDLESS OF THE methodology used to mark up food and beverages, prices charged by commercial food services must not only cover costs but return a profit as well. Pricing is an important function that directly influences customer counts and sales revenue. The optimum price must not only include some contribution to profit, it must also be deemed fair and reasonable by the public.

One cannot remain in business long if costs are not covered. However, costs are not the sole consideration in determining menu prices. Costs must be known in order to measure profit contribution on each sale. Some costs can be accurately calculated and assigned to specific menu items, while other costs must be subjectively allocated across-the-board. At most, costs serve as a reference to begin developing a pricing strategy.

Many operators are experiencing intense competition, rising operating costs, labor shortages and falling customer counts. Such factors will definitely impact on profits. Therefore, the pricing policy is a major factor in developing a strategic plan to meet such obstacles.

Most businessmen seek logical and objective criteria on which to base their pricing strategy. This is the main reason we start with determining the cost of a product or service. There is a tendency to rationalize price as a means of returning an amount that will reflect a fair profit for the time, effort and materials consumed. Of all the business decisions a restaurateur has to make, one that causes much anxiety is pricing the menu. Whenever pricing decisions require raising existing prices, the operator mentally prepares for some adverse customer response. The usual feedback comes in the form of spoken comments and the dreaded dropping customer counts. Consequently, the task of menu pricing is beset with misgivings and uncertainty. Prices that are too high will drive customers away and prices that are too low will sacrifice profit. The main reason for this anxiety may well be the highly subjective methodology used to price the menus in the first place. Anxiety results over which approach to pricing is best or right given the respective menu items, existing market conditions and the operational concept.

Prices partially influence which menu items will sell and therefore impact the overall profitability of the sales mix. Menu items will differ widely in cost, popularity and profitability. Thus, pricing is not a simple matter of cost mark up, but an intricate combination of factors that involve both financial and competitive elements.

What it basically comes down to is that prices can be either market driven or demand driven and depending upon the uniqueness or monopolistic aspects of the menu item and operational concept, the approach to pricing will differ. Prices that are "market driven" must be more responsive to competition. Menu items that are relatively common, found on most restaurant menus, e.g., hamburgers, steaks, fried chicken, prime rib and the like, and in markets where customers have a wide choice on where to go for such items, must be priced rather competitively. This approach must also be used on new items being introduced or tested and before any substantial demand has been established. Prices that are market driven tend to be set on the low to moderate side.

This is contrasted to those prices that are "demand driven" where the customers openly ask for the item and where there are little if any alternatives in the market. Perhaps it is a specialty item or signature food item that can only be obtained at one particular restaurant. Consequently, a monopoly of sorts is created and along with the monopoly comes pricing advantages. Thus prices that are demand driven will be higher, at least until the demand starts to wane due to competitors offering the product or changes in customer tastes. Prices will

eventually stabilize and become more competitive.

Costing out an entree and accompaniments is a relatively objective and logical process. Establishing a price for it is more of an art. Whatever the pricing methodology, there is no *single* method that can be used to mark up every item on any given menu. One must employ a combination of methodologies and theories. Therefore, when properly carried out, prices will reflect food cost percentages, individual and/or weighted contribution margins, price-points and desired check averages, as well as factors driven by intuition, competition, demand and consumer price perceptions.

If pricing were a purely quantitative exercise, a computer program incorporating operating costs, profit objectives and raw food costs could be used to set menu prices. However, such an approach lacks important *qualitative* factors that enter into the pricing decision. It has been said of most retail products and services that the *buyer* determines the price, *not* the seller. Therefore, the seller must be able to offer a product or service and make a profit selling at the price the customers are willing to pay. Value judgments are hard to program into a cost-mark up pricing program.

Minimum profit objectives can be analytically determined, based upon an operation's financial and budgetary idiosyncrasies. However, an operation's financial limitations or profit demands may result in cost standards that

are not compatible or realistic with the existing economic or market conditions. If prices are too high relative to what competition is charging, quality too low or portions so small as to negate the price-value relationship, sales and profit objectives may still not be realized.

What price should be charged? There are two perspectives from which one can approach this question and both are at the extreme ends of the price continuum. Finding the ideal price point is not easy. One perspective says to charge the *highest* price you think the customer is willing to pay. When you take this approach you should expect your customers to be more demanding and critical of the food and service and your operation must be on the "cutting edge" with food, service and ambience.

The extreme opposite approach is to charge the *lowest* price at which you can still make a reasonable profit. When this approach is taken, customers almost always will comment on the reasonableness of the prices, the large portion sizes and the high quality of the ingredients. Therefore, the two perspectives on how much to charge are: charge as much as you can or charge as little as you can. Keep in mind that the success of any pricing methodology is influenced by many factors including, among others, location, competition, clientele and the restaurant concept. What works for one may not work for another.

More often than not, prices are predominantly influenced by competition and/or customer demand. Whenever demand is greater than supply, pricing methodologies that favor higher prices can be used. On the other hand, if customer counts are flat and strong competition exists for the products and services, a different tactic is required.

The market ultimately determines the price one can charge. If you charge too much, your customers will go somewhere else. However, it is important to interject a warning at this point. Lower prices do not automatically translate into *value* and *bargain* in the minds of the customers. Having the lowest prices in your market may not bring customers or profits. Too often operators engage in price wars through discount promotions and find that their market image falls along with their profit on each sale.

White tablecloth restaurants using coupons have quickly learned the pitfalls of discounting (Martin, 1988). Few, if any coupon redeemers return in the future to pay full price. The frugal coupon customer cannot be readily converted to a regular upscale patron and rarely do they spend the entree savings on extras such as desserts or wine. Coupons foster the opinion that white tablecloth menu prices are overstated. When regular customers start redeeming coupons, little is gained.

Every restaurant will be categorized by its customers according to the prices it charges. They will place it into one of three categories: low-priced, moderate-priced and high-priced. Specific numerical check averages are not given because customers, depending upon their income, will apply their own dollar ranges when rating restaurants in each category. A fourth category, ultra-priced (Hayes, 1988), is even mentioned and a price range of $75 per person is indicated. The idiosyncrasies of a given operation, its menu, location and clientele could target a $40 check average as being moderate and a $25 check average as being low. This is very much the case in certain parts of California and New York.

Customers will evaluate a restaurant as a place to *eat-out* or as a place to *dine-out*. If a restaurant is considered an *eat-out* operation during the week (a substitute for cooking at home), customers will be more price conscious. If a restaurant is considered a *dine-out* operation, the visit is regarded more as a social occasion or entertainment and price is not as much of a factor.

Clearly, the eat-out/dine-out aspects vary as much as the check averages. It is difficult for most patrons to accept a $25 check average for just eating-out. In most cases, only dining-out will justify such prices. Restaurant operators are responding to more conservative spending habits by switching their concepts and images from dine-out to eat-out in order to boost the frequency of visitations of "regular" customers.

Knowing how patrons evaluate a restaurant is important to the pricing decision. Rarely will a restaurant be rated in both categories by the same patron. Eat-out operations will experience more frequent visits by patrons than dine-out operations but the average check will be lower per visit. Regular weekday customers may go elsewhere for special celebrations like anniversaries or birthdays. Weekend clientele may differ greatly from weeknight customers. For example, local residents may be the bulk of traffic during the week, while weekends may bring visitors, tourists or people travelling from outside the restaurant's normal market area. Such patrons categorize the operation as a dine-out or special occasion restaurant and will not be as price conscious. The restaurants' menu prices must be in line with the price category in which the majority of its customers place the operation. If prices exceed this range, customers will not purchase many of those items. If prices are too low, there is the danger of lowering the overall image and check average.

What then is the proper price to charge? From the customers' point of view, it is the price that makes them buy. From the sellers' perspective, the best price is the one that moves the product and produces a profit. Prices can reflect such factors as atmosphere, service entertainment and unique product presentation. Customers sense an additional value in being able to receive additional amenities.

One cannot arrive at a selling price without considering some highly subjective factors that have "refined" the interpretation of traditional economic theory on consumer buying behavior. Psychologists are teaming up with marketing analysts and economists to provide some new perspectives on pricing. The methods offered here are largely subjective and for the most part, ignore traditional cost considerations. These "costless" approaches that "fine tune" the actual mark up are (Schmidgall, 1986):

➤ Competitive pricing
➤ Intuitive pricing
➤ Trial and error pricing
➤ Psychological pricing

Regardless of what they are called, these approaches to pricing reflect two of the three critical factors in pricing: demand and competition, the third, of course, being cost.

The "competitive" approach to pricing is very simple. The operator collects menus from competitors and then meets or beats their prices on his menu. This method is highly ineffective because it assumes that the customers make their purchase decisions based on price alone as well as not recognizing the likelihood of cost differences in ingredients, labor and operating expenses incurred in getting the food or beverage to the guest. It also fails to account for the many other factors that influence the purchase decision such as product quality perceptions, ambience, service and even location.

"Intuitive" pricing is practiced by operators who do not want to take the time to gather information from their competitors. They rely instead on what they can remember from past experiences and set prices on what they feel the guests are willing to pay. This method relies on estimating the demand for one's particular products and services.

"Trial and error" claims to be responsive to customer perceptions of prices and is based on customer reactions and comments on existing prices. This can be employed on individual menu items to bring them closer to the price the customer is willing to pay. However, this "wait-and-see" perspective is not practical for new operations and getting a dissatisfied customer to return is very difficult.

The fourth "costless" pricing approach, "psychological" aspects, presents a number of interesting theories that enter into the pricing decision. The first, *buyer price consciousness,* influences the way prices are perceived and the importance of price in the buyer's choice of products or services. Researchers have suggested that *price consciousness* is inversely correlated with social class, implying that price is more a factor with low-income customers and the lower-priced restaurants they are likely to frequent (Gabor and Granger, 1961; Monroe and Kirshnan, 1984).

When the buyer lacks specific qualitative information about a menu item and is unable to judge quality prior to purchase, higher prices are often associated with higher quality in the mind of the customer. *Price perceptions* on the part of the customer are critical. Perceptions are often based on the "last price paid" or *reference price.* The reference price may be the price charged by a competitor and if it was lower other factors will have to be shown by the seller to justify charging more (Monroe, 1973).

The order in which buyers are exposed to alternative prices will affect their perceptions. Buyers exposed initially to high prices will perceive subsequent lower prices as bargains. However, dropping prices to meet a competitor or discounting your regular price is not always effective. Low price does not always result in a dominant market position because people will often refrain from purchasing a product, not only when the price is perceived as being too high, but also when it is perceived to be too low. When prices for two competing products or services are seen to be similar by the customer, the price is unlikely to be a factor when choosing between similar products or services (Della Bitta and Monroe, 1973; Monroe and Petroshius, 1973).

Current evidence would suggest in such cases that it is the buyer's perception of the *total relative value* of the product or service that influences their decision to choose between purchase alternatives and their willingness to pay the asked price. The total relative value consists of such elements as atmosphere, convenience, quality, service and location. The *relative value* is enhanced by either "value analysis" or "value engineering." Value analysis concentrates on increasing perceived value through improving performance (service) relative to customer needs, e.g., guarantees, brand recognition, payment options, carry-out and delivery. Value engineering concentrates on increasing value by decreasing operating costs while maintaining performance standards, e.g., cost efficiencies, purchasing programs and waste reduction (Monroe and Kirshnan, 1984; Monroe, 1986).

The element of customer perception is an important determinant of buyer behavior. Buyers use such cues as product quality, corporate image and name recognition along with price to differentiate among alternatives and to form impressions of product and service quality. Whether the customer will pay the price or balk is the question. Should one start off pricing on the low side and gradually increase prices or start off on the high side and then discount? Precise answers to such questions depend upon one's market position, the demand for the product or service and the stage in the market life cycle of the product and/or operation. Obviously, conceptually obsolete operations and products with decreasing demand cannot command the prices that the trendy and popular operations may be able to charge.

Another psychological theory on pricing looks at the im-

pact of "mental accounting." This theory suggests that as consumers we mentally code purchases into budget categories, e.g. food, housing and entertainment and that each category is controlled to some degree by a budget constraint. Consequently, the amount spent on a meal away from home will vary depending on whether the expenditure is debited to food or entertainment expense. The reference price mentioned earlier also comes into play. For example, while at a football or baseball game, the price we are willing to pay for a Coke and hot dog is going to be higher than the price we would be willing to pay in a neighborhood sandwich shop. This is analogous to eating out while on vacation vs. eating out on a week night in a neighborhood restaurant. Spending is going to be more liberal while on vacation (Thaler, 1961).

If we assume that restaurant expenditures can be assigned to the budget categories of either food, entertainment or recreation, we can approach the pricing decision from the consumers' perspective. The objective is to have the expenditure classified into a higher budget category or combine categories. There is likely to be freer spending from an entertainment budget than from a food budget. The mental budget category can change depending on the occasion and the day of the week. Such considerations may prompt promotions such as early bird specials and discount coupons to entice week-night "eaters" using their food budgets to eat

out instead of at home. Such strategy may not be necessary on weekends, when dining out is done more for entertainment or social purposes and when budget restraints are relaxed.

In any purchase decision there are elements of "pain" and "pleasure" that are derived from the transaction. The pleasure comes from the enjoyment of or benefits derived from the purchase and the pain comes from having to part with one's hard-earned cash. The "pain" aspect of parting with one's money suggests use of one of the two primary ways most menus are priced: à *la carte* and combination pricing (modified *table d'hote*). In price sensitive markets, operators in the low-price units usually price each menu component separately (*à la carte*) to keep prices down and leave it to the customer to decide whether to purchase extra items. Upselling strategy is then employed by servers and order takers to increase check averages, e.g. suggesting large drinks, fries and dessert. The combination pricing (*table d'hote*) charges a higher price but includes accompaniments that otherwise must be purchased separately. The larger, one-time payment is considered less painful than several individual purchase decisions. In addition, the combination price is lower than the sum of the accompaniments purchased separately (Kahneman and Tversky, 1979).

In addition to these pricing perspectives, the practice of using certain combinations of numbers to stimulate sales has been studied. The most popular terminal digits used for prices on restaurant menus are 5, 9 and zero. This "fine tuning" of prices affects only the terminal digits and has little cost purpose. Its greatest impact is on customer perception when contemplating the purchase of two or more competing items. This has been referred to as "odd-cents" pricing. The assumption is that customers perceive a price of $9.95 as being a better buy than $10.00. In addition, the use of odd-cents pricing makes price increases less noticeable (Kreul, 1982).

In the past, operators set menu prices primarily to cover food costs or to achieve certain gross profit margins. The decision was also tempered with what the competition was doing. However, today's operators must study customer demographics, market trends and give greater thought to the wants and needs of their customers. Price-value perceptions are not made from prices alone. It is a feeling that the customers have about receiving their money's worth when they pay their check. It is a combination of price, quality, portions size, ambience, service and psychological factors. Therefore, the pricing of a menu is both a science and an art.

References

Della Bitta, A. J. and Monroe, Kent B. (1973) The influence of adaptation levels on subjective price perceptions. In *Advances in Consumer Research*, Vol. 1, Ward, Scott and Wright, Peter (eds), pp. 353–369. Association for Consumer Research, Ann Arbor, Michigan.

Ferguson, Dennis H. (1987) Hidden agendas in consumer purchase decisions. *Cornell Quarterly* 28, 31–39.

Gabor, André and Granger, Clive (1961) On the price consciousness of consumers. *Applied Statistics* 10, 170–188.

Hayes, Jack (1988) Fine-dining operators shift from chic to casual. *Nation's Restaurant News* 22, 1–232.

Kahneman, Daniel and Tversky, Amos (1979) Prospect theory: an analysis of decision under risk. *Economoetrica* March, 263–291.

Kreul, Lee M. (1982) Magic numbers: psychological aspects of menu pricing. *Cornell Quarterly* August, 70–75.

Martin, Richard (1988) Fine-dining coupons flop. *Nation's Restaurant News* 22, 1–7.

Monroe, Kent B. (1986) Techniques for pricing new products and services. Virginia Polytechnic Institute.

Monroe, Kent B. and Kirshnan (1984) The effect of price on subjective product evaluations. In *Perceived Quality,* Jacoby, Jacob and Olson, Jerry C. (eds), pp. 209–231. Lexington Books, Mass.

Monroe, Kent B. and Petroshius, Susan M. (1973) Buyer's perceptions of price: an update of the evidence. *Journal of Marketing Research* 10, 70–80.

Thaler, Richard (1985) Mental accounting and consumer choice. *Marketing Service* Summer, 199–214.

Menu Pricing

Student may elect to take one of two approaches to exploring menu pricing in commercial foodservice operations: Option I Review of Literature; Option II Pricing Analysis of Existing Operation.

Option I

The substance of the paper is to review the literature for all articles relating to menu pricing and/or markup theories published in trade or academic journals since the mid sixties to the present date. In addition to the literature review, the paper must conclude with the writer's evaluation of the methods citing their strengths and weaknesses. In addition, a recommendation on which method or combination thereof would be used by the writer in pricing a menu today.

Option II

The substance of this paper will be developed through the costing, pricing and analysis of an existing commercial foodservice operation. Paper must include an audit of menu food costs and mark up, menu sales analysis both with spreadsheet and graphic display. The content of the paper shall be 50 percent descriptive and 50 percent analysis discussing the strengths, weaknesses and recommendations for improvement in the prices or mark up.

In both cases, the length of the paper should be between 5000–7500 words excluding graphs, tables, spreadsheets, and appendices.

Purpose of the Exercise

The menu evaluation exercise provides an opportunity for the student to apply the principles and theory of menu design to a working menu. The exercise will test the student's comprehension of the principles of menu design through written analysis and recommendations for improving the menu as a cost control, merchandising, and communication tool.

Guidelines

Select a chain affiliated or independently owned and operated table service restaurant serving dinner and lunch for the purpose of evaluating their printed menu. Your analysis of the menu will assess its effectiveness as cost control, merchandising, and communication tool. You will need to include a copy of the menu when you turn in the written evaluation. Carry-out menus and miniature souvenir menus are not acceptable. If an independent restaurant menu is used ask to talk with someone who was directly involved in designing the menu and writing the merchandising copy to gain actual insights as to their decision making.

The following information should be contained in the evaluation:

Name, location, type of menu, i.e, static, combination, etc. Describe the process used to select the menu items and the overall design and visual appearance of the menu.

In your analysis include a table of menu prices by menu categories, i.e., appetizers, entrees, desserts, etc. Within each category, divide the highest priced item by the lowest priced item and comment on the price spread. Comment on the prices of complete dinners relative to appetizers and dessert prices. Does the menu use à la carte or modified table d'hote pricing? If the restaurant has a wine list, include a pricing table for wines and comment on the price of a full liter of wine relative to the cost of an entree. What is the average food check per person and how does it compare to the prices on the menu?

Evaluate and comment on the menu mechanics. Does the menu have a separate and detachable cover? What information is shown on the cover? Is the menu designed to complement the interior decor and comment on the thematic continuity of the design? Evaluate the type styles and sizes. Is it readable under low light conditions? Are type styles and sizes used to guide your gaze motion to certain items or parts of the menu?

Is the menu professionally printed or printed in-house on a laser printer? Does the menu contain clip-on specials? If yes, comment on the production quality of the clip-on and if it complements or detracts from the rest of the printed menu. Is there a special location designed on the menu to accommodate clip-ons or is it placed over existing menu copy? Comment on clip-on placement relative to menu merchandising effectiveness.

Comment on the descriptive copy used. Is it original or trite? Is it too long or too brief? Is it truthful? Comment on its "sell power."

If the menu contains illustrations, pictures, graphics, screens, color or other visual presentation accents, comment on their use and effectiveness in altering the gaze motion and drawing attention to certain sections or items on the menu. If sales analysis information is available, are the items emphasized typically their most popular items?

List the items that are considered house specialties or signature foods for the restaurant. Are those items given special treatment on the menu to increase their sales? If yes, describe. If they are not given any special treatment, what would you recommend they do to increase their visibility?

Give the menu an overall rating on each of the following areas: cost control tool, merchandising tool, communication tool. Use a scale of 1–10 with a ten being the highest.

What specific suggestions do you have to improve the menu design? You may include a paste up of your new menu design along with your word processed comments. This assignment should be as long as you feel necessary to answer the questions. However, if the analysis is shorter than two pages (approximately 500 words) the analysis may be incomplete.

This assignment will be graded on the following criteria:

1. Depth and breadth of analysis

2. Organization and presentation of the information

3. Application of the principles of menu design as covered in class

4. The specific suggestions given for redesigning the menu

6

QUANTITY FOOD PRODUCTION

Production Planning
Marian C. Spears

Project 1

Project 2

PRODUCTION PLANNING

Marian C. Spears

IN THE SIMPLEST POSSIBLE terms, the objective of food production is the preparation of menu items in the needed quantity and desired quality, at a cost appropriate to the particular service. Quantity is the element that distinguishes production in foodservices from home or family food preparation. Quality, an essential concomitant of all food preparation, becomes an extremely vital consideration in mass food production due to the number of employees involved. Quality includes not only the aesthetic aspects of a food product but also the nutritional factors and the microbiological safety of the product. Cost, of course, determines whether or not a product should be produced for a specific clientele. An example in contrast would be serving filet mignon as a school lunch item—obviously too costly a choice. In the 1990s, foodservice operators are being challenged by rising food, energy, and labor costs. The key to success is flexibility and an effort by managers to change strategies and management styles (Cichy, 1983).

After procurement, production is the next major subsystem in the transformation element of the foodservice system and is highlighted in Figure 1. Because of the increased use of partially processed foods, such as peeled and sliced apples, the small amount of prepreparation will be done in the production unit. *Production* in the generic sense is the process by which goods and services are created. In the context of foodservice, production is the managerial function of converting food items purchased in various states into menu items that are served to a customer, client, or patient.

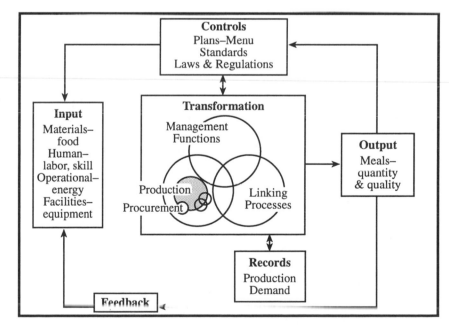

FIGURE 1. Foodservice systems model with the production function highlighted

In foodservice operations today, production is no longer considered as merely "cooking in the kitchen" but involves planning, control of ingredients, production methods, quality of food, labor productivity, and energy consumption.

In essence, foodservice managers responsible for production are resource managers and in some organizations may be so designated. Those who rely on past experience to make decisions could have difficulty surviving in today's competitive market. Innovative approaches to decision making are required for allocation and control of resources (Lambert and Beach, 1980). For example, analytical and computer techniques used in production industries can be adapted by the foodservice manager for determining resource requirements for production.

Planning for production is the establishment of a program of action for transformation of resources into goods and services. The manager identifies the necessary resources and determines how the transformation process should be designed to produce the desired goods and services. Once this process has been developed, planning must be integrated with the other managerial functions of organizing and controlling.

Planning, organizing, and controlling are overlapping managerial functions, however, and cannot be considered separately. For example, the foodservice manager and the production supervisor might have established a schedule of preparation times to prevent vegetables from being overcooked (controlling), but then suddenly must revise the production schedule (planning) because one essential employee went home sick and a critical task had to be reassigned. The content of jobs has to be analyzed to be sure all tasks are covered (organizing).

Production Decisions

Planning encompasses the setting of goals and objectives by top management and the development of policies and procedures by middle management. Eventually, decisions must be made concerning the necessary quantities to produce and the standards of quality that must be maintained within the limitations of costs. In foodservice operations, as in industry, managers must estimate future events. Thus, forecasting, planning for aggregate or total output, and production scheduling are important elements for decision making.

All these planning decisions must be made within the constraints of the existing facility. Much too often, in a hospital or nursing home, the number of patients or residents is increased, but the capacity of the equipment in the kitchen is not. If the anticipated future demand exceeds the present capacity, then the facility must be expanded, future production curtailed, or more ready prepared foods purchased to handle the increased demand.

Production planning primarily is the effective synthesis of quantity, quality and cost objectives. Investigations of the tasks of industrial production managers indicate that most frequently their time is spent on labor relations, cost control, production control (quantity scheduling), and quality. Based on these observations, the secondary production objectives are (Adam and Ebert, 1978):

▶ Determine characteristics of the product.
▶ Determine characteristics of the production process.
▶ Predict quantities to meet the expected demand.
▶ Define the desired quality level.
▶ Correlate the cost elements of labor, material, and facility utilization.

These industrial production planning objectives are equally applicable to foodservice operations. The characteristics of the product or menu items depend upon the type of operation, such as short orders in a quick service restaurant or hotel coffee shop, individual item selections in a full service restaurant, or a fixed menu in a school. For example, a ground meat patty would be served as a grilled hamburger on a bun for a quick service restaurant, a charbroiled ground steak for a full service restaurant, or an oven baked hamburger for school foodservice.

Production process characteristics include the method of food preparation, ranging from grilling to broiling to baking. The process and product characteristics are closely related because the process is actually determined by the product. The process may have a greater bearing on the cost element in planning, though, because of labor, equipment, and energy expenditures.

Obviously, effective planning cannot be done without reasonably accurate forecasting of future demand quantities. Finally, standards of quality must be established for all products that will be produced. Maintenance of quality is a cost factor because of employee training, inventory control of both raw and prepared food items, and sanitation programs.

The cost element in planning is the result of the correlation of initial food item cost, storage, issue, and utilization with the attendant items of labor cost, investment cost in facilities, and utilization of energy. These characteristics must be considered in all planning. Whenever planning goes beyond a day-to-day basis, forecasting becomes absolutely necessary.

Production Forecasting

Forecasting is the art and science of estimating events in the future and provides the data base for decision making and planning. Forecasting [has been] described as a function of production and constitutes the basis for procurement. The specific concern of this chapter, however, is forecasting as applied to food production.

Production Demand

In line with the primary objective of food production— satisfying a quantity and quality demand, at a particular time and cost—the necessity of forecasting food production demand devolves from the facts that food preparation requires a definite length of time, future demand must be forecast, and specific costs are incurred with either over- or underproduction (Konnersman, 1969).

The *length of time* for food preparation is much shorter than it was a few years ago, generally because of the increased use of partially prepared food items, such as cake and bread mixes, portioned meats, frozen vegetables, and ready-to-serve salad greens. Preparation time may be further reduced by using more efficient equipment, including high-speed steamers and powerful mixers. Food production time, however, cannot be drastically reduced by the use of convenience foods unless a total assembly/serve system is adopted.

Production demand for a hospital foodservice probably has the highest degree of uncertainty because of the unpredictable variation in special dietary requirements for patients, food preferences when selective menus are used, and the number of patients, staff, and visitors to be served. A restaurant differs in its production demand because special dietary requirements generally are not considered, or it may have a particular food specialty tending to stabilize the

demand. Customers can satisfy desires for seafood or Italian cuisine by selecting a restaurant specializing in such items, rather than expect to find those foods in all restaurants.

Overproduction generates extra costs because salvage of excess food items is not always feasible. Leftover prepared food spoils easily and requires extreme care in handling and storage. Even though some leftover foods might be salvageable by refrigeration, certain foods may break down and lose quality. A good example of this breakdown is a custard or cream pie that must be held under refrigeration for food safety but could develop a soggy crust and not be salable within a few hours after preparation. Policies and procedures for the storage of overproduced food items should be well defined and rigorously enforced.

Attempts to reduce overproduction costs by using an available high priced food item as an ingredient in a low cost menu item can be very expensive. A typical example is using leftover rib roast in beef stew, soup stock, or beef hash, all of which could be prepared with less expensive fresh meat. In addition to the higher initial costs, planning and carrying out these salvage efforts incur higher labor costs that would have been avoided had the overrun not occurred. Customers are generally quick to suspect the use of leftovers, which certainly can be damaging to the image of a foodservice operation.

Underproduction can increase costs as much as overproduction. A diner unable to secure a desired menu item, whether hospital patient or restaurant patron, will be disappointed and often have difficulty in making another selection. Furthermore, satisfying the customer demand in case of underproduction may involve both additional preparation costs and often the substitution of a higher priced item.

A wise manager will insist that a similar backup item be available when underproduction occurs. For example, in a university residence hall foodservice, if an undersupply of country fried steak occurs, an excellent replacement would be frozen minute steaks, quickly grilled. Such a substitution certainly would increase customer satisfaction.

Demand Forecasting

The desire for an efficient foodservice operation generates the need for production *demand forecasting*. Good forecasts are essential for managers in planning smooth transitions from current to future output, regardless of size or functional type of the foodservice (i.e., schools, hospitals, or restaurants). Forecasts vary in sophistication from those based on historical records and intuition to complex models requiring large amounts of data and computer time. Care must be exercised to choose a forecasting model that is suitable for a particular situation.

Historical Records

Adequate *historical records* constitute the base for most forecasting processes. This is especially true of foodservices in which records of the past have been used to determine food production quantities long before sophisticated forecasting procedures were available. In fact, such historical records are the root of most of these procedures. Such records must, however, be accurate and complete, or they cannot be extended into the future with any reliability.

Effective production records, in addition to listing food items, must be identified by date and day of the week, meal or hour of service, special event or holiday, and even weather conditions if applicable. An example of an historical record for a catered engagement announcement party is shown in Figure 2. This seasonal menu also could be used for a June wedding reception, a graduation party, or even Father's Day. Caterers, either independent or employed by an organization, must keep accurate records of the amount of food for each event to prevent underproduction or overproduction of food items on the next similar occasion. Catering is a profit enterprise, and

---

ENGAGEMENT ANNOUNCEMENT
COCKTAIL PARTY

Date: June 17, 1989—Saturday   **Weather:** 80°F and sunny
Time: 5:00 p.m.   **Special Notes:** Serve on patio in parents' home

Iced Shrimp (3)* with
Tangy Cocktail Sauce

Guacamole
Cherry Tomatoes (2)*
Tortilla Chips

Thin Slices of Rare Beef Tenderloin (2)*
Cocktail Buns Horseradish Sauce

Chicken Liver Pâté with Pistachios (2 pâtés)
Tiny Melba Toast

Assorted Raw Vegetables (3)*
Curry Dip

Whole Strawberries with Stems (2)*
Sour Cream and Brown Sugar Dip

Butter Cookies (2)*

Champagne

*per person

FIGURE 2. Example of an historical record

---

reliable past records are essential because events are not repetitive and elaborate forecasting methods generally are not feasible.

Although the production unit records reveal the vital information on food items served to consumers, it is by no means the only organizational unit that should keep records. Only by cross-referencing records of sales with those of production can a reliable historical base for forecasting be formalized. In foodservices in which meals are sold, as in restaurants, hospital employee and guest cafeterias, and schools, records of sales will yield customer count patterns that can be useful for forecasting. These data can be related to the number of times customers select a given menu item or the daily variations induced by weather or special events.

Historical records in the production unit provide the fundamental base for forecasting quantities when the same meal or menu item is repeated. These records should be correlated with those kept by the purchasing department, which include the name and performance of the vendor and price of the food items.

Forecasting Models

CRITERIA FOR A MODEL

Numerous forecasting models have been developed during the past three decades, but, as one might expect, the trend has been toward sophisticated models using computer-based information systems. According to Fitzsimmons and Sullivan (1982), the factors deserving consideration when selecting a forecasting model are cost, required accuracy, relevancy of past data, forecasting lead time, and underlying pattern of behavior.

Cost of Model. The cost of a forecasting model involves the expenses of both development and operation. The developmental costs arise from constructing the model, validating the forecast stability, and, in the case of large operations, writing a computer program. In some cases, educating managers in the use of the model is another cost element. Operational costs include the cost of making a forecast after the model is developed, which is affected by the amount of data and computation time needed. More elaborate models require large amounts of data and thus can be very expensive.

Accuracy of Model. The quality of a forecasting model must be judged primarily by the accuracy of its predictions of future occurrences. An expensive model that yields very accurate forecasts might not be as good a choice as a cheaper and less accurate model. This is a decision the foodservice manager must make.

Relevancy of Past Data. In most forecasting models, the general assumption is that past behavioral patterns and relationships will continue in the future. If a clear relationship between the past and the future does not exist, the past data will not be relevant in developing forecasts. In these cases, subjective approaches, such as those that rely heavily on the opinions of knowledgeable persons, may be more appropriate.

Forecasting Lead Time. The forecasting lead time pertains to the length of time into the future that the forecasts are made. Usually, these times are categorized as short-, medium-, or long-term. The choice of a lead time depends on the items being forecast: a short-term lead will be chosen for perishable produce, a medium- or long-term lead for canned goods.

Pattern of Behavior. As stated above, many forecasting models depend on the assumption that behavioral patterns observed in the past will continue into the future and, even more basic, that actual occurrences follow some known pattern. These patterns, however, may be affected by random influences, which are unpredictable factors responsible for forecasting errors. Not all forecasting models work equally well for all patterns of data; therefore, the appropriate model must be selected for a particular situation.

TYPES OF MODELS

Forecasting techniques have been categorized in numerous ways, but the three most common model classifications are time series, causal, and subjective. A model in one of the classifications may include some features of the others. In all methods of forecasting, trends and seasonality in the data must be considered.

Time Series Model. The frequently used *time series model* involves the presump-

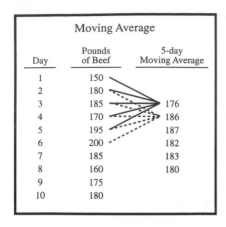

Moving Average		
Day	Pounds of Beef	5-day Moving Average
1	150	
2	180	
3	185	176
4	170	186
5	195	187
6	200	182
7	185	183
8	160	180
9	175	
10	180	

FIGURE 3. Example of moving average

tion that actual occurrences follow an identifiable pattern over time. Although time series data have a specific relationship to time, deviations in the data make forecasting difficult. To reduce the influence of these deviations, several methods have been developed for smoothing the data curve.

The time series models are the most suitable for short-term forecasts in foodservice operations. They are based on the assumption that actual occurrences follow an identifiable trend over time. Actual data may indicate a trend in a general sense but not give forecast information. To make the past data useful, the variations must be reduced to a trend line that can be extended into the future. Moving average and exponential smoothing, both time series models, are used more frequently in rationalizing foodservice data than any other type, although causal models may be used as well.

The most common and easiest of the smoothing procedures is the **moving average method**, which can be used only on items that are of the same kind. The process begins by taking the average of a group of five or ten data for the first point on a forecast line. The second point on the line is made by dropping the first item in the beginning group, including an additional one to make up the same number, and taking an average. The repetitive process is continued for all the data.

An example of the moving average method is shown in Figure 3. The data are for roast beef and cover a ten-day period in the past. A five-day moving average is used. The first five-day moving average is calculated by adding the demand for those days and dividing by five, giving an average of 176 pounds. The next moving average is calculated by adding the demands for days 2 through 6 and dividing by five. The procedure is repeated by dropping the earliest day's data and adding the next for a total of five days. The demand data values and the moving average values plotted on the graph (Figure 4) illustrate the smoothing effect of the method. Note that the smoothed data curve eliminates the daily variations in demand and thus indicates a trend of the past. This averaging process, when continued, yields data points that smooth out the data to a comparatively constant pattern for use in the forecast.

Exponential smoothing is a popular time series procedure for which standard computer software is readily available. It is very similar to the moving average concept ex-

cept that it does not uniformly weight the past observations. Instead, an exponentially decreasing set of weights is used, giving more recent values more weight than older ones. Also, the only data required are the weight (alpha) that is applied to the most recent value, the most recent forecast, and the most recent actual value or demand, thus eliminating storing historical data (Wheelwright and Makridakis, 1989).

The mathematical expression for exponential smoothing contains a judgment factor, alpha (α) which is a number between 0 and 1. Alpha is used to adjust for any errors in previous forecasts and is the weight assigned to the most recent observation, and the $1 - \alpha$ is the weight for the most recent forecast. When alpha has a value close to 1, the new forecast will include a substantial adjustment for any error that occurred in the preceding forecast. Conversely, when alpha is close to 0, the new forecast will not

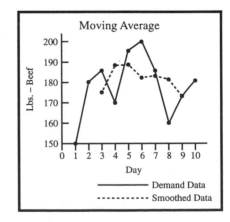

FIGURE 4. Graph illustrating moving average smoothing effect

show much adjustment for the error from the one before. In forecasting for foodservice, alpha generally is 0.3. The most recent forecast values are multiplied by the 1 - α quantity which places a greater weight on recent values. The 1 - α quantity acquires exponents in increasing order as the forecast is repeated, thus decreasing weights of older values and having a lesser influence on the trend curve than more recent data. The mathematical expression for this smoothing method is

- ► The model can be easily programmed and is inexpensive to use.
- ► The rate at which the model responds to changes in the underlying pattern of data can be adjusted mathematically.

Causal Model. Causal models are based on the presumption that an identifiable relationship exists between the item being forecast and other factors. These factors might include selling price, number of customers, market availabil-

The cost of developing and using causal models is generally high, and consequently they are not used frequently for short-term forecasting, such as perishable produce. They are, however, popular for medium- and long-term forecasts, such as canned goods.

The most commonly adopted causal models use **regression analysis.** Following standard statistical terminology, the items being forecast are called dependent variables and the factors determining the value of the dependent variables are called the independent variables. Regression models require a history of data for the dependent and independent variables to permit plotting over time. Once this is done, the regression process involves finding an equation for a line that minimizes the deviations of the dependent variable from it. The two principal kinds of regression models are linear and multiple.

In linear regression the word "linear" signifies the intent of the analysis to find an equation for a straight line that closest fits the data points. In conventional statistical terminology, the item being forecast is called the dependent variable (Y), and the factors that affect it are called independent variables (X).

In the analysis, historic demand data for a single variable will result in a derived equation from a linear regression process in the form of a straight line

$$Y = a_o + a_1X$$

$$S_t = \alpha A_t + (1 - \alpha)S_{t-1}$$

where

α = a constant usually between 0.1 and 0.3 (judgment factor)

S_t = smoothed value at time t (new forecast)

A_t = actual observed value at time t (last demand)

S_{t-1} = preceding smoothed value (last forecast)

Stated in words, this forecast equation is

$$\text{New forecast} = \begin{bmatrix} \text{judgment} \\ \text{factor} \end{bmatrix} \begin{bmatrix} \text{last} \\ \text{demand} \end{bmatrix} + \begin{bmatrix} 1 - \text{judgment} \\ \text{factor} \end{bmatrix} \begin{bmatrix} \text{last} \\ \text{forecast} \end{bmatrix}$$

Fitzsimmons and Sullivan (1982) summarized exponential smoothing as a popular technique for short-term demand forecasting for the following reasons:

- ► All past data are considered in the smoothing process.
- ► More recent data are given more weight than older data.
- ► The technique requires only a few pieces of data to update a forecast.

ity, and virtually anything else that might influence the item being forecast. As with time series models, the assumption is that relationships identified from past data will continue in the future. Causal models vary in complexity from those relating only one factor, such as selling price, to items being forecast to models utilizing a system of mathematical equations that include numerous variables.

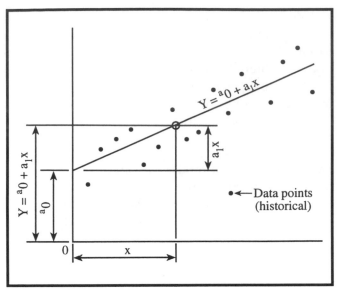

FIGURE 5. Typical regression line

in which a_o and a_1 are numerical constants determined by the regression analysis. As shown in Figure 5, a_o is the intercept of the line on the Y axis and a_1 is the slope of the line. In use, X will be a single independent variable quantity. The data points in the figure are the Y (dependent variable) values for specific values of X (independent variable). Preliminary plotting of the variables on graph paper would be advisable to ascertain if they could be represented reasonably by a straight line. The forecasting value consists of the assumption that the linear relationship between the variables will continue for a reasonable time in the future, or quite simply that the line may be extended. Use of the equation requires only substitution of an anticipated future value for X and then solution for Y, which is the forecasting quantity.

Examples of independent variables in hospital foodservice are total number of patient trays served, patient census, cafeteria customer capacity, number of employees, number of patients on regular diets, and the number of patients on each modified diet. For example, roast beef might be a popular item for a foodservice, and the relationship between the historic number of patient trays and the pounds of roast beef could yield a regression equation. To forecast beef demand, an anticipated future count of trays would then be inserted into the equation as X to solve for Y, the pounds of roast beef needed.

If determination of the effects of more than one independent variable ($X_1, X_2, \ldots, X_n$) on the dependent one is desired, the process is called *multiple regression* and the derived equation will have the following form:

$$Y = a_o + a_1X_1 + a_2X_2 + \ldots + a_nX_n$$

Multiple regression analysis is quite complex, and a good computer program is needed for the solution.

Subjective Model. A *subjective model* is generally used when relevant data are scarce or patterns and relationships between data do not tend to persist over time. In these cases, little relationship exists between the past and the long-term future. Forecasters must rely on opinions and other information, generally qualitative, that might relate to the item being forecast.

One of the subjective forecasting models is the *Delphi* technique, which involves a panel of experts who individually complete questionnaires on a chosen topic and return them to the investigator. The results of the first questionnaire are summarized and returned to the panel for revision. The questionnaires are revised successively until some degree of agreement is reached. The Delphi method can be time-consuming and expensive and is not especially suitable for foodservice forecasting.

Other qualitative forecasting techniques include market research, panel consensus, visionary forecast, and historical analogy. *Market research* is a systematic and formal procedure for developing and testing hypotheses about actual markets. *Panel consensus* is based on the assumption that a group of experts can produce a better forecast than one person. This differs from the Delphi method by requiring free communication among the panel members. A *visionary forecast* is characterized by subjective guesswork and imagination. The *historical analogy* involves comparative analysis of the introduction and growth of new items with similar new product history.

Planning for Total Output

Decision levels within an organization may make the separation into detailed and overall planning desirable. Forecasting models previously discussed are related to detailed planning and generally are used at the operating level. Higher levels of management are concerned with overall or aggregate planning for total output.

Aggregate planning, often described in industrial management literature, is distinguished by planning for gross variable elements by top managers with detail left to the lower echelon managers. In the context of current literature, "aggregate" means overall or nonspecific. The process usually consists of planning in a specific time frame for the elements of product, inventory, and labor.

Foodservice operations are rarely amenable to such an aggregate planning device because of the fundamental differences in technological processes and products that exist between industrial manufacturing organizations and foodservice systems. The industrial manufacturer transforms raw materials by several distinct processes into a finished product that is stored in inventory or shipped to the customer for use at a later time. This inventory can be used to protect the manufacturer from stockouts in periods of increased demands.

By contrast, in foodservice operations, the raw material transformation occurs typically in the same facility in which the product is consumed. Because the finished product is perishable, no such finished goods inventory can be maintained to meet future demand. A large hospital using ready prepared or assembly/serve foodservice systems could possibly utilize aggregate planning, if a high-capacity computer were available. Connell et al. (1984) investigated the use of aggregate planning in large medical center foodservices. The essential element was the aggregate demand consisting of the total services, nourishments, and meals provided by the foodservice system in a production period with labor costs.

Production Scheduling

Production scheduling in foodservice operations can be defined as the time sequencing of events required by the production subsystem to produce a meal. Scheduling occurs in two distinct stages—planning and action—and is essential for production control.

In the planning stage, forecasts are converted into the quantity of each food item to be prepared and the distribution of the items to super-visors in each work center. As an example, 500 servings of roast beef, scalloped potatoes, broccoli, tossed salad, dinner rolls, and cherry pie have been forecast for a special dinner. The foodservice director assigns the production of the 500 servings of beef, potatoes, and broccoli to the supervisor of main production, the tossed salad to the salad unit, and the rolls and cherry pie to the bake shop.

Supervisors in each unit assume the responsibility for the action stage by preparing a production schedule. Each item is assigned to a specific employee and the time to start its preparation is recorded on the schedule. Careful scheduling assures that the food is prepared for service without lengthy holding and deterioration in quality. The supervisors give feedback to the manager by writing comments on the production schedule.

In small operations in which only one cook and perhaps an assistant are on duty at a time, the foodservice manager might also need to assume the responsibility for the action stage. No operation, however small, can avoid the necessity for a production schedule.

Production Schedule

The *production schedule,* frequently called the production worksheet, is the major control in the production subsystem because it activates the menu and provides a test of forecasting accuracy. The menu, of course, must be based on standardized recipes.

The production schedule is highly individualized in various foodservices and may vary from a single sheet for manual completion to a computer program printout. Regardless of the form, certain basic information must be included on each schedule: the unit, production date, and meal should be identified, as well as other pertinent information, for example, actual customer count, weather, and special events. In addition. the following information must be included to make it a specific action plan:

▶ Employee assignments
▶ Menu item
▶ Quantity to prepare
▶ Actual yield
▶ Special instructions and comments
▶ Preparation time schedule
▶ overproduction and underproduction
▶ Substitutions
▶ Additional assignments
▶ Prepreparation

The sample production schedule in Figure 6 is from a large university residence hall foodservice. Note that the general information previously mentioned is displayed at the top of the worksheet and that the production area is marked as the specific destination for this schedule. The meal count at the conclusion of production is also recorded, which validates this schedule as part of historical data. The specific headings previously listed constitute the column headings.

The production schedule generally is posted on a bulletin board in the unit. The name of the *employee* in the left hand column readily enables personnel to find designated duties. The *menu item* column identifies the recipe

by name. Often the unit supervisor will distribute the recipes, either in card form or as a computer printout, to the appropriate employees at the time the schedule is posted.

The *quantity to prepare* is the forecast amount for each menu item. The *actual yield* is the portion count produced by the recipe. Current practice is to include portion size and count on the recipe. If not contained on the recipe, this information should be placed on the production schedule. Note that the actual yield indicates overproduction for some items and underproduction for others. The *instructions* column, completed by the unit supervisor, gives special information and comments on equipment to be used and service instructions. In addition, this column should contain any specific information not included in the recipe, such as that indicated for refried beans and for broccoli: "Add bean liquid as needed to maintain a moist product" and "season with melted butter."

The *time schedule,* completed by the unit supervisor, is intended to assure that the various menu items will be produced for service at the desired time. It also has references to preparation methods standardized in this main production unit for a particular item, such as the country fried steak and Mexican rice.

The *leftover amount* column indicates over- or underproduction. Underproduction is indicated by zero leftover and a time entry in the *runout time* column. The substitution column is used when an item is

underproduced, as in the case of the broccoli spears.

In this residence hall foodservice, *cleaning assignments* are in addition to regularly scheduled cleaning and the name of the person responsible is recorded. Instructions for *prepreparation* for the following meal, whether the same day or next, are in the same form as the production schedule, beginning with the name of the person, and followed by the menu item, quantity, and special instructions. The items listed under prepreparation will be on the schedule for the following meal.

The emphasis in this text on production scheduling is justified by its importance as an element of production control with important hearing on the cost of materials, labor, and energy. Regardless of the perfection of the schedule and the assignment of employees to implement it, however, the production employees are the ones who make the schedule work. Realization of this simple fact implies the value of production employee meetings.

Production Meetings

Foodservice managers in small operations, or unit supervisors in large ones, should hold a meeting daily with employees in the production unit. Ordinarily, these *production meetings* can be rather short but, at a cycle menu change, more time is required to discuss new recipes and employee assignments. In foodservice operations serving breakfast, lunch, and dinner,

		Unit	Main Production					

Date ___1/24/90___

Meal Count ___2153___
Weather ___Fair___

Meal ___ Bkf. ___ Lunch __x__ Dinner

Comments ___Basketball Game___

Employee	Menu item	Quantity to prepare	Actual yield	Instructions	Time schedule	Left over amount	Run-out time	Substi-tution	Cleaning assignment
Wege Whatley	Country Fried Steak	1200	1220	Use 2 tilting fry pans and oven number 3	Begin frying 2:15 See Frying Time schedule	35 servings	—	—	Whatley— tilting fry pans
Lundin	Giant Rolled Tostados	1000	1020	Serve open face on cafeteria line and clientele will roll their own		50 tortillas 10 lbs meat mixture 1 gal cheese sce.	—	—	Lundin— slicer and attachments
McCurdy	Whipped Potatoes	1200	1150	If necessary use instant as a back up	Begin steaming potatoes at 3:00	12 lbs	—	—	
McCurdy	Cream Gravy	2000	1600	Make 4 batches 600—600—400 —100 (if needed) Serve over both steak and potatoes		2 gal	—	—	
Wege	Mexican Rice	900	900	Use 12 × 10 × 4 pans	See Baking Time schedule	18 lbs	—	—	
Mockery	Refried Beans	850	850	Add bean liquid as needed to maintain a moist product		12 lbs	—	—	Mockery— oven number 1, shelves and doors
Mockery	Broccoli Spears	1000	850	Season with melted margarine	Begin 4:00 Prepare based on demand	0	6:00	2 1/2 lbs Aspara-gus Spears	
Mockery	Yogurt Cup	20	20	Serve whole container— blueberry, cherry, rum raisin, plain		8			

Prepreparation:

Employee	Menu item	Quantity	Instructions	Employee	Menu item	Quantity	Instructions
McCurdy	Roast Beef	600 lbs	Pan beef in baking pans, cover and refrigerate	Lundin	(Omelet) fresh eggs	1 case	Break into 60 qt mixer bowl
Mockery	Hard Cooked Eggs	5 doz.	For garnish on spinach	Wege	Ham	10 lbs	Dice for omelets

Source: Used by permission of Kansas State University Residence Hall Foodservice.

FIGURE 6. Residence hall foodservice production schedule

these meetings are generally scheduled after lunch, when activity in the production unit is minimal.

During these meetings, production unit employees can be encouraged to discuss the effectiveness of the schedule just completed. Problems such as underproduction and suggested corrective measures should be recorded for the next time the menu appears in the cycle.

The meeting should conclude with a discussion of the production schedule for the following three meals. At this time, the employees should review recipes for the various menu items, possible substitutions, and prepreparation for the following day. Free discussion of workloads is appropriate for such meetings and can be a morale builder for the employees who really make the schedule work.

Summary

The objective of food production is the preparation of food items in the needed quantity and desired quality at a cost appropriate to the particular service. Production is the second subsystem in the transformation element of the foodservice system and generically is the process by which goods and services are created. In foodservice, production is the managerial function of converting food items purchased in various states into menu items that are served to a customer, client, or patient.

Production planning in manufacturing industries primarily is the effective synthe-sis of quantity, quality, and cost objectives. These objectives are applicable to foodservice operations in which the product or menu items depend on the operation. Forecasting is a function of production and provides the data base for decision making and planning. Production demand has a degree of uncertainty and varies with the type of foodservice operation. Overproduction generates extra costs because salvage of extra food items is not feasible; underproduction also can increase cost because of additional labor for preparation and often the substitution of a higher priced item.

Good forecasts are essential for managers in planning smooth transitions from current to future output, regardless of size or type of foodservice. Historical records constitute the base for most forecasting processes. Forecasting models are categorized as time series, which involves the presumption that actual occurrences follow an identifiable pattern over time; causal, in which the presumption is that an identifiable relationship exists between the item being forecast and other factors; or subjective, which is used when relevant data are scarce and patterns between data do not tend to persist over time. The exponential smoothing model in the time series category currently is the most applicable to foodservice operations because computer software is available. To initiate the program, only a judgment factor for smoothing errors, the most re-cent actual demand, and the most recent forecast are required. In addition, historical records are an integral part of the exponential smoothing model, thus eliminating storage of vast amounts of data.

Forecasting models are related to detailed planning at the operational level. Higher levels of management are concerned with overall or aggregate planning for total output, which usually consists of planning in a specific time frame for the elements of product, inventory, and labor.

Production scheduling in foodservice operations is defined as the time sequencing of events required by the production subsystem to produce a meal and occurs in two distinct stages. In the planning stage, forecasts are converted into the quantity of each food item to be prepared and the distribution of the items to supervisors in each work center. Supervisors in each unit assume the responsibility for the action stage by preparing a production schedule on which each item is assigned to a specific employee and the start time for preparation is recorded. The production schedule activates the menu and is highly individualized in various foodservices and may include quantity to prepare, actual yield, additional assignments, and special instructions and comments. Production meetings should be held daily by the supervisor with the employees in the unit. The meeting should conclude with a discussion of the production schedule for the following meal or meals, review of recipes, and prepreparation. Employee workloads also should be discussed.

References

Adam, E., and Ebert, R. *Production and Operations Management.* 3rd ed. Englewood Cliffs, NJ: Prentice-Hall, 1986.

Armstrong, J. S. The ombudsman: Research on forecasting: A quarter-century review, 1960–84. *Interfaces* 16:89, 1986.

Buchanan, P. W. *Quantity Food Preparation: Standardizing Recipes and Controlling Ingredients.* Chicago: American Dietetic Association, 1983.

Chandler, S. J., Norton, L. C., Hoover, L. W., and Moore, A. N. Analysis of meal census patterns for forecasting menu item demand. *J Am Diet Assoc* 80(4):317, 1982.

Cichy, R. Productivity pointers to promote a profitable performance. *Consultant* 16(1):35, 1983.

Connell, B. C., Adam, E. E., and Moore, A. N. Aggregate planning in health care foodservice systems with varying technologies. *J Operations Manag* 5(1):41, 1984.

Cullen, K. O., Hoover, L. W, and Moore, A. N. Menu item forecasting systems in hospital foodservice. *J Am Diet Assoc* 73(6):640, 1978.

Dougherty, D. A. Forecasting production demand. In Rose, J. C., ed., *Handbook for Health Care Food Service Management.* Rockville, MD: Aspen Systems Corp., 1984.

Finley, D. H., and Kim., I. Y Use of selected management science techniques in health care foodservice systems. *J Foodserv Systems* 4(1):1, 1986.

Fitzsimmons, J. A., and Sullivan, R. S. *Service Operations Management.* New York: McGraw-Hill, 1982.

Forecasting: An effective tool to improve decision making. *Small Bus Report* 11(8):71, 1986.

Georgoff, D. M., and Murdick, R. G. Manager's guide to forecasting. *Harvard Bus Rev* 64(1):110, 1986.

Konnersman, P. M. Forecasting production demand in the dietary department. *Hospitals* 43(18):85, 1969.

Lambert, C. U., and Beach. B. L. Computerized scheduling for cook/freeze food production plans. *J Am Diet Assoc* 77(2):174, 1980.

MacStravic, R. S. *Forecasting Use of Health Services: A Provider's Guide.* Rockville, MD: Aspen Publishers, 1984.

Messersmith, A. M., Moore, A. N., and Hoover, L. W A multi-echelon menu item forecasting system for hospitals. *J Am Diet Assoc* 72(5):509, 1978.

Miller, J. L., and Shanklin, C. S. Forecasting menu item demand in foodservice operations. *J Am Diet Assoc* 88(4):443, 1988.

Sill, B. A formula for forecasting. *Restaur Bus* 86(6):179, 1987.

Wheelwright, S. C., and Makridakis, S. *Forecasting Methods for Management.* 5th ed. New York: Wiley, 1989.

Wood, S. D. A model for statistical forecasting of menu item demand. *J Am Diet Assoc* 70(3):254, 1977.

As a graduate of a prestigious hospitality management program you have decided to open a restaurant. You are confident of your ability but need a silent partner to provide financial backing. Your instructor has agreed to become your investor. He/she has always wanted to do something like this but needs to know all about the operation before committing to the idea. It is your job to describe the operation completely and make your investor thoroughly understand the business. Only then will he/she fork over the big bucks (they will take the form of grade points).

You have already done some preliminary work on this project and have provided your investor with the following:

Restaurant: 90 seats open to the public, full bar for service with meals only
Hours: 5:00–10:00 pm six days a week and Sunday 11:00–2:00; reservations requested
Theme: Old West
Service: Casual family, modified table d'hote; soup, salad, appetizer (choice of two), entree (choose from three available), vegetables (choose from three), starchy item, bread, dessert (choose from three).
Other Info: Marketing based on family trade; does not serve barbecue and trimmings because a barbecue restaurant already exists in the next block in a strip shopping center; this is a free standing building with adequate parking.

Based on the above information you will develop a prospectus for your investor. Items requested are listed below. Since this operation currently exists only on paper and in your mind, thorough and accurate descriptions are important. Help your investor actually "see" this restaurant in action. Be creative with this project and have fun.

Requirements

1. Design a dinner menu and a bar menu. Describe how they will be produced, maintained, changed. Do you expect any special problems or costs. Submit the menus in the finished, usable form.

2. Describe the location and the building. Why did you choose this particular place? Will you need to remodel? Do you own the building or lease it? What is the cost?

3. Describe the kitchen. Based on the menu what are your equipment needs? How is it scheduled to meet menu demands? Is current equipment adequate? Diagram work and traffic flow.

4. Develop the menu (remember target market). Provide recipes. Cost out recipes. Forecast sales for individual items and total sales. Write a purchase order for one week.

5. Describe the staffing plan. How many employees will be needed? What positions must be filled? What type will you need (ex: female, singers, mature)? Where will you find your employees? What is the hiring process? Who will actually spend the time recruiting, interviewing, selecting, and training initially and during regular operation?

6. Describe your personnel policies. How will you evaluate, reprimand, reward, promote, dismiss your employees? Provide a one week work schedule for your restaurant. Write a job description for one person in each position (i.e., cook, waiter, assistant manager, etc.)

7. Project sales and expenses for a typical week. Generate a profit and loss statement.

Grading

You will be given grades on two different aspects of your project. The first is for content and completeness. Can your investor completely understand this restaurant and feel confident about investing? The second part is presentation. Correct spelling and grammar are a must. The ability to express well organized thoughts clearly is expected. Neatness, creativity, and attention to detail will also be rewarded.

The Heritage Squire Restaurant Complex is located in a resort area on the Gulf of Mexico. The Complex is a large central restaurant with four specialty shops and a souvenir boutique for the convenience of patrons. It is in an historic building built around a courtyard which attracts visitors and local citizens alike. The restaurant has a long history of successful operation. During the last ten years, however, the restaurant complex has suffered from new competition in the area. During this time a management company has been in charge of running the property. Managers have shown a distinct lack of interest in this older operation, often using it as a holding place while waiting for a "better" assignment. Business is severely down. Employee morale is low and service is poor. Employees have been laid off Some of the better employees have quit to work at a new restaurant down the beach.

Recently, Mr. R.E. Model has purchased the restaurant complex. He is a local boy who made good. When he was a child and a young man he often dined at the restaurant with his dear departed parents and has fond memories of how things used to be. After the purchase, Mr. Model fired the management company. However he retained several department supervisors because he remembered them from his childhood. These supervisors have been there for years without advancing any further. They have strong cliques among themselves and the employees. They also have strong contacts with influential people in town.

You have been hired by Mr. Model to turn the restaurant around and return it to its former glory. He has given you a good deal of control but has put some limits on what you can do without checking with him. The restaurant and shops are to be closed for one month for cleaning and refurbishing. Employees are to be used for the cleaning detail and outside decorators are working on the dining room, shops, and general theme. The kitchen, with twenty-five year old equipment is to be left alone.

Before you arrive on the property, the chef and dining room manager quit (they were local people who did not work for the management company). Mr. Model has requested that you not dismiss any current employees because they are needed to clean during the one month closure. You quickly discover that the employees are very unhappy about the cleaning assignment, feeling it is beneath them. The only reason they don't quit is that Mr. Model pays better than the newer restaurants. It doesn't take long for the employees to realize that you are not going to fire them, at least not at first. They also have the idea that this is a rich, snooty restaurant and that clients expect to be treated in a snobby manner.

As you work through the remodeling and approach the opening day, you are having continual battles with the old line supervisors. Mr. Model still likes them, often having dinner or meetings with them to discuss old times. The supervisors clearly resent you. They thought one of them should have been promoted, not bring in some young know-it-all from the outside.

Mr. Model has agreed to hiring a new chef and dining room manager. You have located an excellent chef who was recommended by your advisor at school. He is very talented but quite temperamental. He has already offended some of the kitchen staff and is complaining about the old equipment. Applicants for dining room manager include someone you knew at school though not well. He seems well qualified and is interested in moving to the area. However, you are concerned that two managers from the same school might be perceived as "ganging up" by the current employees and maybe by Mr. Model who has no college education. Again, the current employees are resentful of the outside hire rather than promoting from within. You are increasingly concerned about the attitude of the employees and how this will impact your efforts to revitalize the restaurant.

Given this environment, what is your mission as manager of the Heritage Squire Restaurant Complex? How do you plan to fulfill that mission?

What problems will you face the first week on the job? What are your goals? What will you do to address the problems while trying to fulfill the expectations of Mr. Model?

What problems will loom after one month on the job? Will past issues mesh with current difficulties? How will you keep going and keep your job?

What situation will you be in after six months on the job? What have been your successes? What have you been able to change? How can you work and grow within the current situation?

Please be creative and thorough when thinking this through.

7

EQUIPMENT AND DESIGN

The Principles of Design
J. C. Birchfield

Space Analysis
J. C. Birchfield

Project 1

Project 2

THE PRINCIPLES OF DESIGN

J. C. Birchfield

Basic Design Principles

ALTHOUGH THERE ARE significant differences in the physical layout, menu, and method of service of various food facilities, there are underlying design principles that are followed by a food facilities designer in any type of situation. These principles lead to efficiency and a pleasant environment for the worker and customer, but do not result in one particular layout. Prototype restaurants of the three leading hamburger chains are quite different in layout, each for its own reason, but all follow a set of design principles.

A common misconception about design is that there is only one "right" way to lay out the equipment and arrange the space. There are, in fact, many designs that would be acceptable and workable for the same facility. A competent designer will approach a facilities design project knowing that in each project a different set of variables will prevail. Each food facility is treated as unique, with its own design problems to be solved.

The reader should understand the difference between "design" and "layout." Design encompasses the entire facility, with all the considerations [of] concept development. Layout involves a consideration of each small unit or work space in a food facility. In the field of architecture or food facilities design we speak of "designing" a building or a foodservice operation and of "laying out" a range section or bakery.

Compromise

In every design project, conflicting needs will give rise to a series of compromise conditions that the designer must be able to work with. Certainly the number of compromises should be kept to a minimum, but it is certain that they will always exist. For example, in the design of a dining area, it might be highly desirable to include a private dining room that could be closed off for special groups. Should this room be near the customer entrance for easy public access or near the kitchen for convenience to the hot food production area? The answer might be "both"! However, if placing the private dining room near both the entrance and the kitchen interferes with other major components of the design, the best alternative may be to move it to another part of the dining area. Conflicting needs always arise in the design process, and only the skilled and experienced person will be able to balance priorities so that the resulting compromises are logical and defensible. Since the owner's priorities may not be the same as the designer's, frank discussion and give-and-take by all parties are often needed to create a satisfactory working relationship.

Each design professional has a set of guidelines that he or she has found helpful in approaching the design of a food facility. Thus, while certain principles are universally accepted, there is no standard set of design rules for all professionals working in the foodservice field. The following principles, which are based on the author's own experience as a food facilities design professional, are intended to provide a general framework for approaching the design process. The design should:

► Have flexibility and modularity
► Have simplicity
► Create efficient flow of materials and personnel
► Facilitate ease of sanitation
► Create ease of supervision
► Use space efficiently

The Principle of Flexibility and Modularity

The use of heavy-gauge stainless steel in the construction of kitchen equipment is almost universally accepted by the foodservice industry. Stainless steel does not rust, is easy to clean, is not porous, and does not easily wear out. Stainless steel has the major fault of being very inflexible, however. A stainless steel table in the kitchen cannot be modified easily to accommodate a change in the design. If, for instance, a work area 14 feet in length is required, the principle of flexibility would lead the designer to specify two tables, one 6 feet long and one 8 feet long. These two lengths would permit rearrangement of the kitchen, without the necessity of cutting the table to accommodate a new design. The principle of flexibility requires components that can be rearranged to meet changing conditions, such as new management, different methods of service, a new menu, or a new preparation method. Design-

ing for change is the primary means of achieving flexibility.

In the dining area, flexibility can be achieved by dividing movable walls. In the service area, the space can be divided to accommodate both table service and buffet service.

An inflexible construction method that was popular in the past was the construction of concrete pads as a base for kitchen equipment. These bases were used in the place of legs for refrigerators, ovens, or other heavy pieces of equipment to eliminate the difficulty in cleaning under the equipment. The problem with these bases is that as the equipment was replaced or the kitchen was rearranged, the bases were then the wrong shape or were in the wrong spot. A concrete base is difficult to eliminate and almost impossible to move. Concrete bases are now infrequently seen in commercial kitchens.

Modularity in design provides standardized sizes and functions of space and equipment. For example, in the construction industry doors are "modular" because they are sized according to an industry standard. Reach-in refrigerators in the foodservice industry usually are modular in size and function. In a free-flow or "scramble" cafeteria, the service components should be modular, so that the service lines can be easily shifted, as menu and customer tastes change. Modular range sections, which are commonly used, permit the designer to select from many types of equipment and to arrange these in a

smooth and continuous lineup. "Quick disconnect" utility lines that allow inexpensive changes and easy disconnection of the equipment are an excellent example of flexibility and modularity. The modular pieces can be designed for "off-the-floor" installation, with the entire range section mounted on legs for ease in cleaning. In future years, if a piece of equipment needs to be replaced, the modular unit can be removed without disturbing other pieces of equipment.

The Principle of Simplicity

In the designing of a food facility, striving for simplicity offers a great many advantages. Foodservices facilities seem to invite clutter, and clutter leads to poor sanitation, confusion, and inefficiency in the work areas, as well as an environment that customers may find uncomfortable and overcrowded.

The principle of simplicity can be incorporated into the design of foodservice components and systems in various ways. Some examples are:

► Clean uncluttered lines for range sections
► Simple wall-hung tables in areas where a heavy grease or soil condition exists
► The use of modular or drop-in cooking equipment that eliminates corners, edges, and unnecessary under-shelves or overshelves
► The elimination of wheels on equipment that will seldom be moved
► The elimination of utility connections that penetrate

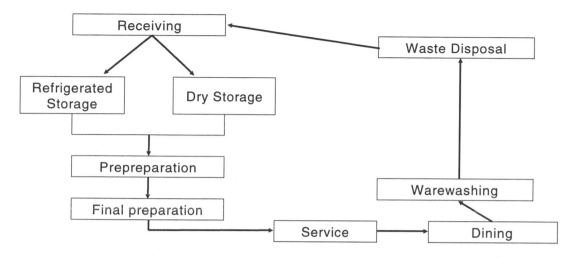

FIGURE 1. The Flow of Materials and Personnel.

the floor (rather than the wall behind the equipment), creating dirt pockets and clutter

➤ The selection of a piece of equipment without unnecessary accessories

➤ Convenient waiter/waitress stations near the serving area in the dining room

➤ The arrangement of tables in the dining room to create natural and comfortable aisle space for waiters and guests

Examples of the violation of the principle of simplicity exist in many restaurant kitchens. For instance, the large stainless steel equipment stands for fryers and grills sold by equipment manufacturers are very expensive and difficult to clean. A better solution is a simple, flat stainless steel table with drop-in fryers and grills. This would save thousands of dollars in the original installation and make the cleaning process much simpler for the employees.

The Principle of Flow of Materials and Personnel

The movement of food through a foodservice facility should follow a logical sequence beginning with receiving and ending with waste disposal. Since both receiving and waste disposal usually occur at the back dock of a food operation, the food moves through the food facility in a circle, as illustrated in Figure 1.

If the food does not move in the order shown, then backtracking by the personnel will occur, resulting in lower productivity and wasted labor.

The following are examples of some flow considerations in design:

➤ The movement of employees from one section of the kitchen to another

➤ The flow of dishes through the dishwashing system, back to the service area.

➤ In a restaurant, the flow of customers from the entrance to the cocktail

lounge and/or to the main dining room

➤ In a cafeteria, the flow of customers from the entrance through the service cafeteria to the dish drop-off point

➤ The flow of raw food ingredients through the main traffic aisles of the kitchen to the preparation area

It is helpful for the designer to diagram the flow patterns on the preliminary floor plan, showing the movement of customers, food, dishes, trash, and garbage. Color coding the flow-lines makes the patterns easier to distinguish and assists the designer in arriving at a design solution that accommodates the proper flow of materials and personnel.

The Principle of Ease of Sanitation

In virtually every type of facility, more employee labor hours are spent cleaning the food operation than are spent preparing the food. A food facility designed with sanitation

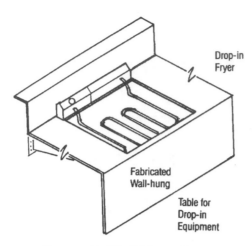

FIGURE 2. Wall-Hung Fryer.

in mind can be cleaned more quickly and easily and thus require fewer labor hours for this aspect of operation. Some examples of sanitation design considerations are described below:

▶ *Building finishes* that are durable and easy to clean. Structural glazed tile on the walls is the most desirable building finish because of ease of cleaning and damage resistance. Ceramic tile is easy to clean and can be purchased in colorful patterns that make the kitchen a pleasant place to work. Epoxy paint on cement block is the least expensive wall finish, but will turn brown around areas that are exposed to high heat. The painted surface is also easily chipped by rolling equipment. The use of bright colors in the kitchen will improve the general appearance of the space and encourage cleanliness. Quarry tile is the standard floor finish for the industry because it does not wear, is grease resistant, and is less slip-

pery than other floors when wet.

▶ *Wall-hung equipment.* The use of equipment that is attached to the wall, eliminating the use of legs, makes an excellent sanitation design (Fig. 2). A space is created under the equipment, allowing for ease of cleaning.

▶ *Equipment racks* with a minimum number of legs.

▶ *Garbage disposals* in work areas to facilitate waste disposal.

▶ *Shelf storage design.* Portable storage shelving systems and open shelving under tables can be cleaned easily.

The Principle of Ease of Supervision

Many hotels and foodservice institutions built during the 1920s and 1930s had vegetable preparation areas that were remote from the main kitchen or separated by partitions and were therefore difficult to supervise. The open type of design, which is now preferred, allows the supervisor to oversee the production

areas more efficiently. The elimination of walls and partitions also permits workers to move and communicate with each other more easily and tends to reduce the number of people needed.

The separation of production areas by floor level not only violates the ease-of-supervision principle by increasing the amount of supervision needed, but it also creates cumbersome flow patterns between the floors. The designer should avoid separating the production areas by floor whenever possible.

It is often desirable to put a half-wall under hoods and between work departments. A 4-foot half-wall provides separation and defines workspace, but does not block the view of the supervisor, who needs to maintain contact with production workers. A half wall is also very useful as:

▶ A place to attach wall-hung equipment
▶ A sanitary site for utility connections
▶ A containment device for spilled water (around stock kettles)

The Principle of Space Efficiency

As costs of building construction and maintenance rise, designers are constantly striving to incorporate space-saving ideas into their work. In this case, necessity can be turned to advantage—space saving is translated into space efficiency in the design of a small, well-equipped food facilities work area.

The principle of space efficiency can, of course, be carried to the extreme. Small, efficient kitchens are a pleasure to use, but kitchens that are too small can be most unpleasant for cooks and other kitchen workers. How can the designer know the difference between "small and efficient" and "too small"? Providing the following components will help ensure that each section of the kitchen has the necessary equipment and storage space to enable employees to work efficiently:

▶ A work surface (table)
▶ A sink
▶ A cutting surface
▶ Storage for utensils
▶ Storage for pans
▶ Storage for raw ingredients
▶ Storage for the finished product
▶ Proper aisle space for movement

If each work area includes the above features, and the work area is arranged efficiently and is adequate for their utilization, the food facility will be space efficient.

SPACE ANALYSIS

J. C. Birchfield

HOW LARGE SHOULD A FOOD facility be? Should the kitchen be half the size of the dining room? How much space will be needed for warewashing and storage? These and related questions must be answered during the early phase of the design project, since the answers will determine the size and thus the total cost of the facility. By knowing space requirements in advance, the owner or architect can make realistic preliminary estimates of construction costs.

It is the design consultant's job to determine the space requirements for each section of the foodservice facility before the actual design can begin. This early but difficult estimate of space is achieved by gathering basic data about the nature of the planned food operation. Once this information has been obtained, the space requirements of each functional part of a foodservice facility are analyzed. The areas that need to be considered are the following:

Receiving
Storage
  dry storage
  paper and cleaning
    supplies storage
  refrigerated storage
  utensil and cleaning
    equipment storage
Office
Preparation areas
  prepreparation
  hot food preparation
  cold food preparation
  final preparation
Bakery
Employee locker room toilet
Service areas
Dining rooms
Warewashing

For purposes of easy reference, the description of each of these functional foodservice areas is divided into four sections entitled:

▶ General Description of the Space
▶ Relationship to Other Areas
▶ Amount of Space Needed
▶ Special Design Features

Receiving

General Description of the Space

The receiving area is located with easy access to driveways and street entrances to the property. Usually the architect will decide where major ingress/egress for people, delivery trucks, and service vehicles will be located. The food facilities design consultant must work with the architect to be sure that sufficient space is allocated for the movement of large tractor-trailer trucks and other vehicles that need access to the receiving area. Consideration must be given to proper screening of the receiving dock and especially to trash and garbage storage containers. It is desirable to screen the receiving area so that persons looking out of the building windows or walking along the street will not have a full view of the receiving dock and garbage containers.

Relationship to Other Areas

The primary relationship of receiving is to the storage areas, which are often scattered and may in fact be located at different building levels. Regardless of the location of storage, easy access must be available for the movement of heavy materials from the receiving dock. The receiving dock must also be accessible to the kitchen for the following reasons:

➤ Many food products will go directly from receiving to the production areas in the kitchen.

➤ Refrigerated storage areas are often located adjacent to the kitchen and will be stocked directly from the receiving dock.

➤ Since in small- to medium-sized foodservice facilities, supervisory personnel such as the chef, manager, or assistant managers will personally be responsible for receiving the food, easy access from the kitchen to the dock is highly desirable.

Other important relationships for the receiving area include access to trash containers, washdown rooms, and cleaning equipment.

Amount of Space Needed

Space needs in the receiving area vary with the volume of food to be received, frequency of delivery, and the distance between the receiving area and the storage spaces. If the receiving clerk must transport food products great distances before placing them in storage, the accumulation of food products on the back dock may require the allocation of additional space. Often, too much space is provided for the receiving dock, resulting in the accumulation of miscellaneous equipment and debris that add clutter to the food operation. The following chart provides general guidelines for allocating the proper amount of space for the receiving dock.

Type of Food Operation	Space Needed[a]		Number of Trucks
	Sq. Ft.	(Sq. M.)	
Fast-food	40–60	(3.72–5.58)	1
Small restaurant (under 75 seats)	60–80	(5.58–7.44)	1
Medium restaurant (75–150 seats) OR Small institution (300–1,000 meals per day)	80–100	(7.44–9.30)	1
Large restaurant (150–400 seats) OR Medium institution (1,000–2,000 meals per day)	120–150	(11.16–13.95)	2
Large institution (over 2,000 meals per day)	150–175	(13.95–16.28)	2
Large hotel, restaurant or institution with complex menu, catering facilities, snack bars	175–200	(16.28–18.60)	3

[a] Does not include space for trash removal truck or trash container. Space for this equipment (approximately 40–60 sq. ft.—3.72–5.58 sq. m.) should be added to the receiving dock.

Special Design Features

The receiving dock can be designed as an elevated platform for tractor-trailer trucks, at street level, or at any level in between these two heights. The decision on receiving dock height will probably be determined by the architect on the basis of site development and the placement of the building on the property. The depth of the dock (distance from front to back) should permit a person to walk back and forth, with space for goods stored temporarily on wooden pallets. Usually 8 or 10 feet is sufficient. The length of the dock should accommodate the number of delivery trucks that are likely to be unloading at one time. For most foodservice operations, a receiving clerk can check in only one or two trucks at a time, and a single or at the most a double truck width is usually sufficient. A third truck width for a trash/garbage vehicle is also desirable. A range of 10 to 15 feet per truck should be used as a standard, depending on the angle for backing to the dock (Fig. 1).

The following design features must be considered in the planning process for the receiving area:

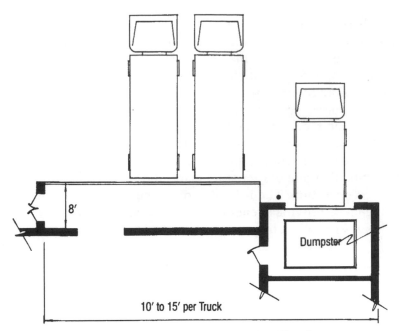

FIGURE 1. Layout of Receiving Dock

- control
- protection from the weather
- scales
- materials handling equipment

Control. The control of food and supplies moving in and out of the receiving area will be of concern to the foodservice management staff. Visibility of the receiving area from an office window is highly desirable if the food facility is large enough to justify a receiving office. For a small food facility that does not have a receiving office, visual control from the kitchen or manager's office should be a design consideration. It is often necessary to construct a stairway at the back dock for the use of employees coming and going from the workplace. This presents a serious control problem because it permits easy access to food and supplies by employees as they enter or exit the building. If possible, a separately controlled entrance for employees should be incorporated into the building design. If this is not possible, the next best solution is to design a separate door and connected corridor from the receiving area to the interior of the building.

Protection from the weather. Receiving personnel must be protected from rain, cold, and excessive heat as they perform their duties on the back dock. Typical architectural solutions include a simple roof overhang, placement of the receiving dock in a recess under the exterior wall of the building, or the enclosure of the entire receiving area with a heavy-duty folding door. Unless weather conditions are extremely severe, the enclosure of the entire receiving area is excessively expensive. The door from the receiving area should be 5 feet wide when two doors are used and a minimum of 4 feet wide for a single door entrance. Double

entry doors should be used for proper screening to prevent flies and other insects from entering the food production area. Air curtains, which are simple centrifugal fans located over the door entrances, are somewhat effective in discouraging the entry of flies.

Scales. The importance of scales adjacent to the receiving dock is often overlooked by many foodservice managers. Meats and most products are often prepackaged and weighed, with the weights clearly marked on the meat containers. It is often assumed—falsely—that these weights are always accurate. All foodservice facilities should have a scale for use by the receiving clerk to verify the weights of foods that are purchased by the pound or kilogram. The location of the scale should be in the breakout area inside the building, so that the scale is protected from the weather.

Materials handling equipment. Several types of materials handling equipment are commonly used in foodservice receiving areas for efficient transport and to avoid stress and injury to employees. Hand trucks (two-wheeled vehicles for moving small stacks of case goods), platform hand trucks (four-wheeled flat vehicles) that are strong enough to hold the weight of fifteen or twenty cases of food goods, and wooden or steel pallets are all a part of the equipment needs for the receiving clerk. Large numbers of wooden pallets (skids) often accumulate in the receiving area because they are commonly used in the food distribution industry for holding and moving large quantities of case goods. Large foodservice operations may want to consider the design of storeroom spaces to hold these large pallets, so that the double handling of hand goods is minimized. These pallets must be moved with either a hand-operated forklift device or a forklift truck.

Other Functions of the Receiving Area

The need for a separate receiving office, breakout area (a small space just inside the receiving doors for checking in and separating foods before putting them into storage), washdown room, or garbage room will depend on the size and complexity of the foodservice operation. These functions are usually carried out in the receiving area, and if space is not provided, they may encroach on other space. Office space should be small (50 square feet), and the washdown area and garbage room should also be limited in size: a range of 50 to 80 square feet should be sufficient. A small area just inside the receiving door can be allotted for breakout space. The following chart can be used as a guideline in deciding whether or not special rooms are needed.

Storage

General Description of the Space

The amount of storage in a foodservice facility is primarily influenced by the number of meals per day served, the number of items that appear on the menu, the frequency of delivery, and the operating policies of the management staff. It is considered good management practice to turn the inventory over twelve times per year (once a month). Turnover for perishable products should, of course, be at least twice per week, and turnover for such items as paper and cleaning supplies may be infrequent. The attitude of management toward inventory turnover should always be discussed prior to beginning the design. The construction of a large canned goods storeroom, for instance, might be viewed by one manager as too small, because he likes the idea of keeping a large par stock of inventory on hand. Other management people might prefer to keep the par stock very low so that cash is not tied up in inventories. The use of computers in the foodservice industry has greatly enhanced the ability of managers to forecast the precise amount of food needed for each meal and, therefore, decrease the

amount of food that must be kept on hand at any one time. Computers, more efficient distribution of food products by vendors, and high interest rates have all contributed to a trend toward smaller storage spaces.

The four categories of storage that must be available in all food facilities are:

▶ dry storage
▶ paper and cleaning supplies storage
▶ refrigerated storage
▶ utensil and cleaning equipment storage

Relationship to Other Areas

Storage areas should be well ventilated, dry, and constructed of easy-to-clean surfaces. Concrete or tile floors, cement block walls with epoxy paint, and acoustic ceilings are common for all storage areas except those that are refrigerated. Large access doors and a high level of security must be included as part of the design. The most important relationship in the design is easy access from the storage area to both food production and receiving. The number of trips that will be made to the production area from the storage area will far exceed the number made from the receiving dock. It is therefore important to be sure that the staff in food production areas have short distances to travel to refrigerated storage and canned goods storage spaces. It is often possible to locate a produce walk-in refrigerator in the immediate vicinity of the cold food preparation department, so that few

Space Needed			
Number of Seats	Office	Washdown	Garbage
Under 50 or fast-food	no	no	small
50–100	no	small	small
100–175	no	yes	yes
175–250	yes	yes	yes
250–500	yes	yes	yes
More than 500	yes	large	large

steps are necessary to procure salad materials and other frequently used perishable items.

Dry Storage

Standard weight and volume of cases of canned goods can be calculated easily. A case of 6 no. 10 cans weighs approximately 48 lbs. (21.8 kg) and occupies about 1 cubic foot (.028 cu. m) of volume. The maximum stack of cases of 6 no. 10 cans should be no more than 7 feet (2.1 m) in height.

Calculating a standard amount of dry storage space is difficult because of the many variables that affect the need. The method that is often used is to consider the many variables that cause fluctuations in the quantity of food to be stored and simply make an educated guess. It is usually better to estimate space needs on the basis of the industry's experience with different types of facilities. The following chart can be used as a rough guide for determining dry storage needs (assuming that deliveries are made twice per week, and that cleaning supplies and paper are stored separately).

Paper and Cleaning Supplies Storage

The storage of paper supplies can be a very large space problem for food operations that use a large quantity of disposable cups, plates, napkins, and plastic ware. No standard space requirement is possible because the extent of the use of disposables and the frequency of delivery are different for each food operation. Paper supply companies and paper manufacturers tend to give significant price breaks for larger orders of paper goods, and the food operator is, therefore, forced to accept large quantities in order to purchase economically.

Cleaning supplies must be stored separately from food supplies to prevent contamination and accidental mixing of detergents with foods. A separate storeroom for cleaning supplies should be large enough to handle 55-gallon drums, cases of dishmachine detergents, and other cleaning items. A space 6 to 10 feet wide and 10 to 15 feet deep will handle the storage needs of most small- to medium-sized operations. A guide for cleaning supplies is as follows:

Type of Food Operation	Size of Storage	
	Sq. Ft.	(Sq. M.)
Fast-food	60–100	(5.58–9.3)
Small restaurant	75–120	(6.98–11.16)
Medium restaurant or small institution	120–175	(11.16–16.28)
Large restaurant or medium institution	175–250	(16.28–23.25)
Large institution with simple menu	250–300	(23.25–27.90)
Large hotel, restaurant or institution with complex menu, catering facilities, snack bars	300+	(27.90+)

Refrigerated Storage

Space needed for bulk storage of frozen and refrigerated foods should be determined at this stage.

A bulk freezer should be selected on the basis of the menu and frequency of delivery. For instance, if the menu contains a large number of food items prepared from frozen food products, the need for freezer space will obviously increase. A fast-food restaurant or college cafeteria will usually use a large number of frozen french fries, and the college may also use large quantities of frozen vegeta-

Type of Food Operation	Range of Size of Dry Storage	
	Sq. Ft.	(Sq. M.)
Fast-food	50–125	(4.65–11.63)
Small restaurant	100–150	(9.30–13.95)
Medium restaurant or small institution	200–300	(18.60–27.90)
Large restaurant or medium institution	400–1,000	(37.20–93.00)
Large institution with simple menu	1,000–2,500	(93.00–232.50)
Large hotel, restaurant or institution with complex menu, catering facilities, snack bars	3,000+	(279.00+)

bles. A seafood restaurant may use large quantities of frozen fish, french fries, onion rings, and perhaps no frozen vegetables at all. A hotel or large catering operation may use smaller quantities, but might stock a large variety of frozen foods.

Frozen foods are usually shipped in rectangular cartons that are easily stacked, and the height of the freezer is therefore an important part of the calculation. The size of a freezer should be determined on the basis of cubic feet of space needed. The following is an example of freezer size calculations based on the following assumptions:

▶ The facility is a small restaurant with delivery of frozen foods once per week.
▶ Frozen hamburgers, french fries, and onion rings are a significant part of the volume of the business.
▶ The menu contains five or six additional items that are purchased frozen.
▶ Ice cream, in six flavors, is a popular dessert.

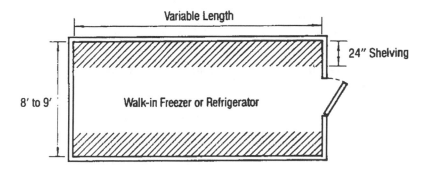

FIGURE 2. Usable Space in Walk-In Cooler.

Walk-in refrigerated storage space is very expensive because of the amount of building space that walk-ins occupy, and because of the high cost of the equipment. A careful calculation of the amount of space needed is therefore strongly recommended.

Assuming a 7-foot, 4-inch high standard walk-in is used, it can only be filled to a height of 6 feet. In fact, less than 50 percent of the space in the walk-in is usable, as shown in Figure 2. Therefore, the total cubic feet of storage, per linear feet of walk-in freezer is: 6 feet (height) times 2-foot shelves times 2

(one on each side) equals 24 cubic feet per linear foot. To determine the necessary length, divide the total cubic feet needed by 24 cubic feet. In the example shown, the length of the walk-in would be:

$$\frac{283\,\text{cu.ft.}}{24} = 11.79 \text{ feet}$$

The walk-in should be 12 feet long by 9 feet wide in this example. The 9-foot width provides space on both sides for shelving and an aisle space of 3 1/2 to 4 feet.

The size of a walk-in refrigerator is determined in a similar manner, but is more difficult to calculate because the products stored are not in rectangular boxes. The bulk cartons of milk, produce, fresh meats, foods that have been prepared, and other miscellaneous items that need to be stored under refrigeration are difficult to measure in cubic footage.

Small fast-food operations or restaurants with very limited menus may only need one walk-in refrigerator. Medium-sized operations may wish to separate meat produce and dairy products. Large hotels,

Food Item	Purchase Unit	Cubic Feet/ (Meters)		Total Per Week	Cubic Feet/ (Meters)	
French fries	case	1.8	(.050)	25	45	(1.260)
Hamburgers	case	1.2	(.033)	30	36	(1.008)
Onion rings	case	2.0	(.056)	20	40	(1.120)
Vegetables	case	1.5	(.042)	15	22.5	(0.630)
Hot dogs	package	.2	(.006)	35	7.0	(0.196)
Roast beef	12 to 15 lbs.	1.0	(.028)	30	30.0	(0.840)
Ice cream	3 gal.	1.5	(.042)	45	67.5	(1.890)
Miscellaneous	case	1.0	(.028)	35	35	(0.980)
		TOTAL cubic feet			283	(7.924 cu.m.)

restaurants, or institutions may need three or four large walk-in refrigerators, located in different sections of the kitchen. The following chart may be used as a general guide for determining the amount of space needed for walk-in refrigeration.

amount of space. Country clubs that hold private functions, buffets, and receptions and that need to store substantial quantities of Christmas decorations and other special events materials may require an extremely large storeroom with movable metal shelving.

Type of Food Operation	Number of Walk-ins	Total Square Feet/	(Sq. M.)
Fast-food	1	90–120	(8.4–11.2)
Small restaurant	1	120–150	(11.2–14.0)
Medium restaurant or small institution	2	180–240	(16.7–22.3)
Large restaurant or medium institution	3	240–400	(22.3–37.2)
Large institution with simple menu	3	400–600	(37.2–55.8)
Large hotel, restaurant or institution with Complex menu, catering facilities, snack bars	4	600–900	(55.8–83.7)

Utensil and Cleaning Equipment Storage

Food facilities that do not include a storage space for infrequently used utensils, backup utensil supplies such as knives and serving spoons, and cleaning equipment such as buffing machines and steam cleaners often are plagued with a considerable amount of clutter in the work areas. For instance, a restaurant that occasionally serves buffets for private parties may want to keep chafing dishes, punch bowls, and serving platters in a utensil storage room.

The amount of space needed is so variable that a standard cannot be easily established. For the small- to medium-sized foodservice facility, a closet with built-in shelving that can be easily secured provides a sufficient

For the large food facility, the separation of cleaning equipment storage from utensil storage is recommended for reasons of security.

Office

General Description of the Space

Offices are needed for the manager, assistant managers, chef or food production manager, and clerical staff. The justification for these spaces is to provide a private environment for talking with employees, vendors, and other business people and to be sure that the management staff has a reasonably quiet place to work.

Relationship to Other Areas

The offices of the general manager and catering manager need to be accessible to the public without the necessity of having customers walk through the kitchen. Office space for managers and assistant managers who have infrequent contact with the public in the office area should be located in a highly visible and easily accessible part of the food facility. Small foodservice operations often have the office located near the receiving area so that the movement of employees and of food in and out of storage areas and the building can be observed. Office space for receiving clerks, store room supervisors, and service supervisors should obviously be located in their respective work areas. Often these office areas are simple enclosures or spaces set aside without doors or four walls.

Amount of Space Needed

Small office areas are usually in a range of 60 to 80 square feet (5.58 to 7.44 sq. m.) and can be increased from this size as space and funds permit. Combination offices in which the clerical staff are adjacent to a manager's office and separated by a partition require additional space to accommodate door swings and extra office equipment such as computers, copy machines, and word processors.

The number of office spaces that may be needed for supervisory and management personnel will depend on the complexity of the organization. For instance, in a fairly complex operation, office space may be needed for:

► accounting and payroll personnel
► catering manager
► sales manager
► executive chef
► production manager
► dietitian
► assistant manager
► purchasing manager
► receiving supervisor
► maître d'hôtel

Special Design Features

Carpeted floors, light-colored walls with chair rails, and acoustical ceilings with fluorescent lighting are desirable surfaces in an office. The location of telephone and electrical outlets on all four walls will permit maximum flexibility as personnel and space needs change. Management and supervisory personnel often prefer an office with many windows for purposes of supervisory control. Clerical employees, on the other hand, often dislike windows that create distractions from their work or that do not provide a sufficient amount of privacy.

Preparation Areas

General Description of the Space

In a well-designed kitchen, the food preparation area is divided into four general areas. Although in a small kitchen these areas are often combined, recognition of each of the areas is an important part

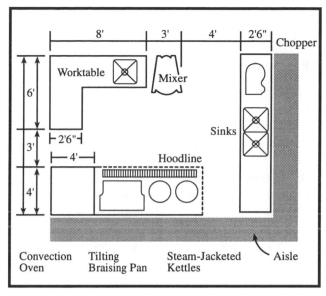

FIGURE 3. Prepreparation Area for a Small Restaurant.

of the design. The four working areas of a kitchen are:

► prepreparation
► hot food preparation
► cold food preparation
► final preparation

Prepreparation

The prepreparation area of the kitchen is where foods are processed, mixed, combined, held, cleaned, or otherwise worked with before the meal period begins. Chopping celery, mixing meatloaf, simmering broth, peeling potatoes, and making salad dressing are all prepreparation activities. Sinks, large work surfaces, and all of the equipment necessary to accomplish food prepreparation tasks are a part of this area of the kitchen.

The prepreparation area usually includes all of the equipment needed to process foods before the meal begins. Typical equipment located in the prepreparation area includes:

► choppers
► work tables
► ovens
► utensil storage
► mixers
► kettles
► vertical cutter/mixer
► racks
► ranges
► tilting fry pan
► sinks

The amount of equipment in this area, and especially the amount of table surface needed, will be determined by the amount of hand preparation that is dictated by the menu and by the volume of food being processed. The layout and dimensions of a prepreparation area for a small restaurant are illustrated in Figure 3. Note in the figure that the total space for prepreparation is 13 feet by 17 feet, 6 inches, or 227.5 square feet. The addition of an aisle on two sides of this would increase the needed space by approximately 90 square feet, to a total of 317.5 square feet (rounded to 320).

Hot Food Preparation

The "range" section of a kitchen is usually considered the hot food preparation area. Since this is where heat is applied to the food product, the space must be extremely resistant to soiling from grease and high levels of heat. Also necessary are elaborate (and expensive) ventilation systems above the cooking surfaces. The area must be designed to meet the demands of the menu, and equipment should be selected accordingly. The most frequent design error in the kitchen is to select "generic" equipment that is manufactured to cook all foods under all circumstances rather than pieces best suited to preparing the foods served in the particular facility.

Cold Food Preparation

In small and medium-sized kitchens this area is the "pantry," where salads are assembled, desserts dished up, and appetizers made ready for service. For a large restaurant or hotel, a separate *garde mange* department may be required for the preparation of cold food appetizers, entrees, and beautifully decorated items for buffets. Typically most of the prepreparation and final preparation for cold foods will occur in the same general area. Worktables and refrigerated storage should be accessible to all food preparation personnel located in this area. A pickup station designed as part of cold food preparation gives easy access to the waiters and wait-

resses. In European kitchens, the traditional layout included a cold kitchen as a separate area.

Final Preparation

The final preparation area is the space in which foods are prepared very close to and during the meal period. It is important in the design to define this space carefully and to be sure that all equipment located within it has to do with final preparation. Foods usually cooked in this area include french fries, fried eggs, toast, hamburgers, frozen vegetables, and other similar items that can be prepared quickly and that will deteriorate rapidly if cooked ahead of time. In a successful restaurant the final food preparation area is the most carefully attended and supervised part of the entire kitchen. Foods prepared in this area must be held a very short period of time before being presented to the guest. Successful fast-food chains have designed elaborate means to be sure that foods are not held more than 5 to 6 minutes in the final preparation area before being

served. The final preparation area typically includes a range, grills, fryers, steamers, and broilers. Obviously, some small amount of prepreparation also occurs in this area, but in an efficient operation, it is kept to a minimum.

Relationship to Other Areas

The flow of people and materials from storage to prepreparation to final preparation can best be illustrated by a simple diagram (Fig. 4). Although this diagram seems very simplistic, the concept that it illustrates is extremely important if good kitchen design is to be achieved. Frequently kitchens are laid out with steam jacketed kettles (a prepreparation piece of equipment) in the final preparation area or fryers (a final preparation piece of equipment) located in the prepreparation area. Although these arrangements may save some duplication in equipment, they tend to cause congestion in the flow of materials and personnel.

Figure 5 shows how preparation spaces relate to the service components of a food facility. The reader should also bear in

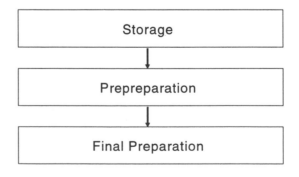

FIGURE 4. Relationship of Final Preparation Area to Prepreparation and Storage.

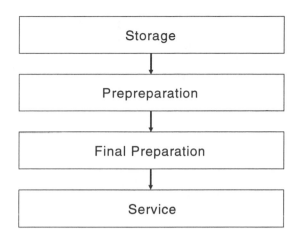

FIGURE 5. Relationship of Prep Spaces to Other Parts of Food Facility.

mind the comprehensive picture of a facility, with the kitchen at the center of all the functional spaces. The design should always reflect these relationships and facilitate the movement of employees and food between functionally related areas. For instance, the distance between the final preparation area and the customer should be short because the time that it takes to move the food is critical. On the other hand, the relationship of the preparation area to the employee locker room is not critical and these spaces could be a considerable distance away from each other.

Vertical as well as horizontal space relationships must be considered. As a general guideline, when spaces must be located on different floors, the following functional areas may be at a different level from the kitchen.

▶ bulk dry storage
▶ bulk frozen storage
▶ paper and utensil storage
▶ employee locker rooms
▶ receiving

The following functional areas must never be located at another level from the kitchen:

▶ warewashing
▶ dining room
▶ service areas

This guideline is often violated in large hotels and institutional kitchens, where it is quite common to see dishwashing located at a different level from the dining room. Architectural limitations at times make it necessary to violate this rule, but there is always a cost in labor, efficiency, and effectiveness of supervision.

Amount of Space Needed

The size of the different preparation areas will be determined by the menu, volume of food produced, and cookery methods used. A common method of establishing the space requirement is to list the needed equipment and make templates of each piece, using a scale of 1/4 inch = 1 foot. The templates are shifted on a drawing board to arrive at a satisfactory arrangement, and the overall space is measured. In developing an equipment list, the food facilities design consultant will discuss the menu and equipment preferences with the owner, manager, or chef (or all three). A checklist for final preparation equipment is as follows:

	Item	Quantity	Capacity Or Size
( )	Convection oven		
( )	Fryers		
( )	Grill		
( )	Kettles, table top		
( )	High-pressure steamer		
( )	Broiler		
( )	Reach-in refrigerator		
( )	Reach-in freezer		
( )	Hot top range		
( )	Open top range		
( )	Pickup table		
( )	Steam table		
( )	Worktable		
( )	Spreader plates		
( )	Beverage pickup		
( )	Plate storage		
( )	Other		

The most frequently asked question concerning the kitchen by the client or architect at the beginning of a project is "What is the ratio of space for the kitchen to space for the dining room?" The food facilities design consultant will usually answer "It depends." First of all, no clear standards for a ratio between dining and kitchen exist, and secondly, different types of operations have different requirements. Space needs depend on:

▶ The size of the menu (number of items)
▶ The use of convenience foods versus cookery from scratch
▶ The complexity of the preparation required (fast-food versus expensive table service)
▶ The foodservice functions provided by a single kitchen (which may include banquet service, coffee shop service, and main dining room foodservice)

Arthur Dana, a highly respected foodservice consultant who practiced in the New York City area during the 1940s, wrote one of the first books on food facilities design (*Kitchen Planning,* published by Harper & Brothers in 1945). Concerning the relative size of dining and food preparation areas, Dana had this to say:

Because of the many variations within each type of restaurant design, a particular restaurant may not necessarily conform to a fixed percentage relationship between the seating and service areas.

About 20 years ago, designers allotted kitchen space for table service dining rooms equivalent to one-third to one-half of the dining area. As time went on it became apparent that more space for kitchen purposes was necessary to provide efficient service.

Recently, a well-known kitchen equipment engineer cited an example in which the kitchen (exclusive of storage and employee facilities) was equivalent to two-thirds of the dining area. Expressed in terms of 100% street level area available, the dining room took 60% of the space and the kitchen, 40%. Other facilities were located in the basement. Every expression of opinion, however (when it is possible to get one), is qualified by references to physical differences, varying needs and a myriad of operating ideas from the owners.

Comparisons of different types of facilities designed by Birchfield Foodsystems may be helpful in establishing guidelines for the size of the kitchen as it relates to the dining room. A comparison of kitchen sizes and dining room capacity can be made from the chart below.

The chart indicates the range of space requirements in different types of food facilities. Because of the extreme variability in space needs, the owner or manager should look to the design consultant for professional advice before deciding on the amount of space to allot to the food production area.

Special Design Features

Since food production areas are continually subjected to heat as well as soiling from grease and spilled foods, dam-

Type of Food Operation	Meals Per Day	Dining Room Size		Preparation Area Size[a]	
		Sq. Ft.	(Sq. M.)	Sq. Ft.	(Sq. M.)
Restaurant table service—100 seats	1,000	1,400	(130.20)	1,300	(120.90)
Restaurant table service—175 seats	1,800	2,625	(244.13)	2,000	(186.00)
Country club—200 seats	600	3,400	(316.20)	1,288	(119.78)
Hospital, cafeteria, and 200-bed tray service	1,400	2,250	(209.25)	2,300	(213.90)
College cafeteria—350 seats	2,400	4,200	(390.60)	1,500	139.50)
University cafeteria and catering department	4,000	5,625	523.13)	2,530	(235.29)
Coffee shop—100 seats	800	1,225	(113.96)	850	(79.05)

[a]Does not include bakery, storage, and dishwashing.

age-resistant, easy-to-clean surfaces are essential. Equipment surfaces of stainless steel are the most practical. Floor finishes of Carborundum chips in quarry tile will provide a slip-resistant, easy-to-clean surface. When made of ceramic tile or structural glazed tile, walls behind the equipment will withstand the combination of heat and grease. Epoxy paint on cement block is not recommended, because the high heat will discolor and/or darken the painted surface. To avoid sanitation problems, careful attention should be given to eliminating cracks and spaces around equipment.

Mechanical engineers and architects working on a food facilities project are encouraged to give special attention to room air supply and exhaust because of the increased use in recent years of compensating hoods that bring a large percentage of makeup air (air that replaces exhausted air) into the hood itself. The kitchen must be well ventilated without complete dependence on the hood system to exhaust the air.

Warewashing

General Description of the Space

The one word that best describes the environment in the warewashing area is "wet." With the exception of the hot food preparation area, warewashing equipment and surrounding areas receive more wear and abuse than any other section of the food facility. Water on the floor, spilled

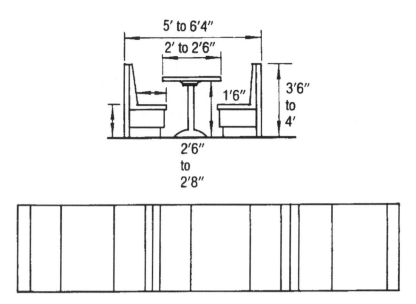

FIGURE 6. Booth Seating.

food, steam and high humidity, and the striking of carts and utensils against the walls and equipment are often a common part of the warewashing environment. Food facilities designers, architects, and engineers should make every effort to eliminate the wet conditions while recognizing that the floor, walls, and ceiling must be constructed to withstand a large amount of moisture.

Health department standards for the equipment and interior of warewashing rooms have become increasingly stringent because of the potential for spreading food-borne diseases. In designing the warewashing area so that it is easy to sanitize and will withstand the wet conditions, the use of slip-resistant quarry tile floors, ceramic or structural glaze tile walls, and moisture-resistant acoustic ceiling is recommended.

Relationship to Other Areas

The most important relationship of the warewashing space is to the dining room. The design should facilitate the movement of soiled dished from the dining room to the warewashing area. In many institutions where self-bussing of dishes is encouraged, the warewashing space must be located adjacent to the exit form the dining room. Without this convenient feature, customers are unlikely to cooperate in bussing their own dishes.

The primary problem with the close proximity of warewashing to the dining area is the noisiness of the former. Conveyor belts for soiled dishes, screening with masonry walls, or the use of double sets of doors to isolate the warewashing area are all common solutions to the noise problem.

Warewashing must also have a close working relationship with the main kitchen, especially if pots, pans, and utensils are washed in the warewashing area. The warewashing room may be designed with three-compartment pot sinks, potwashing machines, or it may be the practice of management to have most small and medium-sized utensils washed by the standard dish machine. If pots and utensils are to be washed in this area, the distance between the primary food production spaces and the warewashing unit should be reasonably close.

Amount of Space Needed

Warewashing machine ratings are usually based on the number of standard 20-by-20-inch racks or the number of dishes per hour that can be processed through the machine. Since neither the machine or the machine operator can operate at 100 percent efficiency, an efficiency factor of 70 percent is normally used. The following chart provides a range of square footage requirements for several different styles of dishwashing systems. The data was determined under the assumption that a three-compartment pot sink with drain boards is included in the warewashing space.

Special Design Features

Nowhere in the design of a foodservice facility is an understanding of time and motion in the work environment more important than in warewashing. A dishwasher usually works in a restricted area with a minimum amount of walking. Good warewashing design must include a study of each move that the dishwasher makes so that the dishes can be handled in the most efficient means possible. The basic steps that are normally taken in washing dishes are:

1. Separation of dishes from paper, trays, and so on
2. Scraping (prerinsing may be done in step 2)
3. Stacking or accumulating
4. Racking
5. Prerinsing (if not done in step 2)
6. Washing
7. Air drying
8. Removing clean dishes

The design principle of simplicity discussed earlier is important to keep in mind when designing warewashing systems. Elaborate conveyor and "bridge" systems for soiled dish tables often add to the clutter and expense of the warewashing area and create barriers that are difficult to move around. At the other extreme, designs that do not provide sufficient space for soiled dish accumulation or warewashing rooms that have insufficient cart storage space for clean dishes are to be avoided.

Sound-absorbing materials on the ceiling, a high level of lighting (80 to 100 ft. candles), and the use of bright colors on the walls and ceiling are desirable design features. One frequent mistake in the engineering of warewashing areas is to provide inadequate circulation of air. The vents and small hoods required by the health department on dishmachines are not sufficient for the removal of moist air from the space. Supply and exhaust equipment that will accomplish 60 air changes per hour is recommended.

Summary

A general description of the primary spaces of a foodservice facility has been included to provide the food facilities planner with general guidelines concerning the spaces needed. Each of the spaces should work in harmony with other functional areas so that a high level of efficiency is achieved. The penalty for ignoring space relationships is an increase in labor and other operating costs. Food facilities owners and managers are encouraged to visit existing operations to familiarize themselves with a variety of design alternatives and to see how

Type of Dish System	Dishes Per Hour	Size of the Space[a]	
		Sq. Ft.	(Sq. M.)
Single tank dishwasher	1,500	250	(23.25)
Single tank conveyor	4,000	400	(37.20)
Two-tank conveyor	6,000	500	(46.50)
Flight-type conveyor	12,000	700	(65.10)

[a]Including space for dish carts, empty racks, and pot washing. The size of the space will vary significantly on the basis of the layout of the soiled and clean dish tables. For instance, a single tank dishwasher located along a flat wall in a small restaurant might only occupy 125 sq. ft. (11.63 sq. m.).

others have dealt with spatial relationships.

The amount of space needed for each area will vary. Some spaces may be "squeezed" and others made larger, depending on the special circumstances of the design or the desires of the owner or manager. The special design features presented for each of the spaces reflect solutions to problems that are frequently encountered by the author in the process of planning and designing foodservice operations.

Develop a serving facility design for a college dining hall to accommodate 500 students for each of three meals daily. You may select either a "board plan" or "cash" operation. Support kitchen location to be defined, but not designed.

Design Considerations to Include

1. Customer flow

2. Method of customer verification or payment

3. Product offerings/appeal

4. Labor efficiency

5. Customer self-service

6. Ease of selection/service

7. Menu flexibility/diversity

8. Replenishment

9. Sanitation

10. Serviceware handling

Project Deliverables

1. Program narrative describing the serving line operation.

2. 1/4″ = 1′0″ scale floor plan, itemized to an equipment schedule.

3. One page of utility information, or 1/4″ to 1′0″ scale mechanical and electrical utility connection drawings of (an approved) service or production counter.

4. Identification of special building requirements.

5. 1/2″ = 1′0″ scale elevation of a custom fabricated service or production counter (worker side).

6. Itemized specification for minimum of three pieces of equipment (two buy-out and one custom fabricated).

Develop a design for a production kitchen that will serve lunch and dinner for a 250-seat dining room and lounge with bar. Level of service and menu offerings will dictate some kitchen design features, and are at the student's discretion. Dining room layout to be defined, but not designed.

Design Considerations to Include

1. Concept and menu development

2. Foodservice equipment needs and placement

3. Utility load design and requirements

4. Itemized specifications of equipment

5. Work station placement and design

6. Traffic flow within the kitchen and to the dining room

7. Renovation concerns

8. Project cost estimates

9. Bid evaluation and consulting fees

Project Deliverables

1. Project narrative describing kitchen design and operation.

2. 1/4" = 1'0" scale floor plan, itemized to an equipment schedule.

3. One page of utility information, or 1/4" = to 1'0" scale mechanical and electrical utility connection drawings.

4. Identification of building special requirements.

5. 1/4" = 1'0" scale drawing showing traffic patterns and workstation areas.

6. Itemized specification for minimum of three pieces of major equipment (two buyout and one custom fabricated).

8

FOOD AND BEVERAGE CONTROLS

A Strategic Approach to Managing Costs
K. Michael Haywood

Project 1

Project 2

A STRATEGIC APPROACH TO MANAGING COSTS

K. Michael Haywood

The greatest challenge facing most firms in the hospitality industry continues to be the management of costs. Even the success of firms such as Marriott and McDonald's is as much dependent on managing unit costs as it is on customer service, development and marketing. In fact, the inability of accommodation and foodservice firms to improve productivity has become a primary issue among executives and economists (Haywood, Patterson and Upton, 1985; Witt and Witt, 1989). Companies are being urged to implement strategies that will increase productivity and reduce unit costs. Unfortunately, little has been written on what such strategies involve, and how they can be implemented successfully.

This article describes the key elements of a comprehensive cost management strategy. Readers will learn how one company is implementing such an approach to ensure that it becomes and remains a low-cost provider of hospitality services. Although the strategy provides some short-run cost reductions, it is primarily aimed at preserving long-term competitiveness by maintaining cost management activities. The essential features of this strategy are: committed management, supervisors and employees; implementation of the best possible technologies; and vigilance in achieving measurable cost reductions and productivity gains year after year.

Cost Challenges

HOSPITALITY INDUSTRY executives generally pride themselves on being cost conscious. Yet corporate performance and executive reaction to continually prevalent cost challenges suggest otherwise. The most pressing cost challenge, of current concern, arises from declining margins as the industry matures and the fight for market share intensifies. The response to this challenge, as noted in a recent editorial appearing in *Nation's Restaurant News,* is either "to reduce costs and expenses and ride out the storm until better days arrive," or "to provide better or more service, marketing and promotions to generate more customers and increase sales." As options of choice the editorial depicts cost-cutting as a hard-nosed, short-term, repugnant task destined to short change the customer. In contrast the service improvement, marketing solution is linked with a long-term, future-oriented approach that will "maintain sales momentum in the midst of a marketing crunch" (Bernstein, 1990, p. 31).

This view of cost control as a crisis, project-oriented activity is worrisome. Once costs have been reduced by the agreed-upon amount or percentage, everyone breathes a sigh of relief and is thankful that the purge is over. Why? First of all, few CEOs and senior executives view cost management as their prime responsibility; cost management is the job of operating managers. Secondly, operating managers and supervisors have learned to hate cost management. Too frequently they are uninformed about overall costs until there is a crisis, and are put on trial to explain variances that may be insignificant or difficult to trace. Cost management often results in clerical drudgery; lacks challenge or reward; and, during crisis, encourages increased direct management control. When cost management is done in a hurry, little time is spent in explaining or communicating effectively.

Cuts are made hastily, often without clear reasons, on discretionary items such as advertising, market development, training and maintenance, all of which have little short-term effect on corporate competitiveness, but for which the company is often penalized heavily in the long run. For example, Carlzon, in his book *Moments of Truth,* reports how indiscriminant cost cutting almost ruined Scandinavian Airlines:

SAS top management at the time used the standard weapon: the cheese slicer, which disregards marketing demands and instead cuts costs equally from all activities and all departments. The cheese slicer did succeed in cutting some costs that the company could forgo during a slump. But it also eliminated many services that customers wanted and were prepared to pay for while retaining others of little interest to the customers. In cutting costs, the company was,

in effect, slicing away its own competitive strengths. The internal effects of the cuts were just as serious: staff members were sapped of their initiative. In the end, no one felt responsible for controlling costs (Carlzon, 1987, p. 22).

Layoffs generate similar effects. Productivity increases but morale, employee burnout, service levels and customer satisfaction are all adversely affected in the long-run unless appropriate management follow-up is taken (Krichel, 1985, p. 28).

It is interesting to note, however, that Michael Porter in his book, *Competitive Strategy,* identifies overall cost leadership as a generic strategic approach to outperforming other firms in an industry:

Cost leadership requires aggressive construction of efficient-scale facilities, vigorous pursuit of cost reductions from experience, tight cost and overhead control, avoidance of marginal customer accounts, and cost minimization in areas like R&D, service, sales force, advertising, and so on. A great deal of managerial attention to cost control is necessary to achieve these aims. Low cost relative to competitors becomes the theme running through the entire strategy, though quality service, and other areas cannot be ignored (Peter, 1980, p. 35).

Cost leadership as a central strategic thrust demands that top-level executives take a leading role and make cost management a valued activity. But cost management in com-

panies pursuing other strategies also plays a leading role. For example, senior executives have to adopt an integrated perspective for the entire business and take actions aimed at gaining cost advantages from major strategy shifts within the industry.

An integrated perspective demands that various categories of costs be included in the development of management strategy. Exhibit 1 reveals four major categories of operating and strategic costs that need to be addressed. The top left hand quadrant identifies the usual hard operating costs that are more easily measured and managed. In crisis situations these costs are frequently reduced further along with postponement of direct, strategic expenditures in the top right hand quadrant. However, by deferring these more tangible strategic expenditures that focus on facility, product, market and employee development, it is likely that a firm may incur some important intangible strategic costs identified in the bottom right hand quadrant. Indeed, failure to consider these less easily measured, operating and strategic costs, as well as the effect of each category of cost on other cost categories puts firms at a competitive disadvantage regardless of the type of business strategy being pursued.

In recent years, a fashionable argument has been that firms can survive and grow if they differentiate their products and services from those offered by the competition. But events of the last decade

EXHIBIT 1. OPERATING AND STRATEGIC COSTS

	Operating Costs	Strategic Costs
Hard Costs	**1.** Labor Food and beverage Supplies Energy	**3.** Facility investments Product/market development Service/employee development
Ephemeral Costs	**2.** Absenteeism Low morale Turnover Slow service delivery Poor Quality	**4.** Poor facility location Technological obsolescence Poor positioning

have proved that differentiation alone is not sufficient. There is not a single, well-differentiated firm in the industry that can afford to ignore costs.

No company, whether industrial, high-tech or service, can succeed over the long term unless it is a lower cost supplier than all others providing equivalent products or services. Short-term survival might be possible but not long-term success. Proprietary advantage never lasts. Maturity and decline come to products and businesses as they do to life, and prices and margins inevitably succumb to pressures. As competitive product distinctions fade, prices become increasingly important in buying decisions. The more effective suppliers will constantly improve productivity and reduce costs. Thus, even when price pressures get intense, margins will at least be maintained. When this is not done profits and market position almost certainly fall (Ames and Illavacek, 1990, p. 140-1).

A comprehensive approach to cost management has to be implemented if short-term gains are to be made while also ensuring long-run improvements. While attention to productivity improvement, service quality and delivery systems (Haywood and Pickworth, 1988), and technology (Haywood, 1990) can contribute to the process, a total view of all costs affecting the firm must be taken into account. In addition to production, overhead and other measurable costs, which are the focus of most traditional cost management approaches, emphasis must be placed on identifying the true cost and profit picture for each product and service, for each product/service market segment and for all key customers. Businesses should also concentrate on cash flow and balance sheet strengths as much as on profits (Ames and Hlavecek, 1990, p. 141). Costs, many of which are not easily measurable, also have to be identified and controlled. For example, there are costs associated with poor market positioning, poor quality, dissatisfied customers, bad employee relations, technological obsolescence, poor unit locations, absenteeism and high turnover.

Traditional Approaches to Cost Implementation

Hospitality firms utilize a variety of methods to reduce systematically costs on an ongoing basis, all of which have limitations from a strategic perspective:

► professional cost control systems;
► capital/technologically intensive investments; and
► mergers and diversification.

Professional cost control systems are prevalent in most companies, but there are firms in which the systems dominate the minds and actions of managers to the point where the implicit corporate strategy becomes "lean and mean." Reliance is on controls which are centralized among professional staff, usually supported by sophisticated computer-based systems. Major problems encountered include "systemitis" or "programitis" in which managers adopt a bewildering array of control systems without any sense of priority or cost effectiveness (Gall, 1978). Systems-maintenance requirements may exceed the capability and resources of the organization; and, if operators have no confidence in the systems, they may retain their own manual control, thereby resulting in costly "double-tracking." Employees begin to feel alienated and resentful when they are not in control and operational activities have to be tailored to system constraints. As a consequence, increased lead times and service delivery delays become commonplace. Customer satisfaction is affected. The system really breaks down, however, during periods of change, when the red tape and procedures necessary to maintain system integrity result in inertia, bottlenecks and spiralling costs.

In manufacturing industries the dominant approach to cost reduction tends to be capital-and-technology-intensive. Closing down old facilities and replacing them with newer, better-designed facili-

ties utilizing financial arrangements that minimize risk and commitment of capital is possible. However, this option is not readily available or appropriate for many hospitality businesses. New investments require large profits and, as life cycles shrink, last payback is unlikely to be realized, especially in mature hospitality markets characterized by deep discounting and continuous cost cutting. In other words, capital-intensive cost-reduction strategies require the right conditions to be truly successful.

New product/service and process technologies can be important to cost reductions and need not be capital-intensive. The stumbling block, however, is lack of a sound technology strategy. Consequently, few firms commit money to research and development activities, and give little thought to a coordinated approach in choosing new and/or appropriate technologies (Haywood, 1990). For many hospitality businesses the main challenge is how to maintain a stream of incremental technological innovations, keep up with the pace of change in computers, process and service delivery techniques, and generate a climate for change and continuous improvement (Haywood, 1988).

Merger and diversification activities represent a way for some firms to achieve better economies of scale and thereby reduce costs. In those situations in which a merger provides a good "fit" of resources, properties and people, it is possible to reduce op-

erating budgets and overheads. Too often, however, instead of enhancing strengths, the mergers compound weaknesses and generate managerial conflict. Even moves to diversify are likely to meet with disaster. Core hospitality businesses can quickly become starved for cash in order to modernize and reduce costs.

Initiating Strategic Cost Management

In the fall of 1987 executives of a leading Canadian lodging corporation met to discuss operating results of its hotels scattered across the country. Of particular concern was the poor financial performance of a number of properties that were generating above average occupancy rates. It was decided to focus attention on one of these hotels for intense study. An in-depth analysis of operating costs revealed that there were disturbing discrepancies in certain cost categories when comparisons were made with costs at similar properties. Discussions with the hotel's manager and accountant failed to resolve some key questions. As a consequence a consultant was hired to review the cost-control system.

The consultant's report pointed to some unsettling problems not commonly identified or mentioned during financial audits. For example, while it was noted that the gospel of cost management was being preached it wasn't being practiced in the executive suite. Not only did a cost management credibility gap exist, but operating managers and supervisors were expressing a high degree of cynicism in regard to cost management programs. In his report the consultant indicated the following: "The approach to cost management is totally unsystematic and arbitrary. No thought has been given to the impact of cost-cutting measures on employees, staff morale, or guest service." Costs had been cut in some areas in which the long-run impact had been ignored. For example, the training budget for fiscal year 1987 had been slashed by 75%.

The consultant also singled out budgets. They were being used to control negative behavior (spending too much) while ignoring positive behavior (building the business). For example, consideration of a point-of-sale computer system was being based on a predetermined budget with insufficient regard to use, value, customer requirements, and maintenance costs. The consultant noted that "the worst budgets set targets only, leading managers to control how much their operation spends and to ignore how much it earns. By controlling the money going in rather than controlling something like the P and L, an organization turns inward; it values rule above initiative; and, it leads controllers to query every little variance in a department's budget."

Criticism was levelled at cost management that was limited in scope. Management had concentrated on food and labor costs, contract services,

and supplies. However, it was discovered that one-time reductions were neither followed up nor maintained. The consultant noted that no pressure for tight performance regarding marketing and overhead costs had been applied. Inflation was also identified as a problem. Room rates had been raised as costs went up, because demand was strong and no new rooms were being added to the supply base in the region. This situation had led to laziness in lowering room division costs. "Logic suggests that, over time, the real, inflation-adjusted costs of doing business should be downward, because as organizations learn how to do things better, they also get more efficient. This is the underlying principle of the experience curve, and it really works" (Ames and Hlavacek, 1990, p. 141).

Following the consultant's advice corporate executives decided to embark on the implementation of a total cost management strategy. They sought new ways to manage costs that would not involve large amounts of capital and would take advantage of the apparent benefits of employee involvement. What follows is a condensed, and somewhat generic version of the strategic process.

The first move taken was similar to that of a crisis activity approach. Hotel management reduced work force levels through early retirements and layoffs (where unavoidable) to levels at which it felt lean on manpower. During this step the hotel chain asked

the consultant to advise on required staffing levels and organizational changes that would focus individuals and departments on creating value-producing activities and on directing costs into revenue-producing activities. This action was taken because management recognized that once employee involvement was sought, future work-force reductions or organizational changes would come slowly through either attrition, early retirement, market or technology realignment.

Shortly afterwards, senior management, from the hotel as well as corporate headquarters, met to establish a framework for its cost management strategy. Management continued to work with the consultant in order to implement a comprehensive cost reduction strategy. The following six key elements of the strategy were established.

1. *Objectives:* Management articulated its long- and short-run objectives. Long-run objectives reflected the way management saw the challenge of remaining competitive in the long-term. Short-run objectives were stated as targets for specific total costs and unit or departmental costs.
2. *Structure:* Recognizing that champions are necessary for an effective activity, the hotel appointed a full-time cost-management coordinator, and appointed part-time coordinators in each major department.
3. *Communications:* A central part of the strategy

EXHIBIT 2. COST MANAGEMENT OBJECTIVES, ACTIVITIES, RESULTS

Annual operating budget of hotel	$6.9 million
Number of employees (full-time equivalent)	210
Objectives	Profitable position, 12 month cost improvement targets by department.
Structure	Full-time coordinator, departmental coordinators, departmental committees.
Communications	Monthly cost review meetings for all employees, newsletter and cost-saving idea bulletin.
Major activities	Suggestion plan, employee meetings, cost-management seminars.
Rewards	10% of first-year saving to originator, 5% shared among implementing staff, recognition.
Results for fiscal year 1988/1989	Cost saving of $350,000, or 3–10% in various departments.

was a commitment to provide every employee with monthly information on company and departmental cost performance. This task was done on company time and provided opportunities for employees to respond.

4. *Education:* Training programs were developed to provide coordinators, supervisors and many employees with skills in managing costs. Typically, these were two-day programs with a focus on implementation. Also, courses were required to improve professional and supervisory presentation and problem-solving skills.

5. *Activities:* Management developed an initial set of activities, relevant to the cost structure of the hotel, to involve employees in managing costs. This set

of activities grew as the strategy was implemented and employees suggested new approaches.

6. *Rewards:* The hotel developed a system for rewarding employee involvement in cost management. Monetary rewards were on both an individual and group basis. Recognition and other non-financial rewards were also given.

These six elements were rapidly communicated during an initial information blitz to make employees more aware of the need to manage costs and the role they could play. A summary of the objectives, activities and results is contained in Exhibit 2.

Making the Strategy Work

Senior executives within the chain were most concerned about employee attitudes and beliefs. These had to be changed; and it was realized that this would be a time-consuming process. Managers and professional staff had to believe that employees and supervisors could act responsibly and make substantial cost reductions. Since a crisis activity approach had prevailed, time would be needed for strategic cost management to be seen as a challenging and valuable activity. Employees would have to be persuaded that cost reductions do not always mean layoffs. And, in a company in which control would have to be tight, supervisors and employees would need time to gain confidence in taking action on their own.

So emphasis was placed first on obtaining management and then on gaining supervisory involvement. One of the activities included an intensive two-day course on comprehensive cost management. The coordinators, who also attended, were given the task of removing obstacles to implementing ideas, and to focus employee efforts on high-cost problem areas.

A budget established specifically for cost management activities was established. Management allocated a significant part of this budget to coordinators and supervisors for their own discretionary use, which was a novelty. Initially, there was some reluctance to use the funds, but gradually the coordinator started to use them for such things as small rewards to work groups for outstanding efforts; employee expenses in travelling to other hotels in the chain from which they brought back ideas; dinner meetings at which employees discussed operating problems and opportunities; and small purchases that would be difficult to obtain through normal approval channels.

During the implementation of the cost management strategy, management started to consider the process of technical change. Emphasis was placed on having technical groups act as gatekeepers, evaluating cost-saving technologies from various outside sources. For example, the method of integrating a technical/ equipment decision, a point-of-sale system, with the cost management strategy in-volved multi-disciplinary groups of managers, technical staff, supervisors and employees, who analyzed operating problems and were responsible for implementing the new system.

But, undoubtedly the single most important influence on the success of the cost management strategy was the commitment and involvement shown by the chief executive officer of the hotel chain and the hotel's general manager. The strategy was implemented quite rapidly and effectively because each of them was frequently seen in the various hotel departments supporting the activity, seeking employee input, sponsoring new initiatives, and working with professional staff to change attitudes.

Strategic Focus

Implementing a cost management strategy has made management in this hotel much more conscious of where its efforts should lie. By examining cost structures in strategic terms, new ways of managing unit and departmental costs have been suggested. For example, the consultant recommended that the hotel management carefully review both corporate and business strategies and, taking a note from Michael Porter (1985, pp. 33–118), conduct a value analysis of all primary and support activities to determine fundamental strengths and weaknesses so as to improve cost competitiveness. The resulting information was passed on to the coordinators to help them and employees further identify and focus on major areas for cost improvement. In addition, control systems were evaluated for their contribution to overall cost effectiveness. This led to a complete reorganization, reordering and reformulation of financial data to better determine costs and profits for a number of discrete product/market businesses. The result has been an improved full-cost allocation scheme that is becoming of immense help in selecting products/services, markets, and customers for emphasis.

In any hotel a large portion of operating expenses can be attributed to food purchases. An analysis of cost management techniques in this area revealed that little effort was being devoted to supplier costs, whereas great effort was put into managing food waste, which was already minimal. As a result, a total reorganization of supplier management is currently underway. A supplier development program is being implemented, in which purchasing and senior kitchen staff work with suppliers to cut costs and improve quality. Attempts to standardize foodstuffs and other items is being intensified, and a vendor certification process is being improved; that is, suppliers are being investigated and are undergoing investigation to ensure that they meet the hotel's requirements.

Analysis of the total cost picture has revealed new insights that are allowing major payroll savings to be made. Safety was found to be a major cost. In addition, excessive absenteeism was found to have resulted in over-staffing, and correspondingly high compensation costs. Now identified, those costs are rapidly being reduced by adopting various employee suggestions, which supervisors and even employees are often able to implement themselves.

Increased focus has also been put on equipment availability and utilization. Once employees understood the impact these factors had on costs, customer satisfaction and competitiveness, equipment abuse declined markedly. Employees have became interested in doing their own routine maintenance; and co-operation is being encouraged between maintenance and operating employees.

The common theme in all these examples is that implementing a cost management strategy has allowed efforts to be focused on the really important costs. Less time is being spent by management chasing employees over low-cost items, such as small, informal inventories of supplies (which were often found to be cost-effective because of time saved). Now, more people are becoming involved in cost management because it is challenging and rewarding.

Where To in the Long-Run?

These are turbulent times in the hospitality and tourism industry, and in the scramble for short-term profitability managers sometimes make decisions that compromise strategic direction, competitive advan-

tage and long-run viability. Industry shake-outs accompanying severe competition, rapid change and new economic realities mean that weaker firms are being forced out.

To be among the survivors, a strategic approach to cost management is going to have to become a way of life for managers and employees alike. However, this approach will not occur if cost management continues to be seen as a no-win game or as a choice between low cost and high quality. The challenge facing hospitality businesses is to turn cost management into an exciting and rewarding activity for everyone—an activity that can increase quality and simultaneously lower costs.

The experience of implementing a comprehensive cost management program suggests, however, that businesses have to learn (though "re-learn" may be a better word) how to simultaneously manage for both effectiveness and efficiency. Perhaps the only way to build a sustainable competitive advantage is to ensure that everyone in an organization is provided with the opportunity to continually expand their capacity to create the results truly desired, to nurture new and expansive patterns of thinking, and to continually learn how to learn together. In other words, the future belongs to those companies that struggle to find ways to institutionalize learning within their organizations (de Beus, 1988). Problematic will be the difficult task of building a shared vision that fosters genuine commitment rather

than compliance, and the task of developing team learning that utilizes shared information and dialogue, and works toward systems thinking—the real essence of an effective strategic approach to cost management.

References

Ames, B.C., and Hlavacek, J.D. (1990, Jan–Feb). Vital truths about managing your costs. *Harvard Business Review,* pp. 140–141.

Bernstein, C. (1990, July 30). Profit margin dilemma: Cut costs or boost service. *Nation's Restaurant News,* p. 31.

Carlzon, J. (1987). *Moments of truth.* New York: Harper and Row.

de Geus, A. (1988, March/April) Planning as learning. *Harvard Business Review,* pp. 70–74.

Gall, J. (1978). *Systemantics: How systems work and especially how they fail.* New York: Pocket Books.

Haywood, K.M. and Pickworth, J.R. (1988). Connecting productivity with quality through the design of service delivery systems. *Proceedings of the International Conference on Service Marketing.* Academy of Marketing Science: Cleveland State University, 261–273.

Haywood, K. M. (1990). Managing technology: A strategic approach. *Cornell Hotel and Restaurant Administration Quarterly, 31* (1), 39–45.

Haywood, K. M., Patterson, J.W. and Upton, E. (1985).

Improving productivity in the foodservice industry. Toronto: Canadian Food-service and Restaurant Association.

Haywood, K.M. (1988). Managing strategic change. *F.I.U. Hospitality Review, 5* (2), 1–12.

Krichel, W. (1985, October 28). Managing a downsized operation. *Fortune.*

Porter, M. (1980). *Competitive strategy: Techniques for analyzing industries and competitors.* New York: The Free Press.

Porter, M. (1985). *Competitive advantage: Creating and sustaining superior performance.* New York: The Free Press.

Witt, C.A., and Witt, S.F. (1989). Why productivity in the hotel sector is low. *Contemporary Hospitality Management. 1* (2), 28–35.

In this project you will study some aspect of an organization using concepts developed in this course. The objective is to prepare a written analysis that includes a description of what you studied, an explanation of what you saw, and practical suggestions for improving the organization.

What You Should Study and How to Study It

You should study some event or practice in the normal operations of a hospitality organization, including (but not limited to) manager/worker training for job specific job procedures; standard cost controls and their effect on the organization; policy/procedures related to cost controls and their effect on customer service; the influence of cost control policy/procedure on organizational decision making/communications.

You should focus on how the event or practice actually (or normally) occurs in the organization. This means you must be able to observe or reconstruct the interaction between people or person/technology involved in the practice of cost controls. Several methods are available for gathering data: (1) Direct observation. Here you would observe the practice and write down notes about it. These notes would include typical accounts of behavior in practice. (2) Interviews. You might interview participants about cost control procedures/practices and summarize their responses. (3) Other records and artifacts. These include manuals and policy/procedure descriptions, newsletters, minutes of meetings, journals, newspaper articles, and other organizational records.

The Report

The finished paper will be 10–15 pages in length and will consist of two parts:

Description

In this section you should describe the practice, with special attention to the role cost control plays within the organization. Your description should attempt to convey the "color" and "life" in the organization.

Analysis

Your analysis should convey an understanding of how the phenomenon you study operates. Specific concerns might include, but are not limited to:

a. Technology factors that shape the organization's cost control practices.

b. Describe the interaction between employees and the specific control procedure.

c. Which "type" best helps you understand the organization and the practice? How does the organization deviate from the type? Is the deviation helpful or harmful?

Grading Criteria

Insight/Depth: Demonstration that you have a clear understanding of the controls used in the organization.

Clarity: Could someone who intends to work with the organization read your report and understand the nature of the control practices?

Evidence: Do you provide evidence for your claims? You should draw on observations to make your points and back them up with data and samples.

PROJECT 2

In this project you will research and apply a decision making process used to purchase computer hardware/software for controlling costs in a foodservice/restaurant environment. The objective is to use prior knowledge of cost control systems to plan and prepare for installing and implementing computer technology in a restaurant/foodservice environment. A written analysis that includes a description of what you studied, an explanation of what you learned, and recommendations regarding the purchase of computer hardware/software and how it relates to cost control systems is required.

The project must include the following:

1. Review the major steps in selecting and implementing computer hardware/software for a restaurant/foodservice environment based on a review of the professional literature. Include a description of the type of business in which the proposed system will be used.

2. Research and analyze three leading hardware/software vendors specializing in restaurant/foodservice software; include copy of demo software/documentation and other related literature.

3. Raise relevant questions/answers for evaluating hard/software that should be considered during the purchasing process. These questions must be based on written criteria. They will include, but are not limited to, a) type of data to process; b) description and justification for various cost control reports; b) information formats; c) hardware configurations; d) training; and, e) installation factors and costs.

4. Make recommendation (with rationale) on which system to purchase.

There is no minimum required page length for the report. However, the report must clearly assist the reader in the decision making process. It must cover the above four points.

9

FAST FOOD

Multi-Unit Management: Managing at a Distance
W. Terry Umbreit

**A Study of Opinions and Practices of Successful
Multi-Unit Fast Service Restaurant Managers**
W. Terry Umbreit, and Don I. Smith

Project 1

Project 2

MULTI-UNIT MANAGEMENT: MANAGING AT A DISTANCE

W. Terry Umbreit

Restaurant chains don't always know what attributes to look for when hiring multi-unit managers or what training to provide them, because this position in the corporate structure has never been well defined

MULTI-UNIT MANAGERS OF restaurant franchises in the U.S. number about 15,000, according to recent estimates. Yet, there is only a vague notion in the literature about what multi-unit management entails. For example, executives polled by *Restaurants & Institutions* magazine indicated that the role of multi-unit managers is one of the most difficult in the organization to define. Managers participating in an attitude survey noted that multi-unit managers are caught between two conflicting roles: the hands-on unit manager and the modern-day analyst of restaurants, people, and ideas. The researchers who conducted the study attributed this role confusion to restaurant companies' failure to define clearly multi-unit managers' responsibilities. Responses given by the multi-unit managers who participated in the study supported that view. Many respon-

dents indicated that they were unsure of what was expected of them. Half said that they received neither training for the position nor an evaluation of their performance.

Since specific job descriptions developed by fast-food companies are proprietary, it is difficult to establish an accurate definition of the multi-unit manager's position or to determine whether multi-unit managers and corporate executives define the responsibilities of the position in the same way. But both fast-food companies and educators could use a clearer concept of the multi-unit manager's role, so I conducted a study among corporate executives and current and former multi-unit managers to learn more about the nature of the multi-unit manager's position.

A Working Definition

Prior to designing the study, I developed a general definition of the multi-unit manager's role, based on job descriptions obtained from several fast-food companies. These job descriptions indicated that multi-unit managers are responsible for policy implementation, sales promotions, facility appearance and maintenance, financial control, and human-resources management. The companies that provided this information appeared to view multi-unit managers as an important conduit between superiors, who need to know what is going on in the field, and unit managers, who are expected to achieve corporate goals.

However, the company job descriptions provided no information about the specific tasks multi-unit managers perform, how they allocate their time, or how they accomplish their objectives. A more comprehensive view of the multi-unit manager's job would enable food-service firms to develop appropriate selection criteria and training program. Hospitality educators would find such information useful for developing courses on multi-unit management and enhancing students' awareness of the management opportunities that exist in the fast-food industry.

In this article, I will describe the results of my study of these managers. The goals of the study were to formulate a comprehensive definition of the job based on what multi-unit managers actually do, to isolate the skills and personal characteristics required for the job, and to determine appropriate recruitment and training strategies based on the findings.

Panel of Experts

In the first phase of the study, a panel of five executives in the chain-restaurant industry developed a job description for multi-unit managers. The executives I selected for the panel were either former multi-unit managers or current supervisors of multi-unit managers.

Using the nominal group technique, the panel identified five job aspects of multi-unit management, namely: finance, restaurant operations, marketing and promotion, facilities and safety, and human-resources management. After developing a general job description, the panel members provided examples of task ac-

tivities for each major element of the job.

View from the Top

To cross-validate the panel's work, I randomly selected 300 firms by size from *The Directory of Chain Restaurant Operators,* and asked the vice president of operations of each firm to evaluate the job aspects developed by the panel. I also asked the executives to evaluate the importance of each job aspect and task activity and indicate whether the task activities developed by the panel were appropriate on the multi-unit management level. Finally, I asked the respondents to identify transitional problems experienced by newly promoted multi-unit managers.

I obtained a total of 73 usable questionnaires, which were representative of the sample in terms of size and type of company. I received 28 responses from firms operating 50 units or fewer, 27 responses from firms operating between 51 and 200 units, and 18 responses from firms operating in excess of 200 units. Although the response rate was low (24.3 percent), perhaps due to the length of the questionnaire, the objective of this phase—obtaining a review of the panel's work and additional information from individuals with knowledge of the job—was achieved. Over 70 executives responsible for multiple units reviewed the job content developed by the panel and made changes that were incorporated in the final job description. The job as-

pects and definitions that emerged from this effort are shown in Exhibit 1.

In addition to questions concerning the roles and functions of multi-unit managers, the questionnaire sent to corporate executives contained questions about how their organization fills multi-unit manager positions. Over 35 percent of the executives who participated reported difficulty in finding competent individuals for these positions. Unit managers were identified as the primary source of supply, and over 82 percent of the respondents said that promotion of unit managers within the company was their preferred method of filling this job. Most respondents said that the estimated turnover rate for multi-unit managers in their company was between 10 and 15 percent per year. Forty-four percent of the executives attributed the turnover to lack of human-resources skills and 25 percent blamed job stress.

The Inside View

I developed a questionnaire for multi-unit managers using the job description in Exhibit 1 and performance-evaluation information obtained through telephone interviews with corporate fast-food executives from 10 firms randomly selected from *The Directory of Chain Restaurant Operators.* This questionnaire was modified to include questions about how multi-unit managers spent their time, the emphasis they placed on each job aspect, their training needs, the unique demands of their position, and the relative importance of each of the *outcome measures* (e.g., sales growth, increase in earnings, employee-turnover rate) for which they are held accountable.

From the 73 firms that returned phase-two questionnaires, I randomly selected 10 to participate in the final phase of the study. I asked executives from these firms to distribute the modified questionnaire to their multi-unit managers. The executives distributed 309 questionnaires, and I received 161 usable responses.

Weighing the job aspects. I asked the respondents to rate the importance of each of the five job aspects identified earlier in the study (finance, restaurant operations, marketing and promotion, facilities and safety, and human-resources management) by distributing 50 points across all the aspects based on the weight they believed each aspect should have in assessing a multi-unit manager's performance. Each aspect was to be assigned at least one point, and the total points assigned to all aspects were not to exceed 50. The vice presidents of operations who participated in the second phase of the study also rated

the importance of these five job aspects. A comparison of these groups' ratings is shown in Exhibit 2.

Both corporate executives and multi-unit managers rated restaurant operations as the most important job aspect, closely followed by human-resources management. Facilities and safety management received the lowest overall weight. The results of an analysis of variance (ANOVA) test indicated that differences in the executives' and the multi-unit managers' responses were statistically significant for three of the five job aspects rated.

EXHIBIT 2. IMPORTANCE OF MULTI-UNIT MANAGER'S JOB ASPECTS

	Mean weightings	
Job aspects	Executives	Multi-unit managers
Restaurant operations	14.3	13.1
Human-resources management	13.0	12.9
Financial management	10.1	12.0
Marketing and promotions	6.9	5.8
Facilities and safety	5.7	6.2
	50.0	50.0

Executives and managers were asked to rate the importance of each job aspect by distributing fifty points across all job aspects, according to the weight they attached to each. The mean weightings assigned by each group are shown above.

Multi-unit managers attached more weight to the finance component, while executives assigned greater weight to restaurant operations and marketing and promotions. These findings suggest that while corporate executives may feel that they do not over-stress the importance of financial management, multi-unit managers are hearing something different. In many cases, the marketing function is handled at the executive level, which may explain why the corporate executives attached more importance to that component. It is noteworthy that both groups agreed on the importance of human-resources management.

Measuring managers. I listed 16 outcome measures commonly used to evaluate multi-unit managers and asked the manager group to answer three questions: (1) which job aspects affect that outcome measure; (2) how strong the relationship is between the outcome measure and each job aspect that affects it; and (3) how long it typically would take for changes in the manager's performance in each job aspect to result in changes in that outcome measure.

The outcome measures and their degree of relationship to each aspect of a multi-unit manager's job are presented in Exhibit 3. I listed only the mean values of the outcome measures that at least 75 percent of the multi-unit managers identified as being related to a job aspect. The respondents identified at least two outcome measures with mean ratings of 4.0 or above for each job dimension, and some

job aspects, such as human-resources management and restaurant operations, had at least six related outcomes with mean ratings above 4.0.

Many aspects of the multi-unit manager's job appear to be linked with "sales growth," "employee turnover," and "quality-service-cleanliness." Perhaps these measures are most generic in evaluating district and regional managers.

Multi-unit managers indicated that they can bring about change in a short period of time, as shown in Exhibit 3. The managers indicated that changes in their performance can bring about changes in nine of the outcome measures within one month, six of the outcome measures within three months, and one of the outcome measures within six months. These responses suggest that the focus of multi-unit management is short term and individuals on that management level can exercise substantial control over most of the important outcome measures related to their job performance. The respondents said that it takes longer to bring about changes related to sales growth; improvement in units' earnings; shoppers' reports; and employee turnover, promotions, and terminations.

The time period required to bring about measurable changes in outcomes should be taken into consideration during the appraisal process. Since multi-unit managers agree that they can bring about changes in outcome measures in six months or less, firms should consider reviewing their performance

EXHIBIT 3. RELATIONSHIP OF OUTCOME MEASURES TO JOB ASPECTS

Outcome measure	Degree of relatedness (mean values, scale of 1–5)	Time lag
Aspect 1—Financial Management		
Food cost	4.706	1 month
Labor cost	4.578	1 month
Earnings improvement	4.230	3 months
Controlling manager turnover	4.113	3 months
Sales growth (from previous period)	3.964	3 months
Semi-variable expenses	3.650	1 month
Controlling employee turnover	3.378	3 months
Aspect 2—Restaurant Operations		
Quality-service-cleanliness	4.843	1 month
Unit inspections	4.404	1 month
Sales growth (from previous period)	4.340	3 months
Food costs	4.316	1 month
Controlling manager turnover	4.213	3 months
Labor cost	4.185	1 month
Shopper's report	3.956	3 months
Customer comment cards	3.951	1 month
Weekly customer counts	3.913	3 months
Controlling employee turnover	3.814	3 months
Executing sales promotions	3.642	1 month
Aspect 3—Marketing and Promotions Management		
Executing sales promotions	4.691	1 month
Sales growth (from previous period)	4.386	3 months
Weekly customer counts	4.296	1 month
Aspect 4—Facilities and Safety Management		
Frequency of employee accidents	4.605	1 month
Unit inspections	4.150	1 month
Aspect 5—Human-Resources Management		
Controlling manager turnover	4.699	3 months
Controlling employee turnover	4.523	3 months
Quality-service-cleanliness	4.465	1 month
Number of employees promoted	4.232	6 months
Number of employees terminated	4.231	3 months
Labor cost	4.197	1 month
Sales growth (from previous period)	4.071	3 months

semiannually. The reported links between job aspects and outcome measures may provide the basis for an improved performance-appraisal system in which multi-unit managers can gain a better understanding of how their behaviors influence outcomes.

Have expertise, will travel. Multi-unit managers also answered questions about the unique characteristics of the job (see Exhibit 4). Not surprisingly, the results indicate that multi-unit management is a demanding job. These managers supervised from four to eight units and worked over 50 hours per week. Nearly 25 percent said they worked over 60 hours per week. They spent most of their workday within the units, visiting with managers, solving problems, implementing new sales-promotion programs, and dealing with personnel issues.

Approximately half of the respondents spent less than two hours traveling between units on a given workday. Nearly 38 percent spent between two and three hours driving from unit to unit, greatly reducing the time they could spend in direct unit management, and a small percentage reported that they spent over three hours of their workday on the road. The average distance between units varied considerably. Forty percent of the managers said that the distance between their units was less than 10 miles, but another 26.4 percent reported that the units they managed were over 20 miles apart.

The respondents indicated that they spent over half their time on problems related to restaurant operations and human-resources management. Perhaps a more interesting finding was that over 40 percent of the multi-unit managers reported that they were spending more time on human-resources management than they did in the past. Due to current labor-market conditions, they have been forced to spend more time finding competent unit managers, assisting unit managers with personnel staffing, motivating and training supervisors, and helping to establish performance goals.

Growing pains. Asked to indicate the most difficult aspect of the job for unit managers making the transition to multi-unit responsibility, 62 percent of the corporate executives and 65 percent of the multi-unit managers named human-resources management. (A summary of the transitional problems is shown in Exhibit 5.)

One corporate executive said, "It's easier to teach someone the operational or financial aspects of the job, but the management of human resources requires patience, maturity, trust, and determination." New multi-unit managers often discover that the motivational techniques they used successfully with hourly employees in the units are not successful with unit managers, who are likely to be older and more motivated than hourly workers. Many of the respondents said that a common problem among new multi-unit managers was the tendency to over-control and

not permit unit managers to make their own decisions. Some respondents observed that multi-unit managers have to learn to work through their unit managers to achieve results, and they must learn to step back and allow their managers to make mistakes so the management team can learn and grow from these experiences. Respondents defined the functions of the multi-unit manager as coaching, motivating, and following up to see whether instructions were understood and correctly implemented.

The chief transitional problem is often one of management style. As one executive noted, "Promotable single-unit managers are usually very good at understanding their market, but they tend to develop a one-dimensional management style after assuming multi-unit responsibilities." This same executive concluded that management style is very difficult to teach and even more difficult to change.

Twenty percent of the corporate executives and 14 percent of the multi-unit managers selected restaurant operations as the area presenting the most difficulty for individuals moving from single-unit to multi-unit management. Some of the study participants cited delegation of responsibilities as the major problem. Multi-unit managers newly promoted from an individual unit are accustomed to jumping in and solving problems rather than standing back and helping others to devise solutions. On this section of the question-

EXHIBIT 4. CHARACTERISTICS OF A MULTI-UNIT MANAGER'S JOB

Percentage of time spent on each job aspect

Aspect	Percentage of time
Financial management	22.3
Restaurant operations	32.7
Marketing and promotions	9.6
Facilities and safety	10.6
Human resources	23.3
Other	1.5

Job aspects on which managers are spending increasing time

Aspect	Percentage of managers
Financial management	18.1
Restaurant operations	23.1
Marketing and promotions	10.6
Facilities and safety	1.9
Human resources	43.8
Other	2.5

Number of restaurants managed

Units	Percentage of managers
2 to 3	4.3
4 to 5	29.2
6 to 8	59.0
9 to 12	5.6
Over 12	1.9

Hours worked in typical week

Hours	Percentage of managers
40 to 44	.6
45 to 48	6.2
49 to 55	32.9
56 to 60	35.4
Over 60	24.9

Hours spent in units per day

Hours	Percentage of managers
Under 2	.6
2 to 4	6.3
5 to 6	21.9
7 to 8	55.6
9 to 10	15.6

Time spent traveling between units

Hours	Percentage of managers
1 to 2	52.8
2 to 3	37.3
3 to 4	5.0
4 to 5	1.9
Over 5	3.0

Average distance between units

Miles	Percentage of managers
Under 2	1.3
2 to 5	12.6
6 to 10	27.0
11 to 15	19.5
16 to 20	13.2
Over 20	26.4

EXHIBIT 5. SAMPLE LEARNING PROBLEMS OF THE TRANSITION TO MULTI-UNIT SUPERVISION

Human Resources

How to manage managers
How to use different motivational
  techniques
How to work with diverse personalities
How to read behaviors
How to communicate effectively

How to solve problems through people
How to coach and develop subordinates
How to evaluate performance and take
  disciplinary action
How to get unit managers to achieve high
  performance standards

Restaurant Operations

How to delegate
How to deal with unstructured time
How to recognize problems in units quickly
How to develop quality visitations

How to set priorities
How to enforce standards in multiple units
How to recognize the differences in each
  unit's operational situation

---

naire, one corporate executive wrote, "The key for the new multi-unit manager is to learn to delegate responsibility quickly, for it is impossible for an individual to spend as much time in each unit on day-to-day details as before." Each new multi-unit manager must learn the secret of managing remotely, which involves learning how to deal with unstructured time, establishing priorities, and making each visit to individual units a high-quality, productive visit.

Training needs. Approximately 42 percent of the multi-unit managers selected human-resources management as the area in which they would most like further training (see Exhibits 6 and 7). Many respondents were concerned with enhancing their motivational and leadership styles. Some respondents expressed interest in the personnel process of locating, hiring, training, and evaluating unit managers.

Many were quite specific about their training needs in the human-resources area, stating that they wanted to learn how to get along with different types of managers, how to get their subordinates to be more creative in problem solving, or how to improve their communication skills to become more effective leaders.

After human-resource management, marketing and promotions was the next most popular choice for further training. Thirty-six percent of the respondents chose this area—an unexpected development considering their responses concerning marketing and promotions management earlier in the questionnaire. The multi-unit management group did not rank marketing and promotions management high in importance or time commitment, and marketing and promotions management was not cited as a problem area during transition or an

area that required more time than the respondents were able to devote to it. The preference so many respondents expressed for training in marketing and promotions management might reflect these respondents' interest in moving up the corporate ladder, since most marketing activities for restaurant chains are handled at the top corporate level. On the other hand, the high level of interest in marketing and promotions management might indicate that a substantial number of the respondents believe such training is necessary to survive competitively. Corporate executives in the fast-food industry should focus on this perceived training need identified by multi-unit managers in view of the tremendous demands already placed on individuals occupying these positions. More training in marketing and promotions management may provide an

EXHIBIT 6. TRAINING PREFERENCES OF MULTI-UNIT MANAGERS

Job aspect	Percentage of managers
Human-resources management	41.9
Marketing and promotions	36.9
Financial management	11.9
Facilities and safety	3.7
Restaurant operations	1.2
Other	4.4

EXHIBIT 7. TRAINING NEEDS IDENTIFIED BY MULTI-UNIT MANAGERS

Human Resources

Motivating and managing managers
Team building and performance orientation
Recruiting, hiring, and training managers
Evaluating manager performance and handling terminations
Reading managerial behaviors and developing appropriate training strategies
Developing communication skills including effective public speaking

Marketing and Promotions

Implementing local-store promotional programs
Determining the effectiveness of promotional programs
Identifying the appropriate products to promote
Developing economic profiles of market areas and assessing competition
Developing radio ads and buying media
Developing in-house marketing and promotion programs

important competitive edge in the future, since multi-unit managers are in the best position to assess changes in consumer purchasing behavior and the effects of competitors' promotional campaigns.

A Starting Point

Although the study described in this article was an exploratory investigation and further research is necessary to validate the results, the information gleaned from the questionnaires is immediately useful in shedding light on some aspects of multi-unit management in the fast-food industry.

Both the corporate executives and the multi-unit managers who participated in the study emphasized the extent to which supervisors of multiple units are really human-resources managers. Multi-unit managers spend a great deal of time on this job component, and veterans in the position report that the time they devote to human-resources management has increased steadily in recent years. Multi-unit managers, typically promoted from single-unit manager positions, experience the greatest difficulty dealing with human-resources management, and they want more training in this job aspect. The importance of human-resources management to this position has implications for the selection, training, and development of future multi-unit managers.

The reasons for the divergent views of corporate executives and multi-unit managers concerning the relative importance of each job aspect must be explored. This lack of consensus on the nature of the job among individuals in the position and their superiors suggests that the role of multi-unit managers is in a fluid stage influenced by the competitive environment. However, firms that develop a comprehensive definition of the job will be able to design more effective recruitment and training programs.

Corporate executives would benefit from responding to the need identified by multi-unit managers for more training in marketing and promotions management. These individuals are in a position to monitor customer preferences and the impact of competitors' marketing strategies, and firms that tap their multi-unit managers' potential as observers and advisers might enjoy a competitive edge.

The information obtained through this seminal study establishes the groundwork for further research. Field research using such methodologies as direct observation, behavioral sampling, and diary keeping would provide additional information on multi-unit management and empirical data against which to measure the responses provided by the participants in this study. Further examination of this important level of management in the fast-food industry would prove useful to firms in their recruitment and skill-enhancement efforts and to hospitality educators responsible for educating potential candidates for management positions in the fast-food industry.

A Study of Opinions and Practices of Successful Multi-Unit Fast Service Restaurant Managers

W. Terry Umbreit and Don I. Smith

Introduction

LARGE RESTAURANT CHAINS continue to dominate the fast-service restaurant segment in sales growth and volume. These chains are highly sophisticated and complex organizations. They are team dependent and comprised of many specialists in the areas of planning, development, real estate, construction, management information systems, accounting and human resource management. However, experienced executives agree that a chain of restaurants is an organization of standards. And its day by day success depends upon the execution of those standards. Getting thousands and hundreds of thousands of youthful, often first-time employed people to deliver those standards flawlessly is the responsibility of a management function called "operations."

Operational managers will tell you that the restaurant manager and assistant are the key to organizational success. The above individuals run the restaurant daily and are responsible for maintaining standards and achieving unit profitability. While no one can argue with the importance of unit management personnel, perhaps an overlooked individual in today's highly competitive market place is the multi-unit supervisor. Multi-unit managers are responsible for supervising between five and seven units and are called District Manager (D.M.) or Area Manager (A.M.). Their duties include hiring, training and motivating unit managers and assistants. More importantly, they are the operational linch-pin responsible for almost all communications between the organization and the restaurants. Until the early 1980's, little distinction was made between the technical, managerial and educational qualifications of restaurant managers and managers of restaurant managers. In fact, not much information had been published on multi-unit managers until Umbreit's seminal work (1987). Umbreit (1989) identified the major job dimensions of multi-unit managers and the unique characteristics of the position. Additionally, he found that single-unit managers comprise the primary recruiting pool for multi-unit managers and experienced transitional problems when making the change in duties.

Further research needs to ask: are the skills, knowledge and interpersonal communication skills of successful restaurant managers the same as those required for success as a multi-unit manager? Information on successful multi-unit managers would add to our knowledge of the position and help identify the important skills necessary for success in today's difficult operating environment. This paper reports on a study designed to gain insight into the beliefs, opinions, and practices of successful multi-unit managers (1989). Since the fast-service segment is facing unprecedented problems such as saturation, an unpredictable economy, a severe labor shortfall and the changing expectations of both consumers and workers, it would appear to be beneficial to study successful multi-unit managers to find out how they succeed in today's difficult operating environment. This information should help hospitality educators in curriculum design and preparing students for the challenges they face in assuming managerial positions in fast-service restaurants.

Survey Methodology

A 39-item questionnaire and self-addressed envelope was given to 60 successful multi-unit managers by their immediate superiors. Multi-unit managers selected by their immediate superiors were chosen on the basis of their above-average performance in supervising fast-service restaurants in their districts. The multi-unit managers were asked to be candid in their responses and not to identify themselves. They were assured that their confidential remarks would be merged with others and that no one involved with their organizations would ever see their responses. The questions were developed by the principal researcher based on his extensive knowledge and experience in restaurant operations and information developed on

multi-unit management by Washington State University. Multi-unit managers in the survey were asked a series of questions about their job responsibilities, important tasks they perform, knowledge and skills necessary to satisfactorily complete the job and how they handle certain situations.

Thirty-one completed surveys were returned for a response rate of 51.7%. A framework for understanding the survey responses was greatly aided by two video discussions. The first was a focus group composed of former multi-unit managers who have since been promoted because of their effectiveness. In the first group, discussion centered around the differences in management emphasis between unit management and multi-unit management. The second tape was a lengthy discussion of restaurant managers' perceptions of the strengths and weaknesses of multi-unit managers.

Results and Discussion

Changes in Management Emphasis

The videotaped discussions and survey responses permitted the researchers to formulate a profile of the differences between single-unit and multi-unit management. Basically, the major difference was a shift in management emphasis in a number of areas which are outlined below:

1. A shift from technical trainer to manager developer.

   Responses from the multi-unit managers revealed the strong need for them to become developers of managers rather than focusing on the training of technical skills.

2. A shift from receiver of information to communicator of information.

   Single-unit managers can often lead by example rather than by language. Multi-unit managers are far more dependent upon both spoken and written language and need to develop communication skills. They must be understood by a broad range of people from a variety of professional, educational and social backgrounds. Multi-unit managers are required to conduct group meetings, use audio-visual aids, and be effective one-on-one counselors and coaches.

3. A shift from a structured to an unstructured work environment.

   Time management and self-discipline are very important to the success of multi-unit managers. The schedule of unit managers is mostly regimented but multi-unit managers must learn how to allocate their time, where to travel and how much leisure time to allow.

4. A shift from "doer" to delegator.

Unit managers are involved with all aspects of their operations, and they take upon themselves many tasks on a daily basis. Multi-unit managers on the other hand must delegate and begin to trust others in accomplishing tasks rather than themselves. Multi-unit managers must learn to enhance the self-confidence of their managers which requires a great deal of self-control and patience.

5. A shift in influencing and motivating techniques.

Survey results revealed the need for multi-unit managers to understand motivational techniques and how their communication styles impact other people. Single-unit managers use their authority to get things done but multi-unit managers are supervising individuals who are highly motivated and require different techniques to enhance their productivity. Multi-unit managers must learn how to bond with a variety of different people,

6. A shift to new business knowledge and skills.

Multi-unit managers must learn new business skills to be successful including financial analysis, business precision and accuracy, computer applications, and personnel management. Multi-unit managers must understand how to analyze the operating results of many restaurants and provide solutions to problems identified in their review process.

7. A shift from a supportive, one-boss environment to a more political and peer-interdependent environment.

Unit managers can find support and guidance from their multi-unit managers. However, when they become managers of multiple units they become dependent on many others for support, achievement and advancement. Multi-unit managers must develop political skills and learn how to succeed in a competitive environment.

Successful Management Strategies

Successful multi-unit managers responded to a number of questions dealing with how they approach their job responsibilities which provided meaningful insights as to their success strategies. When asked to prioritize their job responsibilities, the respondents listed the following in order of importance: (1) management development, (2) maintaining quality/service/cleanliness (QSC) standards, (3) achieving financial goals, (4) customer satisfaction, (5) training, (6) communicating company goals, (7) recruiting, (8) administration and paperwork and (9) assisting in advertising and promotion. The survey revealed that successful multi-unit managers place a high value on the development of managers including the training and recruiting functions.

The survey asked the successful multi-unit managers to indicate what they did to make their restaurants more successful than others in their region. The important responses centered again around the strategy of supporting managers. Specifically, the successful multi-unit managers identified the following: (1) supporting managers and allowing them to manage their own restaurants, (2) letting managers establish their own goals, (3) developing managers, assistant managers and crew, (4) motivating and establishing pride and team spirit, and (5) modeling the work ethic. It was very clear from the comments that the multi-unit managers surveyed believed they were successful because they spent a great deal of time developing their management team, constructing a positive work environment and instilling a sense of pride and team spirit in their units.

This approach was very evident when the multi-unit managers were asked to indicate the four factors that motivate their unit managers. The most important factor was the genuine caring for managers or the act of taking a personal interest in the well-being of the individual. One of the most interesting remarks was: "understanding each individual as a person." Unit managers were also motivated by winning and competition, recognition including positive feedback, money, participation in decisions and opportunities for advancement. When asked to identify the keys to team building, multi-unit managers listed in order of importance: (1) communication, (2) team sharing and involvement in goals, (3) effective delegation and follow-up, (4) public praising of individuals, (5) recognizing individual strengths of managers, (6) meetings in and out of units, (7) making individuals feel that they contribute to the team's success and (8) setting the example.

Successful Management Practices

Multi-unit managers as part of the survey were asked to answer several questions about how they would deal with certain management situations. This information provided an insight into the practices of successful multi-unit managers. Percentage responses did not always add up to 100% because of multiple answers. In the first question, multi-unit managers were asked to indicate the first thing they do when visiting one of their restaurants. Seventy percent stated that they made certain to say hello to everyone followed by 30% who would call managers and crew members by name. Over 30% indicated they would first talk to people to get a reading on the restaurant's climate. Others indicated they would check the grounds first. When posed with another question dealing with a serious problem that involved one of their restaurants closing 35 minutes early, 85% of the multi-unit managers followed a similar procedure

which involved taking the manager into the office, determining the reason, explaining the policy on closing and mentioning the situation should not happen again. Seventy percent of the multi-unit managers would document the incident. Several multi-unit managers indicated they would terminate the individual responsible.

A third question required the multi-unit managers to indicate their response to a situation where the manager is out of the unit for a legitimate business reason when they arrive in the restaurant which appears to be operating in good order. Over two-thirds of the multi-unit managers stated that they would compliment the manager when he or she returned without asking questions. About 15 percent of the multi-unit managers wanted to see if the manager left someone in charge before leaving the restaurant. One multi-unit supervisor said they would have filled in while another would have discussed priorities when the manager returned.

A fourth question required the multi-unit managers to respond to a situation when they walk into one of their restaurants and finds the managers and crew behind in customer service. Sixty percent of the respondents mentioned they would "jump in" and help out immediately followed by 30 percent who would ask the manager's permission first. The remaining respondents indicated they would do nothing at the moment. All would take action later to avoid a recur-

rence. In a fifth question multi-unit managers were asked to indicate how often they hold manager meetings. Over 70 percent of the multi-unit managers held manager meetings weekly while others held them as often as possible. In a sixth question multi-unit managers were told the president of the company was in their community with plans to visit some of the restaurant units. When asked what actions they would take, a high percentage stated they would personally make an assessment of each restaurant and develop an action plan. Other responses included: "go help shine the restaurants up," and "call all restaurants and ask for them to call the multi-unit manager when the president arrived."

The seventh question asked the multi-unit managers to provide responses to a situation where they have been ordered to cut labor cost by one percent which resulted in their restaurants units barely meeting service standards. Most of the respondents indicated that they would take action immediately. Eight multi-unit managers would bring their unit managers together and ask for their ideas and support. Eight more would attempt to determine the problem and then train the unit managers on how to increase productivity. Other multi-unit managers responding to this question stated they would look for areas to cut back on a unit-by-unit basis.

The final question asked the respondents their reaction to a situation where 30 percent of their bonus was tied to their manager turnover rate and they realized that two of their managers were not competent. The multi-unit managers were told in the question that two management candidates were qualified and available for promotion. All of the multi-unit managers revealed they would replace the poor performers. Several of the respondents made interesting comments in response to the question such as: "I make decisions that benefit the business" and "I can make a bonus any time."

A review of the questionnaire responses by successful multi-unit managers reveals a concern for the welfare of their managers and a willingness to get them involved in problems that take place in restaurant operations. Multi-unit managers attempt to solve problems on an even-handed basis by finding out all of the facts before arriving at a decision. The positive approaches the multi-unit managers in the survey take in supervising their subordinates is definitely a contributing factor in their effectiveness.

Successful Management Skills

The third part of the survey was comprised of questions about the skills, attributes and knowledge of successful multi-unit managers together with other aspects of the position. In the opinion of the multi-unit manager respondents, the most important skills required for the position fall into three categories: (1) interpersonal/motivational/leadership,

(2) business knowledge and analytical skills and (3) technical skills consisting of marketing, operations and customer relations. The respondents revealed that their skills would be enhanced through additional training in motivating, communicating with and influencing others, time management, and financial analysis.

Survey respondents when asked to indicate the most satisfying aspects of their job listed the following: having my managers promoted, seeing employees advance and succeed, winning or being the best in my area, being part of a team, recognition from my boss, challenges, customer satisfaction and flexibility of work schedule. The multi-unit managers repeatedly mentioned that the most satisfying aspect of their job was in the development of managers and employees. This consisted of their efforts in training and development, seeing individuals grow and receive promotions and praising managers for their accomplishments. Multi-unit managers like the feeling of being the best in their area and being part of a team.

Multi-unit managers mentioned too much paperwork and administrative requirements as the biggest obstacle preventing them from doing their job better. Some examples of this include: shuffling papers, corporate red tape, unplanned meetings, changing priorities, corporate requests without notice and too many interruptions. Other obstacles involved the time/work relationship dilemma, staffing problems and lack of proper

supervision. Multi-unit managers were critical of their superiors for lack of leadership, too much criticism, not enough support and top down communication.

Conclusions and Implications

This research study on successful multi-unit managers provided a better understanding of a unique position in the fast-service restaurant industry. Managers in the multi-unit environment must develop different skills to be successful. Managers move from a technical focus in single-unit management to a professional business emphasis in multi-unit management. The research findings point out that successful multi-unit managers are people developers, motivators, communicators and delegators. Multi-unit managers in this new environment must acquire special skills and business knowledge, and become more politically adept. These managers are dependent upon many others for support and must learn how to balance their personal and professional needs with those at higher levels including specialists in the organization.

Perhaps the real contribution this research makes is the first-hand information gained on what successful managers actually do and how they perform their jobs. Successful multi-unit managers establish a high priority on developing strong subordinates, providing a supporting work environment, allowing unit management personnel to set their own goals and instilling a sense of pride and teamwork. Multi-unit managers surveyed believe they are successful because of the above approaches. Answers provided by multi-unit managers on the situational questions reinforce their beliefs as many of their practices focus on people development and involving subordinates in the decision-making process. Multi-unit managers participating in this study receive great satisfaction in seeing their managers promoted and being part of a winning team. It appears that this value system contributes to their success.

Research results presented in this paper have important implications for hospitality education. Since this study is one of the first attempts to identify the successful practices of multi-unit managers, educators can utilize the information to reinforce classroom learning on management techniques. Educators can share this information with their students to provide a model for emulation. Textbooks are full of theory, but students must understand how managers function in real situations. The study results provide strong support for the leadership style that recognizes the importance of sound personnel practices and a commitment to human resource development.

Hospitality educators can use the information for curriculum development. The important skills, attributes and knowledge of successful multi-unit managers have been identified. Multi-unit managers revealed the skills required for a successful transition from single to multi-unit responsibility. Information in the paper also discusses the further training needs of multi-unit managers along with obstacles to successful performance. This material should be of value to educators in developing lectures and classroom discussions on current management practice.

References

Umbreit, W.T. (1987). Job responsibilities of the multi-unit manager. *Restaurants USA*, 7, 18–19.

Umbreit, W.T. (1989). Multi-unit management: Managing at a distance. The *Cornell Hotel and Restaurant Administration Quarterly*, 30, 53–59.

Smith, D. and Smith, D.J. (1989). A study of the opinions and practices of successful multi-unit fast service restaurant managers. Presented at the fourth annual Conference on Strategic Issues in the Fast Service Industry. Washington State University, Pullman, Washington, April.

Numerous changes in organization structure have taken place in corporate America in order for companies to remain competitive and maintain successful profit levels. Some of these changes included: downsizing, outsourcing, decentralization, and creation of self-managed teams and autonomous units. The results of corporate and chain structure transformation have made companies smaller, more aware of market trends and customer needs, quality-oriented, better managed, and able to produce goods at lower costs.

Managers of chain restaurant organizations have had to adapt to the structural changes by focusing on leadership, building better unit teams, obtaining employee involvement and commitment, and enhancing customer service. Students preparing themselves for careers in chain restaurant management must understand the impact of the structural changes and how successful managers of multiple-units have adjusted to the new environment.

The objective of this senior project is to provide students with an understanding of the managerial job of supervising multiple units in chain restaurant organizations. The title of this position varies by company but is normally entitled district manager, market manager or area manager. The requirements of the project are outlined below:

1. Students are to make arrangements to spend at least one full day with three separate multi-unit managers as they conduct their job responsibilities. Students during the observation period should take notes on what tasks the manager is performing and how they go about their job assignment.

2. Based on the readings, students should develop a structured interview questionnaire that solicits information from each multi-unit manager about their job duties and responsibilities. Particular attention should be paid on obtaining the opinions and views of the managers on what changes have taken place in recent years to impact their job duties.

3. At the conclusion of the observation sessions and management interviews, students are to write a paper that outlines the job of multi-unit managers including job dimensions, company expectations and managerial use of new technologies and systems. Every attempt should be made in the paper to contrast the difference among the managers in their style and composition of daily activities.

PROJECT 2

The quick-service segment of the foodservice industry continues to grow in sales volume and will become the largest sector in a few years. This segment is dominated by large chain restaurant organizations who are responsible for managing numerous units in geographically-dispersed areas. To remain competitive, chain restaurant organizations must hire excellent unit managers as well as provide overall coordination of multi-units in contiguous market areas.

Because of the size and complexity of the quick-service restaurant segment, this sector provides many opportunities for graduates from hospitality programs. While new management trainees start out in a single-unit operation, companies offer promotions in multi-unit management involving the supervision of many units. In order to prepare themselves successfully, hospitality students must understand the differences between single-unit and multi-unit management as well as gaining an insight into the successful practices of restaurant managers.

This senior project is designed to help students understand the differences between single-unit and multi-unit management. Additionally, students should learn what successful managers do in practice to create winning teams and achieve outstanding sales volumes. The project involves the completion of the following activities:

1. Students are to make arrangements to visit three quick-service units and observe the unit manager's activities. At least four hours should be spent in each unit. In addition, students are to make arrangements to shadow three district managers and spend a typical day with them visiting units.

2. Based on the readings, students should develop a structured interview questionnaire that solicits information from each manager about their job duties and responsibilities. Students should also develop questions that obtain responses from managers as to their successful practices and management techniques.

3. At the conclusion of the observation sessions and management interviews, students are to write a paper that discusses the observed differences between single-unit and multi-unit management. Students should also identify and elaborate on what successful management practices were utilized by managers during observation periods.

10

CONTRACT FOOD SERVICE

Menu Planning and Development
Audrey C. McCod, Fred A. Smith and David L. Tucker

Self-Operating Foodservice Versus Contract Management
Guy E. Karrick

Project 1

Project 2

Menu Planning and Development

Audrey C. McCod, Fred A. Smith and David L. Tucker

MENUS AND THE MENU planning process are different in noncommercial foodservice operations from what they are in the commercial areas of the foodservice industry. Providing foodservices for a school, a corporation, or a hospital requires a different approach to decisions regarding the foods to be served than is required for a hotel dining room or a quick-service restaurant.

The primary difference is that the menus in most noncommercial operations may change daily. This constant change is a great challenge to you, the foodservice manager, as well as to your employees. As the manager, you must meet this challenge by providing menus that are nutritious yet composed of items that are appetizing and appealing to your clientele. Many factors can compound the difficulty of this task. For example, purveyors may not deliver needed products, so the menu must be changed; there are leftovers from previous meals, which must be used imaginatively; guest demands may exceed your forecast for a particular item, leading to shortages and the need to make substitutions. To prevent this task from becoming tedious, you must be innovative, yet careful and creative.

Cycle Versus Set Menus

Two types of menus are most often found in the foodservice industry. These types are the *set menu,* common to the commercial sector and some components of some noncommercial foodservices, and the *cycle menu,* common to other components of the noncommercial sector. It is important to understand the difference between these two menu types, the reasons for cycle menu usage, and the planning process that is required to develop high-quality cycle menus. Because of their unique application to noncommercial foodservices, the focus of this chapter is on cycle menu planning.

The set menu is the type of menu found in restaurants or hotel dining facilities. Such a menu is printed, or posted on a menu board, and does not change from day to day. This type of menu is also used for the grill, deli counter, or the salad bar stations that are often components of cafeterias found in noncommercial foodservices. Restaurants use this type of menu for many reasons, such as to feature their specialty items, facilitate employee training, and realize cost savings. It is expensive to print a new menu every day or to have the large inventory of food on hand that is required for a changing menu. These set menus usually change items to provide menu variety by featuring a daily special or by offering seasonal items (perhaps changing these items every six months). Occasionally major changes are made, and completely new menus are printed. Often the revised menu will incorporate a new fad or trend that has become popular among the restaurant's clientele or will reflect a redecoration or a new ambiance desired by the restaurant.

In contrast, most cycle menus used in noncommercial

foodservices change on a daily basis. The daily change of menu items is necessary, because the clientele served does not change. Herein lies the challenge—to plan and develop menus that will entice the same clientele into the dining facilities day after day.

These menu cycles, as the name "cycle" implies, are usually planned for some predetermined schedule of days or weeks and are regularly repeated over this time period. Typically, a cycle menu will be developed on a three- or four-week basis, but a cycle may be as short as five days or even less. The length of the cycle is primarily determined on the basis of the length of time that the same clientele will be served. A hospital patient, for example, may stay only three to four days, whereas an elementary school child eats in the same cafeteria for a full school year. This daily change and cyclical repetition make the task of menu planning for many noncommercial foodservices difficult and demanding. However, an effective menu cycle is the key to a successful operation in most noncommercial foodservices.

The Menu Planning Process

Planning quality cycle menus is a careful, well defined process that takes time and effort. Effective menus don't "just happen" when the manager or the menu planner has a few hours of spare time one afternoon. Successful cycle menus are the result of carefully following a defined menu planning process.

The first step in the cycle menu planning process is to determine a listing of food items that might be included on the menu throughout the total cycle. Specific items for each day's menu will be selected from this listing. When developing this listing of menu items, it is important to remember that the items selected affect what food inventory must be carried and that other operational constraints (discussed later in this chapter) may restrict the selection of food items.

This listing could be obtained from the foodservice's standardized recipe file or other standardized files available through commercial sources. A manager may also develop a personal recipe listing, including recipes from books, magazines, a variety of recipe files, and other sources of creative menu items. If the foodservice is managed by a contract firm, that firm will probably have a well-tested, standardized recipe file, tailored for that type of foodservice, that would provide an excellent listing of food items to be used for the menu cycle. Several excellent standardized recipe resources are on the market today, such as *Food for Fifty* by Shugart and Molt[1] or *Large Quantity Recipes* by Terrell and Headlund.[2] Table 1 shows how a food item listing might be developed for use in cycle menu planning.

Once the food item listing has been completed, the daily menu planning can begin. Weekly menu planning forms, available from many food product vendors, or other forms tailored to the specific menu pattern for the foodservice can greatly facilitate this step in the menu planning process. Table 2 illustrates such a form. Using this type of form will help you keep the days of the cycle in order and your planning well organized. While you can begin the planning process with almost any component of the menu, most menu planners will start with the entrée items, because the entrées are always the most important components of the menu. It is a good idea to plan the entrées for the entire menu cycle before going on to work on other menu components.

Once the entrées are planned, a good next step is to fill in the starch and vegetable items that blend well with the planned entrées. Soups and salads can be added next, and finally breads and desserts can be planned. Why plan desserts last? They are the "finishing touches" for the menu, and they come in a wide range of flavors, colors, textures, and consistencies. Thus, desserts can be used to add whatever "finish" is necessary to develop a well-balanced overall menu plan for the day.

When completing the menu planning form, consider this basic guideline: *Use many freshly prepared items on Monday*. Monday items should *not* be based on leftovers from Friday or the weekend. Providing freshly prepared items on Monday begins a new week in an upbeat, positive manner—a help to clientele, who may be suffering

TABLE 1. SAMPLE LISTING OF FOOD ITEMS THAT MIGHT BE USED ON A CYCLE MENU

Soups

Cream	*Stock*
Vegetable	Vegetable
Potato	Chicken Noodle
Pea	Chicken Rice
Carrot	Beef Noodle
Chicken	Beef Rice
etc.	etc.

Meats

Beef	*Pork*	*Lamb*	*Veal*
Salisbury Steak	Pork Tenderloin	Leg of Lamb	Veal Patties
Roast Beef	Pork Chops	Lamb Stew	Leg of Veal
Beef Stew	Roast Pork	Lamb Brochette	Veal Stew
etc.	etc.	etc.	etc.

Poultry

Chicken	*Turkey*	*Duck*
Roast Chicken	Roast Turkey	Roast Duck
Chicken à la King	Turkey Pot Pie	Peking Duck
Fried Chicken	Hot Turkey Sandwich	Mandarin Duck
etc.	etc.	etc.

Seafood

Finfish	*Shellfish*	*Crustaceans*
Fried Flounder	Clams	Softshell Crab
Broiled Scrod	Oysters	Broiled Lobster Tail
Poached Salmon	Mussels	Stuffed Prawns
etc.	etc.	etc.

Nonmeat Items

Eggs and Cheese	*Vegetarian*
Eggs à la King	Vegetarian Stir-fry
Cheese Souffle	Pasta Primavera
Macaroni and Cheese	Vegetarian Lasagna
etc.	etc.

Listings would continue to include all categories of food items that might be used on the menu such as starches, vegetables, sandwiches, salads, desserts, etc.

from "Monday Blues." Even though the clientele may have been working or eating in the cafeteria or other foodservice area on the weekend, almost everyone looks at Monday as the start of a new week.

Using "fresh start" items on Monday can also provide planned leftovers for use throughout the week. For example, if roast beef is on the menu for Monday, beef noodle soup, barbecued beef sandwiches, or beef stew could be served on Wednesday. This practice is also cost-effective and will help enhance the menu's variety. Of course, some fresh items should be used in each day's menu, and no one day's menu should be composed only of planned leftovers.

The produce delivery schedule is another "freshness" consideration. Produce quality is

TABLE 2. SAMPLE MENU PLANNING FORM			
Item	Day 1	Day 2	Day 3
Soup 1 (stock)			
Soup 2 (cream)			
Entrée 1	Roast Beef	Braised Pork Chop	Baked Chicken
Entrée 2	Chicken à la King	Spaghetti with Meat Sauce	Beef Stew
Entrée 3	Tuna Salad Sandwich	Vegetarian Stir-fry	Bratwurst with Sauerkraut
Starch 1			
Starch 2			
Vegetable 1			
Vegetable 2			
Salad 1			
Salad 2			
Dessert 1			
Dessert 2			
Bread 1			
Bread 2			

Note: Each category of food item that is to appear on the menu has a space on the form, and there are sufficient spaces for each type of item to list the number of choices that are to be offered for the item. When each space is completed, the total menu has been drafted.

The planning has started with the entrées. The entrée mix is a "piece item" for entrée 1; a mixed item for entrée 2; and a sandwich or variety item for entrée 3. From here, planning will begin on the next category, such as the soups or starches.

Only 3 days are indicated here. The form would be extended to accommodate more days, or the complete listing of items could be repeated for additional rows of days. Several pages of the form may be needed to accommodate the total cycle time period.

best when it is delivered. Therefore, menus should be planned so that special produce items are used as soon as possible after they are received.

Although all the menu item spaces on the menu planning form have been filled in for all of the days in the cycle, the planning work is not finished. To achieve a high-quality menu, the draft menu plan must now be reviewed to search for weaknesses and adjustments made as necessary. During this review, the menu planner will be looking for variety, excessive repetition, appropriate combinations, and whether the menu can be produced and served by the staff in the facility, given the available personnel and equipment. Key aspects to consider in the review of each of these areas will be discussed in this chapter.

When a weakness is identified, one or more food items will need to be changed. Of course, when making the change, it is important to be sure that the new item does not create a new weakness. One area in which problems often occur, but go unnoticed until the menu is implemented, is the joining of the end of one cycle with the beginning of the next. For example, many menu planners forget to consider that week one always comes after week four just as week two comes after week one. They find all at once that roast beef is on the menu for two consecutive days that they had thought were four weeks apart.

Variety Means Cycle Menu Quality

Variety in Food Items

Cycle menu planners will soon discover that variety is the key to success. Variety can be achieved by using different, interesting menu items, products that are new and unique, and items that are especially tasty or eye appealing. Variety is most important in the main entrées. Quality menus use meat, poultry, seafood, and nonmeat *(vegetarian)* items in a balanced, well-thought-out way. A menu that has too many of any one type of entrée—for example, a cafeteria menu that offers a choice of roast beef, Swiss steak, and meat loaf on one day and fried chicken, roast turkey, and chicken à la king on the next day—is a weak, poor-quality menu. Entrée variety would be improved by offering roast beef, chicken àla king, and vegetarian lasagna as the cafeteria selections for the day.

This balance and variety is important not only in entrée items but in all other menu areas, such as soups, salads, sandwiches, vegetables, breads, and desserts, as well. To balance the food items really well, the menu planner will need to count how many times beef appears; how many times fish appears; how many times a sliced entrée appears; how many times green beans are listed; and so forth. Then these counts need to be compared to the relative frequency that is desired for each type of menu item. For example, the foodservice manager may want to serve more poultry than beef or serve pork only twice a week, or have only one sliced item per day but may want to serve peas, beans, carrots, broccoli, and corn an equal number of times on the menu. Without actually counting how items are used, it is surprising how easy it is to plan menus with excessive amounts of the menu planner's or the foodservice manager's favorite items and only a limited number of other items that may be favorites of the foodservice's clientele.

Changes in Texture

Once an appropriate variety of food items is planned, the menus must also be screened for variety in texture. It is a very dull and boring menu that has all the foods of the same consistency or texture. Perhaps a day has been planned that has beef stew, chicken à la king, and chili as the entrées; mashed potatoes and creamed corn as the starch and vegetable; cream of broccoli soup; molded fruit gelatin salad; and chocolate pudding. All of these items together make a weak menu because of their similarity in texture and consistency. An improved menu would offer a solid entrée, perhaps broiled flounder or baked ham, instead of the beef stew; change the starch and vegetable to rice pilaf and steamed broccoli; change the soup to a broth base soup; add a second, "crunchy" salad; and offer fresh fruit as an option for dessert. This menu offers balance both in food types and in the texture of the food items.

Variety in Color

Another variable in menu development, which is very important but often overlooked, is variety in color. Color variety is invaluable for making the food presentation as aesthetically appealing as possible in the noncommercial foodservice environment. Remember that in cafeteria environments the clientele will select food based on how it looks. Furthermore, clientele that is given no choice in the food served will be more likely to eat foods that are appealing and attractively served, and fewer complaints about food will be received. Color variety (along with freshness, portion sizes, and overall quality) will be a major part of the appearance and aesthetic appeal of the meals served.

When planning menus and thinking of new items, it is very easy to forget color combinations and fail to envision what the items are finally going to look like on a steam table, a salad bar, or a patient tray. It is not very difficult to avoid color repetition if the items are color coded as they are selected for the menus. For example, Manhattan clam chowder and minestrone soup at first might be placed on the same day. If these soups were color coded as they were listed on the planning form, it would be easy to see that they were no different in color. In addition, they have the same consistency and are composed of almost the same ingredients. An easy correction for the soup selection for this day would be to change the Manhattan clam chowder to New England clam chowder. By changing the chowder color from red to white and by changing the consistency from stock based to cream based, the result is two very different choices for the clientele.

Soups and vegetables are items where color is easily duplicated without careful consideration. Perhaps peas and green beans are listed as the vegetables for the meal. Both are green. The problem could be resolved by switching the beans with corn niblets from another day. However, with this switch another problem is created, because peas and corn are too close in texture. Another switch will be necessary to finally resolve the problem.

While color problems in any part of the menu contribute to menu weakness, color problems in entrée selections are potentially quite costly. It is easy to overlook the negative impact caused by a lack of color variation when someone is selecting food items to eat, and sales are often lost as a result. Imagine putting macaroni and cheese, tuna and noodle casserole, and cheese strata together on the same steam table in the cafeteria. Is it any wonder that the clientele would consider the food-service dull, boring, and monotonous? Or consider a tray served to a hospital patient where the menu was cream of mushroom soup, tuna and noodles, steamed cauliflower, coleslaw, and rice pudding. How stimulating would this presentation be to the patient's appetite? There is nothing at all wrong with any one of these items individually, but together in these menu combinations they are a disaster!

Variety in Form or Shape

The form or shape of the menu items planned should be considered. Menu items that are all similar in shape or piece size make a plate, tray, or a serving line look monotonous. Within a given meal, food should be presented in several different shapes, such as mounds, cubes, shredded, and whole pieces. When the same item (green beans, for example) is used on different days, it should be presented in different forms (regular cut, French cut, or whole, for example). To illustrate the use of different forms and shapes, a menu combination such as chicken tetrazzini, French cut green beans, coleslaw, and fruit cocktail is composed of items that are all cut into small, similarly shaped pieces. The combination could be improved by substituting whole green beans for the French cut ones, changing the coleslaw to a tossed green salad with tomato wedges, and using peach halves instead of fruit cocktail for dessert. Now there are a variety of shapes in the food products served.

Variety in form or shape may also be introduced through the effective use of garnishes. For example, carrot or celery sticks would lend interest to a cold plate containing mounds, such as a tuna salad plate with coleslaw and sliced tomatoes. A fresh apple wedge might enhance a hot plate, such as roast pork with mashed potatoes and peas. Colorful fruit slices would enhance a pudding dessert.

Variety in Methods of Preparation

It is easy to plan menus that have little variance in the preparation method used, particularly if there are limitations in the available kitchen equipment or if the clientele seems to prefer foods prepared a particular way. However, whenever possible, variety in preparation methods should be considered in the menu planning process, and menus incorporating items all prepared by the same method (e.g., fried) should be avoided. It is also important to be sure that an item is not always prepared the same way each time it is on the menu (e.g., chicken always fried or always baked).

For example, a menu composed of chicken fried steak, fried cod fillet, french fried potatoes, buttered green beans, and french fried zucchini is very poor. All that frying makes the menu monotonous, and it is nutritionally poor as well because of all of the fat in almost all selections. The menu could be improved by having Swiss steak, fried cod fillet, oven browned potatoes, buttered green beans, and steamed zucchini with tomatoes. Lack of variety is most often a problem with the entrées, and preparation methods such as roasting, grilling, baking, creaming, stewing, broiling, braising, scalloping, poaching, and boiling should be considered in addition to frying or pan frying.

Balance Between Light and Heavy Foods

People often talk about having a light or heavy meal. Foods such as deep fried items, fatty meats, potatoes, rice, noodles, spaghetti, macaroni, corn, lima beans, baked beans, breads of all types, pies, cakes, and rich desserts are usually considered to be "heavy" foods. In comparison, foods usually considered to be "light" are items such as soups, fruits, fruit juices, lean roasted or broiled meats, vegetables, salads, many sandwiches, and light desserts such as gelatins, fruits, or sherbets. A well planned, interesting menu achieves a balance between light and heavy foods. However, the proportion of light to heavy foods should take the clientele served into consideration. For example, active young men, such as many college dormitory residents, will require a higher proportion of heavy foods to meet their caloric needs than will residents of a life care facility, who are mostly older women with much lower caloric needs.

An important consideration today in balancing the proportion of light and heavy foods is the need to plan menu options that are low in fat. At least some the clientele of almost all types of noncommercial foodservices now want more healthful foods, particularly foods that are low in fat. Every menu planned should have at least one low fat entrée option as well as one or more "lighter," low fat options in other categories of foods on the menu.

Variety in Kind of Menu Items Served

Clientele boredom (environmental boredom) with the foods served is a significant problem for many noncommercial foodservice managers. Even if the foods served are the clientele's favorites, sooner or later there will be complaints about "always having the same old things," and customer usage of the foodservice will decline. Variety in the kind of menu items served is an important factor in reducing foodservice boredom and criticism of the foodservices. Such variety should be thoughtfully and realistically established to ensure that the menus planned reflect what the clientele wants to eat.

Some ways to enhance menu variety are to avoid the following:

1. Using an overabundance of so-called "starchy" foods
2. Repetition of a single food or flavor, such as cheese in many products or too much barbecue sauce on too many items
3. Serving the same menu items or flavors on consecutive days or meals
4. Serving the same menu item on the same day of the week
5. Serving foods prepared in the same way at the same meal, such as two creamed or two fried entrées
6. Serving a food the same way each time it is put on the menu if there are other popular ways to serve it

Further considerations important for variety today are the inclusion of vegetarian items and other choices perceived as being more healthful. Vegetarian foods, including a wide variety of entrées, are now quite popular. A part of the clientele served by almost all noncommercial food-services now prefers—or expects—a vegetarian option, either because of religious beliefs, concern with health, or an interest in foods with fewer calories. Many tasty recipes, that are readily available and easily prepared, can be used to incorporate vegetarian dishes into the menu.

When considering the clientele's interests in "healthful" foods, it should also be remembered that many persons today do not eat red meat or, at least, would prefer an option to red meat. As a result, the popularity of poultry, fish, and seafood entrées has increased markedly. Every menu should offer one or more non-red meat entrée options for the clientele.

Changing Cycle Regularity

"Boring," "repetitious," and "monotonous" are words that are often mentioned in conjunction with cycle menus. In addition to planning for variety in food items, texture, and color, some other factors must be considered to help improve cycle menu quality. One of the easy traps to fall into when developing this type of menu is putting it on a regular schedule. For example, if a three-week (21-day) cycle is planned, the same menu appears every third Monday or every third Thursday. It does not take long for the foodservice's clientele to become familiar with the cycle and make meal plans accordingly. If customers remember that a particular menu is coming up that they don't like, they will plan to bring their lunch from

Menu Item	Menu A	Weaknesses	Menu B	Strengths
Soups	Manhattan Clam Chowder Vegetable Beef	Consistency and color	Manhattan Clam Chowder Cream of Broccoli	Consistency (stock and cream base) and color
Entrées	Sliced Roast Beef Beef Stew over Noodles Pan Fried Calves' Liver	Color and are all beef	Sliced Roast Beef au jus Tuna/Macaroni en Casserole Chicken Fajitas	Variety (mix of beef, finfish, and poultry)
Vegetables	Whipped Potatoes Buttered Noodles Buttered Wax Beans Cream Corn	No color or texture variety	Whipped Potatoes Oven Browned Potatoes Buttered Green Beans Tex-Mex Corn Niblets	Texture and color variety
Daily Salad Special	Chef's Salad, Julienne	Meat item	Fresh Pineapple Half with Cut Fruit and Cottage Cheese	Nonmeat item
Side Salads	Three Bean Salad Potato Salad	Repeats vegetable; color	Mixed Greens Coleslaw	Texture and color
Daily Hot Sandwich	Sloppy Joe, Special Roll	Beef again	Western Omelette, Special Roll	Egg protein alternative
Desserts	Apple Pie Spice Cake Chocolate Brownies	All heavy, rich items; some flavor similarity in pie and cake	Apple Pie Vanilla Pudding Fruit Compote	Variety in texture and flavor; a light fruit dessert

TABLE 3. A COMPARISON OF GOOD AND POOR MENUS

home or go off-premises to eat that day—and a sale has been lost.

A simple way to avoid the clientele's memorizing a cycle is to make the rotation a little irregular. Instead of using twenty-one days on a cycle, you might use twenty or twenty-two days. Then the same daily menu will not repeat "every third Monday." Consequently, the clientele will have to come to the cafeteria or dining center to find out what is being offered on that day. Once customers are there, they are less likely to leave and eat elsewhere. St. Luke's Hospital in Bethlehem, Pennsylvania, recently reported that when they stopped using a predictable cycle menu, their participation rate in their foodservice rose nearly 20 percent, and their sales increased 35 percent.[3]

Foodservice managers sometimes feel that when the clientele knows what menu to expect, customers will all come when you are serving items they really like and will plan to eat elsewhere on days when items they do not like are served. While it is true that participation rates may be high on days when popular menu items are served, a high participation rate can still be achieved using an irregular cycle by doing a good job of marketing special days to the clientele.

Planning for variety in food items, texture, color, form, shape, and preparation methods; balancing light and heavy foods; and using an irregular cycle will be significant factors in bringing the foodservice's clientele back, day-in and day-out. These variables are easy to put into the menu cycle planning process when the foodservice manager is aware of the impact they have on the operation's success. Table 3 is an example of how the menu planner could see different meal course choices and make adjustments in variety to improve the menu quality.

Constraints in Menu Planning

When you begin to plan a cycle menu, there are several other factors, known *as menu constraints,* that must be taken into consideration. These constraints include (1) equipment available in the production facility; (2) the seasonal availability of food items; (3) the skill level of the production personnel; (4) the type of clientele to be served; and (5) the budgeted food cost allowance.

Equipment Available in the Production Facility

One of the basic mistakes menu planners often make is overloading both the production areas and the equipment needed to produce the menu items. To be effective, a menu planner must know the facility and the capacities of all major pieces of equipment when determining the combination of items for the menu. For example, planning roast beef, baked potatoes, and fresh apple pie on the same menu may produce disaster simply because they all require oven space, and there is only one convection oven to work with.

Timing and the combination of equipment also come into play. The planner must be able to predict production schedules and know when certain pieces of equipment can be available for certain items. For example, production personnel may need to slice luncheon meats for sandwiches early in the day so that the slicing machine will be available later to slice fresh baked ham to order during the meal service. An efficient planner will check the daily menu to avoid overscheduling one work area or certain pieces of equipment.

Availability of Food Items

In this age of fast, efficient transportation systems, most food items are available almost anywhere in the United States. With enough time *and money* to order an item, nearly any type of food desired by your clientele can be provided. However, high prices will be paid if fresh strawberries and cantaloupes are put on the menu in January in a foodservice in the Northeastern part of the United States. Also, the quality level may not be the same as what might be available in June or July. To maintain a cost-effective menu, items that are in season and are readily available should be planned.

Skill of Production Personnel

Creativity and imagination are usually strong points of a good menu planner. However, it is possible to become *too* creative and put items on the menu that are too difficult or too sophisticated for the production staff. Even with standard recipes, the staff may encounter items they cannot easily produce. They may simply be too inexperienced or too unfamiliar with the menu item. The menu planner and the production staff must understand each other's roles and abilities to ensure that the menu planned is the one produced. The menu planner must also know the strengths and weaknesses of the service staff. If a particular item is to be served in a special way, it is important to make sure that the service staff can do what is expected.

Clientele to be Served

Menu planners tend to put items on the menu that they like and are familiar with. They may ignore or forget what their clientele likes. To avoid such oversights, the following clientele demographics should be taken into consideration: (1) age; (2) gender; (3) income level; (4) ethnic background; and (5) geographical location (rural/urban; area of the United States). Even though clientele demographics are considered in the menu planning process, many foodservices regularly conduct food surveys to obtain clientele likes and dislikes. It never pays to *assume* that the menu planner knows the clientele's preferences.

Age. Children attending an elementary school may prefer different foods from college students. While both groups may like pizza, the elementary school children may prefer plain cheese pizza, while the college student may want a variety of toppings, such as a vegetarian pizza. Certainly the portion sizes and total number of foods on the menu will be different. Both groups probably have food preferences that differ from those of older persons in a retirement home. The older persons may prefer foods that are softer and more easily chewed or foods that they have been accustomed to eating throughout their lives.

Sex. You may offer heavier or lighter foods, depending on the male/female ratio. Traditionally, many females prefer lighter food items, such as vegetables, salads, or fruit, and they usually eat smaller portions than do their male counterparts, who may be more likely to eat a meat or poultry entrée with a starch accompaniment. However, this may not necessarily be true for some populations, such as elementary school children. At this age, both boys and girls are quite active and growing and have similar eating preferences.

Income Level. Insofar as income levels are indicative of the budget available for the foodservice's menus or of the type of dining out that the clientele is accustomed to, a menu planner may want to consider the ratio of expensive to less expensive items on the menu. An executive dining room menu with steak, roast prime rib carved at a dining room carving station, fresh seafood, and a choice of good wines would be an example of such consideration. However, budget constraints may prevent the service of tenderloin steaks in a college residence hall dining room, even though the student clientele there would appreciate them very much. On the other hand, residents of an upscale retirement community may have a "steak-level" budget but prefer meat loaf as a menu item because of their chewing limi-

tations and because it was a favorite food that they ate at home when they were young.

Ethnic Background. The ethnic background of the foodservice's clientele is an especially important consideration today. People appreciate foods with which they are familiar, and many of the clientele served may have special foods that they enjoy as a part of their cultural heritage. For example, rice should be a staple on a cycle menu for a foodservice with many Asian customers, or tortillas may be substituted for bread in the Southwest, where a foodservice may be serving people with a Mexican heritage.

Geographical Location. There are differences, in eating patterns and foods eaten, between rural and urban areas as well as between different areas of the United States. An effective menu planner will need to know not only what foods are eaten in these areas, but how preparation preferences differ. Greens steamed tender crisp without fat may do well on a college campus in highly urban Southern California, but unless they are boiled with bacon or salt pork, older people living in a rural Mississippi nursing home may not be at all complimentary about their food. The message here is that a menu planner must be sensitive to the wants and needs of the foodservice's clientele in order to plan high-quality cycle menus effectively. After all, the foodservice is there to please the clientele served.

Budgeted Food Cost Allowance

No matter what the other menu planning constraints may be, the cost of the menu must fall within the allowable food cost. A food item may be a favorite of the clientele; it may be made from readily available foods; and it can be prepared by the foodservice's personnel with the available equipment and facilities. However, if the cost of the product is too high, it is not an acceptable menu item. Many non-commercial foodservices have very limited food cost allowances for their meals. Such limitations are particularly true for correctional foodservices and school foodservices, which often rely on commodity food products as one means of staying within their budgeted food cost allowances. Menus for these foodservices must then include products made from the commodities, because those products are making their foodservices economically feasible. In other situations, a product may be feasible for a menu, but the form in which it is purchased (e.g., purchased frozen, prepared with the price including labor cost, or the components purchased and prepared on-site with labor cost incurred directly by the foodservice) has to be carefully evaluated in terms of the total menu cost.

Inclusion of Fads and Trends in Cycle Menus

Fads

The foodservice industry is ever-changing as people's tastes change. A major advantage that noncommercial foodservices using cycle menus have over commercial foodservices with set menus is the ability to incorporate new fads into their menus quickly and easily (and to drop them just as readily). Fads, which are relatively short-lived ideas, appear frequently in foodservice. "Short-lived" means "here today, gone tomorrow." Nouvelle Cuisine, which was very popular in the late 1980s, is an example of a fad that almost everyone was excited about at that time. However, now it is hardly a part of any foodservices at all. Recognizing and reflecting this rapid change helps keep new items in front of clientele served. To keep abreast of these fads, a menu planner needs to talk to purveyors, read current trade journals and other periodicals, and eat out often, to see what others are serving and what people are buying.

In deciding whether to present the latest fad food, a manager must consider whether the clientele will be willing to adapt to a totally new type of food. For example, college students may have accepted mesquite grilling or Tex-Mex foods much faster than residents of a retirement community did, when these items became fads.

When a fad has run its course, it can simply be eliminated from the cycle and replaced with a new item composed of comparable ingredients. How does one know when a fad has "died"? One rule of thumb that might be used is when the sales of the fad item fall below 10 percent of total sales, this fad has reached its saturation point. It is time to replace it.

Trends

Many people confuse "fads" with "trends." Trends are ideas that are new but that do not necessarily disappear as quickly as fads do. Current trends reflect people's interest in ethnic cuisines, such as Mexican, Italian, and Chinese foods, and in health and wellness. Such ethnic foods are holding their popularity well and show no signs of disappearing from today's foodservices. This ongoing desire for ethnic foods could be related to the wellness and healthy eating trend, since many ethnic foods use fresh ingredients that are low in fat and sodium and are light in texture. The trend toward healthy foods, once considered to be a fad that would soon pass, encourages menu planning that reduces fat, cholesterol, and sodium content; uses grilled rather than fried foods; and emphasizes fruits, vegetables, and grain products. While these are trends in food types, they are also indicative of today's service trends, such as the move toward self-serve and all-you-can-eat buffet service.

A current trend in the noncommercial foodservice market is *branding*. Branding, or the inclusion of brand name products or concepts into the menu or product mix, is now quite popular in all noncommercial foodservice segments. Examples of branding would be using items such as only Oscar Meyer wieners or Pepperidge Farm cookies on your menus or having an outlet for Pizza Hut pizzas in the foodservice facility.

Most national and some regional foodservice companies have developed and marketed their own "brands" that are comparable to popular quick-service food items. In some settings where the products have been well developed and effectively merchandised, these in-house brands have been quite successful for these management companies. The branded concepts have increased sales and helped develop customer loyalty to the foodservice. For example, ARA Services' Itza-Pizza has made ARA the third largest "pizza chain" in the United States. In other cases, however, these items have enjoyed only marginal success. Consequently, more foodservice organizations are now using nationally recognized brands, such as Pizza Hut, Dunkin' Donuts, and TCBY, in some way in their foodservices.

When branding is available, a menu planner will have to work even harder to ensure that the clientele served has a selection of food items. Just because a national brand with all its offerings is available on-premises should not deter the menu planner from planning a full, interesting menu.

The goal should be to keep variety in the foods served, and not let the clientele get "saturated" with burgers or pizzas.

Special Menu Planning Considerations

Some of the segments of the noncommercial foodservice sector have unique features that affect cycle menu planning for those foodservices.

Hospitals

Hospitals may develop two different but related cycle menus—one for their patients and one for the cafeteria—or they may use the same menu for both. One reason for having different menus is that the staff are "always there," necessitating a longer menu cycle to incorporate adequate variety into the cafeteria menu offerings. However, the average patient stay is now five days or less, so a patient menu cycle need be no longer than five days and could be less. Indeed, some hospitals have adopted "restaurant style," or set, menus for their patients, and they are offering other menu innovations, such as room service menus for patients on regular diets, because of this shortened average hospital stay.

Another reason for two separate menus is the need to prepare modified versions of the menu for all of the special diet options offered by the hospital. Menu modifications that may be required might include restrictions in sodium, fat,

sugar or other carbohydrates, protein, fiber, and residue, or combinations of these restrictions. In some cases the texture, or consistency, of the food products may need to be modified because of patients' chewing or swallowing difficulties. The range of menus required in a hospital can vary widely, depending on the types of patients the particular hospital serves.

Some food items, such as roast turkey or green beans, which contain little sodium or fat, are much more adaptable to menus requiring modifications than are items such as baked ham (cured in salt brine) or lima beans (high starch [carbohydrate] content, and cause of gas for many patients). While the registered dietitians on the foodservice staff will write the modified diet cycle menus, food production requirements are simplified if most of the food items used for the regular diets can be readily modified to meet the most frequently used diet restrictions.

Long-Term Care Facilities and Retirement Communities

These facilities, too, have diet modifications that must be considered in planning the cycle menu, although they are fewer in number and less restrictive. However, here the clientele consists of long-term residents, and the cycle must be long enough to reflect adequate variety. The clientele's physical abilities to handle, cut, and chew different foods and changes in their taste sensitivities are also considera-

tions when planning menus for these facilities. Just as for the hospital, the registered dietitian associated with the facility will plan the diet modifications for the cycle menu.

Elementary and Secondary Schools

If a school participates in the National School Lunch Program menus must be planned to meet the required "Type A" lunch pattern. The Type A pattern specifies the types of foods and the serving sizes that are required for the menus, but many food items can be used to meet those requirements. These food pattern and service size requirements are quite specific, and managers will need to be familiar with them when planning school foodservice menus. However, even though the Type A pattern is used as the basis of the menu planning, all the requirements for menu quality, such as variety in texture and color or compatible flavors, must still be considered if the menus are to be well planned.

Schools receiving federal funds for their meal programs also qualify for commodity foods: surplus foods provided to nonprofit meal programs, such as the National School Lunch Program, by the federal government as a part of the U.S. farm price support program. When a school receives such foods or food products prepared from commodity foods, it is often a challenge to incorporate those foods into the menu cycle in a way that will both meet the Type A requirements and offer the children food items that they like. If a school does not participate in the National School Lunch Program, then a manager may plan any type of menus that the children (or teenagers) are likely to accept.

When planning school menus, it is important to remember that children today are enthusiastic patrons of quick-service restaurants and are often quite knowledgeable about foods and sophisticated in their food choices. They need menu variety, choices of healthy and fresh foods, and food that is attractively served. Through efficient menu planning, such menus can be prepared without excessive budget overruns—whether or not the school's foodservices participate in the National School Lunch Program.

Colleges and Universities

College students are a very critical clientele with ready access to many food options. Students of the 1990s are well traveled and rather sophisticated. Thus, offering foods from different parts of the world is no longer something that should be ignored on college campuses.

Planning menus for dormitory residents is particularly challenging, as these students may be paying for three meals per day at the same dining room and comparing the food served with "Mom's home cooking." A wide range of items is needed daily, and the cycle must be long enough to prevent boredom with the food choices.

Business and Industry

The B&I segment is a very competitive market where the foodservice manager must constantly be aware of keeping the participation rates high. The economic climate of the 1990s is making menu planning even more difficult, as the manager faces the "brown bag" competition of meals brought from home as well as the competition from off-premise commercial restaurants for employee dining. These foodservices must offer a wide range of options incorporating a variety of foods that are attractively served and represent current trends and the latest fads in regional and national tastes.

Correctional Foodservices

The overwhelming challenge here is to plan menus that will meet the nutritional standards that have now been, or are being, established by most states for prison inmates-within the budget limitations mandated. Commodity foods are also sometimes available and must be incorporated into the cycle menu when they are provided. Since correctional facilities serve three meals per day to a clientele that is often there for long periods of time, the menus must have sufficient variety and food quality to keep inmates satisfied with the foodservice. A challenge now facing some prisons with aging populations is the need to prepare modified diets similar to those served in health care facilities to meet the medical and physical needs of these aging inmates.

Leisure Facilities

Stadiums and arenas are also participating in the "up-to-date" menu planning trend. They are responding to clientele demands and no longer offer the fan or spectator just a hot dog and a beer. Menus today feature gourmet dogs; grilled chicken; choices of imported beers; the popular finger foods of today such as nachos, fried vegetables, Oriental foods, or individual pizzas; or local favorites such as the Philly cheese steaks served in the Veterans Stadium in Philadelphia.

Inflight Services

Facing some of the most challenging restrictions of all, menus for inflight foods must consider the relatively sophisticated tastes of most airline passengers and the demands for special meals that are becoming increasingly prevalent. Special meals are particularly popular among businesspeople who are frequent flyers, eat many inflight meals, and are often faced with cardiac problems, high cholesterol, or excessive weight. At the same time, foods served must withstand an extended holding and transport period, and hot food products must be in a form that will rethermalize well on board the aircraft. Finally, the food products used must fit into the space allocated for meal storage on the plane. Menu planning here is a very "scientific" process, and most major airlines have people on their staffs who specialize in planning the menus used on their flights.

Truth-In-Menu Guidelines

Foodservices today are legally required to be "truthful" in their menus. Truth-in-menu guidelines have been established to ensure that menus accurately describe the food being served. These guidelines require the food product served to actually be what is listed in the name of the product or in the product description. For example, a menu cannot offer "fresh Maine lobster" when what is being served is frozen Australian lobster tails. A dressing cannot be described as "bleu cheese" if it does not really have bleu cheese in it but is made from other cheeses similar in flavor. Menu planners need to be careful with the descriptive terms used to identify the planned menu items. What is listed *must* be what is served.

Food Presentation

Most noncommercial foodservices serve at least some of their food from steam tables as part of a cafeteria line. Even though color, variety, and texture are effectively incorporated into the menu, the cafeteria service areas or the client trays may still end up offering food that the clientele perceives as dull, boring, or monotonous. It is very important to make the food look attractive while it is being held on the steam table. There are

several ways to enhance the presentation of this food. The following suggestions are some ideas that might be used in a noncommercial foodservice.

Keep Colored Foods Apart

For example, if there are three hot entrées, and two are brown and one is red, the red one should be placed between the two brown ones. Or the stewed tomatoes (red) should be kept away from the Manhattan clam chowder (red).

Garnish the Serving Area

Garnish the steam table and serving shelf with foods and other items to help make the food look attractive. An easy way to give color and eye appeal is to use fresh fruits and vegetables around and between the steam table pans. When the serving day is finished, these fruits and vegetables need not be thrown away but can be very successfully used in the soups and stews of the next day's production. Not only can steam tables be garnished in this way, but salad bars, deli counters, and dessert counters can also use a variety of food items relating to those specific serving areas as garnishes.

Garnish the Food

Garnishing each food product will help make the food look attractive, appetizing and of high quality. This effect can be accomplished by something as simple as shaking paprika (red) on broiled fish (white); by adding some pars-

ley florets (green) beside the fish pieces; and finally placing lemon wheels (yellow) on the fish fillets. Now you have taken a pan of bland, white broiled fish and turned it into something few would pass by without purchasing.

Simple garnishing of all foods should be done and can be done without significantly increasing the food cost percentage. Creamy rice pudding can be made very appetizing with a sprinkle of cinnamon (brown) on top, accompanied by a maraschino cherry (red). An otherwise bland bowl of pasta salad can be highlighted through the use of leafy vegetables around the outer edges and a few well placed tomato wedges.

It is easy to fall into the trap of being boring with garnishes and the use of different foods. Kale, as a leafy vegetable garnish, is great, but after six months of being used in the "same old way," it loses its appeal. There are a variety of foods and other items that can be used. For example, whole fresh fruits and vegetables make the serving line very attractive, and these foods can also be used as display garnishes. It is up to the foodservice manager to see that varied products that can be used for garnishes are always available; that foodservice personnel keep changing garnishes; and that they are creatively working to make the food presentation exciting. Much of the clientele consists of impulse buyers. If the food looks good, there is a much greater chance that they will buy. The only limitations to the presentation possible are the imagination of all the foodservice's staff and their enthusiasm in applying that imagination to their work.

Arrange Foods Neatly

It would be an oversight not to mention the arrangement of foods on the shelves and display areas. For example, many managers will let the dessert items, such as pies and wedge-shaped cake portions, be placed on the shelves "any old way." To keep the foods looking fresh and appetizing, all the points, or the front of the pies and cakes, should be facing the clientele. It is a very small detail, but quality foodservices attractive to your clientele are built on such things. A neat arrangement of foods sends a very direct, positive message to the patrons: "Buy me."

Avoid Wrap

Do not cover and hide food items in plastic food wrap, which sends a message of "nonfresh" or "prepackaged" and "stale" to your clientele. Indeed, one of the largest convention centers in the United States no longer serves any prepackaged sandwiches, for this very reason. Customer satisfaction is much higher, and this satisfaction is reflected in increased sales, when sandwiches are made to order at

deli counters. Even if food products cannot be made to order, foods should be of sufficient quality and freshness that 30 to 60 minutes of exposure to the "elements" will not noticeably reduce their quality. The matter of perception is a strong influence here. A very large grocery store operator used to wrap and cover the fresh fish and then put them in the display area. One day a customer told the operator that he did not buy the store's fish because it didn't "look" fresh. The next day the fresh fish was displayed directly on shaved ice, not wrapped. Fish sales increased fourfold overnight!

Position Desserts First

Offer the desserts as close to the entrance as possible. Desserts are one the food items most persons can "live without." If a guest already has an entrée, some soup, and maybe a beverage, it is easy to walk past the dessert counter without choosing one. It is much harder for the guest to walk past that same dessert counter with an empty tray when the guest is just starting to "eat with the eyes." It's an old trick that still merits use.

Summary

More than ever before, today's clientele is expecting

noncommercial foodservices to serve quality food attractively at a reasonable price. It is up to the foodservice manager and the menu planner to see that these expectations are met. Where the menu planning is done effectively, happy, satisfied clientele will be found. Where it is poorly done, clientele will be disinterested, participation rates will be low, food complaints will be common, and eventual changes will be made. Today's clienteles are too impatient and too demanding to wait long for good variety and high-quality food. It's up to the menu planner to develop cycle menus that will enable the foodservice to meet all expectations and to the foodservice manager to see that these menus are attractively served as planned.

References

1. Grace Shugart and Mary Molt, *Food for Fifty* (9th ed.) (New York: Macmillan, 1989).
2. Margaret E. Terrell and Dorthea B. Headlund, *Large Quantity Recipes* (4th ed.) (New York: Van Nostrand Reinhold, 1989).
3. "Hospital Stops 'Recycling' Its Menus," *Food Management,* 27(10)(1992):88.

SELF-OPERATING FOODSERVICE VERSUS CONTRACT MANAGEMENT

Guy E. Karrick

EXTERNAL GOVERNMENTAL pressure and internal fiscal constraints have forced more and more corporations to reduce the operating subsidy of their foodservice operations and to take a closer look at the bottom line. Corporate cafeterias are not only becoming break-even operations, but many are even expected to show a yearly profit.

As a result, the movement within the industry has been toward hiring foodservice management companies to operate corporate foodservice operations. Most companies are not in the foodservice business, but are in the business of producing something else. Ford Motor Company, for example, is in the automobile industry, not in the foodservice business. That is why corporations ask themselves, "Why do we have to make a commitment to foodservice? Why don't we put the burden on someone else by hiring a foodservice contractor?"

Where does this type of reasoning leave the self-operators? Are companies that contract out not as committed to foodservice? Are self-operators truly becoming a dying breed? This chapter examines the answers to these questions by providing insights of many prominent B&I foodservice managers.

Advantages and Benefits of Self-Operating Foodservice

Although self-ops are becoming few and far between, there will always be a niche for them in the industry. Even though foodservice contractors offer a high level of professional expertise, many corporations who have made a strong commitment to operating their own foodservice in the past will continue to do so. Depending on the corporation, self-ops have the resources and capabilities to do as good a job—and in some cases even better—than a contractor. For instance, "I am

basically providing a level of service and quality of food that would be hard to match by a contractor," says Richard McQueen, manager of foodservices for Bausch & Lomb in Rochester, New York. "We are also meeting all the financial goals with our foodservice." According to Tom Ney, director of the food center at Rodale Press, "We have a very strong corporate philosophy at Rodale where we practice what we publish and translate it into practical sense. Quite frankly, it would be difficult for a contractor to meet the stringent nutritional requirements and aesthetics of our foodservice operation."

Greater control is among the main benefits experienced by corporations that decide to operate their own foodservice. Policy changes and other alterations can be implemented quickly, whereas a contractor may typically need to cut through a myriad of bureaucratic levels to institute changes.

From DINING IN CORPORATE AMERICA: HANDBOOK OF NONCOMMERCIAL FOODSERVICE MANAGEMENT by Joan B. Bakos and Guy E. Karrick. Copyright 1989 by Aspen Publishers, Inc. Reprinted by permission.

"There is generally more red tape to cut through when instigating policy and procedure decisions with a contractor, that I could otherwise make instantly," states Dolores Juergens, manager of foodservices at Northwestern Mutual Life Insurance Company. "In most situations, a liaison must negotiate for certain provisions to which my company has already made a strong commitment."

Craig Smith, manager of food services at Steelcase, Inc. concurs, saying, "Having total control and direct access to the people who are doing the job are the biggest advantages of operating your own foodservice. It's very easy to lose control of your operations when someone else runs your foodservice. You tend to be much more involved when you operate your own foodservice—you have to be," adds Craig.

Foodservice employees working with a self-op environment tend to exhibit more dedication and loyalty toward corporate goals. They are providing foodservice to their fellow employees. They experience none of the conflict engendered by working for one company while being paid by another. Bill Lembach, foodservice director at Eastman Kodak, explains,

By operating our own foodservice, we have a better understanding of the company we work for and show allegiance toward that company. People who actually work for us have allegiance to the company as well. They are company employees.

Gary Gunderson, regional manager in Austin, Texas, for Motorola, Inc., adds, "Our foodservice employees provide personalized service and have a more vested interest in serving their fellow employees."

Another advantage of self-op foodservice is having only one central authority. The contractor must always take direction from its own company procedures, as well as from the client. And, on some occasions, these directions can conflict.

Why Contract Management Companies Succeed

The chief asset of most professional contract caterers is their ability to manage the foodservice at a lower operating cost than a self-operator. Corporations operating their own foodservice must generally pay higher wages and offer benefits comparable with other corporate employees. Contractors are not required to pay these corporate benefits; therefore, they are in a position to present a better financial package to prospective clients.

To complement their own professional foodservice expertise, contractors are able to call on a strong back-up management staff at their company headquarters. According to Martin Cherneff, president of M.H. Cherneff & Associates, "Contractors provide good management depth and solid back-up support for each unit manager. Generally, self-ops have little support or any-

one to turn to. Through the sharing of knowledge, however, professional associations such as SFM can provide self-ops with a viable resource base."

Does the buying power of some of the national contractors give them an advantage over self-ops? Not according to Marty Cherneff. "It doesn't affect the bottom line that much to have the purchasing power of a major corporation versus the astute purchasing ability of a strong foodservice operator."

Michael Barclay, vice president of Southern Foodservice Management, describes the advantages of contractors in this way.

In general, contractors offer the professional expertise of a foodservice management company and in some cases, the ability to purchase on a national scale. However, the single greatest advantage in hiring a professional management company to operate the foodservice is lower labor costs.

Governmental Pressure—Uncle Sam Intervenes

In December 1985, the IRS issued new temporary regulations of the 1984 Tax Reform Act regarding meals provided in subsidized company cafeterias. In 1987, the IRS issued regulations allowing only 80% of all business meals as deductible. Although commercial restaurants have been affected by this legislation, many non-commercial foodservice operators have reported an increase in their in-house corporate dining rooms.

What effect have these two bills and other governmental regulations had on the industry? Although no one can accurately predict the full impact of the new tax bill, companies are encountering increased pressure from the government to operate their foodservice in a profit/loss arrangement, reducing and sometimes even eliminating their subsidy. This competitive environment favors contractors because lower labor costs put them in a better position to reduce the operating subsidy.

If a self-op foodservice can continue to satisfy corporate objectives and meet all financial goals, it will remain self-op. However, if a professional contractor can operate the foodservice more economically, then the trend will continue toward hiring management companies.

Richard McQueen elaborates,

Unless contractors inherit a problem with the IRS, they will continue to grow and consolidate at even greater rates. The efficiency in their sheer numbers in areas, such as test kitchens, centralized menus, and major purchasing programs, will allow them to hold their end up because they can keep the cost down. However, this becomes a labor issue and not a food issue. Foodservice is based on providing quality food and good service, but is not a financial issue. In short, the new tax law means we're all in the same boat to break even.

The new 80/20 bill has provided keen foodservice managers with a tremendous opportunity to promote their own in-house guest or executive dining rooms. By saving an additional 20 percent deductibility, business executives have a financial incentive to entertain in-house, not to mention the time-saving advantages.

Mergers and Acquisitions by National Contractors

What effects have the recent mergers and acquisitions by some of the national contractors had on the industry? Do these rounds of consolidations and mergers signify the end of self-op foodservice?

Although mergers and acquisitions have certainly made contractors more visible, they should not have a dramatic impact on corporations who desire to continue with self-operation. "Mergers and acquisitions have mainly resulted in the development of strong regional management companies," says Marty Cherneff. "But the mergers in no way represent the last vestiges of self-operated foodservice."

Large companies are frequently viewed as being impersonal and unresponsive. The foodservice industry is a very personal business; therefore, responding to the client's individual needs is one of the keys to success. The industry will continue to see the emergence of smaller regional contractors and clients looking for personalized foodservice.

Most large contractors also tend to move their employees around often, resulting in a high turnover of top management. Because management personnel differ in operating philosophy and ability, these moves can potentially affect the client adversely.

Other potential problems can surface in the relationship between the foodservice contractor and the company liaison manager. In many situations, the liaison has come out of personnel, human resources, or even the comptroller's office and has no foodservice experience. "In the end, the smaller regional contractors will prosper and eventually come into their own. Regional contractors have the ability to provide their clients with outstanding, personalized service," says Beryl Yuhas, president of Beryl Yuhas Associates.

How Will Self-Ops Remain Competitive?

In order to survive in an increasingly competitive marketplace, self-ops must continue to offer creative foodservice. Foodservice managers in most self-op situations have a free hand to be creative and make on-the-spot decisions. By taking full advantage of their resources and facilities, self-ops will continue to succeed. Larry Appleton, manager of food and vending operations at Martin Marietta, notes,

Although there have been some challenges set by foodservice contractors, we have become more creative and very competitive in nature. We shouldn't just throw up our arms and say, "Leave it to the foodservice contractor." The self-ops that will be successful will be the ones who are creative, daring and audacious.

Self-ops must turn to other markets, such as carry-out and breakfast programs, to generate additional revenue from their foodservice operations. Such programs as one-stop, take-out dinners for the entire family are a great source of untapped income.

Marketing and merchandising techniques can be used by foodservice managers to increase sales. The bottom line in foodservice is still variety, service, and quality. Those companies that can excel in these areas—going the extra mile and treating their customers like royalty—will succeed. Dolores Juergens of Northwestern Mutual says,

> Everyone in the industry is not solely dependent upon the bottom line. Sometimes service and quality as well as other intangibles overshadow the bottom line; companies develop a strong pride of ownership philosophy. Northwestern Mutual has been self-op since 1915 and we see no reason to change now.

Another area of concern is the number of qualified foodservice managers in the B&I segment of the foodservice industry. Is there a shortage of quality management personnel? According to Craig Smith, there is no shortage.

I am not finding a shortage of good management personnel in the Midwest. A lot of people are looking for jobs in B&I foodservice. For some managers, it's more desirable to work in a self-op environment where you have a greater amount of control. There also tends to be less corporate rules and guidelines to follow, resulting in a greater opportunity to be more creative.

However, Deanna Hormel, director of foodservice at Hallmark Cards, disagrees. "Most foodservice managers are trained for hospitals, hotels, and restaurants. It is vital to contact students and make them aware of opportunities in B&I food service."

Outlook—Where Does This Leave Self-Op Foodservice?

In these turbulent times of increasing governmental regulation and decreasing company subsidies, the trend toward hiring professional contractors will continue. "We will continue to see a trend to hiring contractors, but eventually it will end with those corporations who have made a strong commitment to foodservice and feel it is a vital part of the company remaining self-op," says Craig Smith. Michael Barclay concurs, saying, "The industry as a whole will continue to favor contractors. However, those companies who have professionally trained individuals to manage the foodservice and have made a strong commit-

ment to quality will remain self-op."

Bill Lembach agrees.

More companies will take the easy way out to reduce payroll and labor costs by hiring a contractor to operate the foodservice. Self-ops who want to survive, however, know we must meet our competition head on and Kodak is willing to do that. We're willing to show that we can compete effectively and do a better job than a contractor.

Overall, the B&I segment continues to grow at the real growth rate of 1.3 percent. Although mergers among some of the industry's biggest companies have eliminated some of the players, sales and customer counts are expected to increase.

When deciding whether to operate their own food service or hire a professional contractor, corporations must determine the type of commitment they are willing to make to foodservice. Contractors and self-ops both have the skills and resources to provide quality foodservice, but each one has distinct advantages. Contractors offer lower labor costs; self-op arrangements allow total control of the foodservice operations.

"I am still scratching and clawing at my little corner of the world," says Richard McQueen. "I'm independent and have a free hand to do just about anything that I want. And I'm having fun doing it."

The image and perception of noncommercial institutional foodservice held by many people is that the food is of low quality, usually served cold, and the problems are sustained by boring, monotonous menus. It is the menu which can be the key to successful foodservice operations; keeping customers coming back, keeping the client liaison happy and satisfied, keeping the Director of Food Services challenged, and the foodservice employees motivated and interested—not preparing and serving the same food items day-in, day-out.

In these types of facilities, hospitals, schools (K-12), colleges/universities, and business & industry, the menus are often on a prearranged cycle of 3 or 4 weeks duration. This cycle then perpetuates the negative perceptions of low quality, boring/monotonous, etc.

Until recently, many contract foodservice companies and foodservice directors thought the people (customers) who ate in these cafeterias or dining centers were captive, and had to eat there. These companies and managers are learning very quickly there are no captive customers. Consequently, there has been lots of work and upgrading of menus and food concepts to keep customers coming to the foodservice operation. Not only coming but returning day after day.

With this background information, the project is to find a suitable foodservice facility. Upon finding this facility, do the following activities:

1. Find a history of the company's growth, and consequently a history of on-premise foodservice facilities. Is the foodservice self-op or contracted?

2. Do the statistics and demographics of the facility. Number of client employees, number of meals served, various points of service (catering, private dining rooms, small bars, carts, etc.).

3. Do a menu analysis. Is the menu on a cycle? How often is it changed or up-graded? How often are special days or "monotony breakers" offered in the facility? Evaluate the color, variety, texture of the menu. Make suggestions to improve the menu.

4. Interview the Director of Foodservices. Look for enthusiasm and interest in doing their job. Find participation rate figures. What is being done to increase either participation rate or sales dollars, or both?

In recent years, the Business and Industry segment of the noncommercial foodservice industry has gone through some dramatic changes, especially the lowering of subsidies. Traditionally many companies subsidized the food service operation, in some cases 100% of expenses covered. In the 1990s, many companies are downsizing, re-engineering, laying-off employees, selling un-profitable divisions, etc. leaving the foodservice manager scrambling to cover costs and continue quality foodservice. It has not been an easy environment in which to work. Besides the corporate changes, increasing competition from outside, restaurants up and down the street, "brown bag-gies" bringing food to work, all are working against the foodservice manager. Consequently these jobs are much tougher then they used to be.

Select a Business and Industry foodservice facility and find out the following information:

A. History of the company and facility:
   ➤ when building was constructed
   ➤ growth of building population
   ➤ original or early foodservice objective, i.e. provide quality food, location was far from con-venient to go out for lunch, etc.
   ➤ contracted or self-operated

B. Find recent developments, changes in foodservice:
   ➤ changes in building design or construction
   ➤ declines in building population
   ➤ change from self-op to contractor or vice versa

C. Interview foodservice director:
   ➤ what financial objectives have occurred in past 5 years?
   ➤ what is being done to increase sales?
   ➤ what is being done to control costs?
   ➤ what support does client and/or contract company give director?

D. Interview corporate client liaison:
   ➤ what changes are expected in corporation which will affect foodservices?
   ➤ what will corporation do to ease the pain, if any?

11

HOTEL OPERATIONS

The Revolution in Domestic Hotel Management Contracts
James J. Eyster

**How to Select A Franchise (Steps 1–4, The
  Franchisor-Franchisee Relationship: Stronger
  Partnership . . . Greater Growth)**
*W. Peter Temling, David E. Arnold, Robert M. James and Theodore R.
Mandigo and Dr. Atid Kaplan*

Project 1

Project 2

THE REVOLUTION IN DOMESTIC HOTEL MANAGEMENT CONTRACTS

James J. Eyster

*The changing economic environment of the hotel industry has altered the
traditional relationship of management company and owner. The results
of those changes in relative bargaining strength are reflected in the provisions of contemporary American management contracts*

THE MANAGEMENT
contract has been a cornerstone of the hotel industry's
rapid development of the past
20 years. From its inception,
the concept of separating ownership from operation provided the opportunity for
much-needed capital to fund
the demand for new construction in the domestic and world
markets during the 1970s and
1980s, while creating a vehicle for hotel-management companies to expand their networks and market shares.

Contracts negotiated during
this period of rapid expansion
specifically delineated operator rights and responsibilities
as separate from those of the
owner, providing the operator
the freedom to operate the hotel without interference or significant input from the owner.
The hotel owner and the
lender were passive parties to
the deal.

The financial and operating
projections for these arrangements supported this concept.
This was a period of almost
unbroken economic expansion
with all market segments experiencing unparalleled growth,
both domestically and abroad.
Above-average inflation rates
boosted operating revenues,
cash flows, and property appreciation. Funds to develop
hotels became readily available from both traditional and
non-traditional sources to the
point where money was chasing deals. The belief that this
economic expansion would
continue with only minor fluctuations was prevalent among
all players.

As long as operating results
were strong, the division of
duties and responsibilities
worked, for the most part, to
everyone's benefit. Operators
received healthy management
fees, owners enjoyed positive
cash flows and capital appre-

ciation, and lenders received
above-average fixed and participating interest revenues.

The downside risk, which
was primarily the owner's and
secondarily the lender's, and
the *carte blanche* rights of the
operator were given only cursory attention at first. But, beginning in the mid-1980s, the
relative bargaining power began to shift from heavily favoring the operator to slightly
favoring the owner due to intensified competition among
operators and to increased
owner and lender experience
with hotel management contracts. When the hotel and real
estate industries crashed in
the early 1990s, hotel operating results and cash flows
drastically decreased, owners
and lenders became active in
the monitoring of their properties, and expansion opportunities for operators vanished.
Owner bargaining strength
and owners' and lenders' in-

volvement in operations increased significantly, thus changing radically the way owners, operators, and lenders do business with management contracts.

This article highlights the changes that are occurring in management contracts in the United States and is a supplement to the 1988 basic text on hotel management contracts, *The Negotiation and Administration of Hotel and Restaurant Management Contracts,* which describes more fully contract provisions, changes in those provisions that were underway in 1988, variations within the key provisions, and the major issues that occur for owners, operators, and lenders during the term of the contract. The article concludes with a discussion on the issue of renegotiating existing management contracts.

Shifts in Contract Provisions

Significant shifts have occurred in the following ten major management-contract provisions in the United States: (1) operator loan and equity contributions; (2) initial term and renewals; (3) management-fee structures; (4) operator system-reimbursement expenses; (5) operator performance standards; (6) owner input in operational decision making to include policies, budgeting, and personnel, (7) financial and operational reporting; (8) contract termination at owner's option, on sale, and on foreclosure; (9) restrictive (noncompetition) covenants; and (10)

dispute-settlement mechanisms.

These shifts and the negotiated outcomes are the result of the primary objectives as well as the relative bargaining strength of each of the three parties that have a vested interest in the contract—owner, operator, and lender. These objectives, which often coincide but sometimes conflict, are outlined in Exhibit 1. The most significant change in the negotiating process in the past several years is that lenders have become active players in an effort to protect their objectives, investments, and flexibility.

A. Operator Loan and Equity Contributions

Operator loan and equity contributions have long been a source of negotiation. With heightened competition among operators, loan and equity contributions have increased in recently negotiated contracts. In 1988, chain operators made loans in about 25 percent of their managed properties, and by 1992, that number increased to about 42 percent. During the same period, independent operators (management companies that do not have their own national brand name and reservations system) increased their loan levels from approximately 21 percent to 28 percent.

These loans are subordinate to the property's mortgages, are usually interest-bearing (6- to 8-percent fixed rate), and often nonamortizing. They are usually for an agreed-upon amount lent to the owner at the time the management contract took effect but sometimes are contingency loans with capped amounts to be used only if specified operating cash-flow projections are not obtained.

Equity contributions also increased during the past four years for chain operators, from approximately 28 percent in 1988 to 34 percent in 1992, and for independent operators, from approximately 17 percent in 1988 to 19 percent in 1992. In some cases, operators were able to negotiate a partial or full first-take-out position.

These increases can be attributed to increased competition among operators, greater demands by owners and lenders for operator exposure, and a shrinking of debt financing available, as well as the awareness that operators must become equity partners to obtain a more secure position in the property. Operators that thought themselves secure in previously negotiated long-term contracts found themselves vulnerable to the unilateral termination of their contracts by owners who argued that the contracts, as agency agreements, could be terminated at any time (with the stipulation that the owner is liable to pay negotiated or court-determined damages). To secure a "property interest" in the hotel that would strengthen their position should the owner wish to terminate unilaterally, operators were often willing to make a moderate equity investment in the form of cash or a combination of cash and a contribution of management fees. At pre-

EXHIBIT 2. INITIAL CONTRACT TERMS AND RENEWAL PERIODS			
	Low	Median	High
Chain Operator (with no equity)			
Initial term (years)	5	10	20
Number of renewals	1	2	5
Length of each renewal (years)	3	5	10
Chain Operator (with equity)			
Initial term (years)	10	15	30
Number of renewals	2	3	5
Length of each renewal (years)	5	6	10
Independent Operator			
Initial term (years)	1	3	10
Number of renewals	0	2	3
Length of each renewal (years)	1	2	3
Caretaker Operator			
Initial term (months)	1	3	12
Renewals	1	1	1
Length of renewals (months)	1	2	12

sent, only well-capitalized chain operators can make contributions of any significance. Most independent operators are financially unable to make any contribution.

Owners and lenders have divided opinions as to the advantage of obtaining operator equity contributions. Some believe that the contribution is a benefit because it ties the operator more closely to the project's financial risk, while others believe the contribution is a disadvantageous encumbrance in the event that they might wish to terminate the contract.

Operator loan or equity contributions are seldom included in management contracts with owners-in-foreclosure (lend-

ers who own properties), since operators in these cases are managing the properties on a short-term, caretaker basis until the lender can sell the hotel.

B. Initial Term and Renewals

During the past four years, negotiated lengths of initial contract terms, number of renewals, and lengths of renewal have decreased for both chain and independent operators as the result of increased owner bargaining power. Exhibit 2 summarizes the general tendencies for chain operators, for independent operators, and for operators, primarily independents, that manage properties as caretakers for owners-in-foreclosure. Initial terms for chain operators now commonly run from eight to twelve years, with one or two five-year renewals. Those renewals are often tied to agreed-upon performance levels. For independent operators, initial terms often run from one to three years with possibly one or two two-year renewals. For operators managing for owners-in-foreclosure, contracts usually run on a month-by-month basis with the guarantee that the owner will pay the operator at least one year's basic fee if the contract is terminated short of one year.

Shorter terms, fewer renewal periods, and shorter renewal periods—as compared with past practice—create flexibility for owners but increase uncertainty for operators. With shorter contracts, it is less costly for the owner to remove the operator if the owner wishes to sell the property unencumbered by the contract or to reposition the property in the market using another operator since negotiated operator-termination fees are based upon the remaining term of the contract. Owners also believe that shorter terms increase the operator's sense of urgency to perform well to be renewed. They believe that operators are often more sensitive to owner concerns and communicate more closely with owners if the terms of the contract are shorter than in the past.

On the other hand, operators argue that shorter terms, especially those for independent operators, are detri-

mental to the property and to their own position at the property since it is risky and costly for quality operators to invest the necessary time and energy in improving the hotel's long-term profitability if there is no assurance that they will be able to reap the benefits of their efforts. For an operator, that uncertainty often works against any effort to develop, offer, and expand consistent indepth quality service to the properties being managed. Many operators state that they now must spend more time trying to find replacement properties and less time overseeing their existing contracts, to the detriment of the properties they manage.

The shorter terms and renewals for chain operators, usually up to 15 years, are still long enough to develop a sustained market presence and to generate an adequate return on their investments and management efforts.

C. Management-Fee Structures

Increased owner bargaining power, increased competition among operators, and increased activity lenders in contract negotiations have had a substantial impact on recently negotiated management-fee structures, as summarized in Exhibit 3.

For chain operators, basic management fees have in general decreased from a range of 3 to 4.5 percent of gross revenues to 2 to 3 percent of gross revenues, with fee percentages being smaller for large-volume properties and larger for small-volume properties. For

independent operators, basic management fees have generally decreased from a range of 2.5 to 3 percent of gross revenues to 1.5 to 2.5 percent of gross revenues.

For start-up properties, a basic fee of 3 percent is sometimes graduated, with the first one or two years of operation charged at 2 percent, the next two years at 2.5 percent, the next two years at 3 percent, and the remaining years of the contract at 3.5 percent. Such a graduated formula can be tailored to the individual property's specific operating cash flows to pay basic fees in accordance with the operation's ability to pay the fees. A second trend is to negotiate a deferral or a portion of the basic fee, say, 1 percent of a 3-percent fee, which would be paid once operating cash flow achieves an agreed-upon level. This deferred amount occasionally earns interest. In the event of a sale or refinancing of the property, any existing deferral amount is paid from the proceeds.

Incentive-fee bases, which began in the late 1980s to shift from the gross-operating-profit line to a cash-flow-after-debt-service line or some other negotiated net-profit line, continue to move in that direction. In almost every case today, with the exception of properties managed for owners-in-foreclosure, incentive fees are based on either cash flow after debt service or on a negotiated amount that serves the same basic purpose. In the few cases where gross operating profit or adjusted gross operating profit is used

Chain Operator:	Independent Operator:	Caretaker Operator:
■ 1.5–3% GR plus 8–10% GOP,*	■ 2–4% GR,	■ 1.5–3% GR,
■ 2–3.5% GR plus 8–20% AGOP,*	■ 8–15% GOP,	■ 8–12% GOP,
■ 2–3.5% GR Plus 15–28% CFADS,	■ Fixed monthly amount: $8,000–$15,000,	■ Fixed monthly amount: $5,000–$8,000,
■ 2–3% GR Plus 18–30% CFADSROE, or	■ Fixed monthly amount ($4,000–$8,000) plus 5–8% GOP,*	■ 1.5–2% GR Plus 10–25% IGOP, or
■ 3% GR or 10% GOP whichever is greater, plus 15–30% CFADS.	■ 1.5–2.5 GR+ 5–6% GOP,*	■ Fixed monthly amount ($3,000–$6,000) plus 10–30% IGOP.
	■ 1.5–3% GR+10–20% CFADS,* or	
	■ 2–2.5% GR + 10% AVP.*	

Abbreviations:

GR: Gross revenues

GOP: Gross operating profit (income before fixed charges)

AGOP: Adjusted gross operating profit

CFADS: Cash flow after debt service

CFADSROE: Cash flow after debt service and return on equity

AVP: Appreciated value of property

IGOP: Improvement in gross operating profit

*Deferred to a portion or all of debt service

as the basis for the incentive fee, the payout of the fee is usually tiered from available cash-flow funds. For instance, if an incentive fee of 10 percent of gross operating profit is negotiated, an amount of up to 5 percent would be paid from cash flow available after 50 percent of the debt service is paid, and the remaining 5 percent would be paid from cash flow after the other 50 percent of the debt service is paid. Amounts of the 10-percent incentive fee unpaid in any given year are usually waived but can sometimes be deferred with or without interest.

Operators managing properties for owners-in-foreclosure usually negotiate a basic fee of a fixed amount—the amount depending on the size of the property, or on a percentage of gross revenue, usually 1.5 to 2.5 percent, plus an incentive fee based on the amount the gross operating profit improves after the operator assumes management. For instance, the operator could receive a basic fee of 2 percent of gross revenues plus 15 to 30 percent of the amount by which the gross operating profit improves. The purpose of such an arrangement is to create an incentive for the operator to increase operating profits rapidly, thus increasing the potential sale price of the property.

Both chain and independent operators have been squeezed by decreasing fee revenues, due to lower revenue and profit levels in their older contracts and to the lower fee structures in their recent contracts, and have in many cases pared down corporate and regional staffs in attempts to offset these decreases. They claim that this reduction will adversely affect their ability to provide high-quality service to managed properties. Many owners believe, however, that such streamlining may not have a significant impact, since a portion of those fees were used for operator expansion and development, which have been curtailed for the moment.

With fee revenues down, competition among operators for more contracts has intensified, setting off a fee war among operators who find themselves having to bid lower and lower on fees to obtain additional contracts. As a result, many independent operators are being forced to merge or are being squeezed out of the market altogether.

The industry standards for management fees given here should be used only as guidelines for negotiating the fee structure for a specific property, because each situation is subject to a wide range of factors, all of which must be considered carefully. An owner selecting an operator in today's market should choose one that has solid experience in generating revenues in the hotel's specific market niche and then negotiate a management fee that provides a conservative basic fee with the potential for substantial incentive-fee revenue for meeting attainable profit-improvement goals.

D. Operator System-Reimbursable Expenses

System-reimbursable expenses paid by the owner to the operator for centralized services provided by the operator as part of its system-wide efforts in support of the owner's property have come under increasingly tight scrutiny during the past several years, due to the industry-wide squeeze on operating cash flow. Chain-operator system-reimbursable expenses cover system-wide advertising, national and regional sales offices, centralized reservations systems, and accounting and management information systems, as well as purchasing and procurement services, education and training programs, and such additional services as life safety, energy management, and insurance and risk management. Independent operators offer system services but usually on a less-comprehensive basis.

Two areas of contention often arise during the term of the contract. The first involves disagreements as to which of the operator's corporate expenses can legitimately be billed to the property. The second involves the mechanism for verifying legitimate expense totals and the accurate apportionment of these to the properties in the system. A contract should state clearly which specific operator corporate expenses are reimbursable expenses and should make disagreements subject to arbitration. The contract should also provide for an annual verification of the opera-

tor's total reimbursable expenses and the *pro-rata* calculation by independent means (usually by a public accounting firm).

In the past several years, owners have demanded and received both a clearer definition of system-reimbursable expenses in their contracts and a better method of verifying those expenses than formerly. Some operators highlight their system-reimbursable accounting and tracking systems as a benefit of their services in selling contracts, particularly because owners and lenders realize that those costs can come close to equaling management-fee payments.

Since chain and independent operators use a variety of formats and formulas in calculating their management fees and system-reimbursable charges, the owner must make side-by-side comparisons of these packages to assess them systematically.

E. Operator-Performance Provisions

Inclusion of operator-performance provisions both in chain and independent operator contracts has increased greatly. In chain-operator contracts, the incidence of performance provisions increased from approximately 16 percent in 1984 and 30 percent in 1988 to 37 percent in 1992. In independent-operator contracts, the incidence increased from 11 percent in 1984 and 24 percent in 1988 to approximately 32 percent in 1992 (excluding contracts with owners-in-foreclosure).

Operators are usually willing to agree to a performance provision if it is reasonable and flexible. A provision should include the following components:

► A performance-criteria base: usually an agreed-upon three- to five-year annual projection of gross operating profits;

► A start-up exclusion period: for a new property, one to two years; for an existing property, up to six months;

► A shortfall-deviation allowance: usually 5 to 8 percent on new properties (using five- to ten-year projections), and 3 to 6 percent on existing properties (projections of 3 to 4 years);

► A shortfall time frame: usually two of three consecutive years for new properties and two years for existing properties;

► An operator cure (the ability of the operator to pay the default amount to remain in the contract): usually a mandatory cash cure not to be reimbursed;

► A test for unfavorable economic conditions: an evaluation by an independent third party to determine the performance of competitive properties; performance base criteria would be adjusted for that year to reflect competitive property performance; and

► A contract-renewal hurdle: a requirement that the operator achieve a specified gross operating profit for the overall performance time period to be able to exercise the option to renew.

The recent economic downturn has played havoc with operating projections developed in the late 1980s when ten-year projections were common. As a result, owners and operators have used the shorter projection periods indicated above and have made use of tests for unfavorable economic conditions. To retain their contracts, some operators have renegotiated their management fees, with owners taking a lower basic fee for the short term in exchange for eliminating the performance provision altogether or receiving a higher basic or incentive fee if and when the property achieves improved cash flows.

It appears, however, that the incidence of operator-performance provisions will continue to increase as long as owners hold significant bargaining power in contract negotiations. What has been reinforced in the past few years is the need for the provisions to take into account changing market conditions.

F. Owner Input in Operational Decision Making

Owner input in operational decision making has increased significantly regardless of what is written in the contracts. Driven by the disastrous operating results for hotel properties almost across the board in the past few years, owners, lenders, and their asset managers have taken a much more active role in overseeing their operators and their hotel operations than ever before. With each party

under significant pressure, the owner-operator-lender relationship can be under continual stress.

That change has been met with mixed, mostly negative, feelings from operators. The quality of the revised relationship is influenced by how much pressure is on owners and lenders, the level of understanding owners and lenders have of the hotel business, the operator's responsiveness to owner and lender concerns, and the ability of the operator to put into effect the developed agreed-upon plan of action.

During the late 1980s, owners made inroads during contract negotiations in gaining formal input into operational decision making in three areas: the hotel's operating policies, budgeting process, and personnel selection. That trend has continued during the hotel-industry's severe recession, as owners and lenders more closely monitor and direct their hotel investments.

1: Operating Policies

Operators still hold out for their fundamental right to determine operating standards and policies but are somewhat willing under pressure to allow owners varying degrees of input in developing and monitoring those policies. Operators insist, however, that this input be directed to the operator's corporate office and not to the property's personnel. What creates significant problems in the owner-operator relationship is when the owner decides to place a representative on the property to monitor daily activities and attempts to make suggestions or give advice to the general manager and the staff.

Some operators have negotiated a provision for a policy board consisting of key owner and operator representatives to review, discuss, and, in some cases, determine on a mutually acceptable basis the property's major operating policies, provided those policies are reasonably consistent with the policies and standards of the operator's other properties. Even though provisions of this sort may not be included in the contract, most operators state that owners do provide input and that much of it is constructive. The challenge for both parties is to develop a channel for input, discussion, and decision making that provides well-considered, balanced courses of action.

2: Budget Approval

The approval process for the hotel's operating and capital expenditure budgets can generate controversy, especially when operating funds are limited. Traditionally, the operator had the sole right and responsibility under the contract to develop and implement the operating budget, although operators informally accepted input from owners during the budgeting process.

Beginning in the mid-1980s, owners negotiated for input and approval rights. Those rights have since become much more common in independent-operator contracts than in chain-operator contracts. Within the past two years, the owner's right to pro-

vide input is included in almost every contract, while the right to approve the budget is contained in approximately 85 percent of the contracts. In the past, the owner's ability to disapprove a budget was rather weak, since the contract stated that such approval could not be unreasonably withheld. More recently, owners have negotiated the right to disapprove the budget with the provision that if subsequent agreement could not be reached an arbitrator would settle the differences. Since neither party really wants arbitration, a mutually acceptable budget is usually hammered out even when working capital is severely restricted. Operators do not want to threaten termination of the contract due to the owner's inability to fund the operation for fear of losing market share with so few other opportunities available.

Owners with contracts containing an operator-performance provision must carefully weigh the decision to disapprove the budget submitted by the operator because the owner faces potential liability if the operator subsequently claims that the owner interfered with the operator's best efforts to meet required performance thresholds.

Owners have also more recently negotiated for and received more control with capital expenditure budgets submitted by operators. With replacement budgets for furniture, fixtures, and equipment, owners can generally keep those accumulated-fund balances on-call and have the right to review competitive

bids before purchases are made by the operator. Likewise, with capital-replacement and improvement budgets, owners can keep accumulated fund balances on call and can, in most cases, disapprove requests for expenditures except in emergencies.

With their tightened control of capital budgets, owners are now requiring that operators submit more thorough documentation for expenditure requests to include cost-benefit and net-present-value analyses for proposed expenditures. The major concern voiced by operators is that the majority of their owners have no funds available for replacements and capital expenditures, and that the facilities will deteriorate if refurbishment is delayed for any great length of time.

3: Personnel

Historically, neither the operator nor the owner wanted to be the employer of record for hotel workers. However, under the agency relationships existing in most contracts, line-staff members are the owner's employees. All chain operators and most independent operators insist that the property's general manager and usually all or selected members of the executive staff—resident manager; controller; directors of marketing, human resources, rooms, and food and beverage; housekeeper; chef; and chief engineer—be employees of the operator, but the owner reimburses the operator for the payroll costs associated with these employees.

Owners have attempted to negotiate for the right to approve or disapprove the selection of the general manager and key department heads, but operators have been adamant in retaining this right. Owners can often negotiate the right to interview and provide input into the selection of the general manager, and many operators solicit owner input regardless of what the contract stipulates, believing that to be good business practice. Operators still insist on retaining the right to transfer any management personnel from the owner's property to another managed property.

G. Financial and Operational Reporting

The quality and thoroughness of financial and operational reporting have increased substantially, due to the growing sophistication of operators' management information systems and to the demands of owners and lenders. Exhibit 4 shows operator reporting requirements typically found in the better management contracts negotiated in the past several years and is a standard in today's negotiations.

What is as important as the accurate compilation of mandated reports is the timely manner in which the operator and the owner meet to discuss the strengths and weaknesses of the operating results and the requirements and plans for the upcoming operating period. Owners should focus on the operator's analysis of the just completed operating period, the marketing plan, the strategy to develop revenues during the next period, cost-monitoring mechanisms, and justifications for capital expenditure requests. Both parties should insist upon regularly scheduled monthly or quarterly meetings to discuss the property's most recent operating results, the operating game plan for the upcoming period, capital-expenditure requests, and any other issues either side deems important.

H. Contract Termination at Owner's Option

1: Termination without Cause

The owner's option to terminate without cause is contained in virtually every contract between operators and owners-in-foreclosure but in only about 22 percent of chain-operator contracts and in 31 percent of independent-operator contracts. Such an option can usually be exercised only after a predetermined period of time, ranging from two to five years in chain-operator contracts and from one to three years in independent-operator contracts. A notice period of 90 to 180 days is required for chain operators and 30 to 90 days for independent operators.

Owners must pay the operator a fee when they terminate the agreement. Fees are based upon a multiple of the most recent twelve-months' management fees, the multiple being higher during the early part of the contract's term and decreasing as the term progresses. In a 20-year, initial-term, chain-operator contract, there may be a three-year no-cut period followed by a termination fee that is a multiple of four times management fees for the next three years, three times for the next three years, and two times for the remaining term of the contract. In a five-year independent-operator contract, there may not be a no-cut period, and the termination multiple may be just two times management fees during the first two years, followed by a multiple of one for the remaining term. In chain and independent-operator contracts with initial terms less than those above, the multiple is scaled down accordingly.

In owner-in-foreclosure contracts, operators can be terminated at any time but are paid a termination fee ranging from three months' to one year's management fees. In addition to the termination fees paid, operators often receive a fixed dollar amount determined when the contract is negotiated to assist in relocating any key management personnel who are employees of the operator.

Owners strongly desire to include a termination-without-cause provision in their contracts, since they believe such a clause gives them leverage during the contract's term. They have had limited success in including this provision with chain operators and only moderate success with independent operators because of the uncertainty it introduces for the operators who are attempting to build a stable long-term market presence. The provision does, however, have a significant benefit, and that is that it establishes up

Exhibit 4. Financial and Operational Reporting by Operator to Owner

Financial and operational reporting mechanisms in recently negotiated contracts.

Annually:

Budgets:

▶ Annual operating budget and marketing plan: monthly revenue, expenses, and cash-flow projections.

▶ Projected reserve for replacement expenditures, including justification analysis.

▶ Projected capital-improvement or addition expenditures, including justification analysis.

Financial Statements:

▶ Audited financial statements: balance sheet, income statement, replacement and capital-improvement or addition-expenditure reports, statement of changes in financial position.

▶ Reconciliation of annual basic and incentive management fees.

▶ Calculation and reconciliation of operator system-reimbursable expenses (audited).

Quarterly:

Financial Statements:

▶ Unaudited financial statements: balance sheet, income statement, replacement and capital-improvement or addition-expenditures reports, statement of changes in financial position.

▶ Management-analysis report: review of past quarter's performance to include analysis of variations from budget and overview of upcoming quarter's management plan to achieve projections.

▶ Calculation of incentive management fee (paid quarterly).

▶ Calculation of operator system-reimbursable expenses (paid quarterly).

Monthly:

Financial Statements:

▶ Unaudited financial statements; balance sheet, income statement, statement of changes in financial position.

▶ Management-analysis report: review of past month's performance to include analysis of variations from budget; overview of upcoming month's management plan to achieve projections.

▶ Calculation of basic management fee (paid monthly).

Other:

▶ Additional reports often required include weekly revenue reports, daily or weekly cash deposit and withdrawal reports, and, if applicable, franchisor property-inspection reports.

---

front the specific cost of terminating the contract. Without that guideline, there is no clear estimate of what a unilateral termination will cost the owner and what the operator will receive in damages. That amount can only be determined through a time-consuming and costly litigation procedure or court decision at the end of an often long and acrimonious struggle for both sides.

2: Termination in Event of Sale

Historically, the management contract almost always survived the sale of the managed property, with the purchaser assuming the contract's obligations until its term expired. This condition, in stable times, was usually a benefit to the purchaser who was paying for a stabilized business, the value of which was predicated upon the hotel operator's established position in the market. As real estate began turning over more rapidly—due to the short-term nature of real-estate buying and selling, to new owners' and operators' entering established markets, and to the real-estate crash—hotel sellers and buyers wanted the option to complete the sale transaction with as few encumbrances as possible. As a result, the option to terminate the contract in the event of a sale has increased in frequency.

An owner option to terminate the contract in the event of a sale is contained in 43 percent of chain operator contracts, in 76 percent of independent-operator contracts, and in all owner-in-foreclosure contracts negotiated in the past four years. Chain operators, however, have the right of first refusal or the right of first offer in the majority of these contracts, while independent operators have those rights in a small minority of their contracts.

If the contract is terminated on sale, operators receive a termination fee based on a multiple of the most recent twelve months' management fees as well as relocation expenses for the operator's key property employees. Those multiples are similar to those invoked when the owner terminates without cause.

3: Termination in the Event of Foreclosure

The option to terminate the contract in the event of foreclosure has received great attention during the recent economic downturn. Historically, management contracts sur-

vived foreclosure, and owners-in-foreclosure were either saddled with the contract or had to buy their way out. This situation crippled a lender's ability to sell a nonperforming property or to reposition it with another operator to increase the property's cash flows and boost its value for subsequent sale.

Within the past four years, lenders have insisted that negotiated contracts contain an option to terminate in the event of foreclosure, and they have been successful in including this provision in the majority of cases. Termination fees are paid to the operator either as an agreed-upon fixed dollar amount or a multiple of the most recent twelve months' management fees. That multiple is generally smaller than when termination is without cause or in the event of a sale.

I. Non-Competition Covenants

The importance of non-competition Covenants, in which the operator agrees not to manage or place additional properties within a specified geographical area of the owner's property, has grown substantially in the last six years, as chain operators have introduced market-segmented properties.

Chain operators with market-segmented properties want to negotiate maximum flexibility so they can locate additional managed or franchised properties targeted to identifiably different market segments within the geographic area. Owners, on the other hand, claim that even though

the market-segmented products are somewhat different, they are not different enough to prevent customers from crossing over from one property type to another and diluting occupancy and room rates. Operators counter that this negative effect is minimal and that if they do not build the market-segmented property in the available location, a competing chain will do so, thus increasing the possibility that existing customers will cross over to the competing chain brand and hurt the owner both directly and indirectly.

When introducing new market-segmented products into an existing owner's market area, several chain operators employ consulting firms to conduct impact studies (including the "if we don't build it, the competition will" scenario) to determine the degree of impact the new property will have on the existing one. The operator will build the new property only if the study results indicate that the new property will have negligible negative impact on existing properties. Owners argue that their operators are only adding to the problem and not protecting them. Operators argue that owners are impeding the operators' efforts to build a stronger chain and market share to the ultimate benefit of the owners.

Most contracts negotiated in the past four years contain language that specifically permits operators to introduce other chain-segmented products into the market area and restricting only additional properties determined to be in the same market segment as the existing owner's property. Operators will often give their existing owners the right of first offer to construct and own chain-related properties designed for other market segments within the owners' designated geographic market.

J. Dispute-Settlement Mechanisms

Dispute-settlement mechanisms appear in almost every contract negotiated in the past four years. These usually involve a step-by-step process that begins informally and amicably and then moves to more formal procedures.

Disputes tend to center on the following areas: operating policies, market-plan strategies, operating budgets, capital budgets, personnel hiring and firing, definitions of budgeting terms, and the degree to which economic and market conditions affect operating results. Negotiating owner input in developing operating policies, the budgets, and personnel hiring through the informal mechanism can usually resolve differences of opinion. The major factors in resolving most differences cited by operators and owners are good and frequent communication, sensitive understanding of the other party's objectives and pressures, understanding of hotel operations and the hotel and real-estate industries, and flexibility.

When disagreements are not resolved informally, contracts provide for an arbitrator to handle many types of disputes. Contracts should stipulate the following:

► *Choice of arbitrator:* Owner and operator choose a mutually acceptable person or firm; if owner and operator cannot agree on one person or firm, they each choose one and those two select a third party to arbitrate;
► *Provisions subject to arbitration:* Contracts limit what items are subject to arbitration (generally, budget definitions, the budget-approval process, and tests for unfavorable economic conditions in operator-performance provisions);
► *Process:* Owner and operator each submit one settlement position and arbitrator selects one of those two positions; set a short but realistic time limit for arbitration resolution; and
► *Conditions:* Arbitration outcomes and settlements are private and binding.

Disputes that escalate rapidly or expand beyond the purview of the arbitration provision usually deal with issues that will likely jeopardize the owner-operator relationship and possibly the contract. They are usually characterized by significant misunderstandings, distrust, and accusations of negligence, betrayal, fraud, and ulterior motives. Such situations often involve extreme actions first by one party and then the other and often end in the termination of the contract through litigation. This process is usually disruptive, lengthy, and costly to both parties.

The Renegotiation Question

Given the current economic status of the hotel and real-estate industries, most owners and lenders consider themselves facing lopsided downside risk. Substantial negative cash flows, slow debt-service payments, and property foreclosures have created vast problems for owners and lenders while operators continue to receive fee revenues, albeit at amounts less than they anticipated. A common undercurrent in this dissatisfaction is the belief that operators actively encouraged the rapid hotel expansion that is, in part, responsible for the overbuilt hotel markets.

Owners, in some cases supported by their lenders, are attempting to renegotiate their existing management contracts with varying degrees of success. Their leverage for renegotiation is the existing possibility of being foreclosed upon, in which case the operator's position may go from bad to worse. Owners with old contracts that will soon expire are also trying to take advantage of weakened operator positions to renegotiate concessions in exchange for renewing their contracts with their current management companies.

Operators are trying to hold to their original contract positions, citing that their fees represent a fair return for the services rendered and that their rewards in good times are limited to their management fees. Their position is that they have an agreed-upon contract with certain risks and returns for both parties that were understood when the contract was negotiated and signed. Most operators are also considering that their agency agreements can possibly be terminated and, if that occurs, they must go through time-consuming, costly, and disruptive litigation; lose a location and market share that would be extremely difficult to recapture; incur negative publicity and a damaged reputation; and have no certainty regarding the amount of monetary damages that will be awarded.

On the other hand, an owner that plays brinksmanship with the operator by threatening unilaterally to cancel the contract may well consume time, incur expenses and disruption, and face uncertainty of the outcome of the power play, and still may end up with a new operator that does not manage the property as effectively as did the evicted firm.

When contracts are renegotiated, one or more of the following outcomes may occur:

▶ Lower basic fee in exchange for a higher incentive fee;
▶ Deferral of a portion of the basic fee or deferral of all or a portion of the incentive fee;
▶ Lower basic fee for a specified time period in exchange for a higher basic fee or higher incentive fee later;
▶ Lower basic fee in exchange for an extension of the term of the contract;
▶ Lower basic fee in exchange for receiving a contract on another property;
▶ Limitation of cost of operator system-reimbursable expenses (the operator contributes to the system to make up for shortfalls);
▶ Addition or renegotiation of an operator-performance provision;
▶ Operator equity contribution with first take-out provision;
▶ Operator loan contribution; and
▶ Owner gaining the right to approve operating policies, operating and capital budgets, and selection of general manager and key property personnel (if not already in the contract).

While still somewhat infrequent, the rate at which contract renegotiations will occur in the future depends on the severity and length of the present industry recession. Operators who are willing to be flexible with owners and lenders now and trade present fees for future fees, extended contracts, and goodwill may find themselves in a more advantageous position when the economy rebounds.

Restructuring

The changes that have occurred in management contracts are directly related to the increase in competition among operators; more widespread knowledge about management contracts, the negotiating process, and the administration of contracts; increased owner bargaining strength; the more active involvement of lenders in the negotiating process; and the present deep recession in the hotel and real-estate industries.

With severe strains on operating cash flows, adjustments are being made in the sharing of available cash flow to provide returns to owners, operators, and lenders so that the parties are sharing returns, or lack thereof, more as partners than as three parties that have carefully carved out, independent roles in the same hotel project.

The adjustments that are now occurring in terms of rights, responsibilities, remuneration, performance standards, and the ability to extend or terminate the arrangement will probably carry forward to a great degree into the next economic upswing and contribute to the continuing evolution of the management contract.

HOW TO SELECT A FRANCHISE: STEP ONE—WEIGH THE BENEFITS OF AFFILIATION

W. Peter Temling

HOTEL/MOTEL OWNERS must reach a number of key decisions when they evaluate a franchise affiliation for their property. Although this discussion certainty does not comprise a complete list of the areas that should be analyzed, it does provide an indication of some critical factors that must be considered.

The first—and probably most important—decision is not which franchisor to choose, but whether or not to commit to a franchise affiliation in the first place! You should ask yourself:

Will an affiliation bring me more business than I would have received otherwise? Moreover, will it bring me more bottom-line dollars—after payment of all fees—than I would have received otherwise?

While this may appear to be an obvious first question, it is surprising that property owners sometimes bypass this step and assume that franchising their property is more profitable for them than operating it as an independent hotel/motel. Frequently, they go immediately to what should be the second most important question they should be asking:

Which franchisor should I select?

In searching for answers to these questions, you will look at many of the same analyses and criteria. Nevertheless, you may find it helpful to go through this process in two separate steps:

First—To Franchise or Not to Franchise?

To answer this question, the property owner has to use his/her business judgement to develop a cost/benefit analysis. (In other words, what will it cost, and what will I get for it?)

The *costs* of a franchise are typically the initial license fee, ongoing franchisee fees, reservation fees, and marketing/advertising charges. There may also be higher costs associated with signage and franchise-identity items, such as matches, towels, and in-room promotional products.

The tangible *benefits* of a franchise are the additional room reservations you can expect to receive because of the franchise system. You may also be able to improve the market position of the property and thereby achieve a higher average rate.

Your restaurant outlets could benefit from a franchise name since there appears to be a tendency for the traveling public to eat at locations with known names (the known name implies cleanliness, a "safe" place to eat).

With a franchise you could also spend fewer marketing dollars, for you are, in effect, buying into the marketing efforts of the franchisor—for example, national advertising, and promotion of a toll-free reservation number.

Conversely, without a franchise, you will have to consider the additional payroll, office space, and travel and entertainment expenses for sales representatives you must hire to market your independent property. Your advertising costs could also be higher since you would probably incur expenses to establish customer awareness of your property.

Therefore, assuming that you have now decided that franchising your property is likely to be profitable for you, you will have to select a franchisor. As I indicated earlier, you are going to look at some of the same criteria listed above in this second step of your evaluation:

Second—How to Select a Franchisor

The strength and potential impact on your property of the franchisor's reservation system is clearly the most important and tangible consideration. You may want to consult with others in the industry (accounting firms specializing in the hospitality industry, consultants, management companies) or rely on information and data provided by the franchisor to evaluate the reservation systems potential contribution to your hotel. For example, if you have a property located at an airport, you may determine that Franchise Company A's reservation system has strength in the transient commercial travelers' market. That would be a big plus for that franchisor. Or, if you are located in a resort market, you may determine that Franchise Company B has unique strength and appeal in the vacation market. In that case, Franchisor B may be more appropriate for you. Remember that the traveling public's perception of the franchisor's name plays an important role in this evaluation.

Consider, too, the sophistication of the reservation system: its ability to "upsell," provide comprehensive reports of reservation activity, make it easy for guests to make reservations, and allow the property to "manage" its rooms availability. Look at the franchisor's commitment to upgrade the system as new technology develops.

At the same time that you analyze the strength of the reservation system, industry market segmentation has to be studied to make sure your property fits into the same market segment that the franchisor appeals to. The broad market segments range from budget/limited service properties, to mid-priced, to upscale/first class, to luxury hotels. You will have to decide which is most appropriate for you. For example, if you build a limited-service property, you don't want to consider a franchise that is primarily in the mid-price market.

Joining a well-established franchise chain versus a newer one has to be weighed. Franchise organizations with established names have the obvious benefit of immediate name recognition; but that may also limit your choice since there may already be franchised properties in your area. Looking at franchise companies that are not yet well known may give you more flexibility and choice, and sometimes less cost; however, the drawback is, of course, less product recognition.

Next, you should look at what the franchising company offers for the fees you pay (another cost/benefit analysis is needed here). In addition to giving you a reservation system, an efficient franchisor will offer services from the time you sign up. During the construction phase, the company will assist with plans, concepts, minimum architectural standards, and pre-opening operational assistance. After the property is opened, the franchisor will provide "how-to" manuals, periodic inspections of the property, and generally will work closely with franchisees to help make the affiliation as beneficial as possible.

The periodic inspections are of particular importance if you are a passive owner (that is, an owner who relies on a management company or others to operate his/her property), for such examinations provide another set of eyes that look at your asset and give you periodic and objective reports concerning its physical condition and operation.

Carefully compare what the franchisors you are considering for your property will do to help you and determine how important each element is to you. For example:

▶ Does the franchisor establish regional/district groups or councils that address the specific needs or problems of individual properties in that region/district?

- Does the franchising company have open lines of communication between these regional franchisee organizations and the top echelon of the company?
- Is it likely to react to problems and opportunities on a national scale that will ultimately help the individual franchisees?
- If the franchise company also owns/ operates properties, is it sensitive to the concerns and needs of the franchisees, since they are likely to be quite different from those of the "company" properties?

When evaluating a franchisor, you should look at both the immediate benefits (and, of course, the costs) discussed here, as well as the financial stability and long-range objectives of the franchise company. A franchising affiliation is a long-term commitment and you want to be assured that you can continue to benefit from such an affiliation for a long time. For example, while continued growth of a franchise chain could be an asset to you, it could also mean more competition, particularly if the franchisor allows another property to come into your market or vicinity. This could dilute the primary reason for your affiliation (that is, the reservation system) and make your benefits short-lived.

In sum, undertaking a franchise affiliation is an extremely important decision. Property owners should carefully evaluate all pros and cons in light of this discussion and then seek advice if still uncertain that they have all the facts necessary to reach the right decision.

How To Select A Franchise:
Step Two—Study Your Market's Actual Needs

David E. Arnold

SELECTING A FRANCHISE IS not the first thing to do when you decide to add to existing holdings in the industry.

Even before you put any money up front to option a site that may become your area's next lodging property, you had better do some extensive market research—that is, identify the market, find out what's there, what's coming, what's needed and what will "sell."

Determine whether the area will support high-end, low-end, or a middle-market property. Then break that down within the broad categories noted previously. Is there a need for luxury, middle or economy lodging? Indeed, is there a need for an all-suite property?

Price and product are all-important, too.

Once you determine your segment, you can then decide what end you want to be in—and that determination will clearly establish the package that's right for the product: the quality of the furnishings you'll choose; whether you'll need to plan for a swimming pool (indoor or outdoor); the size of planned rooms; the size and amount of public space; the construction quality of the building itself—and other key factors.

In short, the market will determine the type and cost of your proposed project.

Only now will you be in a position to look at alternative franchise products and programs.

How do you then go about selecting?

What's available? Who is already in your market? What will be acceptable in the market? This really becomes a process of elimination. If one franchise within your market niche already is present in the area, it's quite obvious that you can't put the same product there. So, you have to look at others that fall within the same niche.

Certain franchises, if available, have attributes that make them more desirable than others. For example, one may have a national reservations system, while its alternative may have only a regional system, which may be significant; one may have a stronger image in the area to the travelling public, as well as within the financial community; one may have greater curb appeal (that is, the building, signage, landscaping, etc.), and so may have greater impact on the travelling/motoring public; one may have lesser or greater development costs than its alternative.

Another question: which of the alternatives has the stronger management and marketing support systems in place? And while fees are almost the same across the board, they, too, could have an effect on your decision. However, most experts agree that this should not be a deciding issue.

Although many chains offer and provide extensive support for training and architecture, many franchisees are required to develop their own programs. Often, they also use

---

their own architects, who must comply with franchisors' specifications to meet local zoning and environmental requirements.

Zoning boards in certain markets won't allow "stick-built" properties, for example, and require only brick and cast buildings. So, you may want to choose a franchise based on a prototype design that meets those local requirements. Some franchisors provide alternative designs, while others do not. Some may not be willing to change their design dramatically because changes would materially alter the already established curb appeal and advertised image. These are serious considerations for you to evaluate, for they are based on your own ability to build and your will to move away from rigid offerings.

When selecting your franchise it's important to look for the product that offers the best advertising and promotion support. You should look for the franchisor that has a well-defined marketing plan with both a regional and national orientation. Ideally, the plan should be one that also covers a complete range—from pre-opening strategies through on-going operations, and includes media guides, logos, photostats, slicks for ads, special event programs, seasonal programs, package programs; in sum, an umbrella-marketing concept that offers you, the franchisee, options that you can tie into locally or adjust and refine to meet local needs or customs.

It's desirable too, that the franchisor make available a national and/or regional advertising program of its own. These normally are special programs for which the franchise is assessed a percentage of volume (typically 1–3%), but which can be very effective in advancing the national and/or regional reservations program. These should be viewed only as a supplement to your own local advertising.

Normally, a hotel or motel should dedicate between 5–7% of its volume to marketing efforts. That figure should include all sales salaries, national advertising programs, local and regional promotions, outdoor advertising, print, radio, television and merchandising, as well as public relations fees and out-of-pocket expenses. If you anticipate gross sales of $5 million, then an adequate marketing budget should be in the neighborhood of $250,000 to $350,000 annually. Judiciously budgeted and spent, that amount should be enough to make a meaningful impact.

Strict Inspection Programs

The more effective franchisors also maintain a strict inspection system.

While franchisees often resent the stringent requirements and inspections of the better franchisor companies, it's best to remember that this approach benefits not only the system, but also the individual operator. Strictness enforces the rules. Compliance throughout the system guarantees your image, and provides your guest with consistent service. You may think it is a bother, infringing on your rights and unnecessary, but strict inspection is for your own good.

Historically, inspection checklists concentrated on the physical plant and cleanliness. In recent years, however, we've found that the more innovative chains are initiating quality assurance checklists that concentrate on quality of service and staff. Frequent travellers, particularly, choose a hotel on the basis of service provided. The increasing popularity of special concierge areas is evidence of this trend.

Many chains lease signage to their operators. The chains can "pull the sign" if you don't comply with requirements. That may sound too tough. But, you'll appreciate the result if you hear a customer complain about another franchisee's property where service is poor, quality is below par and the property is deteriorating. Those comments invariably do transfer to you— as part of the chain.

Look closely at a franchisor's track record before committing to its product. That often is reflected in the price you have to pay for the franchise. While many operators are dismayed by what they deem high franchise fees, that high fee could be cheap in the long run—because you're probably buying strength and the company's projected growth, both in your region and perhaps nationally. That strength and ongoing growth translates to profit potential for your unit.

It's important, too, that the franchise you choose provides you and your operations people with detailed manuals of policies, procedures, and standards. The manuals should train not only you but also your key staff members in how to implement those policies and procedures. This guarantees that you know how to operate your property properly, that it meets the high standards that will assure you of repeat business, and assures quality that's expected throughout the chain. You'll also know that other operators within the chain are following the same rules which, over the long term, will generate reservations.

You may want to look into whether the franchisor offers group purchasing programs—programs that aren't necessarily binding upon you, but which could offer you considerable discounts on standard items through mass purchasing.

Moreover, does the company have a strategic plan for growth and profitability? If it does, you can assume that it is in the business for the long haul. The alternative is the firm that jumped into the industry for the short term, to make a quick killing and then sell out.

Ask whether unit operators can offer recommendations concerning operation of the franchise system. There's a lot to learn from the franchisor. However, smart franchisors acknowledge that they can learn a lot from the franchisees, too—from the people in the marketplace who are on the firing line every day of the year. While not necessarily an expert on design, construction, advertising, promotion or operations, the franchisee can often translate and reflect the marketplace better than the franchisor.

While we've discussed the importance of a regional or national reservations system, the prudent franchisee—before committing to any chain—should ascertain the level of services and benefits expected from the chain. You also should be given a vehicle for verification of those services and benefits. If it's not offered, you should retain an independent consultant to assist you in verification.

Reservations System Critical

Some chains obtain a consistently high degree of reservations business through their system, while others fall short. Financing sources are more impressed with strong reservations systems—because that's a faster road to success. It has been our experience that it's extremely difficult to find a lender today if you're an independent hotel operator. And it's almost impossible to secure non-recourse debt without a strong franchisor behind you (a generality, of course).

But, like your own research to determine what's in a market, what the market needs and what's available, financing sources, too, usually approach each market on an individual basis. While you're looking at the market to find your niche, they're looking at your market to ascertain whether that niche will sell and whether their investment will be safe.

In short, it takes a lot of homework before you commit to a product in the hotel/motel field. Do your homework and your chances of success will be magnified.

HOW TO SELECT A FRANCHISE:
STEP THREE—PINPOINT YOUR PRODUCT SEGMENT

Robert M. James

FOR HOTEL/MOTEL OWNERS and developers, franchise selection is no longer a simple, obvious task. In past years, owners could select a franchise from among five or six major chains. In the minds of consumers, each chain was clearly representative of a certain product. Now, however, with the advent of segmentation, product lines have proliferated. Most major chains now offer a variety of products under the same franchise umbrella; upscale, convention hotels, mid-market properties, all-suite hotels, and limited-service properties may all be found within the same franchise family.

As new, highly segmented products continue to be introduced in the market, many fear that franchises may be diluting the very thing that made them so valuable in the first place: a clear product perception. The great challenge faced by franchisors today is maintaining a clear chain perception in the minds of consumers while using a well-known brand name to coattail new products into existence.

In the past, we have witnessed generally unsuccessful attempts by major franchises to introduce upscale products, using a name that was firmly positioned as a mid-market product. At the same time, franchises perceived as upscale were very successful at introducing mid-market and limited service products.

Product-line expansion has greatly complicated the franchise-selection process, introducing many new variables for consideration. Before making a franchise selection, an owner or hotel developer should consider assistance from an unbiased independent with experience in operating various franchises to carefully evaluate the following factors:

The Marketplace

The franchise must be selected on the basis of market needs; therefore, the marketplace must be carefully evaluated prior to franchise selection: What market segments are currently being attracted to and accommodated in the area? What are the needs and wants of each segment? What are these segment members able and willing to pay for the accommodations they desire? What percent of total area demand does each segment represent?

This information enables the hotel owner to eliminate franchises that do not cater to the needs of the specific marketplace. For example, in a market where government/military business represents 60% of area demand for hotel rooms, and assuming this segment operates on a $55 per diem (includes food and lodging), a first-class, luxury perceived franchise would not fit the market. The franchise must provide and support a position that enables the hotel to penetrate the area's major market segments to the fullest extent.

The Competition

What hotels and franchise products are already in the local marketplace? These hotels must be evaluated in order to find a niche or specific area of opportunity. What specific market segments are competitor hotels accommodating and to what degree are they penetrating these segments? What are their strengths? What are their weaknesses? What are they doing specifically to attract each major market segment? Are there opportunities there to attract and accommodate any new segments using a different product or marketing approach? If a downtown metropolitan area is experiencing a 50% occupancy among its upscale, first-class hotels, it simply does not make sense to introduce another upscale franchise product. Your research may, however, indicate that the market could support a high-quality, mid-market property at lower rates. In this case, a franchise with a high quality, mid-market perception should be selected.

Customer Profiling

Franchise selection must help position the hotel to attract targeted segments. Therefore, target segments and sub-segments must be identified and profiled prior to franchise selection. What kind of accommodations will each segment want and expect? What rates can each segment support? What industries do these travelers represent? Are business travelers largely white-collar professionals or blue-collar employees? Are they clients of local companies or are they employees of these local companies? What special amenities and services do they demand? What are their status needs? Are they typically upper management, middle management, or sales people working the territory?

Segment-profile information is vitally important because it enables the hotel to position itself to meet the needs of the area's major market segments. Franchise selection must always serve to support and establish positioning.

In all cases, market needs should dictate the product, and the product should dictate the franchise. There is no such thing as the right franchise in every market; but there is an optimal franchise based on the market to be served and the market's specific needs.

Following are other factors to consider:

▶ **Reservations Contribution.** Most franchises use reservations contribution, or the number of reservations produced through the chain's 800 number, as the measurement of the value of the franchise. However, a closer look at this measurement is recommended. Travel agents always use toll-free reservation numbers when they are available. Individual clients usually also will use a toll-free number rather than pay for the calls themselves. Both types of calls are channelled through the chain's reservation system.

Owners need to evaluate the percentage of reservations contribution that is simply the result of having an 800 number available and the percentage of reservations that is truly the result of brand or franchise loyalty. Recent studies indicate that even satisfied customers switch hotels every third or fourth visit. The real franchise advantage to look for, therefore, is affiliation that helps the customer put you in a category—a name that identifies your product in the customer's mind. The advantage is the franchise's perception or positioning in the market.

▶ **What Franchises Are Available?** Obviously, an owner or hotel developer must start with a basic knowledge of the various franchises available in the marketplace. Information on the various products within each franchise system is also needed.

▶ **Territorial Rights.** Some franchisors limit the number of properties they will franchise within a particular region in order to prevent their properties from having to compete against each other.

▶ **Physical Requirements.** Most franchises have some physical requirements as part of franchise qualification. Some may require, for instance, that their hotels have two restaurants. To add on and operate two restaurants is costly and must first be justified by market demand. Hotel owners must know and evaluate carefully these physical requirements in light of market needs.

► **Financability.** MHM has witnessed many owners and developers select a franchise with the primary objective of fulfilling the lending institution's national franchise-affiliation requirements. Although no one would argue about the importance of financing, the selection of a franchise should be approached from a market standpoint, rather than from a banking standpoint.

► **Royalties and Other Fees.** Royalties and fees vary vastly from franchise to franchise. These expenses naturally must be evaluated based on the estimated benefit of affiliation.

► **Length of Franchise/Conditions for Cancellation.** What is the term of the franchise agreement? Under what conditions can the owner cancel the agreement? Under what conditions can the franchisor's cancel the agreement?

► **Transfer of Franchise Upon Sale.** If the owner decides to sell the hotel, will the franchise automatically transfer in an already-approved state, or must the new owner re-qualify? This affects the salability of the property.

► **Geographic Strength.** Each franchise is usually strongest in its headquarters region or area of origination. For example, if a chain is headquartered on the East Coast, it probably will be strongest and most well-known in the Eastern United States. Hotel owners need to be aware of franchises' geographic strengths in order to weigh these factors into the franchise-selection decision and to identify opportunities available.

► **What Equipment Is Required?** Franchises often have specific equipment requirements. Some chains, for example, require that all of their properties purchase the same computer in order to tie into the chains computer reservations system. Owners need to be aware of these requirements prior to finalizing any franchise agreements.

► **Advertising/Promotional Programs.** How much quality advertising and promotion is really done by the franchise to the consumer? This varies vastly from chain to chain. Some franchises use a percentage of the initial franchise and advertising fee for advertising in the hotel's local marketplace—which is an excellent boost for the property. Other franchises are very weak in the advertising and promotions area.

► **Competing Properties in the Area.** What franchises already operate in the local market? The owner must analyze which properties the proposed hotel will be competing against in order to capitalize on areas of opportunity that exist for his property. The franchise selection, again, should enable the hotel to exploit this area of opportunity.

► **Training.** Some franchises offer excellent sales and management training support for their properties. Many do not. Obviously, the more support and quality training available, the better.

► **Chemistry.** The owner and the franchise must, to some degree, match chemistries . . . that is, the owner needs to feel that he has selected a franchise that is well-managed, competent, and attentive to his needs. He should feel comfortable with franchise people with whom he will be dealing and feel they are people he can work with easily.

Franchise affiliation will become more and more valuable as we proceed to automate society and continue—due to ease of transportation—to expand markets to a truly global nature. As more product fines are introduced in the marketplace, franchise selection will become an even more complex decision-making process.

Franchise information is vast and everchanging, and there is no such thing as the right franchise in every market. Owners must find the optimum franchise on the basis of market-specific needs. The worst possible thing any hotel owner or developer can do is select a franchise that says one thing, a product that says another, and a market that wants something else. A property can be successfully positioned by following these steps:

First: Analyze the market.
Second: Design the product to serve the market.
Third: Select the franchise that supports the positioning.

HOW TO SELECT A FRANCHISE: STEP FOUR— GAUGE THE FRANCHISORS' SUPPORT SYSTEMS

Theodore R. Mandigo

WE ARE CURRENTLY working on two projects that bear directly on the crucial subject of franchising: one to assist an existing downtown hotel—now operating as an independent—to select an appropriate franchise; the second to work with a resort hotel in analyzing the benefits of a franchise to determine whether the current franchise should be renewed or not. Both analyses are targeted at the same end: the determination of the economic benefits of a franchise, and the potential contribution to the properties' profits.

This, in the final analysis, is the deciding point: "Will this franchise improve a property's profitability?"

An interim question, during the development stage, might be: "Will this franchise make this project more attractive to a lender or joint-venture partner?"

Both questions should yield the same answer, although in some circumstances the latter question may be an overriding one in new development, providing a level of assurance to a lender who is unfamiliar with a market or the developer.

The many benefits of a franchise and the points that vary among franchises can be analyzed on the basis of effect on operations. The benefits are many and the selection process is a complex procedure, involving many separate factors. Since the elements that come into play in the decision process are primarily the means to achieve greater profitability, these factors deserve first consideration.

Four areas come to mind when considering a franchise:

▶ "Curb appeal" or the image conveyed by the franchise.
▶ Room nights generated through the reservation system.
▶ Marketing support provided by the franchising company.
▶ And last, but not least, efficiency in operations through systems, analysis, training and management services provided.

All of these considerations are important to an operator and provide "insurance" to the developer. Let's evaluate each factor.

"Curb appeal" relates directly to the image the individual and group traveler has of the franchise. It defines the expectations of the guest in terms of service levels, facilities, rates, and standards of operation. This image is developed by the franchisor through minimum standards in room count, room size, facilities offered and levels of service. It is further enhanced by inspection systems and assistance in upgrade or refurbishment/expansion programs for existing properties, and through a review and approval of development programs for new or prospective properties.

An effective franchisor has a program to weed out those properties that do not conform to standards and create a negative image of the brand name or affiliation. Thus the performance standards and inspection programs that may be a periodic nuisance to an individual operator actually protect the property from the impression created by poor operators flying the same banner.

The site-distribution of existing properties (as well as the marketing program) identifies the level of recognition a particular brand will have. The importance of distribution varies by level of property. For example, a regional budget or limited-service organization may have as strong a customer recognition among its primary market as a nationally recognized luxury hotel has in its market. Therefore, national recognition is not necessarily a determining criterion in the selection of a franchise.

National or regional advertising programs promote the image of the operation and the operating style or philosophy. Such general promotional themes as "A Collection, Not a Chain," "Luxury for Less," and "No Surprises" convey an image and identification appealing to a customer segment without focusing on a specific property. A balanced ad program that fits the image a franchisee is seeking or that a prospective franchisee feels will help in identifying or categorizing his property in the mind of a prospective client helps in capturing off-the-highway business.

Room nights generated through the reservation system are often the greatest selling point for well-established franchisors. Systems generate from 3% to as high as 40% of rooms business. Important factors include the type of reservation system, ranging from the sophisticated Holidex II System, to 800 numbers, to telephone communication among properties for referrals. The former offers two-way communication between properties and the reservation center, access from travel agents and a multitude of variables in guest information. The latter can provide the same service, but obviously at a much less sophisticated level; moreover, the effectiveness depends on the franchisor.

The reservation system is only a part of the ability of a franchisor to generate room nights. Many chains are also noted for specialties in other areas, such as corporate-group meetings programs, convention promotions, tour-group activities, and targeted marketing programs aimed at special-interest groups, such as senior citizens. The breadth of such activities and promotions is a clear point of distinction in selecting a franchise.

In evaluating a franchisor's marketing program, consider head office/parent company assistance, special promotional packages, newsletters, and similar efforts—all enable the local franchisee to tie into national promotions and build business.

Efficiency in operations is an often overlooked benefit of a franchise affiliation. Central purchasing, for example, is common to most franchises, especially in such logo-identified items as towels and soaps. However, the initial savings in furniture and other capital purchases—both in new development and refurbishment—may yield substantial savings to the individual or first-time developer.

Many chain operators provide comparative data on operations, monitoring key ratios such as occupancy and rate; others also run comparisons of overall operating results for the franchisee. These provide the mutual benefit of healthy and well-run properties throughout the franchise group.

Additional operating efficiency, as well as adherence to standards, is provided by training programs, both on-property and through centralized training centers. These teach both management and staff how to do a more effective and efficient job in serving the customer.

An often overlooked benefit of a franchise is the provision of management assistance to address short-term problems. If, for example, sales are slumping, a property owner can either develop his own plan for promotion or tap the resources of the parent company to assist in that program, using tested techniques and experienced staff. Similar assistance should be available in engineering, management, food and beverage operations, accounting, and other specialty areas.

All benefits detailed above are provided at a cost to the developer or operator. These costs are assessed in multiple levels, starting with a base or initial fee, ranging from a flat fee of $250 up to $300 per room, with a minimum of 100 rooms for joining a franchise (due upon application).

The second layer of fees is the annual royalty fee—from 1% to 5 3/4% of room gross; and an advertising fee—from 1% to 3 1/2% of room gross.

A third layer of charges is in the form of a reservation fee—from $1 to $3.75 per reservation, plus equipment charges and other fees.

The final cost of a franchise is the designated signage, logo items, and other in-room and public-area identification of the franchise selected.

The challenge for the operator is to weigh the costs of the franchise against the benefits that particular franchise will deliver, taking into consideration the potential or current operating results without franchise identification versus the performance of the property with the franchise in place. Again, that measurement of benefit is simple and can be interpreted on the basis of increased occupancy and/or rate, and improvement in operating results.

We attempt to measure those contributions by running a comparison of the performance of a franchised property in a similar market versus the total market, and by analysis of the operating performance of a particular franchise operation versus the composite results of a wide variety of properties. This is done with the aid of our annual publication, *Trends in the Hotel Industry,* or other sources of comparative data.

Unfortunately, the wide variety of sizes and types of hotel operations, differences in the composition of markets, and the many other variables in hotel operations make a direct comparison difficult at best. Seldom does the comparison yield a clear black or white conclusion. Therefore, judgement often comes into play in the interpretation of results—with the image of the franchisor conveyed to the developer, consultant, lender or other party playing an equally important role in the process.

Factors that weigh heavily in the franchisor's ability to deliver economic benefits include size of the group, length of experience, number of parent-owned operations, growth rate and expansion plans. All are essential considerations. For a franchise is a long-term commitment to a brand, and a growth-oriented firm with an enviable track record is more likely to provide the necessary benefits than a new franchising group with comparatively few operations.

Obviously, there is a trade-off in cost to obtain the maximum benefits. A smaller, less experienced firm or a firm in an aggressive expansion mode is likely to offer a less expensive franchise than an older, established chain with a large network of existing properties. There is also a price differential in purchasing a franchise for budget versus luxury properties, with the availability of franchise alternatives diminishing as you move up the rate scale. Although there has been some aggressive expansion of franchise opportunities at the luxury end of the market, this segment remains somewhat select because of the national or international recognition necessary to effectively penetrate this market.

Now . . . back to our two projects mentioned at the beginning of this discussion. Although we are not yet finished, the preliminary results indicate that the independent hotel would benefit by approximately $2000 per room through increased occupancy— but a slight reduction in rate— after the cost of the franchise. The franchised property would probably drop about five points in occupancy—but maintain approximately the same level of profitability—if the franchise is not renewed; this is due to a strong level of repeat business and extensive resort amenities. The property's destination orientation and the recognition built up over the years are of greater significance than the advantages the franchise offered during the resort's early life.

The Franchisor-Franchisee Relationship: Stronger Partnership . . . Greater Growth

Dr. Atid Kaplan

IN THE NEXT FEW YEARS AN everchanging and sometimes turbulent economic environment will buffet the lodging industry. In order to focus our energy on this external threat to profits, it is important that franchisors and franchisees understand each other's problems, and cooperate to eliminate the barriers to growth by improving communications and by bolstering joint efforts. The purpose of this discussion, then, is to spotlight a number of common problems and point the way to a more beneficial franchisor-franchisee relationship. This objective can be realized only through greater interdependence on each other's skills, resources, knowledge, and managerial abilities.

The more common day-to-day issues and problems in franchisor-franchisee relationships should be discussed openly so that everyone understands both the pitfalls and the opportunities.

First of all, there has to be a recognition by both the franchisor and franchisee that their profits and growth depend not only on each other's skills, but also on a commonality of goals and objectives.

One major underlying problem is that, in the case of conglomerate and publicly owned organizations (both among franchisors and franchisees), there is a preoccupation with quarterly, short-term results, or "fear-of-the-analyst" syndrome. An understanding and acceptance that long-term planning and results are more important than the instant gratification of quarterly earnings will help both sides focus on long-range goals and objectives.

Franchise contracts and renewal provisions have been causes of concern in the past. Franchisees must now realize, however, that conditions change and that more franchisee suggestions and recommendations are needed to increase the services franchisors provide to franchisees. During the last few years, franchisees have required and demanded more management and marketing support from franchisors. This has involved increased costs, which—in many cases—have been absorbed by the franchisor. The latter must now recoup these costs by higher rates to the franchisee or by in-kind contributions.

On the subject of contracts, perhaps one should add the proviso that they should be written in plain English rather than "legalese." Simple, understandable, clearly written agreements would ensure better communications among all concerned.

We are also observing a change in our basic markets. There is now a move by chains to cater increasingly to specialized market segments. This development has caused many franchisees to fear that the various segmented operations will erode their own prime-target market. This fear may, or may not, be unfounded. Thus, it is important for franchisors to analyze and explain the impact (both positive and negative) of segmentation upon existing franchisees and possibly give them the right of first refusal on new concepts and properties in their areas.

Another major concern, which franchisors will have to allay, is the fear of overbuilding in what may be an increasingly stagnant market. Again, this problem can be alleviated through discussion, analysis and joint participation. On the other hand, franchisees should also do their own basic research to determine whether or not they should participate in new ventures and concepts. Nevertheless, a well-managed property rarely has to fear new and untried competition.

The amount and allocation of chain marketing expenditures is (and probably always will be) a source of friction. Many franchisees feel that they are not benefitting as much as they should from their contributions. Corporate, on the other hand, is faced with countervailing demands and pressure from all sides. This could be alleviated by greater franchisee participation in expenditure allocation.

In addition, franchisees could contribute to the marketing planning process by passing on knowledge of their customer base to assist in the consumer-research process. The use of marketing funds would then be done by a group committed to increasing profitable sales and would ameliorate some of the complaints that franchisees have about the allocation and utilization of such funds.

There has been a fear by franchisees that franchisor units will compete with their properties. While there have been some abuses, it has generally not been a problem. There is always the threat, nevertheless, that these new operations will erode franchisees' market share. However, existing franchisees have frequently benefitted when franchisors have marketed their properties aggressively and thus increased overall market penetration and demand.

One major source of continuing contention centers on inspections and evaluations of individual properties by corporate staff. It is easy to use a standard checklist and evaluation method in a "cookie-cutter" operation. But it is far more difficult where each property was designed and built to serve regional needs within the limits set by the corporate office. While the evaluation may at times be biased and unfair due to the personality of the rater—or because of a clash between evaluator and franchisee—it is not the norm when both sides understand and respect the other's position.

Perhaps we should abolish quarterly and annual ratings by a team of corporate inspectors and substitute a new system using new combinations of people and controls. These could be drawn from a pool of professional evaluators who would provide anonymous ratings. This could be supplemented by continual formal (and informal) monitoring by franchisor/franchisee representatives.

In some cases, the rapid growth in number of units has not given corporate head offices enough time to recruit, select, train and supervise inspectors. It is in everyone's long-term interest to ensure that corporate standards are met and exceeded. Therefore, the franchisee, through regional and district associations, should be involved in the inspection process. Perhaps the use of franchisees' management-trainee staff, as well as retired franchisees, could provide additional experienced and qualified inspectors, who would not only evaluate but also help the operator solve problems. Let's face it, knowledgeable outsiders can sometimes spot problems and come up with solutions that we haven't considered since we're so close to the situation. Control and command of this function could be vested in a group composed of franchisors, multi-unit franchisees, and individual or micro-unit franchisees. A supervising body reporting to all interested parties would serve mutual needs and eliminate a frequent franchisee complaint that different standards are used for their units and corporate units.

A common franchisee complaint has revolved around the issue of franchisee influence on corporate strategy and policy formulation. The franchisee may realize that he cannot make his opinions heard, yet he wants a greater voice in the decision-making process. Many franchisors have made tremendous strides through franchisee advisory groups, yet individual properties that are not involved rarely perceive their potential impact on corporate policy. It is important that franchisees be kept fully informed by their franchisee-association representatives and, equally important, that comments and suggestions be solicited from individual franchisees.

The degree of franchisee-association contributions to policy varies with both the aggressiveness of franchisee representatives and the responsiveness of corporate executives. This, of course, changes with each organization and its executives. However, if franchisees feel they have made effective recommendations concerning such issues as goal setting, strategy formulation and executive selection, it will do much to eliminate griping about so-called "heavy-handed corporate meddling." In addition, it would encourage more informal contact between individual franchisees and corporate executives, which in turn could solve many minor problems quickly—before they blow up into major crises.

A major franchisor-franchisee problem has been a real, or perceived, gap in communications. In order to improve operations, major companies in other fields regularly poll their employees to measure levels of satisfaction, dissatisfaction, and specific areas of concern. Few if any franchisors have done this in the past with their franchisees. While it does not have to be a formal survey, much data could be gathered through informal discussions.

Another approach in improving communications and resolving disputes is through the appointment of an ombudsman. He/she should be selected and paid jointly by franchisee and franchisor, and should have the power to re-solve complaints to the satisfaction of both parties. This person should, of course, have a thorough understanding of field and corporate operations—and human relations. An ombudsman would provide a simple, fast grievance procedure for both parties. In turn, both the franchisee and the franchisor could devote more time for operations.

While many of the issues discussed here have been raised in the past, there is an urgent need to settle differences now—before the critical problems that our industry may well face in the next few years. If we don't act decisively, we'll waste our energy in fratricidal battles. If we do settle these issues satisfactorily—in partnership and harmony—we'll see profits that would make King Midas envious.

PROJECT 1

You have been hired as a consultant by a group of investors that is interested in either buying an existing or building a new 250 room hotel. You have been asked to put together a report which will include the following items listed below. Present a report to the new owner and give scenarios related to an existing property and a new one.

Existing Property

1. Make a recommendation on acquiring a property and give some examples as to properties that are presently on the market in various locations and the asking prices. Describe the present franchise affiliation of these properties, what is the management structure (management contract or independent) and as much information on these properties as you are able to acquire. This would include location and type of property, competition, floor plan, facilities as well as occupancies over the past few years, average room rates, food and beverage sales, the properties present marketing mix, the physical condition of the property, economic health of the community and any other pertinent information.

2. Discuss the total costs of the project. This should include initial purchase costs, any refurbishment or renovation costs etc. Discuss different ways the project could be financed.

3. Make a recommendation as to what to do with the property once you acquire it. Do you recommend keeping the present franchise affiliation if there is one or changing it? Give information on some of the options that might be available and the costs of the other franchises as opposed to being independent if that is an option.

4. Make a recommendation as to how the hotel would be managed. If a management contract company is being considered, review possible companies, track records, fees, costs, contract terms and other pertinent information.

5. Provide projections of income based on at least 3 levels of occupancy and different average room rates for a three year period of time. Also give food and beverage projections as well as other income possibilities.

6. Make recommendations as to how the property should be positioned in the marketplace. Briefly analyze the market and changes that will be occurring.

New Construction

1. Make a recommendation on a specific site, include the specifications on the site, the costs and how the property would be laid out on that site.

2. Discuss the property. What type of facilities and services would it have and what type of market would it be catering to?

3. Discuss the competition in the local market area.

4. Discuss the overall project costs (including the land), pre-opening expenses, etc.

5. Make a recommendation as to a specific franchise affiliation or should the property be independent. If a franchise is desired, what are the possibilities for that market area and what are the costs associated with each franchise?

6. Make a recommendation as to how the hotel would be managed. If a management contract company is being considered, review the possible companies, track records, fees, costs, contract terms and other pertinent information.

7. Provide projections of income based on at least 3 levels of occupancy and different average room rates for a three year period of time. Also give food and beverage projections as well as other income.

8. Make recommendations as to how the property should be positioned in the marketplace. Briefly analyze the market and any changes that will be occurring.

Note to Instructors: This project can be broken down into small subsections by individuals or done in total by a group. The exact amount of detail required can be determined by the instructor.

You have just been appointed General Manager of a 250 room mid-scale hotel that has recently been purchased by a group of investors. This is the third group that has owned the hotel since it has been open. The hotel is 15 years old and situated in a growing suburban area. It was previously a member of an upscale franchise organization and 6 years ago changed to a mid-scale franchise. At one time the hotel was one of the finest properties in the area. During the last 2 years the hotel's occupancy and average room rate have been slowly sinking. Numerous new hotels of all kinds have opened in the last few years in the surrounding area.

The number of repeat commercial/corporate guests as well as group meetings has been steadily declining. Guests complaints have been numerous and customer comments are very often negative. The previous owners spent little or no money on the property and there are many things the hotel needs to do from a maintenance and refurbishment point of view.

As the new General Manager, the new owners have asked you to present a report covering the following things:

1. Analyze the present state of the property and recommend to the owners what you think needs to be done to bring it back to par.

2. Make recommendations as to whether you think the hotel should keep its present franchise or reposition itself with another name to another market. Give your reasons.

3. What changes do think need to be made immediately in the way that the entire operation is run?

4. Design an organizational chart of all positions in the property as you would like to see it evolve. Discuss the major responsibilities of all supervisors and department heads in a way that can later be used to help explain to them what your expectations are of them.

5. What new employee/management communication systems would you employ?

6. What type of new internal and external operational controls would you install to insure that the hotel runs more efficiently and profitably?

12

ENGINEERING AND FACILITIES MANAGEMENT

Environmental Regulation Booms: Are Building Professionals Ready?

Steve Mumford

Over the past several years, building owners and managers and the general public have shown a heightened interest in the environment. Is society more environmentally aware and concerned? Yes. Does environmental sensitivity—recycling, using benign building materials, or conservation efforts—often bring financial benefits? Certainly. But the upsurge of legislation in the environmental arena indicates that regulation is also driving the trend. Facilities professionals who have not already stepped up their environmental efforts will have to kick into high gear to comply.

The most pressing concern, says Jim Dinegar, vice president of Government Affairs for Washington, D.C.-based Building Owners and Managers Association (BOMA) International, is preparing for the Dec. 31, 1955, chlorofluorocarbon (CFC) phaseout. The issue is not new, but many industry professionals are still unprepared.

Dinegar divides those who will be affected into three groups:

1. First is building owners who are keenly aware of the phaseout's implications and have been doing a "yeoman's job" of preparing.
2. The second group has made all of the adjustments currently required—including certification and training for those who work with CFCs—and is complying with anti-venting laws. When it comes to preparation for the phaseout, they project the attitude: "I'll get to it. What do I have, a year and a half?" says Dinegar.
3. The third group "has been living under a rock for the past year," according to Dinegar. "I'd like to say there's hope for those people, but I just don't know what it is."

Obviously, building professionals in all these categories must retrofit or begin refrigerant management programs before time runs out. But the CFC phaseout is not alone on the list of lingering—yet pressing—issues. The specter of poor indoor air quality (IAQ) that has haunted building professionals for years recently made its first appearance in the regulatory arena. The Occupational Health and Safety Administration (OSHA) proposed indoor air quality regulations last month. "It will take two to three years for OSHA to reach the end of its (proposal) process, and perhaps finalize a rule," says Bob Axelrad, director of the U.S. Environmental Protection Agency's (EPA) Indoor Air Division of the Office of Air and Radiation, Washington, D.C.

Meanwhile, BOMA and the EPA have teamed up to provide building professionals with information on voluntary IAQ enhancements. "What we've tried to do is oppose regulation. But you don't just oppose regulation. You have to do something on the positive side," says Dinegar. "We think we have. We've conducted seminars with the EPA under a cooperative agreement to help educate building owners and managers across the country using [the EPA's] *Building Air Quality: A Guide for Building Owners and Facility Managers*, and we've delivered more than 60 programs."

The EPA also has a program in the works that advocates voluntary compliance. Slated to take effect early this fall, about 40 organizations have allied themselves with the EPA. "The basic premise will be to try to get building owners and managers to make commitments as building partners, and to take a series of actions that would be designed to deal with IAQ problems and to prevent them from occurring," says Axelrad. Many of those actions have already been articulated in the air qual-

ity guide that BOMA is helping promote, he adds. Axelrad notes the program will provide recognition for those who comply, and he hopes economic incentives will also be available.

Building owners and facilities managers are not alone in their concern for IAQ. Both tenants and interior furnishings manufacturers have been taking actions to help reduce indoor air pollutants. According to Dinegar, BOMA has circulated about 50,000 copies of *Improving the Great Indoors,* a book of IAQ tips for tenants. "It's a combined effort," he says. Axelrad concurs: "It's definitely agreed that indoor air quality is a shared responsibility."

Long before the air is clear on IAQ, other issues—like identifying and disposing hazardous wastes—will float to the top of owner concerns. Among these is the possibility of a national regulation disal-

lowing the disposal of mercury-laden fluorescent lamps in conventional landfills (precedent has already been set by some states, including California and Minnesota). "The proposed rule goes to the EPA and it's anyone's guess what that rule will be. This July, we should see this proposed rule," says Dinegar, adding that it costs more than 30 cents to remove the mercury from each fluorescent lamp.

If traditional disposal methods are not the answer, what is? One source suggests municipal landfills, unlike private ones, are able to absorb the mercury and prevent it from leaching into ground water. But Michael Italiano. executive vice president and general council for the U.S. Green Building Council, Washington, D.C., says, "Most landfills leak." He agrees that removing mercury for recycling efforts substan-

---

COURSE ADDRESS CONCERNS

A new course, and related 15-chapter textbook, will provide concrete suggestions for protecting workers and the public from potential health and safety hazards that relate to a building's internal and external environment. Among the many topics *Environmental Health and Safety Issues* covers are asbestos, indoor air quality, office ergonomics, and health and safety laws. The course also focuses on how to cope with potential hazardous waste, stormwater/wastewater, storage tanks, and pollution control.

With help from the course, building professionals will better understand government regulations and how to implement them. Guidelines for OSHA and EPA compliance are among the legal topics covered, as well as how to handle environmental assessments, audits and recordkeeping.

Environmental Health and Safety Issues is available to all commercial property professionals for self-study and through classes sponsored by local chapters of the Building Owners and Managers Association. The course was developed by Arnold, MD-based Building Owners and Managers Institute (BOMI), which plans to add it to the core curriculum of its Real Property Administration (RPA) designation program for property managers.

For more information about this references, contact BOMI at (800)235-2664.

tially increases costs, but he cautions: "Trying to say that it's not hazardous when the test shows that it is, is not the way to go. I think, technologically, there are ways to solve the problem. It's a price issue right now."

Contaminated ground water and drinking water are also issues at stake. Italiano says one way to improve water is simple: conservation. "Conservation is important in terms of saving a precious resource, and also in improving water quality, because it improves the efficiency of waste water treatment." Simple conservation methods will help owners use less water, improve water quality, and save money.

For water use outside, Italiano suggests using soaker hoses to water vegetation. These, he says. will cut consumption in half. Inside, low-flow fixtures will help in any conservation efforts.

Finally, a potentially big environmental issue involves changing building codes. "Probably the most controversial issue is changing building codes to reflect environmentally- and energy-efficient building concepts," says Italiano. Why? Because "all of the vested interests are being shaken up."

GREEN EXPECTATIONS

A look at the legislative dockets on national and local levels confirms that this is a year of heightened environmental awareness and activity. Four major pieces of national legislation form the core of this political ground swell: the Resource Conservation and Recovery Act, and reauthorizations of the Superfund, the Clean Water Act, and the Safe Drinking Water Act. Environmental management consultants view the vigorous activity as a chance for the Clinton-Gore Administration and Congress to set new priorities and responsibilities for a greener America.

"There is a lot of interest in reforming Superfund to make it more efficient and effective," says Ira Whitman, PhD, PE, of The Whitman Companies, East Brunswick, NJ. The reauthorization is likely this year, says Whitman, and it will affect vital issues such as owner liability and options for site remediation.

Whitman expects that reform of the Clean Water Act will address "funding for publicly owned water treatment systems and the regulation of non-point sources of pollution. However," he adds, "a lot is still missing, including any attempt to address issues related to wetlands," a topic of great interest to developers.

Short- and long-term environmental expectations will also be shaped by actions in the Senate and the House to boost the development of related technologies, and laws intended to relax the requirements for monitoring drinking water.

Whitman also anticipates headline news stemming from difficulties in implementing the 1990 amendments to the Clean Air Act, and possibly from expenses incurred from clean-up operations at Department of Energy facilities and military bases slated to be closed.

For those with industrial sites in their portfolios, another political move may affect planning in 1994 and beyond: assessment of provisions in the Industrial Site Recovery Act, such as "the certification of environmental professionals, a review of the concept of joint and several liability, and the one in a million cancer risk level for individual contaminants."

—C.C. Sullivan

Getting the Lead Out

Andrew Reinbach

PURE WATER, LIKE CLEAN air, is something most building occupants take for granted. The same goes for building owners and facilities managers—as long as contracting documents are adhered to. But as Washington, D.C.-based Barnes, Morris, Pardoe & Foster Management Services (BMPF), the property management arm of Barnes, Morris, Pardoe & Foster Co., found out, environmental surprises pop up from time to time—even in new buildings.

As related by Kevin C. Wade, a BMPF vice president, one of his environmental teams was conducting a routine testing of the drinking water in a building the company manages, when team members noticed a problem. A small percentage of the samples taken showed lead levels substantially above the 26 parts per billion recommended by the U.S. Environmental Protection Agency (EPA). "We had some pretty healthy spikes in some of the lesser-used hose bibs," he says. "The usual spike was about 85 to 100 parts per billion, but one,

in a very infrequently-used tap, was 680 parts per billion."

Because of the health risks associated with lead, Wade's group immediately turned off the drinking fountains in the 110,000 square foot office building, which was built in 1985. At the same time, he notified building tenants to drink only bottled water and installed portable water coolers.

Following that, Wade and his environmental group conducted a second round of tests, in which they detected high lead concentrations throughout the building. The "spikes" indicating high lead concentrations, however, seemed to move about the building—being present one day, and disappearing the next. The BMPF team flushed all the water pipes and tested a third time. They also removed six soldered couplings from different parts of the building and sent them to a lab for analysis.

The laboratory tests revealed the problem and indicated the likely suspect: The solder was old-fashioned 50/50 lead and tin, while the

construction documents clearly required a solder of 95 percent tin and 5 percent antimony.

"The analysis showed pretty conclusively that it hadn't been the builder's problem—it was the sub-contractor's problem. He'd violated the construction documents, figuring nobody would notice the difference. That cost him $50,000—more than his profit margin, probably—because he had to pay to correct the problem," says Wade.

According to Wade, his group had five options:

1. Do nothing ("Not an option," he says).
2. Provide bottled water forever.
3. Replumb the entire building. This was a real problem, since the building's major tenant was a large law firm that occupied several floors with very high-end interior finishes.
4. Distill the water at all sources of potable water, which was impractical.

5. Isolate the lead by injecting sodium silicate into the pipe system.

Not surprisingly, Wade's team chose option No. 5. over what boiled down to either permanent new expenses—which would *hardly* have delighted the new owner—or protracted litigation. But even more importantly, implementing the decision became an interesting engineering challenge for Wade and his group.

First, certain elements of the piping system that had small openings, which could have been clogged by the coating material, had to be isolated from the main apparatus.

These included the cooling tower, the humidifiers, and the hot water heaters.

Second, the potable water system was isolated from the mechanical system by installing a separate water riser for the mechanical system.

Finally, the injection system itself was installed at the main point of water entry into the building, next to the main water pumps. The injection system, which included a 50-gallon drum of sodium silicate solution, closely resembles an ordinary water treatment system and feeds a steady adjustable amount of solution into the pipes, according to Wade.

The entire process took nine months. As part of it, Wade's engineers had to turn on every water spout in the building to spread the treated water evenly to dis-used areas.

The result? Lead levels that meet the EPA's mandated 26 parts per billion—a reduction of over 75 percent from the average "spike" of 85 parts per billion.

"It just goes to show that a developer needs tight construction specifications," says Wade. "If he hadn't had a good legal group, that builder would've paid for the job himself."

REDUCING RISKS THROUGH HAZARDOUS WASTE DISPOSAL

Andrew Reinbach

IF THE AVERAGE FACILITIES manager thinks disposing of asbestos is a headache, he or she should consider what could be in William O. Floyd's dumpsters: hypodermic needles, deadly poisons, and low-level nuclear waste.

Floyd is director of Plant Operations at Chicago's Michael Reese Hospital and Medical Center, a 1,006-bed teaching facility operated by Columbia/HCA Health Care Co. "No doubt a hospital has more issues to deal with than a shopping center or an office building," says Floyd, "but the issues are there, and they have to be dealt with."

"What's necessary is to have a person on staff who's responsible for environmental safety," he adds. "People don't want to hear this, but it's what's necessary."

To deal with these facts of life, Floyd advocates a formal, structured waste disposal regimen to ensure that:

► All wastes are handled properly.

► Precise inventories are kept.
► No wastes accumulate.
► All wastes are disposed of within 90 days.

Floyd also recommends each facility maintain a hazardous waste subcommittee that meets monthly, conducts regular inspections of the property, and makes sure accumulations are dealt with promptly. To prevent such accumulation, he says, a facilities manager should mandate that:

► Each type of waste is sorted and separated.
► Each type is properly disposed of as per all relevant environmental regulations.
► All paperwork is reviewed by staff.

This regimen, he says, is quite separate from the physical disposal of the wastes themselves. Floyd hires a contractor who does everything from correctly packing, shipping, and disposing of all

waste to completing the actual paperwork.

But even if a facilities professional has a long and good relationship with a contractor, warns Floyd, it essential to constantly review the contractor's work. "We're always responsible," he says. "If the disposal site has a problem. we're still liable for it under the [federal] Superfund [law]." The hospital self-insures for environmental liabilities and carries a supplemental policy as well.

Floyd says his biggest problem came when the hospital was taken over by Columbia/HCA several years ago.

"Over the years, researchers came and went, and they always left a lot of chemicals behind," he says. "We had to bail them all up and ship them to a treatment facility. Some, like the acids and bases, could be neutralized; others had to be stored. And, of course, the EPA has long documents detailing how each chemical has to be handled."

Although Floyd doesn't recall exactly how many gallons of chemicals had to be disposed of, he says. "They'd been piling up for years. We had trucks filled with barrels leaving here for days."

Floyd says infectious medical wastes—including severed limbs—are sent in hard plastic shipping containers directly from patient rooms and operating theaters to a facility that renders the wastes non-infectious.

Floyd, a no-nonsense Tennesseean, is a big fan of facing these issues squarely.

"You cannot stick your head in the sand and ignore these things. They will not go away. You're better off establishing procedures and dealing with them. It's an expense, but it's part of the cost of doing business, and should be looked on that way."

Breathing Easier and IAQ

Andrew Reinbach

"THE BEST WAY TO TELL A building has an indoor air problem is to follow your nose, says Larry Eldridge, director of Engineering for Trammell Crow Dallas/Fort Worth, Inc. "The human nose is hundreds of times more sensitive than the best technology," he says. "You can walk into a lobby or a washroom and know there's a problem. The testing just proves it."

This approach stood Eldridge in good stead not long ago, when he and his team walked into a local office building for which his organization took over management. The building smelled stale. Eldridge and his team went straight to the air handling system.

"We knew there was a problem as soon as we looked at it." he says. "The outside louvers were all shut, and the timers were set wrong. It was a mess."

Investigation showed that engineering mistakes and problems had compounded each other until the whole building was unpleasant. Eldridge and his management team discovered:

▶ The outside air supply was completely blocked, apparently because someone had thought it would improve energy efficiency.
▶ The forced air exhaust systems ran on limited hours. so both fresh air intake and stale air exhaust were limited.
▶ Fresh air intake temperatures ran above the recommended 55- to 60-degrees level, which encouraged mold in the building's ductwork.
▶ Cheap air filters, mistakenly installed as money-savers, constantly clogged, further reducing system efficiency.

Luckily for Crow's client, Eldridge's engineering options were limited—and obvious.

"The primary course had to be to restore the outside air supply," he says. "In a commercial building, there's no alternative to reasonable outside air supply and exhausting.

Anytime that's compromised, it must be restored."

The only wrinkle in restoring the system, according to Eldridge, was in using different levels of filtration and outside air supply. He experimented with various options, after conducting a series of tests with Drager tubes, a hand-operated, ampule-based German air-testing system he favors for reasons of backtracking in case of unusual variations in test results.

Initially, Eldridge opened outside louvers by a factor of 10, which flooded the building with fresh air. His process eventually allowed the building to switch to 100 percent outside air during the winter months, he says, which substantially reduced operating costs by reducing air conditioning requirements. In addition, it lowered the temperature of the outside air intake to 55 degrees, which allowed a reduction of molds in the ductwork.

The process took a total of eight months, according to Eldridge, by which time the air quality was noticeably better. The next scheduled steps were to:

▶ Pre-filter the outside air supply.
▶ Clean mold accumulations from the duct walls.
▶ Retrofit the air-handling system by re-lining ducts to create cleanable surfaces and minimize airborne fibers.

▶ Replace the condensate drain pans, which accumulated water, with stainless steel that had a positive drain.

The result, says Eldridge, would have been optimal air quality. But the building was sold to new investors, and the management contract was awarded to another turn.

However, he says, there had been no reason for the condition to have existed in the first place. "You can measure the effects of good vs. bad maintenance. But the mechanics are very simple; it's mostly a matter of good housekeeping. Responsible design and maintenance in a modern building can give you indoor air quality that's as good as outdoor air."

CLOSING THE LOOP THROUGH RECYCLING

Andrew Reinbach

A "GREEN" MENTALITY isn't only about fixing problems; it's more about avoiding them, partly by creating what the current wisdom calls a "sustainable" economy.

In California's San Fernando Valley, for instance, The Warner Center, a 200-acre office and industrial park in Woodland Hills, is making its contribution to green thinking. At the same time, however, it's making some bucks.

Recycling is part of a successful approach to sustaining resources. By abandoning planned obsolescence for old-fashioned frugality, advocates hope to reduce demand for natural products, like trees and chemicals, by creating new—and profitable—sources of supply.

Paper, for instance, can be made of old paper; old glass can become new glass. Even plastic can be remanufactured.

Unsurprisingly, big facilities like Warner Center, with its 16 property owners and 40,000 employees, are big sources of such "reusable" products. Each year, it casts off—and recycles—2,278 tons of paper, glass, plastic, and other materials, including cardboard, wooden loading pallets, laser toner cartridges, and such so-called green waste as grass clippings.

Of this number, 89 percent—2,027 tons—is paper. At 17 trees per ton of paper, this figure translates into 34,459 trees planted each year. It also means 6,834 cubic yards of refuse that doesn't have to be shipped to a landfill.

The bottom line: "The program makes a $61,000 annual profit and saves Warner Center tenants an additional $73,000 in trash hauling costs and landfill fees, according to Susan Compton, president of RSI Consulting Services, Woodland Hills, which manages the program for the tenant's group, the Warner Center Association.

An added incentive: California law—AB 939—mandates that businesses must reduce their landfill use by 25 percent by 1995, and 50 percent by 2000. The Warner Center project has already reduced that figure to 42 percent, says Compton.

The association contracts with RSI, which acts as a middleman, selling the materials it collects to end-users like paper mills and plastics and glass manufacturers according to Compton, who has been in the recycling consulting business for 15 years. RSI also receives a fee from the association based on how much money RSI saves. Green waste is composted, along with some of the pallets.

Benefits are significant. To bring this into sharper focus. consider one company's experience: The Voit Companies, a local developer that manages three million square feet of office space in 45 buildings in Warner Center, recycled 105.3 tons of paper in 1993, saving $16,786 in fees and diverting 315 cubic yards of trash from the local landfill, according to Jeffrey S. Lapin, a Voit vice president.

But advantage reaches to more than just big firms like Voit. "It's especially valuable for small companies," says Compton. "By grouping together, they get the same deal as companies like Rocketdyne," a large aerospace contractor that has a plant near the Center.

RSI has been managing the Warner Center project since December 1992, and the success it has achieved hasn't escaped notice. Compton is about to extend the program to the entire Woodland Hills Chamber of Commerce, with its 980 companies.

"I was lucky," she says. "I've been working with a very intelligent group of people who were not just concerned with saving the environment, but also understood the advantages of pooling their recyclables."

Greening of the White House: The Federal Government Modernizes with Sensitivity

Andrew Reinbach

IF LEADERSHIP IS THE BEST example, and environmental consciousness a national policy, the White House should be a green machine—to Bill Clinton.

The White House unveiled a plan in March to accomplish this goal calling it the "Greening of the White House," that, in the short term, will cut energy expenditures, improve indoor air quality, increase recycling, save water, and fine-tune environmental management systems in both the Executive Mansion and the Old Executive Office Building. At the same time, the plan is intended to extend these goals as far as possible in the long term.

The fact that such a plan is being implemented doesn't mean the buildings are falling down: The White House was stripped to its sandstone shell and rebuilt in concrete and steel during the Truman Administration: the Executive Office Building is solid granite. "They've been incredibly well maintained, and there's been a great deal of attention paid to environmental issues," says William D. Browning, director of Green Development Services for the Rocky Mountain Institute, Snowmass, CO. "The problem is that some of each building's physical plant is 100 years old. The Executive Office Building, for instance, has no air-handling system, and the White House's heating system is 40 years old; technology has improved some since then," he says.

The program, which is already being implemented, was a managerial nightmare. Four federal agencies are responsible for the two buildings: the General Services Administration; the National Parks Service; the Executive Residence Agency; and the White House Office of Administration. Included in the planning were the Environmental Protection Agency, the Department of Energy, and the District of Columbia. The team also consisted of consultants from Browning's Rocky Mountain Institute, as well as the American Institute of Architects, Washington. D.C.

Phase One moves forward on five fronts:

1. Energy efficiency actions include re-glazing, new lighting, plug load reductions, use of energy-efficient electrical equipment, upgrade of the HVAC system, and, where possible, the use of renewable resources.
2. Building ecology will be improved by generally buying "green." and improving indoor air quality by minimizing volatile organic compounds (VOCs) in the air.
3. The White House's impact on outdoor air and water will be improved through a variety of actions to reduce emissions and conserve water as much as possible, while minimizing the use of pesticides and fertilizers and maximizing the use of native plants.

From BUILDINGS, Volume 82, no. 5, May 1994. Copyright 1994 by Stamats Communications. Reprinted by permission.

4. Sources of pollution will be reduced by managing solid waste (the White House is a volcano of paper) and increasing recycling, as well as reducing hazardous waste (mainly paint and solvents), indoor pesticide use, and the presence of poly-chlorinated biphenyls (PCBs) in transformers.
5. A new energy and environmental management system for the complex will be created that will institutionalize and promote the overall system.

Phases two and three will extend these efforts. Ambient light levels will be reduced from 50 to 30 watts. In fact, the process is already being explored with the installation of a pilot project of task/ambient lighting, using compact fluorescent bulbs in historic-looking fixtures.

In addition, new, non-chlorofluorocarbon (non-CFC) chillers will be installed. Increased use of computers, in general, and green computers, specifically, will reduce paper and electricity use. Waste prevention and hazardous materials programs will be fine-tuned.

The result, in part accomplished via Executive Order, will reduce operating costs and environmental impacts in the nation's most eminent residence. And it will lay the president's money alongside his environmental conscience, putting the federal government's buying power behind the nation's environmental policies.

The American Institute of Architects, Washington. D.C., plans to develop an educational group self-study package that ties in the White House retrofit. The program can be used for demonstration projects to replicate the success of a feasibility study it did for Clinton's energy and environmental upgrade and retrofit. One component of the educational package is an interactive CD-ROM disk that will allow viewers to "tour" the White House and zoom in on any of its many interesting architectural features, as well as receive environmental and technical information geared to their level, education, and proficiency.

Economy and Ecology: A Powerful Coalition

C.C. Sullivan

AFTER THE FIRST HIGH waves of public interest and media subside, we begin to . . . hear from those . . . on the polar extremes of the environmental issue. On the one extreme are those . . . who suggest that we turn our backs on the fantastic benefits we have derived from the use of science and technology, and give it all back to Mother Nature . . . At the other polar extreme [are] those who would treat Mother Nature as if she were the enemy and, clinging to the social economic and environmental views which were in vogue in 1928, would give the earth over to the blind bulldozer. About the only thing these two conflicting groups agree upon is that those of us who labor within society's institutions are not doing things right.

Spoken two decades ago by former U.S. Environmental Protection Agency (EPA) head Thomas F. Williams, and recorded in *BUILDINGS,* these words serve to illustrate profound transformations in American thought. In 1973, environmental concern—considered (then) "a 'now' thing—divided the public into two incompatible and reactionary camps: the "tree huggers" vs. the "blind bulldozers."

Since then, the energy crisis, brimming landfills, oil spills, endangered species, Love Canal, and Chernobyl have led to an "eco-enlightenment" that pervades every sector of our society, from the boardrooms of the Fortune 500 to the living rooms of the American family. Environmental thought has become conventional wisdom and central to discussions (and often, panic) regarding public health safety. This awareness is reflected in the current political climate, which augurs change on the environmental front for building owners and facilities managers.

Since taking the helm, President Bill Clinton has sponsored a flurry of environmental initiatives included in an economic stimulus package, technology research and development programs, and a new White House Office on Environmental Policy (OEP). Widely expected to draft policies on everything from energy efficiency to pollution prevention to global warming, the OEP will reflect the administration's keen interest in the environment.

Interestingly, the OEP's domestic mission is set forth as an economic crusade. In Clinton's words: "We must move in a new direction, to recognize that protecting the environment means strengthening our economy, and creating jobs. And, we must be ready to take advantage of the enormous business opportunities . . . for new environmental technologies that protect the environment and increase profits."

Based on pronouncements and early action, specific effects of Clintonian policy on the commercial real estate industry are being gauged by sources close to the administration. In the energy arena, the spotlight is on efficiency, with incentives and pressures to pursue reduced consumption through demand-side management, utility rebates, and usage of natural gas. The proposed energy tax will undoubtedly spur in-house conservation techniques. Investment in "green" technologies will be pushed by tax credits for capital equipment and by government-sponsored research. New building standards delineated in the omnibus Energy Bill are likely to affect the buildings industry.

Pollution prevention—which in its broadest sense includes efficiency and recycling concerns—is championed by the administration. Building owners will be coaxed to utilize renewable materials, install energy-efficient systems, and reduce wastes. Guidelines on ecologically sensitive construction materials and products will be pushed as standard business practice. On the subject of toxic waste cleanups, Clinton is a pragmatist who will seek effective action with a low price tag.

Other important issues, including the phase-out of chlorofluorocarbons (CFCs), could follow courses outlined over recent years. But the present administration will clearly inaugurate a new age of "green" thought. Public awareness will be enriched, and building professionals will be compelled to reflect on their collective responsibilities and rights.

A common-sense response to the new era of environmental pro-activism materializes: Sharpen your no-lead pencils. Equip your buildings and staff with timely information on key issues, and pursue smart investments in environmentally driven technologies. A solid grasp of the market will help ward off legal action, unnecessary expenditures, and avoidable depreciations of property value.

Do ecologically advanced properties automatically become economically advanced? Maybe, if owners buy carefully and get good advice. The National Audubon Society (NAS) and the West Bend Mutual Insurance Company recently made major investments in new headquarters. These construction and modernization projects incorporate green principles for efficient operations and healthy occupancy. Such noteworthy cases show how common-sense and high-tech environmentalism can help reduce operating costs and maximize profitability.

Recycling buildings is what modernization really means, and the NAS headquarters in New York City show how recycled architecture can afford super-efficient operability. The project relied on life-cycle costing, a novel financial technique in which the costs of producing, transporting, utilizing, and recycling/disposing of building materials are all factored into the owner's purchasing decisions. The result? A thoroughly modern turn-of-the-century classic, boasting universal resource conservation and healthy, cost-effective workspaces.

Romanesque, gargoyled, and massive, the 1891 Schermerhorn building on Manhattan's lower Broadway, designed by the celebrated George Browne Post, provided excellent "bones" for construction recycling. NAS directors hired the Croxton Collaborative and Flack + Kurtz, both of New York City, to develop a "sustainable" building, i.e., one that balances urban demands and existing resources. James A. Cunningham, senior vice president of Finance and Administration at the NAS, points out that resource and energy conservation were design drivers only when deemed cost-effective based on a payback period of three to five years. "We didn't re-invent the wheel," stresses Cunningham. "The resources for this type of project were already there."

The modernization/operational approach was outlined in five steps: (1) recycle the building; (2) recycle demolition material; (3) use recycled post-consumer building materials; (4) install an internal recycling system; and (5) establish purchasing guidelines. The NAS estimates that 300 tons of steel, 9,000 tons of masonry, and 560 tons of concrete were recycled during the renovation. Competitively priced building products with recycled content included steel, gypsum, ceramic tile, roofing felt, insulation, plastics, and carpet underlayment. Purchases of new materials were based on energy efficiency, as well as "cradle-to-grave" issues (such as production-related pollution) and life-safety concerns (such as toxicity and off-gassing).

The project's *piece de resistance* is the proprietary internal high-rise recycling system built into the office walls. Coupled with purchasing managers buying almost nothing but recyclables, the NAS ap-

Unique ownership philosophies dictated many of the selections of materials for the National Audubon Society and West Bend headquarters.

For the West Bend Insurance Co. headquarters, natural materials were favored by the building committee. Natural finishes, like stone, tend to be environmentally benign and have low toxicities.

The headquarters of the National Audubon Society also employ natural materials throughout, but the directors considered the materials and systems from a "cradle-to-grave" perspective. This allowed the participants in the modernization process to learn how materials affect the environment during an entire life cycle.

Here's a brief overview of what materials and systems were actually employed in these projects:

System or Material	West Bend Insurance	National Audubon Society	System or Material	West Bend Insurance	National Audubon Society
Site	Rural	Urban	Paint		Glidden Lifemaster 2000 Spred 2000
Building	1991 Postmodern, 4 stories	1891 Romanesque, 8 Stories	HVAC	Electric	Gas-fired chiller/heater by ParaFlow, Hitachi/York Int'l.
Structure	Local limestone, precast concrete, brick	Recycled steel, cast iron, masonry	Refrigerant	R-22 Freon	Lithium bromide
Roofing	Concrete tiles	BUR tar on felt	Elevators	Otis	Otis
Glazing Technologies	Kawneer double-glazed tinted low-E	Skyline double-glazed with Heat-Mirror inserts by Southwall	Control/security	Johnson Controls	
Insulation	Fiber glass and air pocket detail	Magnesium silicate, whipped sea water	Cabling	IBM	
Carpets, pads	Modular carpeting; Milliken Comfort Plus	Desso wool carpet, wool padding	Recycling system		Midland Metalcraft
Office systems	La-Z-Boy; Invincible Metal	Herman Miller	Utility rebate	Wisconsin Elec. P. Co. (HVAC, light)	Con Edison Brooklyn Union Gas (HVAC, motors, light)
Light fixtures	Ambient: T-8 Octron lamps by Sylvania	Ambient: 30-watt T-8 lamps by Linear and Edison Price	**The Economics:**		
	Task: (Pre-wired partitions have built-in lamps)	Task: Herman Miller Total footcandles: 70	Estimated add'l cost for green systems:	Not calculated	$172,000 or 6%
Ballasts	Electronic	Advance Mark V, VII	Estimated electricity/other savings:	$0.07/square foot or 40% electricity; Productivity gain: up to 15% of salaries	$36,000 total per annum, HVAC; 80% electricity
Walls		Gold Bond sheetrock	Immediate utility rebates:	$200,000	$110,715
Doors/ hardware	LaForce Mfg. and Schlage	Yale	Payback period to recoup:	3.5–5 years	Less than five years

proach could recycle up to 80 percent of its trash, including 42 tons of paper annually.

The NAS headquarters incorporate practical, money-saving technologies that at once address energy conservation, indoor air quality, and the reduction of polluting gas emissions. Energy consumption is cut by maximizing natural illumination, supplementing ambient light with strategically positioned task lighting on occupancy sensors, and taking advantage of rebates from the regional utility company. Upgraded thermal insulation, double-paned glazing with "heat mirror" coatings, and a scaled-down gas-fired absorption heater/chiller slash fuel use. The results, it is calculated, prune energy and electricity consumption by 61 and 68 percent, respectively.

The causes of two major problems related to modern structures—sick building syndrome and CFC emission—are nipped in the bud. A high-speed circulation system provides six air changes per hour (double the highest standard) to prevent bacterial build-up and employee malaise. A CFC-free refrigerant based on water and lithium bromide salts is used exclusively, and the high R-value insulation system comprises magnesium silicate and—surprisingly—whipped sea water.

"Very nice. But how does all this translate into efficient day-to-day operations?" asks an unimpressed, cost-conscious building owner.

Early figures are enough to turn even the most skeptical

head: annual energy savings of $40,000 using natural gas, and 80 cents on the dollar saved on power for lighting. The heating and cooling units emit 62 percent less CO and CO_2, gases associated with global warming. Added to that, zero CFC emission means zero ozone depletion, and no costly retrofitting in the future. The only item that is not cost-effective is the recycling system, but Cunningham points out that, "with mandatory recycling in New York, the system cuts down the time spent carting paper and bottles."

"A short movie and a book will be available," says Cunningham, "so others can benefit from the work we've done." The NAS estimates that the costs of developing and running this robust, highly efficient building are competitive with the costs for new buildings with traditional, less efficient systems. Since operating costs can account for 30 percent of a lessee's total rent, tenants may demand today's attainable levels of efficiency in their buildings. Developers and brokers are already adapting to the new business climate with rental and sales pitches that highlight the eco-friendliness of their portfolios.

A good example of environmentally sensitive new construction can be found in the West Bend Insurance Company headquarters in West Bend, WI. The unintimidating 150,000 square foot facility has postmodern profiles that hug the rolling hills and breach four stories with an un-

derstated octagonal cupola. The modest exterior of local stone, however, belies the new building's boldly intelligent design—a design which makes the structure the ultimate in worker safety and productivity.

Motivated by interest in modern, efficient systems and employee comfort and productivity, West Bend set out to combine the best of both worlds. Using available technologies and innovative design strategies, the company found it could accommodate the dual objective and provide surprisingly effective environmental amenities.

Led by Ronald W. Lauret, senior vice president, the building committee worked with Zimmerman Design of Milwaukee to develop an unusual plan in which workstations are surrounded by a perimeter walkway. "The workstations are fitted with personal environmental modules (PEMs—also known as "environmentally responsive workstations") with individual control panels for each employee. While workers fine-tune their station temperature and airflow, the perimeter walkway is kept at energy-saving temperatures year round. The novel plan—and the cutting-edge, customized PEM micro-environments—were central to attaining the twin objectives of comfort and productivity.

The system effectively paid for itself in a year, according to an independent productivity study. Just as significantly, the scheme, provides a continual windfall in the form of reduced energy consumption. Robert Schmitt, facility manager at West Bend, argues that these factors, combined with significant utility rebates, are a triple incentive for similar projects by other companies. "I calculated that our utilities went from 18 cents [per square foot] per month in our old building to 11 cents per square foot here."

Other architectural elements bolster efficiency at West Bend, including maximized daylighting, high R-value glass, a well-insulated building envelope, and a special raised-floor system. The latest currents in interior lighting control were also incorporated: high efficiency lamps with electronic ballasts to supplement ambient daylight, and motion sensors for automatic shut-off at vacated workstations.

The project's mechanical and electrical engineers added substantially to the building's energy economy by designing features like a partial thermal storage system, heat tracing on hot-water pipes, vane-axial relief fans, and a hill economizer cycle on the chillers for computer support areas. After considering all local heat sources in the building, "[the building committee] decided that we were better off with electric boilers than going with gas boilers," says Schmitt. Are operations affected by this choice of technology? "The building warms up really fast," he boasts, even on frigid Wisconsin mornings.

The finishing touch was provided by Wisconsin Electric's

"Smart Money" program, in the form of utility rebates for energy-saving systems. Flat paybacks were given for qualifying light bulbs and ballasts, and the souped-up mechanical systems were compared to conventional set-ups to calculate kilowatt savings. "We ended up with our entire building project, with close to $200,000, I believe, in rebate money on lighting, windows, and anything electrical," asserts Schmitt.

In its essence, the West Bend facility is a totally electric, highly automated, intelligent structure that responds to employee complaints instantly and silently. Direct digital control provides the "neutral network" for combining all of the systems—systems which give the insurance company a decidedly unique atmosphere. As the project's leadership readily admits, however, the only truly novel technology in the building is the PEM concept. Good engineering is the key driver, from the variable air volume boxes with reheat units in the conference rooms to the "tight" building envelope.

But West Bend's environmentalism doesn't stop at the exterior wall. Schmitt recalls that the overuse, neglect, and pesticide contamination rendered infertile the 160-acre cornfield on which the headquarters now stand. "Basically," laments Schmitt, "the property was becoming useless. Nothing would grow anymore." A desire to bring the plot "back to a more natural state" led to restoration of natural prairie, an on-site tree

nursery, and plantings of 23 flower species and 8,000 trees.

Is this the work of a fanatical group of "tree-huggers"? Not at all, contends Schmitt, who attributes the initiative to concerned officers and employees whose homes—and futures—are right here in this Milwaukee suburb.

Faced with important financial concerns—productivity, total quality, efficiency—and committed to protecting the earth where feasible, West Bend Insurance Company and the National Audubon Society embarked on journeys that taught them a little about good design and a lot about the relationship between people and their environment.

As John Thompson most succinctly observes in his book *The Environmental Entrepreneur*, "In all great problems there are great opportunities. Supply the demands of the market and the riches will flow. In this basic maxim of human enterprise lies the solution to the environmental problem."

Environmental Audits: New Armor for an Old Battle

While Bill Clinton's Office on Environmental Policy (OEP) is a novel initiative, green business and development initiatives embraced by recent presidents and legislators are not new.

Consider the Clean Air Act, first introduced and passed in 1967, and recently expanded by George Bush during his presidential tenure. Another example is environmental auditing, now receiving considerable attention, which—with the controversies it unearths—reminds developers and owners of a similarly contentious issue from the not-so-distant past.

Twenty years ago, *BUILDINGS* reported on "environmental impact statements," the brainchild of the new-fledged U.S. Environmental Protection Agency (EPA). In that article, California was described as "one of the most environmentally conscious states." However, "only a small handful of companies" were qualified at that time to draft environmental impact statements.

Deja vu, say property owners. Today, environmental audits, or "risk assessments," are being conducted by a larger handful of companies. To find suitably qualified auditors, owners and developers tend to rely on referrals from lawyers or other professionals. Alan Riley, a New York City developer, says: "On every single property that we have, we have done an audit with someone recommended to us."

As opposed to impact studies, which gauge the effect of new developments on their surroundings, environmental audits determine the potential hazards of a site to the building and its occupants. Ronald Miller, vice president of VISTA Environmental Information, Inc., an environmental data base service in San Diego, says most real estate transactions should include some type of assessment measures, and that building owners

would be wise to undertake self-audits for existing properties soon.

"There are different kinds of environmental reports," says Miller. "One is referred to as a 'transaction screen,' and the other is called a 'phase I assessment.' New national standards are being published by the American Society of Testing and Materials" (ASTM), governing these reports. "A transaction screen determines, on a preliminary basis, whether there might be environmental hazards such as toxic wastes at the subject site." The screen comprises: (1) a search of government environmental agency records; (2) a questionnaire for the current owner; and (3) a site inspection checklist.

Building owners and facilities managers can conduct transaction screens, but phase I environmental audits must be done by trained "environmental professionals." Phase I investigations involve a visual site inspection, interviews, document reviews, and a report. "The objective of the phase II audit," continues Miller, "is to confirm or deny the presence of environmental contamination" brought to light in the phase I study. Invasive sampling during phase II may demonstrate that remedial designs are needed at the site; the phase III audit provides alternatives for cleanup.

For those who ponder the potential fiscal damage wrought by phased audits, Miller estimates that transaction screens cost less than $500. "Phase I audits typically run between $2,000 and

$4,000, and normally take between three and six weeks to complete." Phase II studies can cost more than $10,000; for phase III, a whopping $25 grand plus.

Recent cases in which tenants illegally used or dumped hazardous substances on a site, show that the owner—even without being aware of these activities—shares responsibility for remediation. Legal precedent was established in *United States v. R.W. Meyer, Inc., et al,* ruled in June of 1991 by federal appeals court in Cincinnati, and also a month later in the New Jersey case *Russell-Stanley Corp. v. Plant Industries.*

Owners not involved in day-to-day operations may not be found liable, but the EPA and other officials will likely seek cooperation and/or remuneration from offenders under the auspices of the Superfund Act. Good judgment suggests that building and sites be assessed forthwith.

But where should the owner or facility manager begin? Miller says that "tenant environmental audits can help (the owner) determine whether the current facility is in compliance with all applicable federal, state, and local laws." He adds that real estate professionals tend not to respect property or tenant audits "until they are burned."

But, as demonstrated in England, clean environmental bills of health for buildings enhance their lease values. Bill Browning of the Rocky Mountain Institute in Snowmass, CO, describes a British assessment technique created by several developers for rating buildings. "The effect is that tenants ask what the rating is, and buildings with higher ratings achieve higher leases per square meter and higher lease rates," says Browning.

Controversy surrounding the efficacy of cleanup efforts at Superfund sites is not likely to curb legal actions against property owners. Recent events encourage owners to learn about standardized site investigations outlined by the ASTM. The Department of Justice has made available typical cases delineating the grounds for criminal prosecution against environmental data bases like the one at VISTA, which lists environmental records of 2.5 million locations in the U.S. and 9.9 million instances of environmental risks.

Introduction

In this exercise the student will formulate a waste management program for an existing full-service hotel in the community or a hypothetical hotel that is representative of a typical full-service hotel in a major metropolitan area. (Instructors: If all hotels in the area have waste management programs in place see the final note at the end of this exercise.) The culmination of the project is a written management report of the waste management program. Address the following steps in the report.

Justification

There are two primary reasons for a waste management program. One is environmental. Landfills must be located and constructed so that their contents do not leach into the groundwater supply. There has been much discussion about the availability of landfill sites and some recent findings have shown that the availability of landfill sites for many communities is not as dire as was once thought, but all will agree that we will eventually run out of space unless we do something now to curtail the contents of our waste stream.

The second justification is economic. Hauling and tipping fees have continued to increase over the past decade. Some operators have seen their prices increase by as much as 500%. The cost of removing and burying solid waste in a landfill is based on number of cubic yards that the operation generates. Another cost associated with solid waste is the cost of unintended throwaways. Unintended throwaways are those items that enter the waste stream that are of immediate value to the property, such as china, glass, and silver.

Steps

1. First, conduct an audit of the existing waste stream. Determine the contents of the waste and estimate the percentage of volume of each major item (e.g. cardboard, aluminum, food scraps, computer paper, etc.).

2. Second, estimate the daily tonnage and volume in cubic yards of waste generated by the property and calculate the costs to haul and bury the current volume of waste.

3. Contact all recyclers in the community to determine what items in the waste stream can be recycled.

4. Conduct a sample of the current waste stream to determine the value of unintended throwaways on a daily, weekly, and monthly basis.

5. Formulate a recycling plan. Include in the plan the training and equipment needed to get recycled materials out of the waste stream and to a central recycling center. Be sure to involve the customer in the process.

6. Conduct a financial analysis of the costs involved in setting up a recycling center. Prepare a list of equipment needed and the cost of such equipment. Also, consider the possibility of contracting the services of a local recycler who would provide personnel and the necessary equipment. Make a recommendation based on your analysis.

7. Estimate the cost savings of establishing a waste management program. Include in your analysis the costs involved in setting up such a program (labor, equipment, and facilities), the savings generated from the reduction in landfill fees, the revenue generated from recycled goods, and the savings that result from recovering unintended throwaways.

8. Describe what departments in the hotel might do to reduce the source of the solid waste being generated and describe waste transformation alternatives (e.g. compactor, pulpers, waste to energy systems, etc.) that are not currently in place in the hotel.

9. Describe how a waste management program can serve as a competitive advantage in marketing the hotel. Include background information on the concept of "green hotels" in your description.

FINAL NOTE. The instructor may wish to turn this project into a simulation exercise and provide all of the data to the students for their analysis. This tactic is recommended after the first time through the exercise in order to avoid annoying local hospitality and recycling businesses.

Introduction

The subject of indoor air quality (IAQ) in general and the presence of environmental tobacco smoke in casinos, hotels, restaurants, and bars in particular promises to be an area of major concern to industry practitioners in the coming years. In this project the student is asked to examine the issues surrounding the topic of indoor air quality and develop a proposal on how to mitigate the problem of unhealthy indoor air,

Students should address the following concerns in their paper:

1. Conduct an exploration of what products in the air may make us sick. Be sure to define the following terms and conditions: (a) bacteria and air born viruses (e.g. Legionnaires Disease, etc.), (b) outside air contaminants, (c) volatile organic compounds (VOCs), (d) environmental tobacco smoke (ETS), (d) sick building syndrome, (e) building related illness. Also, describe the short and long term health issues related to indoor air quality.

2. Identify the stakeholders involved in this issue and what our legal and ethical obligations are to them. Be sure to include in your discussion such terms as "due diligence" and "good faith efforts." Speculate on how current obligations may change if current OSHA recommendations are passed into law. Also, even if the laws do not change appreciably, discuss a hospitality organization's obligation to its stakeholders under common law.

3. Do no-smoking sections in a public facility completely mitigate the problem of environmental tobacco smoke? Defend your response.

4. Explore standards for ventilation that a hotel might adopt in order to meet the obligations outlined in section two. Include in your discussion examples from the American Society of Heating, Refrigeration and Air Conditioning Engineers 62-1989 standards.

5. Explain the part that energy conservation plays in this topic and determine if this is or is not an issue and explain your rationale.

6. Describe how we might increase the dilution of indoor air to help reduce the problem of poor IAQ. Describe engineering equipment components involved in this process.

7. Describe different filtration equipment that could be used to improve indoor air quality and comment on their effectiveness and cost. Be sure to explain why traditional filters on air handlers and fan coils do very little for human lungs.

8. Describe the economic and public relations impact of making a hospitality environment a smoke free area. Are smoke free hotels, restaurants, casinos, and bars a viable alternative to dilution and filtration?

9. Based on your findings in the first eight areas, develop a complete Indoor Air Quality strategic plan for a hospitality property. Be sure to include a proposal on how to conduct an IAQ audit and include a projection of all costs and savings associated with the plan's implementation.

FINAL NOTE. The student should make use of as many sources as possible in preparing this project. Include, if at all possible, information from operators of local, hotels, restaurants, casinos, and bars. Also, use government agencies, local, state, and national hospitality associations, private charities (e.g. American Cancer Assn., etc.), and equipment suppliers.

13

COMPUTER SYSTEMS

Communications Technology
Richard G. Moore and Scott Wilkinson

Probing an Electronic Spreadsheet Decision Support Model
Ron Brathwaite

Project 1

Project 2

COMMUNICATIONS TECHNOLOGY

Richard G. Moore and Scott Wilkinson

Introduction

TECHNOLOGICAL, POLITICAL, and economic forces are causing profound changes in how, what, and when we communicate in our professional and private lives. Communication systems have traditionally played an important role in the operation of hospitality enterprises by enhancing interaction with the guest. Advances in technology, coupled with continuing deregulation and privatization of delivery mechanisms, will have a profound effect on the hospitality sector of the 21st century.

This article has two primary objectives: The first is to explain some of the fundamental concepts in communication theory and technology; the second, to outline several trends in communication technology. These trends include the move to an integrated services digital network; the expansion of cellular communications; the digitization of communication networks; the continuing integration of communications technology and computer technology into a single, holistic technology; and the increasing capacity of our worldwide communications network. We do not address issues related to the capturing of guest data, but rather discusses how this data may be more effectively communicated through a hospitality organization.

For most people, communication is done naturally and without questioning the underlying "how." We pick up the phone; listen to the radio; feel, see, or hear our beeper summon us; log on to an E-Mail system, or receive a fax because of someone's need to communicate. Technology is providing communication options unheard of 10 years ago. Communication at any time, from any place, is the goal of the industry. But before exploring how technology might affect the hospitality industry in the 21st century, a review of some fundamentals is in order.

Basic Concepts of Communications Technology

The dawn of mankind and the origin of communications are coincidental. In the Garden of Eden, Adam and Eve explored some form of communication before the apple interfered with God's plan for perfection. The basic requirements for communicating have not changed since biblical times. In order to have a communication system three requirements must be met: There must be a source that sends information, a medium through which the information is sent, and a receiver of the information (Housley, 1987) (see Figure 1).

A present-day example of a ubiquitous communication system is a television's remote control unit. The hand-held device must be in the line of sight of the TV set. Walking to another room or having the dog walk between the sender and the television destroys one of the necessary requirements for a communication system—the medium.

Basic Characteristics of Communications

Given the simple communication model presented above, the act of communicating maybe further characterized by the needs of the sender and the receiver. The needs of both sides of our communication system define the user's willingness to accept different limitations regarding data flow modes, transmission size, and timeliness. These three concepts and their effect on the possible types of communications are discussed in the following sections.

Communications Flow

Recalling the diagram of the basic communication system (Figure 1), the communications flow may exist in any one of three modes: simplex, half-duplex, or full-duplex (Housley, 1987). Simplex communication exists when data travels in only one direction: The sender is always the sender, and the receiver is always the receiver. Listening to a radio station is an example of simplex, or one-way, communication. If a listener wishes to communicate back to the station, a second medium must enter the communi-

cation system—for example, a phone or a letter. Simplex communication is most effective in communicating with a very large number of receivers.

The second method of communication flow is half-duplex. In a half-duplex mode, the sender and receiver alternate roles, neither having both roles simultaneously. Two CB radio users talking to one another over the airwaves is an example of a half-duplex communications system. Both take turns talking while the other listens. People communicate most effectively in this manner.

The final mode of communication flow is full-duplex. In full-duplex environments, information is sent and received simultaneously. Machines are able to communicate very effectively and efficiently using full-duplex communication, but people cannot.

Transmission Size

The second characteristic of a communication transmission is transmission size. Data transmission size is limited by the medium carrying the transmission, as well as by the protocol used for the transmission. The transmission capacity of a medium is

known as its bandwidth. The concept of bandwidth may best be understood by comparing communication flow to the flow of water through a pipe. In this analogy, the medium is represented by the pipe and the bandwidth by the diameter of the pipe. One way to increase the rate of water flow is to increase the diameter of the pipe. Increasing the bandwidth of a communications line is analogous to increasing the diameter of the pipe.

The column graph in Figure 2 depicts the amount of data that must be transmitted to support four different types of communication (Black, 1987). In the first type, text, in which only letters and numbers are viewed—for example, an online text search using a personal computer—a standard telephone line is sufficient. In the mode, audio communication, a person may be receiving account balance information from the voice answer unit of a bank's computer system. In the third case, single-image communications, a guest may be receiving a picture image of the hotel where a vacation is planned. In the final case, video, a motion-video clip that shows the outdoor activities available at a

FIGURE 1. Diagram of a Basic Communication System

resort is being sent and viewed by a potential guest.

Effects of Time and Distance on Communications

The third characteristic governing communications is reflected by two elements of the communications environment and makes possible eventual universal communication, at any time, from any place. We all make choices concerning the medium of our communications, and the choice is often dictated by the required timeliness of the message and the distance the message must travel to be received. A matrix analysis is useful in exploring these dimensions (see Figure 3). The vertical axis indicates the distance between the sender and receiver. One of two classifications is made: Either the sender and receiver are in close proximity (for people, this would mean face to

face; for machines, it would mean a cable connection), or the sender and receiver are remote (for people, remote could mean in the room down the hall or in an office halfway around the world). Along the horizontal axis, we designate whether communication takes place now (often called real time), or later—a few minutes, hours, or days. One's communication needs, based on distance and timeliness, identify viable modes for a

given message. Some of these options are listed in their respective sectors of the matrix. The trend is to be able to do all communications now, whether remote or face to face. Communication services are moving toward modes that emulate the dynamic, interactive characteristics of face-to-face meetings, presenting the hospitality industry with an interesting dilemma. Exactly how will the demand for

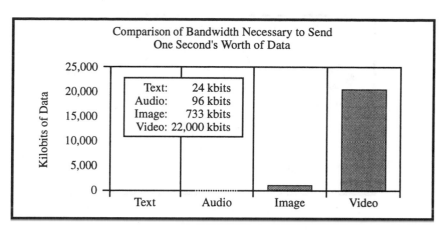

FIGURE 2. Bandwidths of Different Data Sources

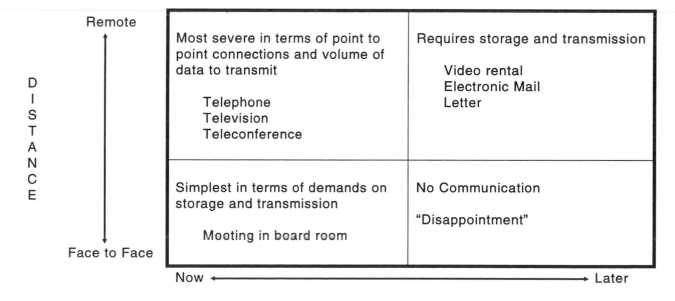

FIGURE 3. Time and Distance Effects on Communication

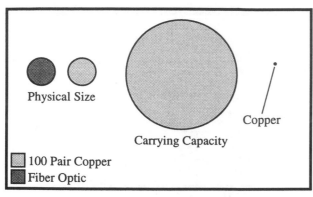

FIGURE 4. Copper Versus Fiber Optic Cable

Trends Changing the Way We Communicate

There are many political and technological factors changing the way we communicate. Three main trends covered in this article are (1) the increasing capacity of the global communication network, (2) the increasing mobility of the communication medium and devices, and (3) the continuing merger of communication and computer technologies.

This article focuses primarily on the technical factors driving change. However, it is important to note that political factors have traditionally played a very important role in determining the extent to which technical progress is made. In the United States, the government has made a major shift in policy for the communication industry. The transition from a regulated environment to a competitive environment has provided an adrenaline boost for the industry. Additional political factors are discussed only in the cases where they directly impede the progress of communication technology.

Increasing Capacity of the Global Communication Network

The capacity of the global communication network is increasing in two dimensions. The first dimension includes technological advancements that better utilize the current communication mediums. The second is the increasing use of new communication mediums, such as fiber optics and a wide range of wireless mediums.

The frequency of communication is increasing because of the increase in the modes of communication available and the ease of their use. Many of these new modes have resulted from the merging of communication technologies and computer technologies (discussed in more detail below). In addition, the digitization of communications networks will allow computer-to-computer communications to utilize more effectively the existing voice network. No longer will separate mediums for data, audio, and video networks be necessary; the same communications channel will carry all digital signals. Extensive digital networks will eliminate the need for modems, one of the limiting factors in the bandwidth capacity of the current communication network infrastructure.

In addition to increasing the efficiency of the current communications medium, the continued introduction and integration of new media will increase the capacity of the global communications network (Dertouzos, 1991). One of the most publicized trends in this area is fiber optic cable. The most obvious advantage of fiber optics is the increase in bandwidth (see Figure 4). However, the advantages of fiber optics over conventional copper mediums extend beyond the dramatic increase in bandwidth. Fiber optic cable is a more secure medium for communications. The additional security is the result of the innate characteristics of fiber optic cable: First, communication over fiber optic cable has a lower error rate, and, second, it is impossible to tap a fiber optic cable without detection.

Another medium through which communication occurs is physical space occupied only by air. The ability to communicate with anyone at any-time can truly be realized only through the use of portable, hand-held communication devices—for example, cellular phones. The traditional limits of telephone communication have been eliminated. The inability to communicate directly with someone is no longer dictated by location, but by an individual's personal decision for privacy. Unless people decide that they not wish to be disturbed, they have perpetual availability to those who attempt to communicate with them.

Proliferation of Mobile Communication

Today, the most common form of mobile communication is the cellular phone. Currently, approximately 2.5% of the U.S. population has access to cellular services; the percentage is approximately the same in Japan (Standard & Poor's Corporation, 1992). The number of cellular phones in the United States is expected to exceed 35 million by the year 2000. Cellular phones travel where their possessors do, but operate only where there is cellular service. To help explain the benefits and limitations of cellular communication, a brief discussion on the workings of such a system is given, followed by several examples of how this relatively new technology has been implemented.

One of the limits of cellular communication is that the Federal Communications Commission (FCC) has allocated only a small range of frequencies for its use. The current frequency range allows for about 60 simultaneous connections for a given cellular source. To cover a large geographical area—that is, a range comparable to that covered by a local radio station—the concept of linking together several small cells is used. Each cell is defined by the area covered by

its transmitter. It would be possible to cover this large area using only a single source; however, the area could not have a large customer base because of the 60-connection limit mentioned above. Dividing larger geographical areas into smaller cells is advantageous because each cell may have 60 simultaneous connections; this means that if a larger area is divided into 4 smaller cells, the number of possible simultaneous connections increases from 60 to 240.

It seems logical that cells could be continuously reduced in size to maximize the number of possible connections in a given geographical region; however, this is not the case. There is an optimal size for each cell. The size is dependent on the customer density for the cell, as well as the physical environment, such as the height of buildings, mountains, and other possible obstacles.

Cellular communication service has not nearly reached full capacity; it is not possible, currently, to have a continuous phone conversation while driving across the United States. Many companies are experimenting with personal communication services. Bell South has a pilot program in progress to receive feedback from consumers (Standard & Poor's Corporation, 1992). The new uses of remote communication technologies extend beyond the traditional use for voice communications. A wireless local area network product is already on the market.

It is important to note that cellular technology is only one form of remote communication. Other technologies have already made an impact on the hospitality industry, such as the use of hand-held ordering devices for restaurant waitstaff. The hand-held devices transmit very low power signals to a receiver in the dining room of the restaurant. The receiver then sends the signal, via a wire medium, to a printer in the kitchen. As this technology matures, these types of devices will become much more prevalent.

Continuing Merger of Communication Technology and Computer Technology

The advent of the first useful computers nearly 40 years ago began an era that has witnessed an exponential increase in the integration of computers into our daily lives. As the number of computers increased, especially during the 1980s with the introduction of the personal computer, it became apparent that much of the data collected and produced by computers were valuable to individuals sitting in front of other computers. The copying of files to disks, and walking or sending the disks to individuals requesting the files, was rigorous and extremely time consuming. In the early days of computing, problems such as these were partially circumvented by the centralized nature of computing; all data were stored on a central mainframe or minicomputer.

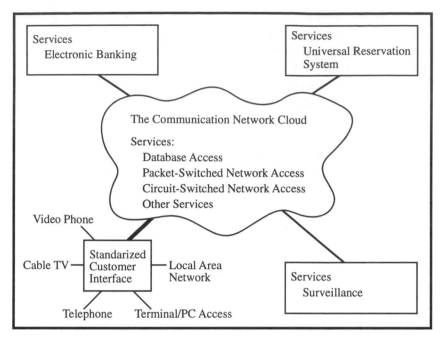

FIGURE 5. The Communication Network Cloud

The idea of linking several computers together to form a network has been around since the beginning of computing, but the problems associated with linking a large number of computers (100,000 to 1,000,000) together into a cohesive network are expansive and have only just begun to be solved. The search for the solution to this immense puzzle is the driving force behind the merger of communication and computer technology.

A result of the merging of these two technologies is the Integrated Services Digital Network (ISDN). The goal of the ISDN is to provide transparent access to a worldwide communications network. It is characterized by a merger between the computing and communications technologies, originating in the field of communications technology. Many of the characteristics of the ISDN are currently found

in the telephone system, and some are already being implemented by hospitality organizations. In the mid-1970s, a need for a worldwide data network was recognized. As a result, large telephone companies began to span the globe with telephone access at that time. It was decided that, rather than build a parallel network for data communications, the data network would "piggyback" on the extensive infrastructure already in place for a worldwide voice network.

According to Stallings (1990):

> The ISDN will be a worldwide public telecommunications network that will replace existing public telecommunications networks and deliver a wide variety of services. This ISDN will be defined by the standardization of user interfaces

and will be implemented as a set of digital switches and [data] paths supporting a broad range of traffic types and providing value added processing services. In practice there will be multiple networks . . . all transparently and uniformly accessible by any user. (p. 421)

A conceptual outline of the ISDN is shown in Figure 5. The largest hurdle in the progression toward the ISDN has been the development of communication protocol. A discussion of this protocol is beyond the scope of this article.

The most fundamental trends in communication technology are for modes of communication to simulate face-to-face communication and for the volume of communications to increase (in terms of volume of data, and number of communication opportunities). The consumers of communication technologies are demanding dynamic, interactive, mobile forms of communication that simulate face-to-face meetings. To support this demand, communications modes are moving toward real time (dynamic) and larger transmission sizes (single images and full-motion video). The increasing transmission size is the driving force behind the conversion of copper-based communication networks to fiber optic. In addition, the proliferation of personal and notebook computers has helped spur the increasing demand for access to diverse and more robust forms of data. The boundaries between formerly distinct types of data (text, audio, image, and full-motion video) are being broken down. User's demand for readily accessible communications, regardless of mode or medium, is a major part of the driving force behind the ISDN.

How Communications Technology May Reengineer Guest Contact

To envision how communications technology may reengineer guest contact, we must first imagine a communications device not yet available, the tele-computer (TC). This new device will represent the complete consolidation of what are now the semiseparate technologies of communications and computing. The TC will result from integration of a television, video camera, telephone, facsimile machine, and most important, the computer. It will be an integrated, all-purpose communications device, able to take full advantage of the benefits that will arise from the communications developments discussed above.

So what will the tele-computer look like? Imagine a computer monitor (the larger, the better) with a video camera in the upper right hand corner. Attached to the side of the monitor will be a removable object that serves as a "remote personal communications assistant," perhaps a cellular phone with a small video display. The hand-held remote personal communications assistant serves numerous functions, all of which increase the organization and

efficiency of the user. The user can jot notes on its screen using a stylus, send a fax, or access a wealth of vital information about his or her schedule and contacts. The remote personal communications assistant can even remind its user of the day's scheduled events. On the lower right-hand side of the monitor there will be a universal slot for, among other things, an identification card. The computer attached to this monitor will have access to a local area network, and the local network will have connections to the outside, ISDN-compliant communication networks (recall the communications cloud in Figure 5).

Let's assume a frequent traveler is calling a reservations service to make arrangements for a trip to Ithaca, New York. To use the communications capabilities of the system, the traveler must first place an identification card in the slot of the monitor of his or her TC. This identification card will contain much more than a single identification number; it will include a RAM chip that can store credit information, as well as schedule and personal information. After placing the card in the slot, the traveler may search a phone directory for the number of the reservations service and then have the TC dial the number. The reservationist answering the call will be able to enable the video portion of the communiqué. The video display of the call will be shown on approximately a quarter of the monitor. A second window on the

monitor would contain an image displaying what is being captured by the local monitor's video camera (for the self-conscious person).

By inserting the card in a reader attached to the monitor, the reservationist's computer system is automatically informed of basic information about the caller—for example, name, company, hotel of preference, and other information regarding the caller's traveling habits. Because the guest's frequent traveler number is sent before the voice call, the reservationist's computer is able to retrieve all pertinent information about the guest. This information would include his or her frequent traveler profile, as well as any reservations on file in order of arrival date. If there is a reservation on file for today, the reservation system's central computer will automatically initiate a link to the local hotel property management computer where the guest is expecting to stay (the guest may wish to check in over the phone). All of this processing occurs as the reservationist picks up the phone, The reservationist will answer with an appropriate reply based on information gleaned from the profile in the frequent traveler master record as well as the individual reservations records for the calling guest.

Now let's assume that the frequent traveler is about to leave the office to go to the airport and wishes to check in now to avoid any hassle. Once the frequent traveler indicates a desire to check in, the clerk can select an icon on the workstation computer and immediately be connected to the hotel's property management system (PMS). In some cases, preferences may have been communicated to the hotel PMS at the time of reservation (special room type or a specific room number). Normally, room selection is done at the time of check-in. The hotel property management computer would then note preferences and privileges (for example, upgrade to junior suite if available, etc.). The most crucial piece of information at this time will be to determine if the guest's length of stay is correct. Length of stay affects everything from booking policies to staffing schedules. The rest of the information then needs merely to be explained to the guest:

We have you arriving on American flight 960 from Orlando at 8:50 today and taking an Avis rental car to our hotel. We have checked you into room 820 on our concierge floor and have assigned your frequent traveler card to the electronic lock. The bed in room 820 has an extra-firm mattress; however, our housekeeping department would be glad to install a bed board if you so desire. Upon your arrival, Mr. John Lee, our executive assistant, would be glad to escort you to your room; however, you may also proceed there directly if you desire. I will send a copy of this check-in to your fax mailbox for reference purposes. Enjoy your stay with us.

In the above scenario, the guest's entire travel itinerary is linked together. There are several reasons for this; one may be the existence of joint frequent traveler programs, in which points must be distributed. More important, though, if the travel itinerary is linked, the frequent traveler's progress over the course of the trip may be monitored; for example, in case flight 960 is delayed and there is need to redirect the guest to another room because of an air conditioning failure in room 820. In either case, the hotel property may need to know when to have the doorman and the bell staff start looking for the expected guest.

With this background, let us explore how a guest might make a reservation over a video/phone computer. All the normal, mundane parts of the reservation have to be processed one way or another. Let us look at where image (pictures) and video technology will have an impact. One way might be to put an image of the reservation (or at least those parts that the reservationist wants the caller to see) on the caller's screen for review. The guest could then save a copy of the screen for future reference. This information may be stored in the traveler's remote communications assistant. The following exchange expands on this theme:

Guest: I will be flying into Syracuse and driving to Ithaca. What's the best way to get to your property?

Reservationist: I am putting a map on both of our

screens. The route you should take will appear as a dotted, red line on your map. Take I-81 south out of the airport. Go about 30 miles south and take exit 12 west, which is the exit for Ithaca. Follow the signs to route 13 and Ithaca. Ithaca is about 18 miles from the town of Homer, through which you will pass. Another town you will drive through on your way to Ithaca is Dryden. I have drawn a circle around Dryden. The speed limit is 30 mph, and the police will pick you up if you go over 33 mph!

We will be having a presentation in the cocktail lounge by a world-renowned physicist at 7:30 p.m. on the day of your arrival. I have attached a 30-second video clip outlining his talk. We look forward to your stay with us.

Admittedly, this scenario will not be possible for several years, yet some of the pieces are already in place. Certainly, there is nothing like the "tele-computer," but AT&T has placed a picture phone on the market. Incorporating a picture phone into a computer monitor will require some clever engineering and software code. Additionally, the capacity to transmit full-motion video over extended geographical areas does not yet exist. However, the move toward the ISDN continues; small pockets of ISDN are beginning to be joined to form a more cohesive integrated network. Perhaps the most important piece of the puzzle is the bandwidth capacity of the communications network. The laying of fiber optic cable continues, but it will still be 15 to 20 years or more before fiber access is as commonplace as copper service is today.

Our worldwide communications network is growing at an astounding pace. With the downfall of both physical and political barriers, billions of dollars are being invested in telecommunications infrastructure in parts of the world that are yearning to "dial direct" to the rest of us. The global communications system is going digital; the bandwidth connecting our systems is expanding enormously, and the trend toward remote communication modes will continue. Digital technology, coupled with wide bandwidths, means that data, audio, images, and video can all be shipped together in the same network. The access to

these networks will be simple, not requiring additional hardware, as has been the case with analog systems. The age of multimedia communication will arrive with fax, data, and video mailboxes as commonplace as the answering machine is today.

From a marketing perspective, the hotel industry must recognize the inevitable negative consequences of such vast improvements in technology. With the capability of more animated and lifelike communication through computers and video screens, the demand for face-to-face meetings will decrease. Rather than fly across the nation to meet with a client, salespeople will be able to do their business in front of computer screens, sitting at their desks at work or home. Hotels will find fewer business travelers coming through their doors, because of the very same technology that will have allowed them to improve the quality of their service.

The effects of this digital revolution on the hospitality industry will be profound. The new age of communication will affect every facet of the guest cycle, from the way hotel properties attract guests to the way in which their needs are served. These new technologies will require training methods as sophisticated as

the products, so that the guest's experience never becomes an impersonal one. The technology must be adapted to enhance the guest's stay, not cause it to be an uncomfortable, peculiar experience. With a smooth transition into the hospitality industry, multimedia communication has an incredible potential to raise service standards to new levels and improve the overall quality of a guest's experience.

References

Black, U. D. (1987). *Data communications and distributed networks.* Englewood Cliffs, NJ: Prentice-Hall.

Cerf, V. G. (1991, September). Networks. *Scientific American,* pp. 42–51.

Dertouzos, M. L. (1991, September). Communications, computers and networks. *Scientific American,* pp. 30–39.

Housley, T. (1987). *Data communications & teleprocessing systems.* Englewood Cliffs, NJ: Prentice-Hall.

Stallings, W. (1990). *Business data communications.* New York: Macmillan.

Standard & Poor's Corporation. (1992, July). *Standard & Poor's Industry Surveys: Telecommunications: Basic Analysis.* New York: Author.

Probing an Electronic Spreadsheet Decision Support Model

Ron Brathwaite

———————————◼———————————

MANY HOSPITALITY management programs are integrating the electronic spreadsheet in courses such as financial management, accounting, foodservice management, and marketing. Miller (1989), in a study on the use of computers in foodservice management education in four-year hospitality management programs, estimated that 96% of the responding programs used computers as a teaching tool. In addition, the study showed that the most used application software was the electronic spreadsheet. Its use in these programs more than doubled the use of its closest rival, database management. Some financial management and accounting textbooks even include electronic spreadsheet templates of topics-related problems as ancillary material to the main texts.

Increasingly, instructors and students are using this modeling tool to create models and to detect, examine, and explain relationships among the models' compo-

nents. When users of a model are compelled to combine data into meaningful information and relate information critically and analytically to form ideas, we witness true learning whereby information is transformed to knowledge and knowledge to wisdom (Cummings, 1992). This article refers to the process of detecting, examining, and explaining these relationships as "probing the model."

In the process of probing a model, an analyst sees relationships among the model's constituent elements differently. By interacting with a spreadsheet model, you notice, for instance, that revenues are sensitive to changes in unit selling price, while depreciation expenses do not respond to unit-price changes. You probably knew about this relationship before from reading about it or hearing it discussed. Now, with an electronic spreadsheet, you're able to simulate the process and "see" the relationship expressed in numbers, text, and

graphs on a computer screen. This type of interaction with the electronic spreadsheet model provides you, the analyst, with the ability to create the scenario on demand, and obtain instant feedback about these relationships. This ability to control the probing process is, in itself, a learning motivator.

Simulating the scenarios and recognizing relationships about the model's parts is not the only payoff from interacting with the electronic spreadsheet. The information you glean from these relationships invites focused questions, which, in turn, elicit direct answers. The answers to first-level questions conjure up second-level and other-level questions. They also suggest new ways of dealing with the elements themselves. For instance, this article illustrates the use of one element in the model to test the accuracy of other key elements within the model. New information, greater knowledge, and, hopefully, wisdom are produced as a net result.

This article demonstrates some techniques for probing a model. It shows how the process highlights relationships among the model's constituent elements and how new information is created in the process. It does this by creating and examining a typical capital budgeting decision-support model for an expansion project.

DSS, EIS, and DSM: How They Relate

It is vitally important for today's students to understand the role of decision support models (DSM) in modern business. DSMs are integral to both decision support systems (DSS) and executive information systems (EIS). A DSS provides management with the timely, relevant, and accurate information it needs to make decisions about the business. Current information technologies have also produced executive information systems, which provide executives with easy access to internal and external information that is relevant to their critical success factor (Crockett, 1992).

These definitions suggest little difference between an EIS and a DSS. In fact, an EIS is considered a form of a DSS (Gallupe, 1991). The major difference between the two systems lies in their end-users (BPP Publishing Ltd., 1991). EISs are used by top-level executives at strategic levels, mainly to make decisions related to unstructured problems. DSSs are used by mid-

dle managers at the tactical level of the decision-making ladder for routine modeling and for analyzing unstructured problem situations for top-level executives.

The heart of the DSSs and EISs is the DSM. According to Gallupe (1991), the modeling component of smaller DSSs and EISs is typically a spreadsheet-based model or simple mathematical model such as linear programming. DSSs and EISs both rely on several spreadsheet-based business DSMs such as budgeting, CVP analysis, regression analysis, and capital budgeting analysis.

Moreover, in some cases, the information executives obtain from the DSS and EIS become the data that is further processed, using electronic spreadsheets, to produce the information they need to answer the questions at hand. Spreadsheets will accept data interactively or import it from files from an accounting or other data base system for further processing. Tunison (1992) described this situation by using, as an example, the Radisson Park Terrace Hotel in Washington, DC:

Topline (an automated value management system) is interfaced with Miracle III Sales and Catering software by National Guest Systems Corp. as well as our property management system, CLS. We use windows as an operating platform so we can have topline, Miracle, CLS, Word-Perfect and Lotus on screen at the same time, and they can transparently share the same data. It's like having

one complete system and the data only has to be entered once. The convenience and efficiency are unbelievable.

As the use of EIS and DSS becomes more widespread, decision support modeling skills will become more important to current and prospective business executives.

The Anatomy of a Decision Support Model

For the purpose of this analysis, the DSMs in Figures 1 and 2 show five separate but interrelated parts. The Decision Section (row 55 to row 58) contains programmed decisions based on the net present value (NPV), internal rate of return (IRR), and modified internal rate of return (MIRR) decision rules that are applicable to the typical capital budgeting decision. Figure 2 illustrates the use of Lotus 1-2-3's @IF function to return an accept or reject decision based on the relationship between the decision criteria and other standards of comparison. For example, the (IRR) decision rule says: accept the project if IRR $\geq$ cost of capital (CC); otherwise, reject the project. In this case, IRR is the decision criterion, and CC is the standard of comparison.

The Decision Criteria section (row 49 to row 53) holds the computed values of the decision criteria, NPV, IRR, and MIRR. Figure 2 shows the formulas and functions the model uses to return these values. This section is the traditional output section of the model—

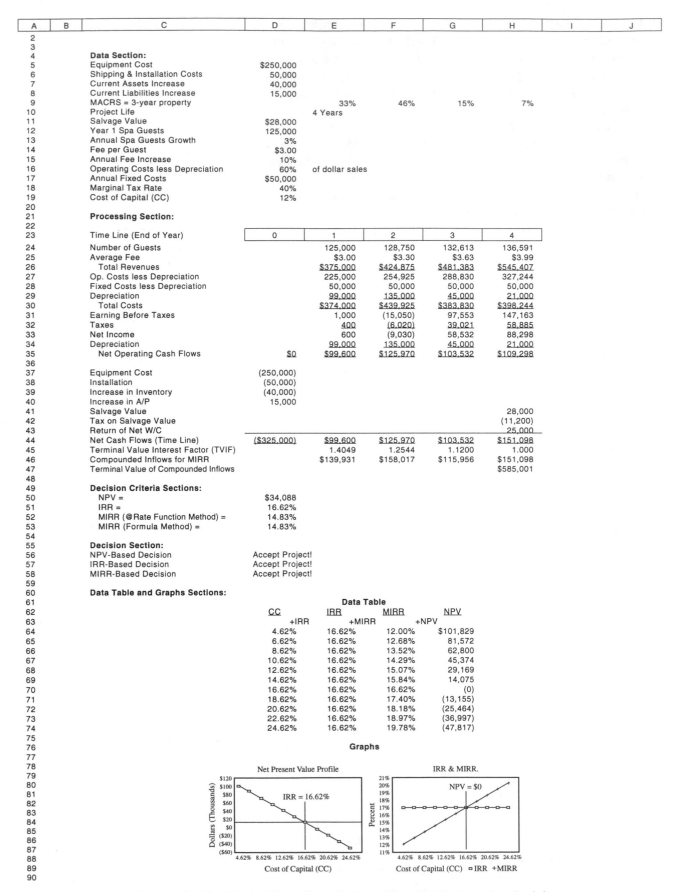

	A	B	C	D	E	F	G	H	I	J

Data Section:

Row			
4	Data Section:		
5	Equipment Cost	$250,000	
6	Shipping & Installation Costs	50,000	
7	Current Assets Increase	40,000	
8	Current Liabilities Increase	15,000	
9	MACRS = 3-year property		33% 46% 15% 7%
10	Project Life	4 Years	
11	Salvage Value	$28,000	
12	Year 1 Spa Guests	125,000	
13	Annual Spa Guests Growth	3%	
14	Fee per Guest	$3.00	
15	Annual Fee Increase	10%	
16	Operating Costs less Depreciation	60%	of dollar sales
17	Annual Fixed Costs	$50,000	
18	Marginal Tax Rate	40%	
19	Cost of Capital (CC)	12%	

Processing Section:

Time Line (End of Year)

	0	1	2	3	4
Number of Guests		125,000	128,750	132,613	136,591
Average Fee		$3.00	$3.30	$3.63	$3.99
Total Revenues		$375,000	$424,875	$481,383	$545,407
Op. Costs less Depreciation		225,000	254,925	288,830	327,244
Fixed Costs less Depreciation		50,000	50,000	50,000	50,000
Depreciation		99,000	135,000	45,000	21,000
Total Costs		$374,000	$439,925	$383,830	$398,244
Earning Before Taxes		1,000	(15,050)	97,553	147,163
Taxes		400	(6,020)	39,021	58,885
Net Income		600	(9,030)	58,532	88,298
Depreciation		99,000	135,000	45,000	21,000
Net Operating Cash Flows	$0	$99,600	$125,970	$103,532	$109,298
Equipment Cost	(250,000)				
Installation	(50,000)				
Increase in Inventory	(40,000)				
Increase in A/P	15,000				
Salvage Value					28,000
Tax on Salvage Value					(11,200)
Return of Net W/C					25,000
Net Cash Flows (Time Line)	($325,000)	$99,600	$125,970	$103,532	$151,098
Terminal Value Interest Factor (TVIF)		1.4049	1.2544	1.1200	1.000
Compounded Inflows for MIRR		$139,931	$158,017	$115,956	$151,098
Terminal Value of Compounded Inflows					$585,001

Decision Criteria Sections:

NPV =	$34,088
IRR =	16.62%
MIRR (@Rate Function Method) =	14.83%
MIRR (Formula Method) =	14.83%

Decision Section:

NPV-Based Decision	Accept Project!
IRR-Based Decision	Accept Project!
MIRR-Based Decision	Accept Project!

Data Table and Graphs Sections:

Data Table

CC	IRR	MIRR	NPV
	+IRR	+MIRR	+NPV
4.62%	16.62%	12.00%	$101,829
6.62%	16.62%	12.68%	81,572
8.62%	16.62%	13.52%	62,800
10.62%	16.62%	14.29%	45,374
12.62%	16.62%	15.07%	29,169
14.62%	16.62%	15.84%	14,075
16.62%	16.62%	16.62%	(0)
18.62%	16.62%	17.40%	(13,155)
20.62%	16.62%	18.18%	(25,464)
22.62%	16.62%	18.97%	(36,997)
24.62%	16.62%	19.78%	(47,817)

Graphs

Net Present Value Profile — IRR = 16.62%

IRR & MIRR. — NPV = $0

FIGURE 1. The Body Shop Spa Project (Capital Budget Analysis)

the area that contains the information on which the decision is based.

The Processing section is the heart of the model, just as the processor or microprocessor is the heart of the computer system. It's based on a system of equations that converts the raw data from the Data section into the information displayed in the Decision Criteria section. Gallupe (1991) referred to this section as the model base, while Hopkins (1991) called it the analysis and format function. Figure 2 shows that this section only contains formulas and functions. Except for constant values as the "one" in the formula $(1+k)^n$, this section does not contain any numbers. This is a basic design rule (Brathwaite, 1992). It is important to the probing process discussed, especially when the investigation involves sensitivity analysis.

The Data section contains all the raw facts the processing section needs to produce the decision criteria. These raw facts are the assumptions on which the model is based. One can never be certain about the assumptions one makes. This uncertainty often requires us to explore the effects changes in data items would have on the decision criteria and, ultimately, the decision itself. The alternative is to embed the data in the formulas and functions themselves. This, obviously, is an inefficient and time-consuming approach, particularly when the user wants to change the assumptions.

A data table and related graph is shown at the bottom of Figures 1 and 2. This section further processes the model's information, the decision criteria, to produce other information. It contains information the analyst can use to identify key relationships, raise questions, and proffer focused answers.

The processing section of this model is not intricate. Figure 2 shows the formulas and functions that support the system of equations used in this section. The remainder of this article will focus on the new information and techniques that result from the probe.

Probing the Model

The MIRR is a relatively new decision criterion; its computation presents properties and relationships that are not yet popular in finance and accounting textbooks. Many texts refer to the inconsistency in decision-making that NPV and IRR decision rules can create when mutually exclusive projects have to be ranked. Differences in the scales of the projects and timing of their cash flows account for these inconsistencies. Thus, situations can arise where an NPV-based decision suggests that we select project A over project B, while, simultaneously, an IRR-based decision recommends that we choose project B over project A. The MIRR eliminates this inconsistency when the scales of the projects do not differ significantly (Brigham, 1992). In other words, it eliminates the decision inconsistency

that results from the difference in timing of cash flows.

The MIRR formula is:

$$PC = \frac{TV}{(1 + MIRR)^n}$$

[where PC = the project cost, TV = the sum of the terminal value of each net cash flow, beginning the end of year 1 and ending the end of year 4; and MIRR represents the unknown value we are trying to find].

Row 45 of Figures 1 and 2 of the models shows the terminal value interest factor (TVIF). This factor compounds each of the net cash flows, beginning at the end of year 1 to return its future value at the end of the project's life, year 4. The TVIF is a variation of the well-known future value interest factor (FVIF) that we use to compound a cash flow to arrive at its future value.

The TVIF formula is derived from the formula:

$$TVCF_t = CF_t(1 + CC)^{(n-t)}$$

[where $TVCF_t$ = terminal value of cash flow occurring at time period t, or the future value of this cash flow at the end of year 4; CC = the discount rate or the weighted average cost of capital; n = life of project; and t = period in which cash flow occurs].

The TVIF is derived from this equation. It is:

$$TVIF = (1 + CC)^{(n-t)}$$

Rows 45 of Figures 1 and 2 shows the TVIFs, while rows

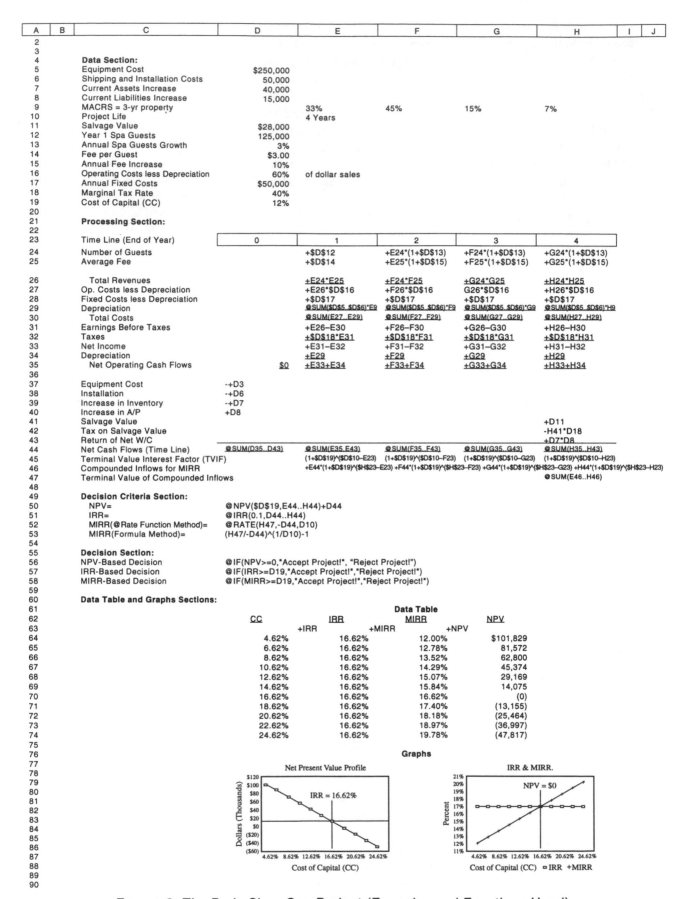

	A	B	C	D	E	F	G	H	I	J

Data Section:

Row	Label	D	E	F	G	H
5	Equipment Cost	$250,000				
6	Shipping and Installation Costs	50,000				
7	Current Assets Increase	40,000				
8	Current Liabilities Increase	15,000				
9	MACRS = 3-yr property		33%	45%	15%	7%
10	Project Life	4 Years				
11	Salvage Value	$28,000				
12	Year 1 Spa Guests	125,000				
13	Annual Spa Guests Growth	3%				
14	Fee per Guest	$3.00				
15	Annual Fee Increase	10%				
16	Operating Costs less Depreciation	60%	of dollar sales			
17	Annual Fixed Costs	$50,000				
18	Marginal Tax Rate	40%				
19	Cost of Capital (CC)	12%				

Processing Section:

Row	Label	D	E	F	G	H
23	Time Line (End of Year)	0	1	2	3	4
24	Number of Guests		+$D$12	+E24*(1+$D$13)	+F24*(1+$D$13)	+G24*(1+$D$13)
25	Average Fee		+$D$14	+E25*(1+$D$15)	+F25*(1+$D$15)	+G25*(1+$D$15)
26	Total Revenues		+E24*E25	+F24*F25	+G24*G25	+H24*H25
27	Op. Costs less Depreciation		+E26*$D$16	+F26*$D$16	G26*$D$16	+H26*$D$16
28	Fixed Costs less Depreciation		+$D$17	+$D$17	+$D$17	+$D$17
29	Depreciation		@SUM($D$5..$D$6)*E9	@SUM($D$5..$D$6)*F9	@SUM($D$5..$D$6)*G9	@SUM($D$5..$D$6)*H9
30	Total Costs		@SUM(E27..E29)	@SUM(F27..F29)	@SUM(G27..G29)	@SUM(H27..H29)
31	Earnings Before Taxes		+E26−E30	+F26−F30	+G26−G30	+H26−H30
32	Taxes		+$D$18*E31	+$D$18*F31	+$D$18*G31	+$D$18*H31
33	Net Income		+E31−E32	+F31−F32	+G31−G32	+H31−H32
34	Depreciation		+E29	+F29	+G29	+H29
35	Net Operating Cash Flows	$0	+E33+E34	+F33+F34	+G33+G34	+H33+H34
37	Equipment Cost	−+D3				
38	Installation	−+D6				
39	Increase in Inventory	−+D7				
40	Increase in A/P	+D8				
41	Salvage Value					+D11
42	Tax on Salvage Value					−H41*D18
43	Return of Net W/C					+D7*D8
44	Net Cash Flows (Time Line)	@SUM(D35..D43)	@SUM(E35..E43)	@SUM(F35..F43)	@SUM(G35..G43)	@SUM(H35..H43)
45	Terminal Value Interest Factor (TVIF)		(1+$D$19)^($D$10−E23)	(1+$D$19)^($D$10−F23)	(1+$D$19)^($D$10−G23)	(1+$D$19)^($D$10−H23)
46	Compounded Inflows for MIRR		+E44*(1+$D$19)^($H$23−E23)	+F44*(1+$D$19)^($H$23−F23)	+G44*(1+$D$19)^($H$23−G23)	+H44*(1+$D$19)^($H$23−H23)
47	Terminal Value of Compounded Inflows					@SUM(E46..H46)

Decision Criteria Section:

50	NPV=	@NPV($D$19,E44..H44)+D44
51	IRR=	@IRR(0.1,D44..H44)
52	MIRR(@Rate Function Method)=	@RATE(H47,−D44,D10)
53	MIRR(Formula Method)=	(H47/−D44)^(1/D10)−1

Decision Section:

56	NPV-Based Decision	@IF(NPV>=0,"Accept Project!", "Reject Project!")
57	IRR-Based Decision	@IF(IRR>=D19,"Accept Project!","Reject Project!")
58	MIRR-Based Decision	@IF(MIRR>=D19,"Accept Project!","Reject Project!")

Data Table and Graphs Sections:

Data Table

CC	IRR	MIRR	NPV
	+IRR	+MIRR	+NPV
4.62%	16.62%	12.00%	$101,829
6.62%	16.62%	12.78%	81,572
8.62%	16.62%	13.52%	62,800
10.62%	16.62%	14.29%	45,374
12.62%	16.62%	15.07%	29,169
14.62%	16.62%	15.84%	14,075
16.62%	16.62%	16.62%	(0)
18.62%	16.62%	17.40%	(13,155)
20.62%	16.62%	18.18%	(25,464)
22.62%	16.62%	18.97%	(36,997)
24.62%	16.62%	19.78%	(47,817)

Graphs

FIGURE 2. The Body Shop Spa Project (Formulas and Functions Used)

46 and 47 show the compounded inflows and their sum—the TV—respectively.

At this stage, we have values for 3 of the 4 unknowns in the equation—PC, TV, and n. We must now solve for MIRR. We can use Lotus 1-2-3's @RATE function to find the MIRR. The syntax of this function is: @RATE(FV,PV,n). To use this function to find the MIRR, substitute TV for FV, PC for PV, and the life of the project, four years, for n.

An alternative method of finding the MIRR is to write a Lotus formula based on the equation:

$$MIRR = \left(\frac{TV}{PC}\right)^{\frac{1}{n}}$$

This equation is a derivation of the general MIRR equation shown above. Row 53 in Figure 2 shows this formula.

This formula has added implications for the teaching of finance. Many instructors shy away from giving examination questions that require students to compute a project's IRR, because this plunges the student into a prolonged trial-and-error process that tests patience and arithmetic skill rather than financial management analytical skill. Based on this equation, the student can compute the MIRR, using a calculator that doesn't have the financial functions.

Data Tables and Graphs

The Data Tables in Figures 1 and 2 were created using Lotus 1-2-3 one-input data table features. This matrix shows the values of IRR, MIRR, and NPV over varying values of CC. In this case, CC is the independent variable, and IRR, MIRR, and NPV are the dependent variables.

This table reveals several interesting relationships. One is that IRR is insensitive to CC, while MIRR and NPV are sensitive to it. The reason: We do not use CC to compute IRR. However, we use CC to discount the cash flows to calculate NPV and to compound the cash flows to arrive at the TV used in determining the MIRR.

Another relationship is that MIRR increases as CC increases, while NPV varies inversely with CC. The reason: MIRR is the end result of a compounding process required to compute the TV, while NPV is the outcome of a discounting process.

A third relationship is seen on row 70 where CC = 16.62%. At this point, CC = IRR = MIRR, and NPV = 0. It's easy to discern some exceptional relationships here. The information on row 70 is comparable to a break-even point or the point of optimum production where the firm's MR = MC and profit from the marginal unit of production is zero. We can reason why this situation exists. NPV accrues when IRR and/or MIRR is greater than CC, since it's the "profits" that accrue after the project has generated enough returns to cover its CC. When there are no "profits"—zero NPV—the firm is just generating enough returns, measured by IRR and MIRR, to cover its CC.

These relationships provide the idea for an important test to determine the accuracy of the model's decision criteria—NPV, IRR, and MIRR. Assuming the NCF computations in row 44 are correct, how do you know that the three decision criteria are correct? The test: Substitute the IRR (formula +D51) for the CC in row 19 of the data section. The same relationship on row 70 of Figures 1 and 2 should result. In this case, when you do the substitution, IRR will remain the same (16.62%) since it's insensitive to changes in CC, and MIRR and NPV will display 16.62% and $0, respectively. This assures you that a critical decision criterion of the model is correct.

A final relationship is that the accept/reject decision is consistent for all values of CC and that we do not have a decision-inconsistency problem. This is simply because the project is an independent one.

The data tables in Figures 1 and 2 provide all the data necessary to graph the relationships. These graphs show information in ways that can provide other ideas for the analyst. The net present value profile graph plots the CC along the x axis and the NPV along the y axis. The NPV profile crosses the zero NPV line at a point equal to the project's IRR. In this case, the IRR is 16.62%.

The IRR and MIRR graph relates IRR and MIRR to CC. IRR is insensitive to changes in CC, while MIRR responds in the same direction to changes in CC.

%Change	Guests +$NPV		Fee +$NPV		CC +$NPV		Equipment Cost +$NPV	
-15%	106,250	($14,992)	$2.55	($14.992)	10.2%	$48,928	$212,500	$59,499
-10%	112,500	1,362	2.70	1,362	10.8%	43,867	225,000	51,022
-5%	118,750	17,715	2.85	17,715	11.4%	38,915	237,500	42,545
0%	125,000	34,068	3.00	34,068	12.0%	34,068	250,000	34,068
5%	131,250	50,422	3.15	50,422	12.6%	29,325	262,500	25,592
10%	137,500	66,775	3.30	66,775	13.2%	24,682	275,000	17,115
15%	143,750	83,129	3.45	83,129	13.8%	20,136	287,500	8,638

SENSITIVITY GRAPH

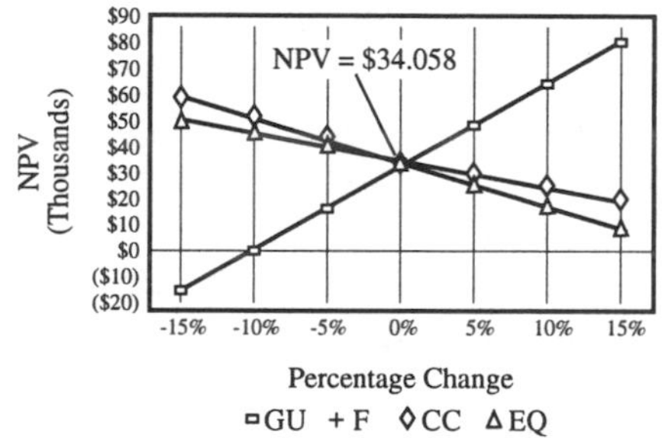

FIGURE 3. Sensitivity Analysis: Multiple Independent Variables

Sensitivity Analysis: Multiple Independent Variables

Lotus 1-2-3 data table features allow a maximum of 2 independent or input variables against which you can test the response of 1 or more dependent variables. Table 3, however, shows how you can test the effect that changes in 4 independent variables will have on 1 dependent variable by using four one-input tables and combining the information on one graph. The table shows the effect on NPV of given percentage changes in number of guests (GU), average fee (F), cost of capital (CC), and equipment cost (EQ).

In this sensitivity analysis, each of the 4 independent variables is changed by five percentage points above and below their original or expected value, holding the other independent variables constant. The model then sets up a matrix that shows the NPV for each of the 4 variables for a range of values.

The sensitivity graph below the table plots the four NPV curves against the percentage changes on the x axis. The slopes of the curves on the graph indicate how sensitive NPV is to changes in the independent variables. The steeper the slope, the more sensitive NPV is to changes in the variable. Figure 3 indicates that NPV is equally sensitive to changes in the number of guests and changes in the fee per guest. A 5% increase above the expected value in either of these two independent variables produces an NPV of $50,422. This curve is also the steepest of the three curves seen on the graph. This indicates that NPV is more sensitive to changes in guest count and guest fee than it is to changes in CC and equipment costs. Since the cost-of-capital curve is the most gradual, NPV is least sensitive to changes in this independent variable.

What is the significance of this test? A 5% decrease below the expected value in guest count and guest fee causes NPV to drop from $34,068 to $17,715, or by 48%. On the other hand, a 5% decrease in CC causes NPV drop from $34,068 to $29,325 (14%), while a 5% increase in equipment causes NPV to drop from $34,068 to $25,592 (25%). The implication: The analyst should spend more time and resources to ensure that the estimates of guest count and guest fee are as accurate as possible. Moreover, management should expend more effort to ensure that the actual guest count and guest fee do not vary much from their expected values over the project's expected life.

One more insight: Why does NPV show the same sensitivity to changes in guest count and guest fee? A one-percentage-point change in guest count, guest fee remaining constant, will produce the same revenue as a one-percentage-point change in guest fee, guest count remaining constant. The same revenue will produce the same NCF, since variable costs and fixed costs are assumed to be the same for the same amount of revenue.

Conclusion

The electronic spreadsheet is perhaps the most popular decision-modeling tool used in today's classrooms and businesses. But creating the decision-support model is just one of the many skills hospitality students will need to enter a business world that is steadily progressing toward the use of decision-support systems and executive information systems. Hospitality students also must learn to probe the created model. It is through this process that they can identify relationships, draw informed conclusions, understand implications, and solve problems.

References

BPP Publishing Ltd. (1991). *Management information systems* (2nd ed.). London: BPP Publishing Ltd.

Brathwaite, R. (1992). Using the electronic spreadsheet to create decision support models. *Hospitality & Tourism Educator, 4*(2), 25–30.

Brigham, E. (1992). *Fundamentals of financial management* (6th ed.). Fort Worth, TX: The Dryden Press.

Crockett, F. (1992). Revitalizing executive support systems. *Sloan Management Review, 33*(4), 39–47.

Cummings, L. E. (1992). Evaluating computer-based educational products. *Hospitality & Tourism Educator, 4*(2), 40–43.

Gallupe, B. (1991). Whatever happened to decision support systems. *CMA Magazine, 65*(8), 26–29.

Hopkins, B. (1991). Executive information systems take off. *CMA Magazine, 65*(8), 31–35.

Miller, J. (1989). Computer applications in foodservice management education in four-year hospitality management programs. *Hospitality Education and Research Journal 13*(2), 1–6.

Tunison, L. (1992). How to put yield management to work. *Lodging, 18*(1), 36–40.

PROJECT 1

As managers in the University Plaza Hotel, you have been assigned the task of investigating the purchase of a computer system for the property. The eventual project will include complete automation of the entire facility, but at this stage you are to investigate only one aspect (system). You have decided that the best approach is to form a task force—the combined efforts of a team will reduce the work load per person, and provide the benefits of mutual wisdom. The ultimate result of your analysis will be a report—both written, and an oral presentation to your board of directors.

Since this is only one component of the final automation project, you will choose one aspect to investigate. Your choices are front office, back office, call accounting, point of sale, or marketing systems.

Your project is to select a system by completing a Request For Proposal (RFP), and then to evaluate **two** alternatives in order to make a recommendation to your owners. As part of your project, your team must evaluate these two systems through live demos.

Each project will have the following sections:

1. A completed RFP to include:

    a. **Sections I—III (10 points)** which are:
    Section I—Background of the property and the project to be communicated to vendors.
    Section II—Bidding Procedures, including due dates, and where bids are to be sent.
    Section III—The Bidding Format listing all relevant sections to be included.

    b. **Detailed property needs,** which will constructed using appendices A and B. Appendix A is the very detailed system requirements for your property. This questionaire allows you to differentiate the vendors' products from one another. Appendix B is your listing of equipment needed. Note that you do not need to specify the exact hardware configuration. Rather, you must select the number of work stations needed, types of printers, and backup systems. Let the vendor suggest the proper hardware platform. (20 points).

2. Other evaluative information to include:

    a. **Vendor comparisons**—which should include some form of rating sheet. Rating would include factors like price, functionality, potential for integration, suitability of vendor. Note for this exercise, you do not have to judge the financial merits of a vendor—you probably cannot get this information in a mock situation. You are expected, however, to prepare some form of reference questionnaire, and to check two references. Also note that to check functionality, the appendices must be checked (through the live sight demos). (20 points).

    b. **Financial Feasibility**—In this section you will use financial techniques like the Payback method, Internal Rate of Return (IRR) and Net Present Value (NPV) that you learned in finance to show if the project is viable. This means that you will have to forecast cash flows from the project. (20 points).

    c. **Summary report**—in which you make your recommendation. This need only be one–two pages. It should, however, use what you learned from the RFP process in making a recommendation. (i.e. do not recommend a system that cannot be cost justified). (20 points).

d. **Oral Presentation**—you get to present to the board of directors (the class, during lab). You select what information should be presented. Each member must present for a grade. An oral presentation is expected to include graphics, preferably prepared and displayed on the computer. The total presentation is not to last over ten minutes. (10 points).

Many reports are prepared in hotels by using spreadsheets. Even though computer systems prepare a wealth of data, this information is often not in a form that is most useful for management. In the case of the PMS and POS systems, the data must be combined to provide a complete picture of the days's activities. On a daily basis, hotel managers may receive a daily sales report, a manager's report, and a daily payroll report, all of which may be prepared on electronic spreadsheets. The daily sales report, if properly designed, can be used to accommodate the needs of both managers and those of the hotel's accountants (who need to prepare an income journal accounting entry). This is the report that we will concern ourselves with.

Instructions

1. Use the attached "Daily Sales Report" formats to prepare a daily sales report.

2. The attached "System Printout" totals are to be used to complete the daily sales report in the computer. All totals should be transferred to the spreadsheet. Note that if the detail is not given, nothing need be put into the associated cell. Your worksheet should use appropriate formulas to accumulate totals. That is, totals should be accumulated by using either addition formulas or sum formulas.

3. The following adjustments will need to be taken into account by subtracting them from the gross totals:

a. Two separate guests complained that their rooms had bugs. Your front office manager processed an allowance for $52.50 **each.** This is broken down into $50.00 room and $2.50 rooms tax. You will need to input the allowance into page one, and subtract the tax allowance from the rooms tax number on page two.

b. Another guest was unhappy with her food in the restaurant. Because she did not take care of it in the restaurant yesterday, it is likewise adjusted at the front desk. The amount was $10.00 food and $.50 sales tax. Again, input the allowance on page one and subtract the tax from the sales tax number on page two.

4. After you have completed page one of the daily report, create a new page for the remaining debits and credits. On the new page create a suitable header (title, page, date). Then insert two columns, one for debits and one for credits. The first entry will be the total credits from page one (total sales for the day). The items from the rooms system and POS system that you did not use will be input here. Thus, sales and rooms taxes will be listed under the credits, and cash will be listed under the debit column. The remaining two totals (guest ledger, and city ledger) may be either debits (if an increase) or credits (if there was a net decrease), and you should use whatever the front office system tells you. Create a total for each column and make sure these totals balance.

5. Create another new page with an appropriate header. On this page, you will prepare statistics for both rooms and food & beverage. You should be consistent here with page one. That is, you should have numbers for today and month to date. All desired statistics are included with the attached data sheets. For example, you should show rooms sold, average rate, and occupancy percentages by room type (for today and month to date). For food and beverage

your report should show sales and average check for food by meal period, and beverage sales by meal period (for today and month to date). Note that I did not specify a prescribed format. Since I did not provide budget numbers, you may omit this column.

HINT: Make sure that your total sales on page three balance to page one.

System Printouts

Front Office System Totals

11/3/93

Transient Room	2,400.00	
Group Rooms	1,500.00	
Restaurant	1,500.00	
Room Service	500.00	
Banquets	1,000.00	
Bar	1,000.00	
Local	100.00	
L Dist	500.00	
Laundry	100.00	
Miscellaneous	100.00	
Rooms Tax	300.00	Credit
Allowances	115.50	Debit
Cash ** (See Note 1)	4,050.00	Debit
Guest Ledger	-2,615.50	Credit
City Ledger	7,450.00	Debit

Statistics

Rooms Sold:

Transient	40
Group	30
Available	100
OOO	5
Vacant	25

Notes

1. Total cash must be the cash received at the front desk, plus the total NET cash from the f&b spreadsheet. Net cash is equal to the total cash less tips paid out.

2. Assume that today is November 3, and that the month to date statistics from November 2 daily report were:

Statistics—MTD 11/2

Rooms sold:

Transient	80
Group	60
Available	200
OOO	10
Vacant	50

SYSTEM PRINTOUTS							
POS System Totals—11/3							
	Covers	Food	Bar	Sales Tax	Tip	Cash	Charge
Restaurant—Break.	100	300					
Lunch	100	500	200				
Dinner	60	800	400				
Total	260	1,600	600	100	200	1,000	1,500
Room Serv—Break.	25	100					
Lunch	10	50	100				
Dinner	8	50	100				
Total	43	200	200	20	80	0	500
Banquet—Dinner	50	600	200	40	160	0	1,000
Bar—Lunch	xxxx		500				
Evening	xxxx		2,000				
Total	xxxx		2,500	300	0	1,800	1,000
Grand Totals	353	2,400	3,500	460	440	2,800	4,000
Memo: Additional information							
The following appeared on yesterday's (11/2) daily report in the month to date column.							
	Covers	Food	Bar				
Restaurant—Break.	200	600					
Lunch	200	1,000	400				
Dinner	120	1,600	800				
Total	520	3,200	1,200				
Room Serv—Break.	50	200					
Lunch	20	100	200				
Dinner	16	100	200				
Total	86	400	400				
Banquet—Dinner	100	1,200	400				
Bar—Lunch	xxxx		1,000				
Evening	xxxx		4,000				
Total	xxxx		5,000				
Grand Totals	706	4,800	7,000				

DAILY SALES REPORT—SAMPLE HOTEL   NOVEMBER 3, 1993

		Today		MTD		Budget
Room Sales						t
—Transient		0		0		h
—Group		0		0		i
—Allowances		0		0		s
Total		0				
						c
Food Sales						o
—Restaurant		0		0		l
—Room Service		0		0		u
—Banquets		0		0		m
—Allowances		0		0		n
Total		0		0		
						w
Beverage						i
—Restaurant		0		0		l
—Room Service		0		0		l
—Banquets		0		0		
—Bar		0		0		b
—Allowances		0		0		e
Total		0		0		
						b
Phone						l
—Local		0		0		a
—L. Dist.		0		0		n
—Allowances		0		0		k
Total		0		0		
Guest Laundry		0		0		
Miscellaneous		0		0		
Total Sales		0		0		
Page 2						
		Credits		Debits		
Credits forward		0.00				
Sales Tax		0.00				
Rooms Tax		0.00				
Cash				0.00		
Guest Ledger		0.00				
City Ledger				0.00		
Total		0.00		0.00		

Page 3—Statistics					
Rooms Sold:		Today	MTD		
Transient		0	0		
Group		0	0		
000		0	0		
Vacant		0	0		
Total Available		0	0		
Average Daily Rate					
Transient		$0.00	$0.00		
Group		$0.00	$0.00		
Total		$0.00	$0.00		
Occupancy Percentage					
Transient		0.0%	0.0%		
Group		0.0%	0.0%		
Total		0.0%	0.0%		
Food Sales		Today	Covers	MTD	Covers
Restaurant		0	0	0	0
—Breakfast		0	0	0	0
—Lunch		0	0	0	0
—Dinner		0	0	0	0
Total		0	0	0	0
Room Service					
—Breakfast		0	0	0	0
—Lunch		0	0	0	0
—Dinner		0	0	0	0
Total		0	0	0	0
Banquets					
—Breakfast		0	0	0	0
—Lunch		0	0	0	0
—Dinner		0	0	0	0
Total		0	0	0	0
Allowances		0	0	0	0
Grand Total		0	0	0	0

Statistics—Continued				
Average Check	**Today**	**MTD**		
Restaurant				
—Breakfast	$0.00	$0.00		
—Lunch	$0.00	$0.00		
—Dinner	$0.00	$0.00		
Total	$0.00	$0.00		
Room Service				
—Breakfast	$0.00	$0.00		
—Lunch	$0.00	$0.00		
—Dinner	$0.00	$0.00		
Total	$0.00	$0.00		
Banquets				
—Breakfast	$0.00	$0.00		
—Lunch	$0.00	$0.00		
—Dinner	$0.00	$0.00		
Total	$0.00	$0.00		
Total Ave. Check	$0.00	$0.00		
Beverage Sales by Meal	**Today**	**MTD**		
Restaurant				
—Lunch	0	0		
—Dinner	0	0		
Total	0	0		
Room Service				
—Lunch	0	0		
—Dinner	0	0		
Total	0	0		
Banquets				
—Lunch	0	0		
—Dinner	0	0		
Total	0	0		
Bar				
—Lunch	0	0		
—Dinner	0	0		
Total	0	0		
Allowances	0	0		
Grand Total	0	0	(Balance)	

14

ACCOUNTING

A Measured Approach to Food-Inventory Management
Behshid Farsad and Stephen LeBruto

A Demand-Based Approach to Menu Pricing
Thomas J. Kelly, Nicholas M. Kiefer, and Kenneth Burdett

Perceived Fairness of Yield Management
Sheryl E. Kimes

Project 1

Project 2

A Measured Approach to Food-Inventory Management

Behshid Farsad and Stephen LeBruto

DO THESE STATEMENTS sound familiar? "We have too much capital tied up in inventory." "We have excessive inventory of certain items." "We are always out of some ingredients." "Our inventory turnover is almost two weeks, but the competition has a four-day inventory turnover." "Every week my managers make several trips to the grocery store to purchase small quantities of out-of-stock items." "We often lose customers because we are out of the menu item they select." They probably do if you are like hundreds of food-service operators around the country. These declarations are indicators of serious inventory problems. What makes this situation so frustrating are the contradictions: having too much inventory of some items but constantly running out of others, or having a slow inventory-turnover rate but at the same time not being able to produce all of the menu items.

Food-service inventory problems are generally related to inaccuracies in determining when to order and how much to purchase, resulting in mistakes in determining the optimum stock that should be on hand for each item or ingredient. The optimum inventory that should be on hand for each item is the amount that is needed to fulfill customer demand between the vendor's scheduled deliveries. Determining the correct inventory on hand is difficult, since there are many factors that influence the process. Those factors include making a correct prediction of the sales mix; maintaining adequate receiving, storing, and issuing controls; vendor reliability and efficiency; correctly predicting customers' desires; and knowledge and application of production controls. This article will address the issue of when to order, leaving the issue of forecasting how much to purchase for another time.

It is possible to reduce the uncertainty of when to reorder foodstuffs by carefully analyzing the answers to such questions as: What is the customer demand for a specific menu item on a particular day or week? Which day of the week generates the most demand for certain menu items? Should a lunch or dinner special be offered to reduce the inventory of specific products? Should dead or slow-moving menu items be removed from the menu or perhaps packaged as a promotion? These questions can be answered with confidence by establishing a systematic and self-correcting management strategy regarding inventory.

Why Have Inventory?

The question of why we need an inventory may seem trivial, but it is a necessary starting point. In most organizations, inventory is needed to protect the supply-production-distribution system from demand fluctuations. Adequate inventories insulate one part of the supply-production-distribution system from the next, allowing each to work independently, absorb the shock of forecasting errors, and permit the effective use of resources when demand fluctuations occur. Furthermore, the correct inventory level helps meet the expected customer demand (distribution), establishes a smoother production process (production), and occasionally acts as a hedge against unexpected price increases or product shortages (supply).

Although it may be a feasible practice for a handful of foodservice establishments to achieve vendor agreements by implementing a modified version of zero inventory, a more realistic situation is that each establishment bears the responsibility of carrying and storing an adequate stock level for all items.

Inventory is considered to be an immediate asset that is reduced during the production process. This reduction is expected to lead to sales, in turn generating revenues and eventually profit. Inadequate control of inventory may result in either an understock or an overstock, either of which bears associated costs. Overstock costs include the opportunity cost of lost investment from using working-capital funds for the asset and the expense of inventory obsolescence, spoilage, and theft. Understock costs include additional handling and transportation costs, gross profit lost on missed sales, and customer dissatisfaction. Overstocking and understocking inventory may be avoided by developing systematic inventory management with the following two objectives:

1. Achieve an optimum (not a minimum) level of inventory, answering the question of how much to purchase; and
2. Reduce operating costs associated with inventory such as the cost of ordering, storage, and maintaining an excess supply (safety stock), addressing the issue of when to order.

While how much to purchase can be answered using a forecasting method, when to order must be answered by determining the correct inventory-reorder point. Even though we have separated them here for ease of discussion, a forecasting method and a reorder point are two inseparable objectives of any inventory-management system since inventory costs are directly affected by the level (amount) of inventory on hand.

Types of Inventory

Accounting for inventories can be perpetual or periodic. The perpetual method (also known as continuous or cumulative) requires additions and subtractions to each product as transactions occur. This method can facilitate management control and decision making through the analysis of interim financial reports, which can be prepared without the benefit of a physical inventory count. Perpetual inventory systems provide information on the current level and total value of inventory for each item, as well as its past usage. Periodic inventory procedures, in which items are counted every so often, do not require this immediate updating of inventory values and quantity levels when an item is added to or subtracted from stock. Financial statements incorporating all changes in the inventory quantities and values are generated when the stock (inventory) is physically counted at the end of a specific period.

Under generally accepted accounting principles (GAAP), use of a perpetual inventory method does not preclude the need for applying a periodic inventory method (physical count) to issue audited financial statements. Most food-service organizations use both a periodic inventory method and a perpetual method, capitalizing on the opportunity to provide timely information to managers through the use of perpetual methods and responding to the requirements of a publicly held corporation by using a periodic method.

Maintaining an accurate inventory level is a difficult and cumbersome process for a food-service organization. It requires a thorough understanding of inventory concepts and maintaining up-to-date periodic-demand estimates. In many food-service organizations, proper inventory-management policies and procedures can be established using elementary management-science or operations-research techniques applied to the inventory. These inventory techniques are classified into two general categories:

1. Techniques using deterministic inventory models; and
2. Techniques using probabilistic inventory models.

Deterministic models represent a general form of inventory-management techniques that are inappropriate for most commercial food-service operations since they do not consider demand fluctuations and usage variations for specific items. In those cases the customer demand or usage rate is known prior to the start of the production process, a situation that may be true for certain food items, catering functions, or institutional food-service operations. Two applications of deterministic models are known as basic economic order quantity and economic production lot size.

Probabilistic models assume that customer demand and usage rates are unknown and that demand and usage can only be estimated by considering a probability of occurrence or weighted value. These models are appropriate for the majority of commercial food-service operations.

Inventory's Anatomy

Historically, most food-service establishments use a modified cyclical process of inventory control where the inventory is built up to a certain level when an order is delivered and depleted as demand occurs. The manager will place another order, the inven-

tory will again be built up, and the cycle starts over. If the establishment runs out of an item before receiving the next delivery, it would attempt either to get it transferred in from another store (if it is part of a chain) or purchase a small quantity from the local grocery store. If the manager is not able to restock the item, all menu items affected by this shortage are struck from the menu.

In this type of inventory system, the answer to the first question of the inventory-management system, how much to purchase, is either "equivalent to the usage during the previous period" or "an estimate based on the manager's value judgment." The answer to the second question, when to order, is either "whenever the vendor agreed to deliver" (e.g., every Monday and Thursday) or "whenever the restaurant ran out of the item." This type of inventory system, which could be called inventory management by gut feeling or simply guesstimation is unfortunately accepted and used by many food-service establishments.

The complexity of the food-service industry mandates the use of more scientific methods to address the many issues of inventory management. The level of management sophistication in the industry has increased dramatically in recent years, primarily due to employing better educated managers and the availability of advanced computer-based equipment. Most food-service managers are using some type of point-of-sale terminals or

computer-based information systems, for example, to generate both daily and periodic information regarding their operations. The inventory model that follows uses some of that technical sophistication to address the issue of when to order.

Constructing a Model

A food-service operator needs fully to understand such factors as reorder point, active stock, safety stock, risk of stockout, demand size, demand pattern, replenishment pattern, and lead time to control and maintain a solid inventory-management system. An inventory model consists of the following five major components:

1. *Maximum inventory level on hand.* This is the maximum or desired level of inventory that can be held on premises. Once this inventory becomes available for production it is called active stock.
2. *Demand and depletion rate.* The inventory is depleted as demand occurs. The higher the rate of demand, the faster the inventory is reduced. Demand rate, referring to the magnitude of demand, has the dimension of quantity. When the demand is the same from period-to-period it is called constant demand (e.g., ten units every week), otherwise it is called variable or fluctuating demand (e.g., ten units one week and five units the next week). The

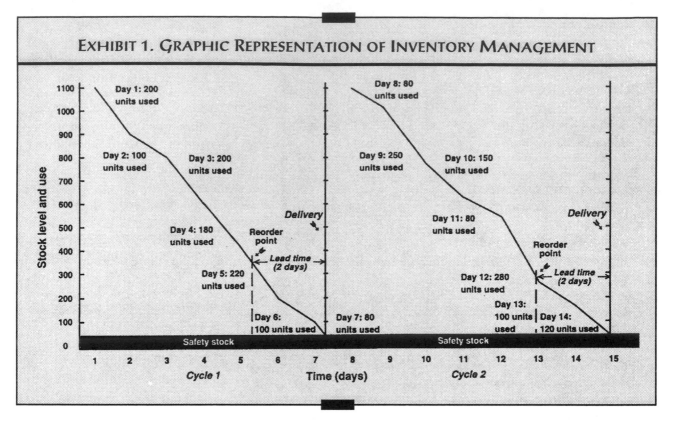

EXHIBIT 1. GRAPHIC REPRESENTATION OF INVENTORY MANAGEMENT

demand size per unit of time is called the demand rate.

3. *Reorder point.* To build an item's inventory to the desired level, the item is replenished periodically. This replenishment takes place when the inventory is reduced to a certain level, called the optimum inventory level on hand. Optimum inventory level and reorder point are the same. A replenishment order should be placed when an item's quantity reaches the optimum inventory level.

4. *Replenishment size, pattern, and lead time.* Replenishment size refers to the quantity or size of the order to be received and added to the inventory, which can be either a constant or a variable amount. Replenishment pattern re-

fers to how the units are added to the inventory (e.g., as part of a batch recipe). Replenishment lead time or reorder lead time is the length of time between the decision to replenish an item and its actual availability for production. This is extremely important for correct calculation of replenishment lead time since a box of frozen steaks, say, cannot be considered as available for production until the steaks are thawed. Therefore, the thawing period needs to be added to the delivery time. In this case if the delivery time is two days and the thawing process will take one day, the total replenishment lead time should be considered as three days.

5. *Safety-stock quantity.* Shortages can be eliminated or at least reduced by deliberately increasing the inventory level above the expected use level. Excess inventory (safety stock) is usable when the actual demand is higher than the estimated demand or the delivery lead time is longer than in the projected (or agreed upon) lead time. A graphic illustration of the item reorder point is shown in Exhibit 1.

What is the optimum reorder point? To answer that question a manager should first look at the four interrelated determinants of the reorder-point quantity. These determinants are: (a) the item's average demand rate (usage between the vendor's scheduled deliveries); (b) the item's reorder lead time (vendor's scheduled delivery days); (c) the type of demand rate and reorder lead time (variable or constant); and (d) the degree of risk that management is willing to take by having out-of-stock items.

Considering those determinants the reorder point is described by one of the following four scenarios. Exhibit 2 shows four possible combinations of demand rate and reorder lead time.

1. In cell one, the item's demand rate and the reorder lead time are both constant. This means that there is no fluctuation in either the demand rate or the reorder lead time, and so there is no stockout risk. This situation is found in certain institutional foodservice operations, such as nursing homes, that have a fixed number of residents or those that operate primarily by reservation only. It is inappropriate, however, to apply this methodology to the vast majority of food-service operations. In this situation the reorder point can simply be computed by multiplying the daily demand (D) by the item reorder lead time (LT). For example, if the demand rate for a certain item (say, ground beef) is 60 pounds per day and the lead time for vendor delivery (including preparation time) is two days, an order must be placed no later than when the on-hand inventory reaches 120 pounds.

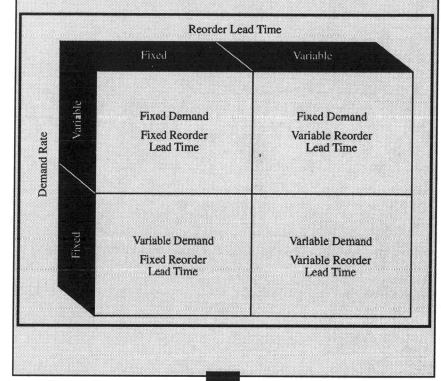

EXHIBIT 2. DEMAND RATE AND REORDER LEAD TIME MATRIX

2. Cell two shows the case where the item's demand rate is constant and the reorder lead time is variable from order to order. Both a constant demand rate and a variable reorder lead time are unusual for most commercial food-service operations.
3. In cell three, the item's average demand rate and the reorder lead time both fluctuate. Although most commercial foodservice operations have a variable demand rate, a variable reorder lead time is unusual.
4. Cell four shows the item's average demand rate varying from day to day while the reorder lead time is

fixed. This is the most common scenario for commercial food-service operations. Most vendors agree to deliver on a particular day of the week and the food outlet must maintain a quantity of safety stock to accommodate demand fluctuations. In this situation it is assumed that item demand during the reorder lead time is composed of a series of independent average daily usages that can be described statistically by a normal distribution. Each product's reorder point (ROP = the optimum level or inventory on hand) can be computed by taking the

Exhibit 3. Sample Z Scores

Probability (%)	Z Value	Probability (%)	Z Value
100	3.09	92	1.41
99	2.33	91	1.34
98	2.06	90	1.29
97	1.88	89	1.23
96	1.75	88	1.18
95	1.64	87	1.13
94	1.55	86	1.08
93	1.47	85	1.04

Shown here are Z scores for the most common percentages used by food-service organizations. Z scores below 85 percent are very close together and those slight differences will not affect the calculated results.

average daily demand ($\overline{D}$) of each product multiplied by the product reorder lead time (LT). For example, if the daily demand rate for ground beef based on the sales analysis of all menu items containing ground beef during the past week was 48, 56, 64, 80, 52, 68, and 52 pounds and the lead time for vendor delivery (including preparation time) is two days, an order must be placed when on-hand inventory reaches 120 pounds. Mathematically, this can be expressed as: ROP = ($\overline{D}$) × (LT), where the average daily demand ($\overline{D}$) equals [(48 + 56 + 64 + 80 + 52 + 68 + 52) ÷ 7], or 60 pounds. Therefore, the reorder point for ground beef is (60) × (2), or 120 pounds.

Safety Stock

Since in this scenario the item demand rate exhibits a degree of variability, a manager must avoid or minimize the risk of running out of stock of a particular item by setting aside an additional amount of product to meet expected but unknown demand variations. That additional amount of inventory is called safety stock. Maintaining safety stock is a survival issue in today's intensely competitive food-service environment, because it helps management avoid disappointing customers due to items' unavailability. Safety stock is computed based on an item's service level, which is the probability that the average demand rate will not exceed the supply on hand during the item's reorder lead time. The amount of safety stock is expressed by a Z score, as we will explain next.

Let us assume that managers of the food-service establishment in our example above decided that they did not want to have a stockout risk of greater than 5 percent on menu items containing ground beef as a recipe component. Turning that around, the managers are saying that they want a 95-percent certainty that they'll be able to serve ground-beef items at all times. Rather than dealing with extremely complex statistics to make that probability a usable number, we can take advantage of the fact that mathematicians have already converted various probability levels to numbers that we can plug into our formula. That statistic is known as a Z score, and it is available from mathematics textbooks or books on managerial statistics (see Exhibit 3). Using the Z scores, the managers find that a 95-percent probability level equates to a Z score of 1.65. The standard deviation of the demand for ground beef usage for the past seven days has been computed to be 10.47 pounds per day (see Exhibit 4).

The safety stock is calculated by multiplying the Z score representing the desired service level by the square root of the lead time (LT) by the standard deviation of the demand during the lead time (σD). Mathematically, the safety-stock level can be expressed as:

$$\text{Safety stock} = [(Z) \times (\sqrt{LT}) \times (\sigma D)].$$

Therefore, the new reorder point, incorporating a provision for safety stock, can be calculated by adding the expected demand to cover the lead time period plus the computed safety stock. Mathematically, this process applied to our example can be represented as follows:

$$\text{Reorder point (ROP)} = (\overline{D} \times LT) + [(Z) \times (\sqrt{LT}) \times (\sigma D)]$$
$$= (60) \times (2) + [(1.65) \times (1.41) \times (10.47)] = 120 + 24.35 = 144.35,$$ or 145 pounds of ground beef.

That amount includes 25 pounds of safety stock that statistically assures the managers that they won't be out of stock more than 5 percent of the time between deliveries. If we were to reduce the expected service level to 90 percent (10-percent stockout risk, Z score of 1.29), the safety stock would be reduced to 19 pounds and the reorder point to 139 pounds, as shown here:

$$\text{Reorder point (ROP)} = (60) \times (2) + [(1.29) \times (1.41) \times (10.47)] = 120 + 19 = 139$$ pounds of ground beef.

EXHIBIT 4. STANDARD-DEVIATION EXAMPLE FOR GROUND BEEF

Day	Daily demand (D)	Mean demand (D̄)	Deviation Deviation (D-D̄)	Deviation squared (D-D̄)²
1	48	60	-12	144
2	56	60	- 4	16
3	64	60	4	16
4	80	60	20	400
5	52	60	- 8	64
6	68	60	8	64
7	52	60	- 8	64
Σ	420	NA	NA	768

N (number of observations) = 7

$\overline{D}$ (Average demand) = 420 ÷ 7 = 60

$$\sigma D = \sqrt{\frac{\Sigma(D - \overline{D})^2}{N}} = \sqrt{\frac{768}{7}} = \sqrt{109.7} = 10.47$$

Worth the Trouble

Inventories are essential to most food-service outlets, and managers cannot escape the need to control this asset. The interrelationships of inventory with each facet of the business environment increases the complexity of solving inventory problems. The approach that we offer here is intended to make the question of when to reorder less of mystery and more of a science. While the statistic may seem initially complicated, a computer spreadsheet will make it easy to calculate the standard deviation of usage for each food item. In a subsequent article, we will deal with the calculations for how much to order each time.

A Demand-Based Approach to Menu Pricing

Thomas J. Kelly, Nicholas M. Kiefer, and Kenneth Burdett

An INTEREST IN MAXIMIZING prices seems to imply an evil intent on the part of the person setting those prices. But setting prices is an important part of product merchandising. We believe that implementation of any restaurant-merchandising concept must be managed through setting prices appropriately. This means restaurateurs must grasp menu-item demand and the elasticity of that demand. That is, not only should they know how strong the demand is for a given item, but they should have an idea of how the demand for that item will change as the price changes. In this context, they should think of menu-item pricing as a method of managing revenue.

Increasing prices without loss of volume is an important method of boosting profitability. Marn and Rosiello point out that a typical manufacturing firm that can achieve a 1-percent improvement in price with no loss of volume will increase profits 11.1 percent. Considering the restaurant industry's high fixed costs, a 1-percent improvement in price can yield as much as a 20-percent improvement in profits. Another reason for paying careful attention to price is that in many cases your customers are focusing on value more than on price. In its publication *Price-Value Relationships at Restaurants,* the National Restaurant Association suggests that "consumers view themselves as being more quality and value conscious as opposed to price conscious—they want quality and are willing to pay for it." That report further notes that consumers generally are in a spending mood when they dine out. Those observations indicate the value of having available a reliable method for determining a menu item's maximum price.

Former Approaches

In many regions of the United States, the demand for restaurant services through the 1970s was strong enough that the old standby of multiplying food cost by a factor of three or even four sufficed.

Some managers viewed price increases in a similar light as taxes—any increase was bad. In either case, profitability was maintained by cutting expenses, often by using inexpensive labor or reducing the quality of food products.

As a result, restaurant managers of the past might be forgiven for not having implemented a sophisticated approach to pricing. Today, however, consumers have many restaurant choices available and menu prices are demand driven as predicated by the consumers' view of restaurant value. In this article, we explain our proposal for achieving appropriate menu prices using experimental data and consumers' responses. At this point, our proposal has not been implemented in a restaurant, but we believe it would be effective, judging from the pilot study described below.

Defining the Ideal Price

Pricing individual items is a problem facing managers in many wholesale and retail businesses. Generally speaking, the price of an item should sufficiently exceed the costs associated with the item to allow for an excess return or profit. Consequently, many purveyors use cost as the basis of price, adding a markup to provide the desired return. Part of the problem with that cost-driven approach is that in many cases the cost of stocking and distributing individual items comprises expenses incurred in common with other items, so individual-item costs are difficult to allocate.

Moreover, pricing based on the amount charged for similar products offered by competitors doesn't work well because the items are often not exactly alike. The restaurant manager who is trying to price menu items faces considerable diversity of product. Other restaurants compete with similar but not identical items, and competitors' decor, selection, service, and quality differ as well. Thus, a restaurant manager is not in the setting of neoclassical economics in which the price is given by the market and the sole decision of the manager is production.

Typical menu pricing schemes include a fixed markup over food cost, a markup over total cost, and pricing to meet a gross-margin requirement. The importance of knowing demand in setting prices also has been noted for some time. Some writers in this journal and elsewhere have proposed taking into account the menu mix (i.e., demand), as well as contribution margins in setting prices. In the end, the effectiveness of any pricing strategy depends on how well managers understand consumers' responses to price changes.

We suppose that an individual entering the restaurant looks at the menu and orders an entrée based at least partly on the prices of all of the entrées. Of course, the decision will depend not only on prices but on the customer's characteristics. However, the kinds of customers entering the restaurant depend largely on marketing decisions other than relative pricing of menu items, so we will assume that the manager is satisfied with his customer mix and is interested in optimizing his pricing for this mix. Additionally, the propensity that any particular item is ordered will depend on the competition. Items that are the subject of fierce competition by local restaurants (e.g., chicken wings, pizza) are likely to be much more price sensitive than signature items that are unique to a particular restaurant.

Modeling the Menu

We attempted to create a mathematical model of the effect of price changes on the likelihood that a customer would order a given item. Although we recognize that changes in the price of one menu item in relation to the others will affect the customers' propensity to order the other items, that change is small. For simplicity, we assumed no such change.

We first built and tested our model to focus on the price and profit effect of a single item, item i. We used π to indicate the propensity or likelihood of an order. The likelihood that an individual entering the restaurant will order item i is given by π_i. The number of orders for i will be equal to π_i times the number of customers. So, if π_i is 0.2 and 100 clients enter the restaurant, we can expect 20 orders for item i.

In simple terms, profits are equal to revenues less costs. In turn, revenues are calculated by multiplying the number of each item sold by its price and then summing all revenues from the items. Costs work the same way. Direct costs are allocated to each item, multiplied by the number sold, and summed over items. Indirect or fixed costs that cannot naturally be allocated to individual menu items must also be considered, but that amount is subtracted after the gross profit (revenues minus direct costs) is totalled for all items.

Mathematically, the above description for calculating variable profits per individual item i is expressed by $\Sigma_i \pi_i (p_i - c_i) - C$, or the sum for all sales of item i of the propensity to order i times the contribution margin, which is price less cost. The term c_i excludes fixed costs, which are captured in total by the extra term, C, that does not depend on prices. The quantity ($p_i -$

c_i) is the contribution margin of item i. For this purpose, we will not consider fixed costs, C.

To determine the appropriate price for item i, consider the effects of a small increase in price from the current level. Two things might occur. The first is a likely decrease in the number of orders for the item. The second is an increase in profit per unit each time the item is ordered. (Although we are not considering the substitution effect, a reduction in the number ordered of item i should result in an increase in other items being ordered.) If the loss in revenue from the decrease in the number of orders for item i is less than the gain in revenue resulting from the price increase in the item, then it may be appropriate to raise the price. Conversely, if the loss in revenue from the decrease in orders is greater than the gain from the increased price per unit, then it may be appropriate to consider a price decrease.

The effects of a change in the price of item i can be summarized in a compact mathematical formula. We will represent the change in price by ∂p and the change in propensity to order as $\partial \pi$. If we continue to assume that the dominant effect of the price (p_i) is on the propensity to order i (π_i) so that we can ignore the "cross price" effect, the optimality condition could be shown by this function that expresses the relative changes in those values: $\partial \pi_i / \partial p_i (p_i - c_i) = -\pi_i$. The change ($\partial$) in the propensity to purchase i (π_i) divided by the change in the price of i multiplied by the contribution margin of i ($p_i - c_i$) equals any reduction in the propensity to purchase item i ($-\pi_i$). Since we expect the accumulated cross effects, though individually small in magnitude, to be positive, a necessary condition for optimality is that the reduction in the propensity to purchase i is less than or equal to the increased revenue resulting from the price change, stated mathematically as:

$$\partial \pi_i / \partial p_i (p_i - c_i) \geq -\pi_i.$$

In this paper we focus on the measurement of π_i and the price effect of the change in propensity to buy against the change in price ($\partial \pi_i / \partial p_i$) for a particular entrée. The π_i is fairly easy to estimate: in a large sample, π_i is approximated by the percentage of customers ordering item i. Though crucial, the other factor is more tricky to measure. That is the effect on π_i of a change in the price of item i. In our example with 100 clients, 100 ($\partial \pi_i / \partial p_i$) represents the change in the number of orders for item i. To measure $\partial \pi_i / \partial p_i$, we collected experimental data on the effects of different prices. This was a pilot study to indicate the feasibility of our approach. The results of our simple design and analysis are useful in pointing the way to more research.

The Restaurant and the Design

Our study was carried out at a medium-price family restaurant that offered a range of entrées (including steak, seafood, and chicken) and specialty sandwiches that are all available at dinnertime. We chose to study the demand for the fried-haddock dinner. This popular item's price, $8.95, was in the middle of the range of entrée prices. After consultation with the restaurant management, we chose to study the effects of raising the price to $9.50, $9.95, and $10.95 on four different menus. We felt that the highest price, more than a 22-percent increase, would be large enough to show a drop in demand (with all other menu prices held constant). The decision to test four price levels was determined in part by convenience. On weekend nights there are four waitstaff members. With four menus, we could assign a menu to each server for the entire evening. To control for the possibility that the waitstaff members would influence orders, we set out a 4 × 4 × 2 Latin-square design, controlling for menu, server, and day of the week (Friday or Saturday). The data were collected over four winter weekends.

At the end of the meal, the customers paid the original $8.95 price regardless of which menu they received and which price they were given at the beginning of the meal. In this way, consumers did not suffer any monetary loss due to our experiment.

EXHIBIT 1. SUMMARY STATISTICS

		Prices				
		8.95	9.50	9.95	10.95	Total
Friday:	Fish	34	58	31	47	170
	Total entrées	240	242	184	200	866
	Proportion	.14	.24	.17	.24	.20
Saturday:	Fish	16	10	9	10	45
	Total entrées	199	143	138	175	655
	Proportion	.08	.07	.07	.06	.07
Total:	Fish	50	68	40	57	215
	Total entrées	439	385	322	375	1521
	Proportion	.11	.18	.12	.18	.14

Data and Analysis

Exhibit 1 shows a summary of the data we collected over the four weekends. Of a total of 1,521 orders, 215 were for the fish fry. The "Friday effect" is easily seen, with the fish fry averaging 20 percent of the orders on Friday and just 7 percent on Saturday. The price effects do not seem to exhibit any specific pattern, certainly not the monotonic decrease in order probability as a function of increasing price that we expected. Orders for the fish fry dropped off at higher prices on Saturday, but the price did not seem to affect order levels on Friday. We judged that waitstaff effects were not systematic and so did not report them.

An analysis of variance (ANOVA) table including all main effects (staff, day, and price) with the dependent variable being the proportion of entrées that are fish is shown in Exhibit 2. The ANOVA ta-

ble indicates that only the Friday effect is statistically significant. That is, the data we see would be extremely surprising if there were no Friday effect ($p < .001$). An interesting question for future researchers is what the data would look like if an item other than the fish fry were tested.

The data clearly indicate that a substantial negative effect of price on the amount of the fish fry ordered is quite unlikely in the range of prices we tested. That means the restaurant might be able to raise its price and its profit without hurting demand. These data indicate no significant systematic price effect. This holds both overall and for each day separately. The apparent small decline in orders on Saturday is not significant.

Reconsidering Prices

The full-service segment of the restaurant industry has experienced little or no real growth in recent years.[7] At 3.2 percent of gross volume, median profits continue to be low by historical standards. This is an appropriate time for restaurant owners and managers to reevaluate their pricing strategies. Clearly, future menu-pricing strategies will incorporate some consideration of the demand function.

The best-known effort that addresses demand issues is the concept of menu engineering as postulated by Kasavana and Smith. This simple model analyzes menu item preference by contrasting popularity of the item (quantity sold) with item contribution margin (profit) in a grid format. The informed restaurateur adjusts menu prices based on this information. As prices are adjusted, the concept of elasticity must be considered. In the Kasa-

EXHIBIT 2. ANALYSIS OF VARIANCE					
Number of OBS = 28			R-SQUARE = 0.5047		
ROOT MSE = .073875			ADJ R-SQUARE = 0.3313		
Source	Partial SS	DF	MS	F	PROB > F
Model	.11121	7	.01589	2.91	0.0286
Price	.01066	3	.0036	0.65	0.5915
Friday	.08442	1	.08442	15.47	0.0008
Staff	.00547	3	.00182	0.33	0.8009
Residual	.10915	20	.00546		
Total	.22036	27	.00816		

Note: The dependent variable is the proportion of fish-fry orders.

vana and Smith typology, for instance, "Stars" are high-margin items for which demand is relatively inelastic. That idea was reinforced by Daniel Nimer, who chastised quick-service restaurants (QSR) for timorous pricing. He stated that the consumer is not nearly as price elastic as most firms in the QSR segment seem to think, given their propensity to merchandise by discounting price. Moreover, based on industry-level data by state, Douglas Brown has observed that restaurants (as opposed to quick-service operations) may experience inelastic demand as an aggregate sector. It is clear that some consideration of the demand function will become increasingly important in restaurant operations.

Our research indicates that an experimental approach is feasible and potentially informative. Restaurateurs may have much more latitude in raising the prices of popular items than is commonly thought. Future research should examine menu-item price elasticity across restaurant categories (quick service, midscale, upscale casual, and upscale formal) and in different geographical markets. Further research should also involve examining the elasticity issue relative to the total dining expense (per-person gross check). In principle our methods and suitable variations could be used routinely by restaurants, especially those with sophisticated point-of-sale systems, to determine the local shapes of demand curves and to set prices appropriately.

Perceived Fairness of Yield Management

Sheryl E. Kimes

As YIELD MANAGEMENT gains in popularity in many service industries, the question of how customers react to yield management remains unanswered. Consumers seem to accept the application of yield management in the airline industry, but little is known about their acceptance of such a policy in other industries.

The airlines have been using yield management longer than other industries, and customers seem to be used to the fact that they are charged different fares for the same flight and that they will receive specific benefits if they accept certain restrictions. In a sense, even though they are buying a similar seat, they are buying different products, because of the associated restrictions.

In other industries, such as the hotel and cruise-line industry, obvious restrictions may not be in place, although customers may pay different prices depending on when they place their reservations. A customer who pays more for a similar service and cannot perceive a difference in the service may view the situation as unfair. If customers view yield management as unfair, the increased revenues resulting from yield management may be short-term. On the other hand, nearly all capacity-constrained service firms should consider adopting a yield-management system if customers can be persuaded that yield-management measures are, in fact, fair.

In this paper I analyze the perceived fairness of yield management in the airline and hotel industries by describing yield management, discussing the concept of perceived fairness, and presenting the results of a survey on the perceived fairness of yield management in the airline and hotel industries.

Yield Management

Yield management is a method that can help a firm sell the right inventory unit to the right customer at the right time and for the right price. It guides the decision of how to allocate undifferentiated units of limited capacity to avail-able demand in a way that maximizes profit or revenue. The question is, how much should one sell at what price and to which market segment?

The concepts behind yield management can easily be seen in the airline industry. The yield is either revenue per seat-mile or revenue per passenger-mile. Airlines typically offer several price classes, such as full-fare, maxi-saver, and supersaver.

Since the airlines cannot fill their planes with full-fare customers, they try to fill them by offering reduced fares. A tradeoff develops between the desire for filling all the seats and the desire for selling seats at the highest price. Owing to the perishable nature of an airline's inventory, an empty seat represents an opportunity lost. The airlines must decide how many discount fares to sell while making sure they have enough seats left to sell to late-booking full-fare passengers.

Many airlines have solved the problem with yield management. They use a combination of seat-inventory management and pricing tools to achieve maximum revenue. Since yield management can provide more revenue from a fixed capacity, it is an attractive option. The airline industry was the first to address systematically the capacity-allocation problem with yield management and has achieved a great deal of success.

Other firms in the service industries, such as lodging, car-rental, cruise-line, and freight-transport firms, have noticed the success of yield management in the airline industry and have tried to adapt yield-management concepts to their industries. In each of those industries, yield is the revenue per available inventory unit. For example, yield for a cruise line is revenue per available cabin. All those industries have a fixed capacity, and all have easily segmented markets and stochastic demand for each type of service.

When service firms are constrained by capacity, financial success often depends on management's ability to use capacity efficiently. Yield management in capital-intensive service industries such as the airline industry is often equated with revenue (or yield) maximization because of the high fixed-cost nature of the industry. The marginal cost of selling another seat and transporting the passenger in it is far less than the marginal revenue. The same is true in the hotel industry, where the cost of filling and then cleaning one more room is far less than the revenue that is generated by selling that additional room. So it

makes a great deal of sense for hoteliers to sell some number of rooms at deeply discounted rates (rooms that otherwise would be vacant) so long as the revenue is greater than the cost of opening the room.

Firms that institute yield-management practices need to be careful, however. Since yield management concentrates on maximizing yield, companies using it may focus on short-term profits, ignoring the long-term profits that could result from improving service or making other product adjustments. The results can be disastrous. Many service organizations are successful because of the high-quality services they offer. Focusing on efficient use of resources may take managerial attention away from service, resulting in a loss of customers at considerable financial cost.

Consumers seem to accept the fact that airlines charge different prices depending on what restrictions are met, but how do customers of other types of services react? In the airline and rental-car industries there are only a few major competitors, but in the hotel industry there are many competitors. A customer who discovers she or he is paying a higher price for a room than a customer who reserved a similar room a few weeks earlier may simply go elsewhere or not come back. That is simply not true of airline passengers, who once in the air cannot so easily change their reservations or the company with which they're doing business.

Perceived Fairness

The issue of fairness has been studied extensively in the field of marketing, and although most studies have involved nontravel products, we can learn from the general issues presented. Several researchers have shown that fair behavior is instrumental to the maximization of long-run profits.

Researchers use the concept of a "reference transaction" when discussing fairness. A reference *transaction* is how customers think a transaction should be conducted and how much a given service should cost. Reference *prices* come from market prices, posted prices, and past experience with the company. For example, customers of a particular hotel may know that they generally pay $80 for a standard room, and so the reference price for a room at that hotel would be $80.

Customers believe that the value to the firm should equal the value to the customer. If that relationship becomes unbalanced by increasing the value to the firm or decreasing the value to the customer, the customer may view subsequent transactions as unfair. For example, if a hotel increases the price for its rooms for no apparent reason, it is increasing the firm value without increasing the customer value. The customer may then view the transaction as unfair. Similarly, if a hotel imposes substantial restrictions on customers in exchange for only a somewhat lower price or without lowering the price at all, customers may view the transaction as unfair.

The principle of dual entitlement holds that most customers believe that they are entitled to a reasonable price and that firms are entitled to a reasonable profit. Three hypotheses emerge from that principle:

1. Customers feel that raising the price to *maintain* profits is fair. If costs increase, customers consider it reasonable for the price of the service to increase;
2. Customers believe that raising the price to *increase* profits is unfair; and
3. If costs decrease, customers believe that it is reasonable for the company to maintain the same price. That may be because the customers are paying what they think they should, or because they believe management should reap the rewards of its cost-cutting efforts.

If the principle of dual entitlement holds true, yield management may be perceived to be unfair. Customers generally view justified price differences (or differences they perceive to be justified) as fair, but they view unjustified price increases to be unfair. If customers believe that the transaction is different from the reference transaction only in price, they may believe that the firm is receiving more than its reference profit and is behaving unfairly.

How to Increase Prices

Several ways of increasing price without incurring customer wrath are available. One method is to increase the reference price. Simply put, that means increasing the rack, or full-fare, rate. Airline records show that 95 percent of the passengers receive some sort of discount. Most hotel customers also receive some discount off the rack rate, and if informed of the discount, may consider themselves lucky to have received it.

Another method of increasing price is to attach additional services or products to the services sold at the increased price. For example, additional amenities, meal or drink discounts, or incentives for future business can be offered. The key is to increase the perceived value of the transaction.

Third, the service can be sold as part of a package, obscuring the price of the service. For example, when a weekend hotel special includes wine and meals, the customer may not know the price of the room. And when a cruise line includes the price of air travel or ground transportation in the cruise package, the customer only knows the total price, not the cost of the individual components.

The fourth method is to attach restrictions to discounted prices so that higher prices (with fewer restrictions) seem fair by comparison. Restrictions may include

1. booking a certain length ahead of time,

2. staying for a minimum length of time,
3. staying over a particular night,
4. having a change or cancellation penalty, and
5. having a nonrefundable reservation. If restrictions are tied to different prices, customers may view the transaction differently and may view the different prices as fair.

Airlines have used that strategy effectively, associating various restrictions with the sale of discounted seats. The more restrictions the customer is willing to accept, the deeper the discount available. Customers are aware of the restrictions and can choose to take advantage of the discounts.

Restrictions and Benefits

If firms offer customers a benefit such as a discount (a net gain to the customer), they may impose restriction that will balance the discount. But if they go too far and impose restrictions that are too strong, that will change the balance of the transaction and be perceived as unfair. That principle works in reverse, too. If a firm wants to impose additional restrictions on customers, it must give the customers something in return for this restriction—for example, a discount, additional amenities, or an upgrade. Again, the question is twofold: How large a restriction is acceptable, and how large a benefit must be extended?

By imposing restrictions, the firm takes away some of the value that customers gain from the transaction and increases the value to the firm. To correct that imbalance, the firm must offer the customer enough to counter the perceived value the firm receives. If the benefit to the customer is not perceived as sufficient, customers will view the transaction as unacceptable.

The Survey

An eight-question survey was administered to a convenience sample of travelers at the Statler Hotel in Ithaca, New York, in November and December 1992. Of the approximately 500 surveys that were left in guest rooms during that time, 118 were returned. Half the distributed surveys dealt with pricing policies in the airline industry, and half dealt with pricing policies in the hotel industry. Of the 118 surveys returned, about half were airline surveys, and half were hotel surveys.

The methodology was based on surveys conducted by other researchers. The survey questions primarily presented different scenarios. Respondents were asked to rate the scenarios on a seven-point acceptability scale in which 1 was highly acceptable and 7 was highly unacceptable.

Of the 118 respondents, about a third were women, about 60 percent did not pay for their own business travel, and about half traveled an average of one to three days a month. How many of the respondents are "frequent flyers" is unknown.

Role of Information

Information plays a large part in determining what the customer considers to be a reference transaction. A firm can greatly influence the amount and type of information its customers receive, thereby influencing customers' notions of what is acceptable. Several questions, therefore, were asked so that I could examine the role of information. The first such question dealt with respondents' reactions when all pricing information is made available:

An airline or hotel increases its price by 10 percent if a reservation is made three days or less before departure. It has advertised this policy and always informs customers that they can receive a lower rate if they book in advance. Lynn calls five days before departure and receives the lower price. Dana calls two days before departure and is quoted a price 10 percent higher than that received by Lynn.

The practice was considered to be moderately acceptable (the mean was 3.67), but opinions varied greatly (the standard deviation was 2.32). The acceptability differed significantly ($p = .0024$) for the airline and hotel industries. Respondents rated the acceptability of the practice as 3.0 for the airline industry and 4.29 for the hotel industry.

A similar survey question used the same scenario except that not all pricing information was made available to potential customers:

An airline or hotel increases its price by 10 percent if a reservation is made three days or less before departure. It has not advertised this policy and does not inform customers that they can receive a lower rate if they book in advance. Lynn calls five days before departure and receives the lower price. Dana calls two days before departure and is quoted a price 10 percent higher than that received by Lynn.

This practice was rated fairly unacceptable (mean, 5.72; standard deviation, 1.88). It was rated equally unacceptable in both industries.

Two other questions also addressed the information issue:

An airline or hotel allows its reservation agents to discount prices up to 20 percent off the regular rate. Customers who do not insist on a lower rate receive no discount. If customers push for a lower rate, they receive a 10-percent discount, and if they threaten to use a competitor, they receive a 20-percent discount.

That practice, common in the hotel industry, was rated extremely unacceptable (mean, 6.45; standard deviation, 1.28). Opinions on the issue did not vary significantly between the airline and hotel industries ($p = .176$).

One other question dealt with information availability and its effect on the reference transaction:

An airline or hotel is advertising a special rate reduction, but if customers do not ask for the special rate, they are charged the normal price.

In that situation the firm is making the information known but not taking the additional step of offering it directly to the customer. That practice was rated highly unacceptable (mean, 6.36; standard deviation, 1.40). Respondents felt more strongly about the use of the practice in the airline industry than in the hotel industry (airline mean, 6.72; hotel mean, 6.03; $p = .0054$)

Imposition of Restrictions

When a firm deviates from its reference transaction it must balance the perceived gains and losses to each party. If the balance seems to be tipped in favor of the firm, customers may view the transaction as unfair. If customers perceive the transaction as balanced, they will view it as fair. Finally, if customers perceive that the balance is in their favor, they will view the situation as highly acceptable.

In a yield-management system the firm can choose to give customers a benefit, but in return for that benefit, it may apply restrictions. How large a benefit should the firm give, and what restrictions are acceptable?

Three questions dealt with the issues of restrictions and benefits. Two of the questions tested the impact of different restrictions, and one question tested the value of one type of benefit. Respondents were asked to rate the acceptability.

Benefits and Penalties

Two questions covered the imposition of cancellation penalties. One question dealt with a 50-percent penalty:

An airline or hotel charges a 50-percent penalty for cancellations. In exchange for imposing this policy, it may choose to extend no benefit to its customers or it may offer a benefit. Please rate each of the following: no benefit, rate reduction of 20 percent, additional 1,000 frequent-flyer miles or free breakfast, class or room upgrade, rate reduction of 20 percent on next purchase.

Respondents rated the *no-benefit* option as extremely unacceptable (mean, 6.36; standard deviation, 1.52). The firm benefited from the transaction, but the customers did not. The practice was viewed as even less acceptable in the airline industry than in the hotel industry (airline mean, 6.72; hotel mean, 6.04).

Respondents rated the option of a *20-percent rate reduction* as moderately acceptable (mean, 4.20; standard deviation, 2.30), with no significant difference between industries (airline mean, 4.28; hotel mean, 4.12). Customers received a benefit in return for the restriction.

The benefit of *additional frequent-flyer miles or a free breakfast* was not a hard-cash benefit, but it did offer customers something in return for the restriction. It was rated moderately unacceptable (mean, 4.94; standard deviation, 2.07), indicating that respondents did not view it as

sufficient. The rating did not vary significantly by industry (airline mean, 5.10; hotel mean, 4.80).

Similarly, respondents did not view the provision of a *class upgrade or room upgrade* as an acceptable trade-off for the 50-percent cancellation penalty (mean, 4.95; standard deviation, 2.09). The rating did not vary significantly by industry (airline mean, 4.91; hotel mean, 4.98).

The benefit of a *rate reduction of 20 percent on the next purchase* was viewed as moderately acceptable (mean, 4.25; standard deviation, 2.35), and it did not vary significantly from the immediate 20 percent off. The rating did not vary by industry (airline mean, 4.31; hotel mean, 4.20).

Benefits and No-Refund Policies

Respondents were also asked to assess the same benefits in return for a no-refund policy on cancellations:

An airline or hotel has a no-refund policy for cancellations. In exchange for imposing this policy, it may choose to extend no benefit to its customers or it may offer a benefit. Please rate each of the following: no benefit, rate reduction of 20 percent, additional 1,000 frequent-flyer miles or free breakfast, class or room upgrade, rate reduction of 20 percent on next purchase.

Again, respondents viewed the provision of *no benefit* as highly unacceptable (mean, 6.46; standard deviation, 1.48), and it was even less acceptable for airlines than hotels (airline mean, 6.92; hotel mean, 6.05).

The option of a *rate reduction of 20 percent* was viewed as moderately unacceptable (mean, 4.75; standard deviation, 2.24), indicating that the respondents did not see it as quite enough in return for the no-refund policy. The benefit was viewed similarly for both industries (airline mean, 4.89; hotel mean, 4.63).

The benefit of *additional frequent-flyer miles or a free breakfast* was viewed as unacceptable (mean, 5.29; standard deviation, 2.11), indicating that the respondents wanted more in return. Attitudes did not vary by industry (airline mean, 5.57; hotel mean, 5.03).

The benefit of a *class or room upgrade* was rated almost the same as the previous benefit (mean, 5.29; standard deviation, 2.07). The rating did not vary by industry (airline mean, 5.49; hotel mean, 5.10).

The benefit of a *rate reduction of 20 percent on the next purchase* was viewed as moderately unacceptable (mean, 4.86; standard deviation, 2.21). It was rated the same as the immediate 20-percent off. The attitude was similar for both industries (airline mean, 4.98; hotel mean, 4.75).

Benefits and Restrictions

We then turned the question around and asked about restrictions in return for a 30-percent-off benefit:

An airline or hotel charges 30 percent less for reservations made 28 days in advance. In exchange for this discount, it may impose a penalty. Please rate each of the following: no refund, 50-percent refund, no refund but can reserve for another date, and no refund but can reserve for another date subject to one of these restrictions: required stay over a weekend day, minimum stay of three days, maximum stay of seven days.

Respondents rated the *no-refund option* as unacceptable (mean, 5.98; standard deviation, 1.75). It was seen as too large a restriction for the 30-percent off. The rating did not vary significantly by industry (airline mean, 5.94; hotel mean, 6.02).

The *50-percent refund* was viewed as a fairly acceptable restriction in exchange for the 30-percent-off benefit (mean, 4.36; standard deviation, 2.00) and did not vary by industry (airline mean, 4.55; hotel mean, 4.20).

The option of *no refund but can reserve for another date* was rated moderately acceptable (mean, 3.36; standard deviation, 2.23). It was significantly more acceptable in the airline industry than in the hotel industry (airline mean, 2.32; hotel mean, 4.29).

The additional restriction in the scenario of *no refund but can reserve for another date subject to restrictions* was associated with a reduction in acceptability (mean, 4.27; standard deviation, 2.19). Again, it was more acceptable in the airline industry than in the hotel industry (airline mean, 3.44; hotel mean, 5.02).

The restriction of a *required stay over a weekend day,* a common airline practice, was rated moderately unacceptable (mean, 4.75; standard deviation, 2.08). It was more acceptable in the airline industry than in the hotel industry (airline mean, 4.10; hotel mean, 5.33).

The restriction of a *minimum stay of three days* was rated moderately unacceptable (mean, 4.70; standard deviation, 2.26), and it was more acceptable for airlines than hotels (airline mean, 4.17; hotel mean, 5.17).

The restriction of a *maximum stay of seven days* was rated unacceptable (mean, 5.49; standard deviation, 1.999). The opinion did not vary by industry (airline mean, 5.31; hotel mean, 5.66).

Perceived Differences

The final question asked the respondents to evaluate one of these scenarios:

(1) Two airline passengers who are sitting next to one another have a conversation on board their flight. It seems that Glen's ticket cost $500, but Pat paid only $400. Pat made a reservation 30 days before arrival, and Glen made a reservation the day before. (2) Two hotel guests have a conversation in the restaurant. Their rooms are identical and next to one another. It seems that Glen paid $100 for a room, but Pat paid only $80. Pat made a reservation 30 days before arrival, and Glen made a reservation the day before.

The situation was rated moderately acceptable (mean, 3.30; standard deviation, 2.23). Respondents considered it more acceptable in the airline industry than in the hotel industry (airline mean, 2.78; hotel mean, 3.66).

Discussion

When the terms of the actual transaction deviate from the reference transaction, customer opinion on the acceptability of the transaction may change. For example, if the associated benefits or restrictions change, or if customer knowledge of the transaction is altered, the opinion on the acceptability of a transaction may change.

Customers view deviations from the reference transactions in the airline and hotel industries differently. One reason for the difference may be the level of customer experience. Customers accept yield-management practices when dealing with airlines because they have been exposed to them. They may not view the practices as just, but they view them as usual.

In particular, practices such as advertising and charging different prices or imposing certain restrictions on discounted reservations are not viewed as particularly unfair in the airline industry, but may be seen as unfair in the hotel industry.

Some of the differences may be due to the differences between the two industries. The airline industry has a small number of competitors, while the hotel industry is very competitive. Also, the typical price paid for an airline seat is much higher than that paid for a hotel room (although not necessarily so for an entire hotel stay) and you can't change seats from one airline to another mid-flight.

Advice to the Hotel Industry

Certain yield-management practices are more acceptable than others. To succeed with yield management, a hotel has to concentrate on the acceptable practices and avoid the unacceptable ones.

Acceptable Practices

Scenarios that were rated fairly acceptable had one or more of these characteristics:

1. Information on the different pricing options was made available,
2. A substantial discount was given in return for cancellation restrictions,
3. Reasonable restrictions were imposed in exchange for a discounted rate, and
4. Different prices were charged for products perceived to be different.

In all cases, there was a deviation from the reference transaction, but respondents viewed the change as acceptable.

First, when a hotel advertises that different prices will be charged based on when people make their reservations, customers view the resulting reference transaction as moderately acceptable, including the reference price. For example, a hotel can advertise the various rates available and the restrictions or benefits associated with each of the rates.

The terms of the reference transaction have been deviated from in that the rules for conducting the transaction have changed, but customers have been informed of the change. Moreover, customers have the option of receiving a benefit: a lower price.

The second acceptable practice is giving a substantial discount in return for cancellation restrictions. By imposing restrictions, the hotel takes away some of the value that customers gain from the transaction and increases the value to the firm. To correct that imbalance, the hotel must offer the guest enough to counter the customer's loss. For example, Marriott offers a substantially lower price for advance purchases. If the benefit to the customer is perceived as sufficient, customers will view the transaction as acceptable.

Third, if a hotel offers customers a discount (a net gain to the customer), it may impose restrictions that will counterbalance the discount. Restrictions that are too strong will upset the balance of the transaction, but acceptable restrictions will create a balance. For example, in this study respondents viewed a broad restriction on the length of stay as unacceptable (e.g., seven days) but a moderate restriction on the minimum length of stay acceptable (e.g., three days).

Fourth, if a firm differentiates its products so that customers view them as different, it can charge different prices for those products. As opposed to the three previous practices, this practice represents a change in the actual reference transaction instead of a change in the balance of the transaction. The entire way in which customers view the transaction is altered because the product they are purchasing is altered. For example, a hotel may charge higher prices for rooms with a view or for rooms on an upgraded floor.

Unacceptable Practices

Yield-management practices viewed as unacceptable included

1. Offering insufficient benefits in exchange for restrictions
2. Imposing too severe a restriction on discounts
3. Not informing customers of changes in the reference transaction. Hotels should avoid those practices

First, if hotels do not offer sufficient incentives to customers in exchange for the imposition of restrictions, customers are likely to view the practice as unacceptable. For example, in this study respondents did not view a free breakfast or a room upgrade as an acceptable tradeoff for cancellation penalties.

Second, if there is too severe a restriction on discounts, customers will perceive that the firm has tilted the transaction in its favor. For example, if a hotel imposes a nonrefundable, nonchangeable restriction on a discounted room, customers may feel they are being taken advantage of.

If firms change the basis of the reference transaction without informing customers, customers have no way in which to assess the fair-market price. For example, many hotels will offer any customer a lower rate if the customer asks for it. If customers do not know that they can ask for and receive a lower price, they may later view the transaction as unacceptable (should they discover the truth after the fact).

Fairness Is Key

The intent of this research was to discover how customers view yield-management practices in the hotel and airline industries. Many common practices used in the hotel industry were viewed as highly unacceptable by the survey respondents.

If a hotel is to be successful with yield management, it must practice it in such a way that customers view the transactions as fair. If a hotel operates in a manner considered unfair, it risks alienating its customers. While the hotel may receive short-term benefits from yield management, it may find the practice to be unprofitable in the long run.

Hotel managers should concentrate on maintaining the balance of the reference transaction. By using the yield-management practices that consumers find acceptable, managers will increase the probability of a successful yield-management system.

If the hotel industry is to pursue yield-management practices commonly used in the airline industry that are viewed as fairly acceptable, hotel managers need to educate their customers about the practice of yield management in the hotel industry. As customers come to view it as usual, they may become more amenable to its use.

This project charges the student with preparing a professional economic feasibility study for a 400 room full service hotel (a fictitious engagement). The project will demonstrate the student's ability to effectively communicate in writing and orally, conduct research, and use technologies while applying principles of hotel management. Specifically, the following elements of an economic feasibility project will comprise the project:

1. Composition of an engagement letter to the developer commissioning the study outlining the undertaking.

2. An analysis of the area and neighborhood focusing on a general description of the region of the country where the project is located and the community.

3. Demographic research on economic factors in the statistical area where the project will be located such as population, effective buying income, retail sales, office space trends, transportation, and tourism.

4. An analysis of the specific location of the property including the legal description of the project site.

5. A conclusion or summary of the area that clearly states estimated growth rates for three market segments that will be attracted to the hotel: the commercial traveler; convention or group business; and the vacation and leisure market.

6. An evaluation and analysis of the direct competition, including a summary of the services and quality of the competing properties in detail.

7. An evaluation and analysis of secondary competition limited to a listing and short summary.

8. A computation of future demand and growth presented in spreadsheet format with a discussion.

9. A computation of the supply, both current and future presented using a spreadsheet. The discussion would include a summary of research indicating other new projects.

10. A computation explaining fair share theory using a spreadsheet and including a discussion.

11. An evaluation and rationale of market penetration factors.

12. Computation of Occupancy for the first year of operation.

13. Determination of the competition's weighted average rate for each market segment.

14. A discussion on facilities and services that the proposed new property should offer based on the competition.

15. Preparation of a Statement of Cash Flows including financial projections and an assumptions narrative.

16. A concluding statement and summary of the findings.

Students are responsible for selecting a full service operating restaurant for the purpose of improving the use of technology in the facility, and applying concepts of food and beverage management to maximize the gross operating profit of the establishment. The student will present him/herself as a professional consultant with the fundamental purpose of the assignment being to assist the operator with increasing profits. The final project will include:

1. A summary of the technology in place at the establishment and a recommendation as to how it can be improved and an estimate of the cost of this implementation. A cost/benefit analysis is to be included.

2. A review of fundamental food and beverage cost control, for the benefit of the operator, including basic concepts of purchasing, receiving, storing, issuing, recipe development, production records, and sales control.

3. An analysis of the current sales from the menu for one week including tracking of customer item selections.

4. A computation of the theoretical cost of goods sold for the chosen week and a comparison with the actual cost of goods sold for the time period, and an analysis of the difference.

5. Preparation and completion of a menu engineering worksheet.

6. Development of a marketing plan to adjust the menu based on the results of the menu engineering worksheet.

15

FINANCE

Market Value and the Valuation Process
Stephen Rushmore

Project 1

Project 2

Market Value and the Valuation Process

Stephen Rushmore

Cost Approach

THE COST APPROACH IS based on the assumption that an informed purchaser will pay no more for a property than the cost of producing a substitute property with equal utility. When the cost approach is applied, market value is estimated by calculating the current cost of replacing the subject improvements and subtracting an appropriate amount for depreciation.

The cost of replacing a property is generally estimated on a square-foot basis using figures from a construction cost manual published by a recognized cost reporting service. The value of the land as if vacant and available for development is then added to the depreciated replacement cost estimate to yield the estimate of value.

Depreciation is defined as a loss in value caused by one or more of the following factors:

► Physical deterioration—the physical wearing out of the property

► Functional obsolescence—a lack of desirability in the layout, style, and design of the property as compared to a new property serving the same function

► External obsolescence—a loss in value from causes outside the property itself

Appraisal literature recommends using the cost approach for new properties, which have not been affected by the various forms of depreciation, and for unique or specialized improvements such as schools and libraries that have no comparable market or income potential.

The cost approach is seldom used to value existing hotels and motels because lodging facilities are particularly vulnerable to physical deterioration, functional changes, and uncontrollable external factors. Sometimes a hostelry can suffer from functional and external obsolescence before its construction is completed. As the building and other improvements age and depreciate, the resultant loss in value becomes difficult to quantify.

Estimating the impact of even minor forms of obsolescence may require insupportable judgments that undermine the credibility of the cost approach.

A more significant reason why this approach is not applied to hotels and motels is that its underlying assumptions do not reflect the investment rationale of typical hostelry buyers. Lodging facilities are income-producing properties that are purchased to realize future profits. Replacement or reproduction cost has little bearing on an investment decision when the buyer is primarily concerned with the potential return on equity.

The cost approach can be useful, however, in determining the feasibility of a proposed hostelry. When applied in conjunction with the income capitalization approach, the cost approach can verify a project's economic feasibility. If the value obtained by applying the income capitalization approach is equal to or greater than the replacement cost plus the land value, the project is usually considered economically feasible. If, however, the value estimated by the income capitalization approach is less than value derived by the cost approach, the investors should either scrap the project, reduce capital costs, or lower their desired return. Moreover, if this is the case, an additional equity investment may be needed to secure sufficient financing.

The data used to estimate the replacement cost of property improvements should come from a qualified source such as an experienced contractor architect, or engineer, or from a construction cost manual. Land value is established by analyzing sales of comparable parcels or by capitalizing the ground rental.

Table 5.1 shows ranges of typical replacement costs, land values, and soft costs for luxury, standard, and economy accommodations.

Sales Comparison Approach

The sales comparison approach is based on the assumption that an informed purchaser will pay no more for a property than the cost of acquiring an existing property with equal utility. When this approach is applied, market value is estimated by comparing the sale prices of recent transactions involving properties similar to the property being appraised. Any dissimilarities are resolved with appropriate adjustments. These differences may pertain to the time, age of sale, the location, construction, condi-

tion, layout, equipment, size of the properties, or external economic factors.

The reliability of the sales comparison approach depends on three factors:

1. Availability of timely, comparable sales data
2. Verification of sales data
3. Degree of comparability, i.e., the extent of adjustment needed to account for the differences between the subject and the comparable property

The sales comparison approach often provides highly supportable value estimates for homogeneous properties such as vacant land and single-family homes when the adjustments are few and relatively simple to compute. For larger, more complex properties such as office buildings, shopping centers, and hotels, the required adjustments are often numerous and difficult to estimate.

For example, assume an appraiser is valuing a motel property by comparing it with a similar motel across the street which was sold last year. In this case the subject differs from the comparable in the following ways:

► Seller will take back purchase-money financing
► Different franchise affiliation
► Better visibility
► More parking facilities
► Larger restaurant and smaller lounge
► Enclosed swimming pool
► Higher-grade furnishings
► Two vanity sinks per guest room

These are just a few of the many potential differences for which adjustments will be needed to make the indicated sale price of the comparable reflect the market value of the subject. In appraising lodging facilities, the adjustment process is often difficult and generally unsupported by market data. The market-derived capitalization rates that are sometimes used by appraisers are susceptible to the same shortcomings inherent in the sales comparison approach. In fact the reliability of the income capitalization approach can be substantially reduced when capitalization rates obtained from unsupported market data are used. This practice not only weakens the final estimate of value, but also ignores the typical investment analysis procedures employed by hotel purchasers.

Although the sales comparison approach is seldom given substantial weight in a hotel appraisal, it can be used to bracket a value or to check the value derived by the income capitalization approach. For example, assume an appraiser is valuing a mid-rate commercial hotel. The appraiser has researched the market and discovered two recent sales. One sale involved a first-class hotel with a value of $90,000 per room. The other sale was of a mid-rate hotel that was obviously less attractive than the property being appraised; it had a value of $45,000 per room.

Although a value estimate based on these data would be difficult to support, a range of values within which the final estimate should fall has been

TABLE 1. HOTEL DEVELOPMENT COSTS (IN DOLLARS PER AVAILABLE ROOM)

	Improvements	Furniture & Equipment	Land	Pre-Opening	Operating Capital	Total
1976						
Luxury	$32,000–$55,000	$5,000–$10,000	$4,000–$12,000	$1,000–$2,000	$1,000–$1,500	$43,000–$80,500
Standard	20,000–32,000	3,000–6,000	2,500–7,000	750–1,500	750–1,000	27,000–47,500
Economy	8,000–15,000	2,000–4,000	1,000–3,500	500–1,000	500–750	12,000–24,250
1979						
Luxury	36,000–65,000	8,000–15,000	5,000–20,000	1,500–3,000	1,500–2,000	52,000–105,000
Standard	25,000–36,000	5,000–10,000	3,000–11,000	1,000–2,000	1,000–1,500	35,000–60,500
Economy	10,000–20,000	3,000–5,000	1,500–6,500	750–1,000	750–1,000	15,750–33,000
1981						
Luxury	45,000–80,000	10,000–20,000	8,000–22,000	2,000–3,500	2,000–2,500	67,000–128,000
Standard	25,000–40,000	7,000–13,000	4,000–12,000	1,200–2,500	1,200–2,000	38,400–70,000
Economy	13,000–25,000	4,000–7,000	2,000–7,000	700–1,200	900–1,200	20,600–41,400
1983						
Luxury	55,000–100,000	12,500–20,000	10,000–24,000	2,300–4,000	2,000–2,800	81,800–151,000
Standard	35,000–50,000	9,000–15,000	5,000–13,000	1,400–3,000	1,300–2,200	51,700–83,200
Economy	18,000–32,000	5,000–8,000	3,000–8,000	800–1,500	900–1,300	27,700–50,800
1984						
Luxury	58,000–110,000	13,000–21,000	10,500–25,500	2,500–4,200	2,000–2,900	86,000–163,600
Standard	37,000–55,000	9,000–16,000	5,300–14,000	1,500–3,100	1,300–2,300	54,100–90,400
Economy	19,000–35,000	5,000–8,500	3,200–9,000	900–1,600	900–1,400	29,000–55,500
1985						
Luxury	60,000–115,000	13,400–30,000	11,000–26,500	3,000–5,000	2,100–3,000	89,500–179,500
Standard	38,000–57,000	9,500–16,500	5,500–14,700	1,900–3,600	1,400–2,400	56,300–94,200
Economy	20,000–36,000	5,000–8,800	3,300–9,500	1,000–1,700	1,000–1,400	30,300–57,400
1986						
Luxury	62,000–120,000	13,700–30,600	11,500–27,800	3,100–5,200	2,200–3,100	92,500–186,700
Standard	39,000–60,000	9,700–16,800	5,800–15,400	2,000–3,800	1,500–2,500	58,000–98,500
Economy	21,000–37,000	5,100–9,000	3,500–10,000	1,000–1,800	1,000–1,500	31,600–59,300
1987						
Luxury	63,000–122,000	13,800–30,900	11,900–28,600	3,300–5,500	2,300–3,200	94,300–190,200
Standard	40,000–61,000	9,800–17,000	6,000–15,900	2,100–3,900	1,500–2,600	59,400–100,400
Economy	21,000–39,000	5,200–9,100	3,600–10,200	1,100–1,800	1,100–1,500	32,000–61,600
1988						
Luxury	65,000–125,000	14,000–31,000	11,900–28,600	3,300–5,500	2,300–3,200	96,500–193,300
Standard	41,000–63,000	10,000–17,100	6,000–15,900	2,100–3,900	1,500–2,600	60,600–102,500
Economy	22,000–40,000	5,200–9,200	3,600–10,200	1,100–1,800	1,100–1,500	33,000–62,700
1989						
Luxury	66,000–126,000	15,000–32,000	11,900–28,600	3,300–5,500	2,300–3,200	98,500–195,300
Standard	41,000–64,000	10,500–18,000	6,000–15,900	2,100–3,900	1,500–2,600	61,100–104,400
Economy	22,000–40,000	5,500–9,700	3,600–10,200	1,100–1,800	1,100–1,500	33,300–63,200
1990						
Luxury	67,000–128,000	15,400–33,000	10,700–25,800	3,500–5,700	2,500–3,500	99,100–196,000
Standard	42,000–65,000	10,800–18,500	5,400–14,300	2,200–4,000	1,600–2,800	62,000–104,600
Economy	22,500–41,000	5,600–10,000	3,200–9,200	1,200–1,800	1,200–1,600	33,700–63,600
1991						
Luxury	65,000–122,000	14,500–31,500	10,200–24,000	3,700–5,900	2,600–3,600	96,000–187,000
Standard	40,000–63,000	10,000–17,800	5,100–13,500	2,300–4,200	1,700–2,900	39,100–101,400
Economy	21,000–39,000	5,000–9,500	3,000–8,600	1,300–2,000	1,300–1,700	31,600–60,800

Source: Hospitality Valuation Services

established. If the income capitalization approach results in a value indication that is outside this range, the appraiser knows that the data must be reevaluated. Occasionally appraisers may apply a gross income multiplier in the sales comparison approach. If this practice reflects the actions of the market, it can be considered in an appraisal.

Hospitality Market Data Exchange

As in all appraisals, the market must be researched to locate comparable sales with which to support the market value estimate. To help appraisers identify comparable sales of hotels and motels, Hospitality Valuation Services has established the Hospitality Market Data Exchange, a central clearinghouse of information relating to hotel and motel transactions.

The Exchange has compiled data on more than 4,700 sales of lodging facilities throughout the United States. The data are categorized by property name, city, and state, and contain pertinent information relating to each transaction.

Every six months the Hospitality Market Data Exchange publishes a cumulative report which contains pertinent information on all the hotel and motel transactions submitted to the Exchange. This report is mailed to each Exchange participant. To become an Exchange participant, an appraiser must submit market data on hotels or motels. Each usable transaction submitted to the Exchange entitles the participant to an additional

six-month cumulative report (i.e., an appraiser who submits four transactions will receive two years of reports).

Current participants of the Hospitality Market Data Exchange include appraisers, assessors, consultants, accountants, lenders, and syndicators as well as hotel owners, operators, investors, and managers.

Usable data on transactions may relate to sales, financing, management agreements, leases, and construction costs of transient lodging facilities. The data submitted must be accurate and sufficiently detailed to benefit other participants. For example, the minimum information for a sales transaction would be the name of the property, its location, the date of sale, the number of rooms, and the sale price. The Hospitality Market Data Exchange assumes that participants submitting data have received the necessary permission and are not violating client confidentiality. Hospitality Valuation Services serves as a conduit for data and assumes no responsibility or liability for data accuracy, usability, confidentiality, or any other matters related to this service.

Table 2 is an annual summary of the sales data compiled by the Hospitality Market Data Exchange from 1980 to 1989.

The table shows the number of sales currently included in the Exchange for each year along with other information such as the total number of rooms represented, the average size of each property, the range in sale price on a per-room basis, and the average

price per room. The data show yearly increases in the average price per room up until 1988; thereafter the hotel market became depressed and prices dropped.

Hotel Valuation Index

A second source of hotel market data is the Hotel Valuation Index (HVI), a sophisticated valuation benchmark showing the indexed market value of a typical hotel located in 24 different regions of the country. This index, developed by Hospitality Valuation Services in association with Smith Travel Research, has been calculated annually since 1986 and reflects value trends over a period of time.

The HVI assigns the greatest weight to the income capitalization approach, with secondary support provided by the sales comparison and cost approaches. Rooms revenue data are supplied by Smith Travel Research and other valuation parameters are provided by Hospitality Valuation Services. Appraisers recognize that hotel values change over time due to differing earnings expectations and capitalization rates. The HVI was designed to illustrate these changes and to quantify the amount of variance attributable to movements in earnings and the costs of debt and equity capital.

While the Hospitality Market Data Exchange records the actual price paid for a hotel unadjusted for nonmarket factors such as favorable financing and unusual motivations which could impact the sale price, the HVI represents the

Year	Number of Sales	Total Number of Rooms	Average Size (in rooms)	Lowest Price Per Room	Highest Price Per Room	Average Price Per Room
1980	211	35,338	167	$1,560	$128,571	$34,480
1981	313	47,523	152	2,000	192,593	34,457
1982	373	54,218	145	1,500	345,000	38,264
1983	451	71,829	159	2,016	595,745	47,723
1984	471	77,784	165	2,459	469,508	55,031
1985	531	86,888	164	3,104	698,148	56,500
1986	621	106,417	171	2,367	517,110	64,340
1987	356	57,475	161	4,565	767,308	81,141
1988	445	78,348	176	1,807	967,742	86,794
1989	360	46,898	130	2,152	1,195,652	75,928

Source: Hospitality Market Data Exchange

property's value under the standard definition of market value.

Table 3 shows the 24 market areas ranked according to their 1990 HVI.

Because of the economic downturn in the lodging industry, hotel values during 1990 declined an average of 50% across the country. The areas that experienced the greatest declines were Philadelphia, Norfolk (Virginia), Boston, Riverside (California), Washington, DC, Anaheim (California), New York, Las Vegas, Los Angeles, and San Diego. On the positive side, hotels in Denver, Houston, Tampa, Atlanta, Minneapolis, Dallas, New Orleans, and Fort Lauderdale experienced value increases during this period.

Hotel values are the highest in Honolulu, New York, San Francisco, and Orlando; similar hotel properties in Nor-folk, Dallas, Denver, and Minneapolis generally command the lowest prices.

Although Houston is near the bottom of the list for value per room, it ranks first in value recovery, gaining 210% between 1986 and 1990. Hotels in Orlando, New Orleans, Honolulu, Tampa, and Miami also experienced impressive gains during this period. The biggest losers were hotels located in Norfolk, which lost 45% of their value during this period, followed by properties in Philadelphia and Boston. The average hotel in the United States experienced a 7% increase in value between 1986 and 1990.

Hotels in Denver and Houston showed gains of more than 40% in 1990, while the economic slowdown in the Northeast adversely affected the values of properties in Philadelphia, Norfolk, and Boston, which declined by 19%, 18%, and 15%, respectively. The upward trend in New York City hotel values ended in 1989, when room revenue increases failed to keep up with inflation and fell 13% during 1990.

Hotels in cities where values fell were generally impacted by declining occupancies and room rates that did not keep up with inflation; areas that benefited from higher occupancies and room rates showed the greatest improvement in hotel values.

Hotel values are still depressed in many parts of the country. For example, the 1990 value of a typical hotel in San Diego is more than three times greater than a similar property located in Dallas. If these hotels were developed at comparable costs, it is evident that the Dallas property is probably experiencing finan-

TABLE 3. HOTEL VALUATION INDEX

	Index Per Room					Annual Compounded Percent Change				
	1986	1987	1988	1989	1990	1986-87	1987-88	1998-89	1989-90	1986-90
Honolulu, HI	3.3571	4.0357	4.6964	5.2857	5.3214	20%	16%	13%	1%	59%
New York, NY	3.5714	4.1071	4.6429	4.5357	3.9286	15	13	(2)	(13)	10
Son Francisco, CA	2.5000	3.0893	3.2500	3.0714	2.9286	24	5	(5)	(5)	17
Orlando, FL	1.5000	1.6429	1.9286	2.5000	2.5357	10	17	30	1	69
New Orleans, LA	1.5357	1.7500	2.2857	2.3929	2.5000	14	31	5	4	63
San Diego, CA	2.8571	2.3571	2.5714	2.6786	2.3929	(18)	9	4	(11)	(16)
Washington, DC	2.1786	2.1786	2.4464	2.6071	2.2500	0	12	7	(14)	3
Los Angeles, CA	2.1071	2.2857	2.3929	2.4643	2.1786	8	5	3	(12)	3
Miami, FL	1.4286	1.6071	1.7321	2.1429	2.1786	12	8	24	2	52
Las Vegas, NV	1.7500	2.1429	2.1786	2.1429	1.8929	22	2	(2)	(12)	8
Boston, MA	2.3571	2.7143	2.6071	2.1429	1.8214	15	(4)	(18)	(15)	(23)
Anaheim, CA	1.7679	1.7321	1.7500	1.8571	1.6071	(2)	1	6	(13)	(9)
Fort Lauderdale, FL	1.4643	1.2679	1.3214	1.4286	1.4821	(13)	4	8	4	1
Riverside, CA	0.9643	1.2143	1.5714	1.7143	1.4643	26	29	9	(15)	52
Chicago, IL	1.4643	1.5000	1.5714	1.5000	1.4286	2	5	(5)	(5)	(2)
Phoenix, AZ	1.2143	1.0714	1.1786	1.5357	1.4286	(12)	10	30	(7)	18
Tampa, FL	0.8393	0.7679	0.8571	1.1429	1.2857	(9)	12	33	12	53
Atlanta, GA	1.0714	1.0179	1.0536	1.0357	1.1429	(5)	4	(2)	10	7
Houston, TX	0.3571	0.4286	0.6964	0.7857	1.1071	20	62	13	41	210
USA	1.0000	0.9464	1.0536	1.1250	1.0714	(5)	11	7	(5)	7
Philadelphia, PA	1.4643	1.5357	1.4286	1.3214	1.0714	5	(7)	(8)	(19)	(27)
Minneapolis, MN	0.7321	0.6964	0.7143	0.7143	0.7857	(5)	3	0	10	7
Denver, CO	0.5357	0.4464	0.4643	0.4821	0.7857	(17)	4	4	63	47
Dallas, TX	0.5536	0.6250	0.6607	0.7321	0.7847	13	6	11	7	42
Norfolk, VA	1.1786	1.0536	0.9286	0.7857	0.6429	(11)	(12)	(15)	(18)	(45)

Source: Hospitality Valuation Services and Smith Travel Research.

cial difficulties even though Dallas-area hotel values are currently rebounding.

In 1990, 19 market areas posted HVIs above the U.S. average and five had HVIs below the average. In 1986, 18 markets outpaced the U.S. average in value while six markets did not.

The HVI is an indexed value based on the 1986 value of a typical hotel in the United States (1986 = 1. 000). Each market area is indexed from this base and assigned a number showing the value relationship of that market area to the base. For example, in 1986 the index for Miami was 1.4286, which means that the value of a hotel in Miami was approximately 43% higher than that of a similar hotel situated elsewhere in the United States. A more meaningful comparison is indicated by the value difference between hotels in two cities. For example, assume a hotel in Fort Lauderdale sold in 1987 for $65,000 per room and a similar hotel in New Orleans would probably command $128,000 per room in 1990. This relationship would be calculated by taking the 1990 HVI for New Orleans and dividing it by the 1987 HVI for Fort Lauderdale to determine the change.

$$\frac{1990 \text{ HVI New Orleans}}{1987 \text{ HVI Fort Lauderdale}} \quad \frac{2.5000}{1.2679} = 1.97176$$

Then the 1987 Fort Lauderdale sale price of $65,000 per room is multiplied by 1.97176 to yield the estimated 1990 sale price for New Orleans.

$$\$65,000 \times 1.97176 = \$128,000 \text{ (rounded)}$$

As long as interest rates remain level, the economy does not decline any further, and owners of distressed hotels do not attempt to dump their properties on the market, hotel values in 1991–1992 should generally remain level for most areas of the country. Because financing is generally unavailable and transactions are difficult to structure, owners of hotels should hold on to their properties for the next two to four years. From a buyer's viewpoint hotel values seem to be bottoming out and investors may find good opportunities to pick up some real bargains.

Income Capitalization Approach

The income capitalization approach converts the anticipated future benefits of property ownership (dollar income) into an estimate of present value. In hotel-motel valuation, this approach typically involves a discounting procedure.

The income capitalization approach is generally the preferred technique for appraising income-producing properties because it closely simulates the investment rationale and strategies of knowledgeable buyers. The approach is particularly relevant to hotel and motel properties, which involve relatively high

risks and are bought for investment purposes only. Most of the data used in the income capitalization approach is derived from the market, which reduces the need for unsupportable, subjective judgments.

The income capitalization approach is applied in three steps.

1. Forecast net income for a specified number of years.
2. Select an appropriate discount factor or capitalization rate.
3. Apply the proper discounting and/or capitalization procedure.

Each of these steps will be discussed in detail.

Forecasting Net Income

Many terms are used to describe the net income that is capitalized into an estimate of value—*net income before recapture, net income before depreciation,* or *net operating income.* All of these terms may be defined as the annual net income before financial charges (e.g., as the recapture of debt service) are deducted. In this book this concept is referred to as *net income before debt service* (after a reserve for replacement).

In the income capitalization approach, the forecast of net income before debt service is based on two assumptions: the income and expenses forecast are expressed in changing dollars and management is competent.

When the first edition of this book was published in 1978, the use of constant dollars in all hotel projections was recommended. As infla-

tion became a more important consideration to both hotel lenders and investors, however, it became apparent that interest, discount, and capitalization rates were being adjusted upward for inflation. Most hotel investors now base their purchases on the property's expected future benefits with inflation built in, so it is also built into the rates.

Forecasts of income and expenses are usually based on competent management because the quality of management plays an important role in the profit potential of a lodging facility. The appraiser must equalize the effects of varying managerial expertise by assuming that the property being appraised will be managed competently. In reality, management quality may be poor, competent, or superior. If the property is currently under poor management, the appraiser is justified in projecting improved operating results based on competent management. If, on the other hand, the subject has superior management, the income and expenses used to estimate market value should reflect less managerial skill—i.e., lower revenue and/or higher expenses. No such assumption is needed if management is fixed by a long-term contract and would not change in the event of a sale, or if the appraiser is estimating investment value rather than market value. Investment value is the value to a particular investor based on individual financial and managerial requirements. It differs from market value in that market value must represent the actions of typical buyers and reflect average, competent management.

The procedure for forecasting income before interest and depreciation has already been described. The appraiser defines the market area, locates and quantifies the demand, and allocates the room nights among the competitive facilities. This procedure provides the information needed to estimate occupancy and average rate. Based on these data, rooms revenue and other sources of income such as food and beverage sales and telephone income can be computed. Expense data can be obtained from actual operating statements if the subject is an existing property, or from comparable properties and national averages if the subject is a proposed facility.

Hotel-Motel Life Cycle

The expected flow of net income before debt service must be assessed to select the appropriate discounting procedure. All real estate investments have specific life cycles that show the rise and fall of net income over the property's economic life. Most income-producing properties reach their full economic potential relatively quickly. This level may then be maintained for a number of years and then gradually decline as various forms of depreciation erode the property's income.

It generally takes some time for lodging facilities to achieve their maximum level of income. A typical hostelry will experience slowly rising occupancy in its first two to four years of operation; often net income does not cover normal debt service during this period. A stabilized level of income normally is reached sometime between the second and fifth years of operation; this stabilized level represents the property's discounted average net income. The income before debt service will usually rise above the stabilized level for a few years, and then gradually start to decline between the seventh and twelfth years because of physical deterioration and/or functional and external obsolescence. This decline continues over the remaining economic life of the property. The life cycle of a lodging facility is not predetermined, however. It can be lengthened or shortened depending on how much maintenance and periodic upgrading the owner is willing to do.

Table 4 shows net income figures for a hotel over its 40-year life cycle. These figures might apply to the 250-room case study property. A sale of the property is assumed to occur at the end of the 40th year, so the income from that year includes both the net income and sale proceeds. The net income figures for Years 1 through 39 are graphed in Figure 1.

Proposed hotels and motels are appraised as of the beginning of their life cycles, but existing lodging facilities may be appraised at any point in the cycle. By estimating a property's position in the life cycle, the appraiser can project future net income before debt service (if adequate market data are available) and select an appropriate discounting procedure.

Selecting Appropriate Capitalization Rates and Discount Factors

Capitalization rates and discount factors are used to convert expected future income into an indication of value. These rates and factors have an interest component, which reflects the return on capital, and a recapture component, which provides for a return of capital.

Theoretically the interest component can be derived through risk and investment analysis. Starting with a base rate that represents the minimal risk of a safe investment such as a federally insured savings account, the analyst makes a series of upward adjustments to reflect different elements of risk and the investment burden. For example, adjustments might be made for the following factors:

	%
Safe rate (minimum risk)	X
Add for general hostelry risk	I_1
Add for management burden	I_2
Add for food and beverage risk	I_3
Add for rapid functional obsolescence	I_4
Add for illiquidity	I_5
Add for other elements	I_6
	Final interest rate

TABLE 4. HOTEL LIFE CYCLE		
	Net Income Before Debt Service	
Year	Inflated Dollars	Constant Dollars
1	$1,634,000	$1,634,000
2	3,322,200	3,164,000
3	4,306,365	3,906,000
4	5,195,125	4,488,000
5	6,060,980	4,987,000
6	6,841,331	5,361,000
7	7,545,223	5,631,000
8	8,162,560	5,801,000
9	8,326,907	5,636,000
10	8,487,284	5,471,000
11	8,642,880	5,306,000
12	8,792,818	5,141,000
13	8,936,143	4,976,000
14	9,071,818	4,811,000
15	9,198,720	4,646,000
16	9,315,633	4,481,000
17	9,421,240	4,316,000
18	9,514,119	4,151,000
19	9,592,733	3,986,000
20	9,655,423	3,821,000
21	9,700,400	3,656,000
22	9,725,736	3,491,000
23	9,729,355	3,326,000
24	9,709,021	3,161,000
25	9,662,331	2,996,000
26	9,586,699	2,831,000
27	9,479,348	2,666,000
28	9,337,295	2,501,000
29	9,157,338	2,336,000
30	8,936,043	2,171,000
31	8,669,724	2,006,000
32	8,354,434	1,841,000
33	7,985,941	1,676,000
34	7,559,711	1,511,000
35	7,070,895	1,346,000
36	6,514,297	1,181,000
37	5,884,362	1,016,000
38	5,175,148	851,000
39	4,380,302	686,000
40	26,550,815	3,960,000

In practice estimating the magnitude of each upward adjustment is too subjective a process to provide a supportable interest rate. A more reliable rate can be produced by utilizing the analytical expertise of the hundreds of money managers who serve the nation's lending institutions.

Generally a hostelry investment consists of a large amount of mortgage money (60%–75% of the total investment) and a smaller amount of equity capital (25%–40%). Thus 60% to 75% of a hotel project's cost of capital is based on the mortgage interest rate, which implies that 60% to 75% of the capitalization or discount rate is determined by the cost of the mortgage financing. The interest rate on a hostelry mortgage is established by the lender, who considers all possible risks. Obviously the mortgagee is in a more secure position than the equity investor but, in the event of a foreclosure, the lender may be forced to assume the equity position.

To develop a capitalization rate, the appraiser first researches the cost of the debt component of the investment by evaluating recent hotel financing transactions. To simplify the calculations for appraisal purposes, the interest rate is generally assumed to be fixed rather than variable. Although variable-rate mortgages are used to finance some hotel projects, it is often possible to have another lending entity fix the interest rate at a specific level, which effectively converts the variable payments into fixed payments.

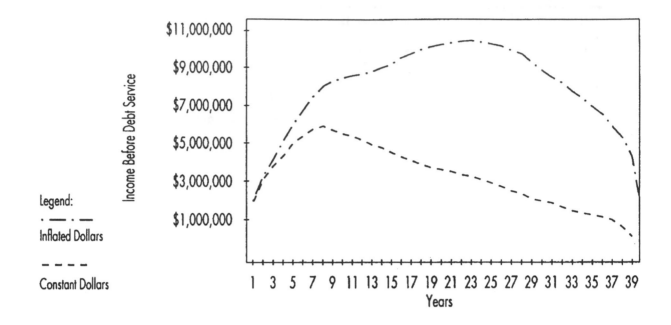

FIGURE 1. Hotel Life Cycle

For the purpose of illustration, a fixed payment mortgage will be used.

The mortgage provision that has the greatest economic impact on an investment is the mortgage interest rate. To assess the cost of mortgage capital, hotel appraisers must know the current lending rates for hotel mortgage loans. In recent years money markets have experienced fast and constant changes. Consequently, there is a critical need for reliable, timely estimates of hotel mortgage interest rates to provide appraisers with a reference point from which to estimate the cost of mortgage financing.

One procedure for accumulating mortgage rate information is to survey lenders actively making hotel loans.

This approach will generally yield results, but the data may not be very accurate for the following reasons:

▶ It may be difficult to find lenders who are actively lending on hotel projects.
▶ Even lenders who are active in the hotel lending market do not make hotel loans on a regular basis. Therefore any information obtained for these sources may be dated, particularly in a fast-changing money market.
▶ Not all lenders are willing to provide data relative to the loans they have made.
▶ A lender who responds to an interest rate survey may provide information that represents the "asking price" or a hotel loan,

rather than the final terms negotiated.

A better, more reliable approach is for the appraiser to obtain accurate information on hotel loans actually originated by lenders. The best source for this type of data is the American Council of Life Insurance. This organization, which represents most of the major life insurance companies, publishes quarterly reports on the hotel mortgages originated by their member companies. Some of the relevant data available to subscribers include the number of loans made, the total dollar amount loaned, the interest rate, the loan-to-value ratio, and the term of the loans.

The primary disadvantage of using information published by the American Council of Life Insurance is that the data are generally four to six months old by the time they are accumulated and distributed. Thus appraisers need to find a way to update the data continuously. Ideally appraisers could use as an indicator some type of money market instrument with a rate of return (yield) that could be obtained on a daily basis. If the movement of this rate showed a high correlation with hotel mortgage interest rates, then a regression equation could be developed to estimate current hotel mortgage interest rates using the known money market instrument.

Several years ago Hospitality Valuation Services attempted to develop such a procedure by running a series of regression analyses. Quarterly mortgage interest rate data supplied by the American Council of Life Insurance were compared with numerous, widely reported money market instruments. Included in this analysis were the prime rate, the federal funds rate, several stock market rates, different types of bond yields, and variety of similar indexes. As a result of this research, a close mathematical relationship was found between the average interest rate of a hotel mortgage and the concurrent yield of a Aa utility bond as reported daily in *Moody's Bond Record.*

Table 5 shows the annual rates for several of the money market instruments that were evaluated. The first column shows the interest rates for ho-

tel mortgages as reported by the American Council of Life Insurance. The other columns contain the comparative rates including the yields on an Aa utility bond, a three-year treasury note, and a 10-year treasury note as well as the federal funds rate, the prime lending rate, the Standard and Poors composite index of 500 stocks, the 30-year corporate bond yield, and the interest rate on FHA-insured home mortgages sold in the secondary market. The table also shows the coefficient of correlation, R, which is derived from the regression analysis used to compare the rates for each money market instrument with the hotel mortgage interest rate. The instrument exhibiting the highest coefficient of correlation (R) provides the

TABLE 5. ANNUAL RATES FOR MONEY MARKET INSTRUMENTS									
	Hotel Interest	Aa Utility Bonds	U.S. Treasury 3 Year	U.S. Treasury 10 Year	Fed Funds	Prime	S&P Composite	30-Year Corporate Bond	FHA-Insured Home Mortgage
1973	9.10	7.79	6.95	6.84	8.74	8.03	3.06	7.20	8.19
1974	9.65	9.04	7.82	7.56	10.50	10.81	4.47	7.80	9.55
1975	10.34	9.44	7.49	7.99	5.82	7.86	4.31	8.35	9.19
1976	10.06	8.92	6.77	7.61	5.04	6.84	3.77	8.30	8.82
1977	9.77	8.43	6.69	7.42	5.54	6.83	4.62	7.95	8.68
1978	9.95	9.10	8.29	8.41	7.93	9.06	5.28	8.25	9.70
1979	11.82	10.22	9.72	9.44	11.19	12.67	5.47	9.10	10.87
1980	12.65	13.00	11.55	11.46	13.36	15.27	5.26	12.30	13.44
1981	14.63	15.30	14.44	13.91	16.38	18.87	5.20	13.00	16.29
1982	15.73	14.79	12.92	13.00	12.26	14.86	5.81	14.00	15.31
1000	12.97	12.84	10.45	11.11	9.09	10.79	4.40	11.00	13.11
1984	9.97	12.94	11.89	12.44	10.23	12.04	4.64	12.60	13.82
1685	12.24	12.06	9.64	10.62	8.10	9.93	4.25	12.50	12.24
1986	9.95	9.30	7.06	7.68	6.80	8.33	3.48	8.50	9.91
1987	9.91	9.77	7.67	8.38	6.66	8.20	3.08	8.00	10.12
Coefficient of Correlation (R)		0.884	0.840	0.837	0.703	0.801	0.649	0.831	0.862

most accurate basis for estimating hotel lending rates.

The table shows that Aa utility bond yields have the highest coefficient of correlation, so this instrument is used to develop the hotel interest rate regression equation. To best reflect the everchanging money market climate, a more comprehensive regression analysis was run using the Aa utility bond yields over an extended period of time. Table 6 sets forth hotel mortgage interest rates and corresponding utility bond yields on an annual basis from 1966 to 1978 and a quarterly basis from 1979 until the first quarter of 1989.

Using the regression command from a Lotus spreadsheet, the following regression output was obtained:

Constant	2.69785
Standard error of Y estimate	.667029
X coefficient	.79497
Standard error of coefficient	.033563
Coefficient of correlation	.95277
Number of observations	59
Degrees of freedom	57

This regression output can be used in the following equation, which calculates the mortgage interest rate (Y) based on the actual yield on an Aa utility bond (X):

$$Y = 2.69785 + .79497\,X$$

Assume that the current yield on an Aa utility bond is 9.39%. Substituting this yield for X and solving for Y results in an estimated mortgage interest rate of 10.16%.

Appraisers using this regression approach to update hotel mortgage interest rates should rerun the regression analysis each quarter when the American Council of Life Insurance releases its latest data on hotel mortgage interest rates.

The real strength of mortgage-equity analysis of a real estate investment is the fact that the mortgage component of the discount rate can be readily supported with current, highly accurate interest rate data. Most investors would agree that it is far better to have 75% of the mortgage-equity discount rate fully supported than to rely on a totally subjective (and usually outdated) overall discount rate.

Other sources of lending information include local banks and insurance companies, real estate investment trusts, mortgage brokers, and regulatory agencies. By comparing the rates derived from several sources, an appraiser can estimate the mortgage interest components with relative accuracy.

The mortgage recapture component, which represents the return *of* the investment, is expressed in the rate of amortization. According to the American Council of Life Insurance, hostelry loans have typically been structured to be repaid over a 20- to 30-year term. The recapture component plus the interest component equals the yearly mortgage constant. The annual debt service is calculated by multiplying the mortgage constant by the original loan balance.

The remaining 25% to 40% of a hostelry investment is equity money. Like common stock, which entitles the owner to the residual earnings after all expenses, including debt services, have been paid, real estate equity investments normally provide overall returns that are higher than those demanded by the mortgage component. The short-term equity return, which is called the *equity dividend* rate by appraisers and the *cash-on-cash return* by hostelry investors represents the annual net income after debt service divided by the value of the equity.

The rate of return that an equity investor expects over a 10-year holding period (the long-term return) is called *equity yield*. Unlike the equity dividend which is a short-term rate of return, the equity yield specifically considers a long holding period (generally 10 years), annual cash flows impacted by inflation, property appreciation, mortgage amortization, and proceeds from a sale at the end of the holding period. Both the equity dividend and the equity yield will produce a good estimate of value when used with the

TABLE 6. UTILITY BOND YIELDS AND HOTEL INTEREST RATES

Year/Quarter	Aa Utility Bond Yield	Hotel Interest Rate
1966	5.222	6.730
1967	5.660	7.220
1968	6.353	7.900
1969	7.344	8.920
1970	8.516	9.780
1971	8.001	9.700
1972	7.602	8.920
1973	7.791	9.100
1974	9.041	9.650
1975	9.435	10.340
1976	8.917	10.060
1977	8.433	9.770
1978	9.097	9.950
1/79	9.777	10.540
2/79	10.020	10.640
3/79	9.803	10.750
4/79	11.297	11.380
1/80	13.080	11.820
2/80	12.400	13.070
3/80	12.620	12.960
4/80	13.890	12.750
1/81	14.430	13.870
2/81	15.240	14.050
3/81	16.050	15.000
4/81	15.460	15.580
1/82	16.130	14.760
2/82	15.300	17.500
3/82	14.770	15.300
4/82	12.960	15.340
1/83	12.810	13.400
2/83	12.500	12.610
3/83	13.030	12.850
4/83	13.000	13.030
1/84	13.240	13.160
2/84	14.500	13.300
4/84	13.050	13.400
1/85	13.020	12.570
2/85	12.500	12.280
3/85	11.620	12.170
4/85	11.090	11.930
1/86	9.860	10.990
2/86	9.200	9.800
3/86	9.120	9.560
4/86	9.020	9.440
1/87	8.650	9.430
2/87	9.460	9.810
3/87	10.140	10.000
4/87	10.840	10.410
2/88	10.447	10.090
3/88	10.650	10.660
4/88	9.830	10.070
1/89	9.960	10.390
2/89	9.730	10.540
3/89	9.280	9.550
4/89	9.260	9.960
2/90	9.750	10.580
3/90	9.750	10.470
2/91	9.200	10.750
3/91	9.090	10.030

Sources: *Moody's Bond Record* and the American Council of Life Insurance

proper technique and supported by appropriate data.

Accurate data relating to equity return expectations are not always easy to obtain. However, since the equity return component represents only 25% of the discount rate (assuming a 75% loan-to-value ratio), the negative impact of any error is reduced. Hotel appraisers typically rely on two sources of equity data—investor interviews and past appraisals.

To obtain data through investor interviews an appraiser surveys actual or potential hotel investors who have recently made or contemplated an equity investment in a lodging facility. Depending on the type of property being appraised, the appraiser should survey either institutional investors or individual investors. The key to obtaining reliable information from investor interviews is to explain carefully the terms *equity dividend* and *equity yield* before conducting the survey. Since many hotel investors are not sophisticated appraisers, these terms may be confused with terms such as *overall rate, capitalization rate,* or *total property yield.* A misunderstanding of terms can distort the appraiser's findings and make the survey invalid. Unless the equity investor has a clear understanding of *equity dividend* or *equity yield,* it is generally best not to include his or her responses in the results of that particular survey. A broad cross section of active buyers must be surveyed because each is influenced by a variety of factors. The results of a limited sample can

produce misleading assumptions. For example, an investor in a high tax bracket may settle for a lower-than-market equity return if the tax shelter benefits of the investment are particularly attractive. Similarly, the opportunity to resell a property after several years for a higher price may induce a buyer to accept a lower equity dividend. Because owning a hotel has a certain amount of status, some buyers may be willing to accept a lower equity return. An active hotel-motel broker, such as a member of the Hotel Motel Brokers Association, can often provide insight into the equity rates of return demanded in the current market. Good sources of equity information include typical hotel buyers and investors, lenders seeking equity participation and joint ventures, and hotel management companies.

The second source of equity return information is readily available to appraisal firms that regularly perform hotel valuations. These appraisers can derive equity dividend and equity yield rates from actual sales of hotels they have recently appraised. This approach differs from deriving an over-all rate from the market in that the appraiser uses the actual forecast of income and expense that was developed in the appraisal immediately preceding the sale. An illustration of this procedure follows.

Example

Over the past 12 months the hotel appraisal firm of Hospitality Valuation Services has ap-

praised more than 400 hotels in most major market areas. In each of these appraisals a similar mortgage-equity technique was used to forecast income into the future and discount it back to present value at rates that reflect the cost of both debt and equity capital. In instances where hotels were actually sold subsequent to the appraisal, equity dividend and equity yield rate were derived from the projection of income and expense by excluding any incentive management fees and then inserting the projection into the valuation model. The appraised value was adjusted to reflect the actual sale price merely by modifying the return assumptions. Table 7 shows a representative sample of hotel sales that were evaluated in this manner and their calculated equity dividend and yield rates.

In addition to quantifying the equity dividend and equity yield, the appraiser sometimes needs to estimate a terminal capitalization rate. When a 10-year forecast is utilized, the terminal, or going-out, capitalization rate is used to capitalize the net income in Year 11 into a reversionary value. It is basically an overall rate that can be estimated with a simple mortgage-equity band of investment using an equity dividend. Note that this rate is applied to the net income before debt service at a point in time 11 years after the date of value; thus it should be adjusted upward somewhat to reflect the fact that the hotel will probably be somewhat closer to the end of its economic life.

		Number of Rooms	Date of Sale	Selling Price	Equity Dividend	Equity Yield
TABLE 7. HOTEL EQUITY DIVIDEND AND YIELD RATES						
Hotel	**City and State**					
Copley Plaza	Boston, MA	397	12/88	$56,000,000	9.8%	17.7%
Logan Hilton	Boston, MA	557	7/88	29,000,000	8.5	20.0
Holiday Inn— Airport	Philadelphia, PA	307	7/88	15,000,000	10.0	21.5
Holiday Inn	Milford, CT	108	6/88	6,500,000	12.5	26.0
Ramada Inn	Kingston, NY	147	4/88	9,100,000	11.5	24.7
Hyatt Regency	Chicago, IL	2,019	9/88	268,500,000	10.0	17.0
LaCosta	Calsbad, CA	482	11/87	250,000,000	10.1	15.6

Applying the Proper Capitalization or Discounting Procedure

Several procedures can be used to combine mortgage and equity data into a discount factor or capitalization rate that will transform a projected net income estimate into an indication of value. The selection of discount factors and capitalization rates depends on many factors, including the length of the income projection period, the age of the property and its position in its life cycle, the nature of the mortgage financing, and the sophistication of equity investors. The following discussion describes the various methods for developing discount factors and their proper application in the valuation process.

Discount Each Year's Income Over the Full Life Cycle

The simplest form of valuation begins with a projection of the property's net income before debt service for each year over the full life of the improvements. Each year's net income is then multiplied by the proper present value of a reversion of one factor and all these discounted net income figures are totaled to produce the overall property value.

Capitalize One Stabilized Year's Income

Instead of projecting net income over the entire life of the property, a single, stabilized estimate of net income can be capitalized at an appropriate rate. The stabilized net income relates to a representative year or, more technically, it is the discounted average net income over the property's economic life. In estimating stabilized earnings, more weight is given to the income expected during the early years of the investment because this income is less affected by discounting.

CASE STUDY

Capitalizing Stabilized Income

The forecast of income and expense developed in a previous case study example indicates that the property will reach a stabilized level of occupancy in the third year of its operation. The net income before debt service as of this point in time is $4,306,000. Deflating this amount back to the opening year at an assumed 5% inflation rate results in an estimated stabilized net income of $3,906,000. (Note that this is only one method for estimating stabilized net income and the appraiser should ultimately attempt to reflect the actions of typical hotel buyers and sellers).

Now the appraiser must develop a rate to capitalize the stabilized net income. One procedure for developing a capitalization rate is the band-of-investment (weighted cost of capital) technique. Combining the weighted average of the return demanded by the mortgage position of the investment with the dividend required by the equity component results in a capitalization rate that reflects the basic financial composition of the hostelry investment.

Using the previously described mortgage interest rate regression formula and a survey of hotel equity investors, the following mortgage and equity terms were established as appropriate.

Mortgage finance terms:
Interest rate	10.5%
Amortization	30 years
Mortgage constant	10.98%
Loan-to-value ratio	75%
Equity dividend rate	10.0%

The band-of-investment technique is used to develop a capitalization rate that is the weighted average of the mortgage constant and equity dividend rate:

	Portion		Rate		Weighted Rate
Mortgage	.75	×	.1098	=	.0823
Equity	.25	×	.1000	=	.0250
	Overall capitalization rate			=	.1073

The stabilized net income is divided by the capitalization rate to produce the capitalized value.

$$\frac{\$3,906,000}{.1073} = \$36,402,000 \text{ (rounded)}$$

The value can be supported with the following calculations:

75% Mortgage	$27,301,000	×	.1098	=	$2,996,000
25% Equity	$ 9,101,000	×	.1000	=	$ 910,000
Value	$36,402,000				$3,906,000

These calculations show that the $36,402,000 value can be divided into a mortgage portion of $27,301,000 and an equity portion of $9,101,000. The yearly mortgage payment, consisting of interest and amortization, is calculated by multiplying the original mortgage balance ($27,301,000) by the constant (.1098), which results in an annual debt service of $2,996,000. The equity dividend is established by multiplying the equity investment ($9,101,000) by the anticipated equity return (.10), which yields $910,000. The annual debt service plus the equity dividend equals the stabilized net income before debt service.

Essentially, the band-of-investment technique works backwards, using the projected stabilized net income to calculate the value that will meet the demands of both the mortgage and equity investors. The components that form the band of investment—i.e., as mortgage terms and equity requirements—can be well documented and supported. However, the stabilized net income used in this approach does not always reflect the potential for low income during the early years of the investment. To get a better indication of the net income of a property in its initial years, the analyst should project several years of income and expenses.

Another way to derive a capitalization rate is to analyze the terms and conditions of actual market sales. For example, assume an investor has recently purchased a motel for $3,000,000. An income analysis indicates that the property has a stabilized income before interest and depreciation of $359,700. The market-derived overall capitalization rate for this sale is:

$$\frac{\$359,700}{\$3,000,000} = 11.99\%$$

To apply this or any other market-related procedure, the appraiser needs a complete understanding of the transaction and the motivations of the parties involved. Adjustments must be made for any unusual factors so that the capitalization rate derived represents normal market conditions. Some questions that the appraiser might ask are

1. Is the stated selling price the market value or has unusual existing or purchase-money financing affected the transaction price?
2. Is the price based on existing or anticipated income?
3. Is the buyer motivated by special factors such as tax shelter or referral benefits?
4. Does the property suffer from deferred maintenance that must be corrected by the buyer?
5. Did the transaction involve a willing buyer and a willing seller, both with full knowledge of all circumstances?
6. Is the comparable property somewhat similar to the property being appraised

with respect to size, location, market, and condition?
7. Does the income statement of the comparable contain a reserve for replacement? If it does not, the subject property's projected income before debt service should also exclude a reserve for replacement.

An appraiser is seldom able to obtain enough data on the sale of a comparable hostelry to derive a meaningful capitalization rate based on the current market. Simply understanding the motivations of the buyer and the seller requires more than a casual observation of the transaction.

Ten-Year Forecast Using an Equity Yield Rate

To eliminate some of the uncertainties associated with excessively long-term net income projections, and specifically to show the normal occupancy build-up for new hotels, most appraisers use projection periods of three to 10 years.

A 10-year projection using an equity yield rate is similar to an Ellwood valuation approach, in which the yearly income to equity plus an equity reversion is discounted at an equity yield rate, and the income to the mortgagee is discounted at a mortgage yield rate. The sum of the equity and mortgage values is the total property value.

The benefits to the equity position include equity dividends from the net income remaining after debt service during the ten-year projection period and the gain or loss realized from the

property's assumed resale. The resale or reversionary benefits include the gain or loss caused by value appreciation or depreciation plus any mortgage amortization. The benefits to the mortgage position are interest and amortization plus repayment of the remaining mortgage balance at the end of 10 years.

Valuation using a 10-year income projection and an equity yield rate is performed in four steps.

1. The terms of typical hotel financing are set forth, including the interest rate, amortization term, and loan-to-value ratio.
2. An equity yield rate of return and terminal capitalization rate are established.
3. The value of the equity component is calculated and added to the initial mortgage amount to produce the overall property value.
4. The value estimate is allocated between the mortgage and equity components.

Researching and analyzing typical financing terms has been discussed in detail, so the next step is to establish an equity yield rate of return. Currently a number of hotel buyers base their equity investments on a 10-year equity yield rate projection that takes into account the benefits of ownership such as periodic cash flow distributions, residual sale or refinancing distributions that return any property appreciation and mortgage amortization, income tax benefits, and nonfinancial considerations such as status and prestige. In addition, the appraiser must estimate a terminal capitalization rate, which will be used to capitalize the Year 11 net income into a reversionary value.

Next, the value of the equity component is calculated by deducting the yearly debt service from the forecasted income, which leaves the net income to equity for each year of the forecast. The net income as of Year 11 is capitalized into a reversionary value. After deducting the mortgage balance as of the end of the tenth year as well as normal legal and selling costs, the equity residual is discounted to the date of value at the equity yield rate. Then the net income to equity for each of the 10 projection years is also discounted. The sum of these discounted values equals the value of the equity component. Adding the equity component to the initial mortgage balance yields the overall property value.

Because the amount of the mortgage and the debt service are unknown, but the loan-to-value ratio is determined in Step 1, the calculation can be solved either with an iterative process on a computer or with an algebraic equation that computes the total property value.

A complex algebraic equation that solves for the total property value using the 10-year mortgage-equity technique was developed by Suzanne R. Mellen, MAI. This equation is known as the simultaneous valuation formula. A complete discussion of this technique is contained in Mellen's article, "Simultaneous Valuation: A New Capitalization Technique for Hotel and Other Income Properties," which appeared in the April 1983 issue of *The Appraisal Journal*. Material from this article has been incorporated into this chapter.

Finally, the value estimate is proven by allocating the total property value between the mortgage and equity components and verifying that the rates of returns set forth in Steps 1 and 2 can be precisely met through the forecasted net income.

Each step in the process will be illustrated using the case study example.

▶ Step 1: Determine the appropriate mortgage financing terms.
▶ Step 2. Estimate an appropriate equity yield rate and

CASE STUDY

Determining Financing Terms

The mortgage interest regression formula indicates a current interest rate of 10.16%. Since the mortgage data reported by the American Council of Life Insurance generally represents investment-grade hotel properties, the appraiser may want to adjust this rate for the location, type of hotel, age and condition of the property, operating history, local supply and demand trends, management expertise and affiliation, and interest being appraised.

It is assumed that the proposed Sheraton Hotel will have new facilities, good management, and a recognized affiliation. Offsetting these positive attributes is the projected downward trend in area occupancies as additional rooms open in the market and become more competitive. In addition to increased competition, the Sheraton will have to survive the normal buildup of occupancy experienced by all new hotels; this risk factor is considered by many lenders. Based on the appraiser's analysis, the following mortgage terms would probably be available for the proposed Sheraton.

Interest rate	10.50%
Amortization schedule	30 years
Payments per year	Monthly
Mortgage constant	.109769
Mortgage term	10 years
Loan-to-value ratio	75%

CASE STUDY

Estimating equity yield and terminal capitalization rates

A survey of hotel investors was conducted to determine their current equity yield requirements. In addition the appraiser reviewed recent appraisals of hotels that sold proximate to the date of value. The range of equity yields for hotels comparable to the proposed Sheraton is 18% to 22%.

Using the same investment criteria employed to determine the mortgage interest rate, a 20% equity yield rate was selected for the proposed Sheraton. The terminal capitalization rate can be estimated with the mortgage-equity band-of-investment utilizing an equity dividend rate. The factors that were considered are set forth on pages 223–224—capitalizing stabilized income.

Loan-to-Value Ratio			Rate of Return		Weighted Average
Mortgage	.75	×	.1098	=	.0823
Equity	.25	×	.1000	=	.0250
					.1073

Adjusting these rates to reflect the tenth year terminal capitalization rate produces a going-out rate of 11% for the proposed Sheraton.

---

a terminal capitalization rate.

▶ Step 3. Estimate overall property value by valuing equity component and adding initial mortgage balance.

By this point in the analysis, the appraiser has made all the necessary subjective and objective decisions. The remainder of the process is purely mathematical. The appraiser must solve an algebraic equation which calculates the exact amount of debt and equity that the hotel will be able to sup-

port based on the anticipated cash flow derived from the forecast of income and expense and the specific return requirements demanded by the mortgage lender (interest) and the equity investor (equity yield).

To solve for the value of the mortgage and equity components, the appraiser first deducts the yearly debt service from the forecast of income before debt service; the remainder is the net income to equity for each year in the forecast. The net income as of Year 11 is capitalized into a reversionary value using the terminal capitalization rate.

The equity residual, which is the total reversionary value minus the mortgage balance at that point in time and any broker and legal cost associated with the sale, is discounted to the date of value at the equity yield rate. The net income to equity for each of the forecast years is also discounted. The sum of these discounted values equals the value of the equity component. Since the equity component represents a specific percentage of the total value, the value of the mortgage and the total property value can be easily computed.

The process described above can be expressed in two algebraic equations, which set forth the mathematic relationships between known and unknown variables. The symbols used to represent these variables are listed below.

NI	=	Net income available for debt service
V	=	Value
M	=	Loan-to-value ratio
f	=	Annual debt service constant
n	=	Number of years in projection period
d_e	=	Annual cash available to equity
d_r	=	Residual equity value
b	=	Brokerage and legal cost percentage
P^*	=	Fraction of loan paid off in projection period
fp	=	Annual constant required to amortize the entire loan during the projection period
R_r	=	Overall terminal capitalization rate applied to net income to calculate total property reversion (sale price at end of the projection period)
$1/S_n$	=	Current worth of 1\$ (discount factor) at the equity yield rate

Using these symbols a series of formulas can be derived to express some of the components comprising this mortgage-equity valuation process.

$$*P = (f - i) / (fp - i) \text{ where}$$
i = the interest rate of the mortgage

Debt service. To calculate a property's debt service, the appraiser first determines the amount of the mortgage, which is the total property value (V) multiplied by the loan-to-value ratio (M). Then the amount of the mortgage is multiplied by the annual debt service constant (f) using the following formula:

$$f \times M \times V = \text{debt service}$$

Net income to equity (equity dividend). The net income to equity (d_e) is the property's net income before debt service (NI) minus the debt service.

The following formula represents net income to equity:

$$NI - (f \times M \times V) = d_e$$

Reversionary value. The value of the hotel at the end of Year 10 is calculated by dividing the net income in Year 11 before debt service (NI^{11}) by the terminal capitalization rate (R_r). The following formula calculates the property's reversionary value in Year 10:

$$NI^{11}/R_r = \text{reversionary value}$$

Broker and legal costs. When a hotel is sold, costs associated with the transaction normally include a broker's commission and attorneys' fees. For a hotel transaction broker and legal costs typically range from 1% to 4 % of the sale price. Because these expenses reduce the proceeds to the seller, they are usually deducted from the reversionary value in mortgage-equity analysis. Broker and legal costs (b) expressed as a percentage of the reversionary value (NI^{11}/R_r) can be calculated with the following formula:

$$(b (NI^{11}/R_r)) = \text{broker and legal costs}$$

Ending mortgage balance. The balance of the mortgage at the end of Year 10 must be deducted from the total reversionary value (debt and equity) to isolate the equity residual. A financial formula is used to calculate the fraction of the loan paid off, which is expressed as a percentage of the original loan balance at a particular point in time. The mortgage interest rate (i) is deducted from the annual debt service constant of the loan over the entire amortization period (f) and the result is divided by the annual constant required to amortize the entire loan over the projection period (sub p) minus the mortgage interest rate. The formula is

$$(f - i) / (f_p - i) = P$$

If the fraction of the loan paid off expressed as a percentage of the initial loan balance is P, then the percentage of the loan remaining can be expressed as $1 - P$. Thus, the ending mortgage balance is the fraction of the loan remaining $(1 - P)$ multiplied by the amount of the initial loan ($M \times V$). The formula is

$$(1 - P) \times M \times V = ending$$
$$mortgage\ balance$$

Equity residual value. The value of the equity when the property is sold at the end of the projection period (d_r) is the reversionary value minus broker and legal costs and the ending mortgage balance. The following formula represents the equity residual value:

$$(NI^{11} /R_r) - (b\ (NI^{11}/R_r)) - ((1 - P) \times M \times V) = d_r$$

Annual cashflow to equity. The annual cash flow to equity consists of the equity dividend for each of the 10 projection years plus the equity residual at the end of Year 10. The following formulas represent the annual cash flow to equity:

$$NI^1\ (f \times M \times V) = d_e^1$$
$$NI^2\ (f \times M \times V) = d_e^2 ...$$
$$NI^{10}\ (F \times M \times V) = d_e^{10}$$
$$(NI^{11}/R_r) - (b\ (NI^{11}/R_r)) - ((1 - P) \times M \times V) = d_r$$

Value of the equity. If the initial amount of the mortgage is calculated by multiplying the loan-to-value ratio (M) by the value of the property (V), then the equity value will be I minus the loan-to-value ratio times the property value. The formula is

$$(1 - M)V$$

Discounting the cash flow to equity to present value. The cash flow to equity for each of the projection years is discounted to present value at the equity yield rate ($1/S^n$). The sum of all these cash flows is the value of the equity $(1 - M)V$. The following formula calculates equity as the sum of the discounted cash flows:

$$(d_e^1 \times 1/S^1) + (d_e^2 \times 1/S^2) + ...$$
$$+ (d_e^{10} \times 1/S^{10})$$
$$+ (d_r \times 1/S^{10}) = (1 - M)V$$

Combining equations: annual cashflow to equity and cashflow to equity discounted to present value. The final step in the process is to make one, overall equation that shows that the annual cash flow to equity plus the yearly cash flows discounted to present value equal the value of the equity.

CASE STUDY

Applying the 10-Year Discounted Cash Flow Valuation Formula

Generally the net income before debt service is projected beyond the stabilized year at an assumed rate of change. By increasing a property's revenue and expenses at the same rate of inflation, the net income expressed as a percentage of total revenue will remain constant and the dollar amount of net income will escalate each year at the rate of change. When a category of revenue or expense is expected to increase at a different rate, the appraiser should reflect this aberration in that specific year's forecast of income and expense. This situation is likely to be the result of contractual changes in a ground rent expense, use of an escalating reserve for replacement percentage, or an expected change in the property tax assessment.

The appraiser finds that hotel investors are using inflation rates of approximately 5%. Table C.S.1 shows the net income of the proposed Sheraton Hotel projected beyond the stabilized year at a 5% rate of inflation.

Solving for Value Using the Simultaneous Valuation Formula

In the case of the subject property, the following variables are known:

Annual net income	NI	See Table C.S.1
Loan-to-value ratio	M	75%
Debt service constant	f	0.109769
Equity yield	Y_e	20%
Brokerage and legal fees	b	3%
Annual constant required to amortize the loan in 10 years	f_p	0.161922
Terminal capitalization rate	R_r	11%

TABLE C.S.1. NET INCOME FORECAST	
Operational Year	**Net Income**
1	$1,634,000
2	3,322,000
3	4,306,000
4	4,521,000
5	4,747,000
6	4,985,000
7	5,234,000
8	5,496,000
9	5,770,000
10	6,059,000
11	6,361,923

TABLE C.S.2. PRESENT WORTH OF $1	
Operational Year	**1/S**
1	0.833333
2	0.694444
3	0.578703
4	0.482253
5	0.401877
6	0.334897
7	0.279081
8	0.232568
9	0.193806
10	0.161505

Table C.S.2 shows the present worth of a $1 factors at the 20% equity yield rate.

Intermediary calculations must be made using these known variables before the simultaneous valuation formula can be applied.

The fraction of the loan paid off during the projection period is calculated as follows:

$$P = (0.109769 - 0.105) / (0.161922 - 0.105) = 0.08378$$

The annual debt service is calculated as $f \times M \times V$.

$$0.109769 \times 0.75 \times V = .082327\ V$$

Next the formula is expressed in terms of V.

$$(1,634,000 - 0.082327V) \times 0.833333+$$
$$(3,322,000 - 0.082327V) \times 0.694444+$$
$$(4,306,000 - 0.082327V) \times 0.578704+$$
$$(4,521,000 - 0.082327V) \times 0.482253+$$
$$(4,747,000 - 0.082327V) \times 0.401878+$$
$$(4,985,000 - 0.082327V) \times 0.334898+$$
$$(5,234,000 - 0.082327V) \times 0.279082+$$
$$(5,496,000 - 0.082327V) \times 0.232568+$$
$$(5,770,000 - 0.082327V) \times 0.193807+$$
$$(6,059,000 - 0.082327V) \times 0.161506+$$
$$(((6,361,923/0.110) - (0.03 \text{ x } (6,361,923/0.11)) -$$
$$((1-0.08378) \times 0.75 \times V)) \times 0.161506) = (1 - 0.75) \times V$$

Then like terms are combined.

$$\$25,814,248 - 0.456133\ V = 0.25\ V$$
$$\$25,814,248 = .070613\ V$$
$$V = \$25,814,248/0.70613$$
$$V = \$36,557,000 \text{ (rounded)}$$

Proof of Value

The value is proven by calculating the yields to the mortgage and equity components over the projection period. If the mortgage receives its 10.5% yield and the equity yields 20% then $36,557,000 is an appropriate value estimate derived by the income capitalization approach.

The indicated market value is allocated as follows:

Mortgage component	.75	$27,418,000
Equity component	.25	+ 9,139,000
Total		$36,557,000
Calculation of annual debt service:		
Mortgage component		$27,418,000
Mortgage constant		× .109169
Annual debt service		$3,010,000(rounded)

Net income to equity is forecast in Table C.S.3.

TABLE C.S.3. FORECAST OF NET INCOME TO EQUITY

Operational Year	Net Income Available for Debt Service		Debt Service		Net Income to Equity
1	$1,634,000	—	$3,010,000	=	$(1,376,000)
2	3,322,000	—	3,010,000	=	312,000
3	4,306,000	—	3,010,000	=	1,296,000
4	4,521,300	—	3,010,000	=	1,511,300
5	4,747,365	—	3,010,000	=	1,737,365
6	4,984,733	—	3,010,000	=	1,974,733
7	5,233,970	—	3,010,000	=	2,223,970
8	5,495,668	—	3,010,000	=	2,485,668
9	5,770,452	—	3,010,000	=	2,760,452
10	6,059,000	—	3,010,000	=	3,049,000

The residual value to equity at the end of Year 10 is calculated by capitalizing the Year 11 net income as follows:

$$\frac{\$6,361,923}{.110} = \$57,835,664$$

Sales proceeds	$57,835,664
Broker & legal fees	1,735,000
Mortgage balance	25,121,000
Net sales proceeds	$30,979,664

The annual cash flow to equity plus the residual equity value is discounted to present value of the equity yield rate of 20% (see Table C.S.4).

TABLE C.S.4. EQUITY COMPONENT YIELD (IRR OF 20.0%)

Operational Year	Net Income to Equity		Present Worth of $1 Factor @ 20.0%		Discounted Cash Flow
1	$(1,316,000)	×	0.833344	=	$(1,147,000)
2	312,000	×	0.694463	=	217,000
3	1,296,000	×	0.578727	=	750,000
4	1,511,300	×	0.482279	=	729,000
5	1,737,365	×	0.401904	=	698,000
6	1,974,733	×	0.334924	=	661,000
7	2,223,970	×	0.279107	=	621,000
8	2,485,668	×	0.232593	=	578,000
9	2,760,452	×	0.193830	=	535,000
10	*34,028,638	×	0.161527	=	5,497,000
Value of equity component					$9,139,000

*Year 10 net income to equity of $3,048,974 plus sales proceeds of $30,979,664
Note: Totals are rounded.

The table demonstrates that the equity investor will receive a 20% yield on the $9,139,000 investment if the annual cash flow and reversion take place as projected. Since the debt service factored into the calculations is based on an interest rate of 10.5%, the required yield for the lender will also be achieved. In addition to the yield to the equity investor, Tables C.S.5 and 6 show the total property yield (14.1%) and the mortgage yield (10.5%).

TABLE C.S.5. TOTAL PROPERTY YIELD (IRR OF 14.1%)

Operational Year	Net Income Before Debt Service		Present Worth of $1 Factor @ 14.1%		Discounted Cash Flow
1	1,634,000	×	0.876157	=	$1,432,000
2	3,322,000	×	0.767651	=	2,550,000
3	4,306,000	×	0.672582	=	2,896,000
4	4,521,300	×	0.589287	=	2,664,000
5	4,747,365	×	0.516308	=	2,451,000
6	4,984,733	×	0.452367	=	2,255,000
7	5,233,970	×	0.396344	=	2,074,000
8	5,495,668	×	0.347260	=	1,908,000
9	5,770,452	×	0.304254	=	1,756,000
10	62,159,974	×	0.266574	=	16,570,000
			Total property value		$36,556,000

*Year 10 net income of $6,058,974 plus sales proceeds of $56,101,000
Note: Totals are rounded.

TABLE C.S.6. MORTGAGE COMPONENT YIELD (IRR OF 10.5%)

Operational Year	Total Annual Debt Service		Present Worth of $1 Factor @ 10.5%		Discounted Cash Flow
1	$3,010,000	×	0.905271	=	$2,725,000
2	3,010,000	×	0.819516	=	2,467,000
3	3,010,000	×	0.741885	=	2,233,000
4	3,010,000	×	0.671607	=	2,022,000
5	3,010,000	×	0.607987	=	1,830,000
6	3,010,000	×	0.550393	=	1,657,000
7	3,010,000	×	0.498255	=	1,500,000
8	3,010,000	×	0.451056	=	1,358,000
9	3,010,000	×	0.408328	=	1,229,000
10	28,131,000*	×	0.369648	=	10,399,000
			Value of mortgage component		$27,420,000

*Year 10 debt service of $3,010,000 plus outstanding mortgage balance of $25,121,000
Note: Totals are rounded.

$$((NI^1 - (f \times M \times V))\ 1/S^1) +$$
$$((NI^2 - (f \times M \times V))\ 1/S^2) + ...$$
$$... +((NI^{10} - (f \times M \times V))$$
$$1/S^{10}) +$$
$$(((NI^{11}/R_r) - (b(N^{11}/R_r)) - ((1 - P) \times M \times V))\ 1/S^{10}) = (1 - M)V$$

Since the only unknown is the property value (*V*), this equation is easy to solve.

One advantage of valuing a hotel with a 10-year forecast using an equity yield rate is that the projection period can specifically show the build-up of net income over the assumed holding period used by most investors. Another benefit is that the value of the mortgage component can be easily substantiated in the market by analyzing current and comparable mortgage terms for similar lodging facilities; assuming a 75% loan-to-value ratio, 75% of the property's market value can be supported.

The difficult part of this approach is estimating the proper equity yield rate. Although many hotel owners have become more sophisticated, they do not always understand the meaning of *equity yield* from an appraiser's point of view. Some still think in terms of *cash on cash or equity dividend* and hold that the reversionary benefits of property appreciation and mortgage amortization are inherently considered in an equity dividend, rather than specifically incorporated into a yield calculation. Consequently, care must be exercised in obtaining yield rates from investors to ensure that their responses represent yields, not dividends.

Even with good data and support, estimating a hotel equity yield rate is a subjective process based largely on judgment. On the other hand, the estimate of a hotel mortgage interest rate can be well documented using the interest rate regression formula described previously and published life insurance industry data. Although an element of subjectivity remains, the value of the mortgage component is largely objective. Thus the capitalization technique produces results that are approximately 75% objective and 25% subjective. In contrast, a 10-year forecast using a discount rate produces results that must be considered largely subjective and do not reflect the investment analysis procedures currently used by typical hotel buyers.

CASE STUDY

Applying a Discount Rate to the Ten-Year Forecast

In the following example, data from the preceding case study is used to illustrate 10-year forecasting using a discount rate.

TABLE C.S.7. DATA AND ASSUMPTIONS	
Year	**Net Income Before Debt Service**
1	$1,634,000
2	3,322,000
3	4,306,000
4	4,521,000
5	4,747,000
6	4,985,000
7	5,234,000
8	5,496,000
9	5,770,000
10	6,059,000
11	6,362,000
Terminal capitalization rate 11% Broker & legal fees 3%	Discount rate 14%

The necessary data and assumptions are set forth in Table C.S.7. The reversionary value is calculated by capitalizing the net income before debt service in Year 11 at the terminal capitalization rate.

$$\frac{\$6,361,923}{.11} = \$57,835,664$$

Sales proceeds	$57,835,664
Less: brokerage & legal	1,735,000
Net sales proceeds	$56,100,664

The net income before debt service for each year plus the reversionary value (net sales proceeds) is discounted to present value at the 14% discount rate. (See Table C.S.5.8.)

TABLE C.S.8. CALCULATION OF DISCOUNTED CASH FLOW

Operational Year	Net Income Before Debt Service		Present Worth of $1 Factor @14%		Discounted Cash Flow
1	$1,634,000	×	0.87719	=	$1,433,328
2	3,322,000	×	0.76947	=	2,556,179
3	4,306,000	×	0.67497	=	2,906,421
4	4,521,000	×	0.59208	=	2,676,793
5	4,747,000	×	0.51937	=	2,465,449
6	4,985,000	×	0.45559	=	2,271,116
7	5,234,000	×	0.39964	=	2,091,716
8	5,496,000	×	0.35056	=	1,926,678
9	5,770,000	×	0.30751	=	1,774,323
10	62,160,000	×	0.26974	=	16,767,038
Total property value					$36,869,041

Ten-Year Forecast Using a Discount Rate

Some large institutional investors who purchase hotels on an unleveraged basis (with no debt capital) will apply an overall discount rate to the 10-year forecast of net income before debt service. To this discounted cash flow they add the discounted value of the property at the end of the tenth year, which is derived by capitalizing the net income in Year 11 at the terminal capitalization rate.

The 10-year forecast using a discount rate does not consider the impact of mortgage debt, leverage, and the specific equity demands of typical hotel investors. Furthermore, it requires a subjective estimate of the entire discount rate, not just the equity portion as in the equity yield approach. Since very few hotel investors purchase lodging facilities on an unleveraged basis, documented support for the discount rate is usually either unavailable or inconclusive.

Conclusion

Of the three valuation approaches available to the appraiser, the income capitalization approach generally provides the most persuasive and supportable conclusions when valuing a lodging facility.

In selecting of a discounting or capitalization procedure, the appraiser considers the market and the techniques used by hotel buyers and sellers in reaching their investment decisions. In the past, various procedures have been employed by hotel investors; their selections have usually been based on factors such as the quality and reliability of the available data, economic conditions, inflation, the availability of financing, and risk.

A brief summary of each technique follows.

▶ Discounting each year's income over the investment's full life cycle. This technique is rarely used because a 40-year forecast of income and expenses is unreasonably long and there is no comparable or support data to derive a 40-year discount rate.

▶ Capitalize one stabilized year. This simple technique works well for an established property that is expected to maintain a stable level of occupancy and net income in the future. It is difficult, however, to establish an appropriate stabilized net income for hotels with occupancies that are increasing or decreasing.

▶ Ten-year forecast using an equity yield rate. This technique is complicated but it most accurately reflects the actions of typical hotel buyers, who purchase properties based on their leveraged discounted cash flow. Often the mortgage component can be fully supported by recent market transactions, so 65% to 75% of the discount rate can be substantiated.

▶ Ten-year forecast using a discount rate. This technique is simple but less reliable because the derivation of the discount rate has little support. Moreover, it is difficult to adjust the discount rate for changes in the cost of capital.

Regardless of the technique applied, the estimate of market value should represent the actions of hostelry investors and provide a basis for comparing investment alternatives.

Developing capitalization rates and applying the proper discounting procedure are crucial to the income capitalization approach. Appraisers should always try to mirror the rationale and actions of typical buyers and sellers in the current market. Although some of the capitalization and discounting procedures described in this chapter were criticized for being overly subjective and contrary to present investment thinking, the analyst should remember the axiom of change. The discounting procedure favored by hotel buyers this year may not be suited to market and investment conditions next year. Appraisers must constantly re-evaluate and update their appraisal procedures to reach supportable estimates of market value.

A corporation can become successful if it manages its resources effectively. The value of a corporation, therefore, depends on how well it manages its financial and human resources. This project concentrates on the financial well-being of a corporation.

At the beginning of the semester, the instructor will assign each student a hospitality corporation and $5,000 in points. The student will need to determine whether he or she should invest in this corporation by completing a finance project. On the basis of the results of the project, if an investment is not made, the student will have the original 5000 points. If an investment is made, and when the stock is sold at the end of the semester, the students will have a point value according to the gain or loss of the investment. All students will receive a grade for the project. The student with the highest points at the end of the semester will obtain either extra credit points or a small reward.

The project should include:

1. Vertical and horizontal analyses on the financial statement of a company for the last two years.

2. Ratios analysis on key ratios of the company for the last two years.

3. Comparison of the company's ratios to industry standards.

4. Required rate of return for investing in the company using the Capital Asset Pricing Model.

5. Equilibrium price of the stock using the Gordon Dividend Model.

6. Written analysis on how the investment decision is reached.

Suggested information sources: CD-ROM on Business Compact Disclosure; Company's Annual Report; 10 K Reports; Host Report by Smith Travel Research and Arthur Anderson; Trends by PKF Consulting; Industry Ratios from Robert and Morris Associates, Dun and Bradstreet, and the Almanac by Leo Troy; Value Line, Standard and Poor Stock Reports, The Wall Street Journal, The New York Times.

This can be done in conjunction with a basic marketing or a marketing strategy class. Most marketing classes require students to compile a marketing plan. This project takes the marketing plan one step further and determines whether the plan is feasible. Students will be required to research and make educated estimates regarding costs and revenues. If the project is done independently in a finance class, the instructor will need to supply some raw data for calculations. These calculations can be set up in an electronic spreadsheet so that the data can be changed easily.

The project will include the calculation of:

1. The cost of debt

2. The cost of equity

3. The weighted average cost of capital

4. The initial investment

5. Depreciation

6. The annual net cash flow

7. The terminal cash flow

8. The capital budgeting decision criteria—payback, net present value, internal rate of return, and/or the modified internal rate of return.

The analysis criteria of payback, net present value, internal rate of return, and/or modified internal rate of return will render a decision regarding the feasibility of the project. A scenario analysis can easily be added if students are required to use electronic spreadsheets for calculations.

16

MARKETING

Marketing Services by Managing the Environment
Bernard H. Booms and Mary J. Bitner

Marketing and Redefining Markets
Melvyn Greene

Project 1

Project 2

Marketing Services by Managing the Environment

Bernard H. Booms and Mary J. Bitner

AT MORGAN GUARANTY and Trust, the desks are of mahogany, the chairs of leather, and the draperies of silk. At Skipper's, a chain of west-coast restaurants, dining areas are furnished with comfortable chairs and divided into small, intimate units by partitions. And at the Library of Congress, the long-closed great bronze front doors have been opened to the public.

These seemingly unrelated organizations have in common the following: Their directors all recognize the power of environment to influence customer perceptions. Elements of a firm's environment can be used to establish or reinforce an image, reposition the firm in customers' perceptions, or influence customer satisfaction or dissatisfaction with the service they receive. At Morgan Guaranty, for example, expensive furnishings project an image of stability, and give clients a sense of importance; at the Library of Congress, open doors symbolize an open, approachable in-stitution; and, at Skipper's, the recently modified decor suggests a relaxed dinner atmosphere rather than a fast-food environment (the firm's previous image).

This article draws on the separate theories of services marketing and environmental psychology to suggest ways in which the physical environment may be used as a marketing tool. Examples of how such service marketers as restaurateurs and hoteliers are currently using the physical environment in their marketing strategies are presented to illustrate how these theories may be put into practice. The implications of the authors' observations—summarized in the final section—should be of interest to service-firm managers in general and restaurateurs and hoteliers in particular.

Using Tangible Clues to Sell Services

Morgan Guaranty, Skipper's, and the Library of Congress are all service firms. The physical environment can be particularly effective as a marketing tool for these firms because the "products" they offer have many intangible characteristics, and they are produced and consumed simultaneously. Because customers must form their expectations about services through means other than actual physical contact with the product they are paying for, their perceptions are influenced by marketing messages (e.g., advertising, publicity, sales promotions) and by tangible clues (e.g., architecture, lighting, temperature, furnishings, layout, and color). These elements communicate information to the customer about how the firm sees itself and about how it wishes its customers to behave. In service marketing, first impressions really count.

For goods manufacturers and distributors, the environments in which the product is produced has little impact on customers; they are often unaware of where the product comes from and how it is produced. Services differ from products, however, in that the customer is present when a service is produced and consumed, and the potential impact of the total surroundings can sharply influence the customer's behavior. As a result of this difference, service marketers must modify conventional marketing-mix theories to suit their own needs. (In Exhibit 1, the authors propose modifications and additions that might be made to a traditional goods-oriented marketing-mix theory.)

Using the Environment to Reinforce or Establish an Image

A service firm that attempts to establish a new image can use the environment to do so. For example, at Speedi-Lube, an oil change and lubricating service recently introduced in the Seattle area, the environment enables the firm to project an image of speed, efficiency, and competence. Attendants are dressed in clean, starched uniforms, and the interior of each revamped Speedi-Lube service station is freshly painted and uncluttered—in contrast to most service stations. Customers are asked to drive their cars over open pits where each car is immediately attended to by several workers. While cars are serviced, customers are served fresh coffee in a clean waiting room whose walls are decorated with a graphic display illustrating the lubrication process. Work is completed within ten minutes, and each customer receives a

friendly reminder three months later that "it's time for another oil change." Here, the environment is used to establish an image of efficiency and confidence, and the reminder card reinforces this image.

Using the Environment to Reposition a Service

Marriott Hotels is using the environment as part of a plan to attract a more upscale business traveler, introducing potential customers to two concepts dependent on new environments—the Marquis Club and the Concierge Level. Guests who have stayed five times at the Marriott hotel are eligible for Marquis Club membership; amenities include large, comfortable guest

Implications for strategy and research

The environment is a critical marketing tool for service managers. *Implications:*
- Include environmental design and analysis in marketing mix for services; research the impact of the environment on customer attitudes, feelings, and behaviors.

The customer perceives the environment as a whole, and all environmental elements are integrated in this whole. *Implications:*
- Make all elements of the environment consistent with the service firm's image.
- Recognize the impact of small environmental changes on customer perceptions.

To be effective, the service-firm environment must elicit approach behavior from potential customers. *Implications:*
- Use the environment to reinforce feelings of pleasure in target markets.
- Use the environment to reduce potential negative responses.

To be effective, the service firm must recognize the emotional needs of its customers. *Implications:*
- Segment the market by emotional needs of clientele for high-load or low-load environments.
- Design the environment to stimulate approach behavior.

The environment influences customer expectations and satisfaction or dissatisfaction with a given service and therefore influences purchase and repurchase behavior. *This intuitive assumption could be tested in the following manner:*
- Studying how customer expectations about services are formed and the role the physical environment plays in this process.
- Pinpointing which areas of service performance consumers have expectations about.
- Researching the standards customers employ to judge service quality and performance.

rooms and express check-out. Concierge Level guests have access to a private lounge area equipped with a color TV, current periodicals, and an "honor" bar. Guests who wish to use Concierge Level facilities merely pay a higher fee than do patrons occupying standard rooms.

Environmental modifications were an important element of the overall repositioning plan when Skipper's Seafood and Chowder Houses changed from a series of fast-food outlets to a group of casual, family-oriented seafood restaurants. Prior to the change, the environment of Skipper's—colors, signage, and dining-room decor—communicated fast food to the customer. When the shift to a dinner-house image was made, interior partitions, softer seating, natural wood textures, decorative photographs, and plants were introduced, and signage was changed from stark (red, white, and blue) to subtle (yellow and brown).

In another successful example of repositioning, the Library of Congress recently opened up its massive bronze doors, set up picnic tables in its courtyard, and installed easy-to-use reader's guides and computer terminals for its patrons. The reason: the new chief librarian wanted to change the library's reputation from that of a "stuffy, closed-off, unapproachable" institution to that of an accessible information source.

Using the Environment to Influence Customer Behavior

Many environmental psychologists contend that the use of particular colors may influence the actions of clients or customers. A California jail and a U.S. Naval Correctional

Center both decided to paint holding cells pink after a study revealed that the color rapidly saps anger and aggression.

The physical environment may also be designed to influence customer behavior by inhibiting or encouraging customer interaction with other customers. At Benihana, the chain of restaurants with Japanese cuisine, customer interaction is encouraged by capacious round-table seating arrangements that permit large groups, whose members are often total strangers to one another, to be seated together. In other restaurants, physical barriers or dim lighting that limit customer interaction and enhance individual privacy help achieve the opposite effect.

Although there are many examples of the use of the environment to communicate the nature of the service experience, there are no established guidelines or marketing strategies that would tie these examples together. In addition to being able to catalog the elements that constitute the service environment and the ways in which they influence customers, service marketers need a framework to guide them in making decisions about the physical environment. The authors propose that a few theories drawn from environmental psychology provide such a framework.

Approach and Avoidance Responses

Environmental psychologist postulate that there are two basic reactions to any environment, *approach* and *avoidance*. Approach behavior involves such responses as physically moving toward something, exploring an unfamiliar environment, affiliating with others in the environment through verbal communication and eye contact, and performing a large number of tasks within the environment. Avoidance behavior includes an opposite set of responses. Because the decision to purchase is considered part of approach behavior, service firms should strive to create an environment that elicits approach behavior from their potential customers.

But to elicit approach behavior, the service marketer must first understand why people react to environments in the ways that they do. Mehrabian and other environmental psychologists assume that people's feelings and emotions ultimately determine what they do and how they do it. They further assume that people respond with different sets of emotions to different environments, and that these reactions, in turn, prompt them to approach or avoid the environments. Service marketers who are able to predict accurately the likely emotional states of their customers, and to provide them with surroundings that set off positive reactions and encourage approach behavior, will profit. Holiday Inns' newly designed guest rooms for business travelers are a good example of this strategy. The firm discovered that its business customers—after a stressful working day away from familiar surround-

ings—were most comfortable in rooms that had all the comforts of home. Accordingly, new rooms were appointed with large beds and colored sheets, telephones with long cords, clock radios (in lieu of a jarring wakeup call), large desks, comfortable, overstuffed chairs, and Home Box Office reception. If the environmental psychologists' theories are correct, these surroundings will inspire approach behavior because they satisfy business travelers' emotional needs for familiarity, security, and relaxation.

High-Load and Low-Load Environments

To design an environment that meets customers' emotional needs, service marketers must first understand the components of the environment as well as the components' impact on customers' behavior. One environmental psychologist uses the terms *high-load* AND *low-load* to describe environments. These terms are based on the concept of "information rate"— the extent of new stimuli in the environment to be processed by the observer. A high-load signifies a high information rate; a low-load represents a low information rate.

Uncertainty, novelty, and complexity are associated with high-load environments; conversely, a low-load environment communicates assurance, homogeneity, and simplicity. Bright colors, bright lights, loud noises, crowds, and movement are typical elements of a high-load environment, while their opposites are characteristic of a low-load environment.

People's emotional needs and reactions at a given time determine whether they will be attracted to a high- or low-load environment. In the Holiday Inns example, the firm assumed its customers would be harried business travelers looking for a low-load environment in which to relax and unwind. Thus, they would seek out familiar surroundings that would not require them to process excessive new stimuli. Vacation travelers, on the other hand, might react more positively to a high-load environment, particularly if it symbolized excitement, new experiences, and change from the home routine.

To elicit approach behavior from customers, the marketer should endeavor to understand their needs and should present them with an environment that caters to these needs. For example, a restaurateur whose dinner customers are professional people, who come directly to his establishment after a long and stressful work day, should design a low-load environment to meet their needs. The same restaurateur could modify the environment through variations in lighting, music, noise level, or temperature to suit a different market segment during the lunch hour or on weekends, when a high-load environment might be more appropriate.

Similarly, a bank might modify its environmental design to suit the emotional reactions of that segment it caters to most often. A downtown bank might experiment with the Morgan Guaranty approach (mahogany desks and silk drapes) to elicit approach behavior from wealthy investors and corporate accounts. On the other hand, a suburban bank, whose customers might feel unpleasantly intimidated by such an environment, could adopt a more casual decor, serve coffee to patrons, or advertise with such slogans such as "person-to-person banking."

Implications for Service Managers

Goods-manufacturing firms are very much aware of the power of packaging as a marketing tool. Market research and careful testing of package designs and increased professionalism among packaging specialists have made packaging "a science, not an art."

For service firms, the physical environment plays much the same role as packaging does for manufactured goods. The total environment, including lighting, decor, temperature, and noise level, constitutes the "package" that cues the customer in to what the service is and what the firm can do. First impressions influence customers' ultimate purchase decisions, in the same way that the design of a package affects a potential customer's decision to purchase a product. Unlike goods packaging, however, the packaging of services is still very much an art. Hospitality firms and other service organizations that successfully meld services-marketing theories with environmental-psychology theories such as those mentioned in this article may be able to convert it into a science.

MARKETING AND REDEFINING MARKETS

Melvyn Greene

What Is Marketing?

IN ORDER TO MAXIMIZE sales *and* net profits, there are three major aspects to be considered on a *continuous* basis:

▶ Marketing
▶ Plan of Action
▶ Sales Techniques

Marketing involves choosing the best and most profitable markets to sell to, taking both a short and long term view-point. It involves continuously defining and, in many cases, redefining markets and sources of business. Following this, a plan of action is required to maximize sales from the defined markets. Lastly, you have to develop the right technique to achieve success from the action plan.

The major difference in marketing hotels as against other consumer products is that after a customer has spent money in a hotel he has nothing physical to show for his money, as compared with buying, say, a television or a refrigerator. Effective market-

ing and dynamic selling is more important with hotels because once you have not sold a seat in a restaurant or a room in an hotel, that income is lost forever. In the case of selling consumer products, if you do not sell a product today, you might sell it tomorrow. A hotel bedroom, or a restaurant seat, has no "shelf life." Unless marketing is understood fully by the executive at the top of an hotel or hotel group, and there is a total commitment to the continuous need to market, the hotel will always experience the worst of the periodic downward cycles that every country, or area, experiences from time to time, and will not maximize profits from new markets and any upturn in a country or region's economy.

This deep understanding of the continuous nature of marketing by the man at the top must be spread down through the organization, through departmental heads to the actual waiter, chambermaid and telephone operator. If a hotel can train the staff who have actual contact with the guest on the

philosophy of marketing, then they will automatically begin to service and sell to guests more effectively. If we add to this basic training in soft sell techniques then the hotel must succeed.

But so often hoteliers explain their marketing by showing you their computer booking service, or the advertising campaign for the coming season. All these are important, but only one part of the continuous circle of marketing. There is a lot of mystique about marketing. Not too long ago every salesman suddenly became a marketing executive. More recently there has been a reaction against the image of the high-powered, business degree type marketing executive, as people have begun to realize that someone, somewhere, actually had to *go out and sell.*

In fact, both are totally inter-related and selling will never be really successful unless markets have been chosen carefully. There are over thirty definitions of marketing. I have chosen five (see following) which I feel are particularly relevant to hotels and food service (and also to travel). In some ways they are views on marketing rather than definitions.

The first definition is by Gerry Draper, and two emanate from my own company. An illustration of the second definition and what we call the "circle of marketing" is shown in Figure 1. By "research" we mean "digging out" facts, information, clues, etc. From this circle one can see that "selling" is just one very essential part of the whole circle of marketing. The fourth definition is by a Swedish firm of advertising agents, Anderson and Lembke. I rather like this view of marketing with its emphasis on beating your competitors. All these definitions have a different emphasis but, read together, they cover our own industry rather than other consumer products. My favourite in many ways is the fifth, by Thomas F. Powers from his book *Introduction to Management in the Hospitality Industry.*

Just think back ten years—which is a relatively short time—to the changes the market demands as a minimum in bedroom facilities and you will see how the market changes. But probably the most rapid changes take place on food and beverage facilities. The capital equipping of a new restaurant may last ten years, but in looking at the feasibility of a new restaurant it is advisable to write the restaurant cost off over, say, only three years, because restaurants become obsolete so fast

FIGURE 1. The Continuous Circle of Marketing

in marketing terms even if they are still satisfactory from an operation viewpoint.

Talk to many business executives who eat out often or stay in hotels regularly, and you will find a significant proportion who suffer from a severe case of "menu fatigue."

Five Definitions of Marketing

No. 1 by Gerry Draper

Ascertaining customer needs, tailoring the product as closely as possible to meet those needs, persuading the customer to satisfy his needs and, finally, ensuring that the product is easily accessible when the customer wishes to purchase it

No. 2 by Melvyn Greene

Marketing is basically seeking out a demand first and then making the product or supplying the service to satisfy that demand. Selling is

rather the other way round—creating a product or service and then trying to find a market for it.

No. 3 by Melvyn Greene

The ultimate in marketing is to establish brand loyalty so that, eventually, the consumer does not only purchase the goods/services once, but continuously. This is achieved only by the producer following the complete process of marketing.

No. 4 by Anderson & Lembke

We believe that the real meaning of marketing is listening to the demands of the market and satisfying those demands at a profit. From this it follows that *superior marketing* is listening to the market more intently than your competitors and satisfying the demands more effectively.

No. 5 by Thomas F. Powers

Marketing is so basic that it cannot be considered a separate function (i.e. a separate skill or work) within the business, on a par with others such as manufacturing or personnel. Marketing requires separate work and a distinct group of activities. But it is first a central dimension of the entire business. It is the whole business seen from its final result, that is from the customer's point of view. Concern and responsibility for marketing must, therefore, permeate all areas of the enterprise.

When they are in their bedrooms thinking of going to eat in your hotel restaurant, or out somewhere in the town, they very often can tell you every item on your menu without looking at it. Good or gimmicky decors pay off sometimes, but if you can regularly try original and fresh menus, dishes and ideas—and promote them in the lobby, elevator and bedroom—the mass market of people who stay in hotels regularly will "beat a path to your door."

As you can see from these comments and five definitions, marketing is a total, all-embracing attitude to life and business, continuously watching for changes in existing markets and searching for new markets, adapting the hotel's facilities and services to the new markets, and setting out to attract the new markets.

Marketing involves a lot of thinking time in pinpointing existing and new sources of business. In no way would I like to imply that selling involves no thinking time or less intellectual input—far from it. This is why a lot of people like it, and rush into it without going through the full process of marketing. If this happens a large proportion of selling effort, time and cost can be dissipated. Carrying out the full process of marketing will enable you to be more selective.

As markets are changing continuously, it is important to redefine markets continuously. This is probably the greatest error of the hotel industry, their designers and architects. Hotels and restaurants are built and designed on a fixed basis for a specific market opportunity. Because they are successful to begin with no attempt is made to redefine their role in the market place. When you have a physical building, it is not too easy to change the "product" to take into account changes in the market. There is, in my experience, a great reluctance to change what *was* a success formula.

But you *can* change the product in various ways, e.g.:

▶ New decor
▶ Special themes
▶ New staff uniforms
▶ Different menus
▶ Change in tariffs and menu prices
▶ New sales literature (hotel and conference brochure)
▶ Grade up more
▶ Grade down slightly

Unless you are continuously reviewing the whole process of marketing there is a danger that present guests and customers may drift away to competitors *and* new customers will not be attracted in their place.

So how do you choose the best markets and sources of business?

Redefining Markets

Most hotels have many and varied potential markets and sources of business. This creates a situation where the hotel management must avoid the trap of selling "a kilometre wide and a centimetre deep," or a mile wide and an inch deep.

It is absolutely essential to decide what the strengths and weaknesses of your product (i.e. hotel) are, bearing in mind the demands and requirements of the different sources of business *and* the strengths and weaknesses of your main competitors. The last point on competitors is a critical factor. In isolation, your own facilities do not matter—they are only relevant when compared with your competition; for example, if you do not have air conditioning this is not a limitation if all your competitors have no air conditioning. For too long many hoteliers have dissipated time and money by not selecting the source of business which they are best suited for and where they have least competition.

What is required is really two things. Firstly, as much information as possible on the hotel, its facilities, occupancy, catchment area, etc. Then a series of objectively prepared league tables grading your hotel's advantages and limitations. In order to assist you in your future marketing, a series of checklists are shown on information required for marketing, redefining markets and the preparation of a sales action plan. They start with a summary of information under eight broad headings. Quite often this information is available already, sometimes it requires some work and research. It is very similar to detailed background information required for an economic and marketing feasibility study for a new hotel, or a new bedroom extension.

The first aspect of the information is basically on the whole catchment area, moves on to the hotel's facilities, competition and present markets. The first four points on the information are broadly required for marketing and selling purposes, the last four are primarily for selling.

Checklist 1: Broad Background Information

Local Community

1. Trend in population and forecasts of population
2. Profile of local residents—age, sex, marital status, etc.
3. Local sports and social clubs, trade and political associations

Local Industry, Commerce and Employment

1. Industrial classification
2. Economic trends

INFORMATION REQUIRED

1. Broad background information:
   a. local community
   b. local industry, commerce, employment
   c. communications
   d. local events and attractions
   e. catchment area
2. Facilities of the hotel
3. Details of competitive hotels
4. Profile of guests
5. Activity levels
6. Employees—selling ability
7. Specific information on local community, industry, events, communications and catchment area
8. Advantage/limitation list—on own hotel
   —on competitive hotel

---

3. Any new factories or offices in last five years
4. Any factories or offices closed in last five years
5. Employment statistics
6. Unemployment statistics
7. Details of main employers:

   Industry Type

   No. of Employees

   Profile of Employers

   Independent or Group

   If Group, Location of H.O. or Branch

8. Statistics on visitors to town or specific attractions
9. Statistics on passengers through airport
10. Airlines and travel companies who use airport
11. Traffic count on local motorways
12. Statistics on bus or railway stations

Communications

This should cover existing and planned developments.

1. Location of hotel
2. Road network: local, national
3. Rail: local, national
4. Airports: local, national, international

Local Events and Attractions

1. Historical, cultural, traditional
2. Scenic
3. Coastline
4. Sports
5. Weather
6. Special events

Catchment Area (C.A.)

If selling, promotion and advertising are to be effective it is essential to define the catchment area (C.A.) for potential markets first, because time and money will be dissipated if you market outside the area.

C.A.'s will usually be very different between bedrooms, restaurants, function rooms and bars.

Usually the C.A. for bedrooms is much wider than, say, a restaurant, in that C.A. for bedrooms may be all of a country or, in some cases, all of the world.

Even with a restaurant, the C.A. may be different for lunch and dinner. At lunch time it may be within a limited circle of local industry and commerce, probably up to a maximum of ten to fifteen minutes driving, or five minutes walk. In the evening it may extend to residential areas within, say, a ten mile radius, or a twenty minute drive. These distances depend on traffic conditions.

Checklist 2: Facilities of the Hotel

Detail facilities sub-divided between:

Areas which produce revenue

Areas which do not produce revenue.

Information on areas which produce revenue:

Number (e.g., 200 bedrooms with private bath, suites, etc.)

Restaurant capacities (number of seats, etc.)

Hours of opening

General appearance and condition.

Tariff for each area.

Source: own knowledge, observation and information

Checklist 3: Competition

1. Existing competitors—hotels, function rooms, restaurants, bars:

Size

Style

Location

Type of business

Prices

Facilities

Background

Any planned expansion

Independently or

group owned

2. Proposed new competition:

Similar information to above

NOTE: It is vital to visit all competition from time to time, in order to assess their facilities, service, etc., compared against your own.

Checklist 4: Profile of Guests

Provide a customer profile separately for each income producing area. In some areas, it is difficult to establish a proper profile, because the market is so varied, or mixed, e.g., function rooms, main bars. Profile should provide information on:

Bedrooms	*Restaurant*	*Bar*
Age bracket	Age bracket	Age brackets
Sex	Sex	Sex
Cash, Card, Charge	Cash, Card, Charge	Type or Group
Type or Group	Type or Group	Mode of transport
Place of employment	Mode of transport	Size of party
Place of residence	Size of party	Drink popularity
Mode of transport	Menu popularity	Any complaints?
Single/Double/Family	New customer?	
Room popularity	First choice?	
New guest?	Any complaints?	
First choice?	Chance or guest	
Length of stay	Average spend	
Any complaints?		
Who made booking?		

In the case of firms who spend a lot of money with you, one would require steady feedback of information on these large sources of income.

Checklist 5: Activity Levels

This information should be analysed by sales area, season, month, day, meal period. One would require:

occupancy statistics—unoccupied rooms

—lost room revenue

Seat turnover percentages by meals and dates

Pattern of empty days for function space, or un-utilized capacity

Pattern of sales in bar

Primarily, the aim is to disclose sales areas which can be improved through a sales effort and where emphasis should be placed.

Source: records, observations, conversation

Checklist 6: Employees—Selling Ability

Analyse list of staff employed between:

Those who have a lot of contact with guests

Those who have some contact with guests

Those who have no contact with guests.

Summarize against the first two groups information and opinion on:

Age

Appearance

Personality

Selling Ability

Training Required

Source: observation, conversation, interview, records

Checklist 7: Specific Selling Information

Local Community

1. Details of local sports and social clubs, trade and political associations:

Name and address

Key contacts

Do they hold functions? If so, what kind, when, how often?

Do they have their own magazine?

2. Details of "influential" local residents, councillors (Mayor, taxi drivers, etc.)

Local Industry and Employment

Details of all main local employers, including any hospitals, universities, etc.

Name and address

Name of managing director

Name of key persons

Who makes bookings?

Do they have a demand for hotel facilities? Number of overnight visitors

Number of functions, etc.

Communications

Names and addresses of airlines and travel companies, if located near airport, and key decision makers.

Local Events and Attractions

List of events, dates, names of organizers and, where applicable, participants.

Competition

Details of all competitive hotels.
Advantage/limitations lists.

Catchment Area

Defined catchment area for accommodation, restaurant and functions, etc. Names, addresses and "key" contacts in local papers serving the catchment area.

Readers will notice in these checklists some interesting points. Under Facilities of the Hotel I am recommending that hoteliers should list areas which do *not* produce revenue. You should then ask "if not, why not?" It is amazing over the last decade how many areas in hotels are now being used to produce revenue, which never produced income in the past, e.g.,

lobbies

basement areas (as meeting rooms, specialty bars, etc.)

car parks and hotel grounds

swimming pool

area surrounding swimming pools

bedrooms.

The list is endless. Think like SPACEMEN.

You are basically in the business of selling space. We have all seen lobbies being used for receptions, dance areas (in Miami), display of new cars. I have seen swimming

CONCIERTOS EN MALLORCA

JOAN MOLL
RECITAL DE PIANO

PIANO RECITAL   KLAVIERABEND   RÉCITAL DE PIANO

I

Obras de compositores mallorquines. Works by Majorcan Composers.
Werke von Komponisten aus Mallorca. Oeuvres de Compositeurs Majorquins

Tema y Variaciones   Miquel Capllonch (1861-1935)
Dos Meteoros   Jaume Mas Porcel (n. en 1909)
— a un bebé alegre
— a una mujer optimista
Bolero del Diablo   Joan Maria Thomás (1896-1966)

II

Obras compuestas por Chopin en Mallorca;   Works composed by Chopin in Majorca
Werke, die Chopin auf Mallorca geschrieben hat;   Oeuvres composées par Chopin à Majorque.

Doce Preludios, del Opus 28   Frédéric Chopin
Scherzo nº. 3   Frédéric Chopin

Domingo 8 Noviembre a las 17 h.	Sunday 8 November at 5 p. m.	Sonntag 8 November um 17 Uhr.	Dimanche 8 Novembre a 17 h.

HOTEL ALBATROS • ILLETAS

PATROCINADO POR:
Consell Insular de Mallorca
Fomento de Turismo de Mallorca
Asociación Empresarial Hotelera de Palma de Mallorca

FIGURE 2. Programme for a Concert in Mallorca

pools with a floor covering which can be lowered from the ceiling so that the swimming pool can be) used for fashion shows or boxing exhibitions. One of our clients had a swimming pool which was not used in the winter, and rented it out to local manufacturers of small sailing dinghies. Let us take a function room or ballroom. Everyone complains that they can only be used on busy nights of the week and certain other periods (i.e. before Christmas).

Take a blank sheet of paper and write down all the activities you have seen, or heard, being used in a function room other than functions. Many of them produce revenue, room hire and rental income and often they can be introduced in the "quiet" periods. They often attract a new market across the threshold barrier of your hotel who have never used your facilities before. Last year I went to stay at the Hotel Albatross in the beautiful location of Illetas in Mallorca, Spain. It was the quiet season. My wife and I walked in on a Sunday and found the lounge areas absolutely full of people listening to a piano recital. Most of the audience were not staying in the hotel and had paid an entrance fee. A good illustration of an independently owned hotel selling empty space. A copy of the publicity is shown in Figure 2.

So please think like SPACEMEN.

Under the heading "Activity Levels" you will notice a case of lateral or reverse thinking. For accounting and control purposes, room and double occupancy is vital. But for marketing purposes what is vital is the reverse—unoccupied rooms, lost room revenue, empty days on function rooms. Information in Checklist 6 spotlights employees who may require further training in social skills and sales ability. Aspects in Checklist 7 are really pinpointing key companies, decision makers, advisers to decision makers, etc., so that mailing and sales target lists can be prepared.

After the gathering of this information, what is then required is a series of "league tables" which show your hotel's (or hotels') position relative to its competition. The objective of the league tables is to put the competition into perspective and to show that for some sources of business there is more competition and for others less. By linking these findings to the respective physical advantages and disadvantages of your hotel and the competition, answers are provided on where to put your sales and marketing effort. We have attended working sessions where just listing the competition for the different sources of business has proved an invaluable exercise.

Examples of the information and league tables required are as follows:

1. Make a list of the hotels which are competitive (and the criteria used)—the list will vary depending on the source of business. It is necessary to visit all these hotels to assess their facilities and to stay the night in hotels where you have not stayed previously. This is a vital first step in assessing your real competition and narrowing down the sources of business where you have least competition.

2. Calculate your market share of the total competitive capacity and your main competitors' share. Usually this can be calculated fairly accurately on Rooms, but has to be estimated on Food and Beverage. Sometimes, independent consumer research just asking for first, second and third choice for:

Bedrooms

Functions

Eating out—Lunch

—Dinner

can provide invaluable clues to your market share.

3. Not all of the following league tables are relevant to all hotels, but examples of league tables required are:

Quoted tariffs (single room)

Single tariffs plus car parking costs

Quoted tariffs (double/twin room)

Double tariffs plus car parking costs

Function charges (food and beverage)

Room hire charges (excluding food)

Inclusive conference rates—daily

—overnight

"Group" rates (tourists, etc.)

The parking costs are relevant to many city centre locations where some hotels have free car parking and others do not.

4. Some league tables are required which do not lend themselves too easily to exact gradings but more to broad groupings (e.g. marketing "muscle"). Examples are:

Site

Location

Car parking facilities

Noise (bedroom guests—meeting rooms)

Sales and marketing capability and "muscle"

Group handling facilities (conventions and tours)

Location convenience to air travellers

Location convenience to train travellers

Location convenience to local attractions and entertainment

Conference packages

Restaurant facilities

Other facilities, e.g., health (swimming pool, gym, sauna, etc.)

5. We often use a popularity score basis in order to produce league tables for:

Businessmen—arriving by train, plane or car.

Individual tourists

Group tourists

Conference delegates

by scoring the grading depending on the demands of the different sources of business. Obviously the grading of the score will usually vary between the different sources of business.

6. The various potential markets have to be considered from a number of points of view, including:

Discretionary or essential spending

Company (expense account) or private

Expanding or contracting market

Repeat business potential

Definite or provisional booking

Seasonality

Effect on other markets (e.g., exhibition running over a number of days)

Potential profitability

If you take the foregoing information and also examine:

▶ Your own internal management information (occupancies, covers, etc.)
▶ Any information you can gather on the trend in the market place (on tourists, businessmen, conferences, etc.)

then by using your own business experience and judgment you should be in a much better position to define more clearly the main sources of business on which your hotel(s) should concentrate marketing efforts. Never neglect established markets and busy parts of the week, month or year. However, many hotels have natural busy periods (e.g., Monday to Thursday nights on rooms, summer season, or function season around Christmas and in the New Year). So try to define markets which will help your quiet, or quieter, periods.

Try this exercise on your own hotel(s), particularly listing the advantages and limitations over your competition for the different sources of business. So often we have found that hoteliers find this fascinating, vital information. It helps to define markets and sometimes just assists a hotelier to get back on the most profitable course. When the markets and sources of business have been defined there is another step which requires careful consideration before you produce a sales action plan. This is to see that the hotel achieves the right *balance* of covers and average spend in the restaurant, and occupancy and average room rate in the bedroom. This aspect of the right balance to achieve maximum profit is elaborated in the next section.

Economic Criteria for Successful Marketing

During the 60s and first half of the 70s considerable worry, effort and attention was concentrated on hotel occupancies. Now, considerable attention is being paid to increasing *average* room rates as well as occupancy. But in a mixed market situation, where there are wide fluctuations in markets and business activity in different periods of the year, how do you ensure that your hotels end up above, or as near as possible to, the right average occupancy and average room *rate* at the end of the year?

The danger is in many ways to oversimplify the objectives. It is too broad an objective to say "we want to achieve an average occupancy of 75 per cent and an average room rate of $55." This does not provide operating management, or marketing people, with the right kind of objectives on *sales mix* and *sources of business* required to achieve a target occupancy and average room rate. Too often in the past marketing people have been blamed for selling at reduced rates, when they have not been given the yardsticks advocated as follows.

Therefore it is strongly recommended that the following economic criteria on room tariffs are calculated for each hotel. These are absolutely essential in defining pricing policy, but consideration should also be given to the comments in the section entitled Pricing Strategies.

1. The total amount of net operating costs (after contribution from the food and beverage departments) of the hotel. One could calculate the *Total:*

   Net operating costs

   Net operating costs plus rent (if payable)

   Net operating costs plus interest

   Net operating cost plus a target return on capital.

2. From this it is possible to calculate the total room revenue requirements (total rooms sales) in order to break even, and to achieve various levels of profit, assuming you know your Rooms Department Cost Ratios, staff numbers and staff standards, etc.

3. On the basis of the foregoing, a schedule should be produced of the average room rates required in order to break even and/or achieve the profit targets at various occupancy levels. At this point, it is very often possible to say that certain levels of profits are achievable, while other levels are impossible. Sometimes in the early years of a new hotel, or where the style and concept demands high operating costs, a calculation will show a target level of occupancy and average

room rate which simple business judgment shows can, or cannot, be achieved.

4. Budgets on room sales have to be produced based on sales mix taking into account the different sources of business. Again, quite often based on this calculation it becomes apparent that a target Net Profit Return on Capital cannot be achieved unless the sales mix is varied by a different marketing emphasis.

5. Then based on the current quoted tariff, it is possible to calculate what percentage discounting factors, *subdivided* between the different sources of business, *must not be exceeded* if the average rate required is to be achieved. This is an extremely vital statistic in setting objectives for sales executives—namely the maximum discounting factors.

The two examples, Tables 1 and 2, are based on a quoted room tariff of $60 single and $80 twin and an average rate requirement per room of $55. It can be seen from the first example that the policy decisions on the discounts shown do not allow the average rate requirement to be achieved at the mix shown, and discounts allowed, the average room rate required comes out at more than $4.48 less—$50.52. However, by fixing lower maximum discounts in the second example the average is $56.64—$1.64 above the average rate required of $55.

TABLE 1					
	Business Mix %	Double Occup. %	Average Quoted rate $	Discount %	Average Room Rate $
Individuals	40	30	66.00	10	59.40
Conferences	10	10	62.00	20	49.60
Groups	50	80	76.00	40	42.36
			$70.60		$50.52

This second example shows maximum discount levels which do allow the average rate requirement to be achieved.

TABLE 2					
	Business Mix %	Double Occup. %	Average Quoted rate $	Maximum Discount %	Average Room Rate $
Individuals	40	30	66.00	5	62.70
Conferences	10	10	62.00	20	49.60
Groups	50	80	76.00	30	53.20
			$70.60		$56.64

6. The information in Tables 1 and 2 should be compared against your own judgment on business mix and average room rate so that you can see whether they are achievable at various occupancy levels. The point behind this exercise is to achieve *both* a target average occupancy and a target average room rate. This is an actual example and the rates may look low to readers through inflation.

Very often these calculations result in a change in marketing direction and a revision in budgets. Sometimes the change is as drastic as management realizing that a source of business is just not worth having. More often it results in a marketing change of emphasis (e.g., the hotel has to achieve 10 per cent more revenue from businessmen), or it produces a more specific policy, e.g., group discounts are not to exceed 30 per cent or the group rate should not be less than $53.00 per room.

Hotels in certain areas may have only one major business source. Examples are: a hotel in the Mediterranean which has only groups of tourists, and a hotel in a commercial town which has primarily overnight business travellers. But even in these types of location hotels often have three sources of business. The tourist resort hotel has group tourists *and* individual tourists and may be breaking into the conference market. The commercial town hotel has businessmen, conference potential and a weekend market different to that of midweek.

Our experience is that most hotels have at least three sources of business while the larger hotels in major cities can have five or six. Further, these sources may differ totally at various times of the year. The variable factors which make these sources different from an economic and marketing viewpoint include:

▶ When they come (time of week, year)
▶ Degree of single, double and multiple occupancy
▶ Degree of price sensitivity
▶ Length of stay
▶ Eating habits (do they eat and drink in the hotel?)
▶ Surplus spending power.

All of these factors must be taken into account if maximum sales and maximum long term profit are to be achieved. The market will ultimately fix prices (see next section) but without these calculations of economic criteria it is quite possible not only to overcharge but to *undercharge* in certain circumstances.

Pricing Strategy— Room Tariffs

The foregoing section sets the economic criteria in order to establish pricing, maximum discount policies, and goals. These economic calculations are absolutely essential in determining pricing policy. But in themselves they should only be used as essential guidelines to room tariffs. The reasons for this are varied. Supposing a hotel costs a

large sum to be built, and therefore its interest charges, or rent, is higher than other competitive hotels. The calculations might show that a certain level of room rate is required to cover rent, or show a target return on capital, but this Average Room Rate Required might be much higher than competitive hotels, or a rate the market will not pay.

Sometimes it is possible that the market would be prepared to pay this higher rate if the hotel is more luxurious, in a better location, or has superior facilities. This may or may *not* be the case. This is where an objective assessment using the league tables as set out in Redefining Markets can be of great assistance. But a higher capital cost is not necessarily a guarantee that one can charge higher prices. Similarly, one hotel may operate with higher costs through inefficiency and this would not justify higher prices. Sometimes the higher costs of, say, payroll could arise through a far older, less cost-effective, design of the hotel. Or the higher payroll may be deliberate policy to provide a higher standard of service which the market might well be prepared to pay for. All these factors should be considered and not just costs. It is the market, ultimately, that fixes prices—not your level of operating costs.

What other factors have to be considered in fixing prices?

For years I have sat at meetings with clients when pricing strategies are agreed for the coming year, or season. It has always appeared to me that there is one significant, un-

known factor which we have always lacked at these meetings, even when independent consumer research has been carried out. The usual factors that everyone looks at are either one or more of the following:

▶ Current charges prior to a review
▶ The estimated inflationary effect on costs for the coming period under review
▶ The general economic situation affecting markets
▶ For hotels attracting foreign tourists during the last five years, the currency exchange trends
▶ The amount of competition and the rate of increase we think competitors are going to charge

In the "good old days" of fifteen years ago—namely the first three years of the 70s when inflation tended to run at 3 to 5 per cent and currency fluctuations were minimal— most of our clients only looked at the first two of the foregoing factors and, depending on how conservative they were, increased their tariffs by 3 to 5 per cent for the coming year, often from the next financial or calendar year. The situation is much more complex now and our clients tend to consider all of these factors, together with the league tables described previously, and to have different strategies on price increases for the busy and quiet periods, and for the different sources of business.

But the one unknown factor which we will never ever obtain an exact answer to is "what tariff increase—if there is to be an increase—will the market bear?"

All hoteliers have a major fear or worry.

There are some consumer industries where they can test market a new product, or a price increase in a geographical region and say that a 5 per cent increase in prices will cause a 3 per cent decrease in market share—or increase in market share if the rate of price increase is lower than that of the competition. The hotel industry is not like this. The fear many hoteliers have is that at some level of price increase the whole market, or a significant proportion of the market, could *disappear*. This is a real worry. We all saw this happen in many European tourist capitals like Paris, and in particular London, when the number of American tourists drastically dropped after 1979 as hotel tariffs were increased and the dollar declined in value at the same time. The market did not disappear totally but the total spend of Americans declined much more than the decline in numbers.

Assuming continued inflation over the next few years, even at a lower level than recent years, we are probably in most cases still talking about fixing a rate of increase rather than a decrease. How do we fix this increase and those prices which will show maximum long term repeat business and profits?

Consumer Research

Some people believe that consumer research will provide the answer. It is my experience that it might provide some clues, but it may well provide the wrong answers. If you approach existing customers or buyers to carry out research, this tends to cover the market you have now but excludes the far larger market which does not use you for a mass of reasons unrelated to price (e.g., they have never heard of you, or The Threshold Barrier).

And if you complete a verbal or written questionnaire with travel agents, or bulk purchasers like tour operators, on their objective opinion of your tariffs, the research *always* shows that your tariffs are too high. I remember a leading travel agent seriously saying in response to a questionnaire for a new hotel in central Edinburgh that the rate should be $25 per room, and this rate would fill the hotel. He said this knowing that the going rate in Edinburgh in the off season was around double this rate and that even if the hotel was full it could never show a profit high enough to be economically viable.

And I am not even sure if the average hotel guest knows what the room rate is. We once carried out an experiment for a client in a large, 3 Star hotel simply by asking a proportion of guests on a series of days what the room rate was as they were leaving, and in fact had only just settled their bills. Around 24 per cent were with groups and so

they had no idea what the room rate was. The remaining 76 per cent were business executives. Only about half had any idea and were prepared to hazard a guess. Out of the total 76 per cent only around one-fifth had any idea of the room rate. The point here is that the vast majority had stayed more than one night and all had incurred extras for meals, telephone calls, etc., which increased the nightly cost. A significant proportion had signed the bill with a credit card, or had a credit account. What guests could give was an impression of "that seemed expensive" or "that seemed reasonable."

Ego Factor

What I do know is that the hotel industry reverses many known marketing rules in fixing prices for a consumer product. In most consumer industries you can increase sales by reducing prices. Assuming the particular firm selling the consumer product is operating above break-even point, the principles of marginal costing pay off higher net profits following the increased sales.

This does not always happen with hotels because although hotels sell a product (in food and drinks) it is one of the few consumer industries which is a combination of product *and* service. In fact, it could be a marketing mistake to reduce prices too far with many hotels, even in cheaper mass hotels, because at a certain level of lower prices the prospective customer gets suspicious, i.e., something must be wrong!

If the Ritz in London, Mark Hopkins in San Francisco and the George V in Paris decided to reduce their quoted tariffs by half, it could well empty the hotels. The normal guest who stays at these hotels would probably switch their allegiances to a more expensive luxury hotel, and the mass of other people would be too overawed to break the threshold barrier and try the hotel. I remember some years ago when the very successful up-market Gosforth Park Hotel north of Newcastle, Britain, opened, that for many years every time they increased their tariffs they expected a slight decline in room occupancy and this did not happen. These are extreme examples of luxury hotels, but to a degree the same point applies to all grades of hotel.

Now bulk purchasers like tour operators will argue the opposite. To a significant extent they are correct in that they must hold down the *total* price of a holiday in order to sell their allocations. But there is a similar point with tour operators in their brochures. For most resorts our "initial" customer, the tour operator, has a series of hotels usually listed in order of total price. Do they automatically sell all the cheapest holidays first, or do they find that their own customers—who are the people who sleep in our rooms—will often avoid the cheapest holiday because they are seeking value for money and not necessarily the cheapest holiday? Digressing

slightly, I always recommend to clients when they are renegotiating next year's price with a tour operator to obtain the current brochure, have it translated if necessary, and see where their hotel is listed and how it is described compared to the competition. This will often provide valuable negotiating clues.

In fact the countries who have gone out to promote themselves as a cheap holiday destination have always lived to regret it. This happened to London after the weak £ and Jubilee Year coincided. It happened to Spain. And I suspect it will happen to Florida, which is currently selling itself in Europe with too much emphasis on just being cheap. This kind of marketing gives you no room for flexibility when the market dips a little and currency rates move against you, as they did for Spain at the end of the 70s.

There is a fundamental difference in the consumer product/service we sell, which we ignore at our peril. It is the only situation where we satisfy some of the basic needs of men and women—a warm, comfortable place to shelter and sleep, food for the hungry, and alcohol for enjoyment and relaxation. So our purchaser (guest) has a totally different reaction to prices in hotels, and prices of other consumer products and services. We satisfy fundamental emotional and physical needs of our customers. This is elaborated more under a later section, "What Motivates People to Buy?"

At the time of writing we are in a business recession and many companies and organizations are being much tougher on their travelling executives' overnight costs. In this situation we may have to provide special price deals, retrospective discounts, etc. for major commercial customers.

The argument is not that hotels should increase tariffs and price themselves out of their different markets, only that we should recognize that low prices lead to lower standards and delays in redecoration and ignores the importance of *the ego factor*. The curtains, carpets and decor, the staff uniforms, the cutlery and glassware we use could be cheap and nasty. But they are usually deliberately the opposite—more luxurious, attractive (and costly) than they need be. Why? Because of the ego factor. By all means reduce prices (or contain price increases) by reducing wastage and increasing productivity. But try wherever possible to avoid reducing the atmosphere, ambiance and service because I *know* people will pay for this.

Factors in Fixing Prices

What we have to think about and consider carefully in these times of rising costs are a series of factors. Firstly, we should have available economic criteria set out in the previous sections. We also need the information listed at the start of this section. Added to this we need:

1. Customer profiles in order to tell us more about the markets we are obtaining now, and provide clues to markets we are missing.
2. A much greater degree of segmentation with a pricing policy taking into account the circumstances of the different segments.
3. Research to ascertain whether the hotel is a first, second or third choice for the different facilities, e.g., rooms, restaurants, bars. This research should be on a regular basis to see that the hotel is not "sliding" in popularity.

An amplification of this information is given below.

Customer Profiles

An indication of the type of information required is as follows:

Rooms

Age Bracket

Sex

Cash, Card, Charge

Business

Tourist

Convention

Type of Group

Employment

Place of Employment

Place of Residence

Mode of Transport

Single/Double/Family

Room Popularity

New Guest?

First Choice

Length of Stay

Who made booking

Similar information is required on the Restaurant(s) and Bars, but normally in not quite the same detail. The information can be gathered from observation, conversation, correspondence, questionnaire and reception records. A well designed guest registration card, guest history records, and information from the Billing Machine, Tab or Computer can supply a lot of useful information. Not all of this information is useful on pricing strategies, but could be important in other aspects of marketing. As an example, place of employment and place of residence (which can be totally different) can help to decide where you are drawing custom from and where to direct advertising and sales effort. Similarly, mode of transport and who made the booking can assist in basic selling.

But many of the other factors can help in pricing strategies. In America credit (or charge) cards are very common and few people carry and pay in actual notes. But in Europe and other parts of the world many hotels still have a high proportion of guests, sometimes over 50 per cent, paying by actual cash. We have found that wherever there is a high degree of payment by cash or cheque, rather than credit card or credit account, there is a greater degree of price sensitivity and more resistance to price increases.

We have also found that the lower the average length of stay, the higher the average rate per night. Naturally this is a generalization, but there is some logic in it. When an hotel (say an airport hotel) has an average length of stay of one night, the rate the hotelier can obtain is often higher than where the average length of stay is longer. Obviously people spending a longer time in an area are more likely to notice the total bill, or to be on a daily allowance. And taking the other extreme of a hotel with a holiday market where the guests stay two weeks at a time, the hotel take per guest may be high but the average room rate earned per night is usually much lower than in other hotels. We have often found a degree of price sensitivity which varies for exactly the same product, and room, within a standardized chain, where the only major difference appears to be a different average length of stay.

Research on guest profiles should be carried out to determine the proportion of guests who have stayed with you before, subdivided between guests booked in by a company or where there is a special arrangement with a company, and "individual" guests. If this research shows a low proportion of repeat business, then the hotel will often have a standards problem related to the price charged. However good the marketing is, it will not become really effective until the reason for the low proportion of repeat business is corrected. One very successful holiday camp company has a 30 per cent repeat potential of people who stay with them *every* year. Presumably there are additional people who return but not necessarily every year. Another exclusive hotel in London has 60 per cent of their guests who have·stayed with them before. The timing of repeat visits is also important. Do guests return every year, or monthly, or weekly, and what are the proportions analysed between individuals and companies who send regular visitors?

Many hoteliers will know this information on guest profiles. But in larger hotels with a mix of markets this information would be invaluable background information where pricing strategies are reconsidered.

Segmentation

It is felt very strongly that we can no longer talk about broad markets of:

Businessmen/women

Foreign tourists

Local tourists

Conventions.

We will have to research these markets in order to find out much more about them in the future. Let us take an example of the business market staying overnight in hotels. Excluding businessmen visiting an area for an exhibition, or convention, broadly, business visitors are visiting:

▶ to buy
▶ or to sell

If they are buying there is a good probability that the local company selling to them will

book them into a hotel, or recommend a place to stay. Are the sellers going to be price sensitive about another $10 on the room rate? No way. Are they going to risk a sale by accommodating their potential buyer in a poor hotel? They will probably consider his age (for the style of hotel), where he will sleep well so that he is less "grumpy" and more receptive to their sales approach the next morning. This is not to say they will always put him in the most expensive hotel because he may not feel at ease there. But they are unlikely to cut their costs by deliberately choosing a cheap hotel, if they are paying. And they are unlikely to bruise the buyer's ego by suggesting too downmarket an hotel if he is paying.

Generally speaking the hotel industry has one great advantage in this buying situation. The total cost of the hotel is usually very small compared to the amount being paid for the product, contract, or service the buyer is there to examine. Think about this point if a large proportion of your overnight guests are business executives, and buyers as well. Most of the invoices and bills from commerce and industry to *their* customers are much larger in value than $100 to $300 for a two-night stay in an hotel.

And what about the business visitor, staying in an area overnight who is selling? There are generally two types of salesmen. Those selling a large, or expensive, product or service. And those travelling on the road many weeks of the year who generally are selling

a large number of smaller value items. Take the first type of salesman selling a product or service of high value. If he knows anything about selling himself as well as his expensive product, is he going to risk the whole sales approach at the end of the day when most local people ask an out-of-town visitor "where are you staying tonight?" Is he going to risk mentioning a cheaper hotel?

Now there is no doubt in the case of the second category of salesperson who is "on the road," that a lot usually have a budget per day to live within and are more price sensitive. But the key point is periodically to analyse and segment your overall business market so you are more aware of who they are, as this information is of paramount importance if you are worrying about whether to increase your tariffs by 3, 10, or 12 per cent, when costs may be climbing at a very unpredictable rate and there is a lot of competition around. Suppose that you find that you get a high proportion of business visitors who are buyers compared with your competitors, or vice versa. Would not this information help you in your pricing strategy?

What Choice Is Your Hotel?

It is possible for a hotel to have a high occupancy and yet be vulnerable to a sudden decline in guests if a significant proportion are not staying in the hotel as a first choice. This decrease in occupancy can arise when there is either an overall decrease in an area's occupancy, so that the first choice competitor has rooms available, or there is a disproportionate increase in tariffs. This situation can arise even where average annual occupancies are *not* high, but where there are peak months of the year when most of the hotels are full, or the city or town is what I call a four-sevenths area and full Monday to Thursday with business visitors.

What we have found very useful is the use of a simple questionnaire (Table 3) just asking the visitor what is the degree of choice of hotels in the town and catchment area, or within a ten mile radius of the factory/office, for accommodating overnight visitors.

Every hotel tends to have a proportion of the overnight visitors who have a preference which is unrelated to price, style or grading. Therefore you will never find 100 per cent of the respondents saying that your hotel is, say, first or second choice. But if you have defined your market segment and pricing strategy correctly, our experience is that around two-thirds (60 to 70 per cent) should rate you as first choice. In fact, it would be very high if as many as 80 per cent rated you first choice although this can happen in a town with only three hotels, say, one motor hotel on the outskirts, one 3 Star, and one 5 Star in the town centre. In an area with a wide connurbation like London or Birmingham in Britain, however successful a hotel is, you will

TABLE 3			
Hotel	VIPs and Top Executives	Middle Management	Other Visitors
First Choice			
Second Choice			
Lower Choice			

usually find the first choice proportion is not much higher than 60 per cent in a busy period, unless you own a unique hotel like, say, Claridges, or Browns Hotel.

This research should be carried out in busy periods because quite obviously the degree of first choice will tend to be much higher in the quiet part of the week or year. The important factor to watch is really the trend and therefore the research should be carried out regularly every year, or six months. If the proportion stating first choice is steadily declining and the second, or lower choice, increasing, then this is a danger signal on standards, pricing strategy, or value for money. Unless corrective action is taken occupancies are bound to decline. This regular research can often help to highlight a problem well in advance before the decline in occupancy and sales starts.

Ask yourself this question assuming costs have been climbing and you are planning a price increase. Would you feel more confident about a price increase if this regular research showed a high rating which was steadily increasing as a first choice?

Although many of the foregoing comments and principles are applicable equally to food and beverage tariffs, there are comments on these areas in the next section. Pricing strategy is a wide, complex subject with no easy answers. I would never underrate basic management experience of the market and the hotel operation. It could seem, that the foregoing information is too much and unnecessary. But if we are in for an inflationary decade during the eighties, and regular constant reviews of tariffs and prices, then the whole decision-making process will be far easier if you have the following back-up information to help you in making the decision:

▶ Economic criteria, estimated sales mix and maximum discounts
▶ Current charges prior to a review
▶ The estimated inflationary effect on costs for the coming year, or period, under review
▶ The general economic situation affecting markets
▶ Currency exchange trends— for hotels attracting foreign visitors (tourists and businessmen)

- The degree of competition and rate of increase competitors have made or might make
- Guest and customer profiles
- Market segments and strategy for each segment
- Market degree of choice, degree of repeat business

This information, together with any further consumer research, number of complaints, trends in occupancy, covers served, etc., is vital and may in some cases lead to a price standstill or reduction not necessarily overall but sometimes for a particular source of business. As an example, a hotel may find it has a high choice rating and no problem on increasing room rates for individual tourists, but is too expensive compared against similar competition for the convention market, and is losing business. In view of the large numbers involved, high spend in bars, etc., a reduction (or no increase) in the overnight convention rate might be justified.

Pricing Strategy— Food and Beverage Areas

Pricing menus and drinks in hotel food and beverage areas to obtain maximum sales *and* profits is a very complex subject and in many ways more complicated than preparing a strategy on rooms. Except in older hotels, many hotels have only three or four types of rooms (singles, twins, suites, front view, back view, etc.) and some new hotels built on a standard module for the bed-

room block have only one type of room. But menus can have dozens of dishes, all with a different food cost, and the food cost is often unrelated to popularity and the price the market is prepared to pay.

What would be useful is if I put forward certain comments, thoughts and suggestions on the main areas in an hotel selling food and beverages. Four points have often puzzled me about this aspect of hotels.

Firstly, why is it that so often the bedroom guest does not eat in the hotel restaurant or coffee shop where there are competitive restaurant facilities near to the hotel? I am not talking about the long stay visitor but the business executive staying in the hotel for maybe one, or two nights. A proportion do eat in, but a significant proportion go out, and a habit has developed with many regular travellers— "sleep in but eat out"—which I would like to see changed. If you have a lot of competitive restaurants nearby a proportion of your guests are going to eat out. But this proportion should be as low as possible. Two main reasons for this situation is the aspect of Menu Fatigue mentioned earlier, and poor In-House Selling.

The second point I have seen developing in the last few years is that where a hotel has two (or more) restaurants that appear to be competing with each other and "splitting the bedroom market down the middle" rather than offering a true price and "experience" alternative to the overnight visi-

tor and the outside business coming into the hotel. This point seems to have developed lately where, say, the hotel coffee shop has been upgraded and the "better" a la carte restaurant has gradually limited its menu to a smaller number of dishes. I could name a number of larger hotels with two restaurants which are directly competitive in average spend, evening opening hours and in every way except decor.

A third point is related to function areas. Except in a recession, if you ask the food and beverage manager, or banqueting manager, if the function areas are busy he will often sigh and say, "Very busy." Functions are, in my opinion, one of the most exhausting and repetitive aspects of hotel life and I fully understand why they say that they are very busy. But quite often the hotel has only one function per day per function room, and some days (e.g., Sunday) or times (e.g., Monday evening) are rarely booked. And where a function room seating 400 people has a function, it is often well below 400 in size.

Most hoteliers would agree that they must have regular room occupancy statistics if they are to set staff standards, operate and market the hotel. But fewer have restaurant "occupancy" statistics (total covers, seat turnover ratios, table turnover ratios per meal, compared against a target) and similar information on function rooms. Very often even if you take a function room as capable of taking one function per day (365 per year) the usage percentage is no more than 35 per cent. And if you compare the covers sold against 365 times the seating capacity, quite often the seat usage percentage is less than 25 per cent.

Profitability by Area

The other major point on the food and beverage areas is that some hoteliers do not know whether the areas selling food and beverage are making a net profit or loss— i.e., a contribution to the total bottom line figure of the hotel as a whole. Hoteliers know the departmental profit (or loss) under the Uniform System of Accounts on:

Rooms

Food

Beverage

Tobacco

Telephones

Shops

Sundries

but often they do not have an indication of whether the restaurant, the function rooms, or the bar make a net profit or a loss, and the *total* sales of a restaurant would be hidden as they would be subdivided in the uniform system under the sources of business for control purposes, i.e.:

Food sales

Beverage sales

Tobacco sales.

These comments are not meant to be a "blanket" criticism of the uniform system of accounts. Most systems in various countries with a developed hotel industry use a uniform accounting system which is based on the American system originally pioneered by the large American hotel accounting firms in the 1930s. No hotel should be without this system, or a variation of it.

But basically it is a control and accounting system and not one designed to assist in policy changes, or marketing. This is why it is recommended that possibly twice a year, or at least annually, the accounts are re-analysed by income producing areas.

In one major London hotel where we first carried out this exercise some years ago, the management was convinced that the function area with sales of around $4 million per year was the biggest area contributor to net profit. In fact it only showed a tiny net profit on a huge sales volume. Our past experience shows that very often many hotel restaurants and many functions rooms operate at a net loss, and this information can be vital in changing policy, creating a greater sense of sales urgency, or in changes in pricing strategy.

Economic Aspects of Food Areas

Most of the broad principles laid down earlier in this chapter on setting room tariffs apply equally to food and beverage prices. You do need similar economic yardsticks to calculate whether it is possible to make a profit.

Even if it is a policy decision that an area cannot make a profit, then you should still be able to measure and control the maximum loss. This policy decision is often made in a hotel where a facility is included to achieve a certain star grading, or it is considered that it is essential to the overall marketing, and achieving a TOTAL hotel profit that certain facilities are included for the guests even if they make a loss.

The economic yardsticks explained in the earlier section on room Tariffs should also be prepared on a restaurant. You generally know your staff standards, food costs and can estimate other operating costs. Added to this you can include an estimate of the area's proportion of energy bills and rates (property taxes) so that you could calculate a reasonable estimate of the total sales required to:

Produce a departmental profit

Break even at house profit level

Break even at net profit

Break even at various net profit levels.

Some further points are made later on menu and bar prices, but most hoteliers have an idea of the average spend, or a range of average spends. Dividing the average spend into the foregoing levels of sales will show the number of covers required to achieve the various levels of sales and profit. Very often this exercise alone will show that the target average spend is wrong, or if it is correct, because of the style creating a low seat turnover ratio and the costs of that particular restaurant, it can never do better, than say, break even at house profit level.

Let us take an example of a 100 seat restaurant in a style and price bracket which dictates that you can only obtain one seat turnover at a busy lunch and at dinner. Your maximum covers is, therefore, 365×200 or 73,000 per year, assuming the restaurant is open for lunch and dinner every day of the year. Assuming that the estimated total costs of payroll, food costs, departmental charges, and a proportion of your undistributed overheads, rents, property taxes, came to $1.7 million, and the maximum average spend was thought to be $20 per cover, net of sales and valued added taxes, but including food, drinks and cigars.

age spend cannot be improved it might be accepted as a policy that the restaurant will not achieve a net profit. Similar calculation to the above (including room rental estimates) should be prepared on function rooms. However, later on I show that through better sales promotion outside the hotel restaurant, and through in-house promotion, most hotels can drastically improve the restaurant results.

Different style restaurants would show totally different results to the foregoing. Generally the lower the average spend, the higher the seat turnover ratio. Higher seat ratios and lower seat areas per seat usually apply in restaurants *outside* hotels where a restaurateur pays rent, interest charges, etc. And the same situation should apply to eating (and drinking) areas within hotels.

Ultimately the market determines whether your restaurant (and bars) charges are value for money and whether you will achieve the target covers at the target average spend.

by the average percentage increase in

Food commodity prices

added to payroll increase

The following factors should be considered very carefully in a hotel restaurant's pricing strategy:

► Economic criteria, target average spends, target covers per meal period
► Current menu and drink prices
► Estimated inflationary effects on *all* costs since last review and in coming period
► Popularity indices for meal periods, and by period
► Average spends (see later comment)
► Competition and what it is likely to do
► Customer segment profile— outside visitors to hotel —guests eating in
► Total cost of staying in room plus average meal

Break even sales $\dfrac{\$1.7\ \text{million}}{\$20} = 85{,}000$ covers

---

In order to break even the restaurant would have to achieve an average seat turnover of 1.16 or increase the average spend by around 16 per cent to $23.2. In many restaurants where there are business executives on their own, or three people eating together, a 100 seat restaurant cannot always achieve 100 covers, and there would also be "quiet" times. In this case if the aver-

But it is worth summarizing again a revised list of the factors which should be considered in changing prices or introducing new menus.

I have often sat at meetings where the prices are increased

The hotelier and restaurateur has to find out more about customers and who they are. I have persuaded many operators to take the time and trouble of carrying out research on their overnight guests, and now I am persuading more hotel clients to do this for their restaurants. In every case the results prove invaluable not just in fixing sales prices but in providing marketing and sales action points.

Let us take the 100 seat restaurant mentioned earlier and assume it achieves 60,000 covers per year. This is a useful accounting and economic yardstick, but it really tells us nothing in marketing and sales terms. Are the 60,000 covers, 60,000 different people who only come once a year? Were there 60,000 bills, or checks, for 60,000 people on their own? Or perhaps 20,000 checks with an average of three covers per check. And out of the 20,000 checks would it be invaluable to know that, say:

---

20 per cent came once in a year
24 per cent came twice in a year
18 per cent came three to five times per year
20 per cent came six to ten times per year
18 per cent were regulars coming more than ten times per year
100 per cent

And how would you react if you carried out this sample research once a year and found that the proportion of regulars was declining? Do you know these proportions in your own restaurants? We must find out more about the people who use our hotels and restaurants, the market segment, their profile, and their spending power. Are they time sensitive but not too price sensitive? What makes them tick? The more we can find out about them the more we can find the right sales and advertising message to attract more of them. And we will be in a better position to choose the most cost effective media to reach the correct market segment.

Average Spends

Most hoteliers and restaurateurs know their average spends on food, and average spends on restaurant-related beverage sales, which provides a total average spend. But by itself this can be misleading because it is only an "average." Averages can provide a false impression in locating your market segments. You all know the old story. Sit down and take your shoes and socks off. Put one foot in a bucket full of boiling hot water. Place the other foot at the same time in another bucket full of freezing cold water.

On average you should feel comfortable!!

It is recommended that you analyse your average spends per meal into price blocks, or groupings. If the average spend is $12 you might analyse the average spends as follows:

	%
up to $8	3
$8 to $10	36
$10 to $12	11
$12 to $14	16
$14 to $16	30
above $16	4
	100%

Suppose the pattern for a meal period tended to show the foregoing percentage proportions. You will see that there are two clear average

market spends, 36 per cent between $8 and $10, and another large group at 30 per cent spending between $14 and $16. In fact, only a minority are spending around the average of $12. More analysis and information would be required to draw conclusions and make decisions on this kind of information but if this was a regular pattern, it would tend to indicate that there were two distinct markets in this restaurant. In some countries "mixing markets" makes little difference. But in many countries "mixing markets" can sometimes be disastrous because it can often drive both markets away.

Past experience shows that this type of spend pattern arises for various reasons. Sometimes the menu prices are structured so that the customer cannot spend at the average level, but is forced into the two brackets because the main entrées are clustered in those price brackets. Usually this arises because management have not really thought out the market segment thoroughly enough. Very often this pattern occurs where there is another higher priced restaurant and the two are competing. Where two restaurants are competing then some of the bracket spending above $14 may have been "taken" from the higher priced restaurant.

Coffee shops, open for long hours, will often show spend brackets which are well apart from the average, and depending on the location, markets may mix amicably, e.g. business executives and people out shopping. It is recommended that periodically this type of average spend is analysed into price bands, together with regular popularity indices on dishes for the various eating areas in an hotel.

Time Sensitivity

Quite often business executives with a high spending power may choose to eat in a coffee shop because they are in a hurry and do not wish to spend more time in a leisurely up-market restaurant. It is customary to assume that the fast food scene is a high volume, low price market but the two do not necessarily go together.

Many businessmen are primarily time sensitive at lunch and may not be price sensitive at all. In fact they might pay more for a good meal served fast. This is not to say that we should turn hotel restaurants into a typical McDonald's fast food restaurant, far from it. But we should find out, through our customer profiles, whether we have a significant proportion of our customers who are time sensitive. We should then systemize and gear the operation to satisfy this market.

We once carried out a popularity study on a restaurant in a famous London hotel. More than half the lunchtime covers were chosen from the trolley even though there was an excellent a la carte menu. The joint on the trolley was not much cheaper than the other entrées so why did customers choose it? The visual display and presentation of the trolley might have been a factor but this restaurant was not famous for its roast joints like, say, Simpsons-in-the-Strand. Besides, the restaurant was so large that most people ordered what was on the trolley without being able to see it clearly. Our research showed that the principal reason was that customers were relatively time sensitive. About 60 per cent ordered from the trolley at lunchtime; this decreased to 15 per cent ordering from the trolley in the evening, when people have more time and when roast dishes may not be so popular anyway.

Fixing a Maximum Spend

Excluding the five star hotel with a superb restaurant and an extensive wine list, let us examine the subject of average spend. Most experienced hoteliers and restaurateurs have a target average spend which they try to improve without affecting sales volume and driving away trade. On the other hand they do not want to have customers coming in during the busy meal periods eating just one course or ordering a cup of coffee. So virtually all restaurateurs introduce a minimum charge in the peak periods; alternatively, they price the menu so that no one spends below a certain amount. This is sound economic sense unless you are very quiet in the usual peak periods.

Many restaurateurs feel that if the customer wants to spend a lot of money, why not give him the opportunity? So they offer various high priced dishes as starters, as a main course, and special desserts (and special coffees and cocktails) in case he is in the mood to spend. I am sympathetic with this as a general policy, but in the mass market of middle-spend customers, isn't there a case for fixing a maximum or ceiling price rather than a minimum? Many people say if you avoid smoked salmon, lobster and the most expensive items, and choose the house wine (which I normally do), two people will leave my restaurant with change from $60 to tip the cloakroom attendant—or words to this effect. The amount of $60 is not as important as the principle.

With one client we decided to take this policy a stage further. The restaurant had a fairly extensive menu but only six wines on the wine list. We specifically planned the pricing strategy so that if a couple had one cocktail, the most expensive dish out of three courses, the most expensive bottle of wine, and coffee, adding taxes and 15 per cent tip they could not possibly spend more than a certain maximum amount. The spend bracket for two people was carefully researched in the catchment area, and the market segment range of spend fixed as a target with a maximum possible spend per couple and naturally half this per cover. The marketing philosophy was that the owners were very happy with the price segment *and* the maximum, and the customer would not experience a shock because he had spent much more than he expected when he walked in. The restaurant was, and still is, very successful.

Inflation meant that after a year the maximum was increased. Then we encountered inflation together with a recession. The decision was made not to exceed the maximum price spend and to hold it at that level whatever the rate of inflation for at least one year. This was done by rethinking and changing dishes, menu specifications, and by better buying, particularly of wines. In a period of inflation *and* recession this policy pays off in repeat business, higher sales volume, and as a bottom line profit.

Food Cost Percentages

Traditionally in hotel food operations we have controlled costs on a percentage basis. We talk about a target food cost of, say, 35 per cent, or in the United Kingdom a target food gross profit of 65 per cent (100 per cent minus 35 per cent). This method of controlling food costs is a useful economic yardstick, but it is totally wrong from the point of view of marketing, pricing strategy *and* net profits. Firstly, once again, it is an average percentage. Secondly, it ignores payroll cost. And, most important of all, it does not take into account what the market is prepared to pay. Let us take an extreme example. The food cost percentage, and therefore gross profit, is usually much better *as a percentage* on a bowl of soup compared with a starter of, say, smoked salmon ("lox"). But

what would you really rather sell in terms of actual *amount of profit?*

Traditionally many restaurateurs and chefs took the food cost of a dish and multiplied approximately by three. Then it became recognized that this priced out of the market certain dishes, where the commodity purchase price was expensive (e.g. lobster, smoked salmon, etc.) Generally throughout the 80s it was recognized that you could not expect to achieve a target food cost percentage of, say, 35 per cent and still find a buyer for these higher priced items. During the next decade the trend will be much more towards establishing a fixed amount of profit per dish which is more related to increasing sales volume, seat turnover ratios and actual amount of profit. Nobody has ever banked a percentage. It is the actual amount of money that counts.

Similarly, as good wines increased in purchase price we persuaded some clients to drop the idea of selling wines on a percentage mark-up basis and to change over more to a standard amount of add-on per bottle. This certainly helped to increase total sales, particularly of the slower moving higher priced wines, and increased overall net profits.

Function Pricing

The right kind of imagination can do a lot to make a routine function something absolutely special whether it be a central feature like an ice carving, attractively produced menus, or something personal-

ized to the name of the company or the people organizing the function. Derek Taylor's excellent book *How to Sell Banquets* is well worth reading on this aspect. Many restaurants can quite honestly obtain higher prices because the food, service, or atmosphere is unique, or just a little better than the competition. This is more difficult with functions. Most functions are fairly routine, and it is difficult to produce a gastronomic experience when you are feeding large numbers. Further, this aspect of a hotel's sales quite often has more competition, particularly on price.

Many of the points raised previously on restaurant pricing strategy are equally applicable to functions and will help to maximize both the number of functions and, where attendance is not compulsory, the numbers who attend. Points like seeking an amount of profit on food and wines rather than a percentage can help to increase sales. I believe that by the 90s food and beverage management will automatically talk about pounds and pence, or dollars and cents, per dish, rather than food percentages. They are going to ask a colleague from another hotel "How many dollars do you make on an eight ounce fillet steak?" rather than "What percentage do you make?"

The other major cost on functions is payroll. Unless the trend moves over totally to self-service buffet style functions, payroll costs are always going to be high. In many countries most of the waiters and waitresses are "casual" employees taken on just for that function or a series of functions. So they are not usually a fixed cost.

Very often a prospective function organizer is offered a series of sample menus covering a range of prices. The prices usually vary depending on the *commodity* cost of the dishes making up the suggested sample menus. Payroll does not enter into the calculations. Most hotels fix a staff standard for functions based on their style of hotel of one waiter to a table of ten people, or one waiter to two tables. And yet payroll is getting more expensive all the time. Where competition is tough, or we in the hotel industry want to stimulate overall growth in the function market, we should consider waiters (as well as food cost) as another "variable" in the pricing strategy. Suppose we said to a prospective function buyer, once the broad menus are agreed:

"Mr. Jones, we have three alternative types of functions where your guests are sitting down to a superb meal, and three different price levels.

"One is our standard function, the other is a function where you are not in too much of a hurry and have more time. And the third is our VIP function."

The first might have one waiter for every ten customers, the one where they have more time might have one waiter for every twenty people, and the VIP might have two waiters per table of ten.

This would be gently explained to the prospective buyer, with the different prices.

In one "slump" year I know one hotelier who decided to take action well before the pre-Christmas office party period, because he feared massive cancellations of functions. He offered local companies who were cutting down on numbers, or thinking of cancelling, the chance to reduce costs by *sharing* a dance or disco with a completely strange company. His argument was that everyone eats in a room with strangers (except at their own table) when they eat in a restaurant, so why not in a large function room? It worked and in fact a number of the companies expressed their thanks to him for trying to save them money. That was pretty radical thinking.

What I am saying is that over the next decade we are going to have to rethink a lot of the ways we fix our pricing strategies because they are based on tradition. Yet the world is changing.

Periodically we should sit down with our team of executives and assume the hotel was *brand new*. We should go through the exercise of fixing room tariffs, restaurant, bar and function prices, and try to forget completely what we are charging now. Assume no prior experience. Look at the competition, find out about the market needs, think fresh. When the exercise is finished we should compare the results with the prices we are charging now and we must consider

carefully, if they vary, why and what we should charge.

Packaging Up in Pricing Strategy

The foregoing sections deal with pricing strategy for room tariffs, restaurant and function prices. At times of recession, or in some circumstances even in busy times, the question of whether to discount on normal quoted tariffs is often raised. Could I make it quite clear that I am not against discounts? There are many circumstances when there is an opportunity to obtain business in a quiet period (e.g., a function on a Monday night). Or there is a possibility of obtaining a booking for a definite large number of people like a group tour with high double occupancy, or an over-night convention, when a discount might be good marketing tactics. In these cases discounting up to an agreed maximum percentage, as shown in the earlier section on Economic Criteria for Successful Marketing, is logical.

But too often I have found on actual consultancy assignments that there is an automatic reaction to put forward a price reduction at once, as the first tactic for obtaining more business. In particular I notice that sales executives in giving a sales presentation sometimes suggest a discount at an early stage where in fact the prospective buyer has not heard the whole presentation, and may not want a discount. And it is not just sales executives who fall into the trap. In obtaining business in a quiet period, or developing new markets (e.g. weekend and short break holidays) the tendency can sometimes be "how competitive (cheap) can we make it?"

The first question about a quiet period should really be why is it quiet? What are the reasons, the problems that prevent business from coming in those periods? Unless there is no business at all, what motivates the present market and custom to use you in the "quiet" times? Very often the different sources of business require a pricing package in order to promote it as this provides the buyer (whether it is a weekend break or a convention) with a chance to fix a maximum budget. It is my contention that this pricing package does not necessarily have to be priced as low as possible, but could be packaged up—or both.

Some years ago I remember the manager of an hotel in the Scottish ski resort of Aviemore telling me he set out to attract more of the honeymoon market than he was obtaining to date. He produced a special brochure and part of the package price was a bottle of Moet & Chandon on ice in the bedroom on arrival. In fixing the price he first thought of including each bottle at cost price only. Then he thought he would see what would happen if he charged the full price for the champagne in the total holiday price and offered both—the basic price with no extras and an alternative with the champagne and other extras. Every couple bought the honeymoon

with the extras. There are many other people who are willing to "trade up" who are not necessarily on honeymoon if it is presented to them in the right way.

Another client was going to enter the weekend break market for the first time and were prepared to invest time and money promoting and developing this market over a three year period. I persuaded them to offer two weekend packages. One was the standard package including accommodation, breakfasts, two dinners, service charges and taxes. The other was a VIP package "for that special occasion" which was the standard package and a half bottle of champagne on ice on arrival— a box of Elizabeth Shaw mints—fruit and flowers in the bedroom—free cocktail before every meal, breakfast in bed, etc. The results were monitored and on average just over a quarter, 27 per cent, purchased the higher priced weekend break.

Another example of a situation which was not creating a new market but was a chance to obtain a bigger slice of business. Our client had a large hotel near a major airport with a number of competitive hotels. Most of them were new and few had significant advantages over the others. All were experiencing low average room occupancies, around 60 per cent. A major international company was launching a new product and wanted to hold the series of launches for their agents world-wide by flying them all to that airport. So the location at the airport was

fixed. They wanted 300 rooms for each series, four days per series, spread over nearly twenty weeks.

The company had asked five or six hotels to quote. Together with the client we worked long hours preparing advantage/limitation lists compared with the competition. And everyone racked their brains to finds ways of quoting the minimum price to obtain this large amount of sales income. I persuaded the client to put forward two quotes and we were told afterwards that we were the only hotel who did.

The first was the Executive Package which was the usual conference rate for an overnight conference reduced "to the bone" and no hidden extras. The second was the VIP conference package including:

Accommodation

All Meals

Use of exhibition and conference rooms

Fruit and flowers in every bedroom

One bottle of gin, sherry and whisky in every bedroom

Opening cocktail party first evening

One evening at the theatre

Last dinner special Elizabethan evening

Complete programme for wives

The total price per delegate of the VIP conference package was nearly twice the price of the lower Executive Package, but the company bought it with hardly any hesitation or alteration.

We often consider packaging up for VIP dinners, conferences, or for a special weekend. But quite often we ignore the opportunity at breakfast. In fact the trend is to move away from including a full breakfast in the room tariff and only include continental breakfast, or nothing in America. Have a look at the breakfast menu shown in Figure 3 from the Ritz Hotel in Lisbon, an Inter-Continental Hotel. This kind of menu could really work successfully where there is room service and the principles would still apply where breakfast is served in a restaurant. I know it works. My wife and I stayed there and we both thought the Sparkling Breakfast was great but did not choose it until Saturday when I did not have to work. We both felt you had to try it.

Many people discount because travel agents and, in particular, tour operators often say the market is very price sensitive. Most tour operators are very shrewd and clever negotiators—if you take a short-term viewpoint.

I always recommend clients to obtain the current brochure when they are renegotiating their price with a foreign tour operator, have it translated if necessary, and see where their hotel is listed and how it is described compared with the competition. That will often provide valuable negotiating clues. For years I have watched "bulk buyers" negotiating prices which are unrealistic considering the long-term future of the product they are buying (i.e., the hotels) and are, therefore, not in their interests.

I would like to put a scenario before you of a hotelier, Sam Salt, negotiating his rates with a tour operator for next winter. The characters are fictitious and so are the rates. John Smith is the tour operator, Ms. Sheraton Hilton is the sales executive, William Black is a competitive hotelier. Sam Salt is speaking.

"I have listened to your remarks, John, about next winter's market, and I agree with most of them: that there is no sign of an end to the recession and that we hoteliers are going to have a tough time next winter. And I appreciate you showing me the market research predicting a bad winter for holidays between your country and London. It doesn't surprise me that my competitors are worried and prepared to give you a rate of $18 per pax (person) double occupancy, including continental breakfast, service charge and VAT. I also agree that there is a mood of panic among some hoteliers because prospects are bad and interest rates high. So your offer of $20 per pax sounds generous. But I have worked out some basic calculations.

"My heat, light and power bill has gone up 38 per cent in three years. My property rates have increased by 72 per cent during the same period. The pattern is the same with most costs, except for repairs and redecorations which I reduced to a minimum last year. It is fortunate that my property is in a good state of repair and décor. I have calculated that I may break even at $20 per pax if I allow a reasonable sum for repairs, renovations and depreciation. In the same very tough years your rate paid to me only increased by 18 per cent.

"I agree that you must hold down the total price of your holidays in order to sell as many as possible and you are correct in pointing out that my competitors would be very happy with $20 . . . you have already shown me the signed agreement with William Black at the Excelsior nearby even though this is confidential.

"I could kick myself for not doing it before, but I got *your* German brochure for this present winter and had it translated into English. You list a choice of eight hotels in London, starting with the highest priced. I find that I am the second most expensive and the Excelsior is seventh, very nearly the cheapest. If your customers' sole criteria was price—as you stress—how is it so many choose *my* hotel?

"What I like best of all is the glowing way you describe my hotel, the friendly staff, the good state of décor and my quiet location. Together with my sales executive, Sheraton Hilton, I have produced a new advantage/limitation list of my hotel *and* my competitors, so we know these glowing comments in your brochure are correct. We have also checked that my breakfast is superior to my competitors.

PEQUENO ALMOÇO Servido entre as 07h00 e as 12h00.	**BREAKFAST** Served from 07h00–12h00

O PEQUENO ALMOÇO REAL — 950$00 — **THE SPARKLING BREAKFAST**

1/2 Garrafa de espumante bruto Salmão fumado da Escócia e espadarte fumado e Bife do lombo grelhado com ovo estrelado e A sua escolha de pequeno almoço Inter-Continental Com morangos ou melão (na época)	150$00 (extra)	1/2 Bottle of brut portuguese sparkling wine Scotch smoked salmon and smoked swordfish and Fillet of Beef with fried egg and Your choice of Inter-Continental breakfast With fresh strawberries or melon (in season)

O PEQUENO ALMOÇO ARISTOCRATA — 500$00 — **THE DUKE'S BREAKFAST**

A sua escolha de pequeno almoço Inter-Continental com Bife do lombo grelhado com ovo estrelado e bacon O·cereal à sua escolha Com morangos ou melão (na época)	150$00 (extra)	Your choice of Inter-Continental breakfast with Grilled minute fillet steak with fried egg and bacon The cereal of your choice With fresh strawberries or melon (in season)

O PEQUENO ALMOÇO TRADICIONAL — 350$00 — **THE TRADITIONAL BREAKFAST**

A sua escolha de pequeno almoço Inter-Continental Escolha de cereais Ovos, à sua escolha, acompanhados com presunto, bacon, salsichas ou cogumelos	Inter-Continental breakfast at your choice Selection of cereals Eggs, any style, served with ham, bacon, sausages or mushrooms

O PEQUENO ALMOÇO INTER-CONTINENTAL — **THE INTER-CONTINENTAL BREAKFAST**

(incluido no preço do seu quarto) Inclui sumo de laranja natural ou qualquer outro sumo, Croissants, pãezinhos ou bolos secos, torradas, Manteiga, compotas diversas ou mel chá, café chocolate ou ovomaltine	(Included in the price of your room) Includes fresh orange juice or other fruit juice, Croissants, rolls and buns, or toast, butter, marmelade, Jam or honey Tea, coffee, chocolate or ovomaltine

Todas as taxas incluidas	All taxes included

FIGURE 3. A Breakfast Menu

"I put it to you, John, that you have been in business for many years, and in your kind of trade a key economic factor is the degree of repeat business and recommendation. I would bet that your CSQs (customer satisfaction questionnaires) rate me as high, if not higher, than many of my competitors.

"After some calculations I have set my new rate at $30 per pax double occupancy. I really want your business, John, but I want it at a profit. I feel that my rate of $30 is good value for money.

"John, we'll have to end our meeting soon because I have an appointment with another tour operator. Sorry to rush you but I don't want to keep him waiting, and you will need a day or so to think this over.

"Give me a call next week."

This little scenario is put before readers to stress some points. Firstly, the hotelier has done some homework. Secondly, he has obviously been on a course on negotiation! Primarily he has planned his tactics and the timing of his next meeting very carefully. He may reduce his price from $30 to do a deal but he will probably achieve more than the tour operator's offer of $20. Obtaining a translation of the tour operator's brochure could be invaluable in negotiations like this. The hotelier is also selling on higher satisfaction for the tour operator's clients and more repeat business rather than selling on price alone.

Although much more extensive, this is very similar to an actual meeting I attended where the tour operator finally agreed $28 per person.

Concentrate on price and you have only one way to go—down. Switch from price to value and you have many paths all of them up.

One of the finest statements I have ever read on the whole subject of price and value was written over one hundred years ago and I have no hesitation in repeating it below.

Value . . .

It's unwise to pay too much, but it's unwise to pay too little. When you pay too much you lose a little money, that is all. When you pay too little, you sometimes lose everything, because the thing you bought was incapable of doing the thing you bought it to do.

The common law of business balance prohibits paying a little and getting a lot. It can't be done. If you deal with the lowest bidder, it's well to add something for the risk you run. And if you do that, you will have enough to pay for something better.

John Ruskin (1819–1900)

Very often in negotiating on price I have read this out and it has helped to win an argument.

Some hoteliers and sales executives automatically assume that the only way to clinch a major deal is to offer discounts. This could be the easy way out—in many situations the buyer would sooner have the proposition "packaged" with a series of extras included, rather than having a reduction in the price. Many people say that the market is price sensitive today. What they mean is that the tour operators say the price is sensitive. Often research shows that the ultimate purchaser (the guest) may show an opposite reaction.

A leading sales executive said to me recently that the only right policy is "pile 'em high—sell 'em cheap," quoting the famous policy statement by the founder of Tesco, a chain of supermarkets. But we are not selling cans of beans, and this attitude may well drive us out of business.

Send sales executives, receptionists and reservation staff out to look at competitors' rooms and list league tables of comparable tariffs. It might dawn on them that your quoted tariffs are not as high as they may seem. I have seen many sales staff and receptionists "breathe in" as they quote the tariff for the room at $40, $60, or more, because they feel it is high. Once they have seen the competition's charges they will have much more confidence in selling their room rates.

Curiously enough, however sophisticated people become, everyone likes something for nothing. And if you include something in a package which appears to be free, people love it. In the Daula Hotel, Kano, Northern Nigeria, we introduced a rose for ladies leaving the dining room. The response was staggering. There are a mass of "small" items which make people think you care and make them return. Too often we have a number of irritating add-ons. The small charge for a morning newspaper or—probably the worst—the cover charge in the restaurant. I know all the reasons for it, but it annoys the majority of customers. I rather like the idea of giving a departing guest a take-away gift which is associated with the area, like a selection of local cheeses, or a paperweight from a local stone, with your own name or emblem on the item or on the wrapping. I have a key ring, a leather coaster for my office desk, and a long shoe-horn which I use virtually every day—all reminding me of the hotels who gave them to me. Naturally the quality of the gift would depend on the style of hotel. Why give a departing guest just a receipted bill and a credit card slip when he leaves after spending possibly $2000 or more on a holiday?

It is a very good rule in obtaining repeat business to give guests something when they arrive and something when they leave.

In good or bad times there are always some people who will spend more money if you give them the chance. And there are always some companies or organizations who are selling a very expensive product, or trying to make a good impression on a product launch, where a hotelier can do the same. Usually the hotel costs are small compared to the overall costs of marketing, in relation to the development costs of a new product, and compared to the sales price of the product.

There is a place for discounts on quiet nights and periods of the year where the market is more price sensitive. Retrospective discounts to major buyers where they have given you more than a certain amount of business in the past years are also useful. But before hoteliers use discounts as a marketing weapon, first:

1. Find out much more about the market, its motivations, price sensitivity, etc.
2. Isolate quiet periods clearly and try some creative selling first, before discounting.
3. Try packaging up rather than pricing down.

What we must avoid is the degree of discounting which lowers the average rate earned per room to a level which is so low that however high occupancy is, the hotel will never show a reasonable profit level. We must not fall into the trap the airlines have fallen into of selling "bottoms on seats" regardless of profits. Belatedly airlines are packaging up with a lot of advertising promoting larger seats, "free" drinks, slippers, etc. The problem is that once the market has got used to low prices, it is very difficult to increase them to an economic level.

Talking about pricing strategy is easier than writing about it, because when you are talking someone can always interrupt, ask a question, and you can cross-fertilize ideas. When I told a friend I was going to write a Section on Pricing Strategy he described it as a "time bomb" where you can never be right. But if this section makes you argue, puts it into perspective, or just provides you with a few clues to your own strategy in the future, I will be very satisfied.

Marketing Plan

The marketing plan project provides an opportunity for students to apply what they learn in class. This project works best when the students have completed at least one marketing course. I have found it useful to limit the plan to one market segment, one outlet in a hotel, or one meal period in a restaurant. This gives the project focus and allows the students to achieve a greater understanding of the process. When students take too broad an approach the plans can become superficial.

There are three ways the students can approach the project. They can work directly with a business. This usually ends up being a present employer, past employer, or a friend. They can do a plan without any direct contact with the management. In this case the students are told to view the project as if they were going to buy the business and develop a marketing plan to use after they take it over. This approach is used when the students want to work on a specific type of business and the owners or managers of the only example of that type of business are not willing to work with the students or when management becomes to busy to work with the students. There are usually several projects each term that fall into the latter category. The students will have a good initial meeting with managers of the business they selected, put a lot of effort into their environmental analysis, and then management postpones the second meeting one or two times due to business pressures. The students panic as deadlines are approaching. One solution is to have the students move to a format that does not require any direct involvement with management. Finally, students who are going into business for themselves can develop an initial marketing plan for their business. I require students in this category to work alone. In this case the students are dealing with a concept, a concept that is well developed in one student's mind, but not well developed in the minds of the other students. This often causes communication problems between the group members.

With the exception of the last category above, this is a group project, groups of 3–4 students work the best. I divide the project into three parts, with parts one and two being due during the course. The grade on these parts is recorded as a homework grade. This gives the students some feedback on how they are doing, helps the instructor identify problems, and spreads the student's work out over the course. The project grade is given on the submission of the final marketing plan. Students are allowed to make changes to the two parts submitted during the term and incorporate these changes into their final project. I use a marketing plan outline adapted from the outline William A. Cohen presents in *Developing a Winning Marketing Plan,* published by Wiley.

This is the description of the plan.

Term Project—Marketing Plan

Students will develop a marketing plan as the term project for this course.

The plan should be for a business that is part of the travel industry. You can work directly with a business, work on your own (without management help) or develop a plan for a business you plan to start after you graduate. The project will be a group project for those working with an existing business. Those working on a proposed business concept will work on their own.

The outline for the marketing plan has been included in the course syllabus. The time table for the marketing plan is as follows;

1. Groups will be formed the second day of class (3–4 people in a group).

2. A proposal of your project will be turned in at the end of the second week of class. This will include the name of the business, and the segment, meal period, or business outlet that you select.

3. Parts three through five of the plan are due at the end of the fifth week of the course.

4. Parts six through eight of the plan are due the tenth week of the course.

5. The completed project is due on the last day of class.

6. During the last week of class a fifteen minute presentation of your plan will be given in class. The grade on the presentation will be fifteen percent of your project grade.

The "Living Case"

This project offers an alternative to a term project. Students enjoy the living case for several reasons. First, students enjoy having the assignments spread out over the entire course. Second, the cases help the students relate the class materials to business applications. Finally, the cases generate interesting class discussions.

I divide the students into four groups so some students have a case for each topic being discussed in the course. For example, in the first week of my course I cover the course introduction, relationship marketing, and marketing strategy. The topics for the next weeks are; the marketing environment, market segmentation, buyer behavior, and marketing information in the fifth week. I start the cases in the second week of class and the case is due on the last meeting of the week. Thus, group one will do a case on the marketing environment, group two will do a case on segmentation, group three will do a case on buyer behavior and group four will be assigned to do a case on marketing information. The cycle will then repeat itself. In a class of forty students ten students will have cases on each topic area, ensuring a good class discussion for each topic. The group assignments are used to decide the topics. All projects are individual work.

Some students have a difficult time grasping the idea of relating an industry practice with the course material. These students will simply write up an experience or recap an article, without tying it back to the marketing literature. To compensate for this I include an example of a good case with the syllabus. I also grade the first case very leniently with a lot of feedback.

The following is the case description, I have also included the grading form I use for the case.

Cases

Each student will hand in three written cases, 750 to 1000 words (two to three double spaced typed pages). The cases will be "living" cases. They consist of a write up of an experience or an article about a firm's effective use of the concepts studied in class, the week the case is due. You can also use examples showing the consequences of not applying marketing concepts.

The purpose of the case is to link the course material with industry practices. The first part of the case should be the example. The second part of the case should link the industry example with marketing theory. The second part of the case requires going to marketing literature other than the text book. Thus, all cases should cite references, other than the text book.

An example of a sample case is provided as part of this course outline. Each student will prepare three cases during the semester. The class will be divided into four groups, with members of each group turning in their case on the due date for their group. The purpose of dividing the class into four groups is to provide cases for class discussion each week. The group membership simply denotes the date the case is due. All cases are to be individual work. All cases are required to be typed. Computers with word processing software and printers are available in the College's computer lab. It is estimated it will take five to eight hours to prepare a case.

Criteria for Cases

1. Must use a company in the travel industry.

2. Should build a case around one company—can be from your experience or an article. If you use an article you might want to use more than one reference.

3. The case is divided into two parts:

Part one is the case

Part two gives marketing implications based on marketing readings in your assigned area. Sources for the readings include: specialized marketing books such as consumer behavior or marketing research texts, service marketing texts, hospitality marketing texts, and journal articles.

Grading Form

Part 1—Case

Case uses business in the travel industry	10 pts _____
Case relates to topic	10 pts _____
Case is well developed	30 pts _____
Case has enough body to support a good discussion	

Part 2—Marketing Implications

References other than class material	15 pts _____
Relevance of references	10 pts _____
Integration of references into the discussion of the case	25 pts _____

17

FRANCHISING

Advantages and Disadvantages of Franchising
Mahmood A. Khan

Going Global
Frank Go and Julia Christensen

Project 1

Project 2

Advantages and Disadvantages of Franchising

Mahmood A. Khan

FRANCHISING IS A UNIQUE and exciting opportunity for both franchisor and franchisee. In actuality there is a symbiotic relationship between franchisor and franchisees. Much of the success of any franchise system depends on how smooth the franchisor-franchisee relationship is. Since both franchisors and franchisees have personal goals that can be achieved at an optimal level by mutual cooperation and trust, it is imperative to have a thorough understanding of all operational aspects of the business. Many franchisor-franchisee relationship problems can be traced to informational imbalance, which could occur before or after entering into contract. Some franchisees do not understand the fundamentals of franchising and at times are impressed with the apparent glamour of successful franchise businesses, which they may observe without being directly involved. The intent of this chapter is to outline the pros and cons of franchising,

viewed from the point of view of franchisees as well as franchisors. A summary of advantages and disadvantages is presented in Table 1.

Advantages to the Franchisee

Several advantages to franchisees result from their participation in a franchise system. The most important ones are discussed below.

Established Concept

The franchisee buys into a business that has an **established concept.** The product or services provided are unique and have potential for success. In business-format franchising, which includes most franchised restaurants, the entire format is available for use. If the franchise has been in operation for some time, consumers are aware of the company, and in many cases the reputation of the product and/or services is well established. Thus a franchisee

is buying into an established business, which is one of the major advantages. In the case of restaurants, if the menu is well known and consumers are aware of the trade-mark, the business is free from start-up uncertainties. Established franchise restaurants have undergone years of rigorous market testing of the products and services so that the concept is so well proven that it is ripe for profitable applicability. Although this advantage is available to the franchisee at the time of initiating the business, further success depends upon the way an individual franchise is operated and managed.

Tools for Success

Franchising does not guarantee success but provides **tools for success.** These tools include: (a) local and national support by the franchisors in vital areas such as site selection, construction, purchasing, equipment selection, operations, training, advertising, marketing, and promotion;

TABLE 1. ADVANTAGES AND DISADVANTAGES OF FRANCHISING		
	Advantages	**Disadvantages**

To Franchisee	Established concept
	Tools for success
	Technical and managerial
	  help
	Standards and quality
	  control
	Minimum risk
	Less operating capital
	Access to Credit
	Comparative assessment
	Research and development
	  advertisement and promotion
	Other opportunities
		Unfulfilled expectations
		Lack of freedom
		Advertisement and
		  promotion practices
		Cost of services
		Overdependence
		Monotony and lack of
		  challenge
		Termination and renewal
		Other problems

To Franchisors	Business expansion
	Buying power
	Operational convenience
	Franchisee's contribution
	Motivation and cooperation
		Lack of freedom
		Franchisee's financial
		  situation
		Franchisee recruitment,
		  selection and retention
		Communication

(b) availability of continuing assistance in various facets of the business from regional or corporate offices of the franchisors.

Many franchisors provide turn-key operations to their franchisees, which avoids the problems associated with starting a traditional nonfranchised restaurant operation. The primary reason why the restaurant business is so challenging is that it is complex and multifaceted. It involves expertise from many different disciplines. An individual alone finds it difficult and cost-prohibitive to afford these tools. Franchisors, due to centralization of collective resources, can provide such services to franchisees. In addition to all these benefits, time and effort needed to establish a new business is lessened by joining a franchise system.

Technical, Operational, and Managerial Assistance

Major advantages of franchising include the technical and managerial assistance provided by the franchisor. This assistance allows even an unexperienced person to enter a business with which he or she is not familiar. Assistance is provided prior to and after opening a business. The on-going assistance program helps in the day-to-day operation of a business as well as during a crisis. Ideally, a communication line is established between franchisor and franchisees with mutually beneficial exchanges.

Several technical and operational areas may need help in any business venture. Some areas of **technical assistance** provided by restaurant franchisors include: market feasibility studies; site selection;

architectural layout and design; and equipment selection and layout. Operational assistance provided by the franchisor includes inventory purchase and control; purchase specifications; production guidelines; operation schedules; sanitation control; and other service parameters. In addition, training and operational manuals provide a continuous source of guidance. Such services make going into business easier for franchisees, although not all franchisors provide all of the above services.

Standards and Quality Control

Advantages of franchising include the availability of standards set by the franchisor and a mechanism for maintaining **quality control.** It is imperative for the success of individual franchising units that they follow these standards for control of the quality of products and services. Established standards are primarily the reason why a hamburger sold in a franchise in California tastes and looks exactly like the one sold by the same franchise in New York. The same is true for the decor, overall theme, and services provided by a franchise restaurant Mutual cooperation and effective administration are essential for the maintenance of uniformity of product and services. Uniformity is essential to retain the image, ensuring return business, and maintaining employee morale and the growth and development of a business. If properly followed, standards also help assure teamwork between the franchisor and the franchisees and their employees. Implementation of standards requires that they be reasonable, flexible, and applicable to specific areas.

Minimum Risk

There is no business without risk—risk being the potential for both success and failure. Franchising reduces the risk of failure to a great extent. The risks involved are substantially lower than when starting one's own business. Since franchising, on the basis of research and expertise, leads to the development of a system that has been proven to be profitable and workable, there is **minimum risk** of failure. To be exact, franchising offers "risk reduction" rather than "risk elimination." Fran-

chising does not guarantee success, and each unit within a franchise faces the possibility of risk. Much depends on how efficiently a franchisee manages business. It is rightly said that when the relationship between the franchisor and the franchisee is set up and operated properly, it is as close to guaranteed business success as one can get.

Less Operating Capital

Compared to independent restaurants, franchise restaurants may require less **operating capital.** In a franchise restaurant certain items, like inventory level, can be forecasted more accurately than in an independent unit. Calculated production and portion control methods reduce the chances of wastage or unnecessary maintenance of stocks. Expenses can be reduced similarly in other aspects of management. Financial credits in the form of inventory or equipment may also be obtained from the franchisor. Ingredients and supplies (particularly during the initial stages of the operation), may be provided on credit by the franchisor. The design of the facilities, well planned by the franchisor's experienced staff, results in increased production and efficient service.

Franchisors may also help indirectly by facilitating the purchase of business insurance, employee health insurance, and other benefit packages. The group buying power and affiliation with insurance companies by the franchisors

can help franchisees reduce their operating costs.

Access to Credit

A major advantage of franchising is the access to financial credit provided by the franchisors. Although this may not apply to a new franchisee, often franchisors provide credit to franchisees for **business expansion,** on much more favorable terms than other financial institutions. This "in-house" support is looked upon favorably by franchisors as well, since it indirectly has a positive impact on their business. Thus there is mutual benefit in this sort of assistance.

Comparative Assessment

A **comparative assessment** of different functional and operational activities of a restaurant is facilitated within a franchise system. Uniformity in operation, unique to franchise systems, facilitates the comparison of one restaurant unit with another and consequent critical evaluation of the business at various levels. Franchisors can provide information pertaining to the successes and new approaches developed by other franchisees within the system. Meetings with other franchisees also help in this evaluation. There are shared benefits from learning the overall experiences of business counterparts.

Benefits from Research and Development

Franchisors have an on-going interest in the development of their franchises, and many maintain permanent **research and development** departments. The fruits of this research and development are shared with franchisees. Research can be in the area of products or services. This type of service is not available to most independents or non-franchised restaurants. Further, acute, individual problems can be referred by the franchisee to these departments for solutions.

Advertisement and Promotion

Funds pooled from all franchisees are available for **advertisement and promotion;** thus wider exposure for advertisements can be provided by the franchisors. Franchisors have combined buying power because of the pooling of resources and possibly by centralized operations. Carefully planned advertising done on a large scale by qualified staff and agencies can be a real asset for a franchisee. Similarly, well-researched promotional efforts can be launched which will enhance the profitability of an operation.

Opportunities

For a franchisee, unique opportunities are provided by franchising. *Opportunity to own one's own business* and the rewards associated with success are both provided by successful franchises. There is a chance to be in business *for* self without having a business *by* self. Independence is intertwined with mutual dependence often referred to as a

"win-win" situation. Such a limited autonomy is desired by many individuals. When franchising is working properly, it offers access to not only the trade-mark and operational aspects, but also the clout and expertise of a large company with proven success, while still allowing the franchisee to maintain his or her entrepreneurial independence.

There is personal satisfaction and pride in being associated with a successful franchise. Franchisees become a part of the overall success attained by a larger, probably well-known and profitable franchise system. Thus an *opportunity to contribute* to the success of the parent corporation is made available to franchisees.

Franchising also provides an *opportunity for personal growth* and advancement in business knowledge. This may result from the extensive training seminars, meetings, continuing education, and operational information provided by the franchisor. Hands-on-experience can lead to further personal growth and advancement. An *opportunity to meet other franchisees* within the franchise system can lead to the exchange of ideas and a comparative assessment of the operational status of the franchise.

The *opportunity to work with people and for people* is considered an asset by many franchisees. People include customers, restaurant crew, community groups, vendors, and purveyors. Further *business growth opportunities* are provided by the territorial

rights that may be granted by the franchisors. Expansion can result from buying, subfranchising, leasing, operating, or converting other restaurants into franchises.

The above advantages are common to most franchises. Although these are underlying advantages, none of these are guaranteed. In short, franchising helps franchisees to remain competitive in business when compared to independent or nonfranchised operators.

Disadvantages to the Franchisee

Ideally, franchising agreements are designed to develop a mutually satisfying relationship between franchisor and franchisee. However, much depends on a smooth franchisor-franchisee relationship. There are certain disadvantages to franchising which are primarily caused by an uneven franchisor-franchisee relationship, leading to dissatisfaction for either or both of the parties.

Unfulfilled Expectations

Franchisees build certain expectations before getting into the business and expect them to be fulfilled when undertaking the venture. Franchisors at times may present a picture of the business that is unrealistic. Contract clauses may be interpreted inaccurately by franchisees, thereby building false expectations. Any of these aspects may lead to dissatisfaction.

Some franchisees fail to read or understand the implications of some of the contract clauses and rely on the sales or promotional literature provided by the franchisors. Franchisees may also fail to understand the upper hand that most franchisors enjoy in a franchise system. A disadvantage may be rooted in the disparity of bargaining power that often occurs in franchising. Since franchisors are financially strong, legal battles may prove to be long and expensive for an individual franchisee.

Lack of Freedom

In spite of its advantages, franchising poses restrictions and limitations which may cause a franchisee to feel a **lack of freedom**. Franchising contracts may contain restrictions on territorial expansion or may limit potential customer contact. Territorial rights may be inequitably distributed, or a territorial overlap may interfere with the prosperity of a franchisee's business. An entrepreneur may have ideas which can be severely hindered by the restrictions imposed by a franchisor. For example, an enterprising foodservice manager may have proven creative menu ideas for regional consumers which cannot be implemented due to the franchisor's restrictions. A franchisee may find food delivery to customers to be a profitable venture for a restaurant, but that venture may not be allowed because of the policy of the franchisor.

Advertisement and Promotion Practices

Although advertising and promotion are listed as advantages of franchising, under certain circumstances they can prove to be a disadvantage for a franchisee. A franchisee may be paying fees for advertising that is impractical or not applicable to the local market. At times it may not even reach consumers within the territorial expanse of the franchisee. In other words, a franchisee may be paying for advertisements directed toward other franchisees. Similarly, promotional methods selected by the franchisor may not be applicable or profitable for a franchisee's operation. For example, coupon sales promoted by franchisor may not be necessary for a restaurant and selling discounted items, even if sold in large quantities, may impose financial and operational burdens on the franchisee.

Services Provided by the Franchisor

Franchisees must pay service costs, and if the services provided are not up to par, they may suffer a considerable financial loss. After a certain period of time franchisees may feel that the franchise fees and royalty fees are not justifiable. It may become psychologically difficult for a franchisee to continue to pay a fixed percentage of gross sales to the franchisor. Franchise fees and royalty fees take a bite out of the return on investment and are always po-

tential sore points in the franchisee-franchisor relationship.

Overdependence

In a franchise system, a franchisee may develop **overdependence** on the franchisor. On such aspects as operations, crisis situations, pricing strategy, and promotions, the franchisee may come to rely too much on the advice of the franchisor. In addition to slowing down the decision-making process, overdependence may become costly for a franchisee. On certain matters, local franchisees can make better decisions than the franchisors. Franchisees may, for example, depend completely on promotional practices of the franchisors, or similarly, may rely too heavily on the judgment of the franchisor for management decisions.

Monotony and Lack of Challenge

After a certain period of time, franchisees may feel a sense of **monotony**. Particularly for an entrepreneur, a franchise system may become routine with a lack of challenge and creativity. An enterprising franchisee may want opportunities for advancement not provided by the franchisor. This may encourage franchisees to diversify their business investment, which may lead them to other type of businesses or even to a competitor franchise.

Franchise Termination, Renewals and Transfers

Franchise termination is the single most crucial issue for franchisees, whose capital investment, years of service and/or livelihood in a franchise are dependent upon franchisors. The franchisor's power to terminate, to decline to renew, or to deny the franchisee the right to sell or transfer a franchise has always been a sore point in the franchisor-franchisee relationship. The report by the Congressional Committee on Small Business (1990) states:

In order to avoid the implicit "threat" of termination, franchisees feel compelled to comply with all directives and instructions of the franchisor, no matter how unreasonable, invalid or arbitrary they may be. Most prevalent forms of abuse in this regard involve: required purchases of inventory and equipment from the franchisor at above market prices; required testing of unproven products without allowance for potential loss; required investment to alter the design or appearance of the franchise location; "voluntary" contributions for special promotional campaigns; alteration of exclusive marketing or territorial rights; and extension of noncompetition agreements to apply to franchise operations or to unrelated business activities of franchisees.

Franchisors feel that termination power is essential to the efficient operation of a franchise system. Thus a franchisee's right to a franchise may be invoked if any of the provisions of the franchise agreement are not followed. This is considered a major disadvantage by many franchisees, particularly those who have stayed with a system for a considerable period of time or those who have invested substantially within a franchise system.

Franchisees' and Franchise System Performances

Once into the system, a franchisee's success is dependent on the performance of other franchisees within that system. If the quality and service of any franchisee is not up to standard, it may have a negative impact on the entire system and thereby affect the sales of other franchisees. Often consumers associate blame for negligence with the entire system rather than an individual franchisee. This may also occur, for example, if the franchiser does not maintain quality standards uniformly among franchisees. An outbreak of a food-borne illness at one unit may have an impact on all franchise stores within that system.

Similarly much depends on the overall performance of a franchise system. Improper management or abrupt changes in management may affect all franchisees within a network. Poor performance of the franchisors may be interpreted by consumers as poor performance of the individual franchisee, irrespective of how successful a restaurant has been in the past. Another aspect of this adverse relationship may be a result of national ranking by industry publications and financial analysts. Poor rating or ranking of a franchise may have a direct impact on sales at individual units. A "guilt by association" phenomenon may occur.

It should be understood that this has been an exhaustive list of the possible advantages and disadvantages of franchising, and one should not assume that all of these will be relevant to a particular franchise system. Further, *advantages* of franchising do not necessarily mean *profitability*, and *disadvantages* may not mean *lack of profitability* of a franchise. On the whole, it is evident that the advantages of franchising far outweigh the disadvantages.

Advantages to the Franchisor

In addition to being a financial asset, franchising provides other advantages and some disadvantages to franchisors, described in the following paragraphs.

Business Expansion

Franchising provides the means for expansion of a business by providing opportunities to franchisees, primarily by territorial expansion agreements. Investment capital for expansion can also be secured by adopting franchising. In fact, franchising is the best way to expand with limited capital investment by the franchisor. The franchisor may choose to invest excess capital for the benefit of the corporation either within the franchise system or in affiliated businesses. Because franchising does not involve elaborate experience in the business, many investors may choose to invest directly in the expansion of a franchised restaurant that has proven success. Thus franchising can attract capital for expansion either by the sale of franchises and/or direct investment by investors.

Potential franchisees may be located in regions with which franchisors are not familiar. Local franchisees are normally familiar with the community, private and public organizations, zoning ordinances, license requirements, and business regulations. The franchisees' knowledge becomes an asset for the expansion of the company.

Expansion of a corporation involves risks and structural modifications, which may become difficult to handle. In franchising, the expansion takes place without significant changes to the organizational structure at corporate headquarters. This allows the franchisor to devote more time and effort to strategic planning, operational planning, market feasibility, and the overall development of the franchise system.

Buying Power

The restaurant business involves large quantity purchase of ingredients, equipment, and supplies. Franchisors may benefit financially from collective and centralized buying for franchisees. Although this advantage may be available in a nonfranchise system, in franchising it is common even

with limited capital investment.

In addition, funds available from fees paid by the franchisees may be used for advertising, promotion, and research development on a well-planned and organized level. Considerable cost savings can be achieved in such large-scale ventures.

Operational Convenience

From the franchisor's point of view, franchising provides **operational convenience** compared to other ways of doing business. A franchisor does not have to worry about day-to-day unit operations or aspects such as employee turnover, benefits, and wages. Single franchise units are usually more easily managed by franchisees than is the management of all units by one corporation. Some chain restaurants which are operated solely by the company face acute human resource problems. Because franchisees have individual vested interests in their unit(s), the operations are handled effectively primarily by the franchisees, except under emergency or critical conditions.

Franchisee Contribution

An advantage that is often underappreciated is the nonfinancial contribution that a franchisee makes to the system. Large franchise corporations have realized that a franchisee can make valuable contributions at the grassroots level. Franchisees are directly involved in day-to-day operation of a unit and thor-

oughly understand its functional aspects. They may provide good solutions to problems, may comment on the applicability of an idea, and may give input on the financial feasibility of a corporate plan. If franchisees are closely involved, many problems can be avoided. Further, when a new idea or change is considered, franchisees serve as a good sounding board. Corporate staffs have made decisions without prior consultation with franchisees, only to regret it. The best franchisors see their franchisees as a tremendous asset bringing creativity, years of hands-on experience, and a drive for success that are invaluable to the system.

Many ideas originate from franchisees, and if carefully tested and adapted may prove to be of lifetime benefit to the corporation. As an example, ideas for McDonald's Big Mac, Filet-O-Fish, and Egg McMuffin sandwiches are all reported to have originated from ideas generated by franchisees.

Motivation and Cooperation

Franchisees are motivated and have vested personal interest in the success of the operation which may be nonexistent in a company-employed manager. The self-direction and motivation of franchisees have led to the success of many franchises. Franchisees are known to the community and may receive cooperation and respect more easily than a company manager. The collective motivation and cooperative power of the franchisees behind the franchisors provide an extra clout in many business and regulatory matters.

Some corporations have franchisee advisory boards which provide regional and national forums for the exchange of ideas between the company and the franchisees. This interaction has positive impact on the business health of a franchise system. Together they create a check and balance system that enables the corporate functional support groups to keep a proper perspective on the business.

Disadvantages to the Franchisor

As with franchisees, there are certain disadvantages of franchising to the franchisor. Most of the disadvantages may be traced to the types of relationships between the franchisors and the franchisees.

Lack of Freedom

Lack of Freedom on the part of franchisors is one of the major disadvantages of franchising. There is no direct control over the units by the franchisors, which makes it difficult to make changes in policies and procedures. Some legal problems and suits by franchisees may hinder, delay, or adversely affect the growth and development of the franchise system. Also, franchisee advisory committees and their groups may become strong enough to interfere in the free operation of a franchise system. It might become difficult for a franchisor to modify

product or processes without the cooperation of the franchisees. Franchisees may not be willing to implement a change which may involve their time, effort and capital, although that change may be beneficial for the corporation on a long-term basis. Often franchisees are interested in the immediate future and a quick return on their investment. Uncooperative franchisees can become a continuous source of problems.

Franchisees' Financial Situation

Franchisees' financial status, which is not under the control of the franchisors, may have an impact on a franchise system. Franchisees, particularly those who own multiple units, may declare bankruptcy, which may jeopardize the operations and overall profitability of the franchisor's corporation. Franchisees also may decide to diversify their investment and spread out so thin that the functional aspects of the units are adversely affected.

Franchisee Recruitment, Selection, and Retention

Franchisee recruitment and selection can become a difficult and time-consuming task, and franchisors must be extremely careful in their selection. It is hard to come up with a profile of a successful franchisee. The glamour of franchising may attract absentee investors who are not interested in the operational aspects of a franchise. Some may use franchising as a tax

shelter. Many lack the motivation or experience needed to be successful in a franchise restaurant business. Some prospective franchisees do not realize the time, work, responsibility, and risks involved in franchising. Such franchisees, if allowed into a system, can become an ongoing source of problems. Franchising is a long-term contract binding both franchisors and franchisees. Some franchisees lose interest after recovering their initial investment, or due to the monotony of activities. Their loss of interest may adversely affect the performance and profitability of the franchise system. Selecting franchisees is like selecting and keeping good employees; while it may be difficult to recruit them, **franchisee retainment** is an equally difficult problem. Constant effort must be directed toward franchisee recruitment selection, and retention.

Communication

Many franchisor-franchisee relationship problems can be traced to communication or its lack. One common problem stems from the misunderstanding of the quality standards or the reasoning behind those standards. Franchisees may not appreciate the methods used to maintain those standards or the inspection procedures used by the franchisors.

Franchisees may also develop a sense of independence and not wish to take advice. They may feel that they are better qualified than staff at the corporate offices. Contract language and other communications may be misinterpreted, resulting in a lack of cooperation from the franchisees. There may be personality differences between the franchisor's regional staff and the franchisees.

Franchisees may be reluctant to disclose their gross sales, on which the royalty fees are based, or may not report those figures accurately.

Noncooperation from franchisees may require policing or may result in long legal battles, with adverse effects on an otherwise healthy business.

As was the case for franchisees, all franchisor advantages and disadvantages may not be present in a particular system. It is generally accepted that the advantages far outweigh the disadvantages both from

the franchisee's and the franchisor's point of view.

Summary

Franchising is an exciting opportunity for both franchisee and franchisor. To be successful, there should be a symbiotic relationship between franchisee and franchisor. Advantages to the franchisee in-

RESTAURANT STUDY—RAX RESTAURANTS, INC.

Building on their proven heritage of roast beef and salads, Rax Restaurants, Inc., claims to continue to appeal to contemporary tastes with the addition of specialty sandwiches such as the Philly Melt, Grilled Chicken sandwich, and a variety of other popular menu items. Being able to respond quickly to the needs of the consumer has been described as a vital part of the RAX formula for success to date.

Rax Restaurants, Inc., has been franchising since 1978. Rax is more than fast food. A Rax Restaurant is a place to go for a good meal, not just a place to stop for a quick bite. Every aspect of the Rax operation—from the layout of the restaurants to its unique specialty sandwiches—evokes an appreciation of quality. Their specialty sandwiches include the Turkey Bacon Club and Beef Bacon and Cheddar that convey value beyond what's usually expected of "fast food." Their approach to dining claims to have appeal to all demographic groups, and to be one that satisfies the tastes and lifestyles of today's consumers.

Quoting from a publication in the franchising package, the following reasons were given as to why Rax is different:

▶ **A Company that Thrives on Changing Tastes**—By continually adapting to meet changing consumer tastes, RAX is positioned for outstanding growth in the decade ahead. Salads were introduced as consumers became more quality-conscious in their eating. And by emphasizing specialty sandwiches, RAX is positioned to capitalize on the fastest-growing segment in the food industry today, while remaining alert to the preferences of tomorrow.

▶ **New Leadership in Corporate Management**—Starting at the top, the new corporate management at RAX is committed to the growth of their franchising system.

▶ **Partnership for Progress**—Through an innovative program, RAX gives franchisees a financial edge during the critical start-up period. Whereas the industry standard for royalties is 4% of annual sales, RAX's Franchisee Partnership Program offers new franchisees a graduated royalty schedule—1% of sales the first year, increasing just 1% each year through the fourth. That means more capital available to reinvest into the restaurant

▶ **Reduced Investment Costs**—The investment costs of starting up a RAX franchise have been substantially reduced through redefined building and operational efficiencies.

▶ **A Company Positioned for Growth in the 1990s**—Varied menu and emphasis on high-quality food meet the discriminating tastes, preference for quality and eating ambience.

Rax Restaurants provide a diversified menu, nutritious food, and a comfortable dining environment. Rax owns, operates, develops and franchises more than 490 fast food restaurants in 29 states and Canada.

clude: involvement in an established concept; provision of tools for success; availability of technical and managerial assistance; use of quality control standards; minimum risk involvement; relatively low operating capital; access to credit; possibility of performance comparison with other units within the system; benefits from franchisor's research and development; professional help in advertisement and promotion; and other opportunities. Disadvantages include unfulfilled expectations; lack of freedom; advertisement and promotion fees; and inadequate services provided. Advantages and disadvantages to franchisors are also outlined in this chapter. Advantages far outweigh the disadvantages to both franchisees and franchisors.

RESTAURANT STUDY—BURGER KING CORPORATION

Burger King Corporation was founded in 1954 in Miami, Florida, by James McLamore and David Edgerton. McLamore and Edgerton, both of whom had extensive experience in the restaurant business before starting their joint venture, believed in the simple concept of providing the customer with reasonably priced quality food, served quickly, in attractive, clean surroundings.

Since its Florida beginnings more than 35 years ago, when a Burger King® hamburger cost $.18 and a WHOPPER® sandwich cost $.37, Burger King Corporation has established restaurants around the world—from Australia to the Bahamas, and from Venezuela to Hong Kong. By 1967, when the company was acquired by the Minneapolis-based Pillsbury Company, 8,000 employees were working in 274 different restaurant locations. Only 20 years later, Burger King® employees number approximately 270,000, in more than 6,200 locations worldwide.

The success and size of Burger King is claimed to be the result of a tradition of leadership within the fast-food industry in such areas as product development, restaurant operation, decor, service, and advertising. According to Burger King, "Just as the WHOPPER® sandwich was an immediate hit when it was introduced in 1957, the company's products—"finger foods" such as CHICKEN TENDERS™ and French Toast sticks—are providing the quality and convenience sought by today's consumers. Still, the WHOPPER® sandwich, one of the best-known hamburger sandwiches in the world, remains a perennial favorite. More than 700 million Whopper® sandwiches are sold annually."

One of the factors that has helped to increase the company's expansion and growth has been the sale of restaurant franchises. By 1961, McLamore and Edgerton had acquired national franchise rights to the company, which was then operating 45 restaurants throughout Florida and the Southeast.

With the expansion of both company-owned and franchise locations, there was a need for providing training. Whopper College, now known as Burger King University, was established in Miami in 1964 to meet this need.

Restaurant decor has traditionally been significant in establishing Burger King image to its consumers. Burger King was the first fast-food chain to introduce dining rooms, allowing customers a chance to eat inside. Drive-thru service was introduced in 1975.

Burger King experienced several milestones in 1985. For the first time, average sales passed the $1 million mark, and a European center to service overseas company and franchise employees was opened. Ground was also broken in that year for a new corporate complex.

In December 1988, The Pillsbury Company and its subsidiaries, including Burger King Corporation, were acquired by Grand Metropolitan PLC for $5.79 billion. The company remains headquartered in Miami. Grand Metropolitan has 5,200 owned or franchised pubs and restaurants in the United Kingdom.

Milestones

1954 James W. McLamore and David Edgerton co-founded Burger King of Miami, Inc., which becomes Burger King Corporation in 1972. McLamore and Edgerton's first restaurant located at 3090 NW 36th Street, Miami, Florida, sells 18-cent broiled hamburgers and 18-cent milkshakes.

1957 WHOPPER® sandwich introduced . . . appears on the menu for 37 cents.

1961 McLamore and Edgerton acquire national and international franchising rights.

1964 "Whopper College," now known as Burger King University, established to provide restaurant managers with technical operational knowledge. Burger King goes international . . . two restaurants open in Puerto Rico.

1967 The Pillsbury Company acquires Burger King as a subsidiary for $18 million.

1975 First European Burger® restaurant opens in Madrid, Spain.

1977 2000th Burger King® restaurant opens in Hawaii, putting locations in all 50 states.

1978 Burger King University established as the company's international training center.

1982 Burger King introduces Bacon Double Cheeseburger.

1983 Salad Bar debuts nationally. First on-campus Burger King opens at Northeastern University, Boston, Massachusetts. First mobile restaurant unit, the "Burger Bus" opened by Ohio franchisee.

1984 "Image '87," interior restaurant design featuring upscale, contemporary interiors is unveiled at International Franchise Convention in Reno, Nevada.

1985 Breakfast debuts nationally with the CROISSAN'WICH® as the key product. Self-serve drinks introduced.

1986 A record 546 new restaurants open worldwide. CHICKEN TENDERS™ debut as one of most successful new products in Burger King history. New breakfast product French Toast Sticks, introduced nationally.

1988 Grand Metropolitan PLC acquires the Pillsbury Company and its subsidiaries for $5.79 billion.

GOING GLOBAL

Frank Go and Julia Christensen

FRANCHISING IS A particularly attractive vehicle for international expansion because it requires substantially less capital than ownership. This article discusses the ins and outs of international franchising, including types of franchise arrangements, timing issues, location considerations, and common pitfalls. The information presented is drawn primarily from the experiences of hotel and restaurant firms that have ventured into the international arena and from a study prepared recently for the International Franchise Association (IFA).

Growth Franchise-Style

Franchising provides the means for firms with limited resources and firms whose resources are directed elsewhere to expand through one of two common arrangements, the trade-name franchise or the business-format franchise. The latter provides access not only to the firm's products or trade name but also to its business plans and corporate support services, including administration, marketing, advertising, and training.

In the U.S., franchised restaurants, hotels, and motels rank among the top ten categories of business-format franchises. In 1985, franchised restaurants, hotels and campgrounds accounted for an estimated $63.5 billion in sales, and by 1990, sales in this category are projected to reach $108.6 billion.

In the restaurant industry, most international franchises are concentrated in the hamburger and chicken segments (see Exhibit 1), but other segments have ventured out successfully. For example, when Ken Gilbert, a U.S. citizen living in Tokyo, joined forces with Nissan in arranging a Taco Time master license for Japan, it was with the understanding that he would open 100 units over the succeeding five years. J. Higby's Yogurt Shoppes seized an opportunity for even greater expansion when it signed a master-license agreement with Japanese investors for the development of 2,000 units over five years.

Most U.S.-based international chains have expanded into other countries through one or more of the following traditional franchising methods:

1. *Master License.* The firm grants a license to an individual or firm in the target territory. The licensee then operates all outlets under its ownership and control, sub-franchises within the territory, or adopts some combination of these strategies.
2. *Direct License.* The franchisor firm grants a license to the operating franchisee and provides direct backup and support, sometimes through the presence of firm representatives in the target territory.
3. *Branch or Subsidiary Operation.* The firm establishes a direct presence in the area by setting up a branch or subsidiary, then it expands in the territory by granting franchises and

EXHIBIT 1. INTERNATIONAL UNITS BY RESTAURANT TYPE 1980–1985

Major activity	Number of U.S. franchise units					
	1980	1981	1982	1983	1984	1985
Chicken	1,299	1,377	1,483	1,621	1,757	1,878
Hamburger	1,887	2,099	2,362	2,811	3,117	3,251
Steak and full menu	396	425	342	470	461	271
Pizza	263	289	410	498	539	578
Mexican	24	60	52	83	90	109
Seafood	57	58	12	18	11	13
Pancake	16	15	14	12	12	15
Sandwich and other	2	2	0	3	3	7
Total	3,944	4,325	4,675	5,516	5,990	6,122

Source: NRA.

providing direct services to its franchisees.

4. *Joint Venture.* The firm establishes a joint company or partnership with a company or individual in the target territory and grants the on-site partner a license to operate its own outlets, sub-franchise, or both.

Two crucial factors often determine the choice of franchising method when a firm expands into other countries. The first is the franchisor's willingness and ability to devote the financial and human resources necessary to provide direct support to its international franchisees. The second is the availability of suitable potential licensees, franchisees, or partners in the target territory.

In North America, many franchisees are entrepreneurs with limited capital, but this is not always the case elsewhere. In Japan, for instance, franchisees are often large trading firms that want to di-versify into the service sector. This type of franchisee generally prefers to operate under a master-license agreement.

To Go or Not to Go Global

Companies participating in the IFA study noted that in addition to growth and increased revenue, international expansion affords the benefits of increased brand recognition and larger market share. International ventures, however, are not without drawbacks. Study participants listed control issues, difficulty in offering adequate support, increased costs, cultural and language differences, difficulty in assessing local needs, varying governmental regulations, and difficulty in repatriating royalties as potential problems in the global arena. Exhibit 2 shows the responses franchisors gave when asked to list the two greatest benefits of international franchising, and Exhibit 3 shows the drawbacks most frequently cited.

The key issue in the decision to venture into the international market, then, is the extent to which your company will experience benefits or the drawbacks associated with international expansion. The franchisors participating in the study provided a list of factors that any company weighing the decision to go global should examine.

Timing

International franchising has mirrored the overall shift to global retailing and marketing in the 1980s. Of the companies who have already taken the plunge, over half launched their first international unit after 1980, and nearly 70 percent said that if they could do it again, they would choose the same timing.

However, not all international firms made a conscious decision to expand on the basis of the global business cli-

Exhibit 2. Benefits of International Expansion

Benefit	Times Cited
Additional growth or expansion	100
Added revenues or profits, improved ROI, or other direct financial gain	99
Larger market, more market penetration, more market share	60
International identity, greater name recognition	37
Less competition	21
Untapped potential	18
Added exposure (in general)	18
Increased service for U. S. & foreign customers	10
Other categories of benefits	52
No benefits	28

Note: Participating franchisors could provide a maximum of two answers. The number of franchisors responding was 354.
Source: Walker, International Franchise Association study.

Exhibit 3. Drawbacks and Deterrents of International Franchising

Drawback or deterrent	Times Cited
Lack of control or accountability	131
Difficulty of supporting or servicing franchisees, operations challenges	53
Cost or expense	50
Distance, time differences	37
Culture or language differences, difficulty in judging local needs	35
Government regulations, laws, difficulty in repatriating royalties	32
Quality control	22
Logistics, supply problems or costs	20
Resource drain, spread too thin	15
Time needed to develop or implement a plan	13
Increased risks or uncertainties	12
Complications or trouble (in general)	11
Adapting product or marketing to new markets	10
Other categories of drawbacks	58
No drawbacks	7

Note: Participating franchisors could provide a maximum of two answers. The number of respondents was 369.
Source: Walker, International Franchise Association study.

Exhibit 4. Reason for Choosing Location of First International Franchise

Reason	No. of U.S. franchisors
First or only inquiry, contact from prospective franchisee	59
Proximity to U.S.	37
Similarities to U.S. (general)	12
No language barrier	12
Qualified prospective franchisee	11
Favorable demographics or market	9
Similar culture, lifestyle, or market	9
Have contacts there	6
Similar business conditions	5
Miscellaneous	12

Source: Walker, International Franchise Association study.

mate. In some instances, the question of timing was actually a question of whether to seize an opportunity when it was offered. Terry Rhoton, vice president of Franchise Sales and Technical Services for Popeye's Famous Fried Chicken, told *NRA News:*

We were approached by food-service operators from Singapore and Malaysia, who expressed an interest in bringing the Popeye's concept to their countries. They were convinced that a market existed for our product. At that time, our restaurants were located in 35 states, and we wanted to concentrate on more development here. But the prime lending rate in the U.S. was 20 percent, while the rate in Malaysia was 8.5 percent, so the company made the decision to expand internationally. Since then, Popeye's has continued its international expansion to a total of 104 units overseas and in Canada.

Whether the timing of a company's expansion was related to a corporate timetable, international business trends, or the availability of an attractive opportunity, companies that succeeded in establishing themselves in the international arena were those that took their domestic strength into consideration when making the decision. A common response among the study participants whose companies had not entered the international arena was that their company was too young and would need to expand more domestically before looking at international growth.

The Launching Pad

The international franchisors in Walker's study indicated that proximity to the U.S. and common language were important factors in choosing a target country. Canada was the launch country

for 57.1 percent of the international franchisors studied, and 81.4 percent currently have units in Canada.

However, nearly half of the participating international companies did not choose a target country—a target country chose them. As Exhibit 4 shows, a contact initiated by a prospective franchisee was the most frequently cited reason for choosing the company's first international site. Many franchisors are approached directly by international investors who have conducted market studies and have already arranged financial backing, as was the case with Taco Time, Higby's, and Popeye's.

Suitable Market

The international franchisors named political stability and the existence of a substantial middle class as the most important factors in predicting whether their product

Factor	Mean
Political stability	3.8
Substantial-size middle class	3.8
High level of economic growth	3.6
Substantial disposable income	3.5
Considerable urbanization	3.4
High level of population growth	3.1
High levels of education	2.9
Substantial consumer mobility	2.8
Substantial proportion of women working outside the home	2.4
Large number of small businesses	2.3
High level of auto ownership	2.1
Widespread use of English	2.1
Relatively short workweeks	1.2

Note: For each factor, respondents assigned a value from 0 to 5, with 5 indicating the most importance and 0 the least importance. The number of respondents per factor ranged from 380 to 389. Factors are ranked by means in descending order.
Source: Walker, International Franchise Association study.

would be acceptable in an international site (see Exhibit 5). Other related factors that the franchisors cited included a high level of economic grow substantial disposable income, and considerable urbanization. Since Japan fulfills these criteria, it is an attractive site for international expansion. Kentucky Fried Chicken (KFC), for example, has been expanding in Japan since 1970 through a joint-venture partnership with Mitsubishi Corporation. KFC-Japan has 758 units, about two-thirds of them franchised, and they have been outperforming other units in the worldwide KFC system.

Making the Move

If your operation is domestically strong and you are interested in moving into the international arena, the ideal situation is to enter into partnership with a franchisee who has approached you with a sound proposal based on positive market studies and established financing.

If you have not been contacted by a suitable franchisee, you should consider such recruitment activities as contacting existing franchisees, advertising in periodicals, giving seminars and presentations, and exhibiting at trade shows. In addition, you might consider using the services of

a franchise-support organization or government-supported associations that offer country-specific information and programs. For example, Fran Corp's "Franchise Japan" program makes arrangements for U.S. franchisors interested in making presentations to interested Japanese investors. The Japanese External Trade Organization (JETRO), which has offices in North America, promotes bilateral trade by offering free information regarding markets and competition and by sponsoring trade shows. Link Consulting of New York holds a database of 14,500 Japanese investors who are interested in purchasing franchises. Link also supplies information on regulatory constraints and provides assistance with market studies, finding suppliers, and acquiring real estate.

Expansion, McD's Style

George Cohon, president and CEO of McDonald's Restaurants of Canada, demonstrated a creative approach to finding international franchisees by contacting Soviet officials during the 1976 Montreal Olympics concerning franchising. After more than a decade of continuing negotiations, Cohon is exporting the Golden Arches to the Soviet Union under a joint-venture agreement with the foodservice administration of the Moscow City Council. Under the agreement, 20 McDonald's units and a food processing and distribution center will be operating in the city of Moscow as of 1989. Most products will be obtained from within the Soviet Union, and the staff members will be primarily Soviet residents, some of whom will receive training at Hamburger University in the U.S.

This Soviet venture is part of McDonald's Corporation's accelerated international development, stimulated by the outstanding performance of the fast-food giant's international units. By 1987, international sales for McDonald's represented over a quarter of system-wide sales, and international restaurants' unit averages and gross sales volumes have consistently exceeded those of their domestic counterparts.

New Game, New Rules

Although the opportunities for growth and increased market share are considerable in the international marketplace, global expansion is not without its pitfalls. A variety of problems rarely experienced by domestic operators can arise due to political and legal hurdles and different customs and tastes encountered in international sites. The key to top performance in the international arena lies in gauging which domestic strategies should be transferred directly to foreign markets, which strategies should be modified for export, and which should not be used at all.

In some cases, it might be necessary to modify your franchise product. You might have to change your facility design, your traditional arrangement with suppliers, your royalty terms, or, in response to local customs or tastes, even the basic product itself.

Ensuring Supply

International restaurant franchisors cite the difficulty of sustaining adequate foodsupply channels as a substantial issue in some markets. Supply problems include variations in quality, consistency, availability, and cost. To gain some control over these variables, many firms include an on-site supplier or producer in their joint-venture agreements, offering that partner a substantial ownership share in exchange for a guaranteed supply of an essential product. In J. Higby's Japa-

nese franchise venture for instance, the Meiji Dairy of Japan is a partner and furnishes the ingredients for the company's frozen yogurt.

The central issue during the 18 months of negotiations that preceded the opening of KFC's first unit in Beijing, China, was the question of supply. China's restrictions on the outflow of foreign exchange required that KFC purchase most of its supplies from within China. The eventual agreement included a 12-percent ownership stake for the Beijing Corporation of Animal Production, Processing, Industry, and Commerce, which arranged with a local farm to guarantee supply of the 700 to 800 chickens per day needed for the Beijing unit. KFC approved this arrangement on the condition that poultry experts from the corporate office would be allowed to work with the local farm for several months to address technological and sanitation concerns.

The International Menu

Menu changes implemented to satisfy international consumers have ranged from such simple alterations as adding new flavors to major changes in basic ingredients. J. Higby's Japanese menu includes two new yogurt flavors—green tea and litchi nut. In Japan, Taco Time offers fewer bean-based products. The company has discovered that smaller portions, attractively presented, appeal to its Japanese customers.

Pizza Time Theatre has made major modifications in its menu in Malaysia and the Middle East due to nonacceptance of pork and dairy products in those regions, and the Swensen's ice cream served in Saudi Arabia is made with a vegetable substitute instead of cream. Popeye's has adjusted its chicken-slaughtering procedures for acceptance in Malaysia.

New Look

High real-estate costs have affected Taco Time's and J. Higby's look in Japan. Both companies have had to redesign their facilities to use more limited space efficiently. In response to the high cost of Japanese real estate, J. Higby's also purchased 100 English-style double-decker buses and converted them into 50-seat mobile restaurants. Adapting their concept to vertical rather than horizontal accommodations presented a design challenge for Pizza Time Theatre. KFC was faced with the same challenge in Beijing, where the Colonel's special recipe is dispensed in a three-story building with seating for over 500 customers and a walk-up, take-out window to serve Beijing's heavy pedestrian traffic.

Teaching the Technique

To ensure that the international product resembles the franchisor's domestic product apart from conscious modifications for a specific market, onsite managers and employees must learn the franchisor's production techniques. Some U.S. fran-

chisors bring their franchisees to the United States to undergo training. McDonald's brings key people to Hamburger University in Illinois, although overseas offices have been established to provide local support. Swensen's has a three-week, U.S.-based training course; Popeye's, a 16-week course; and Burger King requires franchisees to attend a 350-hour course in Florida.

To prepare for the Beijing unit's opening, KFC sent the unit's two assistant managers to Singapore for eight weeks of training. The line workers were prepared with six weeks of in-house training, which included slide presentations, videos, hands-on training, and a written examination.

Although the companies described appear to have dealt successfully with the obstacles presented by international franchising, other companies are not yet convinced that the returns are worth the complications. For instance, an international fast-food chain considering a Shanghai location recently decided not to expand into China due to inconsistency in the quality of local beef, the 360-percent import duty on kitchen equipment, and the excessive rents charged specifically to foreign companies.

The Elements of Success

The franchisors participating in the IFA's study rated the importance of 20 separate factors in achieving success in the international arena. The ratings are shown in Exhibit

6. According to the study respondents, the on-site franchisee is the most crucial element in international expansion. The top four factors cited were supporting, recruiting, training, and controlling the activities of the international partner.

The list reflects many of the complications that challenge international companies, including the need to work with different laws, regulations, tax structures, and currencies; the demands on company resources to provide adequate on-site support; and the need to make alterations in the original concept to accommodate local tastes and customs and to work around local conditions.

Over a third of the study participants said that they had to modify their marketing strategy to succeed in international markets. Specific modifications the franchisors listed were alterations in their promotion approach, pricing strategies, site-location criteria, building design, company or brand name, colors or logo, and the product itself.

The franchisors that have faced and overcome the hurdles inherent in international expansion are reporting unit sales and growth rates unparalleled at home. The figures are compelling, and the question for many domestic franchisors has become not "should I go global?" but rather "where, when, and how?" If you can interest a promising on-site franchisee in your product, your proposed partner may help to answer those questions.

EXHIBIT 6. FACTORS NECESSARY TO ESTABLISH AND OPERATE INTERNATIONAL FRANCHISES

Factor	Mean
Supporting franchisees outside U.S.	4.2
Recruiting enough qualified franchisees	4.1
Training franchisees for units outside U.S.	4.1
Controlling franchisees outside U.S.	4.1
Maintaining adequate quality controls	4.0
Dealing with trademark and copyright regulations	3.9
Committing sufficient managerial resources from headquarters to international expansion	3.9
Satisfying governmental and legal restrictions	3.8
Analyzing potential of different markets	3.7
Arranging sufficient local financing	3.6
Making the product acceptable to foreign consumers	3.6
Repatriating royalties	3.6
Overcoming language and cultural barriers	3.5
Arranging supply channels for inventory and other materials	3.5
Dealing with tax structures and import duties in host countries	3.4
Obtaining enough suitable locations	3.3
Adapting promotional approaches to host countries	3.3
Coping with foreign-currency uncertainties	3.1
Redesigning franchise package to make it salable outside U. S.	3.0
Beating competitors in host countries	2.8

Note: For each factor, respondents assigned a value from 0 to 5 with 5 indicating the highest significance and 0 the lowest significance. The number of respondents per factor ranged from 384 to 395. Factors are ranked by mean score in descending order.
Source: Walker, International Franchise Association study.

PROJECT 1

Select one hospitality franchise for study and obtain all information about that franchise by contacting the headquarters office. This will be your franchise for study for the entire semester and you will be a spokesperson for the franchise. As the topics are covered in class you will complete the assigned aspect in respect to the franchise you have selected. All franchises selected will be discussed during the first week of classes and a final approval is needed before proceeding. The first few minutes of every class will be devoted to a discussion of the franchises that are in the news during that period of time. Collect all information and include in your final report. The following aspects should be studied and included in your report. A final presentation is expected at the end of the semester:

a. Classify your franchise establishment into segment (e.g., for restaurants: hamburger, chicken, pizza, etc.) and describe the current trend of that segment of the industry.

b. Outline the history of the franchise and how the concept was developed.

c. Explore in detail the history of the trademark and record all changes. Attach a copy of the current trademark.

d. List all special features of the franchise.

e. Make a list of all services provided by your franchise (such as site selection, marketing, training, operations, business opening assistance, etc.)

f. Financial status of the franchise. Include stock prices for the semester in a graph format if it is a public company.

g. A thorough analysis of UFOC and franchise package received from the corporation.

h. A detailed description of the financial requirement for acquiring the franchise.

i. Describe the franchisee selection process. Comment on the franchisor/franchisee relationship for your franchise.

j. International franchising and growth of franchises (either for existing or for planned expansion).

k. Number of units: company owned vs. franchised. Comment on the ratio and the trends.

Include all this information in detail. Use AP style guide for writing the final report. Attach all information obtained from the franchise. Attach photos, news clippings, UFOC, reports and other information pertinent to the franchise. Submit on the last day of class.

PROJECT 2

Select five hospitality franchises for study and obtain all information about training in that franchise operation. Contact franchisors or use secondary data for this project. Include all information pertaining to training with special emphasis on the following aspects:

1. Goals and objectives of training

2. Length of training

3. Location of training and duration at each location (units vs. headquarters)

4. Type of training (e.g., skills, knowledge, attitude, etc.)

5. Cost of training (to franchisees/franchisors)

6. Description of trainees (e.g., owner, manager, supervisor, etc.)

7. Qualifications of trainers

8. Materials used in training

9. Specialized training media used for training

10. Evaluation of training

Include all this information in detail. Use AP style guide for writing the final report. Attach all information obtained from the franchisor.

18

SERVICE MANAGEMENT

Service
Suzanne K. Murrmann and Cheri Becker Suttle

Production-Line Approach to Service
Theodore Levitt

Project 1

Project 2

SERVICE

Suzanne K. Murrmann and Cheri Becker Suttle

AT ITS MOST BASIC LEVEL, service is defined as "the act of helpful activity." This definition, however, is somewhat ambiguous. Helpful activity takes many forms and even similar services can be implemented at different levels of intensity. Service is an elusive concept; the *Random House Unabridged Dictionary of the English Language* provides thirty-three separate definitions of service. It is no wonder that communication difficulties arise in discussions of what service is and what service should be. Contemporary views on service are in a state of flux. The only clear consensus on this issue is that service standards are on the decline. Before managers of hospitality firms or other service organizations can hope to improve the public perception of service and service quality, a full understanding of the evolution of the service concept and its multiple components is in order.

Since the 1970s the concept of service and its relative importance as a management concern has undergone dramatic changes. The traditional view of service organizations and service occupations as providing marginal contributions to the general economic well-being of society no longer holds. Today service industries generate more than 71 percent of the gross national product (GNP) in industrialized nations. In the 1980s the growth in service occupations accounted for approximately 93 percent of all new jobs created (Quinn 1988). Available data indicate such trends will continue into the next century; as a result services management has become a primary issue for both the traditional service organization and the general economy. The increased attention to services and service occupations has broadened the traditional definition of service. Today service is viewed as a complex multidimensional concept. Recognizing the various elements involved in producing and delivering satisfying service experiences to customers is the first step in creating a successful service organization.

In the hospitality industry the concept of service has traditionally been confined to those duties performed by individuals who occupy positions as waitstaff or maids. To a large degree such definitions are still foremost in the minds of hospitality executives. This narrow focus limits the management perspective and the likelihood of successful service delivery in today's competitive service-based economy. An understanding of the broader perspective on services and the management of services requires a change in the primary orientation of the service manager; an orientation away from the view of service as an occupation (a kind of work) toward a perspective of service as a technology (a way work is done). As a technology, service work and service output can be differentiated from traditional manufacturing work and manufacturing products based on five major characteristics: intangibility, heterogeneity, inseparability, perishability, and customer participation. Each of these characteristics has serious implications for understanding and effectively managing both service organizations and service employees.

Service Characteristics

Intangibility

Because services include performances as well as products, much of the product-service mix cannot be seen, tasted, or felt in the same concrete manner that can be applied to pure products. Service is experienced by the customer psychologically as well as physically. The intangible nature of the service experience is an elusive element. Intangibility is the most difficult component of the service experience to measure. Unlike manufacturing output where the number of units per hour can be easily counted and the appearance of defects can be observed, the intangible elements of the service experience may be impossible to count. Because of the psychological nature of the service experience, the customer's perception plays a significant role in determining whether a service meets acceptable standards. Since there is often a discrepancy between managerial perception and customer perception, the most effective measurement tool available for service managers is to stay in touch with the customer on a regular basis. Customer feedback provides the only real source for evaluating the elusive, psychological elements of the service experience. Input from customers may be solicited through face-to-face exchanges or through the use of brief questionnaires or comment cards. The appropriate choice will be determined by the type of service being provided and the size of the operation.

Although measurement has traditionally been viewed as the primary problem associated with service intangibility, a second problem of sizeable proportion is related to the use of marketing strategies and advertising copy that make unrealistic promises regarding the intangible benefits of the service experience. In product marketing the use of psychological appeals that promise increased sex appeal as a by-product to using a certain deodorant or a certain toothpaste has become fairly commonplace. Yet it is doubtful that such promises are taken too seriously by most consumers. Such is not the case in services where the experience itself may be paramount. In many services the promise of fun, romance, and excitement may be taken quite literally. Advertising promotions that focus on fulfilling intangible elements based upon the consumer's psychological needs may build up unrealistic expectations—expectations over which the service organization has no control. A promotional strategy that focuses on the concrete benefits associated with the service experience is a safer alternative for any service firm hoping to maximize customer satisfaction and long-term success.

Heterogeneity

Heterogeneity is concerned with the fact that no two service experiences are ever exactly alike. This absence of uniformity is unavoidable since service relies heavily on the input of people and people are unique individuals with different life experiences, different attitudes, and different personalities. Heterogeneity is experienced both at the individual level (in the exchange between customers and service employees) and also at the unit level. In this latter case differences associated with geographic location or individual leadership style may give one chain property a distinction that sets it apart from other affiliates of the same corporation. Although heterogeneity is not always negative, it is unpredictable and as a result it undermines the organization's ability to deliver a consistent service experience to the customer. Heterogeneity can never be completely controlled yet options do exist that minimize any negative impact it might create.

Standardized employee training with intermittent follow-up offers the most basic recourse to combat inconsistency in service production and service delivery. Training is appropriate regardless of the level of service or the type of service organization. The more intense or complex the level of service, the greater the training investment required.

When the type of service being provided is highly standardized, automation provides a solution because it reduces the organization's reliance on people. In large measure the success experienced by McDonald's can be attributed to a systems planning approach that substituted equipment for people and used hard technology to guarantee total product uniformity (Levitt 1972). Because the McDonald's approach greatly reduced the amount of contact time required for service, the influence of employee heterogeneity was also reduced. More recently the widespread success of automatic teller machines in banking has led to the adoption of similar machines in lodging firms where they provide automated check-in and checkout systems to expedite the transaction and eliminate the direct labor costs associated with these procedures.

Highly customized services are really not amenable to automation or rigid standardization policies. Organizations providing such services cannot always predict what kind of special service embellishments a customer might request. As a result it is impossible to provide employees with programmed responses appropriate for every possible situation they might encounter. For such firms the development of a service-oriented organizational climate is one strategy an operation can use to help overcome heterogeneity in employee behavior (Schneider 1980). Orientation of employees can be used to communicate important organizational values related to ex-

pected service standards. Over time as employees are subjected to the socialization process within the organization, these values become ingrained as part of the individual's own value system. Once a value preference has been established, employee behavior is generally more predictable and more likely to meet the standards desired by the organization (Mills et al. 1987).

Inseparability

Because services are first sold, then produced and consumed, the customer and the service provider are often engaged in close contact. In services management this close link between production and consumption, and service customer and service provider, is termed "inseparability." Inseparability creates a situation quite different from that encountered by the traditional manufacturing firm. In the traditional model products are manufactured and assembled in a factory, then sent to retail outlets for customer distribution. In service organizations, particularly those involved in producing and delivering hospitality, it is appropriate to visualize the customer as actually entering the factory and placing an order before the production process begins, then waiting around while the production takes place, and finally consuming the product before leaving the factory premises. The total service experience begins when the customer enters the facility and is not complete until the customer leaves. As a result the

customer's evaluation of the service experience extends to factors such as decor and atmosphere, timeliness of service delivery, and any sounds, smells, or accompanying activity that may occur at any time the customer is on the premises. Special attention to these seemingly secondary elements in the product service mix is extremely important. Controlling these elements provides the service manager with an opportunity to make the service experience more tangible because these elements are experienced through the customer's sensory perceptions. When these elements are selected so that they fit together and create a cohesive organizational image, they reduce the impact of inconsistencies associated with uncontrollable heterogeneity.

Perishability

Perishability refers to the temporal nature of the service product, which can not be inventoried. Hotel rooms not occupied on Monday evening cannot be stored for later use. The same is true of seats on airlines and trains or in theaters and restaurants. For many service providers the effects of perishability are further exaggerated by fluctuating patterns of customer demand. In restaurant operations business peaks at normal mealtimes and dwindles away by mid-afternoon. City hotels may be filled to capacity during midweek when business travelers abound but virtually deserted during the weekend. Demand for tax services, beach resorts, and many types of transportation varies dramatically depending upon the season. Although total control over consumer demand is beyond the grasp of any service manager, strategies for leveling, or smoothing out, extreme fluctuations in demand can be effective.

Discounting is commonly used by service organizations to increase customer demand in nonpeak periods. For years AT&T has varied rates for telephone services to divert customer usage into less busy periods, seasonally affected resorts and transportation systems have commonly offered special off-season rates, and restaurants have used discounting by implementing early bird specials. The fast-food industry met the challenge of building demand in low use periods by expanding services to include breakfast. When fluctuations in consumer demand cannot be managed through smoothing strategies, forecasting provides an alternative. The forecasting of demand patterns provides information that can be used to vary employee schedules and adjust operating hours to correspond with anticipated usage.

Customer Participation

Most services require some level of customer participation. Operations such as cafeterias expect customers to perform self-service tasks. Banking organizations require that customers fill out standardized forms that expedite the service transaction. As

services become more customized the amount of information required to produce the service expected and desired by the consumer increases. As the amount of customer participation increases, the service experience becomes more difficult for the service provider to control. One alternative that allows the service organization to maintain control is to limit customer participation by restricting the number and type of customer requests the operation will accept. Fast-food operations follow such a strategy by standardizing the menu items and limiting the available choices according to the specific meal period. At higher levels of service, interactions between customers and service employees are less structured and less predictable. Customers may make unusual nonstandard requests regarding their expectations for service output. One of the most effective means to maintain control over outlandish customer requests rests in the skills of the service employee. A well-trained service employee has the confidence "to seize the initiative in customer relations—to set the pattern for the relationship" (Whyte 1948:35). The most effective service employees are trained to communicate with courtesy and confidence while simultaneously maintaining control over the service interaction. Evidence suggests that customers react positively when this approach is used (Whyte 1948).

Service Delivery Models

Although the characteristics of service make the job of categorizing service virtually impossible, numerous models have been introduced into the literature on service delivery to help the researcher and service provider identify, in a logical and complete fashion, the most important variables or factors in the process. Although no one model, in and of itself, may be a sufficient framework for providing quality service in every service exchange situation, models do help in understanding the key components of service delivery.

One such model developed by Zeithaml et al. (1990) revolves around the view that the quality of service and service success is a function of the customer's perception of met expectations. Said differently, success in providing quality services is the ability of the service organization and provider to understand the expectations of the customer and to close the important service component "gaps" within the organization for the purpose of achieving expected service. Their model, presented in Figure 1 breaks down service delivery into basic components for individual analysis and identifies the most important gaps between those components that effect the overall mesh between expected service by the consumer and the perceived service they experience. In the model, Gap 1 refers to the discrepancy between customers' service

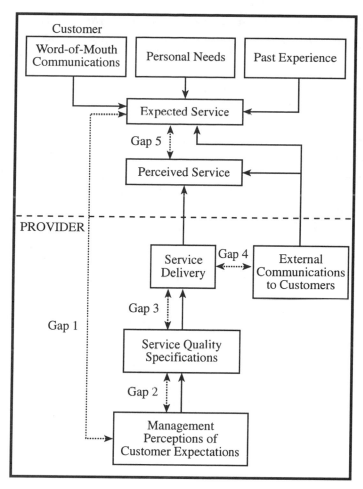

Source: From V. A. Zeithaml, A. Parasuraman, and L. L. Berry. 1990. *Delivering Quality Service: Balancing Customer Perceptions and Expectations.* New York: Free Press.

FIGURE 1. Conceptual Model of Service Quality.

expectations and management's perceptions of those expectations. Best described as "not knowing what customers expect," the gap is attributed primarily to a lack of marketing research or inadequate use of marketing research findings. Closing the gap requires increasing interaction between management and consumers through the use of focus groups, improving upward communication from contact personnel to management, or reducing the number of levels between these two groups.

The second gap identified within the model lies between management's perceptions of customer expectations and service quality specifications, that is, the setting of service quality standards. Thought to be wide in many organizations, the gap is caused primarily by an inadequate commitment to a standard of service quality, inadequate task standardization, and the absence of goal setting. Closing this second gap requires a commitment to quality service, the standardization of tasks, as far as it is feasible within the con-

fines of the service provided through the use of technology, and taking on the task of setting service-quality goals.

The highly interactive, labor intensive nature of service provision often leads to Gap 3, the service-performance gap. Key factors contributing to this gap include the traditional human resource issues of employee role ambiguity and conflict, that is, what is expected of them from both the organization and the consumer of the service they are providing. It is further influenced by poor employee job fit and poor technology job fit, inappropriate supervisory control systems, and a lack of perceived control and teamwork. Good human resource practices including training, conflict management, performance appraisals, and team-building are key management responsibilities necessary to close this gap.

Mention was made earlier to the problems encountered in the marketing of services due to its intangible nature. When promises do not match delivery, a major and often controllable gap occurs between service delivery and external communication to the customer. The key reasons for this occurrence include not only the propensity of the marketing department to over-promise what they cannot or are not delivering, but also inadequate horizontal communication among different functional groups within the organization. Closing this gap requires at the start an understanding and appreciation of the problem. This understanding is equally important in reducing all gaps identified in the model. In addition, there exists the need for opening the channels of communication between advertising and operations, sales and operations, and human resources, marketing, and operations. This can be done through providing opportunities for interaction, such as formal and informal meetings, and providing incentives to employees for engaging in such information exchange.

The gaps discussed previously can be thought of as

key ingredients in a recipe for gaining a good understanding of service quality and its determinants. By breaking down the service delivery process into its basic components, the manager can then use the model to allocate or reallocate the organization's resources in specific areas of the process. By identifying the most significant deficiencies within the organization at these four basic points the gap between expected service and actual perceived service, Gap 5, can be narrowed.

Gap theory is representative of many models that provide a framework for identifying key problem points in the service delivery process. Others are designed to take a more microperspective approach to analyzing specific problems associated with the encounter between the service provider and the customer. The customer service transaction model developed by Barrington and Olsen (1987) provides an excellent example of such models. The service transaction, presented in Figure 2, is partitioned into a three-step process, beginning with anticipation of the experience of the service and culminating in residue. Prior to the actual service experience, customers develop an anticipated expectation of the service they will purchase. Expectation is affected by a variety of factors, the sum of which can be described as their reference bank. Included in this reference bank are their perceptions of the value of the service (utility), past experience with the service (utility), motives for

purchasing the service (occasion), their present emotional state, the amount of risk they are willing to assume, and the anticipated financial cost of the service. Anticipation within the service transaction model closely resembles customer perceptions of expected services within gap theory.

Their feelings about the actual service experience, the second phase of the process, are formulated by the anticipation they carry into the encounter and its congruity or fit with the actual experience. This encounter is made up of four components: service product components, service product characteristics, service product dynamics, and the repertoire produced by the service provider, such as the wait-staff in a restaurant. Service product components are the physical items that surround the customer during this experience, such as lighting, decor, and cleanliness; sensory perceptions caused by these physical items as well as the interactions with service providers; and the psychological experience produced by such components. The encounter and its outcome are likewise products of the characteristics of service described earlier. Service product dynamics reflect the volatile nature of service provision. Although it is difficult for the customer to consciously ascertain these dynamics as a separate component of the service they are experiencing, they are manifested in otherwise good service being provided in a poor manner, primarily because of the inability of man-

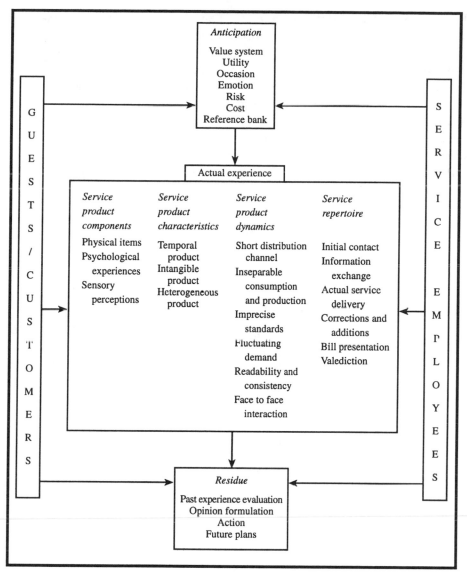

Source: From M. N. Barrington and M. D. Olsen. 1987. Concept of service in the hospitality industry. *International Journal of Hospitality Management Risk* 6(3):131–138.

FIGURE 2. Model of the Hospitality Service Transaction.

agement to anticipate or provide contingency plans for them. One example may be fluctuating demand, poorly anticipated in an organization's employee work scheduling, and culminating in extended waits for service. The fourth component of the service experience is service repertoire. The service repertoire is the framework in which service providers interface with the service consumer. The model assumes the provision of a quality service experience, and consequently, imparts consistency to the interface starting with initial contact and proceeding through to culmination of the service interaction.

Upon completion of the service experience, the final stage of the transaction is completed as the customer evaluates the total service package in relation to initial anticipation. Residue includes the use of this evaluation to formulate the customer's actions and future plans with regard to the service provided.

Such models become very useful for identifying the essential components of the service process. They can be used as a guide for directing organizational resources toward appropriate components, that is, the implementation of quality standards to control service dynamics and training directed at the service repertoire. They also provide a framework for identifying weaknesses in resource development or allocation, such as flawed marketing approaches to influencing anticipation, or lack of empowerment of service providers that can more efficiently affect positive residue.

Summary

This entry provides a basic overview of the important characteristics of services, as well as a discussion of service delivery models. Together they are useful in more clearly articulating the scope and nature of services provided by an organization. Though services differ from organization to organization, it is appropriate and essential to evaluate them in a systematic way, using the concepts discussed here.

References

Barrington, Melvin N., and Michael D. Olsen. 1987. Concept of service in the hospitality industry. *International Journal of Hospitality Management* 6(3):131–138.

Levitt, Theodore. 1972. Production-line approach to service. *Harvard Business Review.* 50(5): 41–52.

Quinn, James Brian. 1988. Technology in services: Past myths and future challenges. In *Technology in Services*, ed. B. Guiles and J. B. Quinn, pp. 16–46. Washington, D.C.: National Academy of Engineering.

Schneider, Benjamin. 1980. The service organization: Climate is crucial. *Organizational Dynamics* 9:52–65.

Whyte, William Foote. 1948. *Human Relations in the Restaurant Industry.* New York: McGraw-Hill.

Zeithaml, Valarie A., A. Parasuraman, and Leonard L. Berry. 1990. *Delivering Quality Service: Balancing Customer Perceptions and Expectations.* New York: Free Press.

PRODUCTION-LINE APPROACH TO SERVICE

Theodore Levitt

Once service "in the field" receives the same attention as products "in the factory," a lot of new opportunities become possible

THE SERVICE SECTOR OF the economy is growing in size but shrinking in quality. So say a lot of people. Purveyors of service, for their part, think that they and their problems are fundamentally different from other businesses and their problems. They feel that service is people-intensive, while the rest of the economy is capital-intensive. But these distinctions are largely spurious. There are no such things as service industries. There are only industries whose service components are greater or less than those of other industries. Everybody is in service.

Often the less there seems, the more there is. The more technologically sophisticated the generic product (e.g., cars and computers), the more dependent are its sales on the quality and availability of its accompanying customer services (e.g., display rooms, delivery, repairs and maintenance, application aids, operator training, installation advice, warranty fulfillment).

In this sense, General Motors is probably more service-intensive than manufacturing-intensive. Without its services its sales would shrivel.

Thus the service sector of the economy is not merely composed of the so-called service industries, such as banking, airlines, and maintenance. It includes the entire abundance of product-related services supplied by manufacturers and the sales-related services supplied by retailers. Yet we confuse things to our detriment by an outdated taxonomy. For example:

The First National City Bank (Citibank) is one of the biggest worldwide banks. It has about 37,000 employees, over half of whom deal directly with the public, either selling them things (mostly money and deposit services) or helping them with things they have already bought (cashing checks, taking additional deposits, writing letters of credit, opening lockboxes, managing corporate cash).

Most of the other employees work back in what is called "the factory"—a massive congeries of people, paper, and computers that processes, records, validates, and scrutinizes everything the first group has done. All the corporate taxonomists, including the U.S. Department of the Census, classify Citibank as a service company.

IBM is the biggest worldwide manufacturer of computers. It has about 270,000 employees, over half of whom deal directly with the public, either selling them things (mostly machines) or helping them with the things they have already bought (installing and repairing machines, writing computer programs, training customers). Most of the other employees work back in the factory—a massive congeries of wires, microminiature electronic components, engineers, and assemblers. All the corporate taxonomists, including the U.S. Department of the Census, classify IBM as a manufacturing company.

Something is wrong, and not just in the Bureau of the Census. The industrial world has changed more rapidly than our taxonomies. If only taxonomy were involved, the consequences of our contradictory classifications would be trivial. After all, man lives perfectly well with his contradictions: his simultaneous faith, for instance, in both God and science; his attachment to facts and logic when making important business decisions, but reliance on feelings and emotion when making far more important life decisions, like marriage.

I hope to show in this article that our contradictory notions about service may have malignant consequences. Not until we clarify the contradictions will companies begin to solve problems that now seem so intractable. In order to do so, they must think of themselves as performing manufacturing functions when it comes to their so-called "service" activities. Only then will they begin to make some significant progress in improving the quality and efficiency of service in the modern economy.

Field Versus Factory

People think of service as quite different from manufacturing. Service is presumed to be performed by individuals for other individuals, generally on a one-to-one basis. Manufacturing is presumed to be performed by machines, generally tended by large clusters of individuals whose sizes and configurations are themselves dictated by the machines' requirements. Service (whether customer service or the services of service industries) is performed "out there in the field" by distant and loosely supervised people working under highly variable, and often volatile, conditions. Manufacturing occurs "here in the factory" under highly centralized, carefully organized, tightly controlled, and elaborately engineered conditions.

People assume, and rightly so, that these differences largely explain why products produced in the factory are generally more uniform in features and quality than the services produced (e.g., life insurance policies, machine repairs) or delivered (e.g., spare parts, milk) in the field, One cannot as easily control one's agents or their performance out there in the field. Besides, different customers want different things. The result is that service and service industries, in comparison with manufacturing industries, are widely and correctly viewed as being primitive, sluggish, and inefficient.

Yet it is doubtful that things need be all that bad. Once conditions in the field get the same kind of attention that conditions inside the factory generally get, a lot of new opportunities become possible. But first management will have to revise its thinking about what service is and what it implies.

Limits of Servitude

The trouble with thinking of oneself as providing services—either in the service industries or in the customer-service sectors of manufacturing and retailing companies—is that one almost inescapably embraces ancient, pre-industrial modes of thinking. Worse still, one gets caught up in rigid attitudes that can have a profoundly paralyzing effect on even the most resolute of rationalists.

The concept of "service" evokes, from the opaque recesses of the mind, time-worn images of personal ministration and attendance. It refers generally to deeds one individual performs personally for another. It carries historical connotations of charity, gallantry, and selflessness, or of obedience, subordination, and subjugation. In these contexts, people serve because they want to (as in the priestly and political professions) or they serve because they are compelled to (as in slavery and such occupations of attendance as waiter, maid, bellboy, cleaning lady).

In the higher-status service occupations, such as in the church and the army, one customarily behaves ritualistically, not rationally. In the lower-status service occupations, one simply obeys. In neither is independent thinking presumed to be a requisite of holding a job. The most that can therefore be expected from service improvements is that, like Avis, a person will try harder. He will just exert more animal effort to do better what he is already doing.

So it was in ancient times, and so it is today. The only difference is that where ancient masters invoked the will of God or the whip of the foreman to spur performance, modern industry uses training programs and motivation sessions. We have not in all these years come very far in either our methods or our results. In short, service thinks humanistically, and that explains its failures.

Promise of Manufacturing

Now consider manufacturing. Here the orientation is toward the efficient production of results, not toward attendance on others. Relationships are strictly businesslike, devoid of invidious connotations of rank or self.

When we think about how to improve manufacturing, we seldom focus on ways to improve our personal performance of present tasks; rather, it is axiomatic that we try to find entirely new ways of performing present tasks and, better yet, of actually changing the tasks themselves. We do not think of greater exertion of our animal energies (working physically harder, as the slave), of greater expansion of our commitment (being more devout or loyal, as the priest), or of greater assertion of our dependence (being more obsequious, as the butler).

Instead, we apply the greater exertion of our minds to learn how to look at a problem differently. More particularly, we ask what kinds of tools, old or new, and what kinds of skills, processes, or-

ganizational rearrangements, incentives, controls, and audits might be enlisted to greatly improve the intended outcomes. In short, manufacturing thinks technocratically, and that explains its successes.

Manufacturing looks for solutions inside the very tasks to be done. The solution to building a low-priced automobile, for example, derives largely from the nature and composition of the automobile itself. (If the automobile were not an assembly of parts, it could not be manufactured on an assembly line.) By contrast, service looks for solutions in the *performer* of the task. This is the paralyzing legacy of our inherited attitudes: the solution to improved service is viewed as being dependent on improvements in the skills and attitudes of the performers of that service.

While it may pain and offend us to say so, thinking in humanistic rather than technocratic terms ensures that the service sector of the modern economy will be forever inefficient and that our satisfactions will be forever marginal. We see service as invariably and undeviatingly personal, as something performed by individuals directly for other individuals.

This humanistic conception of service diverts us from seeking alternatives to the use of people, especially to large, organized groups of people, it does not allow us to reach out for new solutions and new definitions. It obstructs us from redesigning the tasks themselves; from creating new tools, processes, and organiza-

tions; and, perhaps, even from eliminating the conditions that created the problems.

In sum, to improve the quality and efficiency of service, companies must apply the kind of technocratic thinking which in other fields has replaced the high-cost and erratic elegance of the artisan with the low-cost, predictable munificence of the manufacturer.

The Technocratic Hamburger

Nowhere, in the entire service sector are the possibilities of the manufacturing mode of thinking better illustrated than in fast-food franchising. Nowhere have manufacturing methods been employed more effectively to control the operation of distant and independent agents. Nowhere is "service" better.

Few of today's successful new commercial ventures have antecedents that are more humble and less glamorous than the hamburger. Yet the thriving nationwide chain of hamburger stands called "McDonald's" is a supreme example of the application of manufacturing and technological brilliance to problems that must ultimately be viewed as marketing problems. From 1961 to 1970 McDonald's sales rose from approximately $54 million to $587 million. During this remarkable ascent, the White Tower chain, whose name had theretofore been practically synonymous throughout the land with low-priced, quick-service hamburgers, practically vanished.

The explanation of McDonald's thundering success is not a purely fiscal one—i.e., the argument that it is financed by independent local entrepreneurs who bring to their operations a quality of commitment and energy not commonly found among hired workers. Nor is it a purely geographical one—i.e., the argument that each outlet draws its patronage from a relatively small geographic ring of customers, thus enabling the number of outlets easily and quickly to multiply. The relevant explanation must deal with the central question of why each separate McDonald's outlet is so predictably successful, why each is so certain to attract many repeat customers.

Entrepreneurial financing and careful site selection do help. But most important is the carefully controlled execution of each outlet's central function—the rapid delivery of a uniform, high-quality mix of prepared foods in an environment of obvious cleanliness, order, and cheerful courtesy. The systematic substitution of equipment for people, combined with the carefully planned use and positioning of technology, enables McDonald's to attract and hold patronage in proportions no predecessor or imitator has managed to duplicate. Consider the remarkable ingenuity of the system, which is worth examining in some detail:

To start with the obvious, raw hamburger patties are carefully prepacked and premeasured, which leaves neither the franchisee nor his employees any discretion as to size, quality, or raw-material consistency. This kind of attention is given to all McDonald's products. Storage and preparation space and related facilities are expressly designed for, and limited to, the predetermined mix of products. There is no space for any foods, beverages, or services that were not designed into the system at the outset. There is not even a sandwich knife or, in fact, a decent place to keep one. Thus the owner has no discretion regarding what he can sell—not because of any contractual limitations, but because of facilities limitations. And the employees have virtually no discretion regarding how to prepare and serve things.

Discretion is the enemy of order, standardization, and quality. On an automobile assembly line, for example, a worker who has discretion and latitude might possibly produce a more personalized car, but one that is highly unpredictable. The elaborate care with which an automobile is designed and an assembly line is structured and controlled is what produces quality cars at low prices, and with surprising reliability considering the sheer volume of the output. The same is true at McDonald's, which produces food under highly automated and controlled conditions.

French-Fried Automation

While in Detroit the significance of the technological process lies in production, at McDonald's it lies in marketing. A carefully planned design is built into the elaborate technology of the food-service system in such a fashion as to make it a significant marketing device. This fact is impressively illustrated by McDonald's handling of that uniquely plebeian American delicacy, french-fried potatoes.

French fries become quickly soggy and unappetizing; to be good, they must be freshly made just before serving. Like other fast-food establishments, McDonald's provides its outlets with precut, partially cooked frozen potatoes that can be quickly finished in an on-premises, deep-fry facility. The McDonald's fryer is neither so large that it produces too many fresh fries at one time (thus allowing them to become soggy) nor so small that it requires frequent and costly frying.

The fryer is emptied onto a wide, flat tray adjacent to the service counter. This location is crucial. Since the McDonald's practice is to create an impression of abundance and generosity by slightly overfilling each bag of french fries, the tray's location next to the service counter prevents the spillage from an overfilled bag from reaching the floor. Spillage creates not only danger underfoot but also an unattractive appearance that causes the employees to become accustomed to an unclean environment. Once a store is unclean in one particular, standards fall very rapidly and the store becomes unclean and the food unappetizing in general.

While McDonald's aims for an impression of abundance,

excessive overfilling can be very costly for a company that annually buys potatoes almost by the trainload. A systematic bias that puts into each bag of french fries a half ounce more than is intended can have visible effects on the company's annual earnings. Further, excessive time spent at the tray by each employee can create a cumulative service bottleneck at the counter.

McDonald's has therefore developed a special wide-mouthed scoop with a narrow funnel in its handle. The counter employee picks up the scoop and inserts the handle end into a wall clip containing the bags. One bag adheres to the handle. In a continuous movement the scoop descends into the potatoes, fills the bag to the exact proportions its designers intended, and is lifted, scoop facing the ceiling, so that the potatoes funnel through the handle into the attached bag, which is automatically disengaged from the handle by the weight of the contents. The bag comes to a steady, nonwobbling rest on its flat bottom.

Nothing can go wrong—the employee never soils his hands, the floor remains clean, dry, and safe, and the quantity is controlled. Best of all, the customer gets a visibly generous portion with great speed, the employee remains efficient and cheerful, and the general impression is one of extravagantly good service.

Mechanized Marketing

Consider the other aspects of McDonald's technological approach to marketing. The tissue paper used to wrap each hamburger is color-coded to denote the mix of condiments. Heated reservoirs hold pre-prepared hamburgers for rush demand. Frying surfaces have spatter guards to prevent soiling of the cooks' uniforms. Nothing is left to chance or the employees' discretion.

The entire system is engineered and executed according to a tight technological discipline that ensures fast, clean, reliable service in an atmosphere that gives the modestly paid employees a sense of pride and dignity. In spite of the crunch of eager customers, no employee looks or acts harassed, and therefore no harassment is communicated to the customers.

But McDonald's goes even further. Customers may be discouraged from entering if the building looks unappealing from the outside; hence considerable care goes into the design and appearance of the structure itself.

Some things, however, the architect cannot control, especially at an establishment where people generally eat in their parked cars and are likely to drop hamburger wrappings and empty beverage cartons on the ground, McDonald's has anticipated the requirement: its blacktop parking facilities are dotted like a checkerboard with numerous large, highly visible trash cans. It is impossible to ignore their purpose. Even the most indifferent customer would be struck with guilt if he simply dropped his refuse on the ground. But, just in case he drops it anyway, the larger McDonald's outlets have motorized sweepers for quick and easy cleanup.

What is important to understand about this remarkably successful organization is not only that it has created a highly sophisticated piece of technology, but also that it has done this by applying a manufacturing style of thinking to a people-intensive service situation. If machinery is to be viewed as a piece of equipment with the capability of producing a predictably standardized, customer-satisfying output while minimizing the operating discretion of its attendant, that is what a McDonald's retail outlet is. It is a machine that produces, with the help of totally unskilled machine tenders, a highly polished product. Through painstaking attention to total design and facilities planning, everything is built integrally into the machine itself, into the technology of the system. The only choice available to the attendant is to operate it exactly as the designers intended.

Tooling Up for Service

Although most people are not aware of it, there are many illustrations of manufacturing solutions to people-intensive service problems. For example:

Mutual funds substitute one sales call for many; one consultation for dozens; one piece of paper for thousands; and one reasonably informed customer choice for numerous, confused, and often poor choices.

Credit cards that are used for making bank loans substitute a single credit decision (issuing the card in the first place) for the many elaborate, costly, people-intensive activities and decisions that bank borrowing generally entails.

Supermarkets substitute fast and efficient self-service for the slow, inefficient, and often erratic clerks of the traditional service store.

In each of these examples a technological device or a manufacturing type of process has replaced what had been resolutely thought of as an irrevocably people-requiring service. Similar devices or processes can be used to modify and alleviate the customer-repelling abrasions of other people-intensive service conditions.

Consider the airlines. This industry is highly unusual. It is exceedingly capital-intensive in the creation of the facilitating product (the airplane), but it is extremely people-intensive in the delivery of the product (travel arrangements and the customer's flight experience). The possibilities for revenue production that a $20-million airplane represents are quickly vitiated by a surly or uncooperative reservations clerk. The potentials of repeat business that the chef so carefully builds into his meals can be destroyed by a dour or sloppy stewardess.

In fact, stewardesses have a particularly difficult job. A hundred passengers, having paid for reasonable service, understandably expect to be treated with some care. While three young ladies are there to serve them, a number of these passengers must inevitably get their drinks and meals later than others. Most experienced travelers are understanding and tolerant of the rushed stewardesses' problems, but a few usually harass them. The pressure and abuse can easily show in the stewardesses' personal appearance and behavior, and are likely to result in nearly all passengers being reciprocally mistreated. This is human. Besides, the ladies may have been on their feet all day, or may have slept only a few hours the night before.

"More and better training" is not likely to help things very much. When the pressure is on, service deteriorates. And so does a stewardess's cheerful manner and appearance, no matter how well schooled she is in personal care and keeping her cool or how attractively her clothes are designed.

But it might help to put mirrors in the airplane galley, so that each time a stewardess goes in she sees herself. There is some reason to expect that she'll look into the mirror each time she passes it, and that she'll straighten her hair, eliminate that lipstick smudge, put on a more cheerful face. Improvement will be instantaneous. No training needed.

Here is another possibility: the stewardess makes a quick trip down the aisle, passing out rum-flavored bonbons and explaining, "For those who can't wait till we get the ice out." This breaks the tension, produces an air of cheerfulness, acknowledges the passengers' eagerness for quick service, and says that the ladies are trying their hurried best. Further, it brings the stewardess into friendly personal contact with the passenger and reduces the likelihood of her being pressured and abused. She, in turn, is less likely to irritate other passengers.

From the manufacturing point of view, these two modest proposals represent the substitution of tools (or, as I prefer, technology) for motivation. Mirrors are a tool for getting self-motivated, automatic results in the stewardesses' appearance and personal behavior. Bonbons are a tool for creating a benign interpersonal ambience that reduces both the likelihood of customer irritation and the reciprocal and contagious stewardess irritation of others. They are small measures, but so is a company president's plant tour.

In each case there is considerable presumption of solid benefits. Yet to get these benefits one must think, as the factory engineer thinks, about what the problems are and what the desired output is; about how to redesign the process and how to install new tools that do the job more automatically; and, whenever people are involved, about how to "control" their personal behavior and channel their choices.

Hard & Soft Technologies

There are numerous examples of strictly "hard" technologies (i.e., pieces of equipment) which are used as substitutes for people—coffee vending machines for waitresses, automatic check-cashing machines for bank tellers, self-operated travel-insurance-policy machines for clerks. Although these devices represent a manufacturing approach to service, and while their principles can be extended to other fields, even greater promise lies in the application of "soft" technologies (i.e., technological systems). McDonald's is an example of a soft technology. So are mutual funds. Other examples are all around us, if we just think of them in the right way. Take the life insurance industry:

A life insurance salesman is said to be in a service industry. Yet what does he really do? He researches the prospect's needs by talking with him, designs several policy models for him, and "consumer-use tests" these models by seeking his reactions. Then he redesigns the final model and delivers it for sale to the customer. This is the ultimate example of manufacturing in the field. The factory is in the customer's living room, and the producer is the insurance agent, whom we incorrectly think of as being largely a salesman. Once we think of him as a manufacturer, however, we begin to think of how best to design and manufacture the product rather than how best to sell it.

The agent, for example, could be provided with a booklet of overlay sheets showing the insurance plans of people who are similar to the customer. This gives the customer a more credible and informed basis for making a choice. In time, the agent could be further supported by similar information stored in telephone-access computers.

In short, we begin to think of building a system that will allow the agent to produce his product efficiently and effectively by serving the customer's needs instead of performing a manipulative selling job.

Manufacturers Outside the Factory

The type of thinking just described applies not only to service industries but also to manufacturing industries. When the computer hardware manufacturer provides installation and maintenance services, debugging dry-runs, software programs, and operator training as part of his hardware sales program, he acknowledges that his "product" consists of considerably more than what he made in the factory. What is done in the field is just as important to the customer as the manufactured equipment itself. Indeed, without these services there would generally be no sale.

The problem in so many cases is that customer service is not viewed by manufacturers as an integral part of what the customer buys, but as something peripheral to landing the sale. However, when it is explicitly accepted as inte-

gral to the product itself and, as a consequence, gets the same kind of dedicated attention as the manufacture of the hardware gets, the results can be spectacular. For example:

In the greeting card industry, some manufacturer-provided retail display cases have built-in inventory replenishment and reordering features. In effect, these features replace a company salesman with the willing efforts of department managers or store owners. The motivation of the latter to reorder is created by the visible imminence of stockouts, which is achieved with a special color-coded card that shows up as the stock gets low. Order numbers and envelopes are included for reordering. In earlier days a salesman had to call, take inventory, arrange the stock, and write orders. Stockouts were common.

The old process was called customer service and selling. The new process has no name, and probably has never been viewed as constituting a technological substitute for people. But it is. An efficient, automatic, capital-intensive system, supplemented occasionally by people, has replaced an inefficient and unreliable people-intensive system.

In a more complex situation, the A. O. Smith Company has introduced the same kind of preplanning, routinizing, people-conserving activity. This company makes, among other things, grain storage silos that must be locally sold, installed, serviced, and financed. There are numerous types of silos with a great variety of accessories for loading, withdrawing, and automatically mixing livestock feed. The selling is carried out by local distributor-erectors and is a lengthy, difficult, sophisticated operation.

Instead of depending solely on the effective training of distributors, who are spread widely in isolated places, A. 0. Smith has developed a series of sophisticated, colorful, and interchangeable design-module planning books. These can be easily employed by a distributor to help a farmer decide what he may need, its cost, and its financing requirements. Easy-to-read tables, broken down by the size of farm, numbers and types of animals, and purpose of animals (cattle for meat or cows for milk), show recommended combinations of silo sizes and equipment for maximum effectiveness.

The system is so thorough, so easy to use and understand, and so effective in its selling capacity that distributors use it with great eagerness. As a consequence, A. 0. Smith, while sitting in Milwaukee, in effect controls every sales presentation made by every one of its far-flung distributors. Instead of constantly sending costly company representatives out to retrain, cajole, wine-and-dine, and possibly antagonize distributors, the supplier sends out a tool that distributors want to utilize in their own self-interest.

Product-Line Pragmatics

Thinking of service as an integral part of what is sold can also result in alteration of the product itself—and with dramatic results. In 1961, the Building Controls and Components Group of Honeywell, Inc., the nation's largest producer of heating and air conditioning thermostats and control devices, did a major part of its business in replacement controls (the aftermarket). These were sold through heating and air conditioning distributors, who then supplied plumbers and other installation and repair specialists.

At that time, Honeywell's product line consisted of nearly 18,000 separate catalog parts and pieces. The company had nearly 5,000 distributor accounts, none of which could carry a full line of these items economically, and therefore it maintained nearly 100 fully stocked field warehouses that offered immediate delivery to distributors. The result was that, in a large proportion of cases, distributors sold parts to plumbers that they did not themselves have in stock. They either sent plumbers to nearby Honeywell warehouses for pickup or picked up parts themselves and delivered them directly to the plumbers. The costs to Honeywell of carrying these inventories were enormous, but were considered a normal expense of doing business.

Then Honeywell made a daring move—it announced its new Tradeline Policy. It would close all warehouses. All parts would have to be stocked by the distributors. The original equipment, however, had been redesigned into 300 standard, interchangeable parts. These were interchangeable not only for most Honeywell controls, but also for those of its major competitors. Moreover, each package was clearly imprinted to show exactly what Honeywell and competing products were repairable with the contents.

By closing its own warehouses, Honeywell obviously shifted the inventory-carrying costs to its distributors. But instead of imposing new burdens on them, the new product lines, with their interchangeability features, enabled the distributors to carry substantially lower inventories, particularly by cutting down the need for competitive product lines which the distributors could nonetheless continue to service. Thus they were able to offer faster service at lower costs to their customers than before.

But not all distributors were easily persuaded of this possibility, and some dropped the line. Those who were persuaded ultimately proved their wisdom by the enormous expansion of their sales. Honeywell's replacement market share almost doubled, and its original equipment share rose by nearly 50%. Whereas previously nearly 90% of Honeywell's replacement sales were scattered among 4,000 distributors, within ten years after Tradeline's introduction the same proportion (of a doubled volume) was concentrated among only about 900 distributors. Honeywell's cost of servicing these fewer customers was substantially less, its trade inventory carrying costs were cut to zero, and the quality of its distributor services was so substantially improved that only 900 of its distributors captured a larger national market share than did the nearly 4,000 less efficient and more costly distributors.

Again, we see a people-intensive marketing problem being solved by the careful and scrupulous application of manufacturing attitudes. Motivation, hard work, personalization, training, and merchandising incentives were replaced with systematic programming, comprehensive planning, attention to detail, and particularly with imaginative concern for the problems and needs of customers (in this case, the company's distributors).

Stopgaps: Complexity . . .

Exaggeration is not without its merits, especially in love and war. But in business one guards against it with zeal, especially when one tries to persuade oneself. The judicious application of the manufacturing mentality may help the service industries and the customer-service activities of others. Yet this does not necessarily mean the more technology, the better.

Entrepreneurial roadsides are littered with the wrecks of efforts to install Cadillac technologies for people who cannot yet handle the Model T. This point is illustrated by the failure of two exceedingly well-financed joint ventures of highly successful technology companies. These joint ventures attempted to provide computerized medical diagnos-

tic services for doctors and hospitals. The companies developed console hookups to central diagnostic computers, so that everybody could stop sending off samples to pathology laboratories and agonizingly poring through medical texts to diagnose the patients' symptoms.

The ventures failed because of hospital and doctor resistance, not for want of superior or reliable products. The customer was compelled suddenly to make an enormous change in his accustomed way of doing things, and to employ a strange and somewhat formidable piece of equipment that required special training in its use and in the interpretation of its output.

Interactive teaching machines are meeting a similar fate. The learning results they achieve are uniformly spectacular. The need for improved learning is a visible reality. The demand for greater individualization of teaching is widespread. But the equipment has not sold because technologists have created systems employing equipment that is at the cutting edge of technological progress. The teachers and school systems that must use them are far behind, and already feel badly bruised by their failure to comprehend even simple new technologies. For them, the new Cadillac technologies do not solve problems. They create problems.

. . . & Compromise

On the other hand, failure to exploit technological possi-

bilities can be equally destructive. When a major petroleum company with nearly 30,000 retail outlets in the United States was persuaded to pioneer a revolutionary automobile repair and servicing system, compromises of the original plan ensured the system's failure.

The theory was to build a gigantic service and repair system that could handle heavy volumes of continuous activity by using specialized diagnostic and repair equipment. With this equipment (rather than a harried and overworked man at a gas station) pinpointing the exact problems, cars could be shuttled off to specific stations in the repair center. Experts would work only on one kind of problem and section of a car, with newly designed, fast-action tools. Oil changes would be made in assembly-line fashion by low-paid workers, electrical work would be performed by high-paid technicians doing only that, and a post-diagnostic checkup would be made to guarantee success.

Since profitability would require high volume, the center would have to draw on a vast population area. To facilitate this, the original proposal called for a specially constructed building at a center-city, old warehouse location— the land would be cheaper, the building would be equally accessible throughout the entire metropolitan area, the service center's technological elegance and see-through windows for customers would offset any run-down neighborhood disadvantages, and volume business would come from planned customer decisions rather than random off-street traffic.

The original concept also called for overnight pickup and delivery service; thus a car could be repaired at night while its owner slept, rather than during the day when he would need it. And because the required promotion of this service would tend to alienate the company's franchised service station dealers, perhaps driving them into the hands of competitors, it was recommended that the first center be installed in a major city where the company had no stations.

This sounds like an excellent manufacturing approach to a service situation; but the company made three fatal compromises:

1. It decided to place the center in a costly, high-traffic suburban location, on the grounds that "if the experiment fails, at least the building will be in a location that has an alternative use." The results were an awkward location, a land-acquisition cost five times higher than the original center-city location, and, therefore, a vastly inflated break-even point for the service center.

2. It decided not to offer overnight service, on the grounds that "we'd better crawl before we walk. And besides, we don't think people will leave their cars overnight in a strange and distant garage." The fact that the results would be guaranteed by a reputa-

ble, nationally known petroleum company operating an obviously sophisticated new type of consumer service facility was not persuasive to the corporate decision makers.

3. It decided to put the first center in a city occupied by its own franchised dealers, on the grounds that "we know it better." To offset the problem of not being able to advertise aggressively for business, the company offered its dealers a commission to send their repair jobs to the center. The dealers did this, but only with jobs they could not, or did not want to, do themselves. As a result, the traffic at the big, expensive center was miserably low.

Companies that take a manufacturing approach to service problems are likely to fail if (a) they compromise technological possibilities at the conception and design stage, or (b) they allow technological complexity to contaminate the operating stage. The substitution of technology and systems for people and serendipity is complex in its conception and design; only in its *operation,* as at McDonald's, is it simple.

It is the simplicity of mutual funds that, after all, accounts for their success. But the concept is in fact much more complex than that of selling individual stocks through a single customer-man sitting at a desk. Mutual funds are the financial community's equivalent of McDonald's.

They are a piece of technology that not only simplifies life for both the seller and the buyer but also creates many more buyers and makes production more profitable.

Mass merchandising is similar. It substitutes a wide selection and fast, efficient self-service for a narrow selection and slow, incompetent sales-clerk service. The mass merchandising retail store (e.g., general merchandise supermarket) is a new technology, incorporating into retailing precisely the thinking that goes into the assembly line, except that the customer does his own assembling.

Why Things Go Wrong

The significance of all this is that a "product" is quite different from what it is generally assumed to be. When asked once what he did, Charles Revson, bead of Revlon, Inc., made the now well-known reply, "In the factory we make cosmetics, in the store we sell hope." He defined the product in terms of what the consumer wanted, not in terms of what the manufacturer made. McDonald's obviously does the same—not just hamburgers but also speed, cleanliness, reassurance, cheerfulness, and predictable consistency. Honeywell defined it not in terms of replacement parts but, rather, in terms of those needs of its distributors which, if met, would result in substantially larger proportions of patronage for Honeywell. Thus a product is not something people buy, but a tool they use—a tool to solve their problems or to achieve their intentions.

So many things go wrong because companies fail to adequately define what they sell. Companies in so-called service industries generally think of themselves as offering services rather than manufacturing products; hence they fail to think and act as comprehensively as do manufacturing companies concerned with the efficient, low-cost production of customer-satisfying products.

Moreover, manufacturing companies themselves do not generally think of customer service as an integral part of *their* products. It is an afterthought to be handled by the marketing department.

The marketing department, in turn, thinks of itself as providing customer services. There is a hidden and unintentional implication of giving something away for free. One is doing something extra as a favor. When this is the underlying communication to one's own organization, the result is about what one would expect—casual, discretionary attitudes and little attention to detail, and certainly no attention to the possibilities of substituting systems and preplanning for people and pure effort. Hence products are designed that cannot be easily installed, repaired, or modified.

(Motorola's "works in a box" television set, which has been promoted so successfully on the basis of its easy replacement and repairability, is an outstanding example of the sales-getting potential of proper care in design and manufacturing.)

Chill Winds from Ice Cream

An excellent example of the confusion between what a company "makes" and what a customer "buys" is provided by a producer of private-label ice cream products for supermarket chains. Since supermarkets need to create low-price impressions in order to attract and hold customers, selling successfully to them means getting down to rock-bottom prices. The company (call it the Edwards Company) became extraordinarily good at producing a wide line of ice cream products at rock-bottom costs. It grew rapidly while others went bankrupt. It covered ten states with direct deliveries to stores out of its factory and factory warehouse, but continued growth eventually required establishing plant, distribution, and marketing centers elsewhere. The result was disaster, even though the company manufactured just as efficiently in the new locations as it did in the old.

Under the direct and constant supervision of the president in the original Edwards location, an exceedingly efficient telephone ordering and delivery system had been working to meet the supermarkets' rather stringent requirements. Because of limited storage and display space, they required several-times-a-week delivery at specified, uncrowded store hours. To make up for low volume in slow periods, they needed regular specials as well as holiday and summer specials. Over time, these needs had become so automatically but efficiently supplied from the original Edwards factory location that this delivery service became routinized and therefore taken for granted.

In building the new plant, the president and his compact management team focused on getting manufacturing costs down to rock bottom. After all, that is what made the sale—low prices. Not being very conscious of the fact that they had created in the original location an enormously customer-satisfying, efficient, automatic ordering and delivery system, they did not know exactly what to look for in evaluating how well they were working out these "service" details at the plant, distribution, and marketing centers.

In short, they did not know what their product really was (why Edwards had become so successful) and they failed to expand Edwards' success. Service was not considered an integral part of the company's product. It was viewed merely as "something else" you do in the business. Accordingly, service received inadequate attention, and that became the cause of the Edwards Company's failure.

Conclusion

Rarely is customer service discretionary. It is a requisite of getting and holding business, just like the generic product itself. Moreover, if customer service is consciously treated as "manufacturing in the field," it will get the same kind of detailed attention that manufacturing gets. It will be carefully planned, controlled, automated where possible, audited for quality control, and regularly reviewed for performance improvement and customer reaction. More important, the same kinds of technological, labor-saving, and systems approaches that now thrive in manufacturing operations will begin to get a chance to thrive in customer service and service industries.

Once, service-industry executives and the creators of customer-service programs begin seriously to think of themselves as actually manufacturing a product, they will begin to think like product manufacturers. They will ask: What technologies and systems are employable here? How can things be designed so we can use machines instead of people, systems instead of serendipity? Instead of thinking about better and more training of their customer-service representatives, insurance agents, branch bank managers, or salesmen "out there," they will think about how to eliminate or supplement them.

If we continue to approach service as something done by individuals rather than by machines or systems, we will continue to suffer from two distortions in thinking:

1. Service will be viewed as something residual to the ultimate reality—to a tangible product, to a specific competence (like evaluating loans, writing insurance policies, giving medical aid, preparing on-premises foods). Hence it will have residual respectability, receive residual attention, and be left, somehow, for residual performers.

2. Service will be treated as purely a human task that must inevitably be diagnosed and performed by a single individual working alone with no help or, at best, with the rudimentary help of training and a variety of human-engineering motivators. It will never get the kind of manufacturing-type thinking that goes into tangible products.

Until we think of service in more positive and encompassing terms, until it is enthusiastically viewed as manufacturing in the field, receptive to the same kinds of technological approaches that are used in the factory, the results are likely to be just as costly and idiosyncratic as the results of the lonely journeyman carving things laboriously by hand at home.

Review the literature on the management and delivery of services. Based upon your personal interests, select an example of a specific type of hospitality service operation (for example, you might choose a luxury hotel, a casual chain restaurant, or a quick service facility). Develop a proposal for an overall management strategy designed to eliminate the "gaps" that lead to ineffective service delivery and customer dissatisfaction in your chosen operation. Support your proposal with citations from the literature. Identify how the overall strategy impacts upon different functional areas within the organization by separately describing the objectives and action plans for each area: marketing, human resources, operations (including facilities design, productivity, and technology). In the final section of your proposal identify potential areas of conflict which might arise between the separate functional areas as they pursue their individual objectives and describe the techniques which the organization might employ to ensure coordination and cooperation between the functional departments. Your final proposal should include the following components:

1. A title page.

2. An executive summary. A brief summary which highlights the major issues addressed in your proposal (not to exceed 1 page).

3. Body of three part proposal.

   a. Part one: Description of chosen operation and proposed organizational strategy (3 to 5 pages).

   b. Part two: Description of the objectives and action plans for each functional area of the operation (6 to 10 pages). Hint: Using subheadings in this section may help with the organization of the text.

   c. Part three: Identification of potential areas of interdepartmental conflict and proposed mechanisms for managing coordination between functional areas (3 to 5 pages).

4. Reference list. Approximately 10 to 15 references provided in APA format. Use citations within text to support your arguments.

Some hospitality service providers such as quick service restaurants are highly standardized and utilize high levels of customer participation to maintain speed and cost efficiency in the service delivery process. Other operations such as gourmet restaurants and luxury hotels often customize their product-service mix to meet the unique needs and wants of individual consumers. The nature of the primary objectives pursued by standardized versus customized operations are very different. Since ultimately an organization's success depends upon utilizing those strategies which are most appropriate to meeting its own objectives, what leads to success in one hospitality operation may not ensure success in another. Review the relevant literature and write a comparative analysis which contrasts the differences between a standardized operation and a customized operation. Examine the pertinent issues from a managerial point of view to discuss how the strategies in each functional area (marketing, human resources, operations) differ depending upon the overriding organizational objectives (for example, under the human resource functional area, training and selection requirements may differ dramatically depending upon the primary objectives being pursued). Provide a conclusion which summarizes the most important points of your analysis and discusses their implications for the effective management of hospitality service organizations for the future. Your project should include:

1. A title page.

2. An abstract. A brief overview of the topics addressed and the conclusions which resulted from your analysis (not to exceed 1 page).

3. Body of analysis.

   a. Part one: Overview of primary differences between customized and standardized service operations (3 to 5 pages).

   b. Part two: Comparative analysis of the objectives and appropriate strategies for each functional area in customized versus standardized service operations (6 to 10 pages). Hint: Using subheadings in this section may help with the organization of the text.

   c. Part three: Summary of important issues and implications for effective management of hospitality services (3 to 5 pages).

4. Reference list. Approximately 10 to 15 references provided in APA format. Use citations within text to support your arguments.

19

HUMAN RESOURCE MANAGEMENT

Strategic Planning: A Look at Ruby Tuesday
Robert H. Woods

Gender Discrimination and Sexual Harassment as Experienced by Hospitality-Industry Managers
Robert H. Woods and Raphael R. Kavanaugh

Project 1

Project 2

STRATEGIC PLANNING: A LOOK AT RUBY TUESDAY

Robert H. Woods

MUCH HAS BEEN WRITTEN about strategic planning over the past two decades, but little attention has been paid to how the process is carried out in specific hospitality organizations. This article recounts the strategic-planning process carried out by the Ruby Tuesday Group in 1992 and reports on its results.

I am grateful to Morrison Restaurants and to the Ruby Tuesday Group for granting me permission to illustrate important strategic-planning processes and practices by using their organizations' materials. Such cooperation illustrates, I believe, the firm's commitment to hospitality-management education.

Morrison Restaurants

Based in Mobile, Alabama, Morrison Restaurants, Inc., is the oldest food-service company listed on the New York Stock Exchange. First registered in 1920, the company has served various dining segments for the past 70 years. Morrison Restaurants is divided into three divisions that,

combined, generate more than $1.1 billion in annual revenues. The three divisions are Morrison's Hospitality Group, Morrison's Family Dining Group, and the Ruby Tuesday Group.

Morrison's Hospitality Group is a leading provider of contract food services for health care, education, and businesses. Morrison's Family Dining Group includes Morrison's Cafeterias (a dominant cafeteria company in the Southeastern United States), Sadie's Buffets, and Morrison Kitchens (generally found in food courts). The Ruby Tuesday Group comprises four full-service restaurant concepts: Ruby Tuesday, L&N Seafood Grill, Silver Spoon Cafe, and Sweet Peas.

Morrison Restaurants is opening a new full-service restaurant approximately every eight days or gaining a new contract food-service account every four days.

Ruby Tuesday

The focus of this study is the Ruby Tuesday Group. In

1994 this division included some 185 Ruby Tuesday restaurants, 42 L&N Seafood Grills, and 20 Silver Spoon Cafes. In 1993 the company opened 312 Ruby Tuesdays, two L&N Seafood Grills, and five Silver Spoons.

Sweet Peas, a relatively new concept, is reminiscent of a small-town, post-WWII (1940s–50s) restaurant, with ceiling fans, a front porch lined with rocking chairs, and a seasonal vegetable garden in the front of the building. The first location opened in June 1993 and as of April 1994 there were two in operation, with two more scheduled to open later in the year. In 1994 the company will open 40 more Ruby Tuesday restaurants and six Silver Spoons.

Strategic Management

Strategic management is the set of decisions and actions that result in the planning, implementation, and evaluation of strategies designed to achieve the objectives of an organization. The planning proc-

EXHIBIT 1. UNCERTAINTY AND COMPLEXITY VARIABLES INFLUENCING HOSPITALITY BUSINESSES

➤ VARIABLES AFFECTING UNCERTAINTY

Prices charged by suppliers
Pricing by competitors
Labor supply
Products' demand curve
Cost of capital
Financing opportunities
Methods and strategies used by competitors
Regulatory activity within the market area
Industry sales resulting from new-product introductions
Activity caused by competitors entering the market
Fading popularity of standard industry products
The influence of new technology being introduced into the industry

➤ VARIABLES AFFECTING COMPLEXITY

Number of different suppliers for each category of operating materials in the market area
Geographic concentration or dispersion in the market area of:
■ suppliers
■ labor
■ industry sales
■ competitive units
■ customers
Product differentiation in the industry segment in the market area
Socio-cultural diversity in the market area
Diversity of all forms of business in the market area
Volume of business done in all business sectors in the environment
Technological diversity within the industry

ess, one of the first stages of strategic management, is discussed in this article. Developing a mission statement, another step that must be completed early on, is not considered here.

The business environment rules of yesterday may not apply tomorrow and the information that was useful yesterday will likely not be useful tomorrow. The rapid internationalization of industries, the widespread use of computers, and the growth of information transfer have led to radical revisions of how organizations operate. Instead of viewing organizations as closed systems, as they did just four decades ago, today's managers usually view organizations as open systems. The difference between these two definitions is startling.

In a closed system, internal capabilities and information supply all that's needed for success. In an open system, however, a variety of external factors influence organizations and have an effect on the potential for success. As a result, success today depends on close monitoring of both internal and external forces and on being flexible and adaptable to take advantage of them. Exhibit 1 shows several of the forces and factors that can cause uncertainty and complexity in the hospitality environment.

Exhibit 2. Important Variables Influencing All Businesses

Economic	Social	Technological	Political	Ecological
GNP growth	population	R&D activity	wage and price	water quality
purchasing	growth	new products	controls	solid waste
power	population shifts	productivity	social legislation	air quality
inflation	population aging	improvements	tax policy	conservation
interest rates	consumer	product life cycle	government	source reduction
savings rates	activity	patents	stability	recycling
energy costs	environmental	airport regulation	zoning regulation	
disposable	concerns	protectionism	licensing	
income	cultural attitudes			
unemployment				
money supply				

A cursory review of those forces should lead the hospitality manager to conclude that environmental complexity and variability make strategic planning mandatory to maximizing success.

The lists of forces influencing hospitality organizations presented in Exhibit 1 are hospitality specific in the sense that they apply primarily to the hospitality industry. Obviously, a variety of factors in general business environments also influence organizational success. A short list of such factors is provided in Exhibit 2.

Strategic Management and Organizational Performance

Ample correlations between positive organizational performance and strategic management are apparent. For instance, a study of 101 companies over a three-year period showed that improvement in sales, profits, and productivity occurs when strategic management is employed. Another study indicated that most high-performing organi-

zations in the United States use strategic management. In fact, of 20 strategic-management studies reviewed, 12 found that overall organizational performance and bottom-line productivity are significantly improved through strategic planning.

The extent to which business leaders have accepted the notion that strategic management is important has also received considerable attention. Oyeen noted that 91 percent of the CEOs of successful organizations in the United States believe that strategic planning played an important role in their companies' success. Other studies reached similar conclusions; for example, that over 88 percent of U.S. CEOs believe that reducing their company's current emphasis on strategic planning would dramatically hurt their firm's performance.

Strategic Planning

Strategic planning is defined as the analysis of environmental conditions and organizational capabilities and

the formulation of plans to match future capabilities with those conditions.

Strategic planning, sometimes called strategy formulation, is the first step in strategic management. Decisions made during this critical first stage allow organizations to choose which products, services, or markets to abandon or pursue, how to allocate resources, how to design the organization to carry out a chosen strategy effectively, and how to compete.

The *purpose* of strategic planning can be illustrated with the following well-known anecdote.

Two company presidents competing in the same industry decided to go on a camping trip together. They hiked deep into the woods. Suddenly they came upon a grizzly bear that rose up on its hind legs and snarled. Instantly, the first president took off his knapsack and got out a pair of jogging shoes. The second president said, "Hey, you can't outrun that bear." The first president responded, "Maybe I can't outrun the bear, but I can surely outrun you."

Strategic Planning at Morrison Restaurants

Morrison Restaurants is a good example of an organization that believes in strategic management. Morrison has developed and implemented an integrated strategic plan for the organization as a whole and has developed strategic plans for each of its divisions and concepts. The overall plan addresses how the entire company, an organization that operates many different concepts in different segments and markets, will pursue organizational goals, and the divisional plans describe how each division and concept should contribute to the overall plan. In effect, Morrison Restaurants has established a hierarchy of plans linked to one another through supporting goals and objectives.

An integrated corporate plan, such as Morrison's, is complicated by the requirement that it fit with and be in support of each division's plans. Although complicated, it is just as important to overall success as the plan for an organization that operates a single concept in a single market.

Ongoing

This article focuses on the 1992 planning process and results within the Ruby Tuesday Group. Obviously, Ruby Tuesday has since revised its plan to reflect changes both in its environment and among its goals.

SWOT Analysis at Ruby Tuesday

Ruby Tuesday's strategic-planning process starts with the completion of a SWOT (strengths, weaknesses, opportunities and threats) analysis. A SWOT analysis allows organizations the opportunity to identify and rate factors that might influence their success. Such factors are then rated on the basis of

1. Their potential to provide abilities or knowledge,
2. Their requirements for organizational attention,
3. Their ability to provide opportunities to meet strategic goals, and
4. The threat they represent to the organization.

An example of some of the results of Ruby Tuesday's SWOT analysis is presented in Exhibit 3.

The SWOT analysis at the Ruby Tuesday Group is based on market research. As is the case in many organizations, the company hires a market-research firm to collect and analyze data within both the industry and the generic environments that might influence the organization in the future. Data-collection methods used by the market-research firm include

1. Surveys;
2. Focus-group discussions with customers and non-customers;
3. The collection of generic demographic, social, governmental, economic, and technological data from secondary sources; and
4. An overall analysis of the market in which the Ruby Tuesday Group's concepts operate.

A small sample of some of the results of this process are depicted in Exhibit 4.

The results produced by the market-research firm represent only the first step in identifying opportunities and threats to the organization. The second step is asking managers their opinions about factors that may influence the future goals and objectives of the organization. Some organizations believe that strategic planning is solely the responsibility of senior managers. This is not the case with the Ruby Tuesday Group. The strategic planning team comprises 24 key management members including the CEO of Morrison Restaurants; division presidents; concept heads; human-resources personnel from corporate headquarters, the divisions, and the concepts; key managers from the Ruby Tuesday Group; and an outside consultant, whose role it is to guide and facilitate the process.

In addition, the Ruby Tuesday Group collects SWOT data from its managers and district managers through a survey completed by each corporate official, district manager, general manager, and assistant manager within the organization. The survey completed by managers at Ruby

---

EXHIBIT 3. RUBY TUESDAY GROUP SWOT ANALYSIS

STRENGTHS

- ► 10 percent bottom line
- ► Growth rate of 20 percent into the future
- ► Good management team at top (vision)
- ► Fast reaction time from management team
- ► Hands-on leadership
- ► Strong technical skills

WEAKNESSES

- ► Lack of proactive approach (need outside help in developing)
- ► Greater GM autonomy needed to effect regional marketing
- ► Need more management skills at all levels
- ► Internal communications could be improved
- ► Planning system could be better
- ► Need more thorough analysis of stakeholder needs
- ► Need comprehensive review of compensation system

OPPORTUNITIES

- ► Small markets are viable opportunities with smaller units
- ► Delivery and takeout potential good
- ► Technology development in units and at headquarters
- ► New concepts

THREATS

- ► Competition
  - —Direct: Chili's, T.G.I. Friday's, Bennigan's
  - —Indirect: Taco Bell, grocery stores, specialty restaurants
- ► Difficulty in finding new sites (need population of 200,000 to support new site)
- ► Lack of differentiation in markets

Tuesday begins with the question, "As you understand it, what are the primary goals and objectives for the Ruby Tuesday Group on a long-term basis (i.e., three to five years)?" This question is posed first to get managers thinking in strategic terms.

Managers are also asked to respond to questions about tactical issues. Those issues relate to the current effectiveness of key organizational factors. Some of the questions posed in 1992 were:

- ► How do you feel about the menu?
- ► How do you feel about pricing and price-value?
- ► How do you feel about the organizational structure of the company?
- ► Are marketing and other promotional support functions as effective as they should be?

- ► Are there any operational issues that you think need to be addressed?
- ► Are there any areas of human resources, financial management, or planning and control that could benefit from closer attention?

Managers are also asked to identify which elements of the strategic plan they believe to be most crucial. This question was posed in 1992 as follows:

EXHIBIT 4. RESULTS OF THE MARKET RESEARCH FOR RUBY TUESDAY

POPULATION by AGE GROUPS
► U.S. population expected to grow 1 percent per year, 1990–99
► Baby boomers continue to influence population; middle-aged boomers creating a "baby boomlet" (also called a "baby echo")
► Over two-thirds of population will be age 35–54 by year 2000
► By year 2000, 34.3 percent of households will have 35- to 54-year-olds as heads of households (versus 27.5 percent in '85)

AGING HOUSEHOLDS
► The aging population will have an impact on restaurant industry
► 35- to 54-year-old heads of households have median income far in excess of any other age group
► High-income households spend more on food away from home
► By year 2000, over half of food-service sales will be to households headed by a 35- to 54-year-old (versus 49.8 percent in '90)

LABOR FORCE
► Restaurants will employ a diverse labor force by year 2000
► U.S. workforce will have 12 million more females by year 2000 than in '88, a rate of increase much greater than for male workers
► As the percentage of women in workforce increases, so will away-from-home meals eaten by singles, couples, and families
► Training likely to increase in importance as workforce becomes more diverse (icon and bilingual training to become standard)
► Aging workforce
  ■ Almost 50 percent of workers by 2000 will be aged 35 to 54
  ■ There will be a decrease of almost 4 million workers in the 16 to 34 age bracket
  ■ The loss of young workers will influence service staffs and unit managers
  ■ Decreased availability of entry-level employees will increase pressure for simplified unit operations

HOUSEHOLD FOOD EXPENDITURES
► Households with incomes of $50,000+ spend over $6,000 annually in food away from home
► Households with incomes of $40–49,000 spend about $5,000 annually in food away from home
► Households with incomes of $30–39,000 spend less than $4,000 annually in food away from home
► Households with incomes of $29,999 or less spend no more than $3,000 in food away from home

RACIAL AND ETHNIC DIVERSITY
► The U.S. population will continue to become more diverse
► Growth rates of Asian, Hispanic, and African American populations will continue to surpass that of Caucasian population
► In 1990, racial and ethnic minorities were the majority population in 51 U.S. cities (versus 29 cities in 1980)
► Asian and Hispanic population growth will increase opportunities for ethnic foods and for creative menu adaptations by operators

CONSUMER LIFESTYLE TRENDS
► As baby boomers become middle-aged, restaurant industry will need to recognize and cater to consumer motivations, including:
  ■ time constraints
  ■ price-value awareness
  ■ health concerns
  ■ food safety
  ■ social and environmental issues
  ■ easy-to-chew food

CONSUMER PRICE-VALUE AWARENESS
► U.S. consumers are increasingly less likely to accept inferior quality, service, and unreasonable pricing
► Purchasers are sensitized and accustomed to value pricing
► Many consumers are willing to pay a premium for quality
► Consumers expect efficient and courteous service systems to reduce wait times and errors

CONSUMER ATTITUDES VERSUS BEHAVIOR
► What consumers say and do sometimes differ
  ■ In 1991, consumers reported growing concern for health:
    - watching weight: 53 percent
    - eating a balanced diet: 43 percent
    - eating too many high-fat foods: 35 percent
  ■ In 1991, consumers reported these actual behaviors:
    - don't worry about nutrition when eating out: 63 percent
    - percent likely to eat a more healthful diet: women, 38 percent; men, 26 percent

After considering all of your prior comments, if you were asked to identify the three most critical strategic issues, what would these be?

Responses to that question provided the strategic-planning team with a starting point for organizing factors in order of importance.

Data Synthesis and Analysis

The first objective of the strategic-planning team is to synthesize information. At this point in the process, that includes results of the market research and data accumulated from the managers through the internal survey. This information is augmented by the knowledge of the planning-team members, of course.

Planning sessions begin with the facilitator leading a discussion of the various issues already identified. Typically, the facilitator lists all the issues on flip charts that are spread around the room. Once each issue has been discussed the facilitator asks each planning-team participant to complete an individual SWOT analysis and to rank each item. The participants then discuss why they ranked the various issues as they did. Those rankings are posted around the room.

After the individual ranking and ensuing discussion, the facilitator leads the planning team to develop a consensus of what issues are the most important to the company.

Facilitator-led discussions can take a considerable

amount of time to complete. In 1992, for instance, the strategy team at Ruby Tuesday met for two days to discuss and rank each of the issues raised. Such meetings are time-intensive because it is important that the team reach consensus regarding the SWOT factors, namely, which external issues present the greatest opportunities and threats and which internal issues represent the greatest potential strengths and weaknesses.

Group Goals

One of the critical developments that results from team deliberations is the development of organizational goals. The Ruby Tuesday Group team has the additional responsibility of creating goals for the concept that also support the mission statement of Morrison Restaurants as a whole. For example, in 1992 Morrison's mission statement was as follows:

Our mission is to be a great restaurant company that provides the highest quality and greatest value to every guest, every team member, and every shareholder we serve.

Goals developed by the Ruby Tuesday Group's 1992 planning team that supported that mission were worded as follows:

1. We will always exceed the expectations of our guests and thus continually increase the number we serve.

2. We will develop, at all levels of our company, the best service teams in the industry.
3. We will consistently reward our sharcholders.

QVM

Not mentioned in the goals outlined above is a practice used throughout Morrison Restaurants known internally as Quality and Value Management (QVM). QVM is a tool to ensure that quality is assured at all levels of the organization. QVM also serves as a guiding principle throughout the planning process. In 1992 QVM led to charging managers throughout the company with "seeking out every opportunity to hear from those who can best monitor our progress toward these goals and determine any necessary changes."

Operational and Action Plans to Accomplish Goals

Some organizations believe that strategic planning ends with the development of goals for the organization. This is not the case at Morrison, where the planning teams recognize that strategic goals cannot be accomplished without operational plans and action plans. Operational plans represent the means by which goals will be accomplished within the company. Action plans identify specific actions that will be carried out throughout the organization to implement the goals.

Each operational plan developed during the strategy planning sessions is linked directly to one of the three organizational goals. For instance, the first goal, "We will always exceed the expectations of our guests and thus continually increase the number we serve," establishes a goal for the organization in fulfillment of its mission but it does not identify how that goal will be accomplished within the company.

Goal 1: Exceed Guests' Expectations

Operational and action plans to enable each goal revolve around three elements the company recognized as paramount: food, service, and value.

Operational Plans

The following three paragraphs were used in the 1992 operational plan to elaborate on the importance of the first goal.

1. **Food.** We will always produce and protect outstanding food. Outstanding food builds strong guest relationships. Our food will be of the highest quality and consistency. You cannot have one without the other. (There is no quality without consistency.)
2. **Service.** We will provide excellent, caring service for every guest, every time. We will do whatever it takes to keep guests—instantly, before they leave. Great service isn't

enough. We must provide a "WOW" experience.
3. **Value.** We will always give our guests not simply good, but outstanding, value. This will determine how often they spend their money with us versus our competitors. We are committed to providing every guest with a great meal for under $10 ppa (daily per-person average). Whenever possible we will lower prices to increase the value of our meals.

The operational plans identified above establish rules the organization has set for attainment of its goals (e.g., WOW experiences, highest quality food, $10 ppa). However, they do not establish how these goals will be accomplished within the company. That is the role of action plans.

Action Plans

Action plans identify specific desirable and undesirable actions and responsibilities for managers and team members within an organization. For instance, the action plans for the first goal and its three-element operational plan just described can be grouped into four sets, as outlined below. These four parts refer to the issues of food, service, value, and QVM.

1. **Food.** Ruby Tuesday's action plans for food presentation included:

   Guarantee our food—the guests expect it.

   If the quality isn't great, change it. Our food must always be tasteful,

wholesome, and visually appealing. Guests "eat" with their eyes.

Hire and train culinary talent to develop new and existing products. Consumer-test all products before adding to any menu. They're only "great" if the guests say so.

Maintain the right tools to create great food.

Those action plans define exactly how managers and team members should accomplish the first goal and its associated operational plans. They also establish exactly which behaviors are acceptable within the organization and which will be considered deviant. For instance, the second action plan ("If the quality isn't great, change it") empowers managers and team members to replace products that do not meet company specifications. The specific means used to cure problems are what distinguishes a service- and value-driven restaurant company from its competitors. The intangible nature of service, discussed in the second set of action plans (below), is a further example of why organizations must take the time to identify exactly how each goal will be carried out.
2. **Service.** Regarding service, Ruby Tuesday addressed the goals of excellent service and exceeding guests' expectations with

precise action plans, as follows.

Guarantee our service—the guests require it. The response to any guest's request will be, "My pleasure."

Be guest-driven; don't lose a guest over a $9 meal ($3 actual cost). The guest is always right. If you think a guest is wrong, read again.

Do whatever it takes to keep a guest—instantly and before she or he leaves. Create WOW experiences. Turn our infrequent guests into regulars and get the regulars back more often. Service is the key.

Know your guests' names—they love it.

At all times, be happy and smile. Look sharp. Be sharp.

Reduce or remove any administrative or operational functions that keep our management teams from focusing on our guests and team members.

The action plans outlined above for both food presentation and service establish powerful tools for management's use. For instance, consider the three action plans that include the words "Be guest-driven," "My pleasure," and "Reduce or remove any administrative operational functions. . . ." Each of those action plans establishes undeniable rules of operation within the company that empower

managers and team members in specific instances. Each also establishes a philosophy of what will and will not be considered acceptable within the company. For instance, "eliminate administrative and operational functions . . ." sends the message to managers and team members that operations managers should spend their time working with guests and team members to ensure that the highest quality of products and services are provided. This statement also identifies unacceptable behavior by specifically establishing that administrative and operational functions designed to accomplish other tasks should be considered wholly secondary.

3. **Value.** Value was addressed by the 1992 Ruby Tuesday strategic planning team by developing five different action plans.

Provide our guests with outstanding price-value. The guests demand it.

If the value isn't great, change it. If it's not a WOW value, it's not value at all.

Atmosphere adds value. In a competitive industry, it's just as important as food and service. Maintain "clean as you go" habits. Keep the rest rooms sparkling clean and fresh. Always have an "A" rating.

When combined with quality food, service, and atmosphere, the lower the prices, the higher the

guest count. Maintain per-guest check average of $10 or below.

Create better perceived value through menu management and continuous product (new and existing) development.

QVM for Goal 1

As the food and service action plans before it, the plan for attaining value specifically identifies how managers and team members should accomplish operational and organizational goals. Likewise, QVM has three action plans.

During every unit visit all levels of supervisory leadership should talk and listen to guests before leaving the premises; guests inside, team members and coaches outside. Findings should be recorded and communicated to other team members.

Conduct semiannual consumer research to track key measurements of guest satisfaction. Use this data to see how we compare with the competition and whether we're improving. Determine where we stand every six months and measure the change.

Develop programs to identify, recognize, and reward our frequent, most loyal guests. Solicit and track the wants and dining habits of this most valuable group.

It is important to establish specific objectives for managers regarding collection of feedback from team members and guests. It is also important to establish how often such feedback should be collected in order that QVM is assured.

Goal 2: Excellent Guest-Service Teams

The second critical goal ("We will develop, at all levels of our company, the best service teams in the industry") is also addressed specifically by both operational plans and action plans.

Operational plans

In 1992 the operational plans for that goal were as follows.

Our company will be composed of highly motivated, clearly directed, guest-driven teams all working toward the goal of total guest satisfaction. Each and every employee is an important member of the team. Every manager is a solid, supportive team coach or leader. All team members will be focused on serving guests—or serving those who are serving guests.

We will improve the capabilities and enthusiasm of our team members with thorough training, proper recognition and reward, and continuous measuring of team-member satisfaction.

Individual success, and our success as a company, will be determined by:

▶ How well we recruit and select;
▶ How well we train and develop;
▶ How well we monitor every member's performance versus our standards;

▶ How well we coach and counsel; and
▶ How well we motivate and inspire our teams to win.

Action Plans

Ruby Tuesday's service teams are composed of: employees, known as "team members"; key employees, who are called "team captains"; managers, referred to as "team coaches"; and area and regional divisional supervisors, also known as "team leaders."

Ruby Tuesday's service teams' operational plans were supported by the action plans that are presented below.

Overcommunicate

Make a major commitment to open communication to and from every level of the team. Constantly communicate clear, focused, consistent plans. Eliminate guessing. This makes for winners at game time—every meal period.

Sell the company, the concept, the business and principles. Reinforce the company's culture at every opportunity.

Encourage and support suggestions and innovations from all team members. Celebrate team members' successes often and in a highly visible manner.

Coaches and leaders should perform career-development planning with all their team members. Keep everyone informed of where they are in that development track, what they need to do, and where they are going.

Build Loyal, Motivated Teams

Treat all members of the team with dignity and respect. Lead, coach, and counsel with compassion and common sense. We need solid team leaders, not policemen.

Hire the best. Hire experienced managers and trainees. Increase the number of outside hires with district-level experience.

Conduct the best training at every level. Teach, don't just tell, the how and why of every task. Commit to 40 hours of education per year for all levels of leaders (leadership, communication, and team building). Develop all team members to their maximum potential. Raise the standard.

Forge team-member partnerships. Encourage company-wide stock ownership. Support an ownership culture. Fully committed teams will always find ways to build sales.

Quality of life for all team members is important. Foster a healthy balance between work and family or personal interests. This usually means scheduling individuals to work a maximum of five shifts in a regular work week (realizing there may be seasonal- and shortage-related exceptions).

Support Community-Based Teams

Hire experienced leaders from the community who want to stay and actively participate in the community. Encourage and financially support units that are involved in community work.

Don't move top coaches (GMs) unless absolutely necessary; doing so disrupts the team. Implement managing-partner plans to encourage those coaches to remain with the team (e.g., multi-year contracts, fixed base with percentage of profits over and above norm).

QVM for Goal 2

Implement the standards inventory program in all our businesses to objectively account for the standards of productivity, service quality, and overall performance of units and their teams.

Perform annual surveys of team members and coaches to determine menu strengths and weaknesses, service issues, and how to achieve consistent, long-term improvement in team satisfaction.

Ruby Tuesday's action plans stress the need for caring, professional relationships among managers, other employees, and the organization, and they specifically outline guidelines and rules for those relationships. For instance, by first designating that specific terms be used when referring to all personnel within the company, the Ruby Tuesday Group forcefully recognizes the need to treat all participants within the Morrison Restaurants company with dignity. That is then reinforced through additional action plans that outline specifically how this relationship should be conducted.

Goal 3: Maximize Shareholder Value

The final goal established during the 1992 strategy meetings ("We will consistently reward our shareholders") is clarified by an operational plan that reads, "We will maximize shareholder value by executing the Morrison's quarterly business basics. Our team leaders, armed with a strong conviction to these proven business disciplines, will continually grow our businesses and improve our company."

Operational Plans

Operational plans for this goal include:

Increase sales from our existing assets

Achieve 2-percent real growth in same-store sales without increasing average guest checks, and
Achieve revenue growth of 20 percent per year.

Create higher guest value.

Lower the cost of doing business

Reduce below PAC line expenditures (as a percentage sales) and reinvest these dollars toward guest satisfaction programs.

Invest only in high return opportunities

Maintain 20-percent after-tax annual return on all invested dollars.

Action Plans

Those operational plans (above) are supported by the following action plans.

Increase sales from existing assets

Exceed guest expectations on every visit.

Develop additional sales opportunities in all brands, for example:

- Alcohol and non-alcohol beverages,
- Coffee and cappuccino programs,
- Retail items, and
- Focused carry-out programs (Fast Takes) and quality packaging (meal combos).

Involve the entire team in the sales history, profit quotas, and financial goals of each unit. Create incentives for team members to increase their guest counts.

Reduce or remove any administrative or operational functions that keep our coaches from focusing on the team and the team from focusing on the guests.

Hold our average checks at current level ($10 or below daily ppa). Lower the guest check average and the typical guest will return more often. Increase prices by no more than half of the competition's increases. Always know what the competition is doing with pricing and coupons.

Create higher guest value

Build a great product- and menu-development team to create stronger quality and value items as perceived by the guest. Perception is reality.

Focus on menu management. Position food to sell based on lowest cost, best value, or highest gross. Lower prices whenever possible, but maintain gross profit.

Our design criteria (interior and exterior) should be driven by what our guests want and value. The design of all our locations must be kept current and fresh. Ease of cleaning and maintenance should be a design priority.

Lower the cost of doing business

Always look for the better, faster, less costly way of doing things.

Maximize unit-level efficiencies.

Eliminate any and all bureaucratic costs that are not guest driven or do not contribute to the team. General and administrative costs should increase by less than half of sales or profit growth.

Dramatically reduce the cost of moving people. (It's simple; just move fewer people.)

Management turnover should be at 20 percent or less (annualized). Employee turnover should be at 100 percent or less.

Establish a committee of best-unit coaches (GMs) to review all paperwork to validate use. Eliminate paperwork that's of little or no benefit.

Invest only in high-return opportunities

Mandatory after-tax return on invested dollars: 20 percent.

Develop and test food-distribution vehicles in all divisions that are: smaller, more productive, lower break even, and higher return.

QVM for Goal 3

Conduct regular focus groups in selected units (managers and guests) to discuss any food service- or value-related problems or opportunities.

Create and support in-unit quality and value (QVM) circles where coaches and team members can discuss how to improve food, service, safety, and value to guests.

The final set of action plans (above) establishes the high level of professionalism required throughout the Ruby Tuesday Group. As the operational plans indicate, real sales increases (not just price increases), higher guest value, lower costs, and investment in only high-return opportunities serve as guiding economic principles for the company.

The action plans identify specifically how those operational objectives will be carried out in each of the five areas outlined. For the manager, those operational and action plans provide succinct guidelines that reinforce what can and should be done with the considerable assets each manages for the company.

Supporting Materials

The goals, operational plans, and action plans presented on the preceding pages represent key elements in the Ruby Tuesday Group's strategic plan. They also represent a good example of an organization that has established a hierarchy of goals within its strategic plan.

The company also takes other definitive steps to ensure that Ruby Tuesday's strategic plan is widely understood and used. For instance, managers and team members receive several documents that reiterate what is impor-

tant, what should be attempted and what should not be attempted, and how business is to be conducted.

Such materials include a statement of management philosophy; a code of conduct for managers and employees; a pocket-size daily-reminder card entitled "Ten Points of Service," used to remind managers and employees of important organizational objectives (for instance, "teamwork" and "appearance"); and laminated pocket-size daily-reminder cards that on one side reiterate the year's goals and on the other side set forth a managerial philosophy the company calls the "Will to Win." The Will to Win contains only three guiding principles—commitment, execution, and accountability.

Unique and Dynamic

Each organization should have a unique strategic plan that matches its own internal strengths and weaknesses, external opportunities and threats, and culture. There is no chance that any two plans would ever be the same.

Morrison Restaurants realizes that strategic plans are dynamic documents that must change as a company's internal and external environments change. As such, the 1992 plan for Ruby Tuesday presented here serves as a vehicle to illustrate how planning took place in one organization at a particular point in time and it illustrates the type of results, operational plans, and action plans that can be developed to support an organizational strategy. Over the last few years many factors have changed and, as a result, the Ruby Tuesday Group has updated its strategy through subsequent planning sessions similar to those described above.

The timeless factors of the Ruby Tuesday Group's planning process are (1) the company's beliefs about the value of strategic planning, (2) its characterization of the relationships within an organization (for instance, managers as coaches and counselors, not as policemen), and (3) its recognition that it is in a competitive business and that both organizational and individual actions reflect on the degree to which the company can succeed in that environment. At several points in the statement of goals and in the operational and action plans, for example, the company refers to the "highly competitive" or "competitive" nature of the food-service industry. Clearly, Morrison Restaurants and the Ruby Tuesday Group believe that success depends on preparedness, and that strategic planning is the key to ensuring that the company is prepared to meet and to exceed the performance of its competitors.

Gender Discrimination and Sexual Harassment as Experienced by Hospitality-Industry Managers

Robert H. Woods and Raphael R. Kavanaugh

—————◼—————

GENDER DISCRIMINATION and sexual harassment are topics that have recently come to the forefront, in part owing to the Clarence Thomas and Anita Hill confrontations during Thomas's 1991 Supreme Court nomination confirmation hearings in the U.S. Senate. That series of events may also be responsible for the increase in sexual-harassment charges filed with the Equal Employment Opportunity Commission since those hearings—reported to be 53 percent.

The literature on sexual harassment indicates that it is widespread, to the point of being pandemic, and that although it primarily affects women, men are also subject to sexual harassment. Some articles describing how to develop sexual-harassment policies have also appeared. Many of them fall into what has been called the *How to Avoid Harassment Charges* category.

Articles describing the extent of gender discrimination in business in the United States have also appeared recently, many of them focusing on the "glass ceiling," the invisible barrier that has kept women from reaching the top in many management circles. Other studies have prescribed specific actions to be taken by women confronted with sexual discrimination in the workplace.

Despite the thoroughness of those and other studies, none has focused on sexual harassment and discrimination directed toward managers in the hospitality industry. This article reports on research that explored that issue.

Methods

We surveyed managers to collect information about gender discrimination and sexual harassment in the hospitality industry. The questionnaire we developed for the survey included some questions taken from a 1989 study conducted at Wichita State University.

We mailed the 49-question survey to 1,550 hospitality managers in the spring of 1992. All the managers had earned a baccalaureate or masters degree from one of two large hospitality-management programs within the preceding seven years. The two programs from which our mailing list was generated reported that during that period there were about the same number of male and female students enrolled.

Of the 1550 surveys mailed, 613 usable surveys were returned (a response rate of 40 percent). Of the usable responses, 353 (58 percent) were from women.

Although planned in advance, the mailing happened to take place after Clarence Thomas's Supreme Court confirmation hearings in the U.S. Senate. As previously explained, those hearings and the ensuing prime time coverage of the testimony raised the public's awareness of the issues of gender discrimination and sexual harassment in the United States. We believe that the results of the Survey reflect the increased awareness.

Participant Profile

Exhibit 1, shown on the following page, presents an overview of the demographic makeup of the respondents. Most (65 percent) are under the age of 30—as one would expect from a sample population that had graduated from college within the last seven years. About half the men and two-thirds of the women have never been married, perhaps reflecting the difficulty some people in hospitality have in managing both career and marriage.

Many of the respondents work in the hotel industry. In fact, over 45 percent of the men and 51 percent of the women work in hotels. About half as many—24 percent of the men and 27 percent of the women—work in commercial food service. One percent of the men and almost 10 percent of the women worked in contract food service; more than 9 percent of the men and fewer then 2 percent of the women worked in clubs; and a little more than 21 percent of the males and more than 10 percent of the females worked in affiliated industries (e.g., consulting, accounting, supplying).

What is not shown in Exhibit 1 is the number of respondents who do not work in any segment of the hospitality

industry. Knutson found that about a third of hospitality-management graduates left the industry within five years of graduation and that hospitality operations were most likely to lose female managers. Pavesic and Brymer found a similar number (28 percent) of graduates left the industry within five years, and that most of these were women (55 percent).

Twenty-three of the responses were from people who no longer work in hospitality; all but one of them were women. It is interesting that they returned the survey at all, since it did not relate to their current lives. Many of them wrote notes on their questionnaires telling why they had left the hospitality industry. In many cases the reasons involved gender discrimination or sexual harassment.

Respondents were asked to indicate their salaries in terms of specified ranges and from that data we calculated the approximate mean salaries for both males and females. We found that the mean is about $42,300 for men and about $35,900 for women. Also, almost a fifth of the men reported salaries of $55,000 or over, while only two women—less than 1 percent of our sample—reported such salaries. Those data suggest that a salary disparity exists along gender lines (see Exhibit 2).

The mean income for respondents as a whole is approximately $38,500. Using the salary range $35,000–$39,999 as the midrange for the entire group, we find that 43 percent of the men have

salaries below the middle range, and 43 percent have salaries above it. However, 60 percent of the women have salaries below the group's middle range, and only 20 percent have salaries above it. In fact, the middle range for just the women is $30,000–34,999. That finding is somewhat skewed by the fact that male respondents reported having more experience in the industry (Exhibit 1), although experience alone does not explain the gender difference in earnings (see Exhibit 2). Perhaps a more likely cause is the sort of jobs offered to men versus women upon graduation and, if that's the case, the ensuing "fast track."

Gender Discrimination

Each of the respondents answered a single question about the *extent* to which sexual discrimination occurs in the hospitality industry. The results are overwhelming; 80 percent of the male respondents and 90 percent of the female respondents believe that sexual discrimination occurs frequently. Those data appear to contradict recent reports that cracks in the hospitality industry's glass ceiling have been getting bigger.

The male and female respondents have different perceptions about where sexual discrimination is most likely to occur (see Exhibit 3). Of the women, 40 percent reported that it most often is related to promotion, and nearly as many (38 percent) reported that it is most often related to salaries. Male perceptions of

EXHIBIT 1. DEMOGRAPHIC PROFILE OF THE RESPONDENTS				
	Men		Women	
	n	%	n	%
Ages				
20–29	188	72	213	60
30–39	72	28	122	35
40–49	0	0	18	5
Marital Status				
Married	108	42	90	25
Never married	128	49	227	64
Separated	0	0	0	0
Divorced	0	0	15	4
Widowed	0	0	0	0
Living as married	24	9	21	6
Segment of the Hospitality Industry				
Hotel Industry	116	45	181	51
Restaurant industry	62	24	95	27
Contract food service	3	1	35	10
Club management	24	9	5	1
Other*	55	21	37	10
Experience as a Hospitality Manager				
Less than four years	119	46	185	52
Four to five years	53	20	116	33
More then five years	88	34	52	15
Time in Present Position				
Less than one year	160	62	312	88
One to two years	44	17	29	8
Three to five years	32	12	10	3
More than five years	24	9	2	1
Companies Worked For In Past Three Years				
One	125	48	257	73
Two or three	97	37	66	19
More than three	38	16	30	8
Individual Annual Income				
Less than $20,000	20	8	16	5
$20,000–$24,999	8	3	32	9
$25,000–$29,999	28	11	89	25
$30,000–$34,999	56	22	76	22
$35,000–$39,999	36	14	68	19
$40,000–$44,999	4	2	38	11
$45,000–$49,999	40	15	16	5
$50,000–$54,999	20	8	16	5
$55,000–$59,999	24	9	0	0
More than $60,000	24	9	2	1

*Most of these respondents (80.4 percent) work for companies engaged primarily in consulting.

Exhibit 2. Men's and Women's Salaries Compared

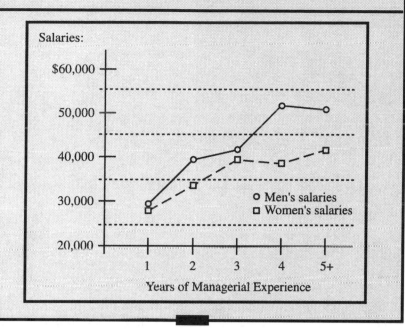

Salaries:

○ Men's salaries
□ Women's salaries

Years of Managerial Experience

Exhibit 3. Responses to the Question, "In what context does sex discrimination occur most frequently?"

	Men		Women	
	n*	%	n*	%
Promotion	40	16	135	40
Salary	62	26	128	38
Selection	67	27	73	22
Responsibility	52	21	1	0
Other	30	12	0	0

*The number "n" refers to those respondents who reported in what areas they believed gender discrimination and sexual harassment occur. The number n does *not* include respondents who believe no discrimination occurs in any of those areas.

the form sex discrimination takes are more evenly spread over various possibilities. Marked differences between male and female respondents are seen in their reported perceptions of discrimination in the areas of responsibility and "other."

Why so many men (12 percent) answered "other," and what those other forms of sex-

ual discrimination are, is a mystery. In retrospect, we recognize that the inclusion of the "other" option was a mistake. It was intended to encourage open-ended responses in which participants would elaborate on their choice, but few did so. As a result, no explanation for those responses is possible. It is interesting to note that not a single woman identified any form of sexual discrimination as "other" than those presented by the research.

Sexual Harassment

Participants were asked how often sexual harassment occurs in the hospitality industry. Nearly a fourth of both male and female respondents completely agree with this statement: "Most women in my field have been subjected to sexual harassment at work" (see Exhibit 4). A much larger percentage of female managers than male managers either completely agree or partially agree with that statement. Almost no female respondents completely disagree with that statement, while 15 percent of male respondents completely disagree.

Defining Sexual Harassment

Sexual harassment is not simply basing employment decisions on an individual's acceptance or rejection of sexual advances. Another form of sexual harassment is the creation of an intimidating, hostile, or offensive work environment. Repeatedly staring

EXHIBIT 4. RESPONSES TO THE QUESTION: "MOST WOMEN IN MY FIELD HAVE BEEN SUBJECT TO SEXUAL HARASSMENT AT WORK."		
	Men	**Women**
Completely agree	25%	24%
Partially agree	14	41
Neutral	22	20
Partially disagree	25	15
Completely disagree	15	0

provocatively and making off-color jokes or remarks are also considered sexual harassment. Harassment does not always involve a superior's behavior toward a subordinate. An employee can charge an employer with sexual harassment as a result of the actions of managers, fellow employees, vendors, and even customers.

Sexual harassment can also occur among seemingly willing participants. For instance, an employee can participate in telling sexual jokes and then later successfully claim that she or he was sexually harassed, because such incidents resulted in the creation of a hostile work environment."

A classic case was *Meritor Savings Bank (of Virginia) v. Vinson.* A female employee had engaged in consensual sex 40 to 50 times over a period of four years before charging her employer with harassment. Vinson, the employee, contended that she had engaged in sex with her boss to get ahead in the company and that failure to do so would have limited her opportunities to succeed. The Supreme

Court ruled that "voluntariness" is not a defense for the employer. The court also ruled that a classic "hostile environment" had been created.

Finally, while sexual harassment is most often a case of a man harassing a woman, that is not always the case. Cases of the reverse and of harassment among same-sex managers, employees, and customers have also occurred.

Discussion

Data presented in this paper support the argument that substantial levels of sexual discrimination exist in the hospitality industry. The data also indicate that male and female managers hold differing opinions about how gender discrimination and sexual harassment are manifested, even though they agree that both are frequent occurrences.

Perhaps more important, the data indicate that both male and female managers believe that sexual discrimination is pervasive in hospitality. Therefore, the data appear to refute others' reports con-

tending that sexual discrimination in hospitality is declining and raise questions about the extent of sexual harassment in the hospitality industry.

The results raise many questions. For instance, why do men and women disagree about where discrimination occurs? Perhaps those questions will encourage others to investigate the issues.

Observations

Before closing, we would like to make three additional observations. The first is the fact that although not a single man wrote comments on his questionnaire, many of the women wrote extensive comments in the margins. Most of the comments were devoted either to relating personal experiences or to emphasizing how strongly they felt about their responses. In short, we struck a nerve with many female participants. For instance, several female respondents not only answered the questions but also related personal experiences of harassment and discrimination to illustrate why they held such opinions. Some of those commentaries were so vivid, in fact, that they included names of perpetrators, dates, and locations of specific incidents.

We hope that the results presented in this paper will help alleviate problems female managers face in hospitality by increasing awareness and illustrating the pervasiveness of those issues and the frequency of their occurrence. If nothing else, perhaps these findings will compel industry executives to institute programs to reduce the likelihood of gender discrimination and sexual harassment.

We would also like to comment on a bias of our own that we learned about while completing the research. It was pointed out to us by several gay and lesbian respondents that we had left them out and that our focus on male-female gender discrimination and sexual harassment was heterosexually biased. Specifically, they told us that discrimination occurs frequently against gay and lesbian managers (by non-gays and non-lesbians) and that the extent of that discrimination should also be investigated. It's true that that issue was not a part of this study, for which we apologize. We challenge our colleagues to further investigate the issue.

Finally, the issues presented in this paper are of immediate concern to us as hospitality educators. Educators must create an environment in which such issues can be discussed. And educators must help break down the barriers to advancement by our students and graduates.

Semester Project (to be completed in teams assigned by the professor. Each student must complete an application for team membership—see attached.)

The semester project will require student teams to conduct a strategic analysis for a selected company. The teams will also have the opportunity to work directly with the company they are analyzing. The three phases of this analysis are as follow:

1. Analyze the company's industry

2. Evaluate the company's corporate level strategy

3. Analyze the company's implementation strategies

Analyzing the Industry

Strategic industry analysis is a complex, and important phase of strategic planning and implementation. Competition within an industry is influenced greatly by the various competitive weapons each firm within that industry utilizes. Competition is also influenced by suppliers, buyers and other stakeholders in that industry and by critical success factors, substitute products and other factors within an industry. Identifying each of these important elements in an industry is the first key step in developing an effective strategic plan.

Some key questions student teams will want to ask include:

1. What are the success factors that companies must satisfy to compete in a specific industry?

2. What are the different segments of the industry, and how much is each segment growing?

3. What stage of the life cycle is the industry in, and how has this stage affected competition?

4. Who are the major suppliers in the industry and how much power do they have relative to the companies they supply?

5. Who are the major buyers of the industry's products and services and how much power do they exert?

6. Who are the other stakeholders in this industry and how much power do they exert?

7. What are the strengths, weakness, opportunities and threats in the industry?

8. How do substitute products threaten this industry?

9. What developing technology could have significant impact on this industry?

10. To what extent are global considerations important in this industry?

11. What legislative and/or regulatory factors threaten this industry?

12. To what extent is the industry subject to the impact of economic recession, inflation and other financial considerations?

13. What trends are observable in the industry which may impact this company?

Corporate Level Strategy

A second step in this project is to analyze the company's corporate level strategy. In effect, this represents top management's game plan for the company. Corporate strategy is concerned with overall purpose, mission and long-term objectives of the company. In firms which compete in only one industry the corporate level strategy is the same as the strategy of the strategic business unit. In companies which operate in several industries, however, this strategy will be different. You should ask yourself to what extent the corporate strategy of the firm you are investigating effectively addresses these and other critical issues discussed below.

Company Mission

1. What is the company mission which describes the product, market and technological areas of emphasis for the business?

2. What are the values and philosophy of corporate top management and how are they reflected in the mission statement or creed?

3. Are there competitive pressures impacting on the firm which might necessitate changing the mission statement?

Company Profile

1. What are the company's various SBUs (if they have them) and how well is each one performing?

2. What are the distinctive competencies of the company as a whole?

3. How has the company performed financially in recent years?

4. Which SBUs have been identified as resource generators?

5. What are common weaknesses that the company currently has in its SBUs (in the company overall)?

6. How does the company stack up against key competitors?

Strategic Choice

1. What long-term objectives have been established by the company?

2. What is the current grand strategy (e.g. concentration, diversification, vertical integration, etc.) of the company?

3. What acquisitions, divestitures, joint ventures, or vertical integration moves would enhance the company's overall position?

4. How should financial resources be allocated among the various SBUs or departments?

5. Which SBUs or departments are most consistent with the company's mission?

6. What key threats and trends from the task and remote environment are affecting the company?

Operationalizing and Institutionalizing the Strategy

1. What are the basic guidelines that the corporate level has established for each SBU?

2. How have key corporate policies and procedures been communicated to each SBU?

3. What sort of formal business plan is each SBU required to submit?

Control and Evaluation of Corporate Level Strategy

1. What quantitative and qualitative measures are used to evaluate each SBU's performance?

2. What rewards and penalties are being used to motivate key SBU managers?

3. Is the desired synergy between SBUs working out as intended?

4. Are interim objectives being met?

Implementing the Strategy

The final phase of the project deals with the issue of strategic implementation. The objective in this phase is to identify methods by which the company is currently implementing strategies and to determine methods by which implementation can be enhanced.

To complete this section students will want to answer the following questions.

1. Is the present strategy capitalizing on the major strengths and distinctive competencies of the company?

2. Is the strategy attainable on the unit and SBU levels?

3. What current trends or threats might make implementation of the strategy more difficult?

4. Does the current strategy offer the desired level of risk/return relationship?

5. Does the company possess the financial and human resources to implement the chosen strategy?

6. What supporting roles must functional areas play to achieve the strategy?

7. How should financial and human resources be allocated among the functional areas?

8. What evaluative mechanisms should be installed to determine how well the company's strategy is being implemented?

Application for Student Teams

The purpose of this application is to create competitive teams. The application is used for no other reason.

Name _____

Classification (Junior, Senior, grad. etc.) _____

Other classes taken _____
_____
_____
_____

Primary industry interest (hotels. restaurants, non-commercial, etc.)
_____

Major field (accounting, finance, human resources, operations, marketing, F & B, etc.) This may be your favorite field or the one in which you consider yourself to be most expert.
_____

Some students receive good jobs upon graduation while others are left to take whatever is offered. This exercise is designed to help make sure that you are one of the students who receives the job offers you want. The exercise consists primarily of identifying companies you want to work for, locating information on those companies, preparing a game plan for introducing yourself to those companies and selling yourself through letters, personal contacts and thorough preparation for and conduct during interviews. Details on the specific "turn-in" requirements of the project will be explained during the second week of class.

Project Requirements

I. Personal Objectives

    1.   Establish personal objectives for 1, 3 and 5 year periods after graduation.

        A.   Objectives should include positions intend to attain, region of country (world) you hope to work in, industry you choose to work in (hotels, restaurants, fast foods, etc.), salary you hope to attain for each period, responsibilities you hope to achieve, etc.

    2.   Identify two companies you are interested in working for upon graduation.

        A.   Select these companies by first determining the industry (hotels, restaurants, institutional foods, fast foods, etc.) that you are interested in.

        B.   After determining the industry—select two companies in that industry.
           (1.) Provide written justification for why you are interested in this industry and these companies (one paragraph or so each). You may wish to rewrite this portion after completing remainder of project.

II. Collect information on companies you hope to work for upon graduation.

    1.   Collect generalized information on these companies, including

        A.   Profitability for minimum of last three years

        B.   Names of corporate leaders (Chairperson, CEO, President, COO, Human Resource Director, Chief Financial Officer, others as appropriate)

        C.   Identify names and titles of regional corporate personnel (in your region)

        D.   Identify (where possible through Career Expo) names and responsibilities of persons attending Career Expo as recruiters for your companies.

        E.   Identify principle long-term objectives of the organization, including plans for expansion/contraction of properties and/or concepts. Pay particular attention to plans for your preferred region.

        F.   Collect published materials (trade journals, national and regional publications, etc.) which relate to policies, procedures, accomplishments or objectives of the companies you have identified.

G. Identify names, addresses and phone numbers of a minimum of three graduates who work for the companies selected (you may wish to consult Alumni records/publication for this information).

H. Write letters of introduction to the six people identified above. Contact is not required.

1. Identify five things you like most and five things you like least about the companies you have chosen.

III. Prepare interview information

1. Prepare a list of questions you intend to ask a recruiter for the companies you have chosen.

2. Prepare a "two minute" (i.e., something you could say in two minutes) commercial on yourself you intend to give recruiter.
(Remember: You have about this long to impress someone.)

3. Be prepared to rehearse the interview and/or commercial in class if asked to do so.

IV. Interview with Student and Industry Resource Center office

1. Schedule an interview with SIRC to collect information/career advice on companies, your options and career objectives.

V. Resumé

1. Prepare a personal resumé designed to catch the attention of the companies you have identified (knowing what you now know about these companies this should be easy).

VI. Interview

1. Sign up for and attend an interview with a company representative during Career Expo.

2. Write a brief (1 page) report on what transpired during interview, what you learned, etc.

VII. Flowchart

Create a flowchart depicting each step in this process. The flowchart should be used as a reminder to you of what must be done to complete the assignment. Use the flowchart to negotiate your way through the project.

VIII. Hand-in requirements

Package and hand in all completed materials called for no later than the first day of Career Expo. These materials should include copies of articles (if copied), notes on companies, information learned from SIRC, report on interview, etc. This packet should clearly inform the reader about what you have learned during the project.

20

HOSPITALITY LAW

Conventional Contracts and the HRI Industry
J.R. Gaston and J.R. Goodwin

Project 1

Project 2

CONVENTIONAL CONTRACTS AND THE HRI INDUSTRY

J.R. Gaston and J.R. Goodwin

Contracts in the Courts

WHEN DECIDING LEGAL controversies, the courts are always watchful to see if a contract was involved in the dispute. If so, the terms of that agreement come to the front and the court will use those terms in deciding the matter. By making a contract, the parties set their own standards. The courts will not change those standards in the absence of fraud or other criminal activity that may have given rise to the contract. The courts do not write contracts—they only use them to resolve disputes. A good way to begin is by an examination of the definition of contract.

Definition

A leading authority on the subject tells us that "a contract is a promise, or set of promises, for the breach of which the law gives a remedy, or the performance of which the law in some way recog-

nizes as a duty." This definition points out that a promise or promises are needed and that the "law" is involved. A contract creates legal obligations when it comes into being; it usually concerns property or something of value, and it creates rights that can be addressed to a court for enforcement. If the contract requires skill, exercise of special knowledge, or judgment, it is a "personal service contract." If it concerns property, it is a "property contract."

Contract Definition and Reservations

Travel Group X makes prepaid reservations at Zero Inn for 50 rooms, two weeks in advance. When attempting to check in, the group is told that no rooms are available. The translation of the above contract definition follows: "A contract is the promise of Zero Inn to have 50 rooms available for Travel Group X on the agreed day. The promise was not kept, thus giving the travel group the right to

seek damages (dollars) in court, or a remedy in equity. If the promise had been kept, the law would recognize that as having been a duty."

Next, it is useful to examine the basic contract classifications.

Classifications

Contracts can be joint or several; bilateral or unilateral; executory or executed; express or implied; and void, voidable, and unenforceable.

Joint or Several

A joint contract is one in which A and B bind themselves to C so that both are responsible for the obligations assumed. Both must be sued by C if they fail to meet their obligations. A "several contract" is one in which either A or B may be sued for breach, at the election of C.

Bilateral or Unilateral

If A and B enter into a contract and each makes binding promises to the other, the contract is "bilateral"—or two-party. If an "offeror"—the one who makes an offer—does not want a promise in return, the situation is "unilateral." For example, A says "cut down that tree at the inn and carry away all debris and I will pay you $200." This is a *promise for an act* and does not create a binding obligation on either—at least not at that point. If B cuts down the tree and removes the debris, the act requested is completed and A must pay the sum promised. The same situation often arises in the making of room reservations.

A Unilateral Reservation Contract

For example, it is late afternoon and the inn is nearing capacity. Ninety percent of the guests have checked in, and an additional 8 percent of the available rooms are out on guaranteed reservations. Assuming the inn has 300 rooms, six rooms remain available.

If a walk-in requests a room, the common-law duty to receive requires acceptance assuming that person is in acceptable condition and able to pay. Five vacancies now exist.

A phone caller then requests a "room for tonight, down and out, arrival at 5:30 P.M." The caller is an American Express card holder who offers to guarantee payment by use of the card number.

Two options now are available. One can accept the reser-

vation unconditionally, reducing the available rooms to four, or accept the reservation with the condition that the traveler arrive by a specified time. The latter is an option since the common-law duty to receive does *not* extend to phone reservations.

One could reply, "We will hold the room for you if you arrive no later than 6 P.M. If you don't, we will sell the room if someone wants it."

A unilateral offer has been created. We have promised to have the room available if that person performs the act of arriving by the stated time. If he or she arrives on time, the sale is made—if not, the room is available for a potential guest, and bookings can reach 100 percent.

Unilateral Contracts: Another Example at the Inn

An employee handbook created by an inn sets forth duties, rights, responsibilities, penalties, and the like. This is an example in which there is only one set of promises and they have been made by the inn. As the employees go about their duties, those acts constitute an acceptance and the terms of the handbook become contractual.

Closely related to the making of reservations in unilateral form is the using of *conditions* when taking reservations.

Conditions on Inn Reservations

When making a reservation contract, it is permissible for the innkeeper to place condi-

tions on that contract. Some examples would be a "cash deposit received in advance," a "minimum stay of three days," and "subject to cancellation if the guest does not arrive by 6:00 P.M." If such conditions are not met, the reservation contract does not come into being. As a judge once said, "Conditions are the arch enemy of the promise," for the more conditions one makes, the less the promise is worth. Thus, their use in HRI operations makes good business sense. Conditions can be "precedent" (meaning something must first happen), "concurrent" (meaning some event must occur at the same time as another event), or "subsequent" (meaning that some event must follow an event).

Another classification is that of executory and executed contracts.

Executory and Executed

An executory contract is one in which one or both parties must yet perform. An executed contract is one that has been performed with nothing left for either to do. A promise to sell land is an executory contract. After the deed is transferred and the price paid, the contract is executed.

Express or Implied

An express contract is one in which the promises and terms are stated by the parties. Implied contracts arise "from mutual agreement and intent to promise but where the agreement and promise have not been expressed in words. Such contracts are true contracts and have sometimes been called contracts implied in fact."

Void, Voidable, and Unenforceable

A void contract is technically no contract at all. It may be a contract that the parties felt was valid but that has been held by a court to be invalid. "Void contract" is thus a redundancy. A "voidable" contract is one that is valid but has built within it the right of one or both of the parties to avoid all obligations under the contract. A, a minor, buys an item from B, an adult. A can void the contract because of A's age and B can do nothing about it. However, until A voids, B is bound to perform with A.

An unenforceable contract is one that, for some reason, cannot be enforced by one against another. A contract may be unenforceable in part and enforceable in the balance. For example, A contracts with B and the contract contains six provisions. Two of these provisions are illegal but the other four are not. The contract is unenforceable as to the two provisions and valid as to the balance. This brings into play the "blue pencil doctrine." If such a contract gets before a court, the judge can "blue pencil" the illegal provisions and enforce the others.

Turning from classifications, it becomes necessary to examine the legal requirements for the creation of a binding conventional contract sometimes called "common-law contracts."

The Statutes of Frauds

The first factor to consider in contract making is the "statutes of frauds," which require certain contracts to be in written form and "signed by the party(ies) to be charged."

Historically such laws were called "Statutes of Frauds," because they were designed to prevent fraud in the use of contracts and they are called this now. Examples of contracts that must be in writing and signed include:

1. Contracts involving the sale of real estate or any interest in real estate.
2. Contracts that cannot be performed in one year.
3. Promises of one person to pay the debt of another.
4. Leases for more than one year.
5. Contracts in which one person promises another money or property if that person will enter into marriage with the other.
6. Promises of those who handle deceased persons' estates to pay the debts of creditors out of their own pockets if there is not enough in the estate for that purpose.

A helpful way to gain an understanding of the statutes of frauds is to ask oneself, "What *isn't* covered?" If a pending contract does not fall into one of the six areas, then the contract *does not have to be in writing to be binding.* A sampling of noncovered areas follows:

1. Personal-service contracts, even though they are to last for more than one year.
2. Providing a service as contrasted to a sale.
3. Leases of real estate for less than one year.
4. The sale of items of real estate which are to be removed from the real estate by the seller.
5. Inn reservations on a short-term basis.

This brings us to the *form* of contracts.

Form of the Contract

No particular words are necessary to show contractual promises or the intention of the parties as they relate to those promises. With the exception of those contracts that must be in writing under the statute of frauds, oral contracts are as binding as written contracts. For example, a hotel manager can hire an assistant manager orally and the terms agreed upon are binding. Employment contracts are an exception to the statute of fraud's one year provision. Even if the employment may last for years, it *could* have ended in the first year by the death of the employee. Therefore, it is *not* a contract that *cannot be performed* in one year—a technical point.

Related to form are time periods in which contracts can be enforced in court.

Statute of Limitations

In each state, a statute of limitations controls the time within which one may sue for breach of contract. The period

Step 1:

$$\text{Offeror} \xrightarrow{\text{Offer}} \text{Offeree}$$

The offeror (or promisor) has made an offer, the form of which is a question: "Here is my offer (or promise). Do you want the benefits of it?"

At this point the offer is a mere Inquiry. In the absence of a standing relationship between the parties, there is no obligation on the part of the offeree to reply. He or she may stand silent and the silence will not constitute an acceptance.

FIGURE 1

of five to ten years is typical and starts when the breach occurs, not from the date of the contract.

Turning from the statutes of frauds and the form of contracts, we next examine the legal requirements of a contract that can be enforced in court.

Requirements of a Binding Contract

The conventional contract has six requirements that must come into being before it becomes legally enforceable. These requirements are offer, acceptance, mutuality (or meeting of the minds, sometimes called "manifestation of mutual assent"), consideration, competent parties, and legal purpose. We will examine each in turn.

Offer

An offer is made by the "offeror" ("promisor") and is most often a statement of what that person is willing to do if the other is willing to do what is requested. While an offer is a promise, it is condi-

tional. The promise may lapse if not accepted within a reasonable time, or it may be revoked by the one who made it, provided the revocation comes before an acceptance. It must come to the mind of the offeree—the one to whom it is directed. An offer may be rejected by the offeree, or the offeree may make a "counteroffer" which is treated as a rejection of the offer. Mere silence on the part of the offeree is nothing at law and thus the offer will lapse after the passage of a reasonable time.

An offer must be definite in its terms. If there is an offer and an acceptance, but the terms are so indefinite that they cannot be determined, the court will hold that there is no contract.

To assist in understanding the process under discussion, the main steps have been placed into a drawing. Examine Figure 1, Step 1.

The offer will not last indefinitely and, if made face to face, ends when the parties part. It can lapse after the passage of time; it can be revoked by the one who makes

it so long as this happens before it is accepted; it can be rejected by the one to whom it is made, thus bringing it to an end; it can end by the making of a counteroffer; it can end by destruction of the subject matter of the offer, by illegal interventions, and by acceptance. An offer also ends upon the death or insanity of the offeror if either event occurs before acceptance. An offer cannot be assigned unless it takes the form of a written option. The brother of the offer is the "acceptance."

Acceptance

Acceptance occurs when there is some assent that the offeree wants to be bound in a contract with the offeror. If the offer specifies a time by which acceptance must be made, an acceptance after that time is ineffective. If no time limit is specified, an offer must be accepted within a reasonable time. Acceptance comes too late if an offer lapses, is revoked, or is rejected. If a dispute arises as to whether or not an offer was ac-

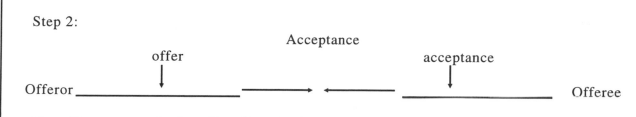

Step 2:

Acceptance

offer   acceptance

Offeror _____   ⟶ ⟵   _____ Offeree

The offeree wants the benefits offered and accepts. The acceptance may be the nod of a head at an auction, or a written acceptance if dictated by the statutes of frauds.

FIGURE 2

cepted, it becomes a question of fact for a jury to determine.

Just as with the offer, an acceptance must be communicated. If the offer is revoked before an acceptance is received, the acceptance fails.

An acceptance can be made in the form in which the offer is made. That is, if an oral offer is made, the acceptance can be oral. If the offer is in writing, the acceptance should be in writing. If an offer is made by mail and acceptance is also made by mail, the acceptance is effective when mailed. The offeror chose the mail, so when the acceptance was mailed it was in the hands of the offeror's agent and thus effective at that time. The rule that acceptance made by mail is good when mailed was laid down in the case of *Adams v. Lindsell*. Thus the rule is part of the common law.

Acceptance can come about by signing a document, by acts where the offer is in unilateral form, by conduct, by trade usage, and even by custom. If the offeror specifies that the acceptance will not be effective until received, then that provision controls. In a face-to-face situation a nod of

the head may be a good acceptance.

An acceptance must conform to the offer, and if it varies the terms of the offer, it will fail. The offer must also be accepted in its totality or not at all. An attempt to accept part would vary the terms of the offer and is not permitted. If parties exchange letters and the terms in those letters are not on "all fours," there is no contract. The letters are merely proposals of each to contract with the other. The court will treat them as "negotiations." If the terms in the letters agree, a contract will result. Examine Step 2, Figure 2.

Mutuality

A contract implies mutual obligations. What "mutuality" means will vary with the types of contract situations and the intention of the parties. It at least implies that the parties have agreed to assume obligations that move from each of them to the other. In a situation where there is a promise for a promise, the mutuality is provided by the mutual promises, spoken of in law as the

quid pro quo. Examine Step 3, Figure 3.

Consideration

Consideration has been defined as "a benefit to the party promising or a loss or detriment to the party to whom a promise is made." It is thought of by the courts as "reasons for enforcing promises," and it does not need to be expressed in, or equated to, economic value. It can be doing nothing if that is what the parties bargain for. For centuries, it has been essential for consideration to be present in traditional contracts (at least Anglo-American contracts). In some states, the applying of a seal to a contract (a formal contract) will supply the consideration. In sales contracts, the law has moved sharply away from consideration.

While consideration must be present, there is no requirement that it be adequate monetarily. The parties to a contract are considered to be the sole judges of value as it relates to consideration. A promise to sell a $10 million hotel for $1.00 would be adequate consideration if that is what

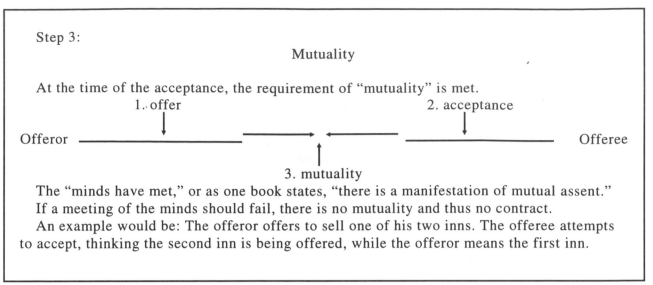

Step 3:

Mutuality

At the time of the acceptance, the requirement of "mutuality" is met.

1. offer   2. acceptance

Offeror ————————————→ →———————← ————————————↓—————————— Offeree

3. mutuality

The "minds have met," or as one book states, "there is a manifestation of mutual assent."
If a meeting of the minds should fail, there is no mutuality and thus no contract.
An example would be: The offeror offers to sell one of his two inns. The offeree attempts to accept, thinking the second inn is being offered, while the offeror means the first inn.

FIGURE 3

the parties in fact bargained for. Contract law does not require that value be given for value, only that consideration, in some form, be present. Anything that confers a benefit on the party to whom the promise is made, or loss or inconvenience to the party making the promise, is sufficient. Consideration could be an extension of payment on a note—or giving up smoking. The consideration does not have to have any interest to the party making the promise. It is sufficient if it affects the interest of the party to whom the promise is made.

As a black letter rule, mutual promises standing alone provide the consideration to support them. However, agreeing to do what one is already bound to do will not supply consideration, since it provides no legal reason to enforce this promise. In addition, something that has occurred before a promise is made will not support that promise. Consideration must

relate to the present or future. Examine Step 4, Figure 4.

Consideration can take the form of an act, a promise, a nonact, a forbearance, cash, or a combination of these elements. One characteristic of it is that there must be some change, no matter how slight or insignificant, in the legal status of the parties. Other matters that supply consideration include support and maintenance, withholding competition, and giving up the right to file a lawsuit.

"Failure of consideration" occurs when what is promised does not materialize as agreed.

In addition to the four requirements just discussed, a contract must be between parties of contractual capacity and have legal purpose. (Our "step" drawings are not necessary here.)

Competent Parties

Both parties to a contract must be of the age of majority; functioning free from du-

ress, fraud, or mistake; and have no mental disabilities that would render them incapable of knowing the nature and consequences of their acts. An incompetent party can cause a contract to be void or voidable, depending upon the circumstances. The following are considered to be incompetent to contract: infants; those who are adjudicated insane; intoxicated persons; those under the influence of narcotics; and those who, because of the nature of the surrounding circumstances, are not capable of exercising normal, rational judgment.

Legal Purpose

A contract must be for a legal purpose. Courts will not force parties to do illegal acts even if they contract to do them. Thus if a so-called contract is for an illegal purpose, it cannot and will not be enforced in court. Illegal bargains, which often involve violations of statutes, include

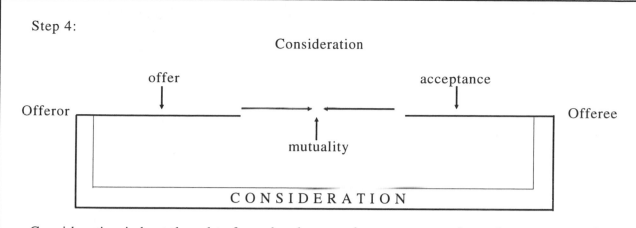

Step 4:

Consideration

offer   acceptance

Offeror   Offeree

mutuality

CONSIDERATION

Consideration is best thought of as a legal reason for a court to enforce the agreement. It can be money, or it can assume other forms at law. It does not have to be adequate—it simply must be present. It supports or holds up the offer and acceptance.

FIGURE 4

contracts of bribery, extortion, gambling, usury, and contracts to violate licensing laws.

Following is a list of inn situations that involve conventional contracts.

Conventional-Contract Inn Examples

1. A requests a room at the inn and the inn accepts.
2. A reserves a room at the inn but it is conditioned upon arrival before 6:00 P.M. A arrives at 5:45 P.M.
3. C agrees in writing to sell her inn to D for $10,000,000.
4. Guest X at Zero Hotel gives his suit to a bellboy for cleaning and pressing and return the next day.
5. Travel Agent Z books T on a trip around the world.
6. Guest H deposits valuables at the front desk of the inn.

7. Traveler Jim leaves his auto with the inn valet.
8. At a restaurant, patron U checks her valuable fur at the check room and pays a $1.00 fee.

It is next necessary to learn something about contract "performance" and "breach."

Performance and Breach

In the countless contracts entered into yearly, most are performed without problems arising. It is to those contracts about which disputes arise that we will briefly turn.

Breach

A breach of contract has been defined as anything so material and important as in truth and fairness will defeat the essential purposes of the parties to a contract.

Where a breach occurs, damages to compensate the other party for loss are generally available. However, the other party may not be able to prove loss and thus recover nothing. It should also be understood that a breach of contract is not a criminal act. It is simply a violation of the civil duty to honor one's promises. The Thirteenth Amendment prohibits "involuntary servitude" and this keeps civil debts from being criminal in nature.

Anticipatory Breach

If one party to a contract has made it clear that he or she will not perform when the time arises, the other party can "anticipate" the breach and sue at once.

Refusal to Perform

If, when time of performance arrives, one party refuses to perform, that party is guilty of the first breach and can be held responsible for loss caused by the refusal. But if one refuses to perform a minor part of a contract, this may not excuse the other party from performing.

If a breach occurs because of fraud on the part of one party, the injured party may sue in tort or contract. If one proceeds in a contract action for the loss suffered, a later tort action will be barred since an "election" has been made. One cannot sue twice on one civil cause of action.

Damages Recoverable

What can be recovered because of a breach of contract are damages that fairly, reasonably, and naturally arise in the course of such breach. One will not be allowed to escape liability where the loss will be substantial but not capable of precise determination. The court will allow a "reasonable standards" measurement to be used with the matter being a question of fact for a jury to determine. If proof of damages must be based on pure speculation, however, the proof will fail. The courts will not permit guessing in the proof of contract damages.

What About Damages to Punish?

Punitive (exemplary—to make an example of) damages are not allowed in breach of contract cases. Yet if the breach is accompanied by a willful or malicious tort, this may create an independent claim for punitive damages that may be allowed by a court.

If a breach of a reservation contract is caused by no-shows, the inn has the right to seek damages. For a case in which a hotel recovered for the cost of 120 rooms not occupied, see *Hotel Del Coronado v. Qwip Systems*.

As a general rule, damages in a court action cannot exceed the assets of the defendants, whether a hotel corporation, chief executive officers at an inn, directors of inn personnel, or others.

What About Custom and Usage?

Can custom and usage be used to defeat a contract action for breach of a reservation contract? A federal judge in Pennsylvania had this to say: "The plain terms of the contract prevail over trade usage or custom. . . . Custom and usage evidence cannot create an ambiguity where none exists."

Nominal Damages

Another type of damages are known as "nominal damages." When such damages are awarded, it means that the winning party has proved liability but has failed in his or her proof of loss. The typical nominal-damages verdict is $1.00. Such an award has the practical effect of placing the costs of the litigation on the losing party. The *USFL v. NFL* litigation ended with such an award.

Liquidated Damages

The parties to a contract may agree in advance as to what the damages will be in the event of a later breach.

Such provisions are enforceable provided that they bear a reasonable relationship to actual loss and are not in the form of a penalty. The term "liquidated" tells us that the damages are "set" and thus not a subject of speculation.

To illustrate, Motel Zero contracts with Ace Construction to remodel the pool. The price agreed upon is $200,000, which includes all costs and labor. The work is to be completed no later than May 31, the customary pool opening date in Eastern states.

The parties agree that, if the work is not completed by that date, the construction firm will forfeit $500 for each day the firm is late. Since the motel sells pool memberships at $100 per family, the agreed-upon damages would be reasonable and would be enforced by the court. If the pool is 30 days late in the completion, the motel can deduct $15,000 from the final payment.

If a liquidated-damage clause is not included in a contract, and even if a completion date is spelled out, the passage of that time without completion of the contract will generally *not* be held to be a breach. The exception to this would be if the contract makes "time of the essence," and contains those words or words to the same effect.

"Time Is of the Essence"

If these or similar words are included in a contract, the courts will treat the date specified as the time by which performance must be completed. Otherwise, the completion date will be treated as an approximate date.

In some contract situations, the legal remedy of damages (dollars) may not be sufficient. A second remedy is provided by "equity."

Specific Performance

If the subject matter of a contract is unique, upon breach by one party the other party may ask a judge to specifically require the breaching party to perform. This remedy is available in real estate contracts where one refuses to perform as promised. Since each parcel of real estate is unique, the remedy of specific performance can be used.

Specific performance cannot be used in personal-service contracts or in any situation in which supervision of the court would be needed to carry out the contract. A court will not place itself in the position of an overseer. The only remedy would be an action for damages in such cases.

To conclude our discussion of conventional contracts, we will examine implied contracts, illegal contracts, and contracts that violate public policy.

Implied Contracts

An express contract must be distinguished from a contract implied in fact and one implied in law. The principle involved in implied contracts is an equitable one that holds that one should not unjustly enrich oneself at the expense of another.

A contract implied in fact is a true contract, the terms of which will be inferred from the circumstances. When one confers benefits upon another, which the other knows of and should pay for, the law implies an agreement that such payment will be made. An express contract is thus distinguishable from one implied in fact. In the former, the terms are agreed upon. In the latter, the terms are implied from the conduct of the parties.

Contracts *implied in law* are not true contracts and are resorted to by the courts for purposes of remedy only. Such situations are often referred to as "quasi-contracts." The widest application would be in situations where, if they were not used, an injustice would occur.

As a general rule, where there is an express contract, an implied contract in fact or in law will never arise. The express contract controls.

Illegal Contracts

An illegal contract is one that has as its object an illegal purpose. As a general rule, an illegal contract is void—not voidable—and cannot be the subject of a court action for breach of that contract. There can be no enforcement of an illegal contract in law or equity whether the illegality existed at the outset or "intervened" later. For example, a subsequent statute may make the terms of a prior contract unlawful. In addition, "when an illegal modification of a lawful contract is attempted, the modification is a nullity and the contract is unscathed."

An illegal contract should be distinguished, however, from one that is against "public policy."

Contracts Against Public Policy

"Public policy" relates to the requirements of the public welfare. "Whatever tends to injustice or oppression, restraint of liberty, commerce, and natural or legal rights; whatever tends to obstruction of justice, or to the violation of a statute; and whatever is against good morals, when made the object of a contract, is against public policy and therefore void and not susceptible of enforcement." Thus, while a contract against public policy may be illegal, it is not so limited because, otherwise, legal contracts may violate public policy.

Whenever a court must look at such a matter, the court will not look for a precise definition of "public policy" and will not hesitate in its practical application to the law of contracts. An example of a contract against public policy would be one in which "a party stipulates for his exemption from liability for the consequences of his own negligence." Such a contract is not permitted at law. Other examples include contracts to influence legislation, the joining of companies to circumvent the effect of restrictive statutes, and a contract by a servant promising to release the master *before* injury occurs to others.

To conclude the chapter, we will examine an old HRI case that still carries an important message.

Ms. Aaron entered into a contractual relationship with a bathhouse at Coney Island, paying 25 cents as the consideration for that contract. The contract was then breached by those in charge of the bathhouse and Ms. Aaron sought damages. The ALI definition of contract told us that, for a breach of contract, the law gives a remedy. That "remedy" is the subject matter of the case.

AARON V. WARD[15]

APPEAL, by permission, from a judgment of the Appellate Division of the Supreme Court in the second judicial department entered March 21, 1910, affirming a judgment of the Municipal Court of the city of New York in favor of plaintiff.

The nature of the action and the facts, so far as material, are stated in the opinion.

In all cases of breach of contract (breach of promise of marriage excepted) the plaintiff's loss is measured by the benefit to him of having the contract performed, and this is, therefore, the true measure of damages. The cases where actions *ex contractu* have been brought against carriers and transportation companies wherein damages have been allowed for humiliation, indignities and mental suffering or anguish are highly exceptional in their character, and arise altogether out of the peculiar nature and character of the particular contract under consideration.

The business conducted by the defendant was purely private in its nature, and the ticket of admission by the plaintiff was entirely revocable at the pleasure of the defendant, and the latter could, if necessary, expel the plaintiff from the premises with all reasonable force.

The trial court having found for the plaintiff it had a right to award the plaintiff compensatory damages and was not limited to the actual loss of money sustained which in this case was twenty-five cents, the price of the ticket. The case at bar is analogous to that of a passenger for wrongful treatment by a common carrier and to that of a guest for injuries to feelings by an innkeeper. The claim that the business of keeping bathing houses for hire is not of the same public nature as that of a common carrier or an innkeeper and may be said to be a private enterprise may be sound without, however, affecting the rule as to the measure of damages.

[The Opinion of the Court Now Follows:]

CULLEN, Ch. J. The defendant was the proprietor of a bathing establishment on the beach at Coney Island. The plaintiff, intending to take a bath in the surf, purchased a ticket from the defendant's employees for the sum of twenty-five cents, and took her position in a line of the defendant's patrons leading to a window at which the ticket entitled her to receive, upon its surrender, a key admitting her to a bathhouse. When she approached the window a dispute arose between her and the defendant's employees as to the right of another person not in the line to have a key given to him in advance of the plaintiff. As a result of this dispute plaintiff was ejected from the defendants premises, the agents of the latter refusing to furnish her with the accommodations for which she had contracted. It is not necessary to discuss the merits of the dispute or narrate its details as the questions of fact involved in that matter have been decided in plaintiff's favor by the Municipal Court, in which she subsequently brought suit, and that judgment has been unanimously affirmed by the Appellate Division. The plaintiff was awarded $250 damages against the defendant's contention that she was not entitled to any recovery in excess of the sum paid for the ticket, and the correctness of the defendant's contention is the only question presented on this appeal.

The action is for a breach of the defendant's contract and not for a tortious expulsion. It is so denominated in the complaint and was necessarily so brought as the Municipal Court has no jurisdiction over an action for tort. It is contended for the defendant that as the action was on contract, the plaintiff was not entitled to any damages for the indignity of her expulsion from the defendant's establishment. It may be admitted that, as a general rule, mental suffering resulting from a breach of contract is not a subject of compensation, but the rule is not universal. It is the settled law of this state that a passenger may recover damages for insulting and slanderous words uttered by the conductor of a railway car as a breach of the company's contract of carriage. *(Gillespie v. Brooklyn Heights R. R. Co.,* 178 N.Y. 347.) The same rule obtains where the servant of an innkeeper offers insult to the guest. *(de Wolfe v. Ford,* 193 N Y 397.) *And it must be borne in mind that a recovery for indignity and wounded feelings is compensatory and does not constitute exemplary damages. (Hamilton v. Third Ave. R. R. Co.,* 53 N.Y. 25.)

It is insisted, however, that there is a distinction between common carriers and innkeepers, who are obliged to serve all persons who seek accommodation from them, and the keepers of public places of amusement or resort, such as the bathhouse of the defendant, theaters and the like. That the distinction exists is undeniable, and in the absence of legislation the keeper of such an establishment may discriminate and serve whom he pleases. [It must be kept in mind that there is no longer an "absence of legislation" because of the *Civil Rights Act* of 1964/72.] Therefore, in such a case a refusal would give no cause of action. So, also, it is the general rule of law that a ticket for admission to a place of public amusement is but a license and revocable. But granting both propositions, that the defendant might have refused the plaintiff a bath ticket and access to his premises, and that even after selling her a ticket he might have revoked the license to use the premises for the purpose of bathing, which the ticket imported, neither proposition necessarily determines that the plaintiff was not entitled to recover damages for the indignity inflicted upon her by the revocation. We have seen that in the case of a common carrier or innkeeper, a person aggrieved may recover such damages as for a breach of contract, while on the other hand, on the breach of ordinary contracts, a party would not be so entitled, and the question is, to which class of cases the case before us most closely approximates. In several of the reported cases the keeping of a theater is spoken of as a strictly private undertaking, and it is said that the owner of a theater is under no obligation to give entertainment at all. The latter proposition is true, but the business of maintaining a theater cannot be said to be "strictly" private. In *People v. King* (110 N.Y. 418) the question was as to the constitutionality of the Civil Rights Act of this state which made it a misdemeanor to deny equal enjoyment of any accommodation, facilities and privileges of inns, common carriers, theaters or other places of public resort or amusement regardless of race, creed or color, and gave the party aggrieved the right to recover a penalty of from fifty to five hundred dollars for the offense. The statute was upheld on the ground that under the doctrine of *Munn v. Illinois* (94 U.S. 113) theaters and places of public amusement (the case before the court was that of a skating rink) were affected with a public interest which justified legislative regulation and interference. In *Greenberg v. Western Turf Assn.* (140 Cal. 357) a statute making it unlawful to refuse to any person admission to a place of public amusement and giving the person aggrieved the right to recover his damages and a hundred dollar penalty in addition thereto, was upheld on the authority of the cases we have cited—a decision plainly correct, because if the legislature can forbid discrimination by the owners of such resorts on the ground of race, creed or color, it may equally forbid discrimination on any other ground. Our statute has since been amended so as to expressly include keepers of bathhouses. On the other hand, no one will contend that the legislature could forbid discrimination in the private business affairs of life—prevent an employer from refusing to employ colored servants, or a servant from refusing to work for a white or for a colored master. So, it has been held that a bootblack may refuse to black a colored man's shoes without being liable to the penalty prescribed by our statute. *(Burks v. Bosso,* 180 N.Y. 341.) Such conduct may be the result of prejudice entirely, but a man's prejudices may be part of his most cherished possessions, which cannot be invaded except when displayed in the conduct of public affairs or quasi public enterprises. That public amusements and resorts are subject to the exercise of this legislative control shows that they are not entirely private. Therefore, though under the present law the plaintiff might have been denied admission altogether to the defendant's bathhouse, provided she were not excluded on account of race, creed or color (*Grannan v. Westchester Racing Assn.,* 153, N.Y. 449), the defendant having voluntarily entered into a contract with her admitting her to the premises and agreeing to afford facilities for bathing, her status became similar to that of a passenger of a common carrier or a guest of an innkeeper, and in case of her improper expulsion she should be entitled to the same measure of damages as obtains in actions against carriers or innkeepers when brought for breach of their contracts. The reason why such damages are recoverable in the cases mentioned is not merely because the defendants are bound to give the plaintiffs accommodation, but also because of the indignity suffered by a public expulsion. In a theater or other place of public amusement or resort the indignity and humiliation caused by an expulsion in the presence of a large number of people is as great, if not greater, than in the case of an expulsion by a carrier or innkeeper, as it is the publicity of the thing that causes the humiliation.

The judgment of the Appellate Division should be affirmed, with costs.

GRAY, WERNER, WILLARD BARTLETT, HISCOCK, CHASE and COLLIN, JJ., concur.

Judgment affirmed.

Objective: Upon completion of this project, the student will have:

1. Selected and researched a pertinent topic of a legal nature applicable to the hospitality industry.

2. Conducted a survey/interview with a hospitality executive to discuss the selected topic and evaluate how he/she has addressed the issue relative to the operation.

3. Presented the documented research and the survey/interview results in a formal report. (Length and format to be determined by the instructor)

Possible Topics

1. Americans with Disabilities Act (1992)

2. Discrimination—Civil Rights Acts (1964, 1991) Title II—Admission, Title VII—Employment

3. Alcohol Service Liability/Server Awareness

4. Liability for the Sale of Foods/Implied warranties

5. Sexual Harassment

6. Risk Management/Crisis Management

7. Swimming Pools/Recreation Facilities Management and Liability

8. Property of Guests—Limiting Liability Statutes

9. Automobiles and Parking Facilities

10. Hospitality Contracts

11. Workmen's Compensation/HazComm/OSHA

12. Personal Injury Liability (Torts) in Hotels/Restaurants

13. Liability for Actions of Employees

14. Security—Internal and External

15. Property Maintenance:
    Snow and Ice Removal
    Hot Water
    Walkways and Stairways
    Glass Doors
    Furniture and Fixtures
    Other

16. Wrongful Firings/Discharge of Employees

17. Duty to Receive Guests—Hotels

18. Rights of Guests to Privacy/Fourth Amendment

19. Grounds for Eviction/Forceful Removal of Guests/Patrons

20. Acquired Immune Deficiency Syndrome in the workplace.

21. Drug Testing

This list is not exhaustive, it is only meant to provide suggestions to the student.

Required

1. The student will select a topic and use conventional research methods to investigate the subject and provide the informative content of the report.

2. The student will conduct an survey/interview with a hospitality executive to discuss the subject matter and its application to the particular operation. Any documentation, journals, policy statements, incident reports, etc., regarding the subject matter provided by the operation should be included in the report.

3. The student will also include his/her individual thoughts and opinions in the report, combining the facts gained through specific research and the results of the interview.

Objective

Upon completion of this project, the student will have:

1. Evaluated a situation/incident which could have occurred in a hospitality operation that may ultimately result in litigation.

2. Identified the specific application of the appropriate area of the law to the situation.

3. Provided an informed opinion based on research of similar cases.

Required

1. In each of the following examples, a certain specific area of the law is applicable. The student will read the "case" and identify the legal subject matter.

2. Using whatever resources available, (textbooks, newspaper, magazine, journal articles, documented court cases, etc.) the student will investigate how the case might be decided, citing examples of similar situations and the application of the laws identified in #1 above.

3. Provide a conclusion based on the information gathered and the student's individual observations.

4. The length of the report should not exceed 2–3 typewritten pages.

Hospitality Law Volume 6, N. 7 July 1991

Drew v. LeJay's Sportsmen's Cafe, Inc. 806 P 2nd. 301, WY. 1191

Eddie Drew and Ted Gonzales went to LeJay's restaurant in Jackson, WY, around 1:30 a.m. after a night of "partying." Drew started choking after only a few bites of his meal.

Gonzales was slow to realize the seriousness of the situation: when Drew could no longer talk and did not move, Gonzales finally sought help. Initially, he simply asked three or four times for a cloth to wipe Drew's mouth, but he testified that he also said several times, "This man is dying over here."

After Gonzales tried several times to summon help, restaurant employees threatened to call the police on him, and Gonzales told them to go ahead. From the testimony, Gonzales talked to waitresses, the cashier and the cook. It is not clear how many times he asked employees for help, or in what order, but he did ask more than once. Some time during this activity, Gonzales asked customers near Drew for help, and they placed Drew on the floor and gave him mouth-to-mouth resuscitation. When the police arrived, they continued giving mouth-to-mouth resuscitation to Drew.

Although Gonzales told the police Drew was dying and to call an ambulance, this was not done right away. It is unclear how long the wait was for an ambulance to be called or who made the call, but by 2:38 a.m. the ambulance was en route to the restaurant. It began its return trip to the hospital by 2:52 a.m., arriving at 2:55 a.m. Efforts during the ambulance ride and at the hospital failed to revive Drew. At the hospital a two-inch chunk of meat, which caused Drew to have cardiorespiratory arrest, was removed from Drew's trachea. Despite a flight for life to a Denver hospital and further medical attention there, Drew was pronounced dead at 5:51 that evening.

Drew's estate filed a wrongful death action against the restaurant, alleging that Drew died as a result of the restaurant's failure to render first aid and summon emergency help after Drew had begun choking.

Hospitality Law Volume 5 N. 4 April 1990

Southern Bell Tel. and Tel. Co. v. Altman, 359 S.E.2N 385 GA 1987

Southern Bell Telephone Co. sponsored an awards banquet, which was attended by Ross Altman, a Southern Bell employee. Alcoholic beverages were served with the meal, and following dinner, more alcohol was available to attendees at their own expense.

Altman, a reformed alcoholic until this night, voluntarily consumed alcohol during and after the banquet. At the request of a Southern Bell, several of Altman's co-workers kept him at the restaurant for almost an hour and a half after the dinner, and got him to drink some coffee.

These co-workers then persuaded Altman to allow them to drive him home. One drove Altman's truck, followed by the two other co-workers in another vehicle. After delivering Altman to his home and parking his truck, the co-workers started to leave; however, they stopped when they saw Altman get into his truck.

One co-worker got out of the car and asked Altman what he was doing; Altman explained he was only backing his truck into the garage. The three co-workers then waited to see Altman back the truck into the garage, exit the truck, and walk toward the front door of the house. Because it appeared someone was in the house and that Altman was going into his home, the three left.

However, Altman subsequently got back into his truck and drove away. Later that night he was killed in a collision. Altman's wife and the other driver filed suit against Southern Bell.

Hospitality Law Volume 5 N. 5 May 1990

Danieley v. Goldmine: Ski Associates, 266 Cal. App. 749 CA, 1990

Vicki Danieley, her husband, and two sons traveled to the Goldmine Ski Area, adjoining Big Bear Lake in the San Bernandino Mountains for a day of skiing. All had been skiing before, at different resorts, for approximately 3 years, although this was both the first time this season, and the first time at Goldmine.

During the morning session, Vicki spent most of her time in the "novice" area, taking several ski runs to "warm up" for the more difficult trails later in the day.

After lunch, she traveled down slopes marked "intermediate" approximately *ten times* with no difficulty. On eleventh run, on a completely different slope also marked "intermediate," Mrs. Danieley lost control of her skis while attempting a turn and collided with a large tree just beyond the groomed edge of the run.

Mrs. Danieley sustained serious injuries, and swift action by the ski patrol *probably saved her life.* Despite these efforts, she is nonetheless suing the ski resort for damages, charging it with negligence in the operation and maintenance of the premises.

Specifically the complaint alleged that Goldmine had failed *"to remove an obstacle (the tree) immediately adjacent to the ski run which presented an unreasonably high risk of harm . . ."*

Answer the following discussion questions in one page or less. (Provided by Instructor)

1. Consider the *elements of a tort of negligence:* Which of the four elements could be considered *questionable*?

2. Which *tests for negligence* could be used to resolve the questionable element(s) in question #1?

3. Which tort doctrine would *most likely be used* to decide the outcome of the case?

Hospitality Law Volume 5 N. 8 August 1990

Fennema v. Howard Johnson Co., 559 So.2d 1231, FL 1990

Robert Fennema and his wife Kimberly moved from Washington State to Dade County, Florida. They travelled in a Chevy Camaro and a rented 24-foot U-Haul truck, which, stuffed full with their belongings, also towed their Toyota Land Cruiser. Upon arrival in Dade County, they pulled in to a Howard Johnson Motor Lodge.

Mrs. Fennema went into the motel office and registered. She told the registration clerk they had a Toyota Land Cruiser towed by a large U-Haul truck containing nearly all of their personal belongings and asked for a safe place to park.

The clerk told her to park in the motel parking lot behind a building where it presumably would be safe from vandalism or theft. That is where they parked. Although there had been numerous incidents of criminal activity, including motor vehicle thefts on or about the motel grounds, the Fennemas weren't given this information or warned of potential risks.

The Fennemas spent the night in the motel and went for a drive in the Camaro the following day. When they returned to the motel at 3 p.m., they discovered the U-haul had been stolen. The Fennemas are suing the hotel for $177,000; the hotel is arguing that a Florida limiting liability statute limits its liability to $1,000.

Hospitality Law Volume 5 N. 7 July 1990

Mayo v. Hyatt Corp., 898 F. 2d 47, LA 1990

Jack Mayo fell down several steps at the Hyatt Regency Hotel in New Orleans, cracked his skull and died three days later.

Tests indicated he had a blood-alcohol level over three times the legal limit for intoxication, and that he had ingested a substantial amount of cocaine.

Mark Heitzmann, a hotel security employee. described the accident as follows:

About an hour before the accident, Heitzmann observed Mayo on the second floor level of Poydras Mall, adjacent to the Hyatt premise. Mayo appeared intoxicated. but asked Heitzmann for directions to a nearby bar. Heitzmann directed Mayo to Georgie Porgie's in Poydras Mall, which is not on Hyatt property. Just before midnight, Heitzmann encountered Mayo again. Mayo told Heitzmann he was a guest at the Hyatt, but didn't know his room number and had lost his key. Mayo was wobbling and having difficulty speaking coherently, leading Heitzmann to believe he was highly intoxicated.

Consequently, Heitzmann offered to assist Mayo to the Hyatt's registration desk on the first floor to help him get to his room. Heitzmann suggested taking the elevator down to the first floor but Mayo refused and began walking to the stairs instead.

Heitzmann accompanied Mayo downstairs, but within a few steps Mayo began to stumble and fail. Heitzmann caught him and interlocked his arm with Mayo's, holding him up. Mayo protested that he was under control and jerked his arm away from Heitzmann.

After breaking away, Mayo began to descend the stairs much more rapidly. A few steps later, he lost his balance, spun around and fell backwards down the stairs, hitting the back of his head on the floor. Immediately after the accident, Hyatt employees secured an ambulance and sent Mayo to a hospital.

Mayo's widow and three minor children sued the hotel, claiming Heitzmann negligently failed to protect Mayo from the consequences of his own intoxication. That theory was premised on the testimony of their expert witness, who suggested that Heitzmann had inadequate training as a security officer and that a more competent security guard would have taken virtually any measure to cajole, persuade, coerce, or forcibly restrain Mayo from approaching the stairs.

(You may assume that the facts are true as have been presented, there is no need to assume anything else.)

WILL THE HOTEL BE FOUND LIABLE IN THIS CASE? WHY OR WHY NOT?

Hospitality Law Vol. 5 N. 11 November 1990

Freeman v. Kiamesha Concord Inc. 351 N.Y.S. 2d 541 NY 1974

Mr. Freeman saw an advertisement in the New York Times indicating that Joel Gray would perform at the Concord Hotel in the Catskill Mountains during the Memorial Day weekend. Freeman made reservations for his wife and himself at the hotel. In response, he received an offer of a reservation for a "three night minimum stay" that contained a request for a $20 deposit. He forwarded the money confirming the reservation.

While driving to the hotel, Freeman observed a billboard, located about 20 miles from the Concord Hotel, indicating that Joel Gray would perform at the hotel only on Sunday. He checked into the hotel even though he claimed to be disturbed, having thought Gray would perform every day. After staying at the hotel for two days, Freeman advised the management that he wished to check out because of his dissatisfaction with the entertainment. He told the hotel that he had made his reservation believing that Joel Gray would perform throughout the holiday weekend. The management suggested that since Gray was to perform that evening, he should remain. Freeman refused and again asserted his claim that the advertisement constituted a misrepresentation. The hotel insisted upon full payment for the entire three-day guaranteed weekend in accordance with the reservation.

Freeman told hotel employees that he was an attorney, and that they had no right to charge him for the third day of the reserved period if he checked out. He pointed out Section 206 of the general business law that read:

". . . no charge or sum shall be collected or received by any hotelkeeper or innkeeper for an service not actually rendered or for a longer time than the person so charged actually remained at such hotel or inn, provided such guest shall have given such hotelkeeper or innkeeper notice at the office of his departure. For any violation of this section, the offender shall forfeit to the injured party three times the amount so charged."

Freeman was offered a one-day credit for a future stay if he made full payment. He refused the credit, paid the full charges under protest and advised the hotel of his intention to sue them, which he did.

Discussion Questions (Provided by the Instructor)

1. Does a valid and binding contract exist in this case?

2. Is the minimum stay policy offered by the hotel valid?

3. Does Section 206 apply in this case?

4. Did Mr. Freeman receive the services agreed upon?

Hospitality Law Volume 4 N. 11 November 1989

EEOC v. Hacienda Hotel, 881 F 2d 1504 CA 1989

Teodora Castro, a Seventh Day Adventist, observed the Sabbath on Saturday. When she worked for the hotel on an earlier occasion she was given Saturdays off. When she was rehired she asked the executive housekeeper for Saturdays off again.

That request was denied and she was fired when she didn't work on a Saturday.

At the same time, another maid was permitted to have both Saturday and Sunday off for a non-religious reason.

Maria Elena Gonzalez was also a maid and a Jehovah's Witness who observed her Sabbath on Sundays, and she requested Sundays off. The request was initially granted, but two days later that was reversed and she was told she must work Sundays.

Gonzalez filed a union grievance and went to the hotel manager. As a result, the executive housekeeper told Gonzalez that since she complained to the hotel manager, she'd never get Sundays off and that she was going to "make life so difficult for her that she would not know her head from her feet."

In the next month, Gonzalez was given four disciplinary warnings and was fired.

Instructor's Note: Looking for disparate treatment regarding religious discrimination.

Hospitality Law Volume 5 N. 10 October 1990

Coleman v. Shaw, 314 S.E. 2d 154 SC 1984

Jacob Coleman, his wife, son and niece were registered guests at the Lodge. On the morning of his death, Mr. Coleman, 29, and the two children left their second-floor room to swim in the motel pool. According to testimony by the niece, Mr. Coleman swam for awhile, stood up near the pool's dividing rope in waist-high water, appeared to regurgitate and fell into the water. He then floated to the surface, toward the deep end of the pool. The niece ran to get her aunt who was sleeping in the room.

Mrs. Coleman testified she looked out her window and saw her son leaning over the pool's edge. She pulled on her housecoat and ran to the pool. When she got there, she saw her husband at the bottom in a crouched position on his side. Because Mrs. Coleman did not know how to swim, she asked a woman standing nearby if she could swim. The woman couldn't, and Mrs. Coleman ran to the motel front desk and asked the employee there for help. The clerk asked what her husband was doing in the pool alone. When she received no assistance, she went into the coffee shop and began asking people there if they could swim.

One of the men volunteered and dived into the pool, capped Mr. Coleman's mouth with his hands, but saw no air bubbles. He then decided Mr. Coleman was dead, and returned to the coffee shop to tell Mrs. Coleman. She continued to ask that her husband be removed from the pool and attempted to do so herself, but was held back. Only then did the motel employee, who was still behind the front desk, telephone a rescue squad.

Rescue workers arrived about 20 to 30 minutes later but made no attempt to revive Mr. Coleman. According to Mrs. Coleman, she requested an autopsy but one was never performed. Further testimony indicated Mr. Coleman had no major health problems, did not appear ill the morning of his death and had not eaten breakfast before his swim.

The state regulation in effect at the time read in part:

". . . no swimming pool shall allow solo bathing. At least one employee, having had first aid training, shall be on hand at all times. A stretcher, two woolen blankets and other emergency equipment shall be provided. There should be a telephone available with a list of emergency telephone numbers."

No such employee was on hand and no emergency equipment was provided.

21

ETHICS

Ethics Without the Sermon
Laura L. Nash

Students' Perceptions of Ethical Issues in the Hospitality and Tourism Industry
Linda K. Enghagen and David D. Hott

Project 1

Project 2

ETHICS WITHOUT THE SERMON

Laura L. Nash

WHETHER YOU REGARD IT as an unchecked epidemic or as the first blast of Gabriel's horn, the trend toward focusing on the social impact of the corporation is an inescapable reality that must be factored into today's managerial decision making. But for the executive who asks, "How do we as a corporation examine our ethical concerns?" the theoretical insights currently available may be more frustrating than helpful.

Many executives firmly believe that corporate operations and corporate values are dynamically intertwined. For the purposes of analysis, however, the executive needs to uncoil the business-ethics helix and examine both strands closely.

Unfortunately, the ethics strand has remained largely inaccessible, for business has not yet developed a workable process by which corporate values can be articulated. If ethics and business are part of the same double helix, perhaps we can develop a microscope capable of enlarging our perception of both aspects of

business administration— what we do and who we are.

Philosophy has been sorting out issues of fairness, injury, empathy, self-sacrifice, and so on, for more than 2000 years. In seeking to examine the ethics of business, therefore, business logically assumes it will be best served by a "consultant" in philosophy who is already familiar with the formal discipline of ethics.

As the philosopher begins to speak, however, a difficulty immediately arises; corporate executives and philosophers approach problems in radically different ways. The academician ponders the intangible, savors the paradoxical, and embraces the peculiar; he or she speaks in a special language of categorical imperatives and deontological viewpoints that must be taken into consideration before a statement about honesty is agreed to have any meaning.

Like some Triassic reptile, the theoretical view of ethics lumbers along in the far past of Sunday School and Philosophy I, while the reality of practical business concerns is con-

stantly measuring a wide range of competing claims on time and resources against the unrelenting and objective marketplace.

Not surprisingly, the two groups are somewhat hostile. The jokes of the liberal intelligentsia are rampant and weary: *Ethics and Business—* the shortest book in the world." "Business and ethics— a subject confined to the preface of business books." Accusations from the corporate cadre are delivered with an assurance that rests more on an intuition of social climate than on a certainty of fact: "You do-gooders are ruining America's ability to compete in the world."

What is needed is a process of ethical inquiry that is immediately comprehensible to a group of executives and not predisposed to the utopian, and sometimes anticapitalistic, bias marking much of the work in applied business philosophy today. So I suggest, as a preliminary solution, a set of 12 questions that draw on traditional philosophical frameworks but that avoid the

private philanthropy is well known and whose concern for social welfare has long been echoed in the company's personnel policies.

In the past, pressure on senior managers for high profit performance had obscured some of these ideals in practice, and the statement of strategy was a way of radically realigning various competing moral claims with the financial objectives of the company. As one senior manager remarked to me, "The values seem obvious, and if we hadn't been so gross in the past we wouldn't have needed the statement." Despite a predictable variance among Lex's top executives as to the desirability of the values outlined in the statement, it was adopted with general agreement to comply and was scheduled for reassessment at a senior managers' meeting one year after implementation.

1. Have You Defined the Problem Accurately?

How one assembles the facts weights an issue before the moral examination ever begins, and a definition is rarely accurate if it articulates one's loyalties rather than the facts. The importance of factual neutrality is readily seen, for example, in assessing the moral implications of producing a chemical agent for use in warfare. Depending on one's loyalties, the decision to make the substance can be described as serving one's country, developing products, or killing babies. All of the above may be factual statements, but

level of abstraction normally associated with formal moral reasoning.

I offer the questions as a first step in a very new discipline. As such, they form a tentative model that will certainly undergo modifications after its parts are given some exercise. Table 1 poses the 12 questions.

To illustrate the application of the questions, I will draw especially on a program at Lex Service Group, Ltd., whose top management prepared a statement of financial objectives and moral values as a part of its strategic planning process. Lex is a British company with operations in the United Kingdom and the United States. Its sales total

about $1.2 billion. In 1978 its structure was partially decentralized, and in 1979 the chairman's policy group began a strategic planning process. The intent, according to its statement of values and objectives, was "to make explicit the sort of company Lex was, or wished to be."

Neither a paralegal code nor a generalized philosophy, the statement consisted of a series of general policies regarding financial strategy as well as such aspects of the company's character as customer service, employee-shareholder responsibility, and quality of management. Its content largely reflected the personal values of Lex's chairman and CEO, Trevor Chinn, whose

none is neutral or accurate if viewed in isolation.

Similarly, the recent controversy over marketing U.S.-made cigarettes in Third World countries rarely noted that the incidence of lung cancer in underdeveloped nations is quite low (from one-tenth to one-twentieth the rate for U.S. males) due primarily to the lower life expectancies and earlier predominance of other diseases in these nations. Such a fact does not decide the ethical complexities of this marketing problem, but it does add a crucial perspective in the assignment of moral priorities by defining precisely the injury that tobacco exports may cause.

Extensive fact gathering may also help defuse the emotionalism of an issue. For instance, local statistics on lung cancer incidence reveal that the U.S. tobacco industry is not now "exporting death," as has been charged. Moreover, the substantial and immediate economic benefits attached to tobacco may be providing food and health care in these countries. Nevertheless, as life expectancy and the standards of living rise, a higher incidence of cigarette-related diseases appears likely to develop in these nations. Therefore, cultivation of the nicotine habit may be deemed detrimental to the long-term welfare of these nations.

According to one supposedly infallible truth of modernism, technology is so complex that its results will never be fully comprehensible or predictable. Part of the executive's frustration in respond-

ing to question 1 is the real possibility that the "experts" will find no grounds for agreement about the facts.

As a first step, however, defining fully the factual implications of a decision determines to a large degree the quality of one's subsequent moral position. Pericles' definition of true courage rejected the Spartans' blind obedience in war in preference to the courage of the Athenian citizen who, he said, was able to make a decision to proceed in full knowledge of the probable danger. A *truly moral decision is an informed decision. A decision that is based on blind or convenient ignorance is hardly defensible. One simple test of the initial definition is the question:*

2. How Would You Define the Problem If You Stood on the Other Side of the Fence?

The contemplated construction of a plant for Division X is touted at the finance committee meeting as an absolute necessity for expansion at a cost saving of at least 25 percent. With plans drawn up for an energy-efficient building and an option already secured on a 99-year lease in a new industrial park in Chippewa County, the committee is likely to feel comfortable in approving the request for funds in a matter of minutes.

The facts of the matter are that the company will expand in an appropriate market, allocate its resources sensibly, create new jobs, increase Chippewa County's tax base, and most likely increase its re-

turns to the shareholders. To the residents of Chippewa County, however, the plant may mean the destruction of a customary recreation spot, the onset of severe traffic jams, and the erection of an architectural eyesore. These are also facts of the situation, and certainly more immediate to the county than utilitarian justifications of profit performance and rights of ownership from an impersonal corporation whose headquarters are 1000 miles from Chippewa County and whose executives have plenty of acreage for their own recreation.

The purpose of articulating the other side, whose needs are understandably less proximate than operational considerations, is to allow some mechanism whereby calculations of self-interest (or even of a project's ultimate general beneficence) can be interrupted by a compelling empathy for those who might suffer immediate injury or mere annoyance as a result of a corporation's decisions. Such empathy is a necessary prerequisite for shouldering voluntarily some responsibility for the social consequences of corporate operations, and it may be the only solution to today's overly litigious and anarchic world.

There is a power in self-examination: with an exploration of the likely consequences of a proposal, taken from the viewpoint of those who do not immediately benefit, comes a discomfort or an embarrassment that rises in proportion to the degree of the likely injury and its articulation. Like Socrates as gadfly, who stung his fellow citizens into a critical examination of their conduct when they became complacent, the discomfort of the alternative definition is meant to prompt a disinclination to choose the expedient over the most responsible course of action.

Abstract generalities about the benefits of the profit motive and the free market system are, for some, legitimate and ultimate justifications, but when unadorned with alternative viewpoints, such arguments also tend to promote the complacency, carelessness, and impersonality that have characterized some of the more injurious actions of corporations. The advocates of these arguments are like the reformers in Nathaniel Hawthorne's short story "Hall of Fantasy" who "had got possession of some crystal fragment of truth, the brightness of which so dazzled them that they could see nothing else in the whole universe."

In the example of Division X's new plant, it was a simple matter of defining the alternate facts; the process rested largely on an assumption that certain values were commonly shared (no one likes a traffic jam, landscaping pleases more than an unadorned building, and so forth). But the alternative definition often underscores an inherent disparity in values or language. To some, the employment of illegal aliens is a criminal act (fact 1); to others, it is a solution to the 60 percent unemployment rate of a neighboring country (fact 2). One country's bribe is an-

other country's redistribution of sales commissions.

When there are cultural or linguistic disparities, it is easy to get the facts wrong or to invoke a pluralistic tolerance as an excuse to act in one's own self-interest: "That's the way they do things over there. Who are we to question their beliefs?" This kind of reasoning can be both factually inaccurate (many generalizations about bribery rest on hearsay and do not represent the complexities of a culture) and philosophically inconsistent (there are plenty of beliefs, such as those of the environmentalist, which the same generalizers do not hesitate to question).

3. How Did This Situation Occur in the First Place?

Lex Motor Company, a subsidiary of Lex Service Group, Ltd., had been losing share at a 20 percent rate in a declining market; and Depot B's performance was the worst of all. Two nearby Lex depots could easily absorb B's business, and closing it down seemed the only sound financial decision. Lex's chairman, Trevor Chinn, hesitated to approve the closure, however, on the grounds that putting 100 people out of work was not right when the corporation itself was not really jeopardized by B's existence. Moreover, seven department managers, who were all within 5 years of retirement and had had 25 or more years of service at Lex, were scheduled to be made redundant.

The values statement provided no automatic solution

for it placed value on both employees' security and shareholders' interest. Should they close Depot B? At first Chinn thought not: Why should the little guys suffer disproportionately when the company was not performing well? Why not close a more recently acquired business where employee service was not so large a factor? Or why not wait out the short term and reduce head count through natural attrition?

As important as deciding the ethics of the situation was the inquiry into its history. Indeed, the history gave a clue to solving the dilemma: Lex's traditional emphasis on employee security and high financial performance had led to a precipitate series of acquisitions and subsequent divestitures when the company had failed to meet its overall objectives. After each rationalization, the people serving the longest had been retained and placed at Depot B, so that by 1980 the facility had more managers than it needed and a very high proportion of long-service employees.

So the very factors that had created the performance problems were making the closure decision difficult, and the very solution that Lex was inclined to favor again would exacerbate the situation further!

In deciding the ethics of a situation it is important to distinguish the symptoms from the disease. Great profit pressures with no sensitivity to the cycles in a particular industry, for example, may force division managers to be ruthless with employees, to short-weight customers, or even to fiddle with cash flow reports in order to meet headquarters' performance criteria.

Dealing with the immediate case of lying, quality discrepancy, or strained labor relations—when the problem is finally discovered—is only a temporary solution. A full examination of how the situation occurred and what the traditional solutions have been may reveal a more serious discrepancy of values and pressures, and this will illuminate the real significance and ethics of the problem. It will also reveal recurring patterns of events that in isolation appear trivial but that as a whole point up a serious situation.

Such a mechanism is particularly important because very few executives are outright scoundrels. Rather, violations of corporate and social values usually occur inadvertently because no one recognizes that a problem exists until it becomes a crisis. This tendency toward initial trivialization seems to be the biggest ethical problem in business today. Articulating answers to my first three questions is a way of reversing that process.

4. To Whom and What Do You Give Your Loyalties as a Person and as a Member of the Corporation?

Every executive faces conflicts of loyalty. The most familiar occasions pit private conscience and sense of duty against corporate policy, but equally frequent are the situations in which one's close colleagues demand participa-tion (tacit or explicit) in an operation or a decision that runs counter to company policy. To whom or what is the greater loyalty—to one's corporation? superior? family? society? self? race? sex?

The good news about conflicts of loyalty is that their identification is a workable way of smoking out the ethics of a situation and of discovering the absolute values inherent in it. As one executive in a discussion of a Harvard case study put it, "My corporate brain says this action is O.K., but my noncorporate brain keeps flashing these warning lights."

The bad news about conflicts of loyalty is that there are few automatic answers for placing priorities on them. "To thine own self be true" is a murky quagmire when the self takes on a variety of roles, as it does so often in this complex modern world.

Supposedly, today's young managers are giving more weight to individual than to corporate identity, and some older executives see this tendency as being ultimately subversive. At the same time, most of them believe individual integrity is essential to a company's reputation.

The U.S. securities industry, for example, is one of the most rigorous industries in America in its requirements of honesty and disclosure. Yet in the end, all its systematic precautions prove inadequate unless the people involved also have a strong sense of integrity that puts loyalty to these principles above personal gain.

A system, however, must permit the time and foster the motivation to allow personal integrity to surface in a particular situation. An examination of loyalties is one way to bring this about. Such an examination may strengthen reputations but also may result in blowing the whistle (freedom of thought carries with it the risk of revolution). But a sorting out of loyalties can also bridge the gulf between policy and implementation or among various interest groups whose affiliations may mask a common devotion to an aspect of a problem—a devotion on which consensus can be built.

How does one probe into one's own loyalties and their implications? A useful method is simply to play various roles out loud, to call on one's loyalty to family and community (for example) by asking, "What will I say when my child asks me why I did that?" If the answer is "That's the way the world works," then your loyalties are clear and moral passivity inevitable. But if the question presents real problems, you have begun a demodulation of signals from your conscience that can only enhance corporate responsibility.

5. What Is Your Intention in Making This Decision?

6. How Does This Intention Compare with the Likely Results?

These two questions are asked together because their content often bears close resemblance and, by most calculations, both color the ethics of a situation.

Corporation Buglebloom decides to build a new plant in an underdeveloped minority-populated district where the city has been trying with little success to encourage industrial development. The media approve and Buglebloom adds another star to its good reputation. Is Buglebloom a civic leader and supporter of minorities or a canny investor about to take advantage of the disadvantaged? The possibilities of Buglebloom's intentions are endless and probably unfathomable to the public; Buglebloom may be both canny investor and friend of minority groups.

I argue that despite their complexity and elusiveness, a company's intentions do matter. The "purity" of Buglebloom's motives (purely profit-seeking or purely altruistic) will have wide-reaching effects inside and outside the corporation—on attitudes toward minority employees in other parts of the company, on the wages paid at the new plant, and on the number of other investors in the same area—that will legitimize a certain ethos in the corporation and the community.

Sociologist Max Weber called this an "ethics of attitude" and contrasted it with an "ethics of absolute ends." An ethics of attitude sets a standard to ensure a certain action. A firm policy at headquarters of not cheating customers, for example, may also deter salespeople from succumbing to a tendency to lie by omission or purchasers

from continuing to patronize a high-priced supplier when the costs are automatically passed on in the selling price.

What about the ethics of result? Two years later, Buglebloom wishes it had never begun Project Minority Plant. Every good intention has been lost in the realities of doing business in an unfamiliar area, and Buglebloom now has dirty hands: some of those payoffs were absolutely unavoidable if the plant was to open, operations have been plagued with vandalism and language problems, and local resentment at the industrialization of the neighborhood has risen as charges of discrimination have surfaced. No one seems to be benefiting from the project.

The goodness of intent pales somewhat before results that perpetrate great injury or simply do little good. Common sense demands that the "responsible" corporation try to align the two more closely, to identify the probable consequences and also the limitations of knowledge that might lead to more harm than good. Two things to remember in comparing intention and results are that knowledge of the future is always inadequate and that overconfidence often precedes a disastrous mistake.

These two precepts, cribbed from ancient Greece, may help the corporation keep the disparities between intent and result a fearsome reality to consider continuously. The next two questions explore two ways of reducing the moral risks of being wrong.

7. Whom Could Your Decision or Action Injure?

The question presses whether injury is intentional or not. Given the limits of knowledge about a new product or policy, who and how many come into contact with it? Could its inadequate disposal affect an entire community? two employees? yourself? How might your product be used if it happened to be acquired by a terrorist radical group or a terrorist military police force? Has your distribution system or disposal plan ensured against such injury? Could it ever?

If not, there may be a compelling moral justification for stopping production. In an integrated society where business and government share certain values, possible injury is an even more important consideration than potential benefit. In policymaking, a much likelier ground for agreement than benefit is avoidance of injury through those "universal nos"—such as no mass death, no totalitarianism, no hunger or malnutrition, no harm to children.

To exclude *at the outset* any policy or decision that might have such results is to reshape the way modern business examines its own morality. So often business formulates questions of injury only after the fact in the form of liability suits.

8. Can You Engage the Affected Parties in a Discussion of the Problem Before You Make Your Decision?

If the calculus of injury is one way of responding to limitations of knowledge about the probable results of a particular business decision, the participation of affected parties is one of the best ways of informing that consideration. Civil rights groups often complain that corporations fail to invite participation from local leaders during the planning stages of community development projects and charitable programs. The corporate foundation that builds a tennis complex for disadvantaged youth is throwing away precious resources if most children in the neighborhood suffer from chronic malnutrition.

In the Lex depot closure case I have mentioned, senior executives agonized over whether the employees would choose redundancy over job transfer and which course would ultimately be more beneficial to them. The managers, however, did not consult the employees. There were more than 200 projected job transfers to another town. But all the affected employees, held by local ties and uneasy about possibly lower housing subsidies, refused relocation offers. Had the employees been allowed to participate in the redundancy discussions, the company might have wasted less time on relocation plans or might have uncovered and resolved the fears about relocating.

The issue of participation affects everyone. (How many executives feel that someone else should decide what is in *their* best interest?) And yet it is a principle often forgotten because of the pressure of time or the inconvenience of calling people together and facing predictably hostile questions.

9. Are You Confident That Your Position Will be as Valid over a Long Period of Time as It Seems Now?

As anyone knows who has had to consider long-range plans and short-term budgets simultaneously, a difference in time frame can change the meaning of a problem as much as spring and autumn change the colors of a tree. The ethical coloring of a business decision is no exception to this generational aspect of decision making. Time alters circumstances, and few corporate value systems are immune to shifts in financial status, external political pressure, and personnel. (One survey now places the average U.S. CEO's tenure in office at five years.)

At Lex, for example, the humanitarianism of the statement of objectives and values depended on financial prosperity. The values did not fully anticipate the extent to which the U.K. economy would undergo a recession, and the resulting changes had to be examined, reconciled, and fought if the company's values were to have any meaning. At the Lex annual review, the managers asked themselves repeatedly whether hard times were the ultimate test of the statement or a clear indication that a corporation had to be able to "afford" ethical position.

Ideally, a company's articulation of its values should anticipate changes of fortune. As the hearings for the passage of the Foreign Corrupt Practices Act of 1977 demonstrated, doing what you can get away with today may not be a secure moral standard, but short-term discomfort for long-term sainthood may require irrational courage or a rational reasoning system or, more likely, both. These 12 questions attempt to elicit a rational system. Courage, of course, depends on personal integrity.

Another aspect of the ethical time frame stretches beyond the boundaries of question 9 but deserves special attention, and that is the timing of the ethical inquiry. When and where will it be made?

The questions offered here do not solve the problem of making time for the inquiry. For suggestions about creating favorable conditions for examining corporate values, drawn from my field research, see Table 2.

10. Could You Disclose without Qualm Your Decision or Action to Your Boss, Your CEO, the Board of Directors, Your Family, or Society as a Whole?

The old question, "Would you want your decision to appear on the front page of the *New York Times?*" still holds. A corporation may maintain that there's really no problem, but a survey of how many "trivial" actions it is reluctant to disclose might be interesting. Disclosure is a way of

TABLE 2. SHARED CONDITIONS OF SOME SUCCESSFUL ETHICAL INQUIRIES

Freed time frame	Understanding and identifying moral issues takes time and causes ferment, and the executive needs an uninterrupted block of time to ponder the problems.
Unconventional location	Religious groups, boards of directors, and professional associations have long recognized the value of the retreat as a way of stimulating fresh approaches to regular activities. If the group is going to transcend normal corporate hierarchies, it should hold the discussion on neutral territory so that all may participate with the same degree of freedom.
Resource person	The advantage of bringing in an outsider is not that he or she will impose some preconceived notion of right and wrong on management but that he will serve as a midwife for bringing the values already present in the institution out into the open. He can generate closer examination of the discrepancies between values and practice and draw on a wider knowledge of instances and intellectual frameworks than the group can. The resource person may also take the important role of arbitrator—to ensure that one person does not dominate the session with his or her own values and that the dialogue does not become impossibly emotional.
Participation of CEO	In most corporations the chief executive still commands an extra degree of authority for the intangible we call corporate culture, and the discussion needs the perspective of the legitimization by that authority if it is to have any seriousness of purpose and consequence. One of the most interesting experiments in examining corporate policy I have observed lacked the CEO's support, and within a year it died on the vine.
Credo	Articulating the corporation's values and objectives provides a reference point for group inquiry and implementation. Ethical codes, however, when drawn up by the legal department do not always offer a realistic and full representation of management's beliefs. The most important ethical inquiry for management may be the very formulation of such a statement, for the *process* of articulation is as useful as the values agreed on.
Homegrown topics	In isolating an ethical issue, drawing on your own experience is important. Philosophical business ethics has tended to reflect national social controversies, which though relevant to the corporation may not always be as relevant—not to mention as easily resolved—as some internal issues that are shaping the character of the company to a much greater degree. Executives are also more likely to be informed on these issues.
Resolution	In all the programs I observed except one, there was a point at which the inquiry was slated to have some resolution: either a vote on the issue, the adoption of a new policy, a timetable for implementation, or the formulation of a specific statement of values. The one program observed that had no such decision-making structure was organized simply to gather information about the company's activities through extrahierarchical channels. Because the program had no tangible goals or clearly articulated results, its benefits were impossible to measure.

sounding those submarine depths of conscience and of searching out loyalties. It is also a way of keeping a corporate character cohesive. The Lex group, for example, was once faced with a very sticky problem concerning a small but profitable site with unpleasant (although in no way illegal) working conditions, where two men with 30 years' service worked. I wrote up the case for a Lex senior managers' meeting on the promise to disguise it heavily because the executive who supervised the plant was convinced that, if the chairman and the personnel director knew the plant's true location, they would close it down immediately.

At the meeting, however, as everyone became involved in the discussion and the chairman himself showed sensitivity to the dilemma, the executive disclosed the location and spoke of his own feelings about the situation. The level of mutual confidence was apparent to all, and by other reports it was the most open discussion the group had ever had.

The meeting also fostered understanding of the company's values and their implementation. When the discussion finally flagged, the chairman spoke up. Basing his views on a full knowledge of the group's understanding of the problem, he set the company's priorities. "Jobs over fancy conditions, health over jobs," Chinn said, "but we always *must disclose*." The group decided to keep the plant open, at least for the time being.

11. What Is the Symbolic Potential of Your Action If Understood? If Misunderstood?

Jones Inc., a diversified multinational corporation with assets of $5 billion, has a paper manufacturing operation that happens to be the only major industry in Stirville, and the factory has been polluting the river on which it is located. Local and national conservation groups have filed suit against Jones Inc. for past damages, and the company is defending itself. Meanwhile, the corporation has adopted plans for a new waste-efficient plant. The legal battle is extended and local resentment against Jones Inc. gets bitter.

As a settlement is being reached, Jones Inc. announces that, as a civic-minded gesture, it will make 400 acres of Stirville woodland it owns available to the residents for conservation and recreation purposes. Jones' intention is to offer a peace pipe to the people of Stirville, and the company sees the gift as a symbol of its own belief in conservation and a way of signaling that value to Stirville residents and national conservation groups. Should Jones Inc. give the land away? Is the symbolism significant?

If the symbolic value of the land is understood as Jones Inc. intends, the gift may patch up the company's relations with Stirville and stave off further disaffection with potential employees as the new plant is being built. It may also signal to employees throughout the corporation that Jones Inc. places a pre-mium on conservation efforts and community relations.

If the symbolic value is misunderstood, however, or if completion of the plant is delayed and the old one has to be put back in use—or if another Jones operation is discovered to be polluting another community and becomes a target of the press—the gift could be interpreted as nothing more than a cheap effort to pay off the people of Stirville and hasten settlement of the lawsuit.

The Greek root of our word *symbol* means both signal and contract. A business decision—whether it is the use of an expense account or a corporate donation—has a symbolic value in signaling what is acceptable behavior within the corporate culture and in making a tacit contract with employees and the community about the rules of the game. How the symbol is actually perceived (or misperceived) is as important as how you intend it to be perceived.

12. Under What Conditions Would You Allow Exceptions to Your Stand?

If we accept the idea that every business decision has an important symbolic value and a contractual nature, then the need for consistency is obvious. At the same time, it is also important to ask under what conditions the rule of the game may be changed. What conflicting principles, circumstances, or time constraints would provide a morally acceptable basis for making an exception to one's normal institutional ethos? For instance, how does the cost of the strategy to develop managers from minority groups over the long term fit in with short-term hurdle rates? Also to be considered is what would mitigate a clear case of employee dishonesty.

Questions of consistency—if you would do X, would you also do Y?—are yet another way of eliciting the ethics of the company and of oneself, and can be a final test of the strength, idealism, or practicality of those values. A last example from the experience of Lex illustrates this point and gives temporary credence to the platitude that good ethics is good business. An article in the Sunday paper about a company that had run a series of racy ads, with pictures of half-dressed women and promises of free merchandise to promote the sale of a very mundane product, sparked an extended examination at Lex of its policies on corporate inducements.

One area of concern was holiday giving. What was the acceptable limit for a gift—a bottle of whiskey? a case? Did it matter only that the company did not *intend* the gift to be an inducement, or did the mere possibility of inducement taint the gift? Was the cut-off point absolute? The group could agree on no halfway point for allowing some gifts and not others, so a new value was added to the formal statement that prohibited the offering or receiving of inducements.

The next holiday season Chinn sent a letter to friends and colleagues who had received gifts of appreciation in the past. In it he explained that, as a result of Lex's concern with "the very complex area of business ethics," management had decided that the company would no longer send any gifts, nor would it be appropriate for its employees to receive any. Although the letter did not explain Lex's reasoning behind the decision, apparently there was a large untapped consensus about such gift giving: by return mail Chinn received at least twenty letters from directors, general managers, and chairmen of companies with which Lex had done business congratulating him for his decision, agreeing with the new policy, and thanking him for his holiday wishes.

The 12 questions are a way to articulate an idea of the responsibilities involved and to lay them open for examination. Whether a decisive policy is also generated or not, there are compelling reasons for holding such discussions:

The process facilitates talk as a group about a subject that has traditionally been reserved for the privacy of one's conscience. Moreover, for those whose consciences twitch but don't speak in full sentences, the questions help sort out their own perceptions of the problem and various ways of thinking about it.

The process builds a cohesiveness of managerial character as points of consensus emerge and people from vastly different operations discover that they share common problems. It is one way of determining the values and goals of the company, and that is a key element in determining corporate strategy.

It acts as an information resource. Senior managers learn about other parts of the company with which they may have little contact.

It helps uncover ethical inconsistencies in the articulated values of the corporation or between these values and the financial strategy.

It helps uncover sometimes dramatic differences between the values and the practicality of their implementation.

It helps the CEO understand how the senior managers think, how they handle a problem, and how willing and able they are to deal with complexity. It reveals how they may be drawing on the private self to the enhancement of corporate activity.

In drawing out the private self in connection with business and in exploring the significance of the corporation's activities, the process derives meaning from an environment that is often characterized as meaningless.

It helps improve the nature and range of alternatives.

It is cathartic.

The situations for testing business morality remain complex. But by avoiding theoretical inquiry and limiting the expectations of corporate goodness to a few rules for social behavior that are based on common sense, we can develop an ethic that is appropriate to the language, ideology, and institutional dynamics of business decision making and consensus. This ethic can also offer managers a practical way of exploring those occasions when their corporate brains are getting warning flashes from their noncorporate brains.

Students' Perceptions of Ethical Issues in the Hospitality and Tourism Industry

Linda K. Enghagen and David D. Hott

From six different hospitality and tourism programs, 349 students responded to a survey asking them to identify what they consider to be the most important ethical issues confronting the hospitality and tourism industry today. Generally, they perceived solid waste disposal, conditions of employment, a variety of employment discrimination issues, employee theft, false advertising, vendor honesty, sanitation violations, and AIDS in foodservice to be today's most compelling issues in this industry. The data collected did not permit many conclusions to be drawn in regard to possible associations between the issues identified and various demographic variables.

Introduction

ETHICS HAS BECOME ONE of the watchwords of the decade as the business world moves from the excesses of the 1980s into a new decade of struggle with the aftermath of insider trading, bankrupt leveraged buy-outs, and a nationwide banking disaster.

Whether, as argued by some, American society in general or American business in particular has achieved a new level of moral decay (Yankelovich, 1981; Josephson, 1990) will continue to be debated in the pages of the popular, academic, and business presses. The more compelling question, however, is not whether the moral lapses of the 1980s have risen to a new dimension; but how to move from the current state of affairs to the creation of a better society, including a better environment in which to do business. The task confronting the business world generally and the hospitality and tourism industry specifically is how to define and act on the ethical issues germane to their respective spheres within society and the business arena.

Toward these ends, this research is intended to begin to define the nature of the ethical issues specifically germane to the hospitality and tourism industry. One perspective of the nature of the ethical issues pertinent to this industry can be gained from students who are pursuing an education in this field but who are not yet immersed in the day-to-day world of a full-time professional. Students, by virtue of studying in this field, exhibit some level of interest in and specific knowledge of its operations. On the other hand, because of their youth and relative inexperience, students are less likely than seasoned professionals to be tainted or jaded by the belief that "it's always been done this way." Consequently, this research seeks to measure whether students share perceptions of the most important ethical issues confronting the hospitality and tourism industry today.

To the extent that perception is reality, measuring perceptions can be an important undertaking. This research intends to measure perceptions only. It should be emphasized that this research makes no claims concerning what, in fact, are the day's most pressing ethical issues in the hospitality and tourism industry. It is intended only to measure what students perceive to fall into that category.

Generally, the purpose of this research is two-fold. The first is simply to determine whether students share perceptions of the most important ethical issues confronting the hospitality and tourism industry today. If the answer to this first question is yes, the second purpose of this research is to determine whether there are any significant differences among students' perceptions on the basis of such variables as sex, race, year in college, institution attended, or anticipated career path (e.g., food and beverage, hotel operations, travel, and tourism).

At the outset, it must be emphasized that this research is exploratory in nature.

Instrument

The instrument developed for this survey represented the culmination of experimenting with five earlier versions administered to small classes of students at the University of Massachusetts at Amherst. The final instrument asked students to provide basic identifying information. In addition to sex and race, students were asked to identify their year in college (e.g., junior) and the area of the hospitality and tourism industry in which they intended to pursue a career. In this last category, the choices they were given were food and beverage service, hotel sales and/or management, travel and tourism marketing and/or operations, I don't intend to work in this industry, and other. Students were not explicitly advised that they might choose to decline to respond to the demographic variable portion of the survey. As will be discussed later, some of the hypotheses of this research involved correlations between demographic characteristics and the particular ethical issues listed. Nevertheless, the confidentiality of responses was ensured. The survey instruments were not coded in any way to enable or permit the identification of individual respondents. The only identification of respondents was on a group basis. That is, when the responses were tested for correlations, one correlation examined was that between ethical issues listed and the group's institutional affiliation.

Following the demographic information, students were asked to list the five most important ethical issues confronting the hospitality and tourism industry today. This was an open-ended question. The only guidance given the students was the request that they be as specific as possible with the following example: ". . . if you believe pollution is a problem are you referring to air pollution, water pollu-

tion, or some other type of pollution." It should be noted that the results must be examined to determine whether this example created any bias in the results.

In developing the survey instrument, consideration was given to inquiring about whether the students had taken ethics related courses. For a variety of reasons, this was not pursued. First, prior research indicates that only 4% of hospitality and tourism programs in the United States offer ethics as a separate course (Enghagen, 1990). Given that so few programs offer a separate course, it was assumed that it was unlikely to reveal any significant results given the sample size used in this research. Second, 73% of hospitality and tourism programs in the United States include ethics in the curriculum as a component of another course (Enghagen, 1990). While this is the case, prior research does not reveal how it is included or how extensively ethics is covered (Enghagen, 1990). Consequently, it was concluded that in this research no significant correlations could be drawn without pursuing, with specificity, the nature of the courses ethics is included in as well as how that is done and to what extent. These matters were beyond the scope of this research.

Methodology

Surveys were sent to eight different hospitality and tourism programs throughout the United States. The eight programs were selected on the basis of two criteria. First, in an effort to obtain a sample representative of all hospitality and tourism students, programs were selected from various geographic regions throughout the United States. The second criterion was access to a willing survey administrator at each institution. The individuals administering the survey were instructed to administer it to groups of students consisting almost exclusively of juniors and seniors in hospitality and tourism or related programs. Juniors and seniors were selected on the basis of the assumption that they were more likely than freshmen and sophomores to possess some practical knowledge of industry practices. Researchers indicated that it was preferable to give the survey in a classroom setting, but that a club meeting was an acceptable alternative. The number of responses sought from each institution was in the range of 50–100 students. Six of the eight institutions provided a sufficient number of responses to be included in this research, with a total of 349 students providing usable data.

While there is some research examining the ethical development of students in hospitality and tourism programs (Freedman and Bartholomew, 1990), no research was found that examines students' perceptions of ethical issues pertinent to this industry (or business generally) through the format of an open-ended question.

TABLE 1. ORIGINAL RANKING OF ETHICAL ISSUES		
Rank	**Issue**	**Response Rate**
1.	air/water pollution	37%
1.	solid waste disposal	37%
2.	conditions of employment	32%
3.	nonspecific discrimination	29%
4.	race discrimination	27%
5.	employee theft	26%
6.	sex discrimination	24%
7.	false advertising	15%
8.	sexual harassment	11%
8.	vendor honesty	11%
9.	sanitation violations	10%
10.	AIDS discrimination	9%
11.	AIDS in foodservice	8%

Results and Discussion

Students' Perceptions of the Most Pressing Ethical Issues In the Hospitality and Tourism Industry Today

Given the open-ended nature of the survey question, the first step was to develop a list of the responses and then to establish appropriate categories. This initial list consisted of approximately 75 completely different issues and was reduced to 25 issues through two means. First, issues listed infrequently were eliminated. Second, a number of related issues were all categorized under the headings "conditions of employment" and "discrimination—nonspecific." For example, issues listed under "conditions of em-ployment" included scheduling, number of hours worked, worker's compensation, medical insurance, minimum wage laws, low wages generally, childcare, respect of workers, maternity leave, merit/promotion, high turnover rates, and lack of or inadequate training. The category of "discrimination—nonspecific" included those who simply listed discrimination as an issue as well as those who listed specific types of discrimination which appeared infrequently (i.e., age, handicap, club membership, marital status, quotas).

Table 1 provides a rank ordering of the issues most frequently cited by the 349 students responding to this survey. (It should be noted that not all students listed five issues.)

Rank	Issue	Response Rate
	TABLE 2. REVISED RANKING OF ETHICAL ISSUES	
1.	solid waste disposal	37%
2.	conditions of employment	32%
3.	nonspecific discrimination	29%
4.	race discrimination	27%
5.	employee theft	26%
6.	sex discrimination	24%
7.	false advertising	15%
8.	sexual harassment	11%
8.	vendor honesty	11%
9.	sanitation violations	10%
10.	AIDS discrimination	9%
11.	AIDS in foodservice	8%

As noted earlier, the results of this research must be evaluated for any bias that may have been created by virtue of the example cited in the survey instrument. That is, when the students were asked to list the five most important ethical issues in the hospitality and tourism industry today, they were also asked to be as specific as possible with the following example: ". . . if you believe pollution is a problem, are you referring to air pollution, water pollution, or some other type of pollution?" It appears that this example did create a bias in that air/water pollution ranked first along with solid waste disposal with 37% of the students listing it as an ethical issue. Consequently, this issue must be eliminated and the results adjusted accordingly. At first glance, the reason for this bias may seem obvious.

Pollution was the example cited in the instructions. However, when earlier versions of this instrument were administered to over 100 students at the University of Massachusetts, no such bias resulted. It was on this basis that the example was used. In the earliest versions of the instrument no example was given and many of the responses were too vague to reasonably categorize. Another problem was that some students had difficulty knowing where to begin. The example was intended to be remote from any obvious or direct connection with the hospitality and tourism industry. That is, air and water pollution would be likely responses if this survey were looking at the ethical issues of the manufacturing or chemical industries. In any event, after the insertion of the example, this was no longer a problem

with the experimental groups. After taking the apparent bias into account, the revised results of the rank ordering of the ethical issues are shown in Table 2.

Given a number of factors, it is not surprising that solid waste disposal ranked highest of all the issues enumerated by the respondents. Earth Day 1990 was the biggest environmental celebration ever, many communities and states now mandate recycling, supermarkets ask customers if they want their groceries bagged in paper or plastic, quick-service restaurants are replacing styrofoam products with paper and/or instituting recycling programs, and advertising is replete with claims about the environmental soundness of its products.

Broadly speaking, the 12 different ethical issues in this ranking can be categorized into three areas: operations (relations with customers, vendors, and regulators); employer/employee relations; and both (those that affect operations and employer/employee relations). Four of the ethical issues enumerated by the students relate specifically to operations: solid waste disposal, false advertising, vendor honesty, and sanitation violations. Six, or 50%, of the issues offered by students specifically relate to the employer/employee relationship: conditions of employment, nonspecific discrimination, race discrimination, sex discrimination, sexual harassment, and AIDS discrimination. The two remaining issues have both operations and employer/employee relations dimensions: employee theft and AIDS in foodservice.

Bearing in mind that these results measure only the perceptions of the students surveyed, we find two disturbing findings in these results. First, the students perceive the employment relationship to be riddled with problems. Though it is impossible to draw any conclusions here, this raises the question of whether there is any correlation between this perception and the high turnover rates among employees in the hospitality and tourism industry. Second, of the six issues falling under the category of employer/employee relations, five of the issues involve discrimination in the employment relationship: nonspecific discrimination, race discrimination, sex discrimination, sexual harassment (legally defined to be one form of sex discrimination), and AIDS discrimination.

It is interesting to note that AIDS appeared as an ethical issue in two different contexts. AIDS was listed as a discrimination issue by 9% of those responding and as a foodservice issue by 8% of the respondents.

Demographic Variable Comparisons

The profile of the students responding to this survey reveals that 58% of the respondents were female and 42% were male. The racial composition of those surveyed is as follows: 81% are white, 5% are black, 7% are Hispanic, 6% are Asian, and 2% are

other. (In some cases the totals are slightly above or below 100% because of rounding.) Of the students 38% are juniors, 60% are seniors, and 1% are other. The intended career paths of those surveyed breaks down as follows: 40% intend to work in the food and beverage service, 40% intend to pursue a career in hotel sales and/or marketing, 7% expect careers in travel and tourism marketing and/or operations, 5% do not intend to work in this industry, and 7% listed other. The six participating institutions are identified as institutions A, B, C, D, E, and F. Their response rates are as follows: 21% of those responding were from institution A, 15% were from B, 19% were from C, 15% were from D, 16% were from E, and 15% were from F.

In the second segment of this research, the data were analyzed to determine whether there were any significant differences among students in their perceptions of the most important ethical issues in the hospitality and tourism industry on the basis of demographic variables. Given that the information collected was nominal data, this segment of the research is based on an assumption. That is, it is assumed that an issue is perceived to be unimportant to a student if that student fails to list it. Unimportant, of course, given the structure of the survey instrument is a relative concept. Students were asked to list only five issues. Therefore, it is assumed that the failure to list an issue means a student did not perceive the issue

to rise to the level of being among the five most important ethical issues confronting the hospitality and tourism today. It is certainly possible that a student perceived an issue to exist but to be of lesser importance.

Before evaluating the responses for associations, we hypothesized that significant differences in perceptions would exist on the basis of the variables of sex, race, and career path. It was further hypothesized that no significant differences would exist in relation to year in college and institution attended. The chi-square test was used to measure possible associations.

Gender

It was expected that gender would be a significant factor in relation to the issue of sex discrimination. However, 26% of the males included it as an issue while only 22% of the females included it in their lists. Females did report sexual harassment as an issue with greater frequency then males (14% and 8%, respectively) but the chi-square test failed to show any association.

Race

Similarly, it was expected that race would be significant in relation to the issue of race discrimination. Again, the chi-square test failed to show any association. In this case, the problem seems to rest with the sample size. The sample was too small to draw any conclusions. Nevertheless, there is some suggestion that a sufficiently large sample would

TABLE 3. INSTITUTIONAL ASSOCIATIONS			
	Discrimination		
	Race	**Sex**	**Solid Waste Management**
A	23%	14%	40%
B	13%	17%	30%
C	54%	43%	12%
D	30%	28%	30%
E	20%	25%	38%
F	15%	12%	79%

render a different result. For example, if we look only at the sample of whites and blacks in these data, 22% of the whites reported race discrimination as an issue in contrast to 44% of the blacks.

Career Path

This sample revealed no association between intended career path and perception of the most important ethical issues confronting the hospitality and tourism industry today. It was hypothesized that such differences would exist by virtue of the differences in the day-to-day operations of businesses in the different facets of the business. Of the 349 students responding, 124 indicated food and beverage service to be their intended career path, while 130 listed hotel sales and/or management. The remaining 95 were split among the other three categories, with the result that there were insufficient responses to evaluate for associations.

Year In College

The only original hypothesis that was supported by these data was that there is no association between a student's status as a junior or senior and his or her perceptions of the most important ethical issues of the day. The category of "other" was too small to evaluate. Given that there is minimal difference between a typical college junior and senior in regard to age, maturity, and professional experience, no significant difference would be expected here.

Institutional Affiliation

The chi-square test did reveal an association between the institution attended and 3 of the 11 ranked issues: race discrimination, sex discrimination, and solid waste disposal. The chi-square test showed no association between the institution attended and the issues of nonspecific discrimination and conditions of employment. The sample size was insufficient to evaluate for each of the remaining issues. Table 3 shows the percentage of students, by institution, listing race discrimination, sex discrimination, and solid waste disposal as ethical issues.

The issue of race discrimination was listed by 27% of the complete sample, but appeared at twice that rate by the students from institution C and slightly less than half that rate (13%) by students at institution B. Sex discrimination appeared at a rate of 24% in the full sample but with a frequency as great as 43% again at institution C and as low as 12% at institution F. The most startling difference is in relation to the issue of solid waste disposal. In the general sample, it ranked first with 37% of the students listing it as one of the most important ethical issues confronting the hospitality and tourism industry today. However, it was reported at over twice that rate, 79%, by the students at institution F. At the same time, it was included by only 12% of the students at institution C.

Given that this finding was not hypothesized, there was nothing in the design of the research seeking to offer an explanation for this result. Consequently, it is possible to speculate only as to the reasons for this conclusion. Perhaps the students from these institutions were drawn from a class in which they were exposed to such issues within an ethical framework. Another explanation might be that the curriculum and/or professors at these institutions sensitized their students to such concerns. Or perhaps there was a self-selected group of students at these institutions or in the classes surveyed that resulted in certain predispositions toward a survey of this type. At this stage of this research, it is impossible to draw any conclusions.

Recommendations

Given the exploratory nature of this research, there are a number of recommendations that can be made relative to future research of students' perceptions of the most important ethical issues in the hospitality and tourism industry.

First, the survey instrument must be further refined to avoid any bias in the results and to offer some insight into the explanation for the association found for institutions. This could be done as a longitudinal study to determine to what extent the issues change over time.

Second, further research might build on this work by providing students with the list of the most frequently cited issues and asking them to rank or rate the issues on an appropriate scale.

Third, similar research should be done with professionals in the hospitality and tourism industry to determine whether their perceptions are similar to those of the students.

Conclusions

The results of this research indicate that students in the hospitality and tourism field do share perceptions of the most important ethical issues in this industry. Whether their perceptions reflect reality or are shared by professionals in the field remains to be seen.

With the exception of institutional affiliation (for some issues only), this research fails to show any association between the demographic characteristics asked of the students and their perceptions of today's most important ethical issues in the industry.

References

Enghagen, L. (1990). Ethics in hospitality and tourism education: A survey. *Hospitality Research Journal, 14* (2), 113–118.

Freedman, A., and Bartholomew, P. (1990). Age/Experience and gender as factors in ethical development of hospitality managers and students. *Hospitality Research Journal, 14* (2), 1–10.

Josephson, M. (1990). The IDI's are coming! The IDI's are coming! *Ethics: Easier Said Than Done,* Issue 10, 34–46.

Yankelovich, D. (1981). *New rules: Searching for self-fulfillment in a world turned upside down.* New York: Random House.

One of the challenges in ethical decision making is to develop standards of ethical behavior which can be specifically articulated. Throughout the history of the development of ethical theory many approaches have been offered. Some have their origins in religious beliefs. Others are from the field of philosophy. Still others evolve from the thinking of those concerned with the practical application of ethical theory to professional, business, and everyday life. Despite the differences in their origins, many of these "competing" theories are not only consistent with one another, but compliment each other as well. Such is the origin of Golden Kantian Consequentialism. This set of standards is designed for application to life in all its dimensions. It reformulates three familiar ethical principles: The Golden Rule, Kant's categorical imperative, and John Stuart Mill's utilitarian principle.

The Golden Rule
Do unto others as you would have them do unto you.

Kant's Categorical Imperative
One must do only that which one would will to be universal law.

John Stuart Mill's Utilitarianism
The ends justifies the means if and only if the ends is the common good.

Noted ethics trainer and consultant, Michael Josephson, blended and reformulated these three principles thereby creating a new standard of ethical analysis known as Golden Kantian Consequentialism.

Golden Kantian Consequentialism

1. All decisions must take into account the interests of all stakeholders (i.e. all those affected).

2. Ethical values and principles always take precedence over nonethical values.

3. It's ethical to violate an ethical principle only when it's clearly necessary to advance another true ethical principle which creates the greatest good in the long run.

Assignment

Select an ethical issue in the hospitality/tourism industry. Write a 10–12 page paper analyzing it under the principles of Golden Kantian Consequentialism.

Socrates, the philosopher, advanced the proposition that "The unexamined life is not worth living." Nathaniel Branden, a psychologist, ascribes to the theory that "A moral life requires serious reflection." For the purposes of this paper, you are to assume each of these propositions to be true. Further, you are to assume they apply to one's professional life as well as one's personal life. With this framework, reflect on the hospitality/tourism industry. Identify the ten most compelling ethical issues facing the hospitality/tourism industry today. Define your criteria for identifying something as an ethical issue. Explain why each issue you selected satisfies those criteria. Discuss what individuals within the hospitality/tourism industry can be to positively respond to these issues. Your paper should not exceed 30 pages.

22

MULTI-CULTURAL MANAGEMENT

Ten Aspects of Culture: Understanding Cultural Programming
L. Gardenswartz and A. Rowe

Demographic Destiny: Work-Force Trends and Their Impact
L. Gardenswartz and A. Rowe

Project 1

Project 2

TEN ASPECTS OF CULTURE: UNDERSTANDING CULTURAL PROGRAMMING

L. Gardenswartz and A. Rowe

HOW FREQUENTLY YOU bathe, how close you stand to someone with whom you are talking, how you address a boss, how you solve a problem, and how you respond to stress are all determined by your cultural programming. For example, the African-American accountant mentioned at the beginning of this chapter was not regarded as a team player because she demonstrated and dealt with her stress differently from her colleagues. Under pressure, her response was to get very quiet, close her office door, and hunker down to work. Her Euro-American coworkers, on the other hand, went around complaining about being overworked and pressured, getting sympathy from one another. It was only when the accountant's boss uncovered the reasons for the conflict that he could correct his own and his staff's misinterpretation of her behavior. Then he could work with his whole team to help them understand one another's behavior and negotiate

a mutually satisfying resolution.

To understand the aspects of cultural teachings, it is helpful to contrast different cultural rules within the 10 areas of cultural programming described by Harris and Moran. However, the risk in doing so is that new stereotypes will develop. The cultural norms described in the following section are generalizations that do not take into account individual personalities or the degree of acculturation to the dominant American culture. For example, while the American culture teaches individuals to make direct eye contact and speak their minds, many Americans are shy, avert their eyes, and keep their opinions to themselves. In addition, there is much variation within any group. The term *Latino* can mean a second-generation Mexican-American, a recent immigrant from El Salvador, a Cuban exile, or a Puerto Rican businessman.

1. Sense of Self and Space

Have you ever felt uncomfortable because someone stood too close when talking with you? Have you ever felt put off when your warm hug was received with a stiff, statuelike response? Or have you reacted to what you consider the pretension of someone addressing others by their titles instead of their first names? Chances are these rubs have their roots in cultural norms.

"Too close for comfort" and "Get out of my space" are common expressions that deal with the issue of space. The dominant American culture teaches us to stay about 1 1/2 to 3 feet, or an arm's length, from people with whom we are talking in a business or friendship relationship. Any closer is reserved for more intimate contact with family, romantic relationships, or very close friends. Maintaining greater distance signifies a desire to stay aloof or protect oneself. When someone steps into your space, you'll probably move back to maintain a comfortable distance. Other cultures have different norms. In the Middle East, people stand close enough to be able to feel your breath on their face and to be able to catch your scent. On the other hand, people in Japan maintain an even greater distance than those in the United States. As for greeting, in Japan it's a bow; in North America a hearty handshake; in Mexico and South America a warmer, softer handshake sometimes accompanied by a hug; and in the Middle East a hug and a ritualistic kiss on each cheek.

These physical aspects of the way we respect an individual's sense of self and space also have a less tangible counterpart in the degree of formality we expect in relationships. Many languages (Spanish, German, Tagalog, etc.) have two forms of the word *you*—the formal and the familiar. In these cultures, the familiar form is reserved for children, family members, close friends, and those below you in the social hierarchy, such as servants. English long ago dropped the familiar *thee and thou,* so we are left with one pronoun, you, for all relationships, whether we are talking with the president, a boss, or a spouse.

"Let's not stand on ceremony" is the dominant American culture's response to what most Americans consider stuffy formality. New acquaintances, bosses, and older individuals are commonly called by their first names. In other cultures, formal introductions using Mr., Mrs., and titles are expected as a sign of respect for both parties.

Since most other cultures are more formal than the dominant American culture, you are safest if you err on the side of formality. Trying to be buddy-buddy with a staff of people from other cultures that expect more formal behavior from a boss is apt to make workers uncomfortable and embarrassed. In business relationships and discussions, keeping a more reserved tone also tends to send the message that you respect the individuals with whom you are meeting. An American employee of a Japanese company doing business in the United States learned the hard way. Well schooled in both the Japanese language and culture, she made a presentation at a meeting. Because the company had succeeded in achieving its goal, she couldn't contain her excitement and she ended her recounting of the success statistics with a "Yeah!" Her Japanese boss told her later that her show of emotion was inappropriate for a formal business presentation.

Suggestions for Managers

▶ Make sure you say good morning and good-bye to each employee every day.
▶ Introduce new employees to their co-workers formally, taking the individual around to meet each new colleague.
▶ Be careful in using first names, especially with older workers.

▶ Ask people what they prefer being called.
▶ Guard against being overly familiar with workers.
▶ Learn to listen and create an atmosphere of trust where you can learn about each other's needs.

2. Communication and Language

It is clear that language differences often accompany cultural differences. However, more is involved than just the specific language an individual speaks. It is estimated that over half of our communication is nonverbal, indicating the significance of gestures, facial expression, tone of voice, and intonation patterns.

The most obvious of the nonverbal signals is eye contact. All cultures use it to send signals. The difficulty comes when the signals are misinterpreted. "Look at me when I'm talking to you!" we were told by our parents when being reprimanded as children. We break eye contact when we want to end the conversation with the bore who has cornered us at a party. We catch the eye of the waiter to let him know we want the check in a restaurant. Not making eye contact in our culture is taken as a sign of deceitfulness, nonassertion, or disinterest. However, in Asian and Latin cultures, averting one's eyes is a sign of respect and the proper behavior when in the presence of an older person or authority figure.

Gestures are another nonverbal communicator, one we often depend on when there is a language barrier. Yet gestures can get us into trouble in multicultural groups. The okay sign, for example, made with the thumb and forefinger, is an obscene gesture in Greece and some parts of South America. Smiling, often considered an international gesture, is another nonverbal cue that can be misinterpreted. The following examples are cases in point:

▶ A bank's customer service representative assists a limited-English-speaking customer in filling out a form. In an attempt to put the customer at ease, he smiles and speaks in a lighthearted manner. He is shocked when the customer calls from home a few minutes later to complain about being laughed at and treated disrespectfully.
▶ An engineering manager asks why the Asian engineers whom he supervises smile so much. "I feel like they are snickering and laughing at me," he says.
▶ A visiting professional from Germany being taken around by his host, an outgoing Texan, is quite impressed. He notices that each time they pass through a tollbooth on the Texas highways, they are greeted by a smiling toll taker who says, "Hi. How y'all doin' today?" At the end of the day, the German says "I'm amazed at how many friends you have."

A smile is seen as a welcoming, friendly gesture in this culture. In Asian cultures, it may be a sign of embarrassment, confusion, or discomfort. In the Middle East, a smile from a woman to a man can be construed as a sexual come-on. In Germany, smiling is reserved for friends and family.

Nodding the head is yet another nonverbal cue that causes problems. Saying no is considered rude, impudent behavior in many cultures because it upsets the harmony of relationships. A nod often means "Yes, I heard you," not "Yes, I understand" or "Yes, I agree."

Perhaps the difference that causes the most difficulty in communication is the subtlest. It has to do with the degree of directness or indirectness, or the amount of information that is stated rather than implied. In Japanese culture, for example, communication is very indirect, depending on subtle contextual cues. An individual would not tell someone to turn the heat on but would instead hug herself. If that did not get a response, she might mention that it was a bit chilly. The other party would immediately pick up the cue and turn the heat on. Japanese employees are not told they must stay at work until the boss leaves, yet only after he has gone through the office saying good night do workers, in order of rank, begin to leave. A manager wanting to tell an employee about some errors on a report might suggest the employee look it over again. If both manager and employee are Japanese, the employee would understand that this subtle suggestion meant something was wrong with the report. This implied direction would be missed by most American employees, who would probably be perplexed by the suggestion.

Contrast this approach with the "Don't beat around the bush" dictum of American culture, which favors a very explicitly stated message. When these two approaches collide, problems can result. The Japanese, for example, are often exasperated at what they see as Americans' "irresponsibility" when they interpret literally an offhand comment such as "I'll give you a call" or "I'll get on that, right away." On the other hand, Americans are just as frustrated when they miss the unstated clues that their Japanese counterparts automatically pick up. "How was I supposed to know I had to wait until the boss left? Why don't they just tell me?"

Suggestions for Managers

▶ When there is a language barrier, assume confusion. Don't take the nod or *yes* to mean the individual understands or agrees. Watch for tangible signs of understanding such as immediately beginning the task and doing it correctly.
▶ Consider that smiles and laughter may indicate discomfort or embarrassment. See if you can identify what is causing the difficulty.
▶ Avoid smiling when giving directions or when having serious work-related discussions with employees, especially when giving feedback

or when conducting performance reviews.

► Be careful not to think out loud. Employees hearing you may take your off-the-cuff comments literally and may even act on them.

► Watch for subtle clues that may be speaking volumes. A comment about another worker's frustrations may be telling you about a work-group complaint. Hints about family members moving in might be couching a desire for a raise.

3. Dress and Appearance

Though we may be taught not to judge a book by its cover, in this culture we do. The problem is that each culture has different rules about what is appropriate. Not only does "dressing for success" mean different things in different cultures, but also within a society rules differ. Pinstripe-suited Wall Street executives dress very differently from their Honolulu counterparts, who wear Hawaiian shirts and muumuus on Fridays, known as Aloha Days in the islands.

A dashiki or a shirt and tie? A bright silk dress or a dark gabardine suit? Which is the best choice for a job interview? It depends on which group you ask. In some cultures clothing is a sign of social class; hence, much money and attention are spent on dressing expensively. In others, clothing offers a chance to express one's personality and creativity, so the brighter and more decorative, the better. In still others, clothing is just a necessity of life, neither a status symbol nor an individual statement.

Take a look at the different workplace implications of dress. One client almost discounted a qualified job applicant because of these differences. The selection committee was interviewing applicants for a community outreach position in which the individual would be developing business with minority-owned firms. When this interviewee arrived dressed in a bright silk dress, lots of jewelry, and long painted nails, the committee collectively gulped. However, they thought about what they had learned in cultural diversity training and realized she was dressing very appropriately for her culture. More important, her appearance might be right in sync with the community members with whom she would be working. In another example, one government agency dealing with the management of state vehicles found that the rift between male and female mechanics was made less of a problem when all wore unisex uniforms that minimized the differences between the sexes and became a badge of their profession.

In still another situation, a draftsman was transferred from the San Francisco office to the Los Angeles office of a large engineering consulting firm. As an immigrant from Europe, used to more formal dress, he had noticed that shirts and ties were the "uniform" for all engineers and draftsmen in this company. He continued to wear what he considered appropriate dress in this new location. It was only when the draftsman was teased about trying to look like an engineer that he realized the rules were different in Los Angeles, where only engineers wore ties while draftsmen wore sport shirts without ties.

Hair can also be an appearance hot spot. Turbans, dreadlocks, Afros, ponytails on men and mohawks are just a few of the different hairstyles that raise eyebrows cross-culturally. Since the days of Samson and Delilah, hair has been a bone of contention. While in many mainstream American companies and in the military hair for men must be above the collar, in other cultures the rules are different. Hindus believe that the hair should never be cut, and the men wrap their heads in turbans. Orthodox Jewish men wear forelocks, while their wives cover their hair in public. Sometimes, hair makes a statement, as in the 1960s when wearing an Afro sent the "Black is beautiful" message or, more recently, when Sinead O'Connor shaved her head to draw attention to her political protests. In many cultures, hair is a symbol of virility for men, femininity for women, and individual dignity for all. Prisoners, for example, are often shorn, thereby stripping them of their individuality and humanness.

Probably one of the most uncomfortable areas to deal with regarding grooming is body odor. The dominant American culture has a near fetish on the topic. We have a deodorant for almost every part of the body. In polite society, we react negatively to the smell of another human being. Not so in other parts of the world. According to Edward T. Hall, in the Middle East, marriage go-betweens often ask to smell the girl before they recommend her as a prospective bride. Also, as mentioned, it is considered a normal part of communication to be able to feel and smell another's breath when talking. In still another cultural norm, Iranians bathe after sexual intercourse so as to be clean and pure for prayers. Body odor, whether from a lack of deodorant use or from diet (as in the garlic-laden kimchi eaten by Koreans), can cause real problems in work teams when people find each other's odors offensive.

Suggestions for Managers

▶ Before reacting to another's appearance, stop to consider the meaning attached to appearance by the individual.
▶ When making assessments about job applicants, consider their cultural norms regarding dress.
▶ Consider the job the individual will be doing and the people with whom he/she will be interacting when determining appropriate dress.
▶ Teach individuals the cultural rules required in your organization regarding dress and grooming.
▶ Remember that body scent is not necessarily a sign of uncleanliness.

▶ Consider uniforms as a way to eliminate differences and build common ground.

4. Food and Eating Habits

While you may know that what we eat, when we eat, and how we eat it are culturally directed, you may ask what food and eating habits have to do with work. When asked about the benefits of living and working in a multicultural environment, food is almost always mentioned high on the list. Most of us enjoy the pot-lucks with exotic and enticing dishes that result from having a diverse staff. Yet in the workplace, differences can cause conflict, as in the following examples:

▶ At a catered lunch at a management meeting, the entrée is quiche lorraine made with ham. Two managers never touch their plates.
▶ Employees at a manufacturing plant complain about the smell of the fish lunches being heated and eaten by their Vietnamese co-workers.
▶ An elderly couple being cared for by a Filipino home health aide nearly starves to death. While their nurse cooks gourmet meals for them, they are unfamiliar with and do not like Filipino cuisine. It is finally discovered that because they really like their nurse they are throwing the food away after she leaves.

Understanding food restrictions and taboos is a starting point. Prohibitions against certain foods are often associated with religious rules. Among the Kosher food laws adhered to by some Jews is the prohibition against eating pork and shellfish. Devout Muslims also refuse pork and alcoholic beverages. Hindu religious beliefs prohibit the eating of meat of any kind. In addition, many individuals choose to eat a vegetarian diet because of ethical considerations, medical reasons, or personal preferences.

Beyond restrictions, cultural norms influence our food preferences. Animals that are pets in one culture may be a food source in another. The American repugnance and outrage at the eating of dog, horse, or cat meat are probably akin to a devout Hindu's feelings about Americans eating beef.

Do you eat with chopsticks or a fork and knife? In which hand do you hold your fork and knife? What do you think about eating with your hands? Chopsticks are the utensils of choice in most of Asia, while holding the knife in the right hand and the fork in the left is proper for Europeans. In parts of the Middle East, eating with the right hand from a communal bowl is the accepted practice.

Smacking one's lips, burping, and picking one's teeth at the table are considered breaches of etiquette in America, yet these behaviors may be entirely acceptable elsewhere. In fact, belching is seen as a compliment to the cook in Asia. Europeans eat with both hands on the table, while Americans are admonished to keep the left hand in the lap unless cutting food. Before you judge others' table manners, stop and think about what might be proper by their standards. Also consider that others may be just as appalled by your table manners.

Suggestions for Managers

▶ When planning catered meals or snacks for meetings and group gatherings, include a variety of foods so there will be something edible and acceptable for all.
▶ Avoid serving food that might be offensive to some staff members.
▶ Have alternate dishes available (e.g., a vegetarian plate or fruit salad).
▶ When choosing restaurants for business meetings, keep individual dietary restrictions and preferences in mind.
▶ Provide well-ventilated or outdoor eating areas for staff where odors can be more easily dissipated.

5. Time and Time Consciousness

When asked about the hardest adjustments they've had to make, Americans who work abroad invariably talk about the differences in time consciousness. The so-called mañana attitude in Mexico and the *Inshallah* of the Arab world clash with the "Time is money" and "The early bird gets the worm" American views of time. In this culture, time is seen as a commodity to be used, divided, spent, and saved. It is linear and finite. However, in other parts of the world, such as Latin America and the Middle East, time is considered more elastic and more relative. Time is used not just to accomplish tasks but also to develop relationships and enjoy oneself. When things happen depends on not just a schedule, but also on other events, priorities, and the will of God. So, *mañana* does not necessarily mean "tomorrow," but sometime in the future. *Inshallah* may mean "whenever it comes to pass."

An American concerned with deadlines is understandably frustrated by what may appear to be a lack of motivation, efficiency, or honesty when encountering such a response. The American, on the other hand, may be seen as always in a hurry and more concerned with tasks than with people.

Suggestions for Managers

▶ Recognize that differences in time consciousness are cultural and are not a sign of laziness.
▶ Allow time in your schedule for the development of relationships.
▶ Make it a point to spend some time each week with each employee.
▶ Explain the reasons for deadlines and schedules.
▶ Explain the part promptness plays in assessment of performance and work habits.

6. Relationships

In the dominant American culture, hiring relatives is considered nepotism and is, in fact, prohibited in many organizations. Yet in most other parts of the world, hiring kin is not only common but also expected. Not to do so would be considered abdicating one's responsibility to one's family. Furthermore, while *family* in America usually means the nuclear group of one's parents and siblings, in other cultures it involves a large network of extended family members—cousins, aunts, uncles, nieces, nephews, and in-laws. Loyalty is expected toward one's kin, and obedience and respect are paid to older family members. Organizational rules or directions that require employees to go against these norms will be circumvented or disobeyed. You might experience an employee who hides the fact that his "friend" is really a relative, for example, or an employee who takes extended leaves to go back to his home village during the holidays.

In most other cultures, families are not egalitarian democracies. There is a definite hierarchy of status, with age being the determiner of power and respect. A definite pecking order exists, for example, with an older brother having authority over a younger one or a grandmother having matriarch status. An employee from such a family would not think of making a work-related decision such as seeking a promotion or accepting a transfer without talking it over with the "head of the family." This same sense of respect may transfer to the work unit, where employees apply a similar hierarchy within the group.

A seminar participant related how she learned about this kinship hierarchy on the job. As a nursing manager, she was in charge of running her unit, which included dealing with patients' family members and visitors. A problem arose one evening when one of her patients, a Gypsy, had the entire extended family, of more than 20 people, visiting. There were complaints from staff and other patients so the manager went in to deal with the problem. Luckily, a security guard accompanied her. Before she could say anything, the guard formally introduced her to the head of the family, explaining that she was the manager in charge. She then explained the situation to the head of the family and asked for his cooperation. She got it. However, she was certain that without the cultural sensitivity and savvy of the security guard, she would not have paid attention to the family hierarchy and probably would not have gotten the quick cooperation she did by respecting the group's cultural norms.

Suggestions for Managers

▶ Recognize that family responsibility and loyalty to kin will be a prime value of many workers. Take this into consideration when identifying rewards and motivators for staff (e.g., hiring relatives and giving time off for vacations and holidays).

▶ Allow employees time to discuss important decisions with family members before they give you a final answer.

▶ Recognize the informal leadership older members may hold in the work unit. Consult with them and seek their cooperation.

▶ Show respect to older employees by addressing them first and giving them formal authority when appropriate.

▶ Recognize that, as the boss, you may be seen as the "head of the work family." Employees may come to seek your advice and counsel about problems in and out of work.

7. Values and Norms

One of the cornerstones of American society is the doctrine of individual freedom. We fought a revolution to attain independence and the inalienable rights of life, liberty, and the pursuit of happiness. The Bill of Rights goes further in specifying the extent of our individual freedoms. The promise of freedom has attracted immigrants to these shores for centuries. In recent times, the idea of personal entitlement has pushed the ideas of individual freedom even further. Not so in most other cultures, where conformity to the group, family, and larger society is the norm. To most Americans, the need to conform—to subjugate one's individual needs to the those of the group—would feel confin-

ing and stifling. To many Asians, on the other hand, the dominance of the group over the individual assures harmony and order, and brings a feeling of stability to life. In an interesting experiment, a group of bilingual Japanese women were given a series of open-ended statements to complete in both Japanese and English. When asked in English to complete the statement "When my wishes conflict with my family's, . . .," one woman responded, "I do what I want." When asked to complete the same statement in Japanese, the response was "It is a time of great unhappiness." In the workplace this difference may show itself in employees' discomfort with individual praise, especially in public; with staff members' reluctance to break rank and blow the whistle; or with workers' difficulty in openly seeking advancement.

Related to this group orientation is another difference: the competition versus cooperation dichotomy. The competitive spirit is an underpinning of American life and the capitalist economic system. However, competition upsets the balance and harmony valued by cultures that prefer cooperation and collaboration. A Japanese high-tech firm doing business in America discovered this difference in attempting to correct a problem. Dismayed to learn of the theft of some expensive equipment, top management assembled a group of middle managers to come up with a solution. The American managers concluded that offering a reward to the individual who reported the thief was the best solution. The lone dissenting voice came from a Japanese manager, whose suggestion that the team that did not whistle-blow and that did not have any theft problem be rewarded was laughed at. Each solution, however, was culturally appropriate.

Another cultural difference that emerges in the workplace regards privacy. To many newcomers, Americans seem naively open. Discussing personal matters outside the family is seen as embarrassing, and opening up to someone outside of one's own cultural group is rare. Thoughts, feelings, and problems are kept to oneself in most groups outside the dominant American culture. Off-the-cuff thinking, shooting from the hip, and giving an immediate response to a question from the boss would be difficult for someone raised with this cultural norm.

On the other hand, when it comes to privacy in space as opposed to thoughts and feelings, Americans are not so open. Perhaps because the United States has had the luxury of vast open spaces, we have a culture that fences off each person's area—children have their own rooms (sometimes with a Keep Out or Knock First sign on the door), backyards are fenced, and office spaces are partitioned into cubicles. In much of the rest of the world, such fencing off is not the case. Families may sleep in the same room, and on the job the work spaces are communal. In Japa-

nese offices, the boss generally does not have a separate office but rather shares a portion of the work space with employees. Likewise, in public areas, a new passenger on a bus or train would generally take a seat next to someone rather than sit in an unoccupied section. That would be considered odd behavior at best, and dangerously threatening at worst, in this country.

Loyalty is still another value that is differently displayed from culture to culture. Most Americans are taught loyalty to such abstract principles as "truth, justice, and the American way" and believe no one is above the law. Mexicans, Filipinos, and Middle Easterners, on the other hand, are loyal to individuals rather than to abstractions. That personal allegiance might mean breaking a rule to help a friend or covering up for a relative's infraction. Employees feeling this personal attachment also tend to give their allegiance to the boss rather than to the organization.

Finally, we get to an issue critical to all human beings— respect. While all of us want to be treated with dignity and respect, we define and demonstrate respect differently. Loss of face is important to avoid in all cultures. In Asia, in the Middle East, and to some extent in Latin America, one's face is to be preserved at all costs. In fact, death is preferred to loss of face in traditional Japanese culture, hence the ritualized suicide, hara-kiri, as a final way to restore honor. Any embarrassment can lead to loss of face, even

in the dominant American culture. To be criticized in front of others, to be publicly snubbed, or to be fired would be hard to swallow in any culture. However, inadvertent slights or unconscious faux pas can cause serious repercussions in intercultural relationships.

In Mexico, the Middle East, and parts of Asia, for example, the separation of the individual from the behavior is not so clear. "I am my behavior and my behavior is me" might be the motto. Criticism of performance may be taken as a personal insult, hence the case of the Indonesian worker who quit because of the loss of face he experienced in being corrected by his boss. In another example, the owner of a large travel agency had decided to reorganize her company, streamlining in the face of an economic slump during the Persian Gulf crisis. In doing her assessing, she noticed that one supervisor's group had slowly dwindled so that there was no one left for the supervisor to manage. The owner, an immigrant from the Philippines herself, called in her Chinese-born supervisor to discuss reorganization plans. While the employee understood the need for the changes, she begged the boss not to take away her title of supervisor and demote her. "I would lose face in my community if I lost my title," she said. The boss, understanding that "face" in this case took priority over a logical organization chart, complied. "What difference does it make to me what her title is? I just care that she is a satisfied and committed employee. If letting her be called supervisor accomplishes that, why not?" she thought.

Suggestions for Managers

▶ Consider giving rewards and feedback to the whole work group rather than to individuals.

▶ Structure tasks to require teamwork rather than individual action.

▶ Give workers time to think about and formulate responses to input requests.

▶ Consider the face-losing potential of any actions you are planning. Seek out ways to achieve your objectives while avoiding diminishing employees.

8. Beliefs and Attitudes

Religion probably comes to mind when you think of beliefs and attitudes with regard to cultural programming. Whether we practice them or not, religions are powerful influencers of our beliefs and attitudes. While the doctrine of separation of church and state is set down in the U.S. Constitution, there is a strong Judeo-Christian foundation in this country, with an emphasis on the Christian part. If you don't think so, look at legal holidays and school vacations.

Given today's pluralistic work force, it is important to realize that everyone does not practice the same religions, celebrate the same holidays, or want the same days off. An observant Orthodox Jew, for example, cannot work during the Sabbath, from sundown Friday to sundown Saturday, so holding important staff meetings on Friday afternoons or scheduling a team-building retreat on a Saturday would exclude this person, as it would a Seventh-Day Adventist. Among Muslim religious observances is the month of Ramadan, during which devout Muslims can have nothing to eat or drink each day from sunup to sundown. This might be a month to avoid holding heavy-duty negotiations or employee recognition luncheons if you have Muslims on your staff. One manager reported that since one of his employees reserved the noon hour for midday prayers, the manager made sure he never scheduled meetings during lunch.

Holiday celebrations are often times when religious differences are inadvertently ignored. In one client organization, management was surprised to find that not all employees appreciated the red poinsettia plants that were purchased to decorate all office cubicles at Christmastime. Many of the staff were not Christians and so did not celebrate Christmas.

In addition to religious views, beliefs about the position of women in society differ among cultures. In some groups, it is accepted that women work outside the home. In other groups, it is seen as a deficiency on the part of the male head of the house if any of the women from his family work. In other cases, while women may work outside the home, they cannot be in a position of authority over men. For a man to take orders from a woman would cause loss of face. This difference may cause problems between bosses and subordinates or between female staff and male clients/customers. In one local city with a large group of residents newly arrived from the Middle East, this problem became acute. Many of the Armenian immigrant men who came to do business with the city utility department were unaccustomed to dealing with women in business and demanded to talk with a man. However, there were no male employees in the customer service department. This culture clash caused much stress for the female city employees. Another situation that highlights the differences in attitudes about the role of women arose in a manufacturing company. The supervisor of one of the shifts was a Latina. Many of the male assembly-line workers refused to work for a woman. The only way the owner could keep her employees was to have segregated male and female work teams. Beyond ethical principles, with today's laws regarding equal employment opportunity (EEO) and affirmative action, organizations need to educate employees about the legal risks involved in discriminating because of gender.

Still another area of cultural programming regards attitudes about social order and authority. In Asia, students don't question teachers, employees don't confront bosses, and children don't talk back to parents. Not so in America, where the culture tends to be more egalitarian than in cultures that have more traditional and hierarchical attitudes about authority. While no society is truly classless, there is a wide range in views about social class, from the social mobility suggested in the "It's not who you are but what you are that counts" motto and Horatio Alger stories popular in America to India's more rigid caste system. Once you understand this difference, you can interpret others' behavior more accurately. You will see differently the housekeeper who calls you Miss/Mr./Mrs. before your first name, the employee who will not participate in group decision making at meetings, or the staff member who will not take direction from a countryman who is younger or on a lower social scale than he.

Suggestions for Managers

▶ Find out what religious holidays staff members celebrate. Keep those in mind when planning work-group activities, holiday celebrations, and individual schedules.

▶ Avoid scheduling meetings and training programs on any religious holidays.

▶ Take advantage of the fact that employees want different holidays, days off, and vacation times (e.g., some people would be willing to work on Sundays or on Christmas day).

▶ Help newcomers understand the reasons for shared decision making and the need for suggestions and input from employees.

▶ Educate employees about EEO and discrimination. Explain the legal liabilities as well as the principles of equality that, though not always adhered to, are foundations of this country.

9. Mental Processes and Learning

Do you prefer getting directions in words or with a map? Do you learn best by listening and taking notes; by being involved in experiential activities; by seeing models, diagrams, and graphs; or by taking part in lively discussions? Do you attribute your successes to your hard work and tenacity, or to luck and fate?

We all have preferences in learning and thinking styles, and some of these preferences are cultural. A few years ago, George Will quipped, in contrasting the United States and the then USSR, that the game that represents the thinking style of the United States is poker, while that of the USSR is chess. These two games represent very different styles of problem solving and thinking. Such different approaches may show up on your staff.

Perhaps the most obvious difference in problem solving has to do with the perception of human control. The dominant American culture professes a "fix-it" approach to problems, one that assumes that we have the power to control our world. Problems are seen as obstacles to be over-

come, and success in doing so depends on our actions. Progress and change are often seen as ends in themselves. In most of the rest of the world, the view is different. Problems are viewed as situations to which one must adapt and the changes required by problem solving are seen as a threat to order and harmony. In addition, fate and luck play a great part in determining the outcome of ventures. Cause-and-effect relationships are less emphasized in this kind of thinking. American culture also has a preference for logical analysis, while other cultures may bring more intuition and holistic thinking to a problem.

Another difference is in learning style. Teaching and learning are generally much more didactic, formal, and one-way, from teacher to student, in most of the rest of the world. There is also more dependence on written information. Therefore, staff from other cultures might feel lost in a typical American training seminar that emphasizes experiential activities and role playing, which require the learner to draw his/her own conclusions. Participants might also want copies of all information charted at the board or easel, or they may ask for lecture notes or outlines.

Suggestions for Managers

▶ Explain cause-and-effect relationships when getting staff members involved in problem solving.

- Ask staff members what they suggest be done about the problems and complaints they express.
- Use nonlinear problem-solving methods such as brainstorming that capitalize on lateral thinking and intuition rather than logical analysis.
- Ask troubleshooting questions such as "What would happen if . . .?" in order to get staff to think about possible consequences.

10. Work Habits and Practices

"The devil makes work for idle hands" exemplifies the Protestant work ethic, a cornerstone of American society. In this view, work is seen as more than a means to survival. It is a divine calling, a "vocation." In today's vernacular we talk about job satisfaction, finding one's magnificent obsession, and creating a career that brings joy, esteem, and achievement. Work is not always held in such high regard in other cultures. In fact, it may be seen as a necessary evil.

The type of work one does may also be seen as a sign of status. In this culture, we make distinctions between blue-collar and white-collar work, manual labor and professional work, and exempt and nonexempt employees. In other cultures, such as in India and the Arab world, for example, working with one's hands has lower status than doing professional work. This may explain why workers balk at certain tasks or prefer one kind of work over another. A physicist who manages an international staff at a premier space and technology research organization related the differences he has seen among members of his multinational staff. From his observation, the Swedish and German scientists love to tinker, work with their hands, and build models. The Indian scientist, on the other hand, disdains working with his hands and finds it beneath his dignity to have to input his own data into the computer.

An area critical to understanding if you are trying to get motivation and commitment from staff is the reward structure. What an employee considers rewarding is in the eye of the beholder, and that eye is cultural. A promotion to management might be considered a reward to one individual and a punishment to another; a bonus for a job well done might feel like a pat on the back to one employee and an insult to another. Paying attention to what individuals consider rewarding is important in any work group, but in a diverse group it may be more difficult to figure out. If you know that an employee has family responsibilities outside of work, allowing a more flexible schedule with staggered hours might be more of a motivator than a promotion would be. If an employee is trying to save money to bring other family members to this country, giving overtime assignments as tangible reinforcers might be appreciated.

Taking initiative and being self-directed are other work habits not universally taught. In most other cultures, workers are not expected to exercise independent judgment, make decisions, or initiate tasks without being directed to do so. When you notice employees waiting for direction, do not immediately assume these employees are unmotivated or lazy. They may be waiting for you to exercise your leadership role.

Suggestions for Managers

- Get to know your employees and find out what place work plays in their lives. Find out what gives them satisfaction on the job.
- Be sensitive to employees' perceptions about the status of certain kinds of work. Explain the reasons for each assignment and its importance in the whole scheme of things.
- Talk to employees and find out what is rewarding to them.
- Understand that taking initiative and making independent decisions may be difficult for some employees. Take time to coach them in this direction.

The chart *Comparing Cultural Norms and Values* gives a brief recap of the major differences between mainstream American and other cultures relative to the 10 aspects of culture discussed. The three tools that follow offer activities that can help individuals learn about cultural differences and apply that knowledge to their own real-life situ-

COMPARING CULTURAL NORMS AND VALUES		
Aspects of Culture	Mainstream American Culture	Other Cultures
1. Sense of self and space	Informal Handshake	Formal Hugs, bows, handshakes
2. Communication and language	Explicit, direct communication Emphasis on content—meaning found in words	Implicit, indirect communication Emphasis on context—meaning found around words
3. Dress and appearance	"Dress for success" ideal Wide range in accepted dress	Dress seen as a sign of position, wealth, prestige Religious rules
4. Food and eating habits	Eating as a necessity—fast food	Dining as a social experience Religious rules
5. Time and time consciousness	Linear and exact time consciousness Value on promptness—time = money	Elastic and relative time consciousness Time spent on enjoyment of relationships
6. Relationships, family, friends	Focus on nuclear family Responsibility for self Value on youth, age seen as handicap	Focus on extended family Loyalty and responsibility to family Age given status and respect
7. Values and norms	Individual orientation Independence Preference for direct confrontation of conflict	Group orientation Conformity Preference for harmony
8. Beliefs and attitudes	Egalitarian Challenging of authority Individuals control their destiny Gender equity	Hierarchical Respect for authority and social order Individuals accept their destiny Different roles for men and women
9. Mental processes and learning style	Linear, logical, sequential Problem-solving focus	Lateral, holistic, simultaneous Accepting of life's difficulties
10. Work habits and practices	Emphasis on task Reward based on individual achievement Work has intrinsic value	Emphasis on relationships Rewards based on seniority, relationships Work is a necessity of life

ations. *Dimensions of Culture* gives you a format to record information about different cultural norms. *Analyzing Cultural Differences helps* you apply that knowledge to specific work relationships. Finally, *Cross-Cultural Hooks* enables you to gain a better understanding of your own intercultural button-pushers.

DEMOGRAPHIC DESTINY: WORK-FORCE TRENDS AND THEIR IMPACT

L. Gardenswartz and A. Rowe

TODAY'S DEMOGRAPHIC revolution is radically transforming society and organizational life. The changes are fundamental and far reaching. How American businesses deal with the dilemmas presented by the five trends we describe will affect not only their success but also the survival of the national economy. The first place to begin in grappling with this massive societal shift is to examine the five major trends impacting the workplace.

1. Increase in the Number of Women

While working mothers, two-wage-earner households, and single parents are commonplace in our society, the Hudson Institute reports that by the year 2000, women will make up almost half (47 percent) of the labor force and 60 percent of the new entrants to the work force. In addition, women are holding a larger share of jobs in management and the professions, especially in fields that have been tradi-tionally male dominated such as law, medicine, and accounting.

Having more women in the work force and more women at higher levels means organizations have to deal with the needs and circumstances of women, who continue to bear the major burden for home and family responsibilities. Organizations have begun to respond with child-care options, flexible scheduling, elder-programs, and cafeteria-plan benefit packages. However, they still need to make progress in creating career development options that meet the needs of women. Once satisfied to merely get in, women, like other previously excluded groups, are cracking the glass ceiling and demanding admittance to the upper echelons of organizations.

2. Increase in the Number of Minorities

Changing demographics are beginning to make the terms *minority* and *majority* invalid and irrelevant in many commu-nities across the country as the percentage of Latinos, African-Americans, and Asians increases. According to Hudson Institute estimates, by the year 2000, nonwhites will make up 29 percent of the work force. In order to capitalize on this sector of the work force, organizations will need to expand opportunities for nonwhites by creating more inclusive environments.

3. Increase in the Number of Immigrants

Immigrants are flocking to America's shores and over its borders in greater numbers than any period since World War I. However, today's newcomers are different from those of the early 1900s, who were mainly Europeans. Today's immigrants are not as visibly assimilable—they look different. They are mainly Latino, Asian and Middle Eastern individuals, who, like all immigrants past and present, want a piece of the American dream, but not at the expense of their unique cultural characteristics and values. This steady flow of one half to three quarters of a million immigrants per year is felt most strongly in California, Texas, and New York, states where well over half of all foreign-born residents live. The range in education, skill level, and ability is wide, from those who are illiterate in their native languages to those who are multilingual and who possess advanced degrees.

Language is one of the greatest challenges immigrants pose for organizations. While some are fluent English speakers, most immigrants are not. Yet a survey of 645 American organizations by Towers Perrin and the Hudson Institute reported that fewer than 10 percent of the companies surveyed had English-as-a-second-language programs for employees. Beyond dealing with language barriers, organizations are faced with the challenge of helping managers understand the cultures of their employees so they can motivate, reward, and build productive work relationships with their diverse staffs.

4. Aging

As the demographic bulge created by the postwar baby boom (1946–1961) passes into maturity, it moves a large proportion of the work force into middle age. While the majority of workers in the next decade will still be in their most productive years (35–54), the labor force is slowly getting older. This means fewer young, entry-level people, as well as more experienced

workers who come with education and training as well as a higher price tag. Organizations will be called upon to help more mature employees maintain the flexibility and energy needed to deal with an accelerated pace of change. In addition, businesses will also have to find ways of dealing with the increased competition among older workers for midcareer promotions and management positions at a time when most companies are streamlining and trimming layers of management.

5. Rise in Education and Skill Requirements

Today's and tomorrow's jobs require a more highly skilled, more educated work force in a society where the education and skill levels of the population are declining. *Workforce 2000* predicts that the majority of jobs from now on will require education beyond high school. This trend may prove a barrier to minority groups who have been educationally disadvantaged and who have traditionally entered the work force through unskilled or semiskilled jobs. Organizations will need to create bold new methods of training employees in both basic and job-related skills and retraining existing workers to keep up with the demands of the workplace.

Aging: Different Generations Equal Different Values

Morris Massey's film *What You Are Is What You Were*

When has cleverly brought the topic of generational values into organizations across the country. With humor and insight he helps people understand how deeply programmed our values are by the era in which we grew up. Those of us with parents reared during the depression of the 1930s undoubtedly grew up hearing them praise thrift, hard work, and perseverance while viewing security as a prime value in a job. On the other hand, those reared in more affluent recent times are accused of being the "me first" generation with no patience for delayed gratification. "Enjoy now, pay later" is the current motto.

When we lead diversity seminars, participants often tell us that one of the hardest gaps to bridge is not one of culture or race, but one of age. Stereotypes, both positive and negative, abound. Younger workers are labeled irresponsible, ill-mannered, undependable, and not willing to pay their dues. Most damning of all, they are thought to have an inferior work ethic. Conversely, older employees are described as rigid, stodgy, uncreative, and resistant to change. While no one person of any generation is a carbon copy of others of the same age, there are values sets that characterize age groups. The differences between generations center on the following values and assumptions.

1. Entitlement

Younger employees have grown up in an era of abundance and a climate of questioning authority. Where mature workers brought up in a more hierarchical and traditional society may follow directions because they are given by a boss, younger employees want to know why. In addition, with less fear of retaliation such as job loss, younger employees find it easier to challenge authority and demand that their concerns be recognized.

2. Security

As older employees approach retirement, they are naturally concerned with making sure they are set for their "golden years." In addition, many mature workers have a tacit "signed on for life" bargain with the organization. They may feel they have traded more lucrative opportunities for the security of a lifetime job guarantee. The threat of a job loss or layoff may be particularly devastating to an older employee who not only feels betrayed, but is at a loss in competing in a job market that discriminates against older workers. Younger employees, on the other hand, come from a generation that expects career mobility, job hopping, and many career moves. These individuals tend to build security through a strong résumé rather than through organizational stability.

3. Achievement

Older workers tend to subscribe to the "work hard and you'll get ahead" school of thought. Achievement rests on stick-to-it-iveness. Their younger counterparts, on the other hand, subscribe to the "work smarter, not harder" theme. Clever thinking is seen as the ticket to success. This may lead to conflicts where older employees see younger staff members as conniving or lazy, while younger employees may see their older colleagues as plodding and unwilling to try new approaches.

4. Loyalty

Perhaps as another legacy of the entitlement era in which they grew up, today's younger generation's loyalty is to themselves and their own prosperity, advancement, and well-being. Older workers tend to show more loyalty to the organization that has given them opportunities and so are willing to do what is asked, go the extra mile, and do more than is on their list of job duties. On the other hand, this same loyalty is often at the heart of the betrayal felt by these long-termers when organizations are forced to downsize and cut staff. The loyalty often brings with it the expectation that the organization will take care of the employee by lifetime employment.

In dealing with a work force from different generations, it is critical not only to recognize the different values set each age group brings but also to find ways of working with rather than against those differences. One way to do that is to consider both the positive and negative aspects of each value in order to deal with the clashes in a more neutral, dispassionate, and objective way. For example, a strong value on personal entitlement may help the individual get ahead by stating desires and preferences clearly and openly. It may also make the individual a more productive team member who takes the initiative to give input and tell the boss about problems and complaints. On the downside, it may cause the individual to ignore the needs of others, causing rifts in a work group. Or it may lead to a reluctance to bear the extra work and pressure of the tough times that are part of every job from time to time. Conversely, a deemphasis on entitlement may make for an employee who is willing to bear any burden without complaint but one whose built-up resentment shows itself in passive resistance or stress-related illness.

Once seen in a more even light with a more neutral perspective, these value variations look less right and wrong than just plain different. What need to be negotiated are the tangibles such as schedules, hours, tasks, equipment, or supplies rather than the values themselves which are personal, deeply held, and powerfully defended.

Feminization of the Work Force

Gone are the Donna Reed days of apron-clad moms greeting their children with milk and cookies after school. Because of economic necessity, increasing options for women and personal career choices, the majority of women in America today work outside the home, making up close to half of the work force. This fundamental societal change has impacted organizations in significant ways.

1. Dealing with Family Issues

Women in the workplace face double jeopardy—the regular pressures and work load of organizational life and the "second shift" they work when they get home. Because women remain the main caregivers and caretakers in our society, organizations have been forced to deal with family issues as strategic business concerns. Child care, return to work, and leave policies, as well as flexible scheduling options such as job sharing, have been organizational responses to the work/home conflicts faced by most working women. However, more progress is needed. A recent Towers Perrin/Hudson Institute survey reports that fewer than 10 percent of the organizations responding provided near-site or on-site day care or sick child care. Fewer than 15 percent had a gradual return to work policy, 20 percent provided paternity leave, and a little over 30 percent allowed sick days for sick children and maternity leave. In competing for employees in the projected tight labor market, attending to these needs can be a strategic advantage for a farsighted organization.

2. Meeting the Varying Needs of Working Women

Working women come in all shapes, sizes, and lifestyles. Some come from dual-career households, while others are single parents. Child care, elder care, or college tuition may be their main concern. Some are midcareer and climbing, aspiring to executive levels, while others are nearing retirement or working to put a child through college. In order to attract and keep competent female employees, organizations have been required to become more flexible and creative in benefits such as health care, retirement, and educational reimbursement; incentives such as stock options and bonuses; and policies regarding leaves, work schedules, and the like. In the same Towers Perrin/ Hudson Institute report, a little over 20 percent of the organizations responding had job-sharing programs, though half offered flextime options.

3. Dealing with the Career Demands of Working Women

No longer content to fill the bottom layers of organizations, women are increasing their share of managerial and professional jobs. According to *Workforce 2000,* women account for nearly half of all professionals. However, in addition to the discrepancy in earning power, women are angry at hitting the glass ceiling when they attempt to move beyond middle management. In order to retain talented female employees, organizations are

recognizing the need to have both genders in the executive suite. Not only does promoting women give other women a sense of the possibilities within the organization, but it brings a different leadership style into upper management. Women at lower levels see that you don't have to be "one of the boys" and lose your own style in order to succeed. Equally important, the organization benefits from the other gender's approach to problems.

Polls continue to report only one or two women at the helm of major U.S. corporations. This area of career pathing for women is the most problematic for organizations and the one where least progress has been made because it deals with a central issue in diversity—power sharing. Making the most of today's and tomorrow's diverse work force depends on the ability of those in power, traditionally Euro-American males, to share power with groups who have been previously excluded from corporate decision making.

Integration and Racial/Ethnic Shifts

If, as one student quipped, "Immigration is the sincerest compliment," then the United States is certainly much admired. The 1970s and 1980s brought the biggest tide of immigration to the U.S. since the great wave of the early 1900s. Changing immigration laws in 1965; the end of the war in Southeast Asia; and political and economic instability in

Mexico, Central America, and the Middle East have resulted in a huge population influx. Somewhere between 500,000 and 750,000 new immigrants are predicted to enter the United States annually for the remainder of the century.

Many of these new Americans bring languages and cultures that are non-European and non-Western. In addition, today's immigrant is generally more concerned with preserving ethnic identity than were many of those early 1900s pioneers who were eager to shed old-world ways. Finally, because of the large concentration of immigrants in certain cities, it is possible for people to continue to live in their native culture and language in this country. Los Angeles, for example, has the largest Spanish-speaking population in the world outside of Mexico City, the largest Filipino population outside the Philippines, and the largest Korean population outside Korea. The Los Angeles Unified School District reports that 80-plus native languages are spoken by its students.

The impact of this influx of newcomers on U.S. business is multifaceted. Immigrants often enter the work force at the lowest levels and provide a ready supply of low-wage workers for manufacturing and service jobs. However, language presents a problem, as newcomers generally lack facility in English. Organizations find themselves searching for ways to teach employees English while they teach supervisors and managers the skills needed to manage non-

English-speaking workers. The mix of languages and cultures in work groups presents additional challenges for employers attempting to create harmonious and productive work teams. Finally, different cultural norms and values impact performance. How to relate to a boss, participate in a meeting, take criticism, solve a problem, or take initiative are all culturally influenced behaviors. What in one culture looks respectful may look lazy in another. What is polite in one may look deceitful in another. What is direct and clear to one person may seem rude and insulting to another. These cultural differences present significant challenges to managers of multicultural work teams.

While immigration has increased the diversity of the work force, native-born non-Euro-Americans also figure into the diversity mix. African-Americans, previously the largest minority, continue to make up approximately 12 percent of the population and will represent around 20 percent of the new entrants to the work force during this decade. However, other groups such as Latinos and Asians are growing at much faster rates due to immigration. This demographic shift has led to a fear expressed by many African-Americans that their hard-won gains in civil rights and EEO in the workplace will backslide and their concerns be preempted by other groups who by sheer numbers may prevail. One African-American woman who called our office expressed it this way:

I'm black and frustrated. It seems to me that the concerns and issues of blacks have been lost in the shuffle due to all the attention focused on new immigrants from Central America and Asia. Our problems have never been fully addressed and now we're still getting the short end of the stick.

It is clear that America's work force is and will continue to be a heterogeneous, multicultural, polyglot mixture. As with any change, this shift brings with it both challenges and opportunities. It is our new reality to do with as we will.

Educational Deficits: The Gap between Organizational Needs and Work-Force Skill Level

The title of one *Business Week* article says it all: "Where the Jobs Are Is Where the Skills Aren't." One of the biggest challenges for American business is the need for increasingly skilled workers in a population with decreasing education and skills levels. It is projected that over half of the decade's new jobs will require post-high school education and a third will require a college degree. As we shift from a manufacturing to a service economy, more brain than brawn will be called for. The fastest-growing jobs necessitate more language, math, and reasoning skills, while declining occupations have low levels of skill requirements. Entry-level workers are increasingly lacking in the basic skills to perform adequately on the job. High school dropout rates and slipping achievement scores, plus the need to import workers from abroad or ship clerical work overseas, demonstrate the educational deficits we are facing. For example, the *Business Week* article mentioned above reported that Chemical Bank in New York interviews 40 applicants to hire 1 who can be trained as a teller and that the New York Telephone Company had to test 60,000 applicants to hire 3,000 people. The scenario is even more bleak for Latinos and African-Americans who have a greater educational disadvantage.

Organizations are beginning to respond by providing basic skills training for employees in reading, math, and other job-related competencies. A recent study reported fewer than 10 percent of companies provide preemployment training, but over 15 percent offer remedial education, over 30 percent partner with high schools and technical schools, and 40 percent offer on-site skill classes. These percentages are bound to rise as organizational skill needs increase and workers' educational levels decline. In addition to bringing education to the workplace, business is going to the schools. In many communities, business/education partnerships are forming, bringing together leaders from both sides of the issue to solve one of society's toughest problems. With additional financial resources from corporations and more accurate

information about the occupational skill needs of tomorrow, schools are trying to equip students for success after graduation.

Identifying Primary and Secondary Dimensions of Diversity

As fingerprints show us, each human being is unique, providing the world with infinite diversity. However, some differences are more important than others in the effects they have on individuals' opportunities in the world. Marilyn Loden and Judy Rosener, in their recent book *Workforce America!,* separate the major dimensions of diversity into two categories—primary and secondary.

Primary Dimensions of Diversity

➤ Age
➤ Ethnicity
➤ Gender
➤ Physical ability
➤ Sexual/affectional orientation

Secondary Dimensions of Diversity

➤ Geographic location
➤ Income
➤ Marital status
➤ Military experience
➤ Parental status
➤ Religious beliefs
➤ Work experience

Primary factors are unalterable and extremely powerful in their effects. Secondary dimensions are significant in

shaping us, but they are to some extent shapable in return, because we have some measure of control over them.

Janet Elsea, in her book *The 4 Minute Sell,* tells us that the nine most important things noticed about people in our society, in order of importance, are the following:

1. Skin color
2. Gender
3. Age
4. Appearance
5. Facial expressions
6. Eye contact
7. Movement
8. Personal space
9. Touch

Upon encountering one another, we notice, make assessments, and make decisions about how to interact with that individual based on these nine factors. How we respond depends on many variables; among them are our assumptions and expectations. For example, an African-American encountering another African-American would undoubtedly have a different reaction and set of expectations than a Euro-American meeting that same person. A man responds differently to meeting another man than to meeting a woman. These reactions, based on split-second assessments of others, influence our relationships. It is as if each of us were a member of an exclusive club in which we were the only member. Each new acquaintance is analyzed to see if there is enough similarity, comfort, and affinity to permit inclusion—or hiring or promotion.

Analyzing Your Organization's Work-Force Trends

Population Demographics

1. What is the projected breakdown of the community's population in 5 and 10 years in such areas as age, ethnicity, gender, and native language?
2. What is the projected breakdown of the local work force in 5 and 10 years by age, ethnicity, and gender?
3. What are the statistics regarding education level of the work force in 5 and 10 years by gender and ethnicity?
4. What different needs will these workers bring? How will they impact the organization?

Organizational Skills Needs

1. What is the projected number of new workers needed by your organization in 5 and 10 years by skill level such as unskilled, semiskilled, managerial, professional, and/or by type of work such as assembly line, clerical, data entry, and so on?
2. What is the projected gain or loss of employees by your organization in 5 and 10 years by department or function such as manufacturing, accounting, data processing, personnel, sales, marketing, and customer relations?
3. What will be the skill requirements of employees in 5 and 10 years, for example, English literacy or computer literacy?

Training and Development Needs

1. What tools do we need to develop to assess individual skill levels and job requirements?
2. What basic and job-specific skills will need to be taught to employees?
3. What managerial skills will need to be taught to those in supervisory and management

---

The first three items on the list—skin color, gender, and age—would fall into the primary dimensions of diversity. They are virtually unalterable and extremely powerful in determining our life situation from where we live and work to whom we marry and how much we earn. The last six on the list are culturally influenced. Whether we give a handshake or a hug, a direct stare or lowered eyes, a nod or a frown is determined by the culture in which we are raised and is influenced by both the primary and secondary dimensions of diversity.

Consider people with whom you work, both those with whom you feel an affinity and those with whom you do not. How many dimensions of diversity do you have in common with each group? No doubt there are more commonalities both in primary and secondary factors among those with whom you feel a connection.

Analyzing Your Organization's Work-Force Trends

Forewarned is forearmed. Understanding the demographic shift at a societal level is a preamble to taking a look at your own specific work force trends. It has been said that to find out who your entry-level workers will be in five years, you need only to go to your local junior or senior high school. However, you may want to conduct a deeper analysis. Questions such as those in the box may help guide your investigation.

A number of resources can help you in your data gathering and investigation. Local governments and organizations such as the Southern California Association of Governments often compile statistics and provide demographic information about the population, as do most school districts. Local colleges and universities generally have sociologists and statisticians who monitor trends in the population. Finally, the U.S. Department of Labor, Bureau of Statistics, offers state-by-state breakdowns from census figures. In addition, profession- and industry-specific associations often chart relevant trends.

Within the organization, information can be obtained from both existing data such as human resource statistics and the company's strategic plan as well as from management staff who can give a bird's-eye perspective on expected changes. The end result of your analysis should tell you what your organization will need and how well the work force will be able to meet those needs. You will then be in a position to strategically plan ways to bring the two closer together.

Myths and Realities about Today's Multicultural Work Force

"It ain't the way it used to be" may be true, but today's reality may not present as dismal a picture as many would paint. Dispelling some of the alarming myths about the diverse work force may help you have more realistic expectations about our future.

1. *Myth:* Immigrants are illiterate and uneducated. *Reality:* Immigrants come with varying skills, talents, and education levels. Some may be rural peasants with little or no education seeking economic advantage in the United States. Others may be highly educated professionals who have come for political freedom and who are working at jobs well below their education level because of limited English skills that prevent them from passing licensing exams in their professions. *Workforce 2000* reports that during the decade of the 70s, 22 percent of immigrants were college graduates, while only 16 percent of native Americans had completed college.

2. *Myth:* Immigrants are a drain on the economy. *Reality:* The fear may be worse than the reality. Los Angeles, where over 1 million immigrants settled in the 70s, is a case in point. During that period, job growth exceeded the national level, while unemployment was below that of the nation as a whole. Manufacturing wages dropped but the wages in the service industry, an area in which native-born Americans were concentrated, grew at a faster rate than the national average. New, young workers may

draw industries that create jobs. *Workforce 2000* also reports that census data and other studies indicate that in 10 to 20 years, immigrants and their children will out-earn comparable native-born Americans. In addition, UCLA's David Hayer-Bautista, in his book *Burden of Support*, gives a fresh perspective about California's large and soon-to-be-majority Latino work force. He projects that this group of younger workers will be supporting a huge population of retired baby boomers through taxes.

3. *Myth:* Immigrants take jobs away from native-born Americans. *Reality:* This complaint about immigrants has been made about every successive group from the Irish and Germans of the 1800s to the Italians, Slavs, and Jews of the early 1900s. While experiences vary from area to area, one report gives another view. A statistical analysis of 247 urban areas determined that black unemployment did not increase in proportion to Mexican immigration in that labor market. Immigration in these cases was complementary rather than competitive with the existing minority work force. However, recent news events have pointed to a rift between African-Americans and both Mexicans and Koreans who live and work in close proximity in many cities. In

tough economic times, conflicts may increase between groups who see themselves in competition for diminishing resources.

Strategic Implications of Increasing Diversity: Challenges and Opportunities

Our demographic destiny presents organizations with both challenges and opportunities. The central issue in dealing with diversity has little to do with language, culture, or other differences; rather, it is about power sharing. Giving every group in society a stake in the system, every group in your organization a "piece of the action," is at the heart of the most significant challenge that diversity presents. Becoming open to differences and creating an inclusive environment means that new groups will need to be let into positions of decision making and influence. It is rare in human nature to find examples of those in power who willingly share it. Managing diversity in a meaningful way demands that organizations deal with this fundamental strategic issue.

Beyond opening the system, organizations will need to create strategies to help staff at all levels overcome their resistance to this demographic transformation and deal with one another in harmonious, cooperative ways. Companies will find it necessary to overcome barriers to communication and create strategic ways to foster synergistic teamwork, educate and retrain em-

ployees, and meet the varying needs of their increasingly multifaceted staffs.

Diversity will also present opportunities for work-force development, service enhancement, and new-business creation. The opportunities to capitalize on a new world of workers is endless. Organizations are finding rich new labor resources among older workers and the differently abled. Creative recruitment strategies can develop pools of talented entry-level workers among many previously untapped groups. Developing the internal pool of existing employees represents another undercultivated resource.

A diverse population also means different needs in the marketplace. The chance to enhance service and thereby capitalize on new markets is wide open. Understanding the needs and preferences of the changing consumer base and responding to it in more effective ways is an important area for growth. Automatic teller machines in different languages and the growth of foreign-language television programming are examples of this service enhancement. Finally, new business opportunities in the form of new products and services are waiting to be created. The last few years have witnessed the growth of check-cashing services for those who have no bank accounts, personal errand runners, and fast-food and take-out restaurants for working singles and dual-career couples. None of these would have been necessary in the America of 20 years ago.

Turning Diversity into a Corporate Asset

Effectively managing diversity and creating an organization in which differences are truly valued is more than just a good idea—it is good business. It is propelled by more than a moral imperative—it brings a strategic advantage. Those organizations that meet the challenges and capitalize on the opportunities presented by a diverse work force will show bottom-line results and a significant edge over the competition.

1. Better Return on the Investment in Human Capital

The management of human resources is often talked about as the "soft" side of business. Yet most organizations spend more on their human capital than on any other resource. Misuse and poor management of this asset costs organizations in obvious and not so obvious ways. In clearly bottom-line-connected ways, the stress claims, grievances, and EEO suits resulting from diversity-related problems cost organizations millions of dollars annually. But there are more subtle costs as well. Absenteeism and turnover are typical signs of the employee dissatisfaction and stress that can result when staff members are blocked from moving up or are forced to fit into an uncomfortable mold. In addition, employees who feel undervalued don't commit their energy, ideas, or full ability to produce top-quality results. On the other hand, when they feel the organization's commitment to them, they reciprocate by giving both their concentration and commitment.

2. Attracting the Best and the Brightest

As the labor force shrinks, the competition will be heated for top-notch talent. As that talent pool becomes more diverse, those organizations with a reputation for meeting the needs of diverse staff and offering the best opportunities to talented, capable individuals of any stripe will be the employer of choice.

3. Increased Creativity

Creativity has sometimes been defined as the act combining old elements in new ways. Yet it is habitual to stick to the tried and true. The influx of new and different people into an organization can bring an infusion of fresh blood. Newcomers, former outsiders, and those who are different from the norm have new perspectives that can be the source of ideas, suggestions, and methods that have not been previously considered. Men and women tend to think and communicate differently. People from other cultures see and solve problems differently. Employees from varied backgrounds bring knowledge and information about the needs of different groups. If tapped, this diversity of style, experience, and knowledge enhances the organization's ability to respond creatively.

4. Capitalizing on a Diverse Market

A diverse population translates into a diverse market for goods and services. Organizations whose work forces mirror the composition of the society at large will be in a better position to understand and reach out to this pluralistic marketplace. Through the sharing of a common language and culture, diverse employees often have the empathy and sensitivity not only to relate to consumers of different groups but also to anticipate needs and suggest ways to reach new market segments.

Experts in the area of cultural studies agree that the best way to understand cultural differences is to study both your own culture and one other. Therefore, the purpose of this assignment is to:

1. Conduct an indepth study of a culture other than your own (preferably one that you are likely to encounter in the workplace).

2. Research your own culture.

3. Compare the two cultures.

In order to conduct a study of another culture it is helpful if you can locate an individual who represents that culture. One good place to look is the international student office. Often these students are interested in practicing their English and are glad to discuss their native cultures. Use this person as your primary resource, to be supplemented by more traditional types of research. The article "Ten Aspects of Culture: Understanding Cultural Programming," suggests areas for initial study.

A study of the workforce reveals the fact that we are experiencing a demographic revolution. Gone are the days of the white male majority in the workplace. Instead that majority is being replaced a large number of minority groups. Each minority brings its own special advantages to the work environment, and has its own special needs.

Conduct a field study in the area of multi-cultural human resource management. Contact major hospitality corporations to determine what programs they have established to accommodate the multi-cultural workforce. Some suggested areas to investigate might include:

1. Training programs at all levels

2. English as a second language

3. Changes in benefits packages

4. Accommodating various lifestyles (for example flextime, four-day work week, job sharing)

5. Recruiting

23

TRAVEL AND TOURISM

Tourism, Development and Tourist Development
D. Pearce

Project 1

Project 2

TOURISM, DEVELOPMENT AND TOURIST DEVELOPMENT

D. Pearce

TOURIST DEVELOPMENT can be defined in different ways and viewed from several perspectives but essentially it is a hybrid term embodying two basic concepts—tourism and development. This book thus begins with a review of these two concepts and the interrelationships between them to set the scene for a fuller discussion of tourist development. Such a review is important at the outset, for relatively few links have been made between the body of literature on tourism and that on development. An outline of the subsequent structure of the volume is then given.

Tourism

Tourism has been defined in various ways but may be thought of as the relationships and phenomena arising out of the journeys and temporary stays of people travelling primarily for leisure or recreational purposes. While writers differ on the degree to which other forms of travel (e.g. for business, for health or educational purposes) should be included under tourism there is a growing recognition that tourism constitutes one end of a broad leisure spectrum. In a geographical sense, a basic distinction between tourism and other forms of leisure, such as that practised in the home (e.g. watching television) or within the urban area (e.g. going to the cinema or a walk in the park), is the travel component. Some writers employ a minimum trip distance criterion but generally tourism is taken to include at least a one-night stay away from the place of permanent residence or origin. The spatial interaction which arises out of the tourist's movement from origin to destination is an inherent and defining feature of tourism and the subject lends itself readily to geographical analysis (Pearce, 1987a).

The travel and stay attributes are also characterized by the demand for and provision of a wide range of goods and services. In terms of the tourist's destination, these can be grouped into five broad sectors: attractions, transport, accommodation, supporting facilities and infrastructure. The attractions help encourage the tourists to visit the area, transport services enable them to do so, the accommodation and supporting facilities (e.g. shops, banks, restaurants) cater for their well-being while there, and the infrastructure assures the essential functioning of all of these. Many of these services may be combined and provided by tour operators located at the destination, origin or with links to both, who offer the traveller a package involving transport, accommodation and perhaps sightseeing or some other recreational activity. Sales of these packages and/or individual travel items are often made through retail travel agencies located in the origins or markets.

There is then no single tourist product, no one commodity or service by which the output of tourism might be measured. Rather, tourists when they

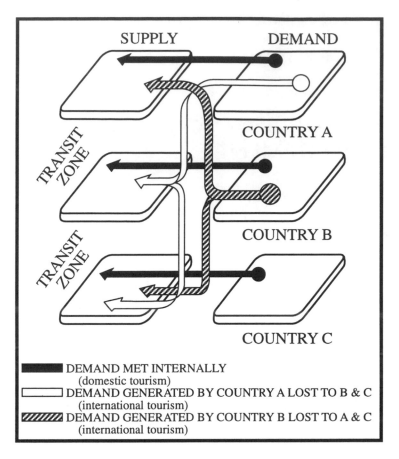

SUPPLY   DEMAND

COUNTRY A

TRANSIT ZONE

COUNTRY B

TRANSIT ZONE

COUNTRY C

■■■■ DEMAND MET INTERNALLY
(domestic tourism)
▢ DEMAND GENERATED BY COUNTRY A LOST TO B & C
(international tourism)
▨ DEMAND GENERATED BY COUNTRY B LOST TO A & C
(international tourism)

FIGURE 1. Schematic representation of the supply of and demand for domestic and international tourism in a series of countries.

travel acquire an experience made up of many different parts, some tangible (transport from A to B, accommodation, souvenirs purchased), some more intangible (the pleasure of an island sunset, the thrill of white-water rafting, the appreciation of works of art, the satisfaction with high quality service in a French restaurant). Much of this experience is acquired at or *en route* to and from the destination. Souvenirs and other goods may be purchased to take home but many of the goods and services demanded by tourists are consumed *in situ,* in the places where they are offered or produced. The degree to which this occurs distinguishes tourism from many other economic activities, such as manufacturing and agriculture. Consumption at the point of production also influences the pattern of impacts which tourism may have.

Tourism is thus a multi-faceted activity and a geographically complex one as different services are sought and supplied at different stages from the origin to the destination. Moreover, in any country or region there is likely to be a number of origins and destinations, with most places having both generating (origin) and receiving (destination) functions (Pearce, 1987a).

Conceptually, many of these elements are brought together in Thurot's multiple origin-destination model. Thurot distinguishes between supply and demand and between domestic (or internal) and international tourism. Part of the demand for tourism generated in country B, probably the larger part, will be fulfilled by that country's tourist facilities with the remainder being distributed to countries A and C. At the same time, part of the demand from country A will be channelled to country B (and to country C), which thereby becomes an international destination as well as a source of international travellers. In contrast, no international demand is shown to emanate from country C, although it may generate domestic tourists and receive tourists from countries A and C. Country C is said to represent certain Third World countries where standards of living may generally be insufficient to generate international tourism (although often a small élite may indulge in a large amount of such travel) and Soviet bloc countries where severe restrictions on international travel may exist.

In the real world, however, the boundaries of tourism are not always neatly confined. On the supply side, for example, facilities and services used by tourists may be purpose-built or designed for them or they may be shared with other users. Facilities built expressly for tourism range from attractions such as Disneyland to resort hotels to ski-field access roads. Others have been transformed from their original function to some tourist use, for example farm cottages have become second homes and old canals and waterways have been restored for recreational boating. In other instances tourism may supplement or complement the original activity—wine-makers have opened their cellars to tourists and Gothic cathedrals today attract the curious as much as the faithful. Or tourists may share their accommodation and transport with other travellers and take advantage of services and infrastructure provided essentially for the resident population.

Classic expressions of tourism include coastal, alpine or thermal resorts such as Benidorm, Chamonix and Badgastein. Less distinct but no less important in terms of tourism are cities such as Tokyo, London and Paris which each year attract millions of visitors and in turn generate millions of travellers. Rural areas, where tourism is often more dispersed and its organization less formal, may also be significant tourist destinations.

Tourism has developed in many different contexts. Modern mass tourism has its origins in the affluence of the industrialized nations of Western Europe, North America and, more recently, Japan. Tourism has also expanded significantly in Eastern Europe and is becoming an important sector in many developing countries in Asia, Africa, Latin America, the South Pacific and the Caribbean. Thus tourism has developed in

liberal Western societies, under centrally planned socialist regimes, as a relatively small part of large industrial economies or again as the leading sector of small developing countries. Likewise, tourism has developed in a wide variety of physical environments— on low islands of the Pacific, in the heart of alpine Europe, in the countryside of the English Lakes District and along the Mediterranean coastline.

Today there can be little doubt that tourism has assumed considerable economic and social significance throughout the world. In 1986 the World Tourism Organization (WTO) estimated the number of international tourist arrivals at about 340 million and receipts from international tourism at 115 billion dollars. Domestic tourists are generally several times more numerous than international tourists in most developed Western States.

Tourism Research

Tourism has been studied by an increasing number of researchers from a variety of disciplines over the last two decades. However, no widely accepted interdisciplinary field of tourism studies has yet been defined and a cohesive body of knowledge which might be thought of as a specialized sub-discipline has been slow to emerge in geography, economics, management, sociology, anthropology and other disciplines.

Pearce (1979a) identified six broad topic areas as constituting the major components

of the geography of tourism: spatial patterns of supply, spatial patterns of demand, the geography of resorts, the analysis of tourist movements and flows, the impact of tourism and models of tourist space. More recent national reviews show coverage of topics varies considerably from country to country and that the literature on tourism is still rather fragmented (Barbier and Pearce, 1984; Benthien, 1984; Duffield, 1984; Lichtenberger, 1984; Lundgren, 1984; Mitchell, 1984; Pearce and Mings, 1984; Takeuchi, 1984). General studies on the geography of tourism (Robinson, 1976; Hudman, 1980) have recently been complemented by major works on more specific areas, with studies on tourism's impacts (Mathieson and Wall, 1982; Murphy, 1985); methodological issues (Smith, 1983) and the spatial structure of tourism (Pearce, 1987a).

In economics, management and marketing, seminal works on tourism appeared comparatively early (Gray, 1970; Baretje and Defert, 1972; Burkart and Medlik, 1974; Wahab, Crampon and Rothfield, 1976), yet in the following decade the literature in these fields appears no more extensive nor cohesive. Booms and Bitner (1980), for instance, argue that tourism enterprises are strictly service enterprises and observe (p. 338) that "with few exceptions, the management literature, management research and management training all focus on manufacturing activities and the problems of goods production." Contributions by economists to tourism research are seen by Gray (1982) to be in the areas of measurement, cost-benefit analysis, resource allocation and the use of public goods in the development of tourism. The balance of payments effect of tourism is the main concern of the special issue of the *Annals of Tourism Research* (Vol. 9, No. 1) devoted to the economics of international tourism.

In a very useful review of the sociology of tourism, Cohen (1984) identifies eight main sociological perspectives on tourism: tourism as commercialized hospitality, as democratized travel, as a modern leisure activity, as a modern variety of the traditional pilgrimage, as an expression of basic cultural themes, as an acculturative process, as a type of ethnic relations and as a form of neocolonialism. Cohen then suggests sociological research on tourism "falls naturally" into four principal issue areas: the tourist, relations between tourists and locals, the structure and functioning of the tourist system, and the consequences of tourism. Anthropologists, according to Grabum (1983), have also focused on the study of the impacts of tourism on host populations as well as on the study of tourists themselves. In his review, Grabum explores the notion of tourism as ritual and play.

The impact of tourism is the most common theme to emerge from these disparate studies, with varying emphasis being given to economic, social, cultural and environmental issues depending on the background of the writers concerned. Each discipline also has its own perspectives on the way in which tourism is organized, with geographers highlighting its spatial structures, sociologists and anthropologists underlining social relationships and economists emphasizing economic attributes.

Development

Recent reviews of the "meaning of development" have highlighted the many ways in which development has been used and the numerous interpretations which continue to be given to it (Goulet, 1968; Seers, 1969, 1977; D. Smith, 1977; Mabogunje, 1980; Unwin, 1983; Thirlwall, 1983; Welch, 1984). Welch (p. 2) considers development "has become a term bereft of precise meaning" and quotes Friedmann (1980) who suggests it "is one of the more slippery terms in our tongue." That there is no single, unequivocal definition of development is due in part to different uses of the term by different disciplines and changes in those uses over time, particularly in the last three decades.

Much of this ambiguity results from the use of the term "development" to refer both to a process and to a state. Goulet (1968), one of the earlier writers in the field, notes (p. 388):

Development has usually been treated as a process, a particular kind of social change. Nevertheless, development is also a state or condition. Whenever a society is called developed or underdeveloped we refer to its present condition. Similarly, when development is declared to be a major goal of Third World nations, the allusion is to a terminal condition, not to a process. Thus the single term "development" refers both to the destination of a journey and to the journey itself.

Development, according to Friedmann (1980, p. 4):

suggests an *evolutionary* process, it has positive connotations . . . And of course, development is always *of* something particular, a human being, a society, a nation, an economy, a skill . . . It is often associated with words such as *under* or *over* or *balanced*: too little, too much, or just right . . . which suggests that development has a structure, and that the speaker has some idea about how this structure *ought* to be developed. We also tend to think of development as a process of change or as a complex of such processes which is in some degree lawful or at least sufficiently regular so that we can make intelligent statements about it.

Rostow (1960), in one of the most widely cited (though not universally accepted) examples of development as process, claimed to identify five successive stages of economic growth: traditional, transitional, take-off, maturity and high mass consumption. Moreover, he suggested societies or nations could be classified according to these stages with the implication that there was a natural path to economic growth which nations follow.

Much of the literature on development as a state has focused on how to measure that state. D. Smith (1977, p. 203) notes that "development is frequently assumed to be an economic condition" and that "the most common measure of development is an economic indicator—GNP per capita." Debate in this area has revolved around whether such measures are adequate indicators of development and if not, as is being increasingly recognized, what other social indicators might complement or replace them. This has given rise to quite an extensive literature on socioeconomic indicators involving such measures as infant mortality rates and levels of protein intake.

There have also been calls for less technical definitions of development. D. Smith (1977) argues for development as "welfare improvement" and suggests (p. 207) "development means a better state of affairs, with respect to who gets what where." Earlier, Goulet (1968) had identified as three major goals of development—sustenance of life, self-esteem and freedom—each broadly defined.

This broadening of the concept of development, both as process and state, away from narrow considerations of economic growth to encompass wider economic then social concerns has contributed significantly to the burgeoning range of definitions of the term in the last two decades. This is not to say that earlier definitions have been completely abandoned. Development is still seen solely in terms of economic growth in some quarters.

As an illustration of the shift in the concept of development, Mabogunje (1980) cites two of the seminal papers by Seers (1969, 1977). In the first, Seers writes:

> The questions to ask about a country's development are three: What has been happening to poverty? What has been happening to unemployment? What has been happening to inequality? If all three of these have declined from high levels, then beyond doubt there has been a period of development for the country concerned.

Eight years later Seers (p. 5) underlines the importance of an additional element, self-reliance:

> On this approach, "development plans" would hence forward not put the main emphasis on overall growth rates, or even on new patterns of distribution. The crucial targets would be for (i) ownership as well as output in the leading economic sectors; (ii) consumption patterns that economised on foreign exchange . . . (iii) institutional capacity for research and negotiation; (iv) cultural goals [e.g. reducing cultural dependence on one or more of the big powers].

Mabogunje then goes on (pp. 36–46) to identify four main ways in which the term development has been used, before introducing a fifth definition of his own. These are:

1. Development as Economic Growth

Mabogunje argues that in the early post Second World War period, development was interpreted narrowly in terms of economic growth with priority given to "increased commodity output rather than to the human beings involved in the production." A common expression of this in the underdeveloped countries was concentration on export production and the emergence of a dual economy.

2. Development as Modernization

Later a social dimension was incorporated. "Development, still in the sense of economic growth, came to be seen as part of a much wider process of social change described as modernization. . . . The emphasis on development as modernisation is . . . on how to inculcate wealth-oriented behaviour and values in individuals." Education was seen to be a critical aspect of societal change but modernization also had a consumption dimensions: "To be modern meant to endeavour to consume goods and services of the type usually manufactured in advanced industrial countries."

3. Development as Distributive Justice

By the late 1960s attention was being increasingly turned

to who was getting, or not getting, the benefits of social and economic change:

> Development came to be seen not simply as raising per capita income but more important, of reducing the poverty level among the masses . . . interest in development as social justice . . . brought to the forefront three major issues: the nature of goods and services provided by governments for their populations; the question of accessibility of these public goods to different social classes; and the problem of how the burden of development (defined as externalities) can be shared among these classes.

The latter factor is an important extension of the concept, incorporating as it does not only who benefits but also who pays for development in terms of such externalities as air and water pollution resulting from industrialization. Regional development planning emerged as an important strategy for distributional justice.

4. Development as Socio-Economic Transformation

This interpretation is attributed by Mabogunje to "scholars of a Marxist philosophical persuasion [who] argue that the questions of distribution and social justice cannot be resolved independently of the prevailing mechanisms governing production and distribution." This interpretation is essentially a critique of the capitalist "mode of production" (those elements, activities and social relationships

which are necessary to produce and reproduce real (material) life). "Basic shifts in any of the aspects of the mode of production can trigger off wide-ranging changes which may culminate not only in the transformation of the mode but also in changes in the relative importance of social classes. It is such a socioeconomic transformation that really constitutes development." This interpretation stresses the interrelationships between development and underdevelopment with developed metropolitan centres becoming enriched at the expense of the "underdeveloped" peripheral regions. As such, it is closely linked to dependency theory.

5. Development as Spatial Reorganization

Mabongunje himself stresses (pp. 65–8) the spatial dimension of development: "spatial reorganization is seen as synonymous with development in the sense that spatial forms represent physical realizations of patterns of social relations." The need for a pattern of social relations which can inculcate new processes of production thus requires the reconstruction of spatial structures both in the rural and urban areas of a country. Mabongunje raises the notion "that certain types of spatial arrangement can be expected to make a relatively better contribution to the attainment of specified goals than others," and underlines the importance of magnitude and the time factor in development.

The development literature discussed here has largely fo-

cused on the underdeveloped countries. Development, nevertheless, does still occur in the developed world. There many of the issues raised above have been discussed within the context of the more specific literature on regional development. Yuill, Allen and Hull (1980), for example, suggest there are three distinct phases of regional policy in Europe. In the first, immediately after the Second World War, the emphasis was on national economic growth with (p. 217) "an increase in the national cake being viewed as far more important than questions of how the cake might be spatially distributed." A second period, from the late 1950s to the early 1970s, is characterized as the heyday of regional development, for with growing economic prosperity came a concern for greater social justice and an evening out of regional inequalities which an increasing number of studies using socio-economic indicators had identified. In the third, most recent period, that following the general downturn in many European economies since the energy crisis of 1973–74, attention has turned once again to the size of the national cake rather than the manner in which it is distributed. As Yuill *et al* (p. 221) put it, "in short, for regional incentive policy the post-1973 period has been very much one of consolidation in a hostile environment."

In the case of France, these different phases can be seen in the changing emphases of the various Five Year Plans of the post-war period. The first three plans (1947–53, 1954–57, 1958–61) were essentially aimed at reconstruction and modernization of key industries. The Fourth (1962–65), Fifth (1966–70) and Sixth (1970–75) Plans became "Plans for Economic and Social Development." A social and regional dimension was incorporated for the first time in 1962. However, by the Sixth Plan, economic growth was once again dominant but "social priorities were not to be sacrificed to the needs of economic progress" (House, 1978, p. 24). The Seventh Plan (1976–80) was characterized by a move to smaller scale projects under the Priority Action Programmes while the Eighth (1981–85) reflected the Socialists' moves towards decentralization.

Development then takes on many meanings, being used to refer both to a process and to a state and to have a range of defining characteristics from narrowly delineated economic ones through broader social values to more general attributes such as self-reliance. Generally the change has been away from narrow economic usage to embrace other attributes. The links between process and state suggested by Goulet (1968) have, however, not always been explicitly made, that is that the state of development derives from the processes which have caused it.

Tourism and Development

The development literature generally ignores tourism and few writers on that subject set their studies in the broader context of development although they may address some of the specific questions raised in the previous section. None of the reviews of the development literature discussed above, for instance, alludes to tourism despite its growing economic and social significance and use in development strategies in many developing countries over the last three decades. In this respect tourism has been treated by development writers in the same way they have ignored other service sectors for much of the development debate has centred on the transition from an agricultural to an industrial society and neglected tertiary activities.

Exceptions to this pattern occur nevertheless, as in several discussions of underdevelopment in the Mediterranean. Schneider, Schneider and Hanson (1972), for example, take tourism as one aspect of modernization, citing the emulation by locals of tourist behaviour as an illustration of the "incorporation of distorted metropolitan lifestyles by dependent regions and issues of economic dependence." For Seers (1979), the centrifugal flow of tourists from Western Europe to countries of the southern Mediterranean is one of the manifestations of the core-periphery relationship between the two regions.

Direct links between tourism and theories of economic development were made in several early tourism papers which have been quoted rarely or have had limited circulation (e.g. Krapf, 1961; Kassé 1973; van Doorn, 1979) as well as in a couple of tourism books which have been widely cited (Bryden, 1973; de Kadt, 1979). A small number of more recent writers have also addressed these issues squarely (Britton, 1982; Erisman, 1983).

In his pioneer paper, Krapf (1961) raises a number of explicit questions. Which are the developing countries? What is the nature of economic growth? What types of aid can be given to these countries? What role can tourism play? Krapf draws heavily on Rostow's model and notes in passing that mass tourism is one consequence of an age of mass consumption. He then goes on to ask whether tourism is an appropriate form of aid; whether the development of a luxury sector is justified when many people do not have the bare essentials of life. Krapf concludes that tourism has a "special function" in developing countries, a function which he defines in terms of a series of "economic imperatives," viz:

► Exploitation of the countries' own natural resources,
► International competitiveness due to favourable terms of trade,
► An ability to provide internally many of the goods and services required,

► Improved balance of payments,
► Social utility of investments in tourism: employment generation and multiplier effect,
► Balanced growth.

Krapf's emphasis is clearly on tourism's contribution to economic growth and the notion that tourism had a special function in this regard appears to be one which was widely held in the 1960s and one which has persisted.

By the early 1970s Kassé (1973) is writing of the emergence of a "theory of the development of the tourist industry in under-developed countries." This he summarizes in terms of tourism's perceived ability to generate, from limited investment in plant and infrastructure, large sums of capital which may be transferred to other sectors of the economy. The theory also underlines the multiplier impact of tourism, the creation of employment, public revenue and foreign exchange earnings. Kassé however, does not take these points for granted but raises two basic questions. What are the real costs of developing tourism? What are the effects, direct and indirect, which tourism has on the rest of the economy? While acknowledging the number of variables which much be taken into account and deficiencies in the data needed to answer these questions, Kassé, drawing on the African experience, suggests the costs of tourism may be greater and the benefits smaller than popularly supposed. Kassé also

broadens the economic argument and discusses some of the social implications of tourist development, citing in particular the work of Ben Salem (1970) in Tunisia.

In a larger, better known study from the Caribbean entitled *Tourism and Development,* Bryden (1973) raises similar issues and attempts to document them more fully. Bryden (p. 218) concludes that "To state that this study has provided a definitive economic case against the further development of tourism in the Caribbean would be going too far," but continues that it does "raise some very serious doubts about the viability of tourist development *in its present form.* " This latter point is an important one as Bryden was one of the first to recognize explicitly that tourism development takes different forms and its impact is conditioned by the context in which that development occurs. In particular, he notes that his general conclusions about the viability of tourism in the Caribbean result from the high degree of foreign ownership and consequent repatriation of profits, the employment of non-nationals with similar results and the real costs to the nation of government involvement in the provision of infrastructure and incentives.

Van Doorn (1979) takes this notion further and argues (p. 5) that "tourism cannot be considered outside the context of the different stages of development countries have reached." He then proposes a typology which combines levels of social and economic de-

velopment based on prosperity and welfare criteria with levels of tourist development derived from the social impact work of Forster (1964) and Greenwood (1972). This potentially very useful typology unfortunately is not elaborated on nor illustrated by empirical examples. It also begs the question of the relationship between the stage of tourist development and the level of socioeconomic development. What did tourism contribute to the country's level of social and economic prosperity? To what extent is the stage of tourist development dependent on more general economic and social conditions?

Van Doorn does, however, go on to suggest that theories of development must be taken into account in the assessment of the impact of tourism (p. 6):

Any effect of tourism, be it raised employment, decreased awareness of cultural identity or the contribution of health facilities must be weighed *explicitly* against the underlying theory of development. Most studies have only an *implicit* notion based on an intuitive feeling of one of the two mainstreams in development theory: the *traditional* and the *modern* theory.

Van Doorn sees the traditional theory being based on "the creation of a Western type of society as a result of a combination of economic, social and cultural changes." Such changes are conditioned by the internal characteristics of the country in question and the solution to underdevelopment is seen to lie in economic injection or in social changes of roles, norms and values. Developing tourism for the reasons outlined by Krapf (1961) is consistent with this theory. For van Doorn, the "leading lady" amongst the modern theories is dependency or core-periphery theory which explains differences in levels of economic development in terms of external factors. Here the "central thesis is that developed countries grow autonomously while the underdeveloped countries show a growth-pattern that has been derived from the developed countries." Examples supporting this concept are drawn by van Doorn from the literature, for example Bryden (1973), but they have generally not been expressed directly in these terms.

Several geographers have been much more explicit in setting their analysis of tourism in the context of modern theories of development. According to Hills and Lundgren (1977, p. 256) "from the viewpoint of geographical theory, a major characteristic of international tourism is the centre-periphery syndrome . . . The periphery is . . . relegated to a subordinate function of the centrifugal process, bringing not only visible physical commodities, in the form of tourists, but simultaneously injecting powerful, and more subtle, hierarchical dimensions." Britton's (1982, p. 332) intention is very direct, that is "to place the study of tourism firmly within the dialogue on development." This dialogue is equated with dependency theory (pp. 333–4). "Dependency

can be conceptualized as a process of historical conditioning which alters the functioning of economic and social sub-systems within an underdeveloped country. This conditioning causes the simultaneous disintegration of an indigenous economy and its re-orientation to serve the needs of exigenous markets . . ."

One of these is the market for international tourism. After examining the organization of international tourism and case studies from the Pacific, Britton concludes (p. 355) that "The international tourist industry, because of the commercial power held by foreign enterprises, imposes on peripheral destinations a development mode which reinforces dependency on, and vulnerability to, developed countries."

Political scientists have examined other aspects of tourism and dependency theory, notably in the Caribbean. Francisco (1983) investigated relationships between levels of American tourist activity and political compliance amongst Caribbean and Latin American nations and concluded (p. 374): "Economic reliance on tourism . . . may result in distorted economic development, foreign economic leakage, domestic social dissatisfaction, and resentment, but it does not result in political compliance at the international level." Questions of tourism and cultural dependency are addressed by Erisman (1983) who recognizes (p. 350) that "the literature contains only implicit theories based on scattered, often random comments." The four most com-

mon implicit theories—Trickle Down, Commodization, Mass Seduction and Black Servility—are then outlined and illustrated by reference to a variety of studies from the Caribbean. Limitations with each are found with Erisman concluding that a Commodization/Mass Seduction synthesis is likely to be the most productive avenue for future research.

Other social and cultural aspects of tourism and development are drawn together by de Kadt (1979) in *Tourism, Passport to Development?* After outlining changing attitudes to development and stressing the importance of social and cultural issues he observed (p. xv): "These social changes, together with important material effects on employment and income, are, of course, precisely the results that determine whether the process of tourism development is judged good or bad by the people affected." De Kadt also recognizes that tourism takes various forms and is one of the few to acknowledge explicitly that the papers in his volume deal essentially with one particular form, namely resort tourism.

Tourist Development

The writers who address directly the relationships between tourism and development in the manner outlined in the preceding section are by and large exceptions. Many of the studies which touch on issues raised in the previous two sections have been phrased in terms of the "impacts of tourism," the area identified earlier as the most extensive in the literature on tourism. Such studies commonly examine issues of tourism-generated revenue or employment, social changes induced by the expansion of tourism or the environmental impacts of tourist projects. These issues are seen in terms of the impacts of tourism but such impacts, as van Doorn (1979) has noted, are not usually set in any broader context of development, however defined. For a variety of reasons, most studies also only focus on a limited range of impacts and few pretend to be exhaustive or comprehensive. Moreover, these impacts are often divorced from the processes which have created them. Many writers speak of the impact of tourism without considering the type of tourism concerned or the way in which tourism has developed. Summing up the 1976 symposium on tourism and culture change held by the American Anthropological Association, Nash (cited by Smith, 1977a, p. 133) noted: "In these papers generally, the causal agent (tourism or some aspect of tourism) tends not to be well delineated or explicated. We have to dig to find out what it is."

Finding out about tourism, the way in which it develops and the effects of that development is what this book is about. It focuses on development both as a process and as a state, the focus broadening with the passage from process to state. That is to say, in terms of tourist development

as a process, the emphasis is on the way in which tourism develops or evolves. Some account must be taken of more general processes of development but the focus is sectoral and the sector examined is tourism. In this respect tourist development might be narrowly defined as the provision or enhancement of facilities and services to meet the needs of tourists. Tourism, however, might also be seen as a means of development in a much broader sense, the path to achieve some end state or condition. It is in this light that the so-called impacts of tourism are re-examined. To what extent do these impacts contribute to the development of countries, regions or communities? Furthermore, what are the relationships between process and state? To what extent does tourism's contribution to the state of development in any area depend on the way tourism there has developed?

This book attempts to answer these and other questions by examining systematically different aspects of tourist development. By identifying the various factors involved and analysing the general relationships amongst them an attempt is made to provide readers with a general appreciation of the subject and a basic framework and methodology with which they may then address particular problems. Many of the basic relationships to be explored and the questions to be examined are outlined or raised in the following review of models of tourist development.

Models of Tourist Development

Miossec's (1976, 1977) model, which depicts the structural evolution of tourist regions through time and space, remains the clearest and most explicit conceptualization of the process of tourist development. In Friedmann's (1980) terms, it is both evolutionary and has a well defined structure. Miossec stresses changes in the provision of facilities (resorts and transport networks) and in the behaviour and attitudes of the tourists and the local decision-makers and host populations. In the early phases (0 and 1) the region is isolated, there is little or no development, tourists have only a vague idea about the destination while the local residents tend to have a polarized view of what tourism may bring. The success of the pioneer resorts leads to further development (Phase 2). As the tourist industry expands, an increasingly complex hierarchical system of resorts and transport networks evolves while changes in local attitudes may lead to the complete acceptance of tourism, the adoption of planning controls or even the rejection of tourism (Phases 3 and 4). Meanwhile the tourists have become more aware of what the region has to offer, with some spatial specialization occurring. With further development, Miossec suggests it is tourism itself rather than the original attractions which are now drawing visitors to the area. This change of character induces some tourists to move on to other areas.

The phases of tourist development are not purely hypothetical as empirical studies have shown different tourist regions throughout the Mediterranean might be equated with the stages of maturity depicted in Miossec's model (Pearce, 1987a). The coast of Provence has undoubtedly reached a very mature stage, being well developed or even saturated for virtually its entire length, with a dense and well integrated transport network being established and tourism coming to shape or even dominate the urban and economic structure of the region. Market specialization occurs, distinct variations in types of accommodation are found and a hierarchy of resorts and urban centres is apparent. Languedoc-Roussillon, the Costa Brava, Costa Blanca and Costa del Sol are at an earlier stage of development. A range of resorts has been developed in each case, the communications network has been expanded to include regional motorways and, especially in the Spanish case, international airports and an overall regional structure is starting to emerge. The Mediterranean coast of Morocco is at an even earlier stage, perhaps Phase 3 of Miossec's model. The number of resorts there has multiplied as package tourism expanded but a coherent, hierarchical regional structure has yet to develop and there are indications that this may not occur given the difficulties experienced by some of the isolated tourist enclaves there.

As a general framework of tourist development, Miossec's model contains several useful points. Firstly, it embodies a dynamic element, the development of the region through time and space. This notion of spatial/temporal evolution is critical, both in analysing past processes and in planning the path future development is to take. Secondly, it attempts an overview of this evolution; changes in the behaviour of the tourists and the local population are related to the growth of resorts and the expansion of the transport network. However, as Miossec notes, each of the four elements need not develop apace and therein lies the source of many of the problems to which tourism may give rise. The key factor is that impact is related to development and, more importantly, particular impacts are related to specific stages of development. Other aspects of the development process are less explicit although they might be incorporated into the model. Some activities are attributed to the local population, for example the provision of supplies and the development of infrastructure, but the actual means of, and the agents for development, are not elaborated on. Who builds the resorts, how, for what reasons and with what results are fundamental questions which must be asked and answered. Likewise, the factors which influence the location of the resorts and the form of the hierarchies which emerge must also be examined. More generally, the context in which this development takes place is also neglected here as is the case of many other models. Tourism has developed in comparatively empty areas such as the Mediterranean coast of Morocco (Berriane, 1978) and developers have actively sought non-settled areas for the construction *ex nihilo* of ski resorts (Pearce, 1978a) but tourism usually develops within an existing socioeconomic structure where some form of urban hierarchy and some transport networks are already found.

Other models place greater emphasis on several of the points which Miossec has not explored, notably the interrelated questions of the extent of local/non-local participation in the development process and changes in the volume and composition of the tourist traffic over time.

Figure 1.2 suggests a general decrease in local participation over time as control of and involvement in the development process passes to regional and national authorities and developers. Drawing on some of the same literature as van Doorn (1979), Stansfield's (1978) study of Atlantic City and Plog (1973) and Cohen's (1972) work on tourist typologies, Butler (1980) has developed a more complex model of the hypothetical evolution of a tourist area.

Six stages are identified in this evolutionary sequence which is based on the product cycle concept: exploration, involvement, development, consolidation, stagnation and rejuvenation or decline. No specific facilities for visitors exist in the first stage, those in the involvement stage are provided primarily by locals but then local involvement and control declines rapidly in the development phase (p. 8):

> Some locally provided facilities will have disappeared, being superseded by larger, more elaborate and more up-to-date facilities provided by external organizations, particularly for visitor accommodation. Natural and cultural attractions will be developed and marketed specifically and these original attractions will be supplemented by man-made imported facilities. . . . Regional and national involvement in the planning and provision of facilities will almost certainly be necessary and, again, may not be completely in keeping with local preferences.

Major franchises and chains in the tourist industry will be represented by the consolidation stage. Local involvement only increases again in the decline stage "as employees are able to purchase facilities at significantly lower prices as the market declines" (p. 9).

In Gormsen's (1981) model of the spatio-temporal development of international seaside tourism, regional participation in the development process is shown to increase not decrease over time. Gormsen's model is based on a study of the historical development of coastal tourism, essentially from a European perspective. Thus the first periphery refers to resorts on both sides of the Channel as

well as those of the Baltic; the second incorporates the coasts of Southern Europe; the third includes the North African littoral and the Balearic and Canary Islands; while the fourth periphery embraces more distant destinations in West Africa, the Caribbean, the Pacific and Indian Oceans, South East Asia and South America. Approximate dates are given for the various stages in the development of each periphery. Thus unlike the models of Miossec, Butler and van Doorn, is time and place specific, although at a fairly general scale. Gormsen also suggests comparable peripheries can be identified for the USA.

According to Gormsen's model, the initiative in the early stages comes from external developers but with time there is a growing regional participation. Gormsen argues that at any given time the outermost periphery will be dependent on "the leading strata of the metropolises" not only to generate the demand but also to develop the facilities, which are usually of a high order. Historically, in the first periphery "the bourgeoisie not only formed part of the tourist élite but also invested in the luxurious palace hotels which were rapidly being built on cliff-tops and along promenades." Villas for the upper classes were an important part of the initial development of the second periphery. The more recent development of the outer peripheries has also seen a dependence on external capital and international investment, much of this tour-

ism being characterized by large-scale hotels and group tours which longer distances and travel to more alien cultures encourage.

Over time, however, changes in demand occur as participation in holidaytaking is extended to other social groups through more general processes of socioeconomic transformation. This may also induce increased regional participation in the development of tourism (p. 162):

> In the peripheries closer at hand, which were opened up at an earlier stage, the proportion of the middle and lower classes among the seaside holiday makers is . . . increasing. This is also true of the regional participation, as with immigration and a certain multiplier-effect the population is gradually becoming involved in independent activities, which are however limited chiefly to secondary, less profit-making tourist services. In some of the countries concerned, general trends in the socioeconomic change are bringing about the formation of a middle-class which now too is participating in seaside tourism in its own country, in which, alongside financial resources and fixed holiday allocations, the adoption of spare-time pursuits from industrialised societies is of great importance. Examples in this category are not only from Spain and other southern European countries but also Mexico where the domestic tourism in many seaside resorts is taking over from the international.

Thurot (1973) sees the early development of international tourism in the Caribbean in terms of class succession. He outlines a process, based on the analysis of the evolution of airline routes, in which the different destinations pass through three successive phases:

Phase 1: Discovery by rich tourists and construction of an international class hotel.

Phase 2: Development of "Upper Middle Class" hotels (and expansion of the tourist traffic).

Phase 3: Loss of original value to new destinations and arrival of "Middle Class" and mass tourists.

Plog (1973), on the other hand, emphasizes not class but the personalities of different types of travellers. From a series of motivational studies, initially of flyers and non-flyers, Plog suggests that travellers are distributed normally along a continuum from psychocentrism to allocentrism. At the one extreme are the "psychocentrics" who tend to be anxious, self-inhibited, non-adventuresome and concerned with the little problems in life. In contrast, the "allocentrics" are self-confident, curious, adventurous and outgoing. Travel, according to Plog, is a way for them to express their inquisitiveness and curiosity. The travel interests and demands of the two groups differ so that different groups of travellers will visit different destinations. Moreover, Plog suggests that the market for a given destination evolves and that the destination appeals to different groups at different times. The destination will be "discovered" by "allocentrics," but as it becomes more well known, develops and attracts more visitors, for example the "mid-centrics," it will lose its appeal and the "allocentrics" will move on. As the population is said to be normally distributed, this means that an area will receive the largest number of visitors when it is attracting the "mid-centrics," that is at a stage when it is neither too exotic nor too familiar. But from this point on, the implication is that the market will decline. According to Plog (p. 16), "we can visualize a destination moving across the spectrum, however gradually or slowly, but far too often inexorably towards the potential of its own demise. Destination areas carry with them the potential seeds of their own destruction, as they allow themselves to become more commercialized and lose their qualities which originally attracted tourists." Thus Butler (1980) associates the growth in the tourist traffic during the development phase of Fig. 1.4 with a broadening of the market base due to the attraction of mid-centrics while in the stagnation phase destinations will draw more on psychocentric visitors.

Reime and Hawkins (1979) argue that decline is not inevitable and might be avoided by more appropriate marketing (p. 74): "By defining the needs of each market segment and translating these needs into elements of a touristic experience, we can prevent those forms of development that incorporate in their very design the decline of the attraction." But marketing alone is not enough (p. 74): "to be successful, tourism development must correspond to the inherent characteristics and needs of the region, its society and the customers sought." Three factors must be taken into account according to Reime and Hawkins: the consumer, the producer and the society at large (p. 68):

The history of tourism development has shown that the three elements are equally important and that long-range objectives cannot be achieved if one element is continually subordinated to the others. Examples of unstructured tourism development abound and the problems encountered frequently outweigh even the most attractive benefits. Social problems emerge as local residents—forced to serve as a cheap labour supply—revolt against the attitudes of the clientele whose demands and behaviour are often foreign to their own way of life. Ecological problems resulting from inadequate infrastructure and planning are also inherent in these unstructured, one-dimensional tourism developments.

A successful tourism development is one in which the attraction serves as a facility for both residents and visitors. The long lived, carefully conceived development does not force the whims and aspirations of a multitude of strangers on a region—it uses the indigenous qualities of the region, whether social or natural, to satisfy the expressed needs of a selective clientele.

Reime and Hawkins then propose a set of criteria for selecting desirable development alternatives:

▶ Is it economically viable?
▶ Is it socially compatible?
▶ Is it physically attractive?
▶ Is it politically supportable?
▶ Is it complementary?
▶ Is it marketable?

With the addition of a further criterion—is it environmentally sustainable?—this might be considered a very useful general set of questions to ask about tourist development.

Summary

The different models and concepts reviewed here are by no means all-embracing and the field of tourist development is yet to be fully supported by a strong theoretical base. Many of the hypotheses incorporated in these models conflict, competing explanations of processes are given and there has been little empirical testing of the ideas and theories advanced. Nevertheless, the review of the models of tourist development, together with the earlier discussions of tourism and development, have raised a series of important issues, many of which are examined further in subsequent chapters.

In order to conduct an in-depth, senior-level study of tourism a multi-faceted approach is imperative. Projects 1 and 2 include elements of the following dimensions of tourism:

► The social, cultural, environmental, economic, and political impacts of tourism.
► The research, planning, and management that is necessary to maximize the positive aspects of tourism and minimized the negative.
► Destination image and life-cycle.
► The often conflicting needs of the visitors, the businesses serving the visitors, the host community, and the host government.

Secondary sources (i.e. journal articles, books, current periodicals and perhaps television) will provide the data for each project. The length of each project should be 20–30 typed, double-spaced pages with appropriate citations.

Project 1: "World Class" Events

There are two possible "world class" event types from which to choose. The first type is a specific "world class" event such as the 1994 Winter Olympics in Lilhammer, Norway or the 1967 World's Fair in Montreal, Canada. The second type is an annual "world class" event such as Mardi Gras in New Orleans or the Boston Marathon.

Once the "world class" event has been selected, two to three weeks will be required to acquire the necessary secondary data sources. Almost every aspect of the hospitality industry can easily be incorporated into the research project.

The introductory part of the paper should include a brief overview of the event. In other words, what kind of event was it, where was it held, how many people participated, how many people attended, was there a television audience and if so what kind of coverage did it get, who were the sponsors, etc.

The second part of the paper should cover subject areas such as the accommodations and food service that were needed by participants and spectators and the advance planning that occurred before the commencement of the event. For instance, were new facilities built, were existing facilities used or redesigned, did one particular food vendor (e.g. ARA) contract all of the food service, were some of the food and beverage suppliers (e.g. Coke) also sponsors, how long did it take to get the site ready for the event, was there a bid process to "win" the event, etc.

The third part of the paper should discuss the social, cultural, environmental, political, and economic impacts of the event. For example, was there community pride in the event, were local people employed as a result of the event, did the city and/or country enjoy political gain from the event, did the physical environment suffer irreparably from the new building and/or infusion of large numbers of people, did the destination become "visible" for the first time or did it gain a new image or improve an old one, etc.

The forth and final section of the paper should discuss the costs and benefits of the event. These would include political, environmental, human, and financial. The concluding remarks should give the author's assessment of whether the over-all benefits of the event outweighed the costs.

"New" Tourism Development

Choose a relatively new tourism development site (e.g. the eco-tourism sites in South America or the Foxwood Casino Complex in Ledyard, CT) or a proposed development site (e.g. Disney's U.S. historical theme park in Haymarket, VA).

Once the "new" tourism development site has been selected, two to three weeks will be needed to acquire the necessary secondary data sources. The data will most often be found in newspapers, magazines, and on television. Other sources, such as journals and books, may provide examples of other similar tourism development sites that were once in the "new" or planning stages. A project of this type will require some deductive reasoning and "educated" speculation on the part of the author.

In part one of the paper give a brief history and description of the "new" tourism development. In other words, what is the development plan? Include in this section, if appropriate, brief examples of a few other sites that have recently (in the last ten years) been in the same stage of development.

The second part of the paper should cover the pros and cons of the "new" development site. It is important to remember that to adequately delimitate the pros and cons an assessment of the social, cultural, political, environment, and economic impacts must be made. In addition, the often conflicting needs of the visitors, the businesses serving the visitors, the host community, and the host government must also be considered. Visitor interest in sites of this type, the current image of the destination site, and the feasibility of new businesses that will serve visitors are somewhat more discernable. Impacts on the host community and government are less visible in the pre or new development stages. Many of the proposed community benefits are only "promises" at this stage of the development. In order to facilitate the illumination of the costs and benefits in these two sectors, it is useful to create a table of tourism externalities with specific examples. The following table is an outline example:

TABLE X. TOURISM EXTERNALITIES AT "NEW" DEVELOPMENT SITE "X"					
Type of Effect					
Sector Affected		**Economic Effects**	**Social & Cultural Effects**	**Environmental Effects**	**Political Effects**
Individuals in Host Community	Benefits	jobs & more transportation service	increased community pride	new public parks and cleaner water	politicians pay attention to constituent needs
	Costs	inflated land costs	increased traffic & discomfort associated with large numbers of visitors who are culturally different	noise, water, and air pollution	political pressure to approve development in order to gain some other community need
Host Government	Benefits	more tax revenue	full employment and reduced loss from migration	preservation of flora & fauna	seen as progressive & innovative
	Costs	more infrastructure demands	more police, fire, sanitation, and health care services	destruction of flora and fauna	power and decision making controlled by a select few—nepotism

Begin with the press coverage and interject lessons from similar development projects that have occurred in the past ten years when there is no current information beyond the "promise" stage for this specific "new" tourism development. The conclusion is the author's assessment of whether or not this is a sustainable tourism site that positively impacts the community in which it is located. To be a sustainable tourism development it must also provide a desirable attraction for visitors and an opportunity for businesses providers to make a reasonable profit.

24

MEETING AND CONVENTION MANAGEMENT

What Meeting Planners Want: The Conjoint-Analysis Approach
Leo M. Renaghan and Michael Z. Kay

A Messy Business
Charles Butler

Project 1

Project 2

WHAT MEETING PLANNERS WANT: THE CONJOINT-ANALYSIS APPROACH

Leo M. Renaghan and Michael Z. Kay

MEASUREMENT CAN BE A major problem for marketers. Most of us are by now familiar with the basic marketing theory that people buy products and services to meet specific needs or wants. In a perfect world, the products or services people purchase would suit their needs exactly. In reality, however, no product meets all the needs a purchaser seeks to fulfill, and the purchasing decision consequently becomes one of making tradeoffs among product features.

In using marketing research, we try to discover what tradeoffs consumers make as they purchase goods and services. The measurement problem is to determine which attributes carry the most weight in the purchase decision, and which ones the consumer is willing to forgo. If we can determine the right combination of attributes, we can unlock the secret of why consumers choose our hotel, restaurant, or airline—or why they patronize our competi-

tors. Moreover, if we can measure the *relative* importance of the attributes consumers value, we can design our hospitality products specifically for purchase by a target group of consumers.

Unfortunately, many efforts to measure the rationale behind a purchase decision fail because they are too simplistic. If we ask people about product attributes, we often get a "top-of-the-mind" answer that doesn't portray the full complexity of the decision. Such research won't really tell managers which attributes should be included in a product or service.

Consider, for instance, a research study recently conducted by a hotel in a large eastern city. Weekend guests were asked to assign an importance rank to ten attributes of their hotel stay. The top-ranked item was "cleanliness of the guest room," followed by "comfortable bed." Such items as "convenience of the location" and "efficiency of checkin" ranked farther down

the list. Based on these rankings, the hotel's sales department was ready to start a new advertising campaign that promoted clean, comfortable rooms for the weekend market. The general manager was hesitant to act on the basis of this information, because the results didn't make sense to him.

The GM was right to want a better study. The design of this research was too simple to capture all the facets of a hotel guest's purchase decision. To begin with, it confused *important* features (some of which any purchaser would simply expect in every hotel room) with *determinant* features—those that separate one hotel from another and actually bring about the purchase decision. Moreover, the study did not begin to approach the thorny problem of how the purchaser weighs the hotel's characteristics—both positive and negative—in making the final decision.

In our research, we were particularly interested in the

Conjoint analysis is a research technique that assesses different product attributes' relative weights simultaneously. The first step in the analysis is to discover the important characteristics or attributes applying to the purchase decision. The best way to do this is through exploratory research involving in-depth interviews or focus groups representing the target market. From this exploration, you can develop a list of the main attributes that influence a purchase decision.

Through application of conjoint analysis, you can learn how the customers consider these attributes in reaching a purchase decision. It is this understanding of the complex interaction of the attributes involved in the decision that is necessary to the design of a successful marketing strategy.

We can learn the importance of each attribute relative to the others being studied and to the entire decision. This is accomplished by calculating a partial worth or *utility score* for each level of each attribute. The higher the score, the more important the attribute.

The utility scores are calculated from customers' evaluations of various sample scenarios or combinations of benefits. Survey respondents give each scenario a score of 0 (absolutely no chance of purchase) to 100 (would definitely purchase). From these rankings, a computer assigns a utility value for each attribute level. The most desirable attributes are those with the highest utility values, and the most desirable product is the one combining the attribute levels with the highest utility values.

To know that an attribute is important in the decision is not necessarily enough. You can also learn which level of an attribute is most preferred by a customer. Many attributes can be offered at different levels, and management needs to know which levels are not preferred. Price is a simple example of an attribute that can be offered at a number of different levels.

A most intriguing use of conjoint analysis is to determine where customers are willing to make tradeoffs among product attributes. Rarely are customers able to make the ideal purchase of an attribute bundle; they are generally forced to make compromises in which they give up some level of one attribute to get more of another. That is the reality of most decision-making. Given the choice, of course, most consumers would take the maximum benefits at the minimum price, and businesses would go broke. By examining utility values, we can gain valuable information concerning the tradeoffs consumers are willing to make—that is, the extent to which they are willing to give up one product attribute or level to gain more of another. In a simple example, a restaurant may discover that a $1.00 increase in entree prices will cut the utility of meals by ten percent. But the same research might show that the addition of inexpensive flowers on the table would increase the meal's utility by 15 percent. The restaurant could probably ameliorate a negative reaction to price increases by adding flowers to the table.—L.M.R.

purchasing behavior of meeting planners (our target market). We wanted to know what meeting planners expected in a meeting facility, which of these attributes were the most important, and which ones they would give up to get something else.

We decided to sort out these factors through *conjoint analysis,* a research technique that assesses different attributes' relative weights simultaneously. In this article, we will describe how we used this technique to gain some insight into the needs of meet-

ing planners. (A description of conjoint analysis appears in the accompanying box.)

Decision-Making by Meeting Planners

In a 1986 study, we researched the factors that are

important to meeting planners when they choose a facility for their clients' meetings. The study addressed the following main questions:

► What combinations of attributes do meeting planners consider important in their selection of conference centers?
► What compromises or trade-offs are planners willing to make if they cannot have their "ideal" combination of attributes (i.e., what are they willing to give up)?
► What problems are frequently encountered in the use of meeting facilities?

Preliminaries

Most hotel firms are aware that meeting planners constitute a specialized market with its own set of wants and needs, but few companies have properly analyzed those needs. In most cases, even the basic building design fails to take planners' needs into account. When designing either new hotels or renovating structures, architects often spend most of their time specifying the types of function spaces and little time on the specific designs and arrangement of meeting areas. Part of the problem is that designers and architects don't have easily accessible means for knowing what meeting planners (or other target markets) might need. Although major hotel corporations provide hotel-design guides, most designers shy away from these highly technical manuals.

Moreover, many architects and designers are concerned more with the aesthetics of their design than with the needs of the people who will eventually be using those spaces. Many rooms are pretty to look at, but awkward to use. Some hotel designers simply apply the same rules of thumb for developing meeting rooms that they use for lobbies or other "problem spaces."

The inadequacies of meeting room design in hotels gave rise to conference centers, which are specifically designed for meetings. These centers have seriously challenged hotels for the profitable meetings market. Conference-center designers pay much more careful attention to the physical design of meeting spaces than typical hotel designers. In true conference centers, the meeting rooms are designed first, and guest rooms, foodservice areas, and recreational facilities are designed around the meeting areas.

Research is scanty on the important factors in meeting planners' facility-selection decisions. From the available material, it is clear that service is high on the meeting planner's facility-selection list. Service embodies such factors as the attitude, availability, and competence of the hotel's employees, as well as the relationship formed by the planner and the hotel salesperson. In a 1982 survey, 300 meeting planners were asked what aspects of a meeting facility they considered essential to the success of a business meeting. Four of the top seven factors were service-related (see Exhibit 1). But service is hard for planners to judge in advance, so it becomes more of a decisive factor when planners are rebooking a meeting than when they are trying a new facility.

Facilities are also important to meeting planners. Since they are more tangible than service, the attributes of meeting facilities are variables that could differentiate a hotel from its competition. In a poll by *Meetings and Conventions*

Factor	Percent of Planners
Front-desk attitude	81%
Conference coordination and staff	76
Meeting-room comfort, and environment	67
Lighting, audiovisual, supplies	62
Follow-through by property staff	61
Abundant and accessible recreation	58
Checkout procedures	51

EXHIBIT 1. FACTORS ESSENTIAL TO SUCCESS OF A MEETING

Source: Survey of 300 meeting planners by Wright in 1982.

Factor	Corporate Planners	Association Planners
EXHIBIT 2. FACTORS IMPORTANT TO THE SELECTION OF MEETING FACILITIES		
Number, size, and caliber of meeting rooms	70%	85%
Quality of food service	76	75
Number, size, and caliber of sleeping rooms	53	71
Efficiency of checkin and checkout	47	58
Efficiency of billing procedures	49	53
Availability of single contact person	45	51
Availability of meeting-support services	46	46
Prior experience with facility and staff	41	42
Provision of special meeting services	26	25
Proximity to airport	23	16
On-site recreational facilities	29	19
Availability of exhibit space	15	46
Proximity to off-site attractions	10	19
Newness of facility	5	4

Source: Mel Hosansky, *Meetings and Conventions*, 1982.

magazine, planners ranked the caliber of meeting rooms near the top of factors important to their site-selection decision (see Exhibit 2).

These studies, being one-dimensional, did not say anything about combinations of factors. But they pointed out directions we might take in a conjoint study.

With this information in hand, our first research step was to interview meeting planners, who are the end-users of conference centers, to learn how they make their site decisions. In these interviews, we asked the planners about the site-decision process, the importance of various facility characteristics or attributes, and their present levels of satisfaction with the sales staffs of existing hotels and conference centers.

Following these interviews, we invited planners to participate in focus groups to identify important attributes, to pinpoint relevant attribute levels, and to explain as much as possible about how meeting planners trade off attributes in making the site-purchase decision. The planners' busy schedules limited the size of the focus groups, but the sessions still provided a wealth of information for the development of the questionnaire that would form the backbone of the study.

Next, we conducted additional interviews that seemed to confirm the appropriateness of the attributes chosen for study in the questionnaire. At this point, ten planners filled out the questionnaire as a pretest.

Mail Survey

We mailed the final questionnaire to 140 meeting planners selected from a pool of 260 names drawn randomly from two groups: members of Meeting Planners International and past users of a well-known conference center near New York City. All planners agreed by telephone to participate in the survey, and 113 eventually returned their surveys. (Two of these surveys were discarded for being incomplete. All respondents lived east of the Mississippi River.)

The respondents represented a full cross-section of the meeting planner market, as shown in the table in Exhibit 3. Most were corporate meeting planners, and all had used a conference center.

Important Attributes

A meeting facility, whether located in a hotel or a conference center, is not a simple product. It has many attributes, and those attributes have many levels or facets. The purpose of the research was to discover the most important attributes, and assess their relative importance. To that end, the questionnaire was limited to the five facility-related attributes that had come through as most important in the preliminary research. They were:

▶ The size of the main meeting room,
▶ The location of breakout rooms,
▶ The complexity of audiovisual equipment,
▶ The control of lighting and climate, and
▶ The price.

For each attribute, the planners could choose among different levels or values, as follows:

▶ *Meeting-room size:* comfortable accommodation of up to 50, or up to 75 (school-room style);

▶ *Breakout rooms:* either adjacent to the main meeting room, or not adjacent;
▶ *AV:* either standard (overhead projector, 16mm film projector, 35mm slide projector, and microphones), or sophisticated (the standard setup, plus rear-screen projection, oversize screens, VCRs, and several TV monitors);
▶ *Climate control:* total control by group from one location, total control by group from several locations, or no control by group;
▶ *Price:* $150, $175, or $200 (per person, single occupancy, full American plan).

There are 72 possible different combinations of the attribute levels listed here, a number too large for consideration in any questionnaire. Because it would be too difficult for respondents to evaluate so many scenarios, the questionnaire was limited to 16 scenarios, chosen in such a way that all five attribute levels presented would be as balanced as possible. (In technical jargon, the scenarios were presented in an orthogonal array, chosen on the basis of a Latin-square design to be statistically significant.)

Five parts

The questionnaire, still a long and thorough one, consisted of five parts. The first part presented the meeting planners with the 16 meeting-room scenarios and the following instructions:

You are planning a three-day training meeting for 50 persons at a 425-room hotel conference center, located in the suburbs of a large city in the southeastern U.S. You need to evaluate the actual meeting facilities, basing your final decision about whether to use the property on the adequacy of those meeting facilities.

Assume that you are in a position to evaluate 16 possible combinations of meeting facilities offered by the conference center. For each of the 16 combinations, indicate on a scale of 0 (definitely would not hold a meeting there) to 100 (definitely would hold a meeting there) how likely you would be to book your meeting in a conference center that offered these attributes.

Rank order

Part two of the questionnaire asked the meeting planners simply to rank 12 features of conference facilities that various researchers had found to be important. This ranking served as a validity check for the responses in part one and allowed us to compare the importance of individual attributes. In sections three, four, and five, we asked the respondents about other meeting-center facilities (e.g., recreation, food service), and about problems they frequently encountered, as well as the categorical questions that yielded the information presented earlier in Exhibit 3.

Individual Attributes

Before we discuss the findings of the conjoint analysis,

EXHIBIT 3. PROFILE OF RESPONDING MEETING PLANNERS

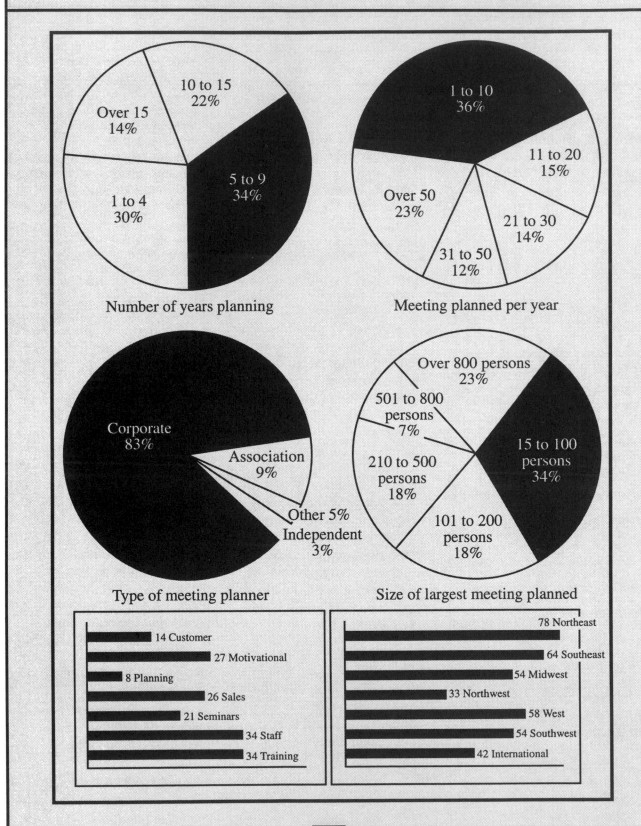

Number of years planning

Meeting planned per year

Type of meeting planner

Size of largest meeting planned

it would be instructive to review the importance rankings of individual product attributes (part two of the survey). The planners' rankings of 12 facility features are shown in Exhibit 4.

These meeting planners considered the size and soundproofing of the meeting room to be of top importance. They ranked audiovisual capabilities, climate and lighting control, and price about equally—just behind the room size. The location of breakout rooms came in slightly behind these three items. Two features—tack-up walls with chalkboards and tiered amphitheaters—were ranked dead last. (Yet these features are commonly promoted by new conference centers as points of differentiation from existing hotel meeting rooms.)

Soundproofing

Nearly 80 percent of the respondents said soundproofing was important, but this feature does not easily lend itself to study in a conjoint tradeoff model—we doubt that planners would give up soundproofing for anything. Moreover, we didn't know how to define or measure "medium" soundproofing. Therefore, we did not include soundproofing in the benefit bundles we tested. We believe that meeting planners simply expect that meeting rooms will be totally soundproof, so the presence of soundproofing will probably not differentiate one conference center from another. The *absence* of this attribute, on the other hand, is

---

EXHIBIT 4. IMPORTANCE OF FACILITY FEATURES (MOST TO LEAST IMPORTANT)

Main meeting-room size
Soundproof meeting rooms
AV capabilities
Climate and lighting control
Price
Location of breakout rooms
"18-hour" chairs
Twelve-foot ceilings in meeting rooms
Recreational facilities
Separate coffee-break areas
Tack-up walls, built-in chalkboards
Tiered amphitheater

---

all most certainly a dissatisfier. If planners find that this feature is absent, they will probably downgrade their consideration of that conference center.

The importance ratings presented here may be deceiving, because planners are evaluating each feature separately, and not in relation to other features. The studies we discussed earlier suffered from the same problem. Booking a conference center constitutes a purchase of many attributes in combination. Knowing that one single attribute is more important than another explains little of how the meeting planner's decision is actually made. Instead, the meeting planner's evaluation almost certainly involves the facility's "package" of features. During this consideration, the importance weight of one attribute may change depending on the presence or absence of other attributes that are, by themselves, less important.

A comparison of the planners' *ratings* of the importance of individual attributes with *rankings* of the same attributes' relative importance (derived from conjoint analysis) demonstrates this point, as is evident in Exhibit 5. When meeting planners

---

EXHIBIT 5. COMPARISON OF INDIVIDUAL AND RELATIVE IMPORTANCE RANKINGS (MOST TO LEAST IMPORTANT)

Relative Importance	Individual Importance
Climate and lighting control	Size of main room
Location of breakout rooms	AV capabilities
Price	Climate and lighting control
Size of main meeting room	Price
AV capabilities	Location of breakout rooms

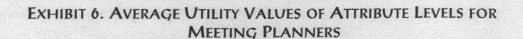

EXHIBIT 6. AVERAGE UTILITY VALUES OF ATTRIBUTE LEVELS FOR MEETING PLANNERS

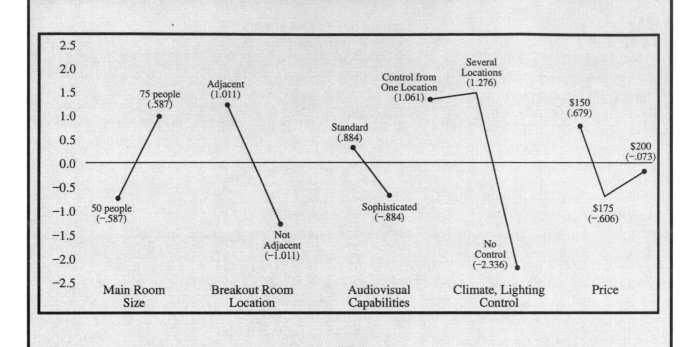

weighed the attribute combinations we offered them, the importance of meeting-room size seemed to shrink compared to that of climate control and lighting. Likewise, planners seemed quite willing to forgo sophisticated AV capabilities rather than give up any of several other attributes.

Because meeting facilities offer a bundle of attributes, then, the planner's decision is almost never based on consideration of single features. Instead, the planner evaluates each center's features as a package. The value of conjoint analysis is in understanding how this evaluation affects the planner's purchase decision.

Conjoint Results

The first step in understanding the tradeoffs involved in a purchase decision is to get an idea of the value or utility of each level of the attributes being considered. These utility scores can be shown graphically, as in Exhibit 6.

Room Size

The utility scores indicate that a planner booking a meeting of 50 people would give greater value to a 75-person meeting room than to a 50-person room. This preference is depicted by the upward slope of the utility line for room size in Exhibit 6.

Breakout Rooms

The average planner perceived adjacent breakout rooms to be more valuable than nonadjacent rooms. In Exhibit 6, this is shown by a descending line from adjacent to nonadjacent rooms.

Price

While planners considered $150 per person the best price, they perceived a greater utility in paying $200 than $175. This result may indicate that some planners perceive a higher price as meaning higher quality. Because the average meeting planner perceives $200 as a price that buys more quality than $175, a conference center might be designed to justify that price level.

AV, Climate, and Lights

Unexpectedly, planners assigned a higher utility to standard AV setups than to a broader offering that included highly sophisticated equipment. The climate-related feature with the greatest utility for planners was total control of climate *by the group* from a number of locations, followed closely by total control from one location. Climate control exclusively by the facility staff had a very low utility.

These meeting planners appeared to have a pronounced desire for control over the environment in which meetings take place. Predictably, they preferred an oversize meeting room and adjacent breakout rooms. But their indifference to costly, sophisticated AV equipment and the strong, sharply negative utility of lighting and climate controlled by the facility's staff clearly indicated their preference for personal control. Another level of the climate variable, control by the group from several places, garnered the highest utility score of all (1.276, compared to 1.011 for adjacent meeting rooms, the next most useful feature). The high score indicates that climate and lighting control is the most important of the five attributes we tested. As we will discuss later, the utility assigned to this attribute was apparently in part a reflection of the planners' assessment of hotel-staff competence. We believe the planners' lack of interest in complex AV equipment could also be rooted in

concern about staff capabilities.

Preferred Combinations

By combining the attribute levels attaining the highest utility scores, one can arrive at the bundle of benefits that is most desirable to this sample of meeting planners. Their ideal conference facility would have the following attributes:

▶ A meeting room that accommodates more people than the number actually attending the meeting (allowing extra space)
▶ Breakout rooms adjacent to the main room
▶ Standard audiovisual capabilities
▶ Total control of the lighting and climate by the group from a number of locations in the room
▶ A low price.

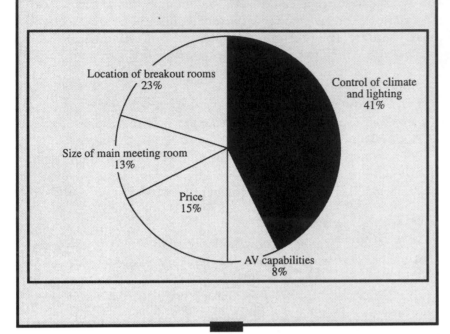

EXHIBIT 7. RELATIVE IMPORTANCE OF FACILITY ATTRIBUTES FOR MEETING PLANNERS

Location of breakout rooms 23%

Size of main meeting room 13%

Price 15%

Control of climate and lighting 41%

AV capabilities 8%

In short, the average meeting planner wants the biggest and best room for the lowest possible price!

Since most hospitality firms do not exist to go out of business, and most want to earn a reasonable return on their investment in a conference center, companies building or operating conference centers must assess the tradeoffs planners are willing to make. Will planners pay a higher price to gain total climate control, for instance? Will they agree to nonadjacent breakout rooms if they can, say, book an oversize main meeting room?

Conjoint analysis allows management to assess the interaction of features and determine how willing meeting planners are to forgo a certain level of one attribute to gain a certain level of another. As long as the *decrease* in utility caused by one change is offset (or more than offset) by the increase in utility caused by another change, meeting planners should be satisfied with the bundle of attributes offered by a given conference center.

We can use utility values to indicate which tradeoffs the planners would be likely to accept. The average planner, for instance, should be willing to allow control of lighting and climate from one location instead of several (a utility decrease of .115) in exchange for an oversize main meeting room (a gain of 1.174), for this combination yields a net utility increase of .959. An increase in price from $150 to $200 (utility decrease of .752) can be counterbalanced by increasing meeting room size, offering breakout meeting rooms adjacent to the main

meeting room, or giving the group control of climate and lighting from a number of locations. But these planners generally will not trade control over the lights (once they have it) for any change in another attribute, even a cut in price.

Importance of Attributes

The range of utility scores for each attribute (the score of the highest level minus that of the lowest) can give an indication of the importance of that attribute. When this range is compared to the total range of utility scores for all attributes, the resulting figure indicates the relative importance of the attribute in the final decision. Exhibit 7 shows the relative importance percentages for the five attributes we have been discussing. For example, the range for the size of the main meeting room is 1.174 (the difference between .587 and -.587). When this is compared to the total range for all attributes (8.781), we can conclude that the size of the main meeting room has a weight of about 13 percent in the final purchase decision.

As you can see, the planners gave control of climate and lighting by far the greatest relative weight in their decision to book a conference facility. (The importance percentage of this feature was nearly twice that of any other attribute.) AV capabilities, on the other hand, seem to play a relatively negligible part in the typical meeting planner's decision.

Problems

This portion of the data supported our suspicions about the planners' assessment of hotel-staff competence. The topmost problem frequently encountered by meeting planners in their use of meeting facilities is staff competence—a factor cited by nearly half the respondents. Two other frequently mentioned problems were with audiovisual support and the physical quality of the facility. Audiovisual support is also partly a reflection of staff competence.

Questions of staff competence and AV support involve the overall service a conference center provides. In the case of meeting planners, the essence of service is that the meeting must go off *exactly as planned*, without a hitch. Because planners are held personally accountable by their clients for the success or failure of a meeting, it is crucial that the planners feel confident that they will receive adequate service support from the conference-center staff whenever they need it. One respondent said that her clients consider the success or failure of a meeting to be a direct reflection of her own competence. She considers it urgent, therefore, that everything go just as she planned it, so that she can look good.

Product: A Successful Meeting

What meeting planners are really buying is not hotel space but successful meetings. They judge conference facilities according to how well a meeting goes, and the planners themselves are judged according to the success of the meetings they produce. The attributes we have discussed are important to the extent that they contribute to that single need. Meeting planners will give up many product attributes, including price, to gain the basic combination of attributes that ensures a successful meeting.

A major theme of the interviews, focus groups, and the questionnaire in this study is that meeting planners do not trust the employees of hotels and conference centers to bring off a successful meeting. During the study, the planners shared anecdotes of promises not kept, of brochures that overrated meeting-room capacity, and of managers who simply did not understand the planners' needs. But the most frequently mentioned problem was lack of competent staff. For the planner, then, the key to a successful meeting lies in his or her ability to control as many of the meeting's variables as possible.

The strategies planners use to exercise that control depend on their experience level and the type of meeting being planned. When we separated planners by their experience levels, we found that the more experienced planners made tradeoffs to gain control of the meeting environment and generally favored *à la carte* pricing, so they could pick and choose the items they wanted. Less experienced planners sought the comparative security of package pricing, and they were less consistent in what tradeoffs they would make to ensure a meeting's success.

Recommendations

We offer the following recommendations, based on these results. To begin with, technology and gimmicks are not necessarily the way to attract meeting business, because planners apparently see complex equipment as merely one more thing to go wrong. Tiered meeting rooms, special chairs, tack-up walls, and sophisticated AV equipment—all items touted in advertising by many conference centers—will probably not increase the likelihood of purchase. They may be useful, visible, and appreciated, but they are not determinant in a purchase.

Providing the greatest ratio of space to participants, on the other hand, is a definite plus. Facilities built with this principle in mind would be differentiated on a tangible and important dimension—one that would be difficult for the competition to duplicate. Moreover, breakout rooms should be situated near main meeting rooms whenever possible.

Inside the meeting rooms, the emphasis should be on giving control to the users. Design and construction should be guided by this principle. The room should be sound-proof, needless to say. Climate and lighting control should be in the group's hands, and not those of the facility's staff.

Meeting facilities need not compete solely on price. The study indicates that planners are willing to pay more to get more, and that price is often taken as an indicator of overall quality. A property that is a price leader, however, must be able to prove to the customer that it can provide a successful meeting.

Although we did not include it in our conjoint analysis, our survey showed food and beverage is also important. Both food and the service that accompanies it should be of high quality, because this factor is crucial to the choice of a meeting facility. Variety of food choices is particularly important. Moreover, food-service delivery often determines whether a planner uses a facility a second time. Menu offerings, including signature items, can also be a point of differentiation from the competition. Creativity in menus can contribute immensely to the perceived success of a meeting.

The meeting planner's decision on which meeting facility to use is a complex one, but the advertising and marketing strategies of most hotels and conference centers are still quite simplistic. Managers who design and communicate an offering based on an increased understanding of the complexity of the planner's decision-making process will increase their chances for winning conference business. It is only with this broadened understanding that properties will be able to meet the increasing competition in the meetings market.

A MESSY BUSINESS

Charles Butler

DEEP DOWN IN THE southwest corner of Georgia, in the tiny town of Cedar Springs, huge metal vats churn from sunrise to sunset inside one building of the Georgia-Pacific paper plant. On this day in May, as on most days of the year, the air near the vats is hot and steamy and smelly. "Smells like garbage" is how one G-P worker describes the lingering odor.

For the folks of the Ace Hardware Corporation, the stench couldn't be sweeter. Inside these vats, the boiling water breaks down cardboard boxes collected days earlier during the move-in and move-out of Ace's 1991 Spring Convention and Exhibit Show, held 280 miles east at the Orange County Convention Center in Orlando, Florida. After collecting and baling the cartons that had contained everything from refrigerators to tool boxes, an Orlando waste and processing company trucked 24.3 tons of cardboard to Cedar Springs, where today, the water inside the vats washes down the cardboard,

dislodging such impurities as glue and staples and adhesive tape.

Through this recycling process, the cardboard will have avoided a fate of slow decomposition in a Florida landfill, and live again as egg cartons and cookie boxes.

A nice ending.

Too bad the prologue stinks.

Ace's road to Cedar Springs, while fulfilling a company wide objective to recycle its trash, became a tortuous and expensive journey. And the trek serves to demonstrate what environmental and hospitality officials say is the inadequate infrastructure now present in the hospitality industry for environmentally conscious meetings and conventions.

Like many other planners who have tried, Ace's convention managers needed to overcome a myriad of roadblocks in their attempt to recycle the refuse accumulated during the company's 9,000-attendee, 1,000-exhibit biannual trade show. They faced a general malaise in municipal recycling programs; nonexistent re-

cycling plans at convention centers; frustrating local bureaucracies; broken promises from suppliers; more than $20,000 in expenses, and their own naiveté. The fact that they survived to tell a "successful" recycling story says plenty for the company's commitment to the environment—but the details of the story expose the lagging environmental consciousness of all sectors of the meetings and convention industry, from planners to suppliers to attendees.

"You have to applaud Ace Hardware for being a concerned company. They really wanted to recycle. They took the difficult and expensive way," says Dale Bilthouse, general manager of Waste Management of Orlando, which hauled and then baled Ace's cardboard before shipping it to Cedar Springs. "I don't expect to be getting too many calls from other companies."

Recycling garbage shouldn't be so offending.

The Need for Recycling

In the past two years, precipitated by the 20th anniversary of Earth Day in April 1990, the call to be environmentally concerned has intensified throughout the United States. There are now more than 1,700 municipal curbside recycling programs nationwide, and over 2,000 environmental bills stand before state and federal legislatures. It's hip—not hokey—to care about the Earth.

Some players in the meetings, convention, and trade show industry have begun to demonstrate a greater sensitivity to the environment, such as Ace Hardware did with its cardboard drive. In 1990, the Air and Waste Management Association, for its first "clean meeting," collected more than 6,000 styrofoam cups used during coffee breaks at its 5,000-attendee convention at the David L. Lawrence Convention Center in Pittsburgh, Pennsylvania. After the meeting, the association shipped the material to a polystyrene recycling center in Massachusetts. The Michigan Townships Association recycled 25 percent of its plastic name badges following its convention last fall. And companies such as DuPont and McGraw-Hill have begun hiring speakers to discuss environmental issues at their sales and training seminars.

Several hotels have aggressively added their support to the effort as well, most notably the Hyatt Hotel Corporation, which has announced plans for each of its properties in the U.S., Canada, and the Caribbean to offer a uniform recycling program by 1992—a program estimated to reduce the company's waste total by 30 percent.

All commendable actions. All on target. And all still not enough to make a dent in the country's—*the world's*—environmental problems. The Environmental Protection Agency estimates that half of the country's existing landfills will close in the next four years, and there is insufficient construction occurring to replace the loss. With 76 percent of the country's garbage now targeted for landfills, and only 11 percent recycled, arithmetic dictates that a change in attitude toward waste disposal take place.

And that includes the hospitality industry.

According to several environmental experts, the meetings and convention industry— a traveling show of trash producers—has so far been satisfied with token gestures of Earth-saving responsibility. Hiett Ives, whose Houston-based consulting business helps trade show organizers establish recycling programs at their events, estimates that only one of every 50 U.S. convention centers is staffed and equipped to recycle trash produced by shows at their facilities. Others suggest that most hotels are more P.R. conscious—not Earth conscious— in their efforts. They point to the press releases hotels mail promoting the installation of water-reducing shower heads—press releases that in most cases are churned out on virgin paper, not recycled paper. And then there are the majority of planners who, environmentalists say, so far have ignored the impetus to recycle the garbage their functions create.

"The meeting planning/convention industry is very much lagging behind other industries in addressing the environment issue," says Marti Wolf, an associate with the Los Angeles-based environmental consulting firm Pacific West Communications Group, and a former president of the International Exhibitors Association. "I think it is a lack of awareness and consciousness."

And leadership. Fact is, planners and suppliers do express interest in recycling trash, perhaps the avenue where the industry can most affect the environment. Problem is, they either don't know how to institute a program at their functions or have been frustrated in trying. They need help, as Carolyn Cooke, director of trade shows and conventions for the International Exhibitors Association, freely admits. "You are talking to a babe in the woods," when it comes to recycling, Cooke says. For that reason, she let the staff of the San Diego Convention Center handle the separation and hauling of paper and aluminum cans during the association's annual convention last month. The San Diego center, equipped with four compactors, is considered to be one of the few convention centers with a well-oiled recycling program in place.

Granted, the country's still-evolving environmental legislation has deterred the industry from establishing a uniform recycling agenda. Environmental laws vary from state to state, change fast and often, and cause values for recyclable products to fluctuate market by market. While 30 states and Washington, D.C. now have comprehensive recycling laws, their stringency varies extensively; 16 states require separation of recyclable products, primarily aluminum cans, glass, and newspapers; the remaining 14 require municipalities only to investigate recycling plans. Only Maine, New Jersey, Pennsylvania, Rhode Island, Wisconsin, and Washington, D.C. require commercial businesses to separate recyclables.

Further complicating the process is the role of the recycling company, which can expedite, muddle, or even ruin a meeting planner's effort. Most environmental consultants agree that if a convention center or hotel uses a disposal company that operates a recycling-process plant, chances increase that collected material will actually be recycled. If the hauler serves as a middleman in the process, be cautious.

"In most cities, it is not in a hauler's financial best interest to say, 'Hey, let's talk about cutting my rubbish revenue by separating the trash,'" says Matt Costello, a Boston-based consultant who advises corporations in establishing in-house recycling programs. "Everyone thinks of recycling as warm and fun and easy. Well, if that were the case,

everyone would be doing it— and few are."

The following examples illustrate the potential hazards a meeting planner faces trying to recycle a meeting—hazards ranging from mismanagement to attendee neglect to fraud:

▶ Several months before her association, the League of California Cities, was to meet at a California convention center last October, planner Kathy Bowman contacted an events coordinator at the center to discuss the possibility of recycling the group's paper and aluminum cans. The coordinator's response: no problem, the center previously has recycled show trash. But just weeks before the convention's start, when Bowman wanted to confirm the logistics of the recycling program, she was told by the coordinator's boss that the center had never attempted such a project. With little time to devise a program on her own, Bowman had to scrap her plans. "The guy at the center offered to put recycling bins out, but he said, 'We'll just end up dumping the stuff in the dumpster in the back of the center,'" Bowman recalls. "I thought, 'If our attendees find that out, they'll be more angry than if we didn't try anything at all.' To me, that looked unethical."

▶ In the past two years, Hiett Ives has designed five recycling programs for such trade shows as the National Solid Waste Management

Association and the National Recycling Coalition. He says he has succeeded only once, when the National League of Cities met at Houston's George R. Brown Convention Center in 1990. At the other shows, Ives says attendees ignored signs to deposit only aluminum cans or paper in specially marked receptacles. Instead, they tossed food and other contaminates into the bins, making the material non-processable to a recycling company. "We literally collected the receptacles and put them right in the dumpster because there were so many contaminates," says Ives, a former employee of Browning-Ferris Industries, a national waste hauler and recycling processor. "Adults are not yet into recycling as part of their psyches."

▶ Several planners report the alleged case of a trade show organizer who scrupulously had aluminum cans, white paper, and newspapers separated for recycling during his show at a Midwest convention center. When the hauling trucks came to collect the material, the planner decided to trail them to the recycling center. To his amazement, the trucks headed straight for a city landfill where the material was unceremoniously dumped.

That incident, along with similar ones that have made the industry's rumor mill, help to explain the trepidation some planners now have toward recycling materials. Sincere motives of saving the Earth are not enough to guarantee an environmentally sound meeting. A lot of sweat, strain and cash will help.

As Ace Hardware discovered.

Worth the Effort

A year ago Ace Hardware, the country's second-largest hardware dealership, instituted a Green Team program at its suburban Chicago headquarters. The program started small, with the company's 600 employees urged to toss soda cans in special receptacles located throughout the building and to separate white paper from colored paper in their offices. The Green Team program quickly took root. The company now collects more than 20,000 pounds of paper and 250 pounds of aluminum cans per month. In a joint effort with Georgia-Pacific, Ace began selling tree seedlings to employees, with profits donated to the Children's Miracle Network charity. In the company's paint manufacturing plant, a process was developed to turn the residue paint accumulated in the cleaning of mixing vats into a low-grade, gray paint suitable for selling. Previously, Ace disposed of the paint with other hazardous chemical waste.

"The recycling culture," says Ace's convention manager Pete Principe, "quickly spread throughout the company"—including to his department. Principe oversees the company's fall and spring trade shows, where Ace dealers come to test the latest in wrenches, air conditioners, rakes, and shovels. During a staff meeting last summer, the idea was conceived to recycle the company's trade show trash, beginning with its October 1990 show at a Southwestern convention center. Principe wanted to concentrate on what he considers "99 percent" of the trade show refuse—the corrugated cardboard left over from the move-in and tear-down of suppliers' exhibits.

A great idea. Little did he and his staff know what awaited them.

"Originally, I didn't think it was going to be as big a project as it turned out to be," says Joanne Shisler, Ace's assistant convention manager who oversaw many of the recycling logistics. "I went into the project with an attitude of 'Why wouldn't anyone want to do this?' That was kind of naive. Recycling is a business, and at the time, I didn't look at it like that." A recycling company made her see otherwise.

Because the center hosting the convention did not offer a recycling program for trade show trash, it provided Ace officials with a list of area recycling companies. Several weeks before the show, Shisler contracted an area recycler to claim the cardboard. That done, the recycling effort appeared set. "But about a week before we left for the show the recycler called to say he couldn't do it—and he wouldn't give me a reason," says Shisler. "But he probably realized that there is no market [in that state] for cardboard." The late cancellation forced Ace to abort its recycling effort, and the cardboard eventually was deposited in a landfill.

Principe and his staff were left disappointed but determined. For the spring show in Orlando, the convention manager bypassed asking the Orange County Convention Center for help, and took total control of the recycling effort. "We were just embarking on a test recycling program, and thought the Ace show would be a good test," says John Smetanka, the convention center's operations manager. "But they ended up handling it all themselves."

Principe instructed Mike Thompson, project manager for Nationwide Convention Systems, the display company responsible for designing and constructing Ace's exhibit hall, to coordinate the recycling project. Thompson first subcontracted the cleaning company, H.K. Associates, to collect and separate the cardboard from the convention center floor during the eight-day move-in. Then, to streamline the trash removal, he hired Waste Management of Orlando, a disposal company that also operates the city's recycling center. (Parent company Waste Management Inc. of Oak Brook, Illinois, is the nation's largest disposal and recycling company.)

With the players in place, the show before the show got under way. The morning of April 20, from the floor of the Orange County Convention

Center's Hall A, an H.K. crewman picked up the first of several hundred cardboard boxes, breaking it down and stacking it. Collecting the cardboard and separating it from other trash had to be precise and speedy, in order not to impede equipment moving about the floor erecting the nearly 1,000 exhibit booths. Every few minutes, a forklift would carry stacks of cardboard to an outside loading dock, depositing them into one of sixteen 22-foot-wide, 7-foot-high containers Waste Management supplied. A Waste Management truck would haul a full container to the city's recycling center, located 45 minutes from the Convention Center. During the show move-in, drivers made 40 such "pulls" to the recycling center, where the cardboard was baled and prepared for shipment to the Georgia-Pacific plant in Cedar Springs. On April 28, the day the show opened, most of the baled cardboard was already en route to Cedar Springs for treatment in the boiling vats. The recycling effort caught the attention of two Orlando television stations, which featured it on their evening newscasts.

Ace continued its recycling campaign during the three-day show, operating its own environmental booth where dealers learned of products with Earth-protecting features, such as low-energy light bulbs. The company also involved several vendors who supplied the convention center's cleaning crew with non-toxic, biodegradable cleaning solutions and trash-can liners

made of recycled plastic, so that "we knew that at least while we were there, no harmful things were done [to the environment] in the cleaning process," says Principe.

Ace's effort did not come cheap, though. With the additional labor required to separate the cardboard, the hauling equipment, and the consulting of Denver-based environmental expert Sally Randel, the bill came to approximately $21,000. At $17 a ton, the 24.3 tons of recycled cardboard earned Ace $462.50. "Recycling is a threat to a show manager because a good intention could come around and hurt you on the backside by increasing your labor and rental costs," says Principe. "So a good intention may not always be enough. In Ace's case, it is."

There's No Choice

The country's decreasing landfill capacity necessitates recycling—voluntarily or mandated. Environmental and hospitality experts say planners, hotels, and convention centers soon will have little choice but to recycle their trash. "Recycling is a big thing to put together. You need the right people working for you," says Ace's Joanne Shisler. "But I certainly don't want to scare anybody, because it is worth doing."

True, but not every convention planner enjoys the financial backbone of an Ace Hardware, which last year had sales of $1.6 billion. Until the majority of the country's meeting facilities are adequately

staffed and equipped for recycling, groups will have to determine on their own the effort and expenses they are willing to commit toward the cause.

Some groups, to start, may have to be satisfied with smaller initiatives, such as using recycled copy paper in their convention programs. Kathy Gilliland, who plans the 2,500-attendee Michigan Townships Association annual conventions, says she was satisfied with her group's effort to reclaim plastic name badges at its last meeting, even though only about 300 were returned. For a first attempt and with little promotion, Gilliland says it demonstrated that meeting attendees are willing to participate.

Then there is the case of the American Society of Agricultural Engineers. Last winter, during its meeting at the Hyatt Regency Chicago, the association spent nearly $6,000 to recycle 1.5 tons of trash. The hotel, which retains a recycling consulting company, did virtually everything for the association, from putting out recycling containers to sorting the trash. Still, says John Hiler, the society's planner, "it was costly, and there's no way to offset the cost except knowing that you are saving the environment. If you're able to sustain that financially, great. But as a businessman, I'm not sure I can afford to do it again." And, Hiler adds, few hotels are as prepared as the Hyatt Regency to handle the task. "Especially in secondary cities, the last thing on a hotel's mind is being environmentally conscious."

Some environmental experts and meeting planners say the only way to enhance suppliers' attitudes is through simple economics: our business for improved recycling programs. In the future, Principe says Ace Hardware will not meet in convention centers that are not willing to participate in Ace's recycling efforts. Other groups may be tempted by a similar strategy. "Meeting planners have leverage. They can tell a hotel or a city, 'it's important to us that we consider the amount of waste we produce,'" advises Ron Kamalyan, who specializes in solid waste management and recycling issues for the Pacific West Communications Group. "They can be proactive in only selecting places that will address recycling issues."

How effectively that stance will play is debatable. While hardly profitable, recycling already provides economic inducements to hotels and convention centers. Separating trash reduces the tipping fees haulers charge businesses, fees based on the weight of the trash. As one consultant says, "Money not spent is money made."

Competition ultimately will drive the hospitality industry toward a greater environmental consciousness—but it may be a competition for prestige, not profit. For Ace Hardware, making the evening TV newscasts in Orlando could prove to be more effective advertising than buying a series of 30-second television spots promoting their stores. Free publicity: You can't beat it. And there's plenty to be had—that is, if planners, hotels, and meeting facilities develop a system, an infrastructure, to make recycling more efficient and less hassle for themselves. "Your return on investment on recycled material is going to be very, very low," says trade show consultant Hiett Ives. "What you get back is image."

Saving the Earth—that's a tough image to knock.

The success of many lodging sites relies on the ability to service specific meeting and conference groups as well as the individual business or leisure traveler. Whoever the customer, some individualization of service is required. In the meetings and conferences market, not only the size of the group, but the purpose of the stay and various ancillary issues must be determined to provide that impressive service. Study the description below to develop a plan of action to host the conference in a particular property.

A national five-day conference for United States governors of all fifty states is held annually in varying geographic locations. The location choice is pending for your region two years from now. The governors may travel with staff members and security as well as spouses and children. Media coverage may include representatives from states, local, national, and international press corps. The headquarters hotel is required to provide the entire hotel—guest rooms, restaurants, all facilities—for the conference and multiple meetings taking place each day.

Considerations in proposing to host such a conference should include:

1. Existing site capabilities

2. Additional sites involvement

3. Special training or services

4. Negotiations with national organization and individual governors' offices

5. Quantity and quality food services

6. Area tourism involvement

7. Access and transportation

8. Strategic staff assignments

Prepare a plan of 20–25 pages which explains how a property can accommodate this five-day meeting. First, develop and define an ideal lodging site as a reference for the study. The body of the report should then identify categories necessary for the conference and how each can be provided by the site. In addition, unique aspects of service or the site for this group should be highlighted. A minimum of ten resources must include literature on successful meeting elements as well as interviews with meeting planners and/or hotel meeting/conference coordinators.

Competitive analysis is a function of any hospitality industry component. Factors reviewed tend to include the physical characteristics of a property, number of fulltime and parttime staff, options of food and beverage outlets and other visible property inventory. With the growth of meeting and conference business within the hospitality industry, more updates of the trends in meetings must be part of competitive analysis.

Each property has varying physical capabilities to service meetings and conferences. However, researching the type(s) of meeting groups hosted within the past year should provide an additional barometer to identify meeting and conference options. A small property with fewer outstanding facilities, for example, may have been more creative in attracting profitable meetings. What meeting or conference clients have been attracted and why?

Assignment

Create an ANALYSIS FORM which will be used for three specific properties which host meetings and conferences:

1. The sites may be a combination of conference or convention centers, resorts, hotels or other sites.

2. Outline the size and description of each property but devote the major part of the form to discover the meeting customers and type(s) of meetings or conferences held during the past year.

Using the completed forms as appendices, complete an ANALYSIS REPORT:

1. Identify the range of meetings hosted as well as observe which property accomplishes the most in facilitating meeting business.

2. Include at least three primary and three secondary resources. Primary resources should be interviews with site staff responsible for meetings and conferences. Secondary resources can include interviews with Convention and Visitors Bureau staff or meeting planners from groups hosted by the site.

3. Include chart or table summaries of (a) meeting types and (b) meetings as percentage of total bookings.

4. The text of the report must be a minimum of 20 pages and a maximum of 30 pages, excluding the appendices.

25

CASINO MANAGEMENT

Gaming in the U.S.—A Ten-Year Comparison
Gary K. Vallen

Casino Operations: Cashing in My Memory Chips, Casino Style
Michael M. Lefever

Project 1

Project 2

Gaming in the U.S.—A Ten-Year Comparison

Gary K. Vallen

IN RECENT YEARS THE growth of legalized gambling in the United States has reached a feverish pitch. Today 47 states allow bingo, 43 have pari-mutuel betting, 35 offer a lottery, 25 allow gambling on American-Indian reservations, and 6 have legalized riverboat casinos. Moreover, given the rapidly changing political climate regarding gaming, those numbers may well have changed with November 1993 elections (the results of which were available too late to be included here).

Many of the negative connotations of gaming have lessened. The proliferation of state lotteries has had much to do with improving the image of gaming. Just 29 years ago, there were no state lotteries. Today the combined national lottery purse exceeds $20 billion annually.

Many experts believe the unparalleled popularity of lotteries has opened the door to other forms of legalized gambling. People who play state lotteries also are attracted to its many other forms: on-line lotto, passive games, keno, on-line numbers, and instant "scratch and win" games. Instant games provide even more excitement and immediate gratification (with or lose) than do lotteries, and are not unlike casino action. In fact the most popular product is the video lottery terminal, which dispenses instant-play lottery tickets. Critics suggest those are scarcely different from casino slot machines. And once someone has played a slot machine, it is a short step to full-scale casino gaming.

Indeed, some form of gambling (including bingo for charity) is now available in 48 states. Only Hawaii and Utah have no legalized gambling, although Utah allows quarter-horse racing provided there is no pari-mutuel wagering. It appears that the United States is entering a new era of gaming morality. The bottom-line is that people enjoy gambling and state governments like and need the revenue.

Even the most stalwart opponents of gambling are breaking down. Louisiana, where the state constitution orders the legislature to "suppress" gambling, decided to call it something else and in less than two years has gone from no gambling to riverboat gambling to approving the largest casino in the world on five riverfront acres in downtown New Orleans. Last fall, the Bible Belt state of Missouri became a destination for riverboat gamblers off the shores of Kansas City and St. Louis. . . . There are efforts to build casinos in downtown Detroit and Chicago, in pastoral New Hampshire and Maine, in the desert elegance of California's Palm Springs, at historic Penn's Landing in Philadelphia, and on the lakefront sites of abandoned steel mills in Gary, Indiana.

And, I might add, large-scale casino-style gambling has been proposed for the nation's capital, as announced in August 1993.

Cause and Effect

Most experts agree there are two basic reasons for the recent explosion in legalized gambling. The first is the Indian Gaming Regulatory Act, which became effective in October 1988. The second is that most states need the revenue.

The Indian Gaming Regulatory Act

The IGRA was based on a 1987 Supreme Court decision (*California v. Cabazon Band of Mission Indians*) that allowed Native American tribes, as sovereign nations, to establish gaming enterprises under certain conditions. The Indian Gaming Regulatory Act gives American Indian nations the right to establish gaming on their own reservations in those states that do not expressly prohibit gaming by statute. Specifically, any state that provides for class-3 gaming must, by federal law, allow American Indian tribes to establish their own gaming without state-government restrictions. Class-3 gaming includes state lotteries, parimutuel wagering, horse and greyhound racing, banking-card games, slot machines, casino games, and jai alai.

The only way a state can prevent Native Americans from opening casinos or providing other forms of gaming on their reservations, then, is to outlaw all forms of class-3 gaming. Nevertheless, even if a state outlaws all forms of class-3 gaming in an effort to restrict or eliminate gaming on Native Americans' reservations, as Arizona did (and has

since recanted), that effort may not have the desired effect because the Indian Gaming Regulatory Act includes a clause that protects existing American Indian gaming operations. Generally, class-3 games on reservations that existed before May 1, 1988, are treated as class-2 games under the IGRA.

Of the 34 states with federally recognized tribal populations, 25 allow some form of gaming on reservations. In 1993 the combined gaming revenues from the reservations of those states approached $5.4 billion.

State Revenues

In 1983, budget shortfalls were the primary catalyst for states' introducing new forms of legalized gambling. The weak condition of the U.S. economy left many state governments with huge deficits and declining revenues. In fact 38 states instituted major budget cutbacks in 1983 to prevent deficit spending the following year. Because most states are constitutionally prohibited from overspending, they must either cut spending or raise revenues.

Ten years later the scenario is unchanged. Most states still face severe budget constraints. Many have turned to gaming legislation as an answer to their plight. "Fueled by state governments' appetite for tax revenue . . . gambling operations are popping up [all over the United States]."

State lotteries alone have experienced a growth of over 100 percent in 10 years. In

1983 there were 17 state lotteries across the United States; by 1993 that number had grown to 35.

Some states limit gaming locations to specific communities where income levels are disastrously low and unemployment rates excessively high. Deadwood, South Dakota, is a good example of a struggling local economy that was improved by gaming:

In an attempt to revitalize a crumbling economy . . . low-stakes gambling was reintroduced in Deadwood in November of 1989.

The regulations in Deadwood are tight, with only blackjack, poker, and slot machines operating. Bets are limited to a $5 maximum and a full complement of games and slot machines is a total of 30 per operator. At the present time there are over 2,100 slot machines and 115 poker and blackjack games in operation in Deadwood (this is roughly equivalent to one large Las Vegas-style casino property). No credit may be extended at any time in Deadwood casino operations.

The results in Deadwood have exceeded all expectations. In its first full year of operations, the city of Deadwood had total casino play of $294 million, and net casino win of $28.5 million. While those numbers are small by Atlantic City or Las Vegas standards, they nonetheless resulted in tax revenue for the state and city of over $2 million in 1990. Considering the restrictions placed on operators of these small casino properties, the results are very positive.

History of the Comparison

Ten years ago I was working in the strategic-planning office of a large casino corporation. The office was in the final phases of the corporate five- and ten-year planning process. A key component of the corporate plan was an understanding of the gaming legislation in each of the 50 states. It was my responsibility to assess, state by state, the status of gaming legislation in the United States.

That assessment was a critical first step in preparing for expansion outside Nevada and Atlantic City. The strategic game, played by all the major casino corporations, was fraught with risk. Although the first operation in a new gaming region stood to gain incredible profits, if the anticipated legalization never materialized, one would be left holding an expensive bag. Some casino corporations actually purchased huge parcels of land in locations that looked promising for new casino legislation. MGM, for example, purchased a vast parcel in Hull, Massachusetts—a gamble that has yet to pay off, inasmuch as Massachusetts still doesn't offer casino gambling.

Data Collection

Summary state-by-state data were difficult to obtain in 1983. There were few reliable sources from which to procure an analysis of gaming legislation in the United States. The few sources that were available provided only overviews, and not the in-depth data required for a casino corporation's long-range plan.

I was therefore forced to assemble primary information with little benefit from existing data sources. Most of the information was collected by telephone calls to governors, senators, representatives, and their aides in each state. Together they provided a wealth of information on the current status of gaming legislation in their states and made predictions about future legislation. As a result, my 1983 long-range-planning document contained 29 predictions, covering the period from 1984 to 1988. Of those predictions, 19 proved accurate (a 66-percent success rate). For example, I predicted that eleven specified states would pass lottery legislation within the following few years. Indeed, that prediction came true for nine of the eleven. (I was wrong about New Mexico and North Carolina but correctly anticipated lottery approvals for California, Florida, Idaho, Indiana, Louisiana, Nebraska, Oregon, South Dakota, and West Virginia.) As for legalized casino gaming, in 1983 I predicted Colorado, Connecticut, Delaware, Massachusetts, New York, and Pennsylvania would institute some form of casino gambling. As it turned out, only Colorado and Connecticut subsequently passed casino-gaming legislation during 1984–1988.

The data-collection process now is significantly less cumbersome. Detailed information is available from many respected sources. Indeed the very fact that so many new sources of gaming-legislation data are available is itself a demonstration of the growth and viability of gaming in America over the past ten years.

A Play-By-Play Analysis

A ten-year state-by-state comparison of gaming legislation yields some interesting results. The decade between 1983 and 1993 has demonstrated growth in every category of gaming legislation except one, jai alai, and many experts predict that the largest growth is yet to come. "The 1990s should show the greatest expansion of legalized gaming ever experienced in the history of North America."

The next section of this article describes the changes in legalized gaming, by category, in the United States over the past decade, October 1982 through October 1992 (see Exhibit 1 as well). The categories below are in order of aggregate growth, from most to least.

Off-Track Betting

Although there is much fanfare associated with high-profile legislation (lotteries, card rooms, and casinos), little is heard about off-track betting. It is therefore interesting that OTB has grown the most during the past decade. In 1983 only 18 states offered OTB; by 1993 that number had risen to 38—for a 111-percent growth rate.

EXHIBIT 1. STATUS OF LEGALIZED GAMBLING IN THE UNITED STATES, 1983–1993

	Bingo	Card Rooms	Casinos	Greyhound Racing	Horse Racing*	Jai-Alai	Lottery**	Off-Track Betting	Other***
Alabama	♦★			♦★	★			★	
Alaska	♦★						★		?★
Arizona	♦★			♦★	♦★		♦★	♦★	?★
Arkansas				♦★	♦★			♦★	
California	♦★	♦★			♦★		★	♦★	?★
Colorado	♦★	★	★	♦★	♦★		♦★	♦★	?★
Connecticut	♦★	★	★	♦★	♦★	♦★	♦★	♦★	?★
Delaware	♦★				♦★		♦★	♦★	?★
Florida	♦★			♦★	♦★	♦★	★	♦★	
Georgia	♦★								
Hawaii									
Idaho	★			★	♦★		★	★	?★
Illinois	♦★	★	★		♦★		♦★	♦★	?★
Indiana	★		★		★		★		?★
Iowa	♦★	♦★	★	★	★		★	★	?★
Kansas	♦★			★	★		★		?★
Kentucky	♦★				♦★		★	♦★	?★
Louisiana	♦★	★	★		♦★		★	★	?★
Maine	♦★				♦★		♦★	♦★	?★
Maryland	♦★	★			♦★		♦★	★	?★
Massachusetts	♦★			♦★	♦★		♦★	★	?★
Michigan	♦★	★	★		♦★		♦★	♦★	?★
Minnesota	♦★	★	★		♦★			★	?★
Mississippi	★	★	★						?★
Missouri	♦★		★		★		★	★	?★
Montana	♦★	♦★			♦★		★	★	?★
Nebraska	♦★				♦★		★	★	?★
Nevada	♦★	♦★	♦★	♦★	♦★	♦★		♦★	♦★
New Hampshire	♦★			♦★	♦★		♦★	★	?★
New Jersey	♦★		♦★		♦★		♦★	★	♦★
New Mexico	♦★				♦★			♦★	?★
New York	♦★				♦★		♦★	♦★	?★
North Carolina	♦★								
North Dakota	♦★	★	★		★			★	?★
Ohio	♦★				♦★		♦★	♦★	?★
Oklahoma	♦★				♦★			★	
Oregon	♦★	♦★		♦★	♦★		★	★	?★
Pennsylvania	♦★				♦★		♦★	♦★	
Rhode Island	♦★			♦★	♦★	♦★	♦★	★	?★
South Carolina	♦★								
South Dakota	♦★	★	★	♦★	♦★		★	★	?★
Tennessee	♦★				★			★	
Texas	♦★			★	★		★	★	?★
Utah					★				
Vermont	♦★			♦★	♦★		♦★		?★
Virginia	♦★				★		★		?★
Washington	♦★	♦★			♦★		♦★	♦★	?★
Washington, DC	♦★						♦★		?★
West Virginia	♦★			♦★	♦★		★	♦★	?★
Wisconsin	♦★	★	★	★	★		★		?★
Wyoming	♦★				♦★			★	?★

KEY: Not legal 1983–'93 except as indicated—
♦ **Legal in 1983**
★ **Legal in 1993**
? **1983 status unknown**

*"Horse racing" may include harness, quarter-horse, or thorough-bred racing. Utah allows horse racing but not pari-mutuel betting.
**"Lottery" may include keno, instant games, on-line lotto, numbers, passive games, video lottery terminals, or pull tabs.
***"Other" may include sports betting, slot machines, or pull tabs; there was limited information about pulltabs for 1983.

One reason OTB leads the list is the number of different activities included in the category: interstate intertrack betting, intrastate intertrack betting, race and sports books, telephone betting, and teletheaters.

State Lotteries

The state lottery has become something of an institution since its introduction in New Hampshire in 1964. In the last ten years 18 states have legalized the lottery, bringing the total to 35 states and the District of Columbia. Of the 15 remaining states, at least four are likely to pass such a referendum in the next two years.

The lottery category includes on-line lotto, passive games, keno, on-line numbers, instant games, and video lottery terminals.

Card Rooms

The card-room category is tied with casinos and horse racing in terms of aggregate growth; 11 new states introduced each category during the past ten years. In 1983 only six states had legalized card rooms; by 1993 that number had grown to 17 (183-percent growth). Experts predict that card rooms will sustain similar growth patterns through the remainder of the century.

Casinos

Casino gambling was legalized in 11 states during the past ten years. In 1983 only two states, Nevada and New Jersey, had legalized casinos. By 1993 that number had grown to 13 (550-percent growth).

Like card rooms, casinos are poised for continued growth throughout the 1990s. However, each state seems to have a different concept of how much casino gambling its constituents will accept. Some states limit the amount an individual can lose or the size of the bet, while others have no discernible limitations whatsoever. Some states restrict casino gambling to remote communities or to riverboats, while others have no restrictions on location.

Horse Racing

More states allow horse racing than any other form of gambling, aside from bingo for charity. Included in the category of horse racing are harness racing, quarter-horse racing, and thoroughbred racing. In 1993, 44 states had legalized horse racing—a 33-percent growth rate over 1983, when 33 states had legalized horse racing. One state, Utah, allows horse racing for sport but prohibits pari-mutuel wagering.

The six states that prohibit all forms of horse racing are Alaska, Georgia, Hawaii, Mississippi, North Carolina, and South Carolina. It is interesting to note that five of those six states, as well as the District of Columbia, also prohibit all other forms of gaming (with the exception of lottery and bingo).

Greyhound Racing

In 1983, 14 states allowed greyhound racing. During the decade five more states legalized it, for a 36-percent increase. All the states that allow greyhound racing also allow horse racing.

Bingo

Bingo, either for charity or for profit, is legal in 47 states and the District of Columbia in 1993, a growth of only three states since 1983. The rate of growth was low (7 percent) because so many states already allowed bingo in 1983.

Bingo, especially for charity, is usually viewed as a mild form of gambling. Many states that are generally opposed to gambling have legalized bingo. There are three states in which bingo is the only legal form of gaming (Georgia, North Carolina, and South Carolina). In just one state, Alaska, and the District of Columbia, bingo and the lottery are the only legal forms of gaming. Only Arkansas, Hawaii, and Utah prohibit bingo, and in Hawaii and Utah that ban is part of a *total* prohibition of gambling.

Inevitability

At least 35 states passed new gaming legislation during the past ten years. They were successful in passing the legislation because gambling is now considered only a "slightly sinful indulgence" and because today it is perceived as just another "extension of the middle-class weekend outing"; indeed, gambling is just another product in the expanding "recreation business."

As I pointed out earlier, the acceptance of gaming is due in part to the rapid expansion of state lotteries over the past 29 years. Today 35 states provide a lottery, and that number is expected to go even higher in the coming years.

The acceptance is also due in part to the proliferation of gaming centers on American Indian reservations. Solidified by the 1988 Indian Gaming Regulatory Act and funded by America's insatiable demand, gambling is spreading rapidly on reservations. More than 170 of the 314 recognized tribes in the United States currently offer gaming. In the last four years the number of tribes providing legalized gaming has grown at a compounded average rate of 15 percent a year. It won't be long before gaming on reservations is as commonplace as amusement parks as a form of recreation.

For many tribes, legalized gaming means economic survival. Following a 25-year period when many American Indians were considered to be among the poorest people living in the United States, today's gaming profits can be a real blessing to Native American nations. With gross revenues from tribal-run gambling projected to grow at approximately $1 billion per year, tribes are able to provide a number of benefits not only to their own people but also to the larger community. Connecticut's Mashantucket Pequot Nation provides an excellent example of careful planning and use of reservation gaming income. The Pequots have been building homes for tribal members, guaranteeing college educations to young tribe members, providing world-travel opportunities for the tribe's elders, and contributing $100 million a year to a state fund for troubled cities and towns.

Not all tribes carry the same favorable long-range view regarding legalized gaming, however. Some tribes see gaming as cultural erosion. Those tribes fear that gambling is

. . . not natural to the reservation [and therefore] may create cultural conflicts. There is another downside to reservation gambling. While it is providing a much-needed source of income to some of the poorest Americans, it has brought unscrupulous investors, corruption, and infighting to many reservations. . . . In Washington State, the Spokane Tribe finished in the red last year amid charges that its gaming commission had grossly mismanaged tribal enterprises. In New York State, the Mohawks dreamed of a Las Vegas-style resort. . . . Instead, they got civil war, a string of failed casinos, and allegations of organized-crime infiltration.

In this era, when most states are overspending and Native Americans are seeking economic independence and stability, it is reasonable to expect that gambling will continue to increase. Gaming legislation, in all its forms, will surely continue unabated for years to come.

Casino Operations: Cashing in My Memory Chips, Casino Style

Michael M. Lefever

As a kid and future casino "executive" growing up at Lake Tahoe, NV, I remember the large brass plaques posted at all casino entrances warning that minors would be arrested immediately if they entered the premises. I imagined predatory security guards dragging minors, kicking and screaming, down into a basement dungeon where they would inflict ancient methods of torture.

But casino management was clever; they provided a well-equipped and supervised game room for minors to stay in while their parents gambled. I found it extremely humiliating to be checked in and out of that game room like a common nuisance.

Spotlights and Showgirls

The one exception to the "no minors" law was that children could attend the early dinner show accompanied by their parents. My parents took me to the Jimmy Durante show on my 10th birthday. Needless to say, I was excited and curious to go beyond those brass plaques and to see for myself if his nose was real.

That evening the parking attendant took our car, and we walked up to the main entrance where the doorman, dressed in top hat and white gloves, said in a schoolmaster's measured voice, "Are you going to the dinner show?" My dad said, "Yes," and we were immediately joined by two beefy security guards. Each took a shoulder and practically lifted me off the floor as they hauled me through the casino toward the showroom. I tried to maintain a shade a dignity by keeping my head high and pedaling my feet even though they only brushed the floor.

I'll never forget Jimmy Durante, because he was the first entertainer I saw in person and because we had front-row seats. In the middle of the show, he reached down toward me with a thousand people watching. I could feel the heat of the spotlights and thought he was going to pull me up on stage. I was so shaken that I jumped back and spilled my third Roy Rogers. I heard my dad shouting, "Shake his hand, shake his hand!" I finally reached up, and there was loud applause. Wow, did I ever feel important as he said "Happy Birthday" into the microphone! Then he did the same thing with two other kids who exhibited much more poise.

After the show, Jimmy invited me and the other birthday kids backstage to his dressing room. He gave us autographed pictures; mine was of me jumping back from his reach during the show. At that moment I became obsessed with casinos and the people who worked in them. They were unquestionably fascinating (as were the scantily-clad showgirls who would step out of one costume and into another in front of everyone backstage!).

Youngest Vice President

In my sophomore year of high school I joined Key Club, an honorary sponsored by the Kiwanis. I became president-elect later that year and began spending much of my time with the Kiwanis advisers. One of the advisers was John, a vice president of the largest, most prestigious Tahoe casino where I had appeared with Jimmy Durante. He was energetic, outgoing, fatherly, and, in my opinion, the pinnacle of success.

I remember the day when I decided to become a casino vice president just like John. After making a speech at the weekly Kiwanis luncheon meeting held upstairs in the casino, I sat down next to John and said, "How long would it take to become a vice president?" John immediately started introducing me to fellow Kiwanians as the casino's youngest vice president.

In the next two years I did everything imaginable to mimic John. I began walking briskly wherever I went and even feigned a slight limp (John had injured his knee in a skiing accident). I talked fast, just like John, and introduced myself to groups of strangers and shook their hands with the confidence of a seasoned casino executive. I even started wearing too much of John's favorite after-shave.

John would send a taxi from the casino to pick me up at the high school to attend the weekly luncheon meetings. The taxis were subsidized by John's casino, and I was always given a "comp," or complimentary, ride. The drivers were always curious how I knew an important person like John. I'd respond in that sullen tone used by important people tired of answering the same personal questions: "Oh, he's my dad?

After a while, I decided to stop riding the bus to school and began calling cabs instead. When a cab arrived outside my house, I'd quickly grab my books, kiss my mother goodbye, and tell my father that I was late for work. I'd clamber in the backseat of the cab and tell the driver it was a comp from John. The drivers were never suspicious, but after a few days my father asked John it he knew about the new chauffeur service he was sponsoring. I was back on the bus the next morning.

But that didn't stop me. I continued taking cabs from the high school to the casino several times a week. The drivers would drop me off at the executive entrance. I'd flash the security guard a hollow smile, nod, and say, "I'm just here to see my dad." By my senior year, I had almost all the security guards convinced that I was John's son. Luckily, John's secretary liked me and let me "study" in John's office when he was out of town. My favorite pastime was propping my feet up on John's big mahogany desk and hiding behind a copy of the *Wall Street Journal*. Other casino executives would pass by and say, "Hi, John," and I'd respond with my best vice-presidential impersonation.

The Catwalk

Once I took a key from John's desk, climbed a secret stairway, and entered the dark and eerie catwalk. The catwalk was the area above the mirrored ceiling of the casino where special security workers watched the activity below from chairs that rolled on rails. Catwalk workers kept a close eye and a camera trained on customers who might be cheating or employees who might be stealing.

The catwalk was probably the most intriguing thing about the casino. It was the heart of casino security and was off limits to everyone except the special catwalk security team and senior casino executives. I was able to enjoy the catwalk only for a short time before a security supervisor asked John if he knew his son was showing up on weekends to watch the ladies play "21" from a revealing vantage point.

Pyramid of Power

About that time, despite the unauthorized wanderings of his adopted son, John was promoted to senior vice president/assistant general manager. John's increase in authority gave me a proportionate increase in confidence and daring. I soon ventured down into the main employee cafeteria where I saw dozens of workers dressed in everything from three-piece suits and conservative uniforms to colorful costumes. There was a separate cafeteria—it smelled sweaty and greasy—

where foodservice workers ate for free and lounges where workers could read, watch television, or sleep. There was even a window where employees could cash in their tips, take a draw on their wages, or receive complimentary breath fresheners.

But the most thrilling thing I discovered under the main casino floor was a large glass-enclosed bulletin board where a pyramid of snapshots set forth the casino executives. Every employee was required to memorize their faces, a formidable job since the casino had a management staff of about 100. In this way, management personnel could comp drinks and meals and escort special guests to the front of lines without question. I would beam with pride as my eyes quickly traveled up and over the faces until they stopped one line from the top. There, from that penultimate perch, John looked down on me and a thousand casino workers with his powerful but subtle grin.

When I wasn't dogging John through the community at casino- or Kiwanis-sponsored events, I was often backstage of the showroom watching the big name entertainers and their showgirls rehearse. I even discovered a special viewing room used by the vice president of entertainment. It was equipped with telephones, binoculars, and a full bar.

The only place I couldn't go was the casino floor itself. Oh, John could quickly steer me through to the dining room or coffee shop without security guards, but I was waiting

for the day when I could wind my way through the crowds as an adult and, someday, as a vice president. What I really wanted was the power of "the pencil" (the ability of senior executives to provide complimentary drinks, meals, rooms, and other services to special guests).

Summer 1: Short Orders and Short Tempers

I asked John for my first summer job after my freshman year in college. I hadn't yet reached the magic age of 21, so my choices were limited to nongaming positions. I sat in his office in one of the comfortable leather chairs and wondered if he knew how much time I had spent sitting in "his" chair with my sneakers resting on his leather writing pad.

John asked, "What would you like to do?" I told him I wanted to work the graveyard shift so I would have all day to lounge on the white sand beaches of Lake Tahoe. He grabbed the telephone in his usual efficient manner and called the director of personnel. A few minutes later, a tired and putty-looking gentleman was shown into John's office by the secretary. He seemed out of breath but immediately increased the wattage on his smile when he saw John.

John asked if the executive chef was available to interview me for a graveyard position. The personnel director said he would take care of everything. A few moments

later I was following him down to the lower level where the executive chef was waiting in his office. The personnel director whispered a directive in the chef's ear and then left the office.

The executive chef announced in a thick, choppy, Austrian accent that I could work in one of the employee cafeterias, one of the snackbars, or one of the coffee shop kitchens. The showroom and posh dining room kitchens were not open during the graveyard shift so I chose to be an apprentice fry cook in the largest and busiest coffee shop.

Going back upstairs to the personnel office to process, I waited in a long line, like everybody else, and was finally given an application and interviewed by a sardonic personnel representative. He said he dutifully interviewed applicants all day who already had their job offers. John was making every effort to make sure that I was treated like other new employees. He obviously knew that I wasn't the type of person who would benefit from too much executive privilege.

My next stop was the Douglas County sheriff's station where I was photographed and fingerprinted, since all Nevada casino employees must be carefully identified and registered with the state and federal criminal investigation agencies. I then was issued a casino work permit. I was very proud of that card, even though the word "minor" was stamped across it in red ink. That stamp prevented me and other minors from cashing our paychecks and receiving two complimentary drink tickets (or "tokes") on the casino floor. They always seemed to be one step ahead of me.

Then I went to the casino wardrobe department. It was a busy place with all kinds of employees rushing in and out. I waited in line as five gray-haired ladies behind a long counter provided uniforms to doormen, parking attendants, cooks, dancers, bartenders, waitresses, cocktail hostesses, maintenance men, restroom attendants, security men, and keno runners. I was allowed to wear the distinguishing chef's hat and neckerchief held in place with a discarded die from the crap tables upstairs. That disfigured and seemingly inconsequential little cube made me feel like an important part of the whole casino operation.

At 11:30 that night I reported to the sous-chef dressed in my white pants, white shift, apron, chef's hat, neckerchief and die. The sous-chef was wearing checkered pants designating him as a supervisor. I was assigned to the three-man short-order grill. My two partners, both about 35 years old, had worked the grill for about 6 months and were just passing through Tahoe. For the next eight hours I "slung" hash-browned potatoes while the other cooks swore at me and told me to hustle. I began moving so fast that the hash browns were being served raw. Then the sous-chef grabbed my neckerchief, twisted it into a noose, and

hissed, "I'd gladly fire you right now if it weren't for John."

The kitchen steward was supposed to clean the grills every four hours. But after my first shift, the sous-chef would send him on a break and make me clean them instead. I briefly entertained the thought of purposely dragging my arm and hand across the hot grill so I could show John the scars. But with my luck, it was going to happen anyway.

Then one night a cook called in sick and I took his place at the egg station. That was the turning point in my first casino job. Soon afterwards, the sous-chef conceded half-heartedly that I was beginning to carry my own weight and ordered the steward to start cleaning the grills again.

It was a long, hot summer working as an apprentice fry cook. John came in to the kitchen only once. He spoke briefly with the sous-chef, sidled over to me, and said, "It sounds like you might make it." After he left, the other cooks asked who he was. I just shrugged and said, "Oh, he works upstairs." The best part of being a fry cook was taking all our personal kitchen knives at the beginning and end of a shift and carefully concealing them in a bar towel. Then we would be escorted the short distance across the casino floor by a security guard. Casino management wasn't fond of letting cooks meander through the casino brandishing butcher knives.

Other than that, I never really saw much of the casino as a cook, except the wardrobe room, the kitchen, and the food-employee cafeteria. Cooks were confined to the bowels of the casino, away from most other workers and far removed from the guests. We protected our domain with knives, hot grease, and ominous-looking grinders and ovens.

Summer 2: One-Armed Bandits

The second summer I found myself sifting in John's office rambling about college life. He asked me where I wanted to work next. I had just turned 21 and was excited about the prospect of working on the main casino floor. I asked if I could be a "21" or "Craps" dealer, but he explained I had just missed the presummer dealer school. The pit department (comprised of "21," craps, roulette, baccarat, and other table games) usually recruited summer dealers from midwestern colleges, because their spring semesters ended in early May instead of late June. This gave casino management a chance to train new dealers before the first wave of summer tourists arrived on Memorial Day. (Despite my choice of a California college, I appreciated those midwestern summer recruits because they were mostly young, attractive, innocent-looking, and female.)

John called the personnel manager. This time when I walked over to his office he said there were openings in outside maintenance, the coin room, the keno department, and the slot department. I chose the slot department, because it was above the others on the casino social ladder (and had the second-highest population of midwestern females!).

I again waited in line, filled out an application, interviewed with the same personnel representative, drove over to the sheriff's station for a work permit (making sure it wasn't stamped "minor"), and then went downstairs to the slot manager's office. He said I could start the next day as a changeperson. I was moving up, albeit slowly, in the casino hierarchy and could begin wearing the prestigious black and white dealer uniform.

The primary responsibility of changepersons was to keep the customers playing as fast as possible. We accomplished that by responding quickly and efficiently to jackpots and changelights. We also were responsible for our change and payoff money. If we balanced within a dollar at the end of a shift, the supervisor would give us two drink tokes. Being careful with my money turned me into a regular barfly.

There were six bars on the main casino floor, but there was only one where slot workers drank and socialized. I was beginning to respect the complexity of the casino worker's culture. Slot workers were certainly ranked above food service workers, but we were at rock-bottom when it came to gaming personnel. So we basically just kept to ourselves. I did, however, often watch for a group of dealers returning from break. As they paraded through the casino, I would calmly glide in behind them in my black-and-whites and then peel off just as they entered the pit.

The best way to determine casino worker rank or status was to observe the employee cafeteria. As a slot employee, I was no longer allowed in the food-employee cafeteria with its free food. Instead, I had to sit with slot employees at unofficially designated slot tables. If, for example, I accidentally sat at a "dealer" table, the dealers would actually get up and move or, better yet, ask me to leave. The most interesting aspect of the employee cafeteria was the complimentary coffee, tea, hot chocolate, and condiment bar. Towards the end of a pay period, down-and-out workers would live for days on hot chocolate and "casino soup" (hot water mixed with catsup and Tobasco).

I had a good summer working in the slot department. What impressed me most was the wide cross-section of people attracted to casino work. I worked alongside a law student, a retired bank president, and a high school principal (off for the summer). They were all drawn by the excitement of casinos and the beauty of Lake Tahoe and the high Sierras.

But the work was tiring, and my lower back has never been the same since packing 20 pounds of slot change around my waist eight or 10 hours a day. Probably more worrisome than permanent back problems was that I was getting into the habit of drinking every night with my fellow workers. We were a pretty close-knit group and even came in on our days off to commiserate around the bar. As I worked I was always amazed at the aggressiveness of the grandmotherly slot players. I saw hundreds of them return each month, cash their social security, welfare, or pension checks, and dump every last nickel into those machines. They would claim an entire row of machines on a busy night and viciously defend their territories against other players and even changepersons who mustered enough courage to remind them of the two-machine limit.

I could always tell how long someone had been playing by looking at their hands. They steadily got dirtier from the coins and were seldom washed. Hard-core players never left their machines, even to visit the restroom: They thought their chances for winning increased with each pull of the handle.

My third summer as a casino worker began as usual in John's office. He had recently moved into an even larger office with two secretaries instead of one. I wasn't surprised when he told me he had been promoted again, this time to executive vice-president/general manager of the growing resort hotel/casino. I bolted downstairs to confirm his promotion with the photo board: There he was, at the top of the heap, not looking a day older.

John said I was ready for the main cashier's office

(often called "the cage"), which pleased me since almost all the casino executives had worked there at one time or another. So off I went to the personnel manager's office. He said the cashier manager wanted to see me as soon as I got processed. I knew the drill all too well.

The cashier manager stood up and politely introduced himself as I entered his office. He asked if I'd like to join him for lunch. I knew instantly that I was going to enjoy the summer. He said that I was obviously being groomed for management and that he was proud to have me in his department.

It was a relief not having to wear the heavy change belt. My new uniform consisted of black and whites with three additional items that marked me as a cashier: a ball-point pen and a mechanical pencil stuck in a protective plastic sheath inside my shirt pocket. I quickly tossed out the plastic sheath and clipped my pen and pencil directly to my white shirt so I'd look more like a pit boss with power of "the pencil," but halfway through my first shift I gladly replaced it after streaking my white shirt with ink and lead.

One of the first things I learned was how to stack and cut chips. It took me most of the summer before I developed enough dexterity and speed to impress the customers. I was even learning how to shuffle two stacks of chips with one hand. On a particularly slow night, I must have been mindlessly shuffling chips at the counter, because a

cashier supervisor rushed up and said, "The catwalk just called, and you're going to get us all fired if you don't stop playing with the money." I resented the complaint; after all, it was only John's money.

I climbed another social rung and received even more prestige than expected as a cashier. We were in constant contact with casino management and this gave us a distinct advantage. I could get a table for any cabaret show and not have to wait in line. I'd simply walk up to the VIP entrance and ask for the supervisor.

Cashiers also didn't have any problems getting drink tokes; we printed and distributed them to the other departments! If our drawer or bank balanced at the end of the shift it was called a "noser" (for "on the nose"), and we got four drink tokes instead of the two issued to changepersons. Even if our drawer was off by a few dollars, we still got two drink tokes. If we wanted more, all we had to do was ask. Yes, the cashiers had their own bar, and all of us met there every night after our shift.

Toward the end of summer, I was assigned (thanks to John) to the special team responsible for the "count." During the shift, six of us would be escorted to a small counting vault deep in the basement. There we put on special pocketless overalls and gathered around a large table covered with green felt. A cashier supervisor then opened the steel drop boxes brought down from the gaming tables and

shook out the currency. We quickly counted the money and recorded the "take" from each box. This was a very sensitive job, and, consequently, we were locked in the vault with an armed security guard posted outside. We also were observed continually by a special catwalk person and his camera located directly overhead behind the mirrors.

The worst part about being a cashier was the constant noise from the casino. The bells, buzzers, music, and screams and shouts of a thousand winners and losers were indescribably annoying when trying to count, make change, speak with a customer, or talk on the telephone. But the summer passed quickly.

Summer 4: Destruction Derby

It was early June, and I had just graduated from college when I returned to the casino for my fourth summer. More than anything I wanted to be a dealer. Craps, "21," and baccarat dealers received the highest respect among hourly casino workers, and they also made the most money in tips. John told me that I'd have to wait for the next dealer school, which started in August. I was deeply disappointed because I had just been drafted and had to report for active duty September 1.

I sat brooding across from John's desk when he said, "How would you like to work in the parking lot?"

"I thought that job was impossible to get," I replied sullenly.

"Well, it's not always easy," John said glibly, "but I'll see what I can do."

Parking attendants had a very private, all-male fraternity, and they often rivaled dealers in the amount of tips they made. But they had to be in peak physical condition and able to jog about 20 miles a day. Not surprising, parking attendants were relatively young, gaunt, and wild-eyed, and spoke in locker-room jargon. I was worried.

The parking lot manager called me a few days later and asked if I wanted a summer job. I couldn't wait to line up at the personnel office and casually mention to others that I, a lowly summer worker, was going to be a parking lot attendant. I was right; everyone wanted to know who I knew.

I went through the processing and uniform routine, only this time I wouldn't be wearing black and white. Instead I was issued cotton Levi's and golf shirts. A wardrobe lady also advised me to invest in a good pair of jogging shoes; I would need about three pairs to make it through the summer, she said.

I had a trainer only for the first day. He showed me how to start, stop, shift, park, and unlock almost every make of domestic and foreign car. The most important thing I learned was to always drive with my left foot slightly above the brake pedal (it the car was an automatic) to cut my reaction time as much as possible. I also developed a knack for opening car doors with a coat

hanger after locking the keys inside.

He explained how it took about six months to master the parking lot. By then a parking attendant was able to locate an empty stall relatively close to the porte cochere, give the customer a receipt, speed off without squealing the tires, and maneuver into the tiny stall without scraping a fender. It was important to learn which stalls were close and which stalls were a half-mile away, because we had to jog to and from the cars. Parking lot supervisors would watch and yell "jog" if they caught us walking. Power-walking did not quality as jogging, and I quickly learned how to kneel down and retie my shoelaces just to catch my breath.

I wasn't a popular person in the parking lot and was nick-named "spook" because my colleagues thought I was a spy for management. The parking lot had long been known as the drive-through pharmacy, but I didn't have much energy to worry about extracurricular activities after jogging 10 hours a day.

I had a pretty good "crash" record for the summer, considering I was a rookie. I smashed the taillights on two cars; "blew" the engine on a Cadillac because I raced it down the ramps of our five-story parking garage without letting it warm up; started an engine fire in a new Jaquar with starter fluid; and crashed head-on into a cement wall when the brakes failed on an older car. I didn't mention in the accident report that I was

speeding, playing with the radio, eating cashews left on the front seat by the owner, and combing my hair in the rear-view mirror when I hit the wall.

Parking attendants were not known for their good manners. We were always too breathless and smelly from jogging to be polite or social. Sometimes if car owners didn't give us a tip we would try to slam the door on their thumb or leg. For a dollar we would gently close their door; for two dollars we would load their luggage or run around to close the passenger's door; and for three dollars we would give them honest directions to the airport.

By the end of the summer I was beginning to drive and jog fast enough to be somewhat accepted by the others. I enjoyed the work because I was outside and could eat continuously while still losing weight. The most memorable parts of the summer occurred in the employee cafeteria when heads turned and the room grew silent as John appeared and sat down with me at a "parking lot" table. However, I was never brought into the attendants' fold because I didn't do drugs and my alcohol consumption decreased dramatically. I couldn't run all day and party all night. I suppose that's what my trainer meant when he said it took six months to master the parking lot.

My wife says I still drive like a parking lot attendant: fast, jerky, and with my left foot always slightly above the brake pedal ready for a cement wall. I never have our car valet parked.

Summer 5: The Pit

I returned from active duty (in worse physical shape than I arrived) and began my fifth summer just in time for the presummer dealer school. Among other reasons, I wanted to be a "21" dealer, since that's how John got his pit experience. I went through all the usual motions of getting processed with the addition of a special test for "21" dealer applicants. It measured our ability to add small groups of numbers in a 10-minute time period. If you could add in your head and not watch the people sitting next to you counting on their fingers, you could pass the test.

The next day we started school in a special roped-off section of the casino. I proudly donned my black and whites and the little apron I purchased from wardrobe; the latter discouraged dealers from stuffing money and chips into their pockets.

We were divided into groups and for the next two weeks practiced dealing to each other under the watchful eye of a trainer. More than anything, new dealers needed practice to increase their speed. It was important to deal quickly to keep the game moving and the cash flowing into the drop boxes.

The casino or house always maintained an advantage and could increase or decrease it by changing the rules of the game such as whether to allow split aces. The main advantage enjoyed by the house was that players would "bust" before the dealer had to take any action.

The trainer taught us to watch for any telltale signs of card counting by the players which could destroy the house advantage. Card counters were asked (or forced) to leave the casino and their names were placed on a statewide "unwelcome list." Card counting became so widespread that we were encouraged to shuffle frequently and began using a "shoe" that held 4–6 decks or packs at once.

The game of "21," unlike craps, keno, slots, and roulette, is not governed by what mathematicians call "independent trials processes." In other words, "21" players can increase their odds of winning by knowing what cards have already been dealt. Basically, a pack rich in fives favors the house and one rich in ten-cards favors the players.

We were instructed to change currency into chips as quickly as possible (players often do not associate chips with hard-earned money) and be pleasant but not overly friendly. Our concentration was supposed to focus on the game, not on the players. An overly friendly dealer would alert pit supervisors to the possibility of complicity.

I was overwrought my first evening in the pit. New dealers were kept away from the highstake tables since we were liable to make more mistakes than experienced players. But I was happy with my $2-minimum table, and I found that the busier I was the better I liked it. We worked 40 minutes on and 20 minutes off every hour.

My biggest disappointment was discovering that summer dealers didn't sit with the year-round regular dealers in the employee cafeteria. It seemed that no matter how far I climbed the social ladder, there was always another group just above me.

Even though management was continually on the lookout, certain dealers were known to cheat. For instance, card bending was a way to mark the pack. Dealers (and players) could "bridge" or slightly bend the ten-cards lengthwise. Then they were easy to spot on the table or in the pack.

The easiest way for a dealer to cheat was to peek at the top card. It was easy to fan the top card slightly forward above the others with a quick kick of the wrist. If it was favorable, the dealer would use it to "hit" himself. If it was unfavorable, the dealer would draw the next card from the pack. This was called dealing "seconds."

Casino management hotly denied the existence of professional knockout dealers. Even so, one method supposedly employed by these "special" employees was to work with a partner in the anchor slot (the position on the dealer's far left). The dealer would peek at the top card and signal the anchor person. If it was a ten-card, the anchor person would always "hit," even if he went bust. Thus, the player sitting next to the anchor often lost his ten-card advantage against the house.

At the table I would stare off into space or hum stupidly to myself when I didn't have any players. I even developed a distinct and intimidating strut that blocked out the rest of the world and allowed me to plow through the soupy casino crowds with little or no resistance. But I spent most of my time waiting for those all-too-infrequent moments when John would walk by my table and give me a reassuring wink.

The highlight of my summer occurred when five massive security guards jumped on a player at my table. He was wrenched off his stool onto the floor and then squashed like a tumbled football. I discovered later that our celebrity was using counterfeit money.

Change of Heart

That fall I went back to college for graduate work and would never return to the casino as an employee. My wife and I, though, did visit the hotel/casino (which by then was a five-star resort) many years later as special guests of John.

As we drove our car up to the hotel entrance, I recognized the doorman as the former security guard who used to stand outside the counting room door. He smiled but looked older. One of my fellow parking attendants had become a bellhop and carried our luggage up to our room. It felt funny giving him a tip. I recognized a room service waiter as the steward who "let" me clean the grills when I was an apprentice fry cook. He pretended not to recognize me. After riding the elevator down to the casino floor, we were greeted by a pit boss who trained with me in dealer school. But standing at the same place, behind the same bar, was my favorite bartender from my main cashier days. Some things just never change.

That evening John took us to dinner in the showroom. The captain was wearing a toothy smile and I recognized him as one of the banquet waiters who used to work the Kiwanis luncheons. We sat near the stage, three tables back from the spot where I sat on my 10th birthday.

It felt strange being in a casino. I didn't feel like an employee and I don't think former casino workers ever feel like ordinary customers. Once you are a casino worker, something changes inside you forever. It's like you've become part of a very special club whose members perhaps have lived too much too fast.

As my wife and I were saying goodbye to John under the porte cochere, I heard the parking attendant squealing down the ramp in our car. I gave her (times had changed!) a good tip so she wouldn't catch my leg or jam my thumb into its socket by slamming the car door. As we drove off I finally realized that my days chasing after John and a career in the casino business were a thing of the past where they belonged.

Guardian Angel

John retired a few years later and moved to southern California with his wife. I haven't seen him for some time, but every now and then I carefully dig out our marriage license, where John signed as best man, and a letter he wrote to me soon after he retired. In it he said he always felt honored that I wanted to follow in his footsteps, but he had decided long ago to let me work only in the summers until I matured and developed a wider range of interests.

You see, summer casino employees often did not make a career of gaming because they never got caught up in the mainstream culture. On the other hand, once someone became a year-round regular worker the casino lifestyle often acted like a narcotic. Even as a summer worker, the casino warmed me with a heady feeling of timelessness, constant acceleration, and the false confidence that I could quit any time. Today, twenty years later, I still get ambushed by the desire to return to Tahoe and the past. But I'll always have my memories.

The following semester project is designed to provide the senior student a more thorough understanding of the role government plays in the regulation of gaming enterprises. This project requires that detailed research be performed in a certain sector of the gaming industry. The specific sector (casino gaming, card rooms, off-track betting, lottery, bingo, etc.) and the state to be researched is ultimately the decision of the student. Choose a topic in which you are especially interested, because you will soon become the expert in this area!

Proposal Submission Process

All projects must be approved by the faculty member within the first three weeks of the semester. Under no circumstance is the student to proceed with the research prior to receiving written commentary and approval from the professor. All projects are approved on a first-come, first-served basis. If your particular project (say casino gaming regulations in New Jersey) has already been selected by a classmate, you may be asked to resubmit. An updated list of approved projects is available outside the professor's office.

Proposals must be submitted in writing—usually one typed page is sufficient. Included in the submission must be details related to methodology of collecting resource materials, initial direction or theme of the paper, examples of interviews to be conducted, and any other information related to the project. In order to ensure availability of data, please consider your proposed topic carefully and prepare some preliminary research prior to submission.

Theme and Concept

This is a semester project, and as such must be a significant work in terms of content and detail. This is not merely a restatement of legislative policies and procedures of a specific gaming category in a given state. Rather, this project develops an understanding of legislation, discusses its effectiveness and compliance, analyzes its inherent cost structure (both to the operation and the state), and makes specific recommendations and conclusions.

The theme of your paper, therefore, should be a reflection of the effectiveness and appropriateness of the state's legislation. Although this theme is based upon your personal perceptions, you must document your findings and opinions. For example, you may be wholly supportive of your state's plan and wish to cite examples of why it appears effective. On the other hand, you may be wholly unsupportive of your state's plan and wish to cite examples of why it is onerous, expensive, and inefficient.

Explain the impact certain aspects of your state's legislation have on the operator. How have specific policies affected the physical design of the operation, staffing levels, internal audit and accounting procedures, ownership, reporting methods, etc.

Sources of Information

Students are encouraged to seek a variety of informational sources as they develop the term project. Indeed, the final grade is based, in part, on the thoroughness and quality of your resources. Personal interviews, state legislative statutes, newspaper, magazine, or journal articles, news reports, and expert testimony are all relevant and worthwhile sources. Be creative, often the hands-on employee has a better understanding of the real compliance with a given statute than the law-maker who introduced the bill.

All references must be cited and documented in APA format. A separate APA style sheet is available from the professor.

Project Submission Requirements

All projects are to be submitted on standard paper, double-spaced, and laser-printed. Each paper must include in-text citations (APA format), page numbers, a title page, section headings, and a reference page. Most projects will have an appendix section and several exhibits.

There is no specific paper length required. A paper must be thorough in breadth and depth, yet concise in verbiage. Good luck.

The following semester project is designed to provide the senior student a more thorough under-standing of the legalized gaming debate. This project requires the student to become familiarized with the societal arguments in favor (or against) gaming in a given community. Each student is re-quired to select a form of gaming (be it casino gaming, card rooms, lotteries, off-track betting, etc.) and argue one side of the debate.

Proposal Submission Process

All projects must be approved by the faculty member within the first three weeks of the semes-ter. Under no circumstance is the student to proceed with the research prior to receiving written commentary and approval from the professor.

Proposals must be submitted in writing—usually one typed page is sufficient. Included in the submission must be details related to methodology of collecting resource materials, initial direc-tion or theme of the paper (pro or con), and any other information related to the project. In order to ensure availability of data, please consider your proposed topic carefully and prepare some pre-liminary research prior to submission.

Theme and Concept

This is a semester project, and as such must be a significant work in terms of content and de-tail. You are preparing a one-sided argument in favor (or against) gaming in your state, region, community, or township. Your paper must stand on its own—it must thoroughly explain your posi-tion, cite real examples from across the United States, analyze societal costs specific to your juris-diction, and convince the reader that your opinion is the most reasonable.

A well-written paper must be pro-active in a sense. It must predict and respond to all possible arguments against your stated position. In other words, the paper will read as a one-sided debate which fields all dissenting points of view.

Included as major subcategories in your treatise will be a number of related topics. Examples of such categories include; the increase in crime experienced by many communities, the increase in related costs—both compliance and law enforcement, the incidence of welfare abuse by local residents who can ill-afford to gamble, the encouragement of problem or compulsive gambling be-havior, and the increase of organized crime associated with legalized gaming.

Sources of Information

Students are encouraged to seek a variety of informational sources as they develop the term pro-ject. Indeed, the final grade is based, in part, on the thoroughness and quality of your resources. Personal interviews, newspaper, magazine, or journal articles, news reports, and expert testimony are all relevant and worthwhile sources. All references must be cited and documented in APA for-mat. A separate APA style sheet is available from the professor.

Project Submission Requirements

All projects are to be submitted on standard paper, double-spaced, and laser-printed. Each paper must include in-text citations (APA format), page numbers, a title page, section headings, and a reference page. Most projects will have an appendix section and several exhibits.

There is no specific paper length required. A paper must be thorough in breadth and depth, yet concise in verbiage. Good luck.

26

CORNELL'S INTEGRATED TEAM PROJECT

The Team Project in Cornell's Redesigned Professional Master's Program

Integration and Interaction in a Graduate Management Program

Appendix: Hotel Americana

THE TEAM PROJECT IN CORNELL'S REDESIGNED PROFESSIONAL MASTER'S PROGRAM

INTEGRATION AND INTERACTION IN A GRADUATE MANAGEMENT PROGRAM

SINCE ITS 1986 INCEPTION, the team project in the Master of Professional Studies in Hotel Administration (M.P.S.) program at Cornell's Hotel School has been a pivotal and differentiating feature. Based on an actual hospitality development proposal or renovation, and integrating five required first-year courses, the team project offers an outstanding educational opportunity. Students interact with industry professionals beginning with their field visit early in the semester to their formal presentations at the semester's conclusion. The teams present a complete hotel development concept including a project design, a marketing analysis and plan, a staffing plan, a restaurant outlet, and financial projections, to actual owners, developers, and managers.

With the faculty selecting a single site, the professional master's students have more opportunity to study a project in depth and to see how subject matter in their required

Food and Beverage Management, Hospitality Financial Management, Human Resources, Marketing, and Property Development courses interrelates. Team work skills are practiced as students work in diverse groups for fifteen weeks. The School's active alumni society affords a selection of projects, and the industry's participation facilitates their getting to know the students and the program. Above all, the professional master's students practice the theory they learn in class and benefit from an intense industry immersion and team experience. This article will discuss the history of the project, the decision to retain and reposition the project in the redesigned program, and pointers for programs considering such an educational approach.

History

The Master of Professional Studies in Hotel Administra-

tion program had its beginning in 1972. Before that time many people were willing to return to school to obtain a second bachelor's degree because there were few schools with the undergraduate hospitality curriculum and none with the master's level curriculum. The faculty decided to prepare and offer a professional master's degree in the field, and the first class graduated in 1974. Group work and actual hospitality projects were hallmarks of the program from the beginning, but it was not until the fall of 1986 that the faculty offered the first integrated group project. It incorporated three of the five first semester courses, Property Development, Food and Beverage Management, and Marketing. The properties professor had included a similar project in the graduate required properties course since 1982. Realizing that students were doing analyses on similar yet disparate and not always real-world projects, he

This chapter was prepared by Sandra K. Boothe, A. Neal Geller, Richard H. Penner, and Glenn Withiam of Cornell University's School of Hotel Administration. Reprinted with permission.

proposed to fellow graduate faculty members that they work together.

Through their consulting and alumni contacts, the faculty knew of two proposed luxury hotel projects in Boston, the suburban Vista Hotel managed by Hilton International and the Pier 4 Hotel planned by restaurateur Anthony Athanas. Students were divided into travel teams, or teams for which the faculty had arranged separate schedules for visits to competing properties and interviews with managers across the spectrum of hospitality functions. Students presented comprehensive development proposals to senior management from Hilton International, the Athanas organization, Laventhal and Horwath, and Pannell Kerr Forster at the end of the semester. The faculty considered the field trip and the entire project to be a success, as was confirmed by a written survey completed by the students early in the following semester.

Seven additional projects have been completed each fall from 1987 through 1993, and each has been considered successful by both faculty and students. With various strengths and weaknesses, each project required an integration of courses, demonstrated the interconnectedness of disciplines, and facilitated in-depth learning. The 1987 project studied the proposed SAS and Meridien hotels in New York City. This market was later considered to be too complex to provide an ideal learning experience and has been avoided since. Projects from the Rittenhouse and Ritz-Carlton hotels in Philadelphia in 1988 included presentations from members of hospitality consulting companies such as Coopers and Lybrand and Pannell Kerr Forster. Students then had the opportunity to compare the points of view of owners, managers, management companies, and economic consultants specializing in the hospitality industry.

The fall 1989 project saw all five required course faculty involved for the first time even though those responsible for three of the courses were new to the project. Two projects proposed by the Desmond Group in nearby Albany, New York, a downtown hotel and a hospital hotel, were chosen, and weekly meetings on the project were initiated. The field trip, tests, case studies, and project deliverables were scheduled to best facilitate student learning, and the students' evaluation of the project that year showed their appreciation of this effort.

The 1990 project in Philadelphia had the benefit of an experienced faculty team plus it was the second project in that city. Appropriately for a recessive year for the domestic hospitality industry, the projects focused on renovations—of the Hershey Hotel in downtown Philadelphia and the CIGNA-owned Conference Center at Eagle Lodge twenty-five minutes from the city. Students stayed at both sites during the field trip and heard presentations by the general managers of both properties, one of whom was expect-ing to have to deal with a strike in a day or two. The Philadelphia alumni chapter hosted a cocktail hour in a new sports bar for the students, and the importance of the networking was illustrated through experience.

Another new development in the 1990 project was the opportunity the students had to make their December group presentations in the Marriott Executive Education Center in the School's teaching Statler Hotel. Outfitted with tiered executive seats and modern media equipment, the Center provided a new opportunity and challenge for the student teams. It was also possible to easily videotape the presentations which added another element of formality and professionalism and provided a learning tool for current and future students.

In 1991 the professional master's curriculum took a further step in preparing students for the global hospitality industry by locating the group project in Ottawa. The site was a proposed hotel at the World Exchange Plaza, a premier downtown location of new office, retail, and entertainment space. The international location, even though accessible by bus, added an element of complexity to both the site visit and the project, but the faculty team had worked together the previous year and could easily accommodate the change. One of the graduate assistants who routinely assist the faculty with the group project required courses organized evening entertainments—a river cruise one night and dancing another night, so the students were able to appreciate the ambiance of the city in ways additional to their hotel visits and dining experiences.

The hotel project itself was in a very early stage even though the attached shopping space was about to be opened. Student proposals ranged from a luxury hotel to a conference center to an athletic club. An additional development was that the group project evaluation, traditionally conducted by the Graduate Office, became a project of the required second-semester Quantitative Methods class. Students working in groups had the opportunity to revise the questionnaire, approach the subject matter from a variety of statistical methods, administer it to their fellow students, and present their results to classmates and project faculty.

The Orlando project of 1992 was a milestone in several ways. Its distance from Ithaca made it necessary to fly down, and, for the first time, an organization valued the input of the master's students to such a degree that they were willing to pay for the cost of the students' and faculty's flight and site visit. Jones Lang Wootton Realty Advisors funded the trip, and the faculty worked to reduce the extra pressure they felt this positive situation might be putting on the students. As is explained to all industry participants, the first and foremost goal of the project is to be a learning experience for the students. The faculty are happy if the industry incorporates the students' suggestions, but the industry is doing the School a service by participating in a project.

The project itself was a proposed renovation for the oldest of three Marriott properties in Orlando, a hotel on International Drive with 16 two-story buildings of both interior and exterior access design on 48 acres. The complex Orlando market was a background that provided not the typical Marriott business person. Attracting price sensitive groups was expected to become more difficult with Walt Disney World opening lower mid-scale resorts. Jones Lang Wootton had also hired Coopers & Lybrand to do a major study of strategic options but wanted the professional master's students to have free reign in examining other Marriott concepts, removing buildings as well as adding new ones, improving operations, and creating new themes and non-traditional approaches.

The site visit went well with the extra dimension of air transportation. The team travel schedules included time for additional exploration at Disney and highlighted a visit to a successful 1961 alumnus of the School who controlled more hotel rooms than any independent hotelier in central Florida. By the semester's end, teams responded to the challenges and opportunities of Orlando with proposals for the International Drive property which ranged from an architecturally unique luxury hotel to a Marriott high-rise to a theme-park hotel for families.

The last project before the introduction of the redesigned curriculum was the Atlantic City Headquarters Hotel project in the fall of 1993. With gaming receiving increased acceptance and revenue worldwide, the Headquarters Hotel project, even though it was to be a non-gaming hotel, exposed students to a hospitality destination which focused on gaming and related issues for hospitality managers. Recognizing that twelve casinos had not improved the decline of the city the way some people had hoped, the New Jersey Casino Reinvestment Development Authority had broken ground on a convention center, obtained $35 million to expand the airport, and was working to develop the rundown central corridor and entrance to the city. The students' project was the proposed headquarters hotel to be the icon of the city at its entrance and joined to an entertainment complex leading to the boardwalk and the casinos.

The project was considered the most successful in the program's history for several reasons. It was a proposal in the early stages of development with few constraints. It also introduced students to gaming—a current opportunity and challenge in the hospitality field. Finally, the involvement of the industry professionals was excellent. Six of them attended the team presentations—the project developer, his financial partner (the CFO of Caesars), the management company (VP-operations of Doubletree), the economic consultant (Coopers & Lybrand), the master plan architect (RTKL Associates), and the chair of the convention center authority. Each of the six commented on and questioned team members after each presentation. A further benefit was that their reaction was generally positive and could be summed up by the Chief Financial Officer's comment that he was impressed by the amount of effort and research that had gone into the projects and that the students would see their ideas in the new Atlantic City headquarters hotel when it was built. The student project considered best by faculty and industry representatives, The Grand Atlantic, is included as an appendix.

Transition in the Redesigned Curriculum

A year-long strategic study initiated by the School in the fall of 1990 highlighted the importance of the professional master's program in maintaining the Cornell Hotel School's worldwide preeminence. With tourism the number one industry in the world economy since 1990, the hospitality industry having become more complex and global, and with most of the 750 existing graduate management programs focusing on manufacturing rather than service and hospitality, the macro environment was extremely positive.

In 1991 the Graduate Faculty was given a mandate to review the professional master's program. The bulk of the work

was carried out by the Graduate Special Committee with review and approval by the Graduate Faculty. A stakeholder survey of industry, alumni, faculty, and students was undertaken to determine what skills and competencies were most important for executives and leaders in the hospitality industry. Dean Scott Cowen of the Weatherhead School of Management at Case Western University was invited to describe and discuss the process of review and implementation for Weatherhead's new and successful program. The literature and other successful graduate management programs were studied. The inadvisability of so many programs having the same general form and content, not focusing on their specific strengths, producing graduates who were low in the ability to implement their knowledge, and not being in touch with the needs of industry or of students were themes that emerged and guided the redesign of the professional master's curriculum.

The team project, with its integration and interaction with the hospitality industry, had always been considered by the faculty and students to be one of the most positive features of the program. For instance, the students rated the overall project even more highly at their pre-graduation interviews than they did in their second semester. The literature of graduate management education continued to support the value of integrated learning as well as interactive real-world experiences. In ad-

dition, the project was an excellent educational method of supporting all seven key themes of the redesigned program: strategic orientation, communication ability, team skills, leadership skills, analytical ability, ethical awareness, and international scope.

At the same time, there were problems with the placement of the team project in the first semester. Some faculty thought that the students did not have a strong enough foundation to benefit educationally from the project that early in the program, and many students tended to agree. The faculty had been trying to address these concerns over the last five years by such means as moving the project field trip later in the semester, coordinating their assignments and schedule of deliverables, and, in the 1993 Atlantic City project, giving students a week of class time to focus on the project after the field trip and making the bulk of the deliverables due in the last month of the semester. These same techniques will still be employed, but it was still decided that the team project would be moved to the second semester in the redesigned curriculum beginning in fall 1994. The students will have a first semester foundation of Competitive Strategy for the Hospitality Industry, Financial Economics, Information Technology for Hospitality Managers, Human Behavior in Organizations, Management Development, and Quantitative Methods before participating in the team project with its historic related required courses in Food and Beverage Management, Hospitality Financial Management, Human Resources, Marketing Management, and Property Development as well as an additional semester of Management Development.

Additional benefits of this adaptation will be that students will have a chance to learn and practice team skills in the first semester, as specifically addressed in the Human Behavior in Organizations course and as experienced in other courses, before they work in teams for the entire second semester. Like many graduate management programs, we were saying that students were learning teamwork skills, while in effect they were put into groups and left to themselves without benefiting from abundant faculty expertise in human relations, management, and leadership. Students will also benefit from an entire semester of personal assessment and individual feedback from faculty and industry on their written communication, presentational speaking, and group process skills before engaging in the team project, and they will continue to receive individual feedback throughout the second semester. The team project experience should now be even more satisfying and professional; there should be few, or ideally no, insoluble group relation problems and no individual who gets low ratings from faculty or teammates on contribution to the group and project.

Two concerns about what would be lost by not having the project in the first semester were that the students would miss an excellent introduction to the industry and the socializing and positive class feeling which were developed on the field trip. Fortunately, the students now enter the program with an average of three years of full-time, hospitality-related work experience. In addition, their first semester course, Competitive Strategy for the Hospitality Industry, will provide a global introduction to the industry. The opportunity for socializing and developing positive class relations will be provided by icebreaker and team building experiences starting at orientation and carried on by such activities as the Human Behavior in Organizations Class adopting the 15th Annual Professional Master's Charity Auction as their class project. There was discussion of moving the team project to the third or fourth semester of the program, but the curriculum is now set up for students to focus on their individual program of study, with the exception of their required Service Excellence for Maximum Profit and Hospitality Management courses. As has been true of all past projects and the program in general, the team project's location in the curriculum as well as all of its other aspects will be continuously evaluated.

Pointers

The main purpose of this chapter was to share with hospitality students and educators the challenges, successes, and failures of the team project in Cornell's master's program. Any of the contributing editors as well as the required course faculty would be happy to provide further information and assistance for programs considering initiating or redesigning a similar project. There are some general suggestions which they hope will be of value and would like to leave you with. The first is that the project would be educationally more valuable if the perfect competitive environment could be designed and controlled. However, the hospitality business environment is complex, and the more controllable and testable the project becomes, the less real it becomes. These parameters are valuable to keep in mind when selecting a project. Another suggestion is to approach a team project integrating a semester's courses from an evolutionary rather than a revolutionary way. A program should build on its own strengths and goals, and tackle only as much as the faculty feels comfortable with for the first project. Finally, acquire the resources needed to execute the project well. Communication with the industry, logistics, and follow-up require extra time. Faculty will also need to meet and communicate more often than they would if their classes were not interrelated. The benefits to students and their positive reactions will help carry the faculty through their extra effort, but the help of graduate assistants and time for one faculty member to be the project coordinator are also valuable.

With higher education having more competition and demands on it than ever, we believe there will be more pressure for curriculum and pedagogy to demonstrate value. Integration within the curriculum and interaction with the hospitality industry are two of the ways that the redesigned professional master's program hopes to exceed the expectations of the more demanding consumer of graduate management education. The past ever-improving success of the team project was an impetus for the value of such well-designed and well-coordinated education, and we expect it to be an outstanding and pivotal feature.

Specific Suggestions and Materials for Organizing the Project

The organization of the project during the semester was much the same as it is now. Perhaps our experience will prove instructive to other educators as they seek new approaches for integrated and industry experiences.

Organization of the Project

The organization of a joint project among five courses, based on a proposed project at a remote site, with a class of 40–50 students may seem a daunting task. But the planning and administration easily can be broken down into individual elements and tasks. In our integrated team project at Cornell one of the core faculty, along with the program director, is assigned the task

of coordinating the project including negotiating with each of the other faculty the deliverables (see sidebar) that they expect from the student teams. Most years it is relatively straightforward and may best be thought of as several discrete steps:

1. Identify the project site, gain approval from sponsors and other faculty, request feasibility and site information.
2. Determine semester schedule, especially the date for the site visit, major class deliverables, and final presentations. Confirm dates with sponsors (availability at project during visit and to attend presentations) and faculty. Arrange transportation, hotel rooms, presentation room.
3. Establish student teams, attempting to balance US/international, skills, and industry background.
4. Develop site visit itinerary, including hotel tours, meetings with department heads at competitive properties, session with such others as financial consultants, visitors and convention bureau, and labor union.
5. Prepare handout with background information: city information, hotel data, feasibility study, etc.
6. Field trip: have fun!
7. Debriefing on return.
8. Complete the semester with individual project assignments in each of the core courses. Students prepare for final presentations.
9. Final presentations and evaluations.
10. Post-semester evaluations (6 to 12 months later).

Scanning this list of steps begins to suggest the type of planning effort required, the amount of lead time necessary, and which tasks are best done by one person, coordinated by the core faculty together, or a larger group.

▶ **Identify the Project Site.** Our experience has been to identify the project site at least three months before the beginning of the semester. While more time might be ideal, development projects often proceed in fits and starts and it may be better to have greater confidence that the project you select will be at a particular stage during the time of the field trip.

Generally the faculty make a number of suggestions based on consulting or alumni contacts, news items they have clipped from the trade press, or other knowledge of what's happening in nearby locations. Several years we have called contacts at such firms as Pannell Kerr Forster, Coopers & Lybrand, or other consulting firms and discussed projects which they know to be proposed in various northeastern cities. Sometimes they have offered to make the first contact with the owner or developer of the proposed hotel.

However, generally, the faculty coordinator begins to solicit interest from, per-

SIDEBAR: DELIVERABLES		
Week	Deliverable	Explanation
4	Field trip	
5	[No project deliverables]	
6	Segmentation Analysis (M)	■ Analyze the lodging market by segment and time period; identify the likely target markets.
7	Preliminary Concept (PD)	■ Identify markets; describe hotel facilities (number of rooms, size of ballroom, etc.); establish quality level, services, and amenities; propose appropriate image.
	Staffing Projections (HR)	■ Quantify staffing by department; establish approximate wage rates.
8	Competitor Analysis (M)	■ Identify major competitors by market segment and rate according to key attributes.
	Financials I (MA)	■ Prepare draft of year 3 financial projections
	Restaurant Concepts (F&B)	■ Prepare outline concept for each outlet; provide operational criteria, preliminary menu, staffing, and financials.
9	[Project Week: no classes or project deliverables]	
10	Facilities Proposal (PD)	■ Provide detailed operational and architectural requirements, design criteria, project budget.
	Staffing Recruitment (HR)	■ Consider overall labor market; identify recruitment methods.
11	Positioning Analysis (M)	■ Describe positioning relative to competitive hotels; propose marketing slogan.
	Financials II (MA)	■ Prepare final of year 3 financial projections
12	Staffing Selection (HR)	■ Propose methods for staff selection.
	F&B Program (F&B)	■ Provide complete program for each outlet, including catering and room service; select one restaurant and prepare detailed operational criteria, menu and wine list, staffing, and financial projections.
13	Financials III (MA)	■ Prepare draft of 10-year financial projections
14	[No project deliverables]	
Presentations:		
	Executive Summary	■ Provide complete summary report for reviewers and faculty. Include market overview and hotel positioning; architectural concept, program, and construction budget; food and beverage concepts and staffing; human resources plans including retention policies; final 10-year financial projections.

Legend: F&B = food and beverage management

HR=human resources management
M = marketing
MA = managerial accounting
PD = property development

haps, several leads and eventually decides on a probable location and project. The coordinator, after checking whether any of the faculty have reservations about the site, makes arrangements with the sponsor. Usually this is the owner or developer of the hotel, sometimes the hotel management company or a real estate firm. We request confirmation in writing that they will allow us to use their project and will cooperate in a number of ways. More specifically, we ask the sponsor to identify a contact person, provide us with site information and a feasibility study (with permission to duplicate and distribute portions to the students), make themselves available during the field trip, and pledge to attend the final presentations on campus at the end of the term.

▶ **Determine the Semester Schedule.** Once we have agreement on a site, the coordinator begins to outline the major dates during the semester, beginning with the date for the field trip. Over the past several years it has fluctuated between the end of the third week to the end of the fifth week of the 14-week term. From an educational standpoint, the later date is better in that the students will have had more class work in each of the core disciplines, more opportunity to prepare, and some chance to develop rapport among members of the project teams. On the other

hand, the earlier date provides more time from the field trip to the end of the semester for the teams to develop their concepts, complete the course assignments, and prepare for the presentations. Some classes have three or four project deliverables, and providing sufficient time, and proper sequencing, in less than about ten weeks is difficult. From a practical standpoint, the trip may be scheduled based on when discounted hotel rooms are available or to meet the schedule of the project sponsor. (One year our group block of about 30 rooms was bumped by the hotel less than a week before the trip. The city, essentially, was sold out. After a frantic half hour, a phone call to the corporate vice-president of rooms was sufficient to reinstate the group.)

Once the trip is scheduled, the coordinator works with the other core faculty to plan the basic project assignments; each course has several other, non-project related cases, papers, and exams in addition to the project work, which varies from about 20% of the course grade in human resources to 40% in property development. The accompanying sidebar illustrates the order of the project assignments during the most current semester.

Arrange for presentation room; reserve hotel rooms; schedule guests and social events.

▶ **Establish the Student Teams.** The organization of the several teams is the one element that has undergone the most evolution since 1986 but still it is likely that there will be at least one "group from hell." The first year the teams were established by the faculty who attempted to get an equivalent mix of US vs. international students, men and women, and students with different industry backgrounds on each team. But we ignored personalities. Since then, the teams have been organized with fewer students (generally 5–6 per group), and only after they have completed the MBTI. One year four of the six members of one team were married—placing a new constraint on the team's ability to easily schedule working meetings; we now spread the married students equally among the teams.

▶ **Develop the Field Trip Itinerary.** The single largest task is to plan the schedule during the field trip. We try to have at least two full business days scheduled with meetings, three to four each day. Typically, we schedule a kickoff meeting for the entire class at which hospitality or economic consultants introduce the competitive character of the local lodging industry. They often provide an overview of the past ten years—for example, how did the addition of a major hotel change the competitive balance; identify the principal market segments, seasonality, price-sensitivity, etc.; briefly describe the competitive set of hotels and their ability to attract the different market segments; and discuss anticipated changes to the market, supply, and demand. Some years other presentations are made to the entire class: by the visitor and convention bureau, by city planners, or by an official of the labor union. In addition, the project sponsor frequently attends to welcome the students and provide background on the actual hotel project.

More complicated is scheduling student hotel tours and meetings with hotel executives. From the first year we recognized that if the student teams went in different directions during the field trip that they would gather more information and gain a wider variety of insights about the competitive situation and needs for the project hotel. Therefore, the "project teams" that will work together during the semester and reorganized into "travel teams"—ideally, there would be the same number of each category, that is, a travel team would consist of one member from each project team. As the travel teams spread out through the city, touring different hotels, meeting with different hotel executives, they would bring back and share with their project team a wealth of information which could be assimilated into the hotel concept.

► **Prepare Background Packet and Hold Briefing Session for Students.** For the trip to be entirely successful, the students need to be prepared before they arrive at the site. For the past several years we have handed out sections of the feasibility study—essentially the local economic and market information, city maps, and data on the competitive hotels. (Some socially-minded student often produces a list of restaurant reviews and suggested attractions; these are, after all, "hotelies.") In addition, the faculty meets with the class to present the schedule, field trip objectives, and general "do's and don'ts" (don't ask the controller for last month's income statement).

► **Conduct the Field Trip.** With Cornell located in rural Ithaca, New York, we have had to travel some distance to each of the project sites. New York, Philadelphia, Albany, and Ottawa are all about four-hours by bus; Boston and Atlantic City approximately six hours. We generally leave early afternoon, arrive about dinner time, and leave the students free to explore the city. Students over the next two days follow very intensive travel and interview schedules.

■ Debriefing
■ Semester Project Deliverables

  faculty coordination
    meetings
  project schedule

■ Final Presentations

  type of room, AV,
    videotaping
  reception

■ Post-Semester Evaluations

Appendix

Hotel Americana

Executive Summary

Presented By:
Cynthia G. Cardenas
Helen E. Haertl
Ali Mutlu
Penelope L. Perlman
William S. Robinson
Kar Tin Teo

QPC Associates Inc.

Contents

QPC
Associates Inc.

121 Pleasant Grove Road

Ithaca NY 14850

Telephone: (607)555-1234

Facsimile: (607)555-2345

INTRODUCTION

Millions of dollars have been spent on casino and community improvement projects in New Jersey since the legalization of gaming. Gaming has not provided Atlantic City with the benefits originally expected, however. Currently, Atlantic City is again trying to broaden and solidify its economic base and redefine its image with the addition of the new convention center, the new headquarters hotel, the Gateway Corridor, and other related development projects.

Before designing a concept for the new headquarters hotel, the needs of the market as well as the goals of the owners and city officials needed to be considered. It was necessary to analyze the existing Atlantic City marketplace and forecast the changes that will occur as a result of the planned developments. These data and projections were used to design a hotel that will meet the needs of Atlantic City officials, other members of the development team, and the hotel's target markets.

DEVELOPMENT GOALS

The construction of the Gateway Corridor, the new convention center, and the headquarters hotel is part of a renaissance program for Atlantic City. The headquarters hotel must serve as an icon for the city's new image and must also complement both the convention center and the Gateway Corridor, helping to make Atlantic City a more attractive destination. The success of the project must be measured by its contribution to the overall economy of Atlantic City, as well as by its internal rate of return. Consequently, the hotel must be large enough to support the convention center, but it must still be financially feasible.

ATLANTIC CITY MARKET

Atlantic City currently hosts regional conventions and a small number of national events at the existing convention hall with the Trump Regency serving as the headquarters hotel. In addition, the Trump Regency and many of the casino hotels host small in-house local and regional conventions. As shown in Table 1 in the appendix, the twelve casino hotels, the Holiday Inn-Diplomat, the Ramada Renaissance, and the Trump Regency all have the facilities to serve the convention market in some capacity. However, the casino hotels are generally reluctant to dedicate a large number of rooms to conventions even during non-peak times. They would prefer to reserve these rooms for their gaming guests and may in fact cancel meetings and banquets with very short notice to accommodate gaining customers or other casino related events.

The new convention center will draw additional conventioneers into Atlantic City each year. National convention attendees tend to be well-educated professionals who demand quality service, but who also place a great amount of importance on value. To serve this group, the hotel will need to provide a wide range of services at a competitive price. As Atlantic City becomes a more attractive vacation destination, these conventioneers may also bring their families and stay over additional nights.

Over 60% of the meetings and conventions currently held in Atlantic City are regional. (Deloitte & Touche, Part II, p. 20) These conventions are fairly limited in scope, however, attracting

QPC
Associates Inc.

121 Pleasant Grove Road

Ithaca NY 14850

Telephone: (607)555-1234

Facsimile: (607)555-2345

blue-collar organizations, sales groups, SMERFS, or governmental agencies with the majority of attendees traveling short distances and arriving by car. Only 20% remain overnight, however. (Laventhol & Horwath, Section IV, pp. 10–11.) It is our hope that a greater percentage will stay overnight if acceptable, convenient accommodations are available. In addition, these consumers are highly value oriented and competitive pricing will be very important.

The addition of the Gateway Corridor will also increase the number of non-gaming leisure travelers to Atlantic City. Convenient access to family entertainment and competitive pricing will be important to this group. However, the gaming industry will continue to play in integral role in the Atlantic City leisure market. The location of the headquarters hotel away from the casinos will weaken its opportunity to capture a large percentage of this segment.

Based on data from Deloitte and Touche and the U.S. Travel Data Center, we have forecasted the future room night demand for each segment, as shown in Table 2 in the appendix. After adjusting this data to reflect the seasonality of demand by segment, monthly occupancy was projected. (See Tables 3 & 4 for more details on the seasonality of demand.)

As shown in Figure 1, the busiest seasons for the national and regional convention segments are Fall and Spring, while the busiest season for the two leisure segments is Summer. Due to the complementary nature of these four market segments, Atlantic City will be able to support a 750-room headquarters hotel.

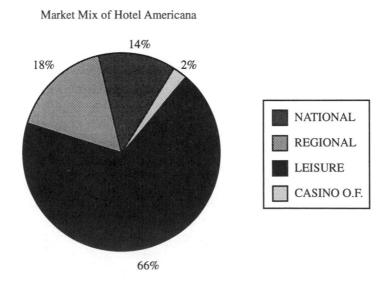

Figure 1.

QPC
Associates Inc.

121 Pleasant Grove Road

Ithaca NY 14850

Telephone: (607)555-1234

Facsimile: (607)555-2345

PROJECTED OCCUPANCIES

Occupancy for the headquarters hotel was then projected based on 750 sellable rooms available 365 days a year and the forecasted changes in demand as shown in Table 2 in the appendix. Fewer rooms will be available, however, in the 7th and 8th years of operation due to planned refurbishments. The growth in supply of 4,000 casino hotel rooms and 3,000 non-casino hotel rooms by the end of the decade was also taken into consideration.

As shown in Figure 2, occupancy in 1996, the hotel's first year of operation, is projected to be 64%, increasing to 72% in 1997 and 78% in 1998 due to the completion of the Gateway Corridor in 1997 which will bring more leisure travelers to Atlantic City. The increasing confidence that meeting planners will have in the new convention center and in the headquarters hotel will also contribute to this increase in occupancy. Occupancy will reach 82% in the stabilized year of operation, 2000. Growth in subsequent years is expected to be small. The spike in occupancy rate in 2002 and 2003 is a result of the decreased number of sellable rooms available during refurbishment.

Figure 2. Changes in Occupancy, 1996-2005

It should be noted that as total occupancy increases to over 95%, the hotel will begin to turn away guests. Preference will be given to conventions guests, then to leisure travelers, and finally to casino overflow guests. For example, in peak convention months (i.e. October) leisure travelers and casino overflow guests may be completely closed out of the hotel. The market mix of the hotel, as shown in Figure 3, takes this into account.

QPC
Associates Inc.
121 Pleasant Grove Road
Ithaca NY 14850

Telephone: (607)555-1234
Facsimile: (607)555-2345

Due to the fact that national and regional convention attendees are projected to be 84% of the hotel's business, the needs of these segments were the primary consideration when designing the headquarters hotel although the needs of the non-casino leisure and casino overflow segments, 14% and 2% of the hotel's total business respectively, were also considered.

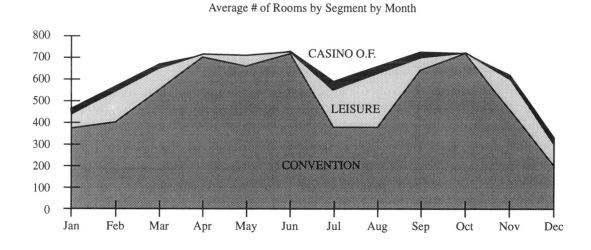

Figure 3.

CONCEPT PROPOSAL

We have developed a concept that incorporates the goals and needs of both the owner/developer and the customer. We have named our project Hotel Americana. We chose the Americana theme not as a political or patriotic statement, but as a celebration of diversity and as a representation of our commitment to excellence. It is also reminiscent of the glory days of Atlantic City and is symbolic of its coming renaissance. As we envision it, the hotel will serve as a physical icon as well as a symbolic one. As visitors come in from the expressway, their eyes will immediately be drawn to the series of American state and territorial flags lining the perimeter of the roof of the 32-story hotel. (See Exhibit 1 in the appendix for a complete site plan.)

Guest Rooms

A 29-story tower will house the guest rooms which includes a large proportion of suites and double/double rooms. This reflects the desires of convention attendees who often need to entertain clients and/or share rooms with colleagues. Twenty-four hour room service will also be available to cater those often impromptu events. The hotel's 750 rooms will be divided as follows:

QPC
Associates Inc.

121 Pleasant Grove Road
Ithaca NY 14850

Telephone: (607)555-1234
Facsimile: (607)555-2345

Kings:	210
Double-Doubles:	460
Handicapped:	15
Junior Suites (2 Bays, 1 Key):	35
Senior Suites (3 Bays, 1 Key):	20
Luxury Suites (3 Bays, Optional Second Bedroom Available):	10
Total (Keys):	750

Meeting Space

Significant meeting space and rooms for small breakouts and banquets are needed to support convention events, as well as small in-house conventions and local special events. To satisfy the preferences of meeting planners, all 34,800 square feet of function space will be centrally located on one floor. The meeting rooms will be flexible as well with

- One 15,000 square foot ballroom divisible into thirds,
- One 10,000 square foot junior ballroom divisible into thirds,
- Two 4,000 square foot banquet rooms each divisible into fourths,
- Two 900 square foot boardrooms, and
- 6500 square feet of pre-function space.

In keeping with the Americana theme, these rooms will be named after national parks, historical monuments, historical figures, or other terms associated with the United States.

Food & Beverage Outlets

Hotel Americana will feature only two restaurants and one multi-purpose lounge because convention attendees are likely to leave the hotel for lunch and dinner to visit the other attractions in Atlantic City. The food and beverage outlets available in Hotel Americana are as follows:

The Bayou Lounge (200 Seats)

Located on the lobby level, this New Orleans style jazz-club, serving breakfast and light lunches, as well as beverages, will provide a meeting place and social center for hotel guests and convention attendees. In the evening, the lounge will serve cocktails and provide live jazz music creating a relaxing and entertaining atmosphere and a good alternative to gaming.

Main Street Grille (250 Seats)

This upscale casual, three-meal restaurant will feature an all-American menu. The facility will be located on the second floor of the hotel, overlooking the lobby, and will be open Monday through Saturday from 7:00 am until 11:00 pm and on Sunday for brunch from 10:00 am to 2:30

QPC
Associates Inc.

121 Pleasant Grove Road
Ithaca NY 14850

Telephone: (607)555-1234
Facsimile: (607)555-2345

pm and for dinner from 5:00 pm to 11:00 pm. Menu items have been carefully chosen to incorporate the diverse ingredients and cooking styles represented in this nation. Posters, pictures, and memorabilia from across the United States and from various periods in this county's history will be displayed throughout the restaurant. The main attraction of the Main Street Grille will be the Broadway bar which will be used at breakfast as a buffet offering a variety of breakfast selections. At dinner, special menu items will be cooked to order at the Broadway bar providing culinary entertainment for the guests. (See Exhibits 2, 3, 4, 5, 6, and 7 for more detailed information on the Main Street Grille concept and menu.)

Sfuzzi's Italian Restaurant (200 Seats)

This leased restaurant will be located on the second floor of the hotel and will have a separate entrance from the Gateway Corridor. Sfuzzi's upscale casual, Italian theme will provide hotel guests with an alternative to the all-American cuisine being served in the Main Street Grille and will also attract Corridor visitors and local residents, as there is a strong need for quality chain restaurants in Atlantic City.

In addition to the food and beverage outlets listed above, revenue will be generated by catering and banquet services and room service.

The distribution of total projected food and beverage revenue between these outlets is shown in Figure 4.

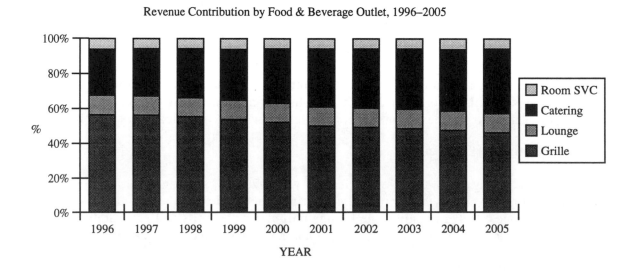

Figure 4.

QPC
Associates Inc.

121 Pleasant Grove Road
Ithaca NY 14850

Telephone: (607)555-1234
Facsimile: (607)555-2345

Other Amenities

The executive business center will cater to the copying, faxing, and secretarial support needs of convention attendees and hotel guests. The hotel also has an executive office which will be rented to business guests. For vacationers and health conscious guests, a health club will be available on the roof of the guest room tower. An indoor pool and deck, an outdoor sun deck, a whirlpool, saunas, and training rooms will occupy 10,000 square feet of space. Several retail shops will border the Gateway Corridor providing guests with the opportunity to purchase various sundries and souvenirs.

(See Table 5 in the attached appendix for a detailed space allocation for Hotel Americana.)

Price/Value

Adequate meeting space, good restaurants, and a health club are appealing to meeting planners and vacationers, but the success of this project will depend on the right price and excellent service. As a result, the Americana theme will be integrated into the Human Resource program. The national and Atlantic City workforce is becoming increasing diverse and managing that diversity effectively will be essential to providing consistent quality service. Extensive training and career development programs will be a part of our efforts to reduce turnover and maintain a satisfied and productive staff. (See Table 6 in the appendix for a detailed staffing plan for Hotel Americana and see Exhibit 8 for a timeline of HR activities.)

A study of competitor prices and market trends, along with our own projected operating expenses, revealed that a $121 ADR was appropriate for Hotel Americana in 1996. The majority of the non-casino hotels in Atlantic City have lower ADRs but do not have the facilities to compete with Hotel Americana. Hotel Americana's higher prices help to differentiate it from these properties. Only one hotel within Hotel Americana's competitive set, the Holiday Inn-Diplomat, has a lower projected 1996 ADR than Hotel Americana. The remainder of the hotel's competitive set have higher projected 1996 ADRS. (See Table 1 in the appendix.) With this pricing strategy, Hotel Americana hopes to position itself as a high quality, competitively priced convention and leisure destination.

POSITIONING

Hotel Americana will be the premier meeting and convention choice in Atlantic City. Conveniently located adjacent to the new convention center and the Gateway Corridor, the hotel's diverse, service oriented staff will meet the needs of regional and national convention attendees, as well as the needs of leisure travelers and casino overflow guests. The hotel's new, four-star facilities include 34,800 square feet of meeting and banquet space, excellent dining facilities, retail outlets, a business center, and a health club. Hotel Americana is dedicated to providing consistent, quality service at a very competitive price. This philosophy and the hotel's dedication to excellence are demonstrated by the hotel's tag line, "When it Comes to High Quality Meetings, We are the New Monopoly in Town."

(See Table 7 in the appendix for an outline of Hotel Americana's promotional strategy.)

QPC
Associates Inc.

121 Pleasant Grove Road

Ithaca NY 14850

Telephone: (607)555-1234

Facsimile: (607)555-2345

PROJECT CONSTRUCTION

We estimate that this project will cost $128.5 million. (See Table 8 in the appendix for a breakdown of project costs.) Recognizing its role in the new Atlantic City package, the hotel will open in early 1996 along with the new convention center.

FINANCIAL PROJECTIONS

Stabilized Year Pro-Forma Income Statement

We have chosen the year 2000 to be the stabilized year of operation for Hotel Americana since it will take time for convention planners to feel comfortable booking a meeting in Atlantic City after the new convention center opens in 1996. Also, non-casino leisure travelers will not visit Atlantic City in large numbers until the Gateway Corridor has opened and has established a favorable reputation. Currently, it is estimated that the Gateway Corridor will be completed in late 1997.

The income statement for the stabilized year has been prepared based on considerations of demand, target markets, proposed hotel facilities, economic data, and the customized base derived from the HOST Report. Also factored into the development of the Pro-forma income statement is the addition of 4,000 casino hotel rooms and 3,000 non-casino hotel rooms in Atlantic City by the end of the decade.

Ten-Year Income Statement

The income statement for the stabilized year was used as the basis for the ten year projection of income and expenses as shown in Table 9 in the appendix. Detailed CPIs over the ten years were determined using regression analysis and were then used to express the ten year income statement in nominal dollars.

All of the hotel's rooms will be refurbished during the seventh and eighth years of operation. In accordance with Generally Accepted Accounting Principles, these costs are capitalized. The effects of the refurbishment program appear in the income statement in the form of increased payroll in the property operations and maintenance department. In order to finance the refurbishment and other ongoing maintenance and replacement costs, it is recommended that Hotel Americana set aside a reserve for replacement of approximately 2.5% of total revenue per year.

As shown in Figure 5, rooms revenue makes up approximately 61% of total Hotel Americana revenue, food and beverage revenue makes up 33%, telephone revenue makes up 2.5%, and rentals and other income make up the remaining 3.5%.

Figure 6 shows the level of Hotel Americana's total revenue for the first ten years of operation, divided into its expense and profit components. Total revenue increases faster than total expense due to the high proportion of fixed costs. (See Table 9 in the appendix for a detailed projection of revenue and expenses.)

QPC
Associates Inc.
121 Pleasant Grove Road
Ithaca NY 14850

Telephone: (607)555-1234
Facsimile: (607)555-2345

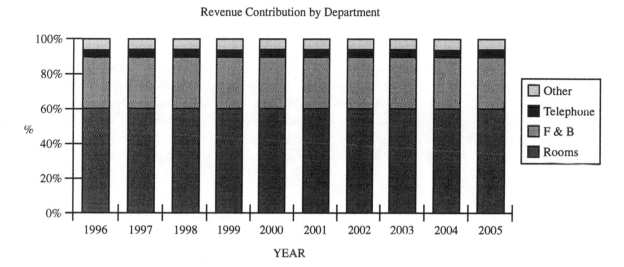

Figure 5.

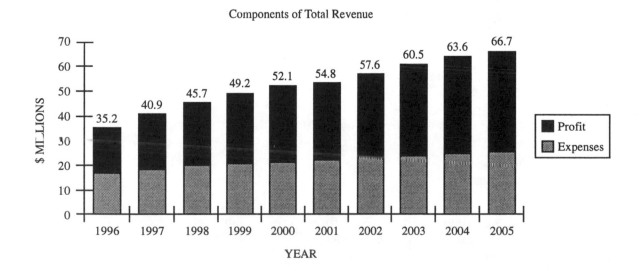

Figure 6.

QPC
Associates Inc.
121 Pleasant Grove Road
Ithaca NY 14850

Telephone: (607)555-1234
Facsimile: (607)555-2345

LONG-TERM INVESTMENT ANALYSIS

The internal rate of return for the project has been determined to be 12.5%. A capitalization rate of 10% was used to estimate cash flows beyond the first ten years of operation as the hotel is expected to generate revenues beyond ten years. Ten percent was chosen as it takes into consideration the risk involved in investments of this nature. The initial cash outlay of $128.5 million was estimated as shown in Table 8 in the appendix. The hotel guest rooms will also be refurbished in the seventh and eighth years of operation at a total cost of $3.96 million. Figure 7 shows the anticipated net cash flows from Hotel Americana over the ten years. The seventh and eighth years reflect cash outflows due to the planned rooms refurbishment. The tenth year includes the simulated sale based on capitalization of eleventh year cash flow at 10%. The positive internal rate of return indicates the profitability of the project.

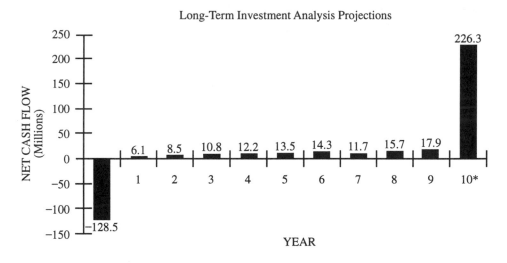

*Includes simulated sale based on 11th year cash flow of $207 million.

*Includes simulated sale based on 11th year cash flow of $207 million.

Figure 7.

CONCLUSION

As discussed, Hotel Americana will be a 750-room, 32-story hotel with two restaurants, a multi-purpose lounge, 34,800 square feet of meeting space, an executive business center, retail outlets, and a health club. These facilities along with a high level of service and the hotel's average daily rate of $121 in 1996 helps to differentiate it from its competition. The hotel has been designed to simultaneously fulfill the goals of Atlantic City and the needs of the market. This proposal, along with the other planned developments, will help Atlantic City capitalize on this opportunity and finally shift its image into a positive direction.

Table 1. Competitive Set

Hotel*	# Rooms	# Suites	Fair Share***	1992 Occ. %	1996 ADR****	# Meeting Rooms	Meeting Rooms Sq. Ft.	% Mtg. Space (Comp. Set)	Max. Capacity (Reception)	# F&B Outlets	Other Amenities (Each hotel has Room Service)
Non-Casino Hotels											
Hotel Americana	750	65	4.24%	N/A	$121	10	34,800	5.29%	1,500	3	Business Center, Health Club, Indoor Pool, Sun Deck, Game Room, Sauna, Whirlpool, Shuttle Service
Holiday Inn—Diplomat	220	8	1.24%	70%	$114	8	9,000	1.37%	300	1	Beach, Outdoor Pool
Ramada Renaissance Suites	296	296	1.67%	56%	$210	6	2,500	0.38%	350	2	Beach, Game Room, Health Club, Outdoor Pool, Spa, Whirlpool, Shuttle Service
Trump Regency Hotel	500	23	2.83%	70%	$143	14	30,000	4.56%	1,600	1	Beach, Health Club, Indoor Pool, Racquetball
Casino Hotels											
Bally's Grand Casino Hotel**	803	233	4.54%	80%	$239	12	22,000	3.34%	1,400	7	Beach, Live Entertainment, Health Club, Indoor Pool, Spa
Bally's Park Place Casino Hotel	1,310	110	7.41%	79%	$183	17	40,000	6.08%	2,050	9	Beach, Live Entertainment, Game Room, Health Club, Indoor Pool, Spa, Racquetball
Caesar's Atlantic City**	1,041	315	5.89%	86%	$169	11	25,000	3.80%	1,000	12	Live Entertainment, Health Club, Outdoor Pool, Spa, Tennis, Mini-Golf
Claridge Casino Hotel	503	56	2.84%	87%	$140	13	25,000	3.80%	1,300	6	Beach, Live Entertainment, Marina, Health Club, Indoor Pool
Harrah's Casino Hotel**	1,145	372	6.48%	88%	$131	9	22,976	3.49%	1,300	9	Live Entertainment, Game Room, Health Club, Indoor Pool
Resorts International Casino Hotel**	919	72	5.20%	92%	$143	12	42,000	6.38%	1,000	7	Beach, Live Entertainment, Game Room, Health Club, Indoor Pool, Outdoor Pool, Spa
Sands Hotel & Casino**	733	69	4.14%	93%	$204	12	25,000	3.80%	700	5	Live Entertainment, Golf, Health Club, Indoor Pool
Showboat Casino Hotel**	1,000	112	5.65%	89%	$135	12	45,000	6.84%	2,200	8	Beach, Live Entertainment, Health Club, Outdoor Pool, Spa
TropWorld Casino & Ent. Resort**	1,355	560	7.55%	89%	$163	29	82,000	12.46%	4,484	8	Beach, Live Entertainment, Health Club, Indoor/Outdoor Pool, Tennis, Spa, Amusement Park
Trump Castle Casino Resort	735	200	4.16%	86%	$129	24	50,000	7.60%	1,730	9	Beach, Live Entertainment, Marina, Game Room, Health Club, Outdoor Pool, Spa, Tennis, Mini-Golf, Running Track, Shuttle Service
Trump Plaza Hotel and Casino**	927	108	5.24%	92%	$175	13	28,000	4.25%	1,000	9	Beach, Live Entertainment, Game Room, Health Club, Indoor Pool, Tennis, Shuttle Service
Trump Taj Mahal Casino Resort**	2,250	450	12.72%	91%	$209	29	175,000	26.58%	2,500	10	Beach, Game Room, Live Entertainment, Health Club, Indoor Pool, Spa

Sources: Greater Atlantic City Convention & Visitors Bureau, Smith Travel Research, Casino Chronicle.

* To be included in the competitive set a hotel had to have over 200 rooms, at least 2,500 square feet of meeting space, and be able to handle receptions for 300+ people.
**Includes proposed additional rooms with the number of suites increasing proportionally.
***Base: 46 hotels/motels in Atlantic City (17,688 rooms). Assumes all proposed new casino hotel rooms will be built.
****Average daily rates were increased by 4.5% each year to estimate 1996 average daily rates. (Based on Smith Travel Research Data & "Detailed CPI Report, August 1993")

TABLE 2. PROJECTED GROWTH IN DEMAND BY MARKET SEGMENT, 1996-2000

Market Segment	1996	1997	1998	1999	2000	2001	2002	2003	2004	2005
Convention	139,443	156,176	171,189	183,728	194,022	196,156	198,314	200,496	202,701	204,931
Percent of Total	78.91%	76.81%	74.00%	74.20%	75.99%	75.87%	75.74%	75.62%	75.50%	75.37%
Percent Growth		12.00%	9.61%	7.32%	5.60%	1.10%	1.10%	1.10%	1.10%	1.10%
Regional	43,227	45,291	46,221	45,932	44,625	45,116	45,612	46,114	46,621	47,134
Percent of Total	24.46%	22.27%	19.98%	18.55%	17.48%	17.45%	17.42%	17.39%	17.36%	17.33%
Percent Growth		4.77%	2.05%	-0.63%	-2.85%	1.10%	1.10%	1.10%	1.10%	1.10%
National	96,216	110,885	124,968	137,796	149,397	151,040	152,702	154,382	156,080	157,797
Percent of Total	54.45%	54.53%	54.02%	55.65%	58.51%	58.42%	58.32%	58.23%	58.13%	58.03%
Percent Growth		15.25%	12.70%	10.27%	8.42%	1.10%	1.10%	1.10%	1.10%	1.10%
Leisure	29,969	39,858	53,012	56,874	54,454	55,543	56,654	57,787	58,943	60,121
Percent of Total	16.96%	19.60%	22.91%	22.97%	21.33%	21.48%	21.64%	21.80%	21.95%	22.11%
Percent Growth		33.00%	33.00%	7.29%	-4.26%	2.00%	2.00%	2.00%	2.00%	2.00%
Casino	7,300	7,300	7,144	6,995	6,852	6,852	6,852	6,852	6,852	6,852
Percent of Total	4.13%	3.59%	3.09%	2.83%	2.68%	2.65%	2.62%	2.58%	2.55%	2.52%
Percent Growth		0.00%	-2.13%	-2.09%	-2.04%	0.00%	0.00%	0.00%	0.00%	0.00%
TOTAL	176,712	203,335	231,345	247,598	255,328	258,552	261,820	265,135	268,496	271,904
Percent of Total	100.00%	100.00%	100.00%	100.00%	100.00%	100.00%	100.00%	100.00%	100.00%	100.00%
Percent Growth		15.07%	13.78%	7.03%	3.12%	1.26%	1.26%	1.27%	1.27%	1.27%

Based on Deloitte & Touche & U.S. Travel Data Center

TABLE 3. HOTEL AMERICANA, STABILIZED YEAR AVERAGE ROOMS PER NIGHT, BY SEGMENT AND MONTH

Month	National Market	Regional Market	Leisure Market	Casino Overflow	Total	Occ. %	ADR
January	289	86	53	7	435	58.06%	$95.20
February	320	96	117	14	547	72.91%	$130.90
March	434	130	105	14	683	91.08%	$130.90
April	548	164	4	0	715	95.33%	$130.90
May	530	158	27	0	715	95.33%	$158.27
June	548	164	4	0	715	95.33%	$158.27
July	289	86	193	26	595	79.35%	$158.27
August	289	86	246	34	655	87.34%	$158.27
September	498	149	68	0	715	95.33%	$158.27
October	675	40	0	0	715	95.33%	$158.27
November	349	104	109	14	576	76.80%	$130.90
December	145	43	105	14	308	41.01%	$95.20
Annual Average	4,913	1,306	1,030	125	7,374	81.93%	$142.56
% of Total	66.6%	17.7%	14.0%	1.7%			

TABLE 4. DEMAND DISTRIBUTION USED TO CONSTRUCT MONTHLY OCCUPANCY

Month	Convention Market	Leisure Market
January	6%	3%
February	6%	6%
March	9%	6%
April	11%	7%
May	11%	11%
June	11%	11%
July	6%	11%
August	6%	14%
September	10%	10%
October	14%	9%
November	7%	6%
December	3%	6%

EXHIBIT 1

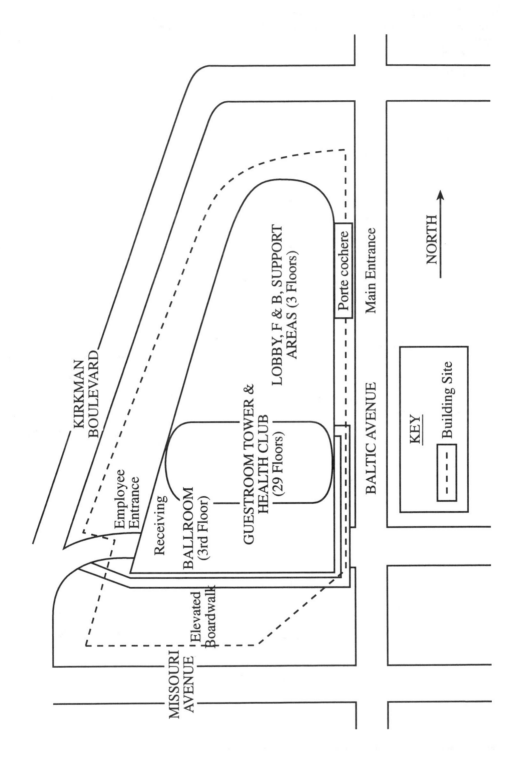

EXHIBIT 2. DEMAND GENERATORS GRID

Hotel: Hotel Americana

Outlet: Main Street Grille

Date: January 2, 1996

Target Markets

Delivery Systems	Weekday					Weekend	
	Monday	Tuesday	Wednesday	Thursday	Friday	Saturday	Sunday
Breakfast	Convention Attendees Meeting Planners Hotel Guests Convention Center Staff Leisure Travelers	Convention Attendees Meeting Planners Hotel Guests Convention Center Staff Leisure Travelers	Convention Attendees Meeting Planners Hotel Guests Convention Center Staff Leisure Travelers	Convention Attendees Meeting Planners Hotel Guests Convention Center Staff Leisure Travelers	Convention Attendees Meeting Planners Hotel Guests Convention Center Staff Leisure Travelers	Convention Attendees Meeting Planners Hotel Guests Convention Center Staff Leisure Travelers Casino Overflow	N/A
Brunch	N/A	N/A	N/A	N/A	N/A	N/A	Convention Attendees Meeting Planners Hotel Guests Convention Center Staff Leisure Travelers Casino Overflow A.C. Residents Corridor Visitors
Lunch	Convention Attendees Meeting Planners Hotel Guests Convention Center Staff Corridor Visitors Purveyors Leisure Travelers	Convention Attendees Meeting Planners Hotel Guests Convention Center Staff Corridor Visitors Purveyors Leisure Travelers	Convention Attendees Meeting Planners Hotel Guests Convention Center Staff Corridor Visitors Purveyors Leisure Travelers	Convention Attendees Meeting Planners Hotel Guests Convention Center Staff Corridor Visitors Purveyors Leisure Travelers	Convention Attendees Meeting Planners Hotel Guests Convention Center Staff Corridor Visitors Purveyors Leisure Travelers	Convention Attendees Meeting Planners Hotel Guests Convention Center Staff Leisure Travelers Casino Overflow Corridor Visitors Purveyors	N/A
Dinner	Convention Attendees Meeting Planners Hotel Guests Corridor Visitors Leisure Travelers	Convention Attendees Meeting Planners Hotel Guests Corridor Visitors Leisure Travelers	Convention Attendees Meeting Planners Hotel Guests Corridor Visitors Leisure Travelers	Convention Attendees Meeting Planners Hotel Guests Corridor Visitors Leisure Travelers	Convention Attendees Meeting Planners Hotel Guests Corridor Visitors Leisure Travelers A.C. Residents	Convention Attendees Meeting Planners Hotel Guests Leisure Travelers A.C. Residents Corridor Visitors	Convention Attendees Meeting Planners Hotel Guests Leisure Travelers A.C. Residents Corridor Visitors

EXHIBIT 3. CONCEPT GRID

Hotel: Hotel Americana
Outlet: Main Street Grille

Date: January 2, 1996

Delivery Systems	Target Markets						
	Conventioneers	Leisure Market	Convention Center Staff	Meeting Planners	Casino Overflow	Purveyors	Atlantic City Residents
	Adjectives						
Breakfast	Quick Service Good Value Good Service Convenience Bright, friendly atmosphere	Good Value Good Service Convenience Bright, friendly atmosphere	Quick Service Good Value Good Service Convenience Bright, friendly atmosphere	Quick Service Good Value Good Service Convenience Bright, friendly atmosphere	Quick Service Good Value Good Service Convenience Bright, friendly atmosphere	Quick Service Good Value Good Service Convenience Bright, friendly atmosphere	Brunch
Lunch	Quick Service Good Value Good Service Convenience Bright, friendly atmosphere	Quick Service Good Value Good Service Convenience Bright, friendly atmosphere	Quick Service Good Value Good Service Convenience Bright, friendly atmosphere	Quick Service Good Value Good Service Convenience Bright, friendly atmosphere	N/A	Quick Service Good Value Good Service Convenience Bright, friendly atmosphere	Brunch Good Value Good Service Convenience Bright, friendly atmosphere
Dinner	Relaxation Entertainment Good Value* Good Service Convenience Bright, friendly atmosphere	Relaxation Entertainment Good Value Good Service Convenience Bright, friendly atmosphere	N/A	Entertainment Relaxation Good Value Good Service Convenience Bright, friendly atmosphere	N/A	Entertainment Relaxation Good Value Good Service Convenience Bright, friendly atmosphere	Entertainment Relaxation Good Value Good Service Convenience Bright, friendly atmosphere

*—Denotes a high (Food + Beverage + Service + Atmosphere) Price

Exhibit 4

Hotel Americana

Main Street Grille

AMERICANA'S GOOD OLD AMERICAN CUISINE

Wake-Up Call

(Breakfast)

Open from 7:00 am - 11:00 pm
Monday - Saturday
Sunday Brunch 10:00 am - 2:30 pm

MAIN STREET GRILLE
AMERICANA'S GOOD OLD AMERICAN CUISINE
WAKE UP CALL

THE BROADWAY BAR   12.50

"Wake up in the City that Never Sleeps":

Includes:

Omelet Bar

Select your favorite toppings and let our chef prepare an omelet fit for the stars. Or have the chef simply prepare your eggs to order.

Yogurt & Fruit Bar

For the healthy at heart, stop at this station on the bar for an amazing assortment of yogurts and seasonal fresh fruit.

Bagel Bar

What would the Broadway experience be without the favorite food of New Yorkers. Choose from a variety of bagels and top with assorted cream cheeses.

Pastry Bar

For your sweet tooth. Freshly baked by our renowned pastry chef.

Juice Bar

Enjoy our variety of fruit and vegetable homestyle juices.

UPTOWN/DOWNTOWN

1. Two eggs any style served with your choice of bacon, sausage or ham, home fries, and toast or biscuits. $7.50

2. Full stack of our famous hot cakes, available with fresh fruit toppings and an assortment of syrups. Served with your choice of bacon, sausage, or ham. $6.00

3. Belgian Waffle with strawberries and whipped cream, or choose from our assortment of syrups. Served with your choice of bacon, sausage, or ham. $6.75

4. French Toast, served with butter and an assortment of syrups. Served with your choice of bacon, sausage, or ham. $6.00

Coffee is included with all entrees and Broadway Bar Selections

MAIN STREET GRILLE
AMERICANA'S GOOD OLD AMERICAN CUISINE
WAKE UP CALL

A LA CARTE:

Egg to order	$2.50
Four Strips of Bacon	$2.00
Four Sausage Links	$2.25
Country Ham	$2.25
Home fries	$1.85
Toast or Biscuit	$1.25
Juice	$2.50
Coffee	$2.00
Tea	$1.50
Milk	$1.50

SUNDAY BRUNCH $18.50

Experierice a feast from our Broadway Bar. Choose from the assortment
of goodies or just have them all. Sparkling wine is included!

EXHIBIT 5

Hotel Americana

Main Street Grille

AMERICANA'S GOOD OLD AMERICAN CUISINE

Town Meeting

(Lunch)

Open from 7:00 am - 11:00 pm
Monday-Saturday
Sunday Brunch 10:00 am - 2:30 pm

MAIN STREET GRILLE
AMERICANA'S GOOD OLD AMERICAN CUISINE
TOWN MEETING

SANDWICH SELECTIONS

Choose from our array of deli fixings, fresh rolls, and scrumptious
toppings from our Broadway Bar. Includes soup of the day and coffee or
soda. $10.50

SOUP SELECTIONS

New England Clam Chowder $4.50
Cincinnati Style Chili $5.00
Farmer's Vegetarian Chili $5.00
Homestyle Chicken Noodle $4.25

FARMER'S MARKET

Cheasapeake Crab Louie $13.35

> Chesapeake lump crab meat over lettuce greens with hard-boiled egg,
> black olives: and tomato wedges. (Seasonal)

California Cobb Salad $9.50

> Chicken, bacon, tomato, and avocado over lettuce greens with fresh
> mushrooms, chopped hard-boiled egg and served with the Americana
> house dressing.

Caesar Salad $10.95

> With your choice of grilled chicken, jumbo shrimp, or steak.

Popeye's Spinach Salad $9.50

> Crisp spinach leave, bacon, fresh mushrooms, and Parmesan cheese
> served with our Americana house dressing.

MAIN STREET GRILLE
AMERICANA'S GOOD OLD AMERICAN CUISINE
TOWN MEETING

MAIN STREET

Philly Cheese Steak	$11.50

Just like they do it in the City of Brotherly Love, sizzlin' steak meat with melted provolone cheese on a toasted roll, with the works!

California Vegetable Garden Pita	$10.50

Mushroom, bean sprouts, green peppers, tomatoes, and onions packed lovingly into a pita pocket and smothered with Monterey Jack cheese.

The Lone Star	$11.50

Pulled barbecue pork with a tangy sauce heaped upon a crusty kaiser roll.

The Loan Shark	$10.50

Just what you need in Atlantic City. White albacore tuna with provolone cheese, grilled on your choice of fresh bread.

City Hall Jumbo Burger	$11.50

This one is full of promises, it will satisfy any appetite. One-third of a pound of ground choice sirloin, served with your choice of toppings.

The Santa Fe Grilled Chicken	$12.00

Lightly grilled chicken breast served with a delectable olive oil, cilantro, and hot chile sauce.

All Main Street items will be served with your choice of
spicy fries, boardwalk fries, cole slaw, or potato salad.

SIDE STREETS

Memphis Onion Loaf	$5.50
Spicy Fries	$3.50
Boardwalk Fries	$3.25
Cole Slaw	$3.25
Potato Salad	$3.75

MAIN STREET GRILLE
AMERICANA'S GOOD OLD AMERICAN CUISINE
TOWN MEETING

LAST RESORTS

Ben and Jerry's Ice Cream $4.75
    Assorted flavors, please ask your server for today's selections.

Billy's Brownies $4.50
    Brownie sandwich with your choice of ice cream and toppings.

Fruity Delight $3.75
    Seasonal fruit compote.

EXHIBIT 6

Hotel Americana

Main Street Grille

AMERICANA'S GOOD OLD AMERICAN CUISINE

Avenue of the Americas

(Dinner)

Open from 7:00 am - 11:00 pm
Monday-Saturday
Sunday Brunch 10:00 am - 2:30 pm

MAIN STREET GRILLE
AMERICANA'S GOOD OLD AMERICAN CUISINE
AVENUE OF THE AMERICAS

ON RAMPS

Buffalo Style Chicken Legs	$9.50
Mozzarella Cheese with Raspberry Sauce	$8.00
Shrimp Cocktail	$10.50
Wisconsin Cheese Plate	$7.50
Clams Casino	$9.50
Potato Skins	$7.50

THE MELTING POT

New England Clam Chowder	$5.75
Chicken Consommé	$5.25
Chunky Vegetable Soup	$5.25
Cream of Broccoli Soup	$5.50
Idaho Potato Leek Soup	$5.50

THE HEARTLAND

Chicken Sesame Salad $11.95

Tender chicken with sweet and sour dressing, toasted slivered almonds, and diced celery over Romaine lettuce topped with toasted sesame seeds.

Shrimp Louie $12.50

Bay shrimp over lettuce greens with hard-boiled egg, black olives, and tomato wedges.

Crab Louie $12.85

Maryland crab over lettuce greens with hard-boiled eggs, black olives, and tomato wedges.

Jambalaya Salad $12.50

Cajun rice with anduille sausage over mixed greens.

Mixed Greens $6.50

Boston Bib lettuce, Romaine lettuce, and Red Tip lettuce served with a fresh array of garden vegetables and topped with Americana's house dressing.

MAIN STREET GRILLE
AMERICANA'S GOOD OLD AMERICAN CUISINE
AVENUE OF THE AMERICAS

ANY TOWN U.S.A.

Northwest Salmon $19.00
> Poached and served with a dill hollandaise sauce.

Maryland Soft Shelled Crab (Seasonal) $20.30
> Batter dipped and gently fried served with a selection of seasoned vegetables.

Marlin Merlot $18.75
> Not quite, but it is an eight ounce tuna steak char-grilled to perfection served with a Merlot sauce.

From the Plains to the Gulf $22.50
> Eight ounce tenderloin served with three jumbo shrimp scampi.

Pork Tenderloin Medallions $19.50
> Sautéed with green onions, tomatoes, and shallots, seasoned with fresh basil.

Southwest Chicken $17.25
> A lightly sautéed eight ounce chicken breast breaded in corn meal, chile, and cilantro.

Pepper Steak $20.50
> A New York steak carefully char-broiled with peppercorns served with green peppercorn sauce.

Stir Fried Vegetables over Linguini or Angel Hair Pasta $15.75
> Your choice of the freshest market vegetables stir fried to perfection and served over a bed of pasta.

All entrees are served with the chef's choice of rice,
potatoes, or pasta and today's vegetable.

MAIN STREET GRILLE
AMERICANA'S GOOD OLD AMERICAN CUISINE
AVENUE OF THE AMERICAS

NO TURNING BACK

Mississippi Mud Pie		$5.75
Concord Grape Pie		$5.00
Shoofly Pie		$5.25
Basket of Jumbo Chocolate Chip Cookies	Per Person:	$2.00
One batch serves the whole bunch.		
All American Apple Pie		$5.25
Served with vanilla ice cream		
Southern Praline Cheesecake		$5.75
Chocolate Mousse Pie		$5.50
Ben and Jerry's Ice Cream		$4.50
Ask your server for today's flavors.		

BEVERAGES

Coffee	$1.75
Tea	$1.50
Soft Drinks	$1.25
Sparkling Waters	$2.50
Juice of the Day	$2.25

Please refer to our wine and beer list to choose from an all
American wine and beer selection.

EXHIBIT 7

Hotel Americana

Main Street Grille

Wine List

MAIN STREET GRILLE
AMERICANA'S GOOD OLD AMERICAN CUISINE
WINE LIST
WHITE WINES

BIN #	HALF BOTTLE	FULL BOTTLE
CALIFORNIA		
1. Chappellet Chenin Blanc Nappa Valley Dry 1991		$18.75
2. Pine Ridge Chenin Blanc		$21.00
3. Pine Ridge Chardonnay 1992	$22.50	
4. Gundlach Bundschu Sonoma County Chardonnay 1991		$30.00
5. Matanzas Creek Chardonnay Sonoma Valley 1991		$43.00
NEW YORK		
6. Wagner Gewurtztraminer Finger Lakes 1989		$25.00
7. Wagner Chardonnay Finger Lakes Barrel Fermented 1988		$32.00
8. Bridgehampton Chardonnay Long Island 1990		$42.90
OREGON		
9. Oak Knoll Chardonnay, Willamette Valley 1990		$30.00
10. Ponzi Chardonnay, Willamette Valley 1990		$30.75
11. Cameron Chardonnay, Willamette Valley 1990		$34.50
WASHINGTON		
12. Columbia Semillon Columbia Valley 1992		$18.00
13. Arbor Crest Semillon Columbia Valley Dionysus Vineyard 1992		$18.75
14. Arbor Crest Sauvignon Blanc Columbia Valley 1990		$19.50
15. Chateau Ste. Michelle Sauvignon Blanc Columbia Valley 1992		$22.50
16. Covey Run Chardonnay Yakima Valley Reserve 1990		$34.25

MAIN STREET GRILLE
AMERICANA'S GOOD OLD AMERICAN CUISINE
WINE LIST
RED WINES

BIN #	HALF BOTTLE	FULL BOTTLE
CALIFORNIA		
17. Iron Horse Pinot Noir 1989		$36.50
18. Audubon Collection Audubon Rouge		$18.00
19. Pine Ridge Rutherford Cabernet 1990		$23.75
20. Clos Pegase Hommage 1990		$43.00
21. Windsor North Coast Petit Syrah 1990		$25.00
OREGON		
22. Firesteed Pinot Noir Oregon 1992		$22.50
23. Sokol Blosser Pinot Noir, Hyland Vineyards 1987		$32.00
24. Veritas Pinor Noir Willamette Valley 1990		$36.50
25. Domaine Drouhin Pinot Noir Oregon 1990		$43.75
26. Seven Hills Cabernet Sauvignon Oregon, Walla Walla Valley 1990		$43.00
WASHINGTON		
27. Kiona Yakima Valley E.B. Lemberger 1990		$24.90
28. Apex Merlot Columbia Valley 1990		$32.00
29. Columbia Crest Merlot Columbia Valley Barrel Select 1989		$32.00
30. Leonetti Merlo Washington 1991		$47.00
31. Columbia Crest Columbia Valley Cabernet Sauvignon 1990		$25.00

MAIN STREET GRILLE
AMERICANA'S GOOD OLD AMERICAN CUISINE
WINE LIST
SPARKLING WINES

BIN #	HALF BOTTLE	FULL BOTTLE
CALIFORNIA		
32. Ballatore Gran Spumante		$12.00
33. Mumm Napa Valley Reserve Cuvee Nape Valley 1989		$38.75
34. Jordan J. Sonoma County 1989		$40.00
35. Iron Horse "Vrais Amis"		$43.00
NEW YORK		
36. Gold Seal Blanc de Blancs American Charles Fournier Special Selection NV		$25.00
37. Glenora Blanc de Blancs 1989		$32.00
38. Chateau Frank Brut Finger Lakes 1987		$38.75
OREGON		
39. Argyle Brut Oregon Cuvee Limited 1987		$39.75
WASHINGTON		
40. Domaine Ste. Michelle Blanc de Noir Columbia Valley 1987		$42.90

MAIN STREET GRILLE
AMERICANA'S GOOD OLD AMERICAN CUISINE
WINE LIST
DESSERT WINES

BIN #	HALF BOTTLE	FULL BOTTLE
CALIFORNIA		
41. Bonny Doon Muscat Canelli Monterey County Vin de Glacier 1992	$32.00	
42. Chateau St. Jean Johannisberg Riesling Late Harvest Alexander Valley Special Select 1989	$41.75	
NEW YORK		
43. Wagner Johannisberg Riesling Finger Lakes Late Harvest Ice Wine 1989	$35.00	
OREGON		
44. Bonny Doon Framboise (Oregon Raspberries)	$18.75	

Wines by the Glass

RED WINES

Hearty Burgundy	Merlot	Cabernet Sauvignon
$4.75	$5.50	$5.75

WHITE WINES

California Chablis	Sauvignon Blanc	Chardonnay
$4.75	$5.50	$6.00

ROSÉ

$4.75

MAIN STREET GRILLE
AMERICANA'S GOOD OLD AMERICAN CUISINE
BEER LIST

BOTTLES

Brooklyn Brown Ale (New York)	$3.75
Ballard Bitter (Washington)	$3.75
Samuel Adams Lager (Massachusetts)	$3.00
Anchor Liberty Ale (California)	$4.00
Dominion Stout (Virginia)	$3.00
Catamount Porter (Vermont)	$3.00
Geary's Pale Ale (Maine)	$3.75
Budweiser	$2.50
Budweiser Light	$2.50
McTarnahan's Scottish Ale (Oregon)	$3.00
Terminator Stout (Oregon)	$4.00
Coors (Colorado)	$2.50
Rolling Rock (Pennsylvania)	$2.75
Garten Brau Wild Rice Beer (Wisconsin)	$4.00
Henry Weinhardt's Private Reserve (Oregon)	$2.75

DRAUGHT

Budweiser	$2.00
Budweiser Light	$2.00
Samuel Adams Lager	$2.75

TABLE 5. HOTEL AMERICANA ARCHITECTURAL SPACE PROGRAM (SQUARE FEET)

Guest Room Mix (Size)	# of Keys	# of Bays	Americana Net	Americana Gross	% of Total Rooms
• King (338 sq. ft)	210	210	70,980		28.0%
• Double-doubles (338 sq. ft)	460	460	155,480		61.3%
• Handicapped (338 sq. ft.)	15	15	5,070		2.0%
• Suites					
– 2-Bay Suites (Total of 35)	35	70	23,660		4.7%
– 3-Bay Suites (Total of 20)	20	60	20,280		2.7%
– 3-Bay Suites (Total of 10)	10	30	10,140		1.3%
(optional second bedroom)					
Total	750	845	285,610	428,415	100.0%

Lobby	Americana Net	Americana Gross	% of Americana
• Flow Area	6,600		
• Seating	1,100		
• Assistant Manager Support	120		
– Bellman Station	120		
– Telephones	75		
– Toilets	500		
Total	7,940	9,925	1.6%

Public Spaces	Americana Net	Americana Gross	% of Americana
• Retail (Second Floor)	1,800		
• Atrium (Second Floor)	4,000		
• Lobby, Toilets, Telephones	2,700		
Total	8,500	9,625	1.6%

Food & Beverage	Americana Net	Americana Gross	% of Americana
• Bistro (Coffee Shop-Second Floor)	4,000		
• Sfuzzi's (Theme Restaurant-Second Floor)	3,800		
• Bayou Lounge	3,500		
Total	11,300	14,125	2.3%

Function Areas—Second Floor	Americana Net	Americana Gross	% of Americana
• Ballroom	15,000		
• Ballroom Foyer	4,000		
• Junior Ballroom	10,000		
• Junior Ballroom Foyer	2,500		
• Banquet Rooms 2 @ 4,000 sq. ft (Each divisible into 4)	8,000		
• Boardroom(s) 2 @ 900 sq. ft.	1,800		
• Support:			
– Business Office	450		
– Function Room Storage	4,000		
– Audiovisual Equipment Storage	150		
– Convention Registration	200		
– Projection Booth	325		
– Banquet Captain's Office	150		
– Toilets, Coats, Telephones	400		
Total	46,975	58,719	9.6%

Administration	Americana Net	Americana Gross	% of Americana
Front Office			
• Front Desk	550		
• Front Office Manager	120		
• Assistant Manager	120		
• Credit Manager	100		
• Director of Rooms	150		
• Reception Secretary	100		
• Reservations Area	225		
• Reservations Manager	120		
• Telephone Operators	175		
• Fire Control Room	120		
• Bellman Storage	250		
• Safe Deposit Boxes	60		
• General Cashier	120		
• Count Room	175		
• Work Area/Mail	125		
• Storage	100		
Sub-Total	2,610	3,263	0.5%
Executive Office (Second Floor)			
• Reception/Waiting	300		
• General Manager	300		
• Executive Assistant Manager	200		
• Resident Manager	200		
• Food & Beverage Manager	170		
• Secretary	180		
• Conference Room	230		
• Copying and Storage	100		
Sub-Total	1,680	2,100	0.3%
Sales and Catering (Second Floor)			
• Reception/Waiting	250		
• Director of Sales	185		
• Sales Representatives	450		
• Director of Public Relations	150		
• Secretary	300		
• Catering Manager	185		
• Banquet Manager	170		
• Banquet Representatives	150		
• Function Book Room	100		
• Beverage Manager	120		
• Convention Services	180		
• Secretary	190		
• Copying and Storage	185		
Sub-Total	2,615	3,269	0.5%
Accounting (Second Floor)			
• Reception Waiting	120		
• Controller	165		
• Assistant Controller/Auditor	110		
• Accounting Work Area	700		
• Payroll Manager	145		
• Secretary	110		
• Copying and Storage	250		
• Computer Room	135		
• Dead Files	160		
Sub-Total	1,895	2,369	0.4%
Total	8,800	11,000	1.8%

Food Preparation	Americana Net	Americana Gross	% of Americana
• Main Kitchen (Second Floor)	10,000		
• Banquet Pantry (Third Floor)	1,500		
• Bayou Lounge Pantry (First Floor)	1,500		
• Sfuzzi's kitchen (Second Floor)	3,500		
• Bakery Shop (Second Floor)	900		
• Room Service Area (Second Floor)	400		
• Chef's Office (Second Floor)	120		
• Dry Food Storage (Second Floor)	1,400		
• Rerfrigerated Food Storage (Second Floor)	1,000		
• Beverage Storage (Second Floor)	1,500		
• Refrigerated Beverage Storage (Second Floor)	325		
• China, Silver, Glass Storage (Second Floor)	750		
• Food Controller Office (Second Floor)	120		
• Toilets (Second Floor)	150		
Total	23,165	28,956	4.7%

Receiving & Storage	Americana Net	Americana Gross	% of Americana
• Loading Dock	600		
• Receiving Area	800		
• Receiving Office	150		
• Purchasing Office	188		
• Locked Storage	188		
• Empty Bottle Storage	138		
• Trash Holding Area	225		
• Refrigerated Garbage	110		
• Can Wash	120		
• Compactor	200		
• Grounds Equipment Storage	350		
• General Storage	3,000		
Total	6,069	7,586	1.2%

Employee Areas	Americana Net	Americana Gross	% of Americana
Personnel			
• Timekeeper	120		
• Security	120		
• Personnel/Reception	175		
• Human Resource Manager	150		
• Assistant HR Manager	120		
• Interview Room	150		
• Training Room	238		
• Files and Storage	90		
• First Aid	125		
Sub-Total	1,288	1,610	0.3%
Employee Facilities			
• Men's Lockers/Toilets	1,300		
• Women's Lockers/Toilets	1,500		
• Banquet/Kitchen Staff Lockers	500		
• Employee Cafeteria	1,400		
Sub-Total	4,700	5,875	1.0%
Total	5,988	7,485	1.2%

Laundry & Housekeeping	Americana Net	Americana Gross	% of Americana
Laundry			
• Soiled Linen Room	250		
• Laundry	3,300		
• Laundry Supervisor	110		
• Valet Laundry	175		
• Supplies Storage	150		
Sub-Total	3,985	4,981	0.8%
Housekeeping			
• Housekeeper	138		
• Assistant Housekeeper	110		
• Secretary	100		
• Linen Storage	2,000		
• Uniform Issue/Storage	650		
• Supplies Storage	150		
• Lost and Found	175		
• Sewing Room	150		
Sub-Total	3,473	4,341	0.7%
Total	7,458	9,323	1.5%

Engineering	Americana Net	Americana Gross	% of Americana
• Engineer	150		
• Assistant Engineer	100		
• Secretary	100		
• Carpentry Shop	200		
• Plumbing Shop	200		
• Electrical Shop	200		
• Paint Shop	200		
• TV Repair Shop	150		
• Key Shop	90		
• Energy Management Computer	120		
• Engineering Storeroom	900		
Total	2,410	3,013	0.5%

Mechanical Areas	Americana Net	Americana Gross	% of Americana
• Mechanical Plant	5,500		
• Transformer Room	1,250		
• Emergency Generator(s)	400		
• Meter Room	125		
• Fire Pumps	150		
• Electrical Switchboard	875		
• Elevator Machine Room	600		
• Telephone Equipment Room	650		
Total	9,550	11,938	2.0%

Recreation	Americana Net	Americana Gross	% of Americana
• Swimming Pool	2,000		
• Pool Including Deck	3,500		
• Sun Deck	2,000		
• Whirlpool	150		
• Lockers, Toilets, Sauna	750		
• Exercise Room	2,000		
• Game Room	400		
• Manager's Office	150		
• Attendant	90		
• Equipment Storage	375		
• Pool Pump/Filter	200		
• Children's Playroom	400		
Total	10,015	12,519	2.0%

First Floor Surface Area (Gross):	58,781	
Second Floor Surface Area (Gross):	53,319	
Third Floor Surface Area (Gross):	58,719	
Rooftop Surface Area (Gross):	12,519	
Single Guestroom Floor Surface Area (Gross):	15,301	
Total # of Guestroom Floors (Excl. Rooftop):	28	

	Gross Area	**% Americana**
Guestroom Surface Area:	428,415	70.0%
Public Surface Area (Including Offices):	106,288	17.4%
Administration:	11,000	1.8%
Back of House:	68,300	11.2%
Kitchens & Storage:	28,956	4.7%
Total Area Gross:	611,753	100%

Assumptions and Calculations Appendix

	Bays
35 * 2 Bay-Suites, 1 rentable unit each:	70
20 * 3 Bay-Suites, 1 rentable unit each:	60
10 * 4 Bay-Suites, 2 rentable units each:	40
Total	170
Add 675 Single Bays, 1 Rentable Unit Each:	675
Total	845
Bay Area Lost Per Floor (Elevator, Ice, Linen):	4
Total Rentable Bay Area Lost Per Building:	112
Total # Bays Needed For the Hotel:	957

Table 6. Staffing Plan

ROOMS DEPARTMENT

Position	# of Emp.	1996 Base Salary	Hours/ Week	Week/ Year	Total Yearly Salary	Total Salary(s) & Benefits	% of Total
Front Office Manager	1	$46,000.00	N/A	N/A	$46,000	$ 57,500	0.5%
Assistant Front Office Manager	1	$25,000.00	N/A	N/A	$25,000	$ 31,250	0.3%
Front Office Supervisor(s)	4	$ 9.50	40	50	$19,000	$ 95,000	0.8%
Cashiers	7	$ 7.50	40	50	$15,000	$ 131,250	1.1%
Front Desk Clerks	20	$ 8.00	40	50	$16,000	$ 400,000	3.3%
Reservations Manager	1	$36,000.00	N/A	N/A	$36,000	$ 45,000	0.4%
Reservations Clerk(s)	4	$ 8.00	40	50	$16,000	$ 80,000	0.7%
Concierge/Guest Services	4	$ 9.00	40	50	$18,000	$ 90,000	0.7%
Chief Bellman	1	$20,000.00	N/A	N/A	$20,000	$ 25,000	0.2%
Bell Captain(s)	4	$ 7.25	40	50	$14,500	$ 72,500	0.6%
Bellmen	15	$ 5.00	40	50	$10,000	$ 187,500	1.5%
Messengers	5	$ 7.00	40	50	$14,000	$ 87,500	0.7%
Doormen	5	$ 5.00	40	50	$10,000	$ 62,500	0.5%
Van Drivers	10	$ 7.00	40	50	$14,000	$ 175,000	1.4%
Telephone Department Head	1	$27,000.00	N/A	N/A	$27,000	$ 33,750	0.3%
Chief Phone Operator(s)	4	$ 9.50	40	50	$19,000	$ 95,000	0.8%
Operator(s)	14	$ 7.50	40	50	$15,000	$ 262,500	2.1%
Head Housekeeper	1	$29,000.00	N/A	N/A	$29,000	$ 36,250	0.3%
Assistant Housekeeper	2	$ 10.25	40	50	$20,500	$ 51,250	0.4%
Floor Supervisors	10	$ 9.25	40	50	$18,500	$ 231,250	1.9%
Maids/Housemen	64	$ 7.65	40	50	$15,300	$1,219,219	9.9%
Laundry Manager	1	$ 10.00	40	50	$20,000	$ 25,000	0.2%
Laundry Supervisors	4	$ 9.25	40	50	$18,500	$ 92,500	0.8%
General Laundry	28	$ 7.65	40	50	$15,300	$ 535,500	4.4%
TOTAL	211					$4,122,219	33.6%

FOOD AND BEVERAGE DEPARTMENT

Position	# of Emp.	1996 Base Salary	Hours/ Week	Week/ Year	Total Yearly Salary	Total Salary(s) & Benefits	% of Total
Food and Beverage Director	1	$70,000.00	N/A	N/A	$70,000	$ 87,500	0.7%
Assistant F&B Director	1	$40,000.00	N/A	N/A	$40,000	$ 50,000	0.4%
Purchasing Agent	1	$35,000.00	N/A	N/A	$35,000	$ 43,750	0.4%
Store Room Clerk(s)	5	$ 8.50	40	50	$17,000	$106,250	0.9%
F & B Support Staff	6	$18,000.00	N/A	N/A	$18,000	$135,000	1.1%
Restaurant Manager(s)	2	$35,000.00	N/A	N/A	$35,000	$ 87,500	0.7%
Supervisors	9	$22,000.00	N/A	N/A	$22,000	$247,500	2.0%
Host/Hostess(es)	8	$ 7.70	40	50	$15,400	$154,000	1.3%
Cashier(s)	10	$ 7.00	40	50	$14,000	$175,000	1.4%
Waiters/Waitresses	90	$ 2.90	40	50	$ 5,800	$652,500	5.3%
Buspeople	28	$ 2.90	40	50	$ 5,800	$203,000	1.7%
Beverage Manager	1	$35,000.00	N/A	N/A	$35,000	$ 43,750	0.4%
Bartenders	9	$ 7.25	40	50	$14,500	$163,125	1.3%
Cocktail Waiters/Waitresses	12	$ 2.90	40	50	$ 5,800	$ 87,000	0.7%
Catering Manager(s)	2	$35,000.00	N/A	N/A	$35,000	$ 87,500	0.7%
Banquet Manager(s)	2	$28,000.00	N/A	N/A	$28,000	$ 70,000	0.6%
Banquet Captains	4	$ 7.70	40	50	$15,400	$ 77,000	0.6%
Room Service Manager	1	$35,000.00	N/A	N/A	$35,000	$ 43,750	0.4%
Room Service Captain(s)	4	$ 9.00	40	50	$18,000	$ 90,000	0.7%
Room Service Waiters	12	$ 3.75	40	50	$ 7,500	$112,500	0.9%
Executive Chef	1	$48,000.00	N/A	N/A	$48,000	$ 60,000	0.5%
Assistant Executive Chef	2	$38,000.00	N/A	N/A	$38,000	$ 95,000	0.8%
Hot Cook	13	$ 9.90	40	50	$19,800	$321,750	2.6%
Cold Cook	13	$ 7.90	40	50	$15,800	$256,750	2.1%
General Prep	20	$ 6.50	40	50	$13,000	$325,000	2.6%
Utility	12	$ 7.50	40	50	$15,000	$225,000	1.8%
Bake Shop	6	$ 8.90	40	50	$17,800	$133,500	1.1%
Executive Steward	1	$27,000.00	N/A	N/A	$27,000	$ 33,750	0.3%
Assistant Steward	4	$ 10.25	40	50	$20,500	$102,500	0.8%
Utility	14	$ 7.50	40	50	$15,000	$262,500	2.1%
TOTAL	294					$4,532,375	36.9%

ADMINISTRATIVE AND GENERAL DEPARTMENT

Position	# of Emp.	1996 Base Salary	Hours/ Week	Week /Year	Total Yearly Salary	Total Salary(s) & Benefits	% of Total
General Manager	1	$114,000.00	N/A	N/A	$114,000	$142,500	1.2%
Executive Assistant	1	$ 31,000.00	N/A	N/A	$ 31,000	$ 38,750	0.3%
Resident Manager (Lives In)	1	$ 83,000.00	N/A	N/A	$ 83,000	$103,750	0.8%
Executive Secretary	1	$ 22,000.00	N/A	N/A	$ 22,000	$ 27,500	0.2%
Receptionist	1	$ 9.50	40	50	$ 19,000	$ 23,750	0.2%
Health Club Receptionist(s)	3	$ 7.50	40	50	$ 15,000	$ 56,250	0.5%
Business Center Receptionist(s)	3	$ 8.00	40	50	$ 16,000	$ 60,000	0.5%
Controller	1	$ 73,000.00	N/A	N/A	$ 73,000	$ 91,250	0.7%
Assistant Controller	1	$ 33,000.00	N/A	N/A	$ 33,000	$ 41,250	0.3%
Auditor(s)	2	$ 22,000.00	N/A	N/A	$ 22,000	$ 55,000	0.4%
Credit Manager	1	$ 25,000.00	N/A	N/A	$ 25,000	$ 31,250	0.3%
Bookkeepers	3	$ 9.50	40	50	$ 19,000	$ 71,250	0.6%
Accounts Payable Clerks	3	$ 9.50	40	50	$ 19,000	$ 71,250	0.6%
Accounts Receivable Clerks	3	$ 9.50	40	50	$ 19,000	$ 71,250	0.6%
Payroll Clerks	3	$ 9.50	40	50	$ 19,000	$ 71,250	0.6%
Director of Human Resources	1	$ 55,000.00	N/A	N/A	$ 55,000	$ 68,750	0.6%
Benefits Manager	1	$ 33,000.00	N/A	N/A	$ 33,000	$ 41,250	0.3%
Recruitment Manager	1	$ 33,000.00	N/A	N/A	$ 33,000	$ 41,250	0.3%
Training Manager	1	$ 33,000.00	N/A	N/A	$ 33,000	$ 41,250	0.3%
Human Resources Staff	3	$ 20,000.00	N/A	N/A	$ 20,000	$ 75,000	0.6%
Secretary	1	$ 19,000.00	N/A	N/A	$ 19,000	$ 23,750	0.2%
Chief of Security	1	$ 40,000.00	N/A	N/A	$ 40,000	$ 50,000	0.4%
Security Officers	12	$ 12.50	40	50	$ 24,000	$360,000	2.9%
TOTAL	49					$1,657,500	13.5%

SALES & MARKETING DEPARTMENT

Position	# of Emp.	1996 Base Salary	Hours/ Week	Week/ Year	Total Yearly Salary	Total Salary(s) & Benefits	% of Total
Director of Sales & Marketing	1	$71,540.00	N/A	N/A	$71,540	$ 89,425	0.7%
Sales Manager	2	$45,045.00	N/A	N/A	$45,045	$ 112,613	0.9%
Public Relations Director	1	$40,000.00	N/A	N/A	$40,000	$ 50,000	0.4%
Convention Services Manager	2	$35,770.00	N/A	N/A	$35,770	$ 89,425	0.7%
Floor Managers	2	$29,145.00	N/A	N/A	$29,145	$ 72,863	0.6%
Administrative Assistant	2	$25,170.00	N/A	N/A	$25,170	$ 62,925	0.5%
Housemen	30	$ 10.60	40	50	$21,200	$ 795,000	6.5%
TOTAL	40					$1,272,250	10.4%

PROPERTY OPERATION AND MAINTENANCE DEPARTMENT

Position	# of Emp.	1996 Base Salary	Hours/ Week	Week/ Year	Total Yearly Salary	Total Salary(s) & Benefits	% of Total
Chief Engineer	1	$59,000.00	N/A	N/A	$59,000	$ 73,750	0.6%
Assistant Engineer	1	$30,000.00	N/A	N/A	$30,000	$ 37,500	0.3%
Maintenance Engineers	17	$ 12.50	40	50	$24,992	$531,081	4.3%
Secretary(s)	2	$ 9.00	40	50	$18,000	$ 45,000	0.4%
TOTAL	21					$687,331	5.6%

GRAND TOTAL:

TOTAL NUMBER OF EMPLOYEES: 615

TOTAL SALARY & BENEFITS: $12,271,674

EXHIBIT 8

TIME LINE FOR HOTEL AMERICANA HUMAN RESOURCE PLANNING

<u>1994</u>

March — Management Company announces:
  General Manager
  Director of Sales and Marketing

August — Executive Committee is announced:
  Director of Food and Beverage
  Director of Human Resources
  Comptroller
  Executive Chef
  Resident Manager
  Chief Engineer
Also announced sales staff

October 1 — Executive meeting to discuss Hotel Americana's philosophy and mission statement.

October — Human Resource department hires:
  Recruitment Manager
  Benefits Manager
  Training Manager

December — Human Resources Department Proposes: Mission Statement
Staffing Proposal approved by Executive Committee

<u>1995</u>

March — Job Analyses and Job Descriptions proposed
Recruitment Plan formalized by Human Resource team.
Begin developing a relationship with local Hospitality Schools and place ads in their Career Development Offices

May — Recruitment for management positions begins
Ads in Trade Associations and Job Banks
Ads in Philadelphia Inquirer, New York Times, Atlantic City Press are placed

June-August — Develop interview questions and standardized evaluation system for management positions
Interviewer training management for Search Committees
Preliminary and Secondary Screening for management positions

August — Candidacy phase for management positions

Sept.-Oct. — Verification and Final selection phases of management positions

October — Management team in place

November — Visit Senior Homes and Group Homes and talk about the job opportunities at Hotel Americana

	Post jobs with counselors Place ads in Newspapers for supervisory positions Develop interview questions and standardized evaluation system for supervisory positions Interviewer training for management staff
December	Preliminary and Secondary Screening and Candidacy phases for supervisory positions

1996

January	Verification of supervisory applicants Place ads for clerical and service craft positions Post jobs listings in libraries and community centers Attend career day at Hospitality Schools in Atlantic City and in Philadelphia.
January 15	Final decision made for all supervisory positions
February 1-8	Supervisory staff in place Place ads on radio stations announcing open house. Place ads in newspapers announcing open house. Develop interview questions and standardized evaluation system for Clerical and Service Craft positions Interviewer training for supervisors Preliminary Screening for Clerical and Service Craft positions
February 8-10	Open House Secondary Screening for Clerical and Service Craft
February 11-15	Candidacy phase for Clerical and Service Craft
February 15-20	Verification and Final Decision is made for Clerical and Service Craft positions
February 20	First round of hires for clerical and service craft will be announced.
March	Second round of recruiting/selection will take place for any remaining positions
March 5-15	Training sessions for all new employees.
March 15	Soft opening of the hotel with initial staff.
March 30-April 15	Training of second round of hires.
April 15	Grand opening.

Dates are only estimates and are subject to change at any time.

TABLE 7: PROMOTIONAL STRATEGIES

Target Market	Elements Used
Convention/Meeting: **Planning Decision Makers** **Senior Secretaries** • Association Directors • Etc.	**Print Advertising** • Convention/Meeting Publications (Meeting News, Meetings and Conventions, Successful Meetings, etc.) • Association Publications (Convene, Executive Update, etc.) **Direct Mail Advertising** • Collateral Materials • Special Incentive Offers **Personal Selling** • National Sales Force • Hotel Americana Sales Force **Merchandising** • Business Center • Health Club • Airport/Boardwalk Shuttle Service **Public Relations/Publicity** • Redevelopment of Atlantic City • Opening of New Convention Center • Opening of Gateway Corridor, etc.
Leisure Travelers **(Non-Casino)**	**Advertising** • Newspaper Travel Sections **Sales Promotion** • Weekend Golf/Entertainment Packages • Room/Meals Packages **Public Relations/Publicity** • Redevelopment of Atlantic City • Opening of Gateway Corridor, etc. **Merchandising** • Health Club • Airport/Boardwalk Shuttle Service
Casino Overflow	**Merchandising** • Airport/Boardwalk Shuttle Service

TABLE 8. HOTEL AMERICANA PROJECT BUDGET OUTLINE

Budget Components	$	% of Total Budget
General Construction		
TOTAL	$73,700,000	57%
Furniture, Fixtures, & Equipment (FF&E)		
Interiors	$13,490,000	10%
Food Service Equipment	$3,329,969	3%
Other	$8,308,638	6%
TOTAL	$25,081,820	20%
Development Costs		
Architectural/Engineering Fees	$5,863,469	5%
Project Manager/Developer	$3,664,668	3%
Other Fees, Permits, Taxes	$6,972,275	5%
TOTAL	$16,500,412	13%
Financing During Construction		
TOTAL	$5,530,268	4%
Pre-Opening & Other Expenses		
Pre-Opening	$3,000,000	2%
Working Capital	$937,500	1%
Reserve Against Operating Shortfall	$3,750,000	3%
TOTAL	$7,687,500	6%
Total Project Cost Excluding Acquisition of Land	$128,500,000	100%
Cost per Guestroom	$171,333	

Assumptions

Guidelines for the project budget were taken from Professor Richard Penner's lecture on November 3, 1993 and from HA 751: Project Development handouts (Fall Semester 1993)

The 6.5% financing rate was taken using current financing fees; it assumes that the inflation rate and the economic situation will remain steady.

TABLE 9. HOTEL AMERICANA PRO-FORMA INCOME STATEMENT

	Schedule #	1996		1997		1998		1999		Stabilized Year 2000	
Number of Rooms		750		750		750		750		750	
Occupancy Rate		64.29%		72.44%		78.07%		80.77%		81.95%	
ARR		$120.93		$126.20		$131.34		$136.81		$142.56	
Revenue											
Rooms	1	$21,282,986	60.53%	$25,025,972	61.17%	$28,069,861	61.48%	$30,251,444	61.50%	$31,975,735	61.39%
Food	2	7,760,108	22.07%	8,971,093	21.93%	10,023,036	21.95%	10,860,197	22.08%	11,591,986	22.26%
Beverage	2	3,223,042	9.17%	3,564,476	8.71%	3,877,584	8.49%	4,150,297	8.44%	4,405,080	8.46%
Other Food & Beverage	2	669,076	1.90%	786,745	1.92%	882,436	1.93%	951,018	1.93%	1,005,225	1.93%
Telephone	3	860,240	2.45%	1,011,529	2.47%	1,134,560	2.49%	1,222,738	2.49%	1,292,432	2.48%
Minor Operated Departments	4	637,215	1.81%	749,281	1.83%	840,415	1.84%	905,732	1.84%	957,357	1.84%
Rentals & Other Income	4	729,839	2.08%	800,628	1.96%	828,436	1.81%	848,650	1.73%	858,163	1.65%
Total Revenue		35,162,507	100.00%	40,909,724	100.00%	45,656,328	100.00%	49,190,075	100.00%	52,085,979	100.00%
Departmental Expenses											
Rooms	1	5,774,136	27.13%	6,609,942	26.41%	7,107,640	25.32%	7,415,726	24.51%	7,623,606	23.84%
Food & Beverage	2	10,563,836	90.66%	11,512,967	86.42%	12,085,454	81.75%	12,572,128	78.77%	13,018,894	76.57%
Telephone	3	593,566	69.00%	697,955	69.00%	782,847	69.00%	843,689	69.00%	891,738	69.00%
Other Departmental Expense	4	597,763	1.70%	695,465	1.70%	776,158	1.70%	836,231	1.70%	885,462	1.70%
Total Departmental Expense		17,529,300	49.85%	19,516,329	47.71%	20,752,099	45.45%	21,667,778	44.05%	22,419,739	43.04%
Departmental Profits											
Rooms	1	15,508,850	72.87%	18,416,030	73.59%	20,962,221	74.68%	22,835,714	75.49%	24,352,130	76.16%
Food & Beverage	2	1,088,390	9.34%	1,809,347	13.58%	2,697,601	18.25%	3,389,383	21.23%	3,983,398	23.43%
Telephone	3	266,675	31.00%	313,574	31.00%	351,714	31.00%	379,049	31.00%	400,654	31.00%
Other Departmental Profit	4	769,291	56.27%	854,444	55.13%	892,694	53.49%	918,151	52.33%	930,059	51.23%
Total Departmental Profit		17,633,207	50.15%	21,393,395	52.29%	24,904,229	54.55%	27,522,297	55.95%	29,666,240	56.96%
Undistributed Operating Expenses											
Administrative and General	5	5,119,775	14.56%	5,693,916	13.92%	6,185,336	13.55%	6,576,028	13.37%	6,915,609	13.28%
Marketing	6	2,242,997	6.38%	2,637,468	6.48%	2,958,261	6.48%	3,188,176	6.48%	3,369,898	6.47%
Energy and Utility Services	7	1,635,557	4.65%	1,915,890	4.68%	2,145,511	4.70%	2,314,674	4.71%	2,451,602	4.71%
Property Operations & Maintenance		1,793,288	5.10%	1,847,086	4.52%	1,902,499	4.17%	1,959,574	3.98%	2,018,361	3.88%
Total Undistributed Operating Expenses		10,791,617	30.69%	12,094,359	29.56%	13,191,607	28.89%	14,038,452	28.54%	14,755,470	28.33%
Income Before Fixed Charges		6,841,590	19.46%	9,299,035	22.73%	11,712,622	25.65%	13,483,845	27.41%	14,910,770	28.63%
Management Fees, Property Taxes and Insurance											
Management Fees		703,250	2.00%	818,194	2.00%	913,127	2.00%	1,320,898	2.69%	1,414,489	2.72%
Property Taxes		2,521,201	7.17%	2,616,886	6.40%	2,708,960	5.93%	2,819,088	5.73%	2,926,507	5.62%
Insurance		175,813	0.50%	204,549	0.50%	228,282	0.50%	245,950	0.50%	260,430	0.50%
Income Before Other Fixed Charges		6,138,339	17.46%	8,480,841	20.73%	10,799,496	23.65%	12,162,947	24.73%	13,496,281	25.91%

TABLE 9. HOTEL AMERICANA PRO-FORMA INCOME STATEMENT

	Schedule #	2001 750 82.48% $148.62		2002 750 89.41% $154.86		2003 696 84.59% $161.29		2004 741 84.13% $167.90		2005 750 84.60% $174.73	
Number of Rooms		750		750		696		741		750	
Occupancy Rate		82.48%		89.41%		84.59%		84.13%		84.60%	
ARR		$148.62		$154.86		$161.29		$167.90		$174.73	
Revenue											
Rooms	1	$33,555,447	61.24%	$35,174,461	61.04%	$36,900,949	60.94%	$38,667,444	60.81%	$40,468,387	60.66%
Food	2	12,297,457	22.44%	13,030,373	22.61%	13,807,550	22.80%	14,614,554	22.98%	15,449,263	23.16%
Beverage	2	4,658,397	8.50%	4,921,632	8.54%	5,198,498	8.59%	5,486,093	8.63%	5,784,119	8.67%
Other Food & Beverage	2	1,054,887	1.93%	1,105,784	1.92%	1,160,060	1.92%	1,215,593	1.91%	1,272,210	1.91%
Telephone	3	1,356,283	2.48%	1,421,722	2.47%	1,491,505	2.46%	1,562,906	2.46%	1,635,698	2.45%
Minor Operated Departments	4	1,004,654	1.83%	1,053,128	1.83%	1,104,819	1.82%	1,157,708	1.82%	1,211,628	1.82%
Rentals & Other Income	4	868,030	1.58%	917,816	1.59%	885,831	1.46%	884,230	1.39%	889,212	1.33%
Total Revenue		54,795,155	100.00%	57,624,917	100.00%	60,549,213	100.00%	63,588,518	100.00%	66,710,518	100.00%
Departmental Expenses											
Rooms	1	7,795,033	23.23%	8,203,461	23.32%	8,193,316	22.20%	8,346,041	21.58%	8,536,325	21.09%
Food & Beverage	2	13,459,076	74.73%	13,915,363	73.02%	14,394,998	71.38%	14,892,023	69.86%	15,405,717	68.45%
Telephone	3	935,835	69.00%	980,988	69.00%	1,029,139	69.00%	1,078,405	69.00%	1,128,632	69.00%
Other Departmental Expense	4	931,518	1.70%	979,624	1.70%	1,029,337	1.70%	1,081,005	1.70%	1,134,079	1.70%
Total Departmental Exense		23,121,462	42.20%	24,079,436	41.79%	24,646,790	40.71%	25,397,474	39.94%	26,204,752	39.28%
Departmental Profits											
Rooms	1	25,760,414	76.77%	26,971,000	76.68%	28,707,634	77.80%	30,321,403	78.42%	31,932,063	78.91%
Food & Beverage	2	4,551,665	25.27%	5,142,427	26.98%	5,771,109	28.62%	6,424,207	30.14%	7,099,875	31.55%
Telephone	3	420,448	31.00%	440,734	31.00%	462,367	31.00%	484,501	31.00%	507,066	31.00%
Other Departmental Profit	4	941,166	50.26%	991,320	50.30%	961,313	48.29%	960,933	47.06%	966,762	46.02%
Total Departmental Profit		31,673,693	57.80%	33,545,481	58.21%	35,902,423	59.29%	38,191,044	60.06%	40,505,766	60.72%
Undistributed Operating Expenses											
Administrative and General	5	7,243,084	13.22%	7,584,902	13.16%	7,939,373	13.11%	8,308,115	13.07%	8,688,644	13.02%
Marketing	6	3,536,382	6.45%	4,077,710	7.08%	4,277,859	7.07%	4,482,645	7.05%	4,691,425	7.03%
Energy and Utility Services	7	2,578,985	4.71%	2,703,831	4.69%	2,847,701	4.70%	2,991,257	4.70%	3,137,125	4.70%
Property Operations & Maintenance		2,078,912	3.79%	2,313,112	4.01%	2,219,952	3.67%	2,271,683	3.57%	2,339,834	3.51%
Total Undistributed Operating Expenses		15,437,364	28.17%	16,679,555	28.95%	17,284,884	28.55%	18,053,700	28.39%	18,857,028	28.27%
Income Before Fixed Charges		16,236,329	29.63%	16,865,926	29.27%	18,617,539	30.75%	20,137,345	31.67%	21,648,737	32.45%
Management Fees, Property Taxes and Insurance											
Management Fees		1,907,720	3.48%	1,995,795	3.46%	2,141,861	3.54%	2,278,638	3.58%	2,416,647	3.62%
Property Taxes		3,037,538	5.54%	3,153,081	5.47%	3,273,139	5.41%	3,396,807	5.34%	3,525,891	5.29%
Insurance		273,976	0.50%	288,125	0.50%	302,746	0.50%	317,943	0.50%	333,553	0.50%
Income Before Other Fixed Charges		14,328,610	26.15%	4,870,131	25.81%	16,475,677	27.21%	17,858,707	28.08%	19,232,090	28.83%

Bibliography

"1982 Benchmark Input/Output Accounts," U.S. Department of Commerce, Bureau of Economic Analysis, 1991.

"1990 Travel Market Report," U.S. Travel Data Center, August 1991.

1991 Study of Media & Markets, Volume P 10: Sports & Leisure, Simmons Market Research Bureau, Inc., 1991.

1991 Survey of Buying Power Demographics USA, *Sales and Marketing Management Magazine.*

Ad $ Summary, BAR/LNA, 1992.

Atlantic City Convention and Meeting Planner, Greater Atlantic City Convention and Visitors Bureau, 1993.

Atlantic City Property Tax Division, Phone Interview, November 1993.

Bally's Park Place Casino Hotel & Tower Public Relations Kit, September 1993.

Borg, Mary O., Paul M. Mason, & Stephen L. Shapiro, "An Economic Comparison of Gambling Behavior in Atlantic City and Las Vegas," *Public Finance Quarterly*, Volume 18, Number 3, July 1990.

Caro, Margaret Rose, " The Meeting Place of the '90s," *Lodging Magazine*, February 1991.

Caruth, Donald L., Robert M. Noe III, and R. Wayne Mondy, *Staffing the Contemporary Organization*, Quorum Books, New York, New York, 1988.

Casino Chronicle, Volume II, Number 14, September 6, 1993.

Circulation '93, Standard Rate and Data Service, 1993.

Condon, Ken, Vice President of Marketing, Bally's Park Place Casino Hotel & Tower, September 22, 1993.

"County Business Patterns, 1990 (CD/ROM)," U.S. Department of Commerce, Census Department, 1992.

D'Amato, Joe, Vice President Finance and Administration, Bally's Park Place Casino Hotel & Tower, September 22, 1993.

Deloitte & Touche, "Atlantic City Convention Center-Project Analysis, Part II, September 1992.

"Detailed CPI Report, August 1993," U.S. Department of Labor, August 1993.

Dev, Chekitan, Lecture Notes, HA 741: Marketing Management, Fall 1993.

Dickinson, Anne, Elizabeth M. Ineson, "The Selection of Quality Operative Staff in the Hotel Sector," *International Journal of Contemporary Hospitality Management*, Volume 5/1, 1993.

Eisen, Jerry, "Hiring Right: You Can Do It The First Time," *Hotel & Resort Industry*, Volume 16/2, February 1993.

Evans, Joel R., Barry Berman, *Marketing*, Fifth Edition, MacMillan Publishing Company, New York, New York, 1992.

Fernandez, Linda, *Now Hiring: An Employer's Guide to Recruiting in a Tight Labor Market*, Bureau of National Affairs, Inc., Washington, DC, 1989.

Fulford, Mark, Lecture Notes, HA 718: Human Resources, Fall 1993.

Gabarro, John J., *Managing People and Organizations*, Harvard Business School Publications, Cambridge, Massachusetts, 1992.

Geller, A. Neal, Lecture Notes, HA 725: Managerial Accounting, Fall 1993.

Goodale, James G., "Improving Performance Appraisal," *Business Quarterly*, Autumn 1992.

"The Host Report, Annual Report for the Year 1992," Arthur Anderson and Smith Travel Research, 1993.

HRM 1993 SHRM/CCH Survey, May 26,1993.

HRM Ideas and Trends in Personnel, Issue No. 278, June 24, 1992.

HRM Ideas and Trends in Personnel, Issue No. 287, October 28, 1992.

HRM Ideas and Trends in Personnel, Issue No. 292, January 6, 1993.

HRM Ideas and Trends in Personnel, Issue No. 312, November 10, 1993.

Human Resources Personnel Practices and Communications Volume I, CCH Business Law Editors, Chicago, Illinois, 1993.

Kelly, Thomas, Lecture Notes, HA 731: Food and Beverage Management, Fall 1993.

Klaas, Brian S., Hoyt N. Wheeler, "Supervisors and Their Response to Poor Performance: A Study of Disciplinary Decision Making," Plenum Publishing Corporation, 1992.

Laventhol & Horwath, "Atlantic City Convention Center: Market and Financial/Economic Analysis, December 1989.

Lewis, Robert C., Richard E. Chambers, *Marketing Leadership in Hospitality*, Van Nostrand Reinhold, New York, New York, 1989.

The Lifestyle Market Analyst 1993: A Reference Guide for Consumer Market Analysis, Standard Rate & Data Service, Wilmette, Illinois, 1993.

Marketing Management Magazine, "Survey of Buying Power Demographics," U.S.A., 1991.

McShane, Kevin, Director of Convention Services, Trump Plaza, October 29, 1993.

Moskowitz, Harvey S., *The New Illustrated Book of Development Definition*, Center for Urban Policy Research, 1993.

The Official Guide to the American Marketplace, New Strategist Publications, 1992.

Official Meeting Facilities Guide: North America, Reed Pubishing (U.S.A.) Inc., Spring/Summer 1993.

Orlando Marriot Village and Towers at International Drive: *Executive Summary*, Crescent Consulting Group, December 10, 1992.

Penner, Richard, Lecture Notes, HA 751: Project Development, Fall 1993.

Platt, Kenneth B., *City of Atlantic City Appendix of Statistical Data 1993*, The Department of Planning and Development, 1993.

Raymos, Donna, PKF, September 20, 1993.

Rosen, David I., "Appraisals Can Make—or Break—Your Case," *Personnel Journal*, November 1992.

RTKI Associates, Inc., *Atlantic City Gateway Corridor*, 1993.

Rushmore, Stephen, "How to Perform an Economic Feasibility Study of a Proposed Hotel/Motel," American Society of Real Estate Counselors, April 1988.

Rutes, Walter A., Richard H. Penner, Hotel Planning and Design, Watson-Guptil Publications, New York, New York, 1985.

Schuler, Randall S. *Managing Human Resources*, West Publishing Company, New York, New York, 1992.

"Sfuzzi to Open Second San Diego Bistro,"The San Diego Union-Tribune, Section C, Page 2, October 8, 1993.

Shifflet, Douglas K, "Focus On Convention Groups," *Hotel & Resort Industry*, April 1993.

Spot Radio Rates and Data, Standard Rate and Data Service, March 1992.

Smith Travel Research, Atlantic City Properties Summary, October 1, 1993.

"State of the Industry Report," *Successful Meetings*, Summer 1993.

Study of Atlantic County Market by the Boyd Company, Inc., Location Consultants, Princeton, New Jersey.

Survey of Current Business, September 1993.

Tony, Richard, Vice President Consumer Marketing and Information Services, Trump's Castle Casino Resort, September 21, 1993.

"Trends in the Hotel Industry—1992," PKF Consulting, 1992.

Trump Castle Employee Handbook

Trump Plaza executives, September 21, 1993

Trump Plaza Promotional Materials, September 1993.

Trump Taj Mahal management, September 22, 1993.

United States Census Data, 1990.

Woods, Robert H., James E. Macauley, "Rx for Turnover: Retention Programs that Work," *Cornell Hotel and Restaurant Administration Quarterly*, May 1989.

INDEX

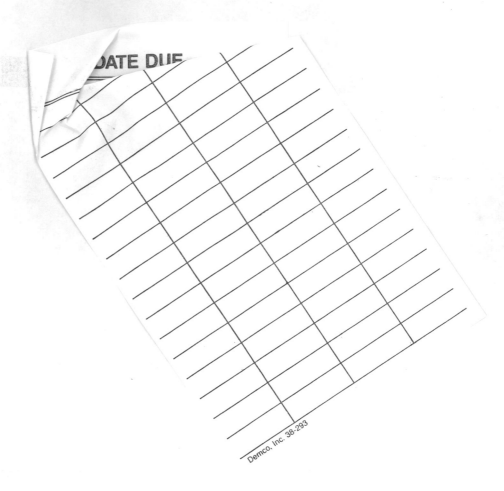

DATE DUE

Demco, Inc. 38-293